D0307511

Kenya

THE BRADT TRAVEL GUIDE

THE BRADT STORY

The first Bradt travel guide was written in 1974 by George and Hilary Bradt on a river barge floating down a tributary of the Amazon, and was followed by *Backpacker's Africa* in 1977. In the 1980s and '90s the focus shifted away from hiking to broader-based guides covering new destinations – usually the first to be published on those places. In the 21st century Bradt continues to publish these ground-breaking guides, along with guides to established holiday destinations, incorporating in-depth information on culture and natural history alongside the nuts and bolts of where to stay and what to see.

Bradt authors support responsible travel, with advice not only on minimum impact but also on how to give something back through local charities. Thus a true synergy is achieved between the traveller and local communities.

*

This Kenya guide brings me back almost to the founding of Bradt Travel Guides. The country featured prominently in *Backpacker's Africa* after George and I had spent over a month exploring Kenya. In those days of budget travel it was the coast that we enjoyed most. We revelled in the ease of travel and the variety of people and cultures from Mombasa to Lamu, not to mention the swimming and snorkelling. A decade later I went back for a few years as a tour leader and discovered the comfort side of Kenya: the superb lodges, the wonderful national parks, the birdlife, the food … everything to make a discriminating visitor happy. I don't remember a dissatisfied tourist; everyone loved each moment and at least one person was changed for ever by the experience. I have been waiting many years to find an author who can do justice to this amazing country. Claire Foottit has risen admirably to the task.

Hilary Bradt

Hilary Bradt

19 High Street, Chalfont St Peter, Bucks SL9 9QE, England
Tel: 01753 893444; fax: 01753 892333
Email: info@bradt-travelguides.com
Web: www.bradt-travelguides.com

Kenya

THE BRADT TRAVEL GUIDE

Claire Foottit

Bradt Travel Guides Ltd, UK
The Globe Pequot Press Inc, USA

First published 2004

Bradt Travel Guides Ltd
19 High Street, Chalfont St Peter, Bucks SL9 9QE, England
www.bradt-travelguides.com
Published in the USA by The Globe Pequot Press Inc, 246 Goose Lane,
PO Box 480, Guilford, Connecticut 06475-0480

Text copyright © 2004 Claire Foottit
Maps copyright © 2004 Bradt Travel Guides Ltd
Photographs © 2004 Individual photographers

The author and publisher have made every effort to ensure the accuracy of the
information in this book at the time of going to press. However, they cannot accept any
responsibility for any loss, injury or inconvenience resulting from the use of information
contained in this guide.

All rights reserved. No part of this publication may be reproduced, stored in a retrieval
system, or transmitted in any form or by any means, electronic, mechanical, photocopying,
recording or otherwise without the prior consent of the publishers.
Requests for permission should be addressed to Bradt Travel Guides Ltd,
19 High Street, Chalfont St Peter, Bucks SL9 9QE in the UK;
or to The Globe Pequot Press Inc,
246 Goose Lane, PO Box 480, Guilford, Connecticut 06475-0480
in North and South America.

British Library Cataloguing in Publication Data
A catalogue record for this book is available from the British Library

ISBN 1 84162 066 1

Photographs
Front cover Claire Foottit (Early morning, Masai Mara)
Text Claire Foottit (CF), Ariadne Van Zandbergen (AZ), Nick Garbutt (NG)

Illustrations Rainee Anderson, Annabel Milne
Maps Steve Munns

Typeset from the author's disc by Wakewing
Printed and bound in Italy by Legoprint SpA, Trento

Author/Dedication

AUTHOR

Claire Foottit was born in Kenya and, although she now lives in the UK, has made numerous return trips to Kenya and other parts of Africa. An Edinburgh University graduate in geography and landscape studies, she has worked in design and PR in the environmental field. Currently working as a photojournalist specialising in African tourism and conservation, she has an in-depth knowledge of Kenya's tourism, wildlife conservation and cultural issues and a comprehensive understanding of the country, based on ten years' experience in the Africa travel industry. She has had over 60 articles published in newspapers and magazines that include *The Times*, *The Scotsman*, *The Herald*, *Wanderlust*, *Travel Africa* and *Geographical*, as well as the in-flight magazine of Kenya Airways, *Msafiri*. She is also a Fellow of the Royal Geographical Society.

DEDICATION

In memory of my pioneer grandmother, Connie Findlay, Waitangi, Kiambu; my parents, Betty and Derek Foottit, for giving me an idyllic early childhood in Kericho and for their love, encouragement and interest in my ceaseless wanderings in Africa; my aunt and uncle, Joan and Phil Wise (formerly Sotik), for their support and kindness to 'the elephant's child'; cousin Jock Dallas, Migaa, Kiambu, whose generous legacy assisted me while researching and writing this guidebook; and Bunny and Hugh Morton, Limuru, who introduced me to safaris and provided a home from home whenever I was in Kenya.

Contents

LIST OF MAPS

Preface

Jake Grieves-Cook, Chairman, Kenya Tourism Federation

The Kenya Tourism Federation represents all the private-sector companies within Kenya's tourism industry, comprising hotels, safari lodges and camps, beach resorts and coastal tourism, air operators, travel agents, tour operators and eco-tourism.

We greatly welcome the publication of this excellent new travel guide which provides such a well-researched background on the history, geography, peoples and wildlife of Kenya, with extensive details of all the diverse attractions available for the visitor and useful travel information. It will prove invaluable to anyone planning a trip to Kenya who wishes to make the most of the time spent here.

The recent election of a new government in Kenya, committed to democratic principles and better governance, marks the start of a new era for this country and there is a growing sense of optimism for the future. Tourism in Kenya has the potential to make an important contribution to our national economy and to provide new employment opportunities and livelihoods for our citizens. This country is blessed with a wealth of natural features ideal for tourism, such as a pleasant climate, spectacular landscapes including vast wilderness areas, views of snow-capped mountains and the great Rift Valley, as well as the largest diversity of wildlife species in the world and the attractions of the white, palm-fringed beaches of Kenya's Indian Ocean coastline. These attractions, combined with a population known for its friendly, easy-going nature and characteristic hospitality, make Kenya an ideal holiday destination.

In today's world it is now more important than ever that security of visitors is given a high priority at a time when there is an increased threat from global terrorism affecting many countries worldwide. The Kenya Tourism Federation wishes to reassure our tourist visitors that we have confidence that the new government in Kenya has fully recognised this increased global terrorist threat and we are aware that effective action has been taken to put in place greatly enhanced security measures around vital installations, airports, tourist resorts, urban centres and foreign embassies, for the increased safety of visitors to Kenya. We would like to assure our visitors that they can expect to receive a friendly welcome from all Kenyans involved in our tourism industry and that Kenya continues to offer a first-class holiday experience for overseas tourists.

We hope that the publication of this new Bradt Travel Guide will enable visitors to make the most of their stay in Kenya by providing a useful insight into the wealth of attractions that awaits them here.

Acknowledgements

While researching this guide to Kenya, I have drawn on knowledge gleaned over a period of many years as well as during the research trip. I am indebted to many individuals, companies and organisations, both in Kenya and the UK, who have helped me, giving generously of their time, expertise and hospitality, some over many years. It is not possible to thank everyone individually, but I extend a collective and sincere thank you to all concerned.

I would especially like to thank the Kenya Tourist Board, the Kenya Wildlife Service, the National Museums of Kenya, the Kenya Association of Tour Operators, the Kenya Tourism Federation Safety and Communication Centre, AirKenya, Safarilink, the Africa Travel and Tourism Association and Tourist Maps [K] Ltd for their assistance, together with the following tour operators and hoteliers who merit a special mention:

African Horizons Travel & Safari, African Quest Safaris, As You Like it Safaris, Basecamp Travel, Bush Homes of East Africa, Chameleon Tours, Charlie Claw's Wasini Island Restaurant and Kisite Dhow Tours, Cheli & Peacock Safaris, Diani Marine, Eco-Resorts, Gamewatchers Safaris, Heritage Hotels, Hoopoe Adventure Tours, Journeys by Design, Kwa Kila Hali Safaris, Let's Go Travel, Marich Pass Field Studies Centre, Serena Hotels, Southern Cross Safaris, Taita Discovery Centre and Wilderness Kenya.

My thanks too to travelling companions Julie Njeru, Simon Mwoki, Joseph Kinuthia, Stephen Waweru, Wilfred Makori, Andy Reynolds, Hugh, Alex and Iain Foottit who accompanied me on various research trips.

While writing the book, close friends and family have given stalwart support, and my grateful thanks to them for their kindness and patience when for months on end my life revolved around hours at the computer.

Last, but not least, my thanks to the team at Bradt Travel Guides: Hilary Bradt, Tricia Hayne, Debbie Everson, Adrian Phillips, Selena Dickson, Debbie Hunter, Henry Stedman, Barry Kew, Sally Brock, Dr Felicity Nicholson and Steve Munns.

RESEARCH ASSISTANTS

My thanks to the many people, among them Sheels Ballard, Rona Birnie, Rufus Carr, Alan Dixson, Paul Easto, Leigh Ecclestone, Malcolm Gascoigne, Sarah Higgins, David Lovatt Smith, Maria Mario, Melinda Rees, Dr David Roden, Annette Ruthman and Kristofer Zachrisson, who contributed snippets of information for the book. I am particularly indebted to the generous assistance of the following people:

Philip Briggs, an Africa specialist and author, who provided an excellent basis for the *Wildlife Guide* and Language appendices, where Angeline Barrett also gave expert comment.

Duncan Dalzel-Job, an architect, who diligently researched and wrote most of the history section.

Angela Robertson, for her cheerful demeanour and enthusiasm, getting me through the mid-term blues while writing the book. She meticulously researched passenger schedules for the *Planning and Preparations* chapter, drew up tables, proofread copy and gave secretarial back-up.

Ulrika Sandberg, a human rights lawyer with a particular interest in indigenous peoples, who wrote much of the section on tribes.

Fiona Laing, a PR professional and journalist, gave helpful comment and also contributed to the *Planning and Preparations* chapter.

Olive Pearson, a cartographer and designer, who helped out on designing advertising copy and gave me useful pointers for drawing maps.

SPECIAL CONTRIBUTORS

My thanks to all those (many who are experts in their field) who have kindly provided box pieces for this guide: Dr David Roden, Alan Dixson, Vivien Prince, Chris Campbell-Clause, Andrew Nightingale, Dr Louise Leakey, Susie Weeks, Richard Lumbe, Peter Faull, Hassan Sachedina, Dr Karen Ross, Yasmin Galani, Steve Curtis, Dr David N M Mbora, Ali Halkano, Beatrice Mungai, George Ngure, Francis Mungai, Dr Lawrence Frank, Dr Robin S Reid, Michael Rainy, Virginia Luling, Lucy Vigne, Richard Zanre, Will Knocker, Anthony Childs, Binyavanga Wainaina, Philip Briggs, Wilfred Makori Mogire, Lawrence Mogire Onyoni, Dismas Mose Mogire, Ben West, James Foottit, James Munyugi, Sally Crook and Philippa D'Arcy Ryan.

A special thank you, too, to wildlife artist, Rainee Anderson, for the use of her exquisite line drawings in the guide.

Introduction

The eminent palaeontologist, Dr Richard Leakey, once put forward the notion that our genetic memory embraces the origins of man, enhancing the appeal of Kenya even to those who have never visited Africa before. It is an interesting concept, echoed in the writings of the psychologist Carl Jung, and not beyond the realms of possibility. Kenya is rich in prehistory, and even today the search is on for the 'missing link' in man's evolution.

My own introduction to Kenya was through my family. My Scottish grandparents were among the first coffee planters at Kiambu who arrived with all the accoutrements of Victorian settlers, not dissimilar to the *Out of Africa* genre; my mother nursed in Nairobi and my father was an agriculturalist under the colonial administration, being trained at Egerton College, which is now a thriving university. We left after independence in 1963 and as a young child I can remember well the *Uhuru* (freedom) celebrations in Nairobi when a sense of euphoria gripped the people. Although much has changed in 40 years, I still had a sense of déjà vu observing the December 2002 election results.

It is this underlying, palpable energy, the assault on the senses – vibrant colours, a myriad of sounds, the smell of rain on dust, vast horizons and wilderness – together with the vitality and humour of the Kenyans, which has drawn me back time and time again. As a student I arrived overland from South Africa, driving a truck from Botswana, through Zambia and Tanzania to Kenya. This was followed after university by another overland trip through Egypt and Sudan to Kenya, after which I backpacked around the country and worked at the Ark (a tree hotel in the Aberdares) and as a volunteer with Limuru Boys' Centre. It was at this time that I had the opportunity to go on camping safaris and to taste tropical ice on Mount Kenya – wildlife in natural surroundings and stunning scenery (Kenya is one of the best places to witness the scale of the Rift Valley), together with fascinating tribespeople, gave me a further appreciation of the wealth of Kenya's natural and cultural heritage.

It's the combination of friendliness, magnificent wildlife viewing (undoubtedly among the best in Africa) and dramatic scenery which has formed the foundation of Kenya's tourism industry. Tourism, wildlife conservation and the welfare of local people now verge on being symbiotic. This has made for some fascinating changes in the tourist industry over the past decade, where mass tourism has been superseded by a growth in ecotourism and community tourism enterprises. The transformation has given rise to a wide spectrum of choice, not only in accommodation, but also in how to experience a safari and the different options available. I have attempted to portray these aspects in this guide.

Over the years, Kenya's fortunes have wavered, from a thriving economy to the crippling effects of corruption and latterly the threats of international terrorism, but it has never lost its spirit. A new era dawned in 2003 with the election of Mwai Kibaki as Kenya's third president. It's an exciting time of challenge and opportunity where Kenya, a peace-loving nation, can bring a greater balance of wealth to its people and fulfil its economic potential. It is a beautiful country with a warm heart, and I have little doubt that any tourist or traveller will enjoy and be enriched by time spent in Kenya.

CAN YOU HELP?

Dear Reader,

Although I have attempted to be as up to date and accurate in the guide as possible, it is in the nature of guidebooks that things change. If you have any comments or new information I would greatly appreciate your assistance in updating the next edition of the Kenya guide and any help will be acknowledged. If you would like to help, please email: info@bradt-travelguides.com or write to Bradt Travel Guides Ltd (Kenya Guide), 19 High Street, Chalfont St Peter, Bucks SL9 9QE, UK. In the meantime, safe travels – *Safari njema*.

Claire Foottit
December 2003

Part One

General Information

KENYA AT A GLANCE

Location East Africa; one of 53 countries on the African continent, straddling the Equator. Borders Ethiopia and Sudan to the north, Uganda to the west, Tanzania to the south and Somalia and the Indian Ocean to the east.

Size 586,000km², of which about 10,700km² comprise the lakes of Victoria and Turkana. It compares in size to France or Texas. The tropical coastline stretches for about 480km.

Climate Tropical to alpine – averages dry temperate; two rainy seasons

Time GMT +3

Electricity 220 volts

Weights and measures Metric

International telephone code +254

Status Republic

GDP US$375 per capita (2000)

Currency Kenya shilling (KSh); coins: 50cts, KSh1, KSh5, KSh10 and KSh20; notes KSh50, KSh100, KSh200, KSh500 and KSh1,000. *Exchange rate April 2003*: US$1 = KSh76; £1 = KSh119; ∈1 = KSh81

Population 30.7 million (2001)

Population growth per year 2%

Life expectancy in years at birth 46

Infant mortality 7.8%

Economy Major earners: tea, coffee, horticulture, agriculture, tourism

Capital Nairobi; population about 2.2 million

Main towns Mombasa, Kisumu, Eldoret, Nakuru

Language English (official), Kiswahili (national), multiple ethnic languages (Bantu, Cushitic and Nilotic language groups)

Religion Christianity, Hinduism, Sikhism, Islam and traditional beliefs

Flag Red, black and green, shield and crossed spears

Public holidays January 1 (New Year's Day), February/March (*Idd il Fitr*), March/April (Good Friday, Easter Monday), May 1 (Labour Day), June 1 (Madaraka Day), October 10 (Moi Day), October 20 (Kenyatta Day), December 1 (Jamhuri Day), December 25 (Christmas Day), December 26 (Boxing Day)

Sites of international importance Three World Heritage Sites; five biosphere reserves; two RAMSAR sites

National parks and reserves 54 – terrestial and marine; about 10% of land area

History and Economy

HISTORY
The Cradle of Mankind (6,500,000–50,000BC)

Kenya has played a key part in the research of man's genealogy. By examining the age characteristics and surroundings of ape-man fossils discovered all over the world, anthropologists have now reasoned that man originated in Africa.

Initially, discoveries of fossils vital to drawing up mankind's birth line were to be found in Asia. The first major find to indicate that the 'missing link' between man and ape was to be found in Africa was discovered in 1911. A German entomologist, Professor Kattwinkel, fell down Olduvai Gorge (in Tanzania) to be confronted by the rock face of a fossil bed. This accidental discovery helped refocus the search to the African continent. The skull shape and bones together with shaped tools indicated the 'lifestyle' of each fossilised man.

In 1924 Charles Darwin's *Origin of Species* helped to develop this line of theory. Prior to the major advances of Kenyan palaeontology (the study of how human ancestors lived) by the Leakey family there had been a wide range of evolutionary theories as to the origins of man. The great force in East African anthropology started in 1931 with Dr Louis Leakey's study, with his then fiancée Mary, of the 1911 Olduvai Gorge site.

In 1959 they made a key discovery: 400 skull fragments of a pre-hominid, *Zinjanthropus boisei*. In 1961 this was dated to 1.75 million years old, although later re-dated. This gave a strong foundation for the Cradle of Mankind lying in East Africa. Furthermore, in 1960, the Leakeys found the remains of *Homo habilis*, an evolved hominid capable of carving stone axes, whose age was estimated at 1.4 million years.

Throughout the 1970s and 1980s there were many fossil discoveries of ancient man boosting palaeoanthropological knowledge. Mary Leakey discovered the Laetoli footprints and fossils of 3.6-million-year-old hominids near Olduvai Gorge. Her son Richard, continuing both the Leakey and *hominid* family line, explored the Koobi Fora site, close to Lake Turkana in northern Kenya, with a Kenyan palaeontologist Bernard Ngeneo, discovering the two-million-year-old remains of *Homo habilis*. Ten years later, in 1984, Richard Leakey found an almost complete skeleton of a *Homo erectus*, the famous 'Turkana boy', a 1.6-million-year-old hominid, more evolved and considered to be a possible direct ancestor of modern man, *Homo sapiens*.

Before the East African digs, the generally accepted theory was that the ancestors of modern humans were of the *Australopithecus* species. The Leakey discoveries suggested that the modern *Homo sapiens* were descendants of *Homo habilis* and that although the two species had lived together, *Australopithecus* had in fact died out.

Each fossil discovery helped to fill gaps in the evolutionary path. In 1995, at the Turkana site, Meave Leakey, Richard's wife, in co-operation with Alan Walker, discovered what is now the oldest of the *Australopithecus*, *A. anamensis*, an elderly

EARLY MAN AND THE RIFT VALLEY MIGRATIONS
Dr David Roden

Apart from its physical uniqueness the Rift Valley is a site of major developments in human evolution, warranting the label 'Cradle of Mankind'. Great local variations in relief have resulted in a wide range of climate, soils and vegetation from arid lowland plains to highland rainforest, all in relatively close juxtaposition. Evidence from several important fossil sites along the valley floor in Kenya (both east and west of Lake Turkana), Ethiopia and Tanzania suggests that here, on well-watered plains teeming with game, the transition from ape to biped human hunter took place between seven million and one million years ago.

More recently, during the last three millennia, the eastern Rift has been a significant line of human movement south from the Ethiopian highlands and the Middle Nile basin (in what is now Sudan), details of which remain scarcely understood. One example has been the successive migrations of cattle herders from the Nile region, presumably in response to pressure on resources. Coming in waves over the last 2,000 years, Nilotic pastoralists moved into different environments in Kenya and Uganda, assimilating existing peoples, imposing their own social organisations and languages, adopting new cultural traits themselves (particularly from Cushitic peoples) and modifying their economies. The Kalenjin speakers, who probably started drifting south about 2,000 years ago through what was then light woodland on the plains west of Lake Turkana, eventually moved up on to the high plateaux west of the Rift escarpment. There, in fine grasslands and forest, they adopted a more agricultural lifestyle, in some areas on or immediately below the escarpment, taking over or developing intricate furrow irrigation systems to supplement rain-fed cultivation. The Turkana-Karamajong peoples and the Luo followed southwards from about the 15th century AD. The former have remained primarily cattle (and camel) herders on what are now semi-arid plains in northwest Kenya and northeast Uganda. The Luo filtered along rivers and through swamps to settle around the northeastern shore of Lake Victoria, gradually developing a more mixed farming and fishing economy.

The last major Nilotic migration along the Rift Valley were the Maa-speakers, the Maasai and Samburu. They were well organised for rapid expansion and over the 200 years up to the mid-19th century were able to occupy some of the best grazing lands in the Rift Valley and the highlands to the east, even expanding at the expense of the Kalenjin speakers to the west. The Maasai and Samburu are still largely herders today.

The Rift Valley and associated uplands have continued to be a focus of economic and political activity in modern Kenya. Ecological variations meant that fine pastures adjoined fertile hills or montane forests. Productive cultivation has developed close to specialised livestock rearing. These were the main areas of European agricultural settlement in the early 20th century, and have remained the main areas of inter-ethnic competition today – for farmland in the uplands and grazing on the drier plains.

Dr David Roden is director of Marich Pass Field Studies Centre.

man 4.2 million years old, judged to be the ancestor of *A. afarensis*. In 1998 and 1999, Maeve Leakey and colleagues made another significant find, unearthing fossils belonging to a new genus of human ancestor, *Kenyanthropus platyops* between 3.5 and 3.2 million years old.

This discovery shed new light on the early stages of human evolution, dismissing the previous scientific assumption that there was a single common human ancestor and revealing that at least two lineages existed as far back as 3.5 million years – *Australopithecus afarensis*, (of which 'Lucy', the partial skeleton discovered in Ethiopia in 1974, is best known) and *Kenyanthropus platyops*, both of which are from the same time interval but are significantly different. For example, the *Kenyanthropus* skull has a flatter face and smaller teeth than *Australopithecus*, suggesting that they had a different diet and therefore did not compete for food resources, enabling them to co-exist.

In November 2000, a French–Kenyan team led by Drs Martin Pickford and Brigitte Senut found the remains of the six-million-year-old hominid *Orrorin tugenensis*, dubbed 'Millennium man', at Kapsomin in the Tugen Hills.

Younger fossils have also been unearthed along the way. As with the homonids who lived on earth more than a million years ago, there are still differing opinions as to mankind's evolutionary path within the last 200,000 years. With each evolutionary find, history becomes more clear, yet the key primeval link between man and ape still lies waiting to be discovered.

Early settlers (50,000BC–AD500)

From around 50,000 years BC, early humans lived as hunter-gatherers, developing tools and speech, and learning how to make fire. As small communities, their movements were dictated by climate and the surrounding land, occasionally staying put for generations. Few clues exist as to how these hunter-gatherers lived, except that they were similar to the Khosian Bushmen people of southern Africa, with a 'click' language, and ancestors of the present day Boni, Wata and Wariangulu peoples. Iron Age and neolithic prehistoric sites may be found around Hyrax Hill, near Nakuru.

From 2000BC, as the inhabitants of East Africa evolved, a greater number of immigrants appeared in Kenya. From Ethiopia came the southern Cushites, who settled around Lake Turkana in the north, later moving south to Lake Victoria and Tanzania. They came from pastoral tribes, and with their mixed farming were technically and militarily superior to the existing tribes. From 1000BC the Yaaku, an eastern Cushitic tribe, moved south to central Kenya, assimilating the agricultural lifestyle and speech of local tribes. Between 500BC until AD500 the Bantus entered from the west along with the Nilotes from southern Sudan, again drawn south by a better climate. Both these peoples were transient, settling only from AD1500 onwards.

Migrants from overseas started to arrive on the Kenya coast from 500BC, mainly traders and explorers. The first documentary evidence is a description of Mombasa in AD110 by a Greek called Diogenes. He included descriptions of two great lakes supplied by a snowy range of mountains that might feed the Nile. Ptolemy collected this, and other information, for his map of AD150 creating the legend, regarded as improbable for many years, of the Mountains of the Moon (the present-day Rwenzoris in Uganda).

Swahili coast (AD500–1498)

The development of maritime trade led to the Kenya coast becoming a vital trade link between the Mediterranean, Europe, West Africa and the East Indies. The Arabs and Persians were first to have a major trade impact from around AD500.

Rather than conquer as they did in Spain and North Africa, they had a peaceful and prosperous effect on the East African coast. To this day Arab and Persian influences can be seen in the architecture of Mombasa, Malindi and Lamu. Further indication of this intermarriage of African and Arabic cultures is found in the present-day Swahili community whose language became the most widespread in East Africa. The word Swahili derives from the Arab word *Sahel*, meaning 'coast'.

This trade expanded sea routes to India and China and developed paths into the African interior, transporting goods, ivory, slaves and, centuries later, European explorers. As the Arabs brought textiles and other goods to the East African coast so the slave trade transported Kenyans throughout the coastal areas of the Indian Ocean. This grim but peaceful relationship lasted until the arrival of the Portuguese at the end of the 15th century.

Portuguese rule (1498–1698)

As the Spanish began their near monopoly of South American colonisation, the Portuguese looked to improve their trade routes towards India. The coast of East Africa was a valuable foothold in the Eastern trade routes, Mombasa especially so because of its ivory resources. The Portuguese navigator Vasco da Gama was commissioned by his king, Manuel I the Fortunate, to gain control. He successfully navigated the Cape of Good Hope in 1498, arriving in Mombasa on April 7. The Arabs promptly attacked, cutting the ship's anchors. Although the expedition continued north, Mombasa and much of the coast (except their original landing point, Malindi) suffered at the hands of the Portuguese for two centuries. They ruled with economic and religious oppression, building Fort Jesus in Mombasa as a military headquarters in 1593.

On March 11 1696, seven Omani ships, along with an army of 3,000 soldiers, entered the port of Mombasa. The Portuguese gathered 2,500 men to defend Fort Jesus, suffering disease, hunger and bubonic plague. By the end of 1696, only 50 Portuguese survived. Amazingly they resisted for nearly two more years, reinforcements arriving in September and December 1698, but by December 13, the Sultan of Oman had learned that only 20 survived. The Omanis scaled the walls and finally, after a 33-month siege, Fort Jesus fell to the Sultan of Oman. Following the fort's defeat, Portuguese control receded, their legacy to Kenya being new crops introduced from South America – corn, manioc, cashew and tobacco – and a few new additions to the Swahili vocabulary.

Omani domination (1698–1856)

After the Omani victory at Fort Jesus in December 1698, the cities of the Swahili coast came under the governance of Muscat. Although trade continued, it never matched the early levels of prosperity due to a more oppressive control. Under the Sultan Saif of Oman, authority became fractured, with neighbouring cities fighting for control and independence. The Mazrui dynasty, a Swahili family, was appointed to govern the island of Mombasa in 1741. The Omani Sultan Saif was murdered and succeeded by Sultan Said al Busaidi. Not always following the new Sultan's orders from Muscat, the Mazruis failed to maintain a steady hand. Revolts sprang up and the Mazruis often had disagreements among themselves. In 1784, Sultan Busaidi's brother invaded the coast to the south of Mombasa, taking Zanzibar and Kilwa. The Sultan reacted swiftly, retaking the area and other unruly cities at the same time. This peace lasted until the early 1800s when the Mazruis retaliated with attacks on coastal cities. A power struggle ensued back in Oman, during which time Sultan Busaidi was murdered by his brother Seyyid Said, who assumed control.

The defeat of the French emperor, Napoleon, in 1815 gave the British the upper hand around the Indian Ocean. They were now competing with the French for East Indian trade routes and also wanted to abolish the highly prosperous slave trade. Allying themselves with Sultan Said, the British began to put pressure on him to end this trade – a difficult decision, as it was the source of much of his wealth. The British did, however, have an ulterior motive, as this act would reduce the supply of slaves to the French West Indies. In 1822 the Anglo–Omani alliance was tested when a British ship arrived briefly to help the besieged Mazruis in Mombasa. Although not effectual, this event marked the first British involvement in Kenya. The Mazruis were finally defeated and deported from Mombasa in 1837. Recognising the need for greater dominance in the region, Sultan Seyyid Said moved his power base from Muscat to Zanzibar and by 1840 the entire East African coast was under Omani rule. The export of ivory, cloves and slaves developed further. The last still occurred, despite a number of slave-trade agreements signed between the Omanis and the British. In 1856 the Sultan died, leaving his two sons disputing control. Thuwani stayed in Oman and Seyyid Majid, his brother, who was supported by the British, gained control of Zanzibar and the East African coast. This separated East Africa from direct Omani rule.

European exploration of Kenya (1844–92)

It was two German missionaries, Johann Ludwig Krapf and Johannes Rebmann, who in 1844 were the first Europeans to venture into Kenya's interior. Other explorers, Richard Burton and John Speke, the Scots missionary Dr David Livingstone and Henry Stanley, had all opted to take the longer, southern route through Tanzania (or Tanganyika as it was then), from Zanzibar to Lake Victoria, in their quest for the source of the Nile. This avoided crossing the inhospitable Taru Desert and the lands of the Maasai, whose warriors had a fearsome reputation. Unlike those who followed, Krapf and Rebmann were not colonial explorers but their quest to convert Kenya, and indeed East Africa, to Christianity led them to many parts that no European had seen before. They left from their mission base at Rabai near Mombasa, armed with a Bible and a sunshade. In 1848 Rebmann spotted Kilimanjaro, and the following year, Krapf observed Mount Kenya. A third missionary, Jacob Erhardt, drew a 'slug map', which showed two snow-capped mountains and a large inland sea – Lake Victoria – based on their evidence and information about the lake gleaned from Arab traders. Their observations were scoffed at by the scientific fraternity in Europe at the time who judged it impossible for there to be snow on the equator. Further exploratory journeys led Krapf to the Tana River, crossing Tsavo to the Yatta Plateau and venturing as far as the Rift Valley. European explorers continued to probe the unknown areas of Kenya.

It was Joseph Thomson, a Scottish geologist and naturalist, who in 1882, at the age of 25, was sponsored by the Royal Geographical Society to lead an expedition deep into the Maasai lands. Rather than opt for a threatening army, as advocated by Stanley, Thomson adopted a lighter tactic: incursion. He took a few armed men and an impressive array of tricks, such as removing his false teeth or making water fizz by adding Epsom salts. The expedition successfully made its way through Maasai territory north of Kilimanjaro, where at the time the Maasai were suffering from cholera and smallpox. Thomson's cautious style kept the Maasai at bay. He travelled to what is now Nairobi and on to Lake Naivasha, passing Mount Kenya and the Aberdare Mountains (which he named after the president of the Royal Geographical Society) before cutting west to Lake Victoria, thereby pioneering the shortest route from the coast at Mombasa to Uganda. The return journey was more eventful: Thomson was gored by a buffalo, contracted dysentery and the expedition was subjected to Maasai raids.

Although he died in 1895, still a young man, Thomson's travels had broken new territory. Others were inspired to explore further. James Hannington, the ill-fated Anglican Bishop of Kampala who was murdered on the shores of Lake Victoria by the king of Buganda, was the first European to discover Lake Hannington (now Lake Bogoria).The Austrian-Hungarian count, Samuel Teleki, and Ludwig von Höhnel attempted to climb Mount Kenya and continued north to discover the last of the Great Lakes, which Teleki named Rudolf (now Lake Turkana) after the then crown prince of Austria.

The partition of East Africa (1856–91)

The period of successive expeditions into the 'Dark Continent' raised the stakes in terms of politics, power and commerce. Kenya was no longer an unknown quantity – its value to other nations, Arab or European, could now be appreciated in terms of raw potential. Although separated from the Middle East, the Sultan of Zanzibar still had considerable power in Kenya through control of much of the coast. The British continued their diplomacy in search of a beneficial alliance. An attack by the local Mazruis, led by Mbarak, forced Sultan Seyyid Bargash to ask for support from the British in 1882. Mbarak was defeated, strengthening British diplomatic power.

By the end of the 1800s, under a period known as the 'Scramble for Africa', Britain, Germany and Italy had all created protectorates and colonies in East Africa while the Turks controlled Egypt and Sudan. The initial driving force in the colonisation of East Africa came from individual businessmen like the German, Karl Peters, and the Scot, William Mackinnon. Peters set up the Witu German Company at Witu, south of Lamu, while Mackinnon founded the British East Africa Association in 1887 which later became the Imperial British East Africa Company (IBEAC) in 1888. As business groups they became ambassadors, sending out representatives to sign territorial agreements with African leaders in exchange for European authority. Sent on imperial missions for their countries both companies competed for dominance of Uganda.

With the creation of these companies, national interest grew, finally compelling governments to act. The carving up of the territories commenced in 1885 with a treaty between England, Germany and France. The Germans took Tanganyika (present-day Tanzania, which includes Zanzibar), the British assumed control of Kenya and Uganda and the French received the island of Madagascar. The once powerful Omani era withered. The Sultan relinquished power of the coastal strip to his allies, the British, under leasing agreements which gave rights to his territories in return for an annual fee.

Protectorates and the *Lunatic Express* (1891–1902)

Britain was now committed to East Africa, declaring Uganda a protectorate in 1894. Lugard and Mackinnon believed a railway to be essential to developing Uganda, and the government was grudgingly persuaded to undertake a feasibility study. The response was favourable: the government commissioned the railway and formed the British East Africa Protectorate in 1895 to protect their assets. Henry Labourchere was among several radical politicians who were strongly opposed to the building of a railway in what amounted to the middle of nowhere in a foreign country, and to the high costs involved. A satirical poem summed up their views:

The Lunatic Line
What it will cost no words can express
What is its object no brain can suppose
Where it will start from no-one can guess:
Where it is going nobody knows.
What is the use of it none can conjecture:
What it will carry there's none can define:
And in spite of George Curzon's superior lecture,
It is certainly naught but a lunatic line.

Subsequently the Uganda railway was dubbed the *Lunatic Express* in Charles Miller's book of the same name.

Work on the railway started in 1896 under the supervision of George Whitehouse, the chief engineer. It cost over £3 million along with the lives of many Indians – 'coolie' labour imported from India to work on the railway – who fell casualty to numerous diseases. But it was a pair of man-eating lions, nicknamed 'the ghost' and 'the darkness' by the terrified Indian workers, that provided one of the biggest obstacles. Attacking at night, 28 men were dragged from their tents and killed in the African bush. Colonel Patterson, an engineer working on the Tsavo bridge, despatched the pair, and the railway continued (see box page 221). Whitehouse established a railhead upon reaching a Maasai waterhole known as *Nyrobi* (Nairobi) in 1899, which soon became the new centre of administration and is today's capital city.

The railway finally reached Port Florence (present-day Kisumu), named after the chief engineer's wife, Florence Preston, on Lake Victoria on December 20 1901. It had taken five years and four months to complete this magnificent feat of engineering, a 1,000km track crossing hostile terrain, climbing 1,150m in one section and traversing the 600m-deep Rift Valley. The railway became the communications artery of Kenya; its Indian workers remained, creating a new community, and towns sprung up along the railway line. This enterprise had also disrupted the lives of the tribes across whose land the railway cut: Giriama, Taita, Kamba, Kikuyu, Kisii and Nandi.

Settlers and hunters (1902–20)

The completion of the railway to Uganda ended the great era of exploration. The train journey from Mombasa only took a few days to reach areas that were previously undiscovered by Europeans 20 years before. Kenya's price for a protectorate was the influx of settlers encouraged by the chance to make a fortune in the exciting but undeveloped land now made accessible.

Mainly arriving from Britain, but also from other countries, settlers like Lord Delamere acquired sizeable estates to supplement their own back in Britain. Attracted to East Africa for its hunting, Delamere bought a farm in 1903, eventually cultivating, although with mixed early success, crops and profitable livestock herds (see box page 288).

As Delamere's success brought more Europeans to the British East Africa Protectorate, it was officially declared a British East Africa Colony in 1905. Fresh territory was needed for settlers to make the railway a profitable investment in Kenya. Spreading out from Nairobi, there were two options: to take land from the Kikuyu or the Maasai. The Maasai's reputation had been tested by the late 19th-century explorers, so the government opted to sign an agreement in 1911 with Maasai chief Lenana, to buy parts of Maasai land in return for the Maasai moving south. The Kikuyu became labourers with restricted rights and access. This

LORD ERROLL

The murder of Josslyn Hay, Earl of Erroll, in 1941, scandalised colonial Kenyan society at the time. A notorious womaniser, especially of other men's wives, he eloped to Kenya with Lady Idina Gordon (then twice married and eight years his senior) and married her at the age of 23. It was Lady Idina's debauched house parties that gave rise to the now infamous Happy Valley set and the wise crack, 'Are you married, or do you live in Kenya?', which infuriated many of the hard-working, upright settlers who were tarred with the same brush.

Subsequently, Erroll had an affair with his married neighbour, Alice de Janzé, divorced Idina and broke up another marriage to then marry Molly Ramsay-Hill of whom he soon tired, leaving her to drown her sorrows in morphine and drink from which she later died. His saving grace was a flair for politics, being a natural and talented leader, but he continued with his illicit affairs. During this period he became involved with Diana Broughton, the wife of Sir Jock Delves Broughton. Sir Jock became the prime suspect for his murder, thought to have been a *crime passionnel*, although nothing was ever proven. Erroll is buried in St Paul's churchyard in Kiambu – the verger will show you the grave (a donation to the church is appropriate). On a hefty tombstone, his poignant epitaph reads:

In loving memory
of
Josslyn Victor Hay
Twenty-second Earl of Erroll
Hereditary High Constable of Scotland
Born 11th day of May 1901
Met his death on 24th day of January 1941

Thy will be done

The mystery and intrigue surrounding Erroll's death has been the subject of two excellent books, *White Mischief* by James Fox, and *The Life and Death of Lord Erroll: the Truth Behind the Happy Valley Murder* by Errol Trzebinski. In a bizarre and cruel twist of fate, Trzebinski's son, Tonio, was found dead in a Nairobi suburb in 2001 – a murder perceived by some to have uncanny parallels to Lord Erroll's demise.

instilled the resentment and violence that would trouble Kenya's history until independence in 1963.

The injustice felt by the indigenous tribes around Nairobi was amplified by World War I. Although there was little fighting in Kenya, some 200,000 conscripts were sent to fight the Germans in Tanganyika. Following the war, the Tanganyika colony came under British rule. The British government initiated the Soldier Settlement Scheme encouraging further settlement to make their colonies more profitable. By 1919 there were around 10,000 white settlers in Kenya.

Suffering of the tribes local to Nairobi, particularly the Kikuyu, continued. Struck by the injustice that this swift colonialism had brought, a few settlers took a conscientious approach, raising an awareness of potential social problems. Others took direct action, such as schooling the local children.

For others their attitude towards hunting changed. With vast expanses of wilderness and prolific trophy animals, game shooting had become Kenya's biggest attraction. Famous names such as Ernest Hemingway, Winston Churchill and Theodore Roosevelt all came to experience the macho destruction of wildlife. Experienced hunters, like Denys Finch-Hatton, Philip Percival and Frederick Selous, concerned about the indiscriminate slaughter of animals, created the Hunters Association in 1920 – the start of the hunter-conservationist.

African nationalism (1920–47)

In 1920, the Colony of British East Africa became the Kenya Colony. Although subdued, African nationalism was fostered in the 1920s by unofficial political parties; unrest surfaced although it was quickly and violently restrained. As these movements began, a key figure emerged in Kenyan politics, Johnstone Kamau Wa Ngengi, more commonly known as Jomo Kenyatta. Educated by European missionaries, he followed Christian and nationalist paths, affiliating with the East Africa Association, and later became the general secretary of the Kikuyu Central Association. He attempted to broadcast the unjust situation developing in Kenya to England and later Europe, becoming a driving force in Kenyan nationalism. He settled in England from 1931 to 1946, studying and later teaching linguistics and anthropology.

Fighting under the British in World War II gave Kenyans an insight into European life, providing them with a greater understanding of politics. By the end of the war Kenya had its first political party, the Kenya African Union (KAU). Nationalism was dividing into two paths: violent and political. While criminal gangs developed themselves into political terrorist groups, Jomo Kenyatta returned in secrecy to lead KAU for six difficult years.

By 1947 one of the strongest of these anti-colonial societies, the Forty Group, had intensified their actions into the start of the Mau Mau rebellion, using violence and prostitution to gather weapons and power in the name of freedom.

Mau Mau and the end of the Colony (1947–63)

Although Kenya's political transformation was to lie with the path taken by Jomo Kenyatta, it was the horror of the Mau Mau terrorists, today regarded as freedom fighters, that characterised Kenya's worst moments in colonial history. For those opposed to African nationalism it was easy to obscure colonial mistreatment when such atrocities were carried out by Kenyan against Kenyan. The movement's initiation ritual demonstrated much of its Kikuyu origin; blood from a goat was mixed with that of the person taking the oath and then poured over banana leaves and mixed with earth. Initiates had to vow to oppose colonisation and anyone who supported it, such as fellow Africans loyal to the colonialists. The two main strongholds for the Mau Mau were around Mount Kenya and the Aberdare Mountains. It is thought that the name 'Mau Mau' derived from the Kikuyu word 'Uma' which means 'get out'. Look-outs posted to watch for the police at the first illegal oathings would shout, 'Uma, uma' to warn the oath administrators to leave. When said fast, 'uma, uma' sounded like 'mau mau' with the result that the authorities mis-interpreted the call as 'Mau Mau'.

During this troubled period, in 1952 Princess Elizabeth (of Great Britain) and her husband, Prince Philip, came to Kenya on a royal visit. They were visiting Treetops Hotel in the Aberdare Forest when her father, King George VI, died and she became Queen Elizabeth II.

At the end of 1952 the Mau Mau had become so fierce that an emergency was declared and troops were brought from Britain to suppress Kenyan nationalism as

HISTORICAL TIME CHART

6m years BC	Age of hominid fossil 'Millennium man' discovered in 2000 by a Kenyan–French palaeontological team in the Tugen Hills.
4.2m years BC	An elderly man dies leaving fossils to be discovered in AD1995 creating a key link in the charting of man's evolution
1.75m years BC	Age of fossils discovered by Louis Leakey in 1959 linking the Cradle of Mankind to East Africa.
1.6m years BC	Age of *Homo erectus* skeleton 'Turkana boy' discovered nearly complete in 1984 near Lake Turkana by Richard Leakey, son of Louis.
1.4m years BC	Period of *Homo habilis* or 'Handy Man' capable of making and working with tools.
50,000 years BC	Early humans lived as hunter-gatherers.
2000BC	Immigrants arrive in Kenya from the north, bringing advanced farming techniques.
500BC to AD500	Traders and explorers arrive from outside Africa.
AD110	Greek explorer Diogenes visits Mombasa.
AD150	Ptolemy creates a map of East Africa using Diogenes' information and his own exploits.
AD500	Arabs and Persians begin to trade with East Africa, creating trade routes to carry textiles in and slaves out.
AD9th century	Malindi and Lamu founded by Arabs.
AD14th century	Mombasa founded by Persians.
1498	Portuguese explorer Vasco da Gama arrives in Mombasa, beginning 200 years of oppressive control.
1593	Fort Jesus built by Portuguese in Mombasa.
1696	Omanis arrive in Mombasa attacking Fort Jesus. They defeat the Portuguese in 1698.
1741	Omanis enlist help of Swahilis, the Mazrui family, to control East African coast.
1815	Defeat of Napoleon in Europe strengthens English prospects around the Indian Ocean.
1822	English ship arrives in Mombasa to briefly aid Mazruis besieged by disgruntled Omanis.
1844	Two German missionaries, Krapf and Rebmann, venture into the Kenyan interior.
1856	Sultan of Oman dies. The resulting split puts the East African coast in control of a pro-British sultan.

a whole. Laying the blame upon the politicians as well as the Mau Mau, the governor arrested 150 people, including Jomo Kenyatta. He was imprisoned until 1960. After this, the British government, which had come to regard Kenya in its political instability as an economic liability, agreed to grant the Kenya Colony independence from Britain.

Kenyan politics had developed throughout the 1950s. Figures such as Ronald Ngala, Tom Mboya and Daniel Arap Moi rose through the political ranks; the last would become prime minister after Jomo Kenyatta. The final downfall of the Mau Mau began in 1953 with the infiltration of the guerrillas, although it was not until independence that the last fighters gave up their weapons to Jomo Kenyatta. The

1882	Scottish geologist, Thomson, breaks new territory exploring Kenya.
Late 1800s	Partition of East Africa between Britain, Germany, Italy and Turkey, creates commercial competition between nations.
1885	Britain takes Kenya as a protectorate in an East African treaty.
1894	Britain gains control of Uganda inspiring the *Lunatic Express* railway.
1899	Railway reaches Nairobi refocusing administration on the area.
1901	Railway reaches Lake Victoria leaving an East Indian workforce to create a community and speeding expansion of white settlement.
1919	Number of white settlers reaches 10,000. Major injustice felt by African Kenyan WWI war veterans returning from Tanganyika.
1920s	Birth of big-game hunting and African nationalism along with Jomo Kenyatta's political life.
1931–46	Jomo Kenyatta settles in England.
1947	Birth of Mau Mau.
1952	Elizabeth becomes queen while at Treetops Hotel in the Aberdare Forest; British troops brought in to quash African Nationalism; Kenyatta jailed.
1960	End of state of emergency, Kenyatta freed.
1963	Kenyatta leads Kenya into independence or *Uhuru*.
1978	Jomo Kenyatta dies. Daniel Arap Moi takes over KANU and the leadership, *Nyayo*
1980s	Unrest and coups against Moi. Richard Leakey appointed as head of Kenya Wildlife Service.
1983	Moi wins elections after supposed conspiracy plot.
1987	Moi 'wins' single party, single candidate elections.
1991	FORD opposition movement set up.
1992	Moi wins corrupt elections.
1995	Richard Leakey attempts politics.
1997/8	Major rains and droughts.
1998	US embassy in Nairobi bombed.
1999	Richard Leakey appointed head of Civil Service.
2002	Moi's KANU candidate Uhuru Kenyatta loses election to the Rainbow Alliance Coalition – NARC. Mwai Kibaki becomes Kenya's third president.

violent civil war had taken the lives of 2,000 loyalist Africans, 11–30,000 Mau Mau and perhaps treble that were arrested and held in prison camps. In 2002, Mau Mau veterans were suing the British government for ill treatment in the detention camps.

Uhuru, Jamhuri, Harambee (1963–78)

The Lancaster House agreement in 1962 set a date for independence. Kenyatta was effectively the only choice to lead Kenya after independence and on June 1, *Madaraka* day, he became prime minister of a coalition government between his party, the Kenyan African National Union (KANU), and the Kenya Africa Democratic Union (KADU). The declaration of independence took place on

December 12 1963, *Uhuru* day, resplendent with all the panache and protocol of the dying days of empire. The British flag was lowered and the new Kenyan flag hoisted, its colours representing green for the land, black for the people and red for the blood shed in pursuit of freedom.

From the start, Kenyatta's approach to leading Kenya was conciliatory in that he realised the economic benefits of including whites and Asians in the modern Kenya. He had remarkable charisma and as with another African statesman, Nelson Mandela, a seeming lack of bitterness for his years spent in detention. Often sporting a *kofia*-style hat and brandishing a giraffe-tail fly whisk he was a passionate orator and rallied people to a national mantra: *harambee*! encouraging everyone to 'all pull together' for the national cause. In theory this was an effective policy but it made him and his Kikuyu tribesmen very powerful, while his opposition were made to seem unpatriotic to the extent that in 1964 the opposition party dissolved themselves to become part of Kenyatta's KANU party, leaving a de facto one-party state.

Within East Africa economics, trade and utilities were unified and by the end of the 1960s a land redistribution policy, the 'million acre' scheme, was set up – although again the Kikuyu elite seemed to benefit the most. The country began to attract international investment and tourists, and a structured education system was established. Although there was some dissent from those supported by the Luo and Gusii tribes, much of this was quashed through undercover methods, and Kikuyu strength was increased within the national administration and security forces. Any insurrection towards the ruling party was countered with a firm hand – often death under mysterious circumstances, such as the fate of J M (Josiah Mwangi) Kariuki, an opposition MP. Although Kenyatta may have instigated a firm hand to maintain power and control, it is unlikely that he fully appreciated the insidious, avaricious corruption starting to permeate the country. No-one was prepared to risk accusations of interference, although the corruption became noticed beyond Kenya's borders. The economy suffered and the East African Community, a liaison between Kenya, Tanzania and Uganda, initiated in 1967 to share communications and transport, finally fell apart in 1977. Kenyatta died on August 28 1978, aged 86.

Nyayo (1978–90)

As the man who had led Kenya from colonialism to independence, many respected Kenyatta, but his death brought an anticipation of change from one man's single-mindedness and control. As expected, Daniel Toroitich Arap Moi, the leading KANU party's vice-president, took power. Although a Tugen from the Kalenjin tribe, support from the Kikuyu ensured his success. Starting with a seemingly non-tribal, non-corrupt stance he later showed that, having helped form Kenya's politics both before Kenyatta and in his shadow, he was not going to turn his back on retaining power for himself. As his election cry of *Nyayo!* – implying 'follow in his footsteps' – showed, he too was content to oppress non-conformists; the crushing of student protests and the closure of the university frequently occurred. Dissent grew, and in 1982 Charles Njonjo, the attorney general, reformed the constitution, effectively establishing a single party. Three months later there was an Air Force-backed coup. Violence ensued, unchecked and sometimes perpetuated by the Army, until much of Nairobi had been pillaged, the Asian minority suffering the worst. The economy suffered, and forthcoming foreign investments were frozen. In 1983 there was another alleged plot, blame being laid on Njonjo who was dismissed from parliament. On the international stage, this period saw a growth in Islamic and communist activity. Moi developed ties with US, granting facilities for the American Navy in exchange for grain.

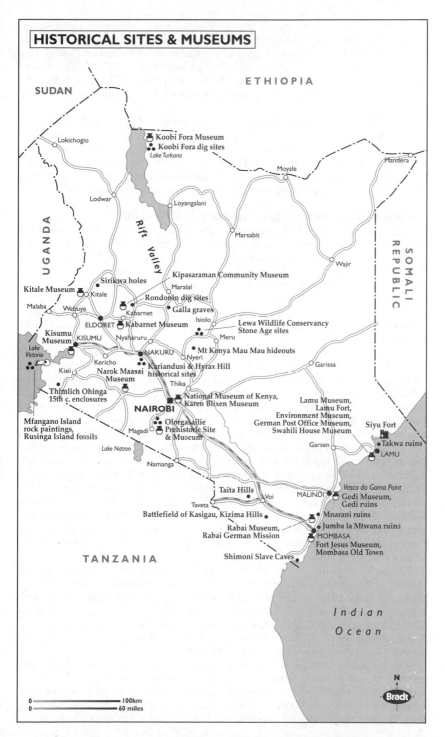

HISTORICAL SITES & MUSEUMS

SUDAN

ETHIOPIA

Lokichogio

Koobi Fora Museum
Koobi Fora dig sites
Lake Turkana

Moyale

Mandera

Lodwar

Loyangalani

UGANDA

Rift Valley

Marsabit

Wajir

SOMALI REPUBLIC

Kitale Museum
Sirikwa holes
Kipasaraman Community Museum
Maralal

Kitale

Malaba

Webuye

Rondonin dig sites

Kabarnet
Galla graves

ELDORET
Kabarnet Museum
Isiolo

Lewa Wildlife Conservancy
Stone Age sites

Kisumu Museum
KISUMU
Nyaharuru
Meru

Lake Victoria

Kericho
NAKURU
Nyeri
Mt Kenya Mau Mau hideouts

Kisii
Narok Maasai Museum
Kariandusi & Hyrax Hill historical sites

Garissa

Thimlich Ohinga
15th c. enclosures
Thika

Mfangano Island
rock paintings,
Rusinga Island fossils
National Museum of Kenya,
Karen Blixen Museum

Lamu Museum,
Lamu Fort,
Environment Museum,
German Post Office Museum,
Swahili House Museum

NAIROBI

Olorgasailie
Prehistoric Site
& Museum

Magadi

Siyu Fort

Takwa ruins

Lake Natron

Garsen

LAMU

Namanga

Taita Hills

Voi

MALINDI

Vasco da Gama Point
Gedi Museum,
Gedi ruins

Taveta

Battlefield of Kasigau, Kizima Hills

Rabai Museum,
Rabai German Mission

Mnarani ruins

Jumba la Mtwana ruins

MOMBASA
Fort Jesus Museum,
Mombasa Old Town

Shimoni Slave Caves

TANZANIA

Indian Ocean

N

Bradt

0 — 100km
0 — 60 miles

While its human rights record was atrocious, Kenya's policy on conservation became exemplary, largely due to the appointment of Richard Leakey, son of the palaeontologist, Louis Leakey, as head of the Kenya Wildlife Service (KWS). In a dramatic anti-poaching action he supervised President Moi's US$3 million ivory pyre, raising awareness about ivory poaching, generating millions of dollars for conservation and helping to bring about the CITES ban on the ivory trade (see page 47).

In 1987, Moi expanded his presidential powers with further amendments to the constitution. For example, he had the power to dismiss judges if he so wished. He became masterful at preventing ministers from gaining too much power by regularly swapping their portfolios. The ethnic clashes which started to take place (and which continued through the next decade), particularly when electioneering was in progress, reflected a shrewd tactician in the art of 'divide and rule'.

Kenya at the turn of the century (1990–2000)

Despite international pressure and some indications of change from effectively a one-party state, the political regime maintained its grip until the end of the 20th century. Murders and deaths in dubious circumstances continued and were often followed by protests and retaliatory police violence. Prominent political figures like Robert Ouko, the popular foreign minister or religious figures critical of the police or government such as Bishop Alexander Muge were among the victims. Even where evidence developed, the suspects responsible were sacked and often later reinstated. Media were suppressed and protest against the government was met by arrests and shootings.

An effective political opposition finally took shape in 1991 with the establishment of the Forum for the Restoration of Democracy (FORD) by Oginga Odinga, a veteran of post-colonial Kenya. Despite his opposition to Kenyatta's KANU and later Moi, Oginga Odinga, with the help of his son Raila Odinga, created a movement effective enough to worry Moi. The International Monetary Fund (IMF) threatened the suspension of international aid pending political and economic reform in the shape of multi-party democracy. Moi, finding himself cornered, responded by amending the constitution to legalise the election of other parties. The possibility of losing power rattled KANU, prompting some ministers to move to FORD or to set up independent parties. A split later emerged within FORD itself – those who believed in a non-tribal balance of power between all the ethnic groups supported FORD-Kenya with Odinga and those who preferred a Kikuyu-centred opposition followed FORD-Asili and Ronald Matiba, another former minister who had lost his seat in the 1987 election. Mwai Kibaki, the current president of Kenya, resigned his position in KANU and formed the Democratic Party (DP).

The build up to the December 1992 elections was violent. KANU, although accused of instigation, was not directly involved in the disruption caused by ethnic clashes between tribal groups in the Rift Valley and western Kenya. Pre-election activities were corrupt, with counterfeit money funding KANU, slow electoral administration in non-KANU areas and a last minute change of the electoral date, which resulted in many people being in a different polling region (and therefore denied a vote) due to the Christmas holiday period.

A democratic victory for KANU was sustained, but ironically Moi was put in a position of having to reinstate defeated cabinet ministers who had defected to different parties before the election. International aid was reinstated, but the scale of corruption had risen to dizzy heights with the revelation of the Goldenberg scandal. Between 1990 and the end of 1992, a paper company, Goldenberg

International, theoretically exported gold and diamonds from Kenya (only small amounts of gold and no diamonds are mined in Kenya). Claiming to have exported over US$75 million, the company was granted a 35% export bonus by the government, amounting to over US$26 million. The impact of this was disastrous, devaluing the Kenya shilling. In 1993 Richard Leakey (still head of KWS), was involved in a plane accident (although it might have been sabotage), in which he lost both legs and in 1994, as an incorruptible head of the KWS he fell out of favour with Moi and proffered his resignation.

After the election the opposition parties had gradually fallen into disarray. Leakey formed a political alliance in 1995 with a former FORD-Kenya leader Paul Muite, creating a party called Safina. In the run-up to the 1997 election, Leakey was publicly beaten at an election rally in Nakuru. Ethnic violence again surrounded the election, this time with brutal clashes at the coast, the Likoni Riots, which were beamed into living rooms worldwide, with a disastrous impact on tourism and coastal tourism in particular. Kenya's position on the world stage was tarnished and Moi widely perceived as a despot. Despite plenty of hostility towards Moi and his KANU government, the opposition was divided, possibly due to individual politicians all aspiring to be president. Some 26 parties stood for election, with the inevitable result that KANU was re-elected. With Kenya's fall from grace and increasing corruption, the international community pressurised Moi to clean up his act.

Moi invited Leakey to take the position of Head of the Public Service and Secretary to the Cabinet in 1999 – a cunning move to appease international donors. Kenya was then struck by drought and the deluge of El Niño rains in 1997 and 1998, which wrought havoc to the infrastructure: property and roads were damaged, bridges swept away and crops destroyed. While reeling in the aftermath, to compound matters, in August 1998 the US Embassy in Nairobi was bombed by terrorists linked to Osama Bin Laden's al-Qaeda network, killing some 250 people, mostly Kenyans, and wounding 5,000. On a more positive note, the East African Community between Kenya, Tanzania and Uganda was revived in 1999.

Victory to the people and Kenya today (2000–03)
The beginning of the 21st century saw Kenyan politics focusing on the December 2002 elections. The economy was severely debilitated, corruption was still rife (according to the watchdog, Transparency International, Kenya ranked 84th out of 91 countries on the corruption scale in 2001) and the majority of the population were oppressed due to political mismanagement. The question on everyone's mind was whether Moi would relinquish his hold on power and make way for new blood. True to form, Moi kept people guessing until the last few months before the elections. Younger politicians, like Uhuru Kenyatta, son of the first president, were coming into the limelight, and again questions were asked – would the new government favour the old guard or the 'young turks'? In a surprising choice which split the KANU party, Moi selected Uhuru Kenyatta as his successor. Kenyatta had the charisma, but had a limited political track record. The build up to the the election saw political manoeuvring on a grand scale. Lessons had been learned from the previous two elections, and there was a flurry of politicians switching parties and forging new alliances. Mwai Kibaki, leader of DP, the main opposition party, linked with FORD-Kenya, led by Kijana Wamalwa, and some 12 other parties to form the National Alliance Party. Defectors from KANU formed the Rainbow Alliance headed by Raila Odinga (son of Oginga Odinga), which included political

MWAI KIBAKI - KENYA'S THIRD PRESIDENT

Emili Mwai Kibaki, a Kikuyu, was born in 1931 and brought up on the slopes of Mount Kenya. An economist, he studied in Uganda and London before entering politics in 1960. Elected into parliament in 1963, he helped to draft Kenya's post-independence constitution. In the KANU party, under Kenya's first president, Jomo Kenyatta, he was minister of finance throughout the 1970s and served for most of the 1980s as vice-president under President Moi. When the ban on opposition parties was lifted in 1991, Kibaki left KANU to found the Democratic Party (DP). He stood against Moi in the 1992 and 1997 elections. A keen union with other political parties – firstly forming a National Alliance of 14 parties, which joined with the defective KANU ministers in the Rainbow Alliance to form the National Rainbow Coalition (NARC) – gave him the vote to oust the KANU party at his third attempt in the 2002 presidential election, when President Moi stood down. NARC won 125 out of the 240 parliamentary seats, with an additional seven MPs nominated by Kibaki, giving the government a majority of 132 seats against 90 seats in the opposition. Kibaki won a landslide victory, polling 3,646,713 votes (62%) against his closest rival, Uhuru Kenyatta, running for Moi's KANU party, who polled 1,834,468 (31%). A keen golfer with a fine sense of humour, Kibaki has a ministerial team with the ability to realise the full potential of Kenya's economy and to stem corruption.

heavyweights like Professor George Saitoti. The National Alliance and Rainbow Alliance then merged to form the National Rainbow Coalition (NARC) as the main opposition to KANU. In this amalgam of parties the ethnic race card was no longer an issue.

In the run up to the elections, tragedy was to strike again at the coast, with another al-Qaeda terrorist attack on November 28 2002, this time targeting Israeli tourists. A car bomb exploded in the reception of the Paradise Hotel north of Mombasa, killing Kenyans and Israelis, and an abortive missile attack was launched on an Israeli airliner leaving Moi International Airport. It was another major blow to tourism which was only just starting to recover in the aftermath of the September 11 2001 bombing in New York.

As election day drew closer, the country was overrun with election fever. International media, predicting chaos, were waiting in the wings ready to announce any civil unrest, which never happened. The election, held on December 29 2002, was conducted with dignity, NARC winning a landslide victory over KANU, Moi and Kenyatta gracefully conceding defeat. The people were euphoric. There was dancing in the streets and a new era in Kenyan politics dawned. The people had spoken with one voice: true Kenyan democracy, a long time in waiting, was established.

Mwai Kibaki was duly sworn in as president on election pledges to reform the constitution within 100 days, to provide free primary education and to stamp out corruption. The mantra had a ring of déjà vu and many are still sceptical as to whether NARC can deliver, citing that there are many old, familiar faces in the new regime: wolves in sheep's clothing, old wine in a new bottle. Despite being confined to a wheelchair after a road accident, 71-year-old Kibaki has set about his reform programme with vigour. First on the agenda was revitalising the economy and complying with IMF and World Bank requirements for donor funding. Since

NARC came to power, an anti-corruption commission has been established under John Githongo, a former executive director with Transparency International. Encouragingly, donor funding has been pledged for providing free primary education. Anti-corruption legislation was passed in April 2003 and the completion of constitutional reform scheduled for November 2003. Being a coalition of different political parties also brings its problems; the Liberal Democratic Party (LDP) under Raila Odinga has given disgruntled rumblings at as-yet-unfulfilled pre-election promises of more prominent involvement in NARC. However, so far these have been dismissed, and it's thought that Odinga is a likely candidate for prime minister, a new post proposed in the revised constitution. Inevitably, the people have given Kibaki a mantle of huge expectations. Having inherited a poisoned chalice, a legacy of mismanagement, it will take time for the new government to make good its election promises. Stamping out the corruption which permeated all levels of society, improving economic growth and providing new jobs are undoubtedly the key to its success.

ECONOMY
History

At independence in 1963, the British legacy to Kenya's economy was a good transport infrastructure and an economy founded on agriculture. The settlers who had been brought in to make the railway economical had, through trial and error, together with the investment of great personal fortunes, experimented with crop and livestock production in the tropics. Their efforts, combined with cheap labour, resulted in sound land management and a flourishing agricultural economy. The country was self-sufficient in food and the export of prime quality tea and coffee brought in substantial foreign exchange. Multinational companies like Brooke Bond were already well established. In addition, the colonial administration had been involved in teaching the small-scale Kenyan farmers the rudiments of soil conservation to combat erosion – such as contour ploughing and not planting next to water courses, to prevent the first deluge in the rains washing away topsoil into the rivers.

Although not endowed with a wealth of mineral resources, Kenya does have small-scale mining of gold and rubies. There is quarrying for soda ash at Lake Magadi, and fluorspar in the Kerio Valley together with limestone at Bamburi at the coast. A controversial project to mine titanium in Kwale on the south coast was stymied in 2003. Since independence several large hydro-power schemes have been built on the Tana River and the Turkwel Gorge, together with the development of geothermal power at Lake Naivasha.

Apart from mismanagement and corruption, the largest contributing factor to the lack of economic development since independence has been the 400% increase in population which has inevitably placed an enormous strain on resources.

The 21st century

Even now, Kenya's economy is dominated by exports of agricultural and horticultural products – primarily tea, coffee, cut flowers and vegetables, earning over 60% of foreign exchange and employing about 80% of the labour force – together with tourism. In 2000, tea earned US$463 million, horticulture US$270 million (of which US$110 million was for cut flowers, Kenya being the world's top exporter of roses), tourism US$250 million and coffee US$154 million. Oil exploration off the Kenya coast is due to start in 2004. The adverse effects of terrorism on the tourism industry caused by the Mombasa bomb in 2002 and the terrorist alert in 2003 are yet to be realised, but they have inevitably had a knock-on effect throughout the sector and service industries, where one tourist is thought to support around 30 jobs. The industrial sector of the economy is poorly developed and foreign exchange is primarily dependent on commodities and tourism, both of which are sensitive to fluctuations on the world market. GNP per capita is US$330 but income is poorly distributed: the top 10% earn 48% of the income (World Bank 1998). During 2002 GDP was static, forecast to grow by 1.8% in 2003 and 3% in 2004 (Economic Intelligence Unit 2003). Once donor confidence is restored, the Kenyan economy has the potential to grow sustainably. An economic growth rate of 5–7% is needed to impact on the country's poverty levels and to give an increase in per capita growth. A fairer distribution of wealth needs to be forthcoming. Since NARC came to power, Government ministers have awarded themselves a 26% pay increase (a move to curtail the incentive for corruption) but teachers, the health service and various sectors of the civil service and industry are demanding a substantial pay review.

Turning from the macro-economic factors, on a smaller scale, Kenya has an interesting informal sector within the economy, which shows a great deal of enterprise. Known as *Jua Kali*, which literally translates as 'hot sun', these are the traders which you see at the roadside, with small businesses such as welding, mechanics, woodwork or plant nurseries. Another versatile area is in self-help projects, often run by women's groups (perhaps with the support of an NGO). These might include knitting, crochet, rug-making and beadwork projects. The significant impact of these projects is that they are giving women an economic freedom and power which traditionally they did not have. The social impact of this can be considerable – for example, in one instance in a Maasai's women's group, one woman's husband wanted to marry off their teenage daughter. Funds from the women's group enabled the woman to act independently. She insisted that her daughter continued with her schooling and provided the funds to pay for the school fees.

Another factor which can impact on micro-economies is the environment – the costs of flood or drought. Unseasonally heavy rains in 2003 displaced a million people in the Lake Victoria region of western Kenya. Severe droughts, such as that experienced in northern Kenya in 2000, can attract famine relief. In this instance, well-intentioned food aid programmes provided maize which was distributed free or at low cost to famine-struck areas (although sometimes there's a fine line between a severe drought and famine). In areas with a marginal rainfall, free or cheap handouts of maize can have an adverse effect on the local economy in several ways. Local farmers have no incentive to grow maize, as the costs of production outweigh the market price, giving a reliance on food aid. Local people receiving handouts no longer have to sell a goat or two to raise the money to buy maize – so the goats breed causing further environmental damage to land which is already beyond its optimum carrying capacity for livestock, and local ranchers are deprived of an income from buying goats from the local people, to fatten on for market.

Tourism

In 1963, Kenya had a fledgling tourism industry which had evolved from the big-game hunting era in the first half of the 20th century. There were seven main game parks – Nairobi, the Aberdares, Mount Kenya, Meru, Tsavo East and West and Amboseli. It was the start of the photographic safari, so named because you went shooting with a camera, although hunting safaris continued until the hunting ban in 1977.

As with the phenomenal growth in tourism worldwide, tourism in Kenya developed exponentially, cashing in on the 1970s and 1980s boom in package and long-haul holidays catering for the mass market. Laissez-faire policies towards tourism development made Kenya a victim of its own success. Large lodges sprung up with little consideration for an area's carrying capacity for tourists, which resulted in overcrowding in the tourism 'hot spots', rampant off-road driving which gave the vegetation a hammering, and numerous vehicles in pursuit of the wildlife, especially predators where it was not unusual to see up to 50 minibuses around a single lion. This type of tourism was boom heading for bust. At the coast, large visitor numbers heralded beach vendors, opportunists in search of a slice of the tourism cake, who were perceived as a nuisance and the source of robberies. Come the early 1990s, the tourism industry was complacent and caught resting on its laurels as other southern African destinations like South Africa and Zimbabwe came on-stream post apartheid.

This heralded a new approach in the Kenyan tourism industry. Government policy turned on its head, seeking to attract the quality end of the tourism market as had been successfully achieved in Botswana. In 1994, visitor arrivals in Kenya were 863,000, a 4.5% increase on the previous year, but with a 17% increase in spending. A detailed market-research survey in 1994 undertaken by the Kenya Wildlife Service (under the director of that time, Dr David Western) revealed that 80% of visitors to Kenya came to see the wildlife – this was even the case for those on a beach holiday. Other attractions which they rated highly were the beautiful scenery, the friendliness of the people, the richness of the local culture, the climate and the high standard of food and accommodation.

Over the past decade, the Kenyan tourism industry has set out to capitalise on these attributes, particularly highlighting the country's diversity, with the marketing slogan 'All of Africa in one country'. New activities, adventure and special-interest holidays (see page 107) have been encouraged, aimed at dispersing tourists away from the 'hot spots'. New tourism circuits have been developed and a greater emphasis placed on ecotourism (see page 54). The majority of visitors to Kenya come from Europe (about 57%) of which about half are British, together with around 29% from Africa, 8% from America and 6% from the rest of the world.

Nevertheless, internal political unrest, with the Likoni Riots in Mombasa before the 1997 election, together with the El Niño floods in 1997–98, made a significant dent in tourist arrivals, the coast in particular being hit hard. In 2001 tourist arrivals were fewer than 500,000, almost half that of a decade before, which was also reflected in reduced tourism revenue. The terrorist attacks in 1998 and 2002, together with the high security alert given in 2003, only compounded the vulnerability of tourism to a worldwide phenomenon. It was a shattering blow to Kenya's tourism industry: in May 2003 it was estimated to be losing US$1 million a day. The NARC government and Kenya's tourism industry responded swiftly to the security alert (see page 157), although the UK government, responding to a direct threat to British Airways flights, implemented a flight ban for all UK airlines. Kenya Airways and other international carriers continued flying to Kenya, with 'business as usual'. Kenya has been selected as a key strategic regional partner in the National Security Strategy set up by the US to counter terrorist activity in Africa. Of the US$20 million earmarked, Kenya is expected to receive US$15 million, which will help to rebuild consumer confidence. It will take time to diminish the perception of Kenya as a high-risk area, but it's important to keep a sense of perspective on the matter, as the threat of international terrorism is not restricted to Kenya alone, but can equally apply to destinations worldwide. People are by nature resilient; no-one wishes to kowtow to terrorism, and it is forecast that tourism in Kenya will recover by 2004.

People and Culture

Kenya is a multicultural society, reflecting the patterns of human settlement since the origins of early man in the Cradle of Mankind. The earliest *Homo sapiens* were hunter-gatherer Khoisan peoples, akin to the Bushmen, today seen in remnant groups – the Ogiek, Dorobo and Boni. Waves of migrations followed – the Cushites from Ethiopia, Nilotics who travelled south from the Nile, and the Bantu who moved in from the south and west. (See box on the Rift Valley migrations, page 4.) The Cushitic-speaking peoples account for about 3% of the population. They include the Boran, Dassenich, el Molo, Orma, Rendille and Gabbra. Around 65% of the population is Bantu-speaking, among them the Kikuyu, Luhya, Embu, Gusii, Kamba, Taita and Pokomo. The Nilotic speakers account for around 30% which include the Luo, Kalenjin (comprising the Kipsigis, Nandi, Marakwet, Pokot, Tugen and Sabaot), Maasai, Samburu, Il Chamus and Turkana. They make up the 42 tribes found in Kenya (some sources cite over 70, but many of these are subtribes). From AD700 the Arabs plied their trade along the Kenyan coast, intermarrying with the local people to form the Swahili. European immigration started in the 15th century, with Portuguese settlement at the coast followed by a period of exploration in the 18th century culminating in the formation of the British East Africa Protectorate in 1894 (Kenya and Uganda) and superseded by a separate Kenya Colony in 1920. Europeans predominantly settled in the Central Highlands, known for a time as the White Highlands. Asians, initially brought in to work on the railway, settled in the main business centres – Mombasa, Nairobi, Nakuru, Eldoret and Kisumu. After independence in 1963 further nationalities were drawn to Kenya, working in the diplomatic or aid sectors, and at certain periods refugees have filtered into the country from Uganda (during the Idi Amin era) and in more recent years from the strife-riven regimes of Sudan and Somalia.

LANGUAGE
English is the official and Kiswahili (often shortened to Swahili) the national language. In addition numerous tribal languages are spoken. A pure form of Kiswahili is dominant at the coast, while inland it's a *lingua franca*. English is spoken in the main urban areas, but spasmodic elsewhere. It's not unusual for Kenyans to speak several languages – English and Kiswahili, together with a couple of tribal languages, and at the coast many have a good grasp of German, Italian and French. (See page 459 for further details on speaking Swahili.)

POPULATION
Kenya's population has increased dramatically since the early 1960s, when it stood at 8.2 million, and the population growth rate is only now beginning to bottom out. In 2001 the population was 3.7 million with a 2% growth rate. The annual forecast growth rate of 1.3% reflects the expected increased death rate due to AIDS. Over two million Kenyans are infected with the HIV virus. Forty-two per cent of the

population is under 15. Most people live in the high rainfall, arable areas of the Central Highlands and western Kenya. In the north and east, 20% of the population lives on 80% of the land. Of the ethnic mix around 22% are Kikuyu, 14% Luhya, 13% Luo, 12% Kalenjin, 11% Kamba, 6% Gusii, 6% Meru and 15% other Africans, while Asians, Europeans and Arabs account for about 1% of the population.

EDUCATION

Kenya has a literacy level of 83% for those over 15, considerably higher than in neighbouring countries. The National Rainbow Coalition government is committed to providing free primary education; fees must be paid for secondary and tertiary education. There are universities in Nairobi, Njoro and Eldoret. Education is seen as a passport to a better future, and it's not uncommon to be approached by children with sponsorship forms seeking funding for their education.

RELIGION

The majority of Kenyans, about 66%, are Christians and there are numerous different sects, many with a distinctly African flavour. It's a reflection of a strong missionary heritage. Church-building appears to be a national pastime and church services a popular Sunday occupation. Other religions are Islam, both Sunni and Sh'ia (Ismaili being practised by the followers of the Aga Khan who has supported many worthwhile projects within the country), Hinduism and Sikhism, together with a smattering of traditional and animist beliefs.

INTERACTING WITH LOCAL PEOPLE

The Kenyans stand out for their genuine friendliness, helpfulness, humour and easy-going nature, which is a pleasure when travelling around the country. Attempts to speak Swahili, or even one of the tribal languages, is appreciated by

TEACHING IN KENYA
Philippa D'Arcy Ryan

'Why Kenya?' friends and family asked. Volunteer teaching in Zimbabwe post university was my first step into Africa and initiated the desire to return to teach once qualified and experienced. After two years of teaching in England, I chose to apply for jobs in Kenya, inspired by a few books I had read, and stories heard. I was attracted to Greensteds School, a private boarding school near Nakuru for many reasons, but particularly its location 'overlooking the Rift Valley'.

Adapting to school life was relatively easy, once I was used to the slower pace of life. The primary school children were enthusiastic, motivated and great fun. My memories include running between classrooms in downpours of afternoon rain or stopping the lessons as we listened in awe as the rain beat down on the tin roof; living by candlelight during frequent power cuts and the excitement of receiving 'post' in the late afternoon. Then there was Friday morning flag-raising assembly, followed by a quick change for whole-school cross-country running – teachers too!

We made links with the Nakuru Street Children's Refuge Centre. Any visit for necessities into Nakuru would involve contact with boys living on the street: faces pressed against car windows; requests; begging and glue sniffing, I would often feel so helpless as I witnessed aspects of their lives. It was encouraging to find out about this centre and to know that there are several projects organised

those who speak little English. It might seem an obvious thing to say, but common courtesy will stand you in good stead wherever you go. When meeting tribal peoples and visiting their homesteads, take your lead from them – for example, wait to be invited into their hut rather than barging in. Take a little time to introduce yourself and ask people's names – it makes for a rewarding cultural exchange, as they are as fascinated by our culture as we are with theirs. The same goes for taking photographs – ask for permission first. If you have a digital camera, showing your models their photographs causes much hilarity, and breaks down cultural barriers. If on a village visit, it helps the women and the local community if you buy their trinkets which they make especially for tourists, rather than buying from one of the large curio stalls where the middle man makes the money. You may also be offered artefacts of a cultural significance. Think twice about the ethics of purchasing these. In many parts of the country you will come across extreme poverty – from beggars in the street to schools where children still write on slates and the entire class shares a text book. If you want to help, the *worst* thing you can do is to give children money, pens or sweets. This just encourages a begging mentality, which is degrading to their culture. There are numerous organisations and charities in the country which help. A donation to one of them (or to individual schools) is far more apt; several are listed within the guide.

CULTURAL DOS AND DON'TS

At the coast, there is a Muslim culture, but a dress code is not vigorously endorsed, tourists having been part of the beach scene for so many years. Nevertheless, topless sunbathing is illegal in Kenya. If visiting Mombasa, Malindi and Lamu, it is befitting to cover up – skimpy shorts and vests are offensive – a shirt with sleeves and a wraparound *kanga* or *kikoi* will suffice.

in Nakuru to assist the children (see box on SCANN, page 290). I have vivid memories of 60 boys lined up in foot size order to estimate how many pairs of flip-flops we needed to buy of each size! They were as excited about the plastic wrapping as they were about the shoes.

Living on campus and mixing with other British and Kenyan teachers provided a good base for friendships and travels. There was always the need to be well prepared for any journey. Fortunately I had only good experiences, including being helped out one night when my car broke down in a fairly desolate spot. Out of the darkness we saw glimmering torches as people came towards the car and offered to help. While two men stayed with the car, another walked with us up the road until we came to a hotel where we could make a telephone call. Nearly two years later a man knocked on my door. 'Do you remember me? I helped you with your car.' He was trying to get a job as a chef at our school and wanted me to recommend him to the head of school. It was a great lesson in how one favour deserves another.

I left Kenya with a new sense of 'home' and some firm friendships, knowing that I had just scraped the surface of a country but feeling a sense of belonging that no time could take away.

To teach in Kenya, look for advertised positions in the Overseas Section of 'The Times Educational Supplement'. To apply for volunteer work contact organisations such as Skillshare International, www.skillshare.org.uk.

SPONSORING A CHILD IN KENYA
Ben West
Sponsoring a child in Kenya has for me been an especially rewarding way of
gaining an insight into the country and helping a poor community in Kisumu.

For about seven years my family have been paying £15 a month to sponsor
a boy, Dawo, through the relief and development agency, World Vision.
Sponsorship pays his school and medical expenses and helps his family and the
community at large with health care and schemes to assist destitute families in
moving towards self-reliance through income-generating projects. Occasionally
we receive letters from Dawo, and it is wonderful to see how he is progressing.
For my children, sponsorship has made it far easier to relate to this distant land.

Several years ago I asked World Vision whether I could visit Dawo's
community, to see where my money was going. They couldn't have been more
helpful. Their staff met me at Kisumu airport and drove me to his home. When
we arrived we were surrounded by a choir of children, all obviously dressed in
their very best clothes. 'Praise God, Hallelujah, I love this earth,' they sang in
perfect harmony, dancing with precision. After a couple of minutes the tempo
altered. The lyrics changed to variants of 'Mr Ben West from London, you are
most welcome on this happy day.' What had I done to deserve this
overwhelming reception? Donated a vital organ? Pledged eternally my life and
possessions to the impoverished of Kenya? Frankly, I felt embarrassed by such
kindness.

I instantly recognised Dawo from the photograph I'd been given by World
Vision. Dawo's mother led us to her house with a small bedroom, living-room
and bare kitchen. Dawo and his two brothers sat next to me. I asked his mother
her age. 'I am very old,' she said solemnly. 'I'm 38.' Well, I suppose that is
elderly in a continent where life expectancy lies most commonly in the 40s and

TRIBES

Many individual tribal members are highly educated and occupy positions of
authority in government and the professions. This section aims to give a brief
synopsis of some of the main tribal groups and their traditons which you may
encounter while travelling around the country. Among Kenya's diverse tribal mix,
some, like the Maasai, Samburu and Pokot, still retain a strong traditional culture,
whereas others like the Kikuyu have assimilated into a more Western lifestyle.

South and eastern Kenya
Kamba (Akamba)
Kenya's fourth-largest ethnic group, the Kamba comprise around 2.5 million
people, with subgroups including the Kitui, Masaku and Mumoni. A hunting
people, from the Tsavo area, famine and drought forced the Kamba to migrate
north to the east of Nairobi, where they settled as farmers. Many fought (and died)
for the British colonial forces in World War I.

Traditionally, the Kamba had a high level of organisation, structured by rituals
such as the initiation rite to adulthood at the age of 12. They have a specific elder
system. Young parents are known as junior elders with responsibility for the
upkeep of the village. When children are old enough to become junior elders, a
ceremony marks their parents' transition to medium elders. In time they become
full elders, with responsibility for death ceremonies and law administration, before

50s. She said that sponsorship had improved their outlook considerably. One of the World Vision staff explained the health risks Dawo's compound faced. Possibly two of the 40 occupants would die during the year from typhoid alone. There's also dysentery and cholera to contend with. Malaria is also a particular problem. Treatment costs around US$65, far more than the average Kenyan can afford.

The children of the compound enacted a couple of hilarious plays they'd concocted, and several recited poems. I was struck by their impressive performing skills and ingenuity.

We returned to Dawo's house for lunch, a huge spread that would have severely dented his mother's resources. There was chicken, beef, rice, salad, chapati and the omnipresent *ugali* to soak it all up. Dawo eagerly stuffed the food into his mouth with both hands.

There was time to see Dawo's school and give presents before we left. I'd been able to dispel any suspicions I may have had that my money was being squandered. I could find no fault in World Vision's work. I had met the chief recipients of my donations and seen for myself that such gestures transformed these people's lives far more than I could have imagined back in Britain.

As we drove away, Dawo stood there, clutching his new football, as his friends laughed and waved, singing 'Farewell, fare thee well'. After this brief excursion, for me many times more memorable than a two-day game safari to the Masai Mara, I was on my way back to the grey skies of Gatwick.

Charities sponsoring children in Kenya include:
Plan International web: www.plan-international.org
Action Aid web: www.actionaid.org
World Vision International web: www.wvi.org

graduating to senior elders with a responsibility for holy places. The Kamba traded extensively with their neighbours, the Kikuyu, Embu and Mijikenda, and as far afield as the coast, Lake Victoria and Lake Turkana. Traditionally they bartered ivory, beer, honey and iron weapons. Skilled in pottery, metalwork and basketry, today they are especially renowned for their exquisite carvings and beautiful inlaid woodwork, selling to the domestic and export markets.

Taita
Numbering around 218,000, this Bantu group lives in the fertile Taita hills and Taveta district. Divided into seven clans, they are farmers with a strong spiritual connection with the land. Sacrifices and supplications are performed to collections of skulls, symbolising ancestral spirits, in order to improve cultivation. Traditionally the crops grown by the Taita were millet, beans, cassava, sweet potato and sugarcane, with the help of irrigation. Nowadays these are augmented with cash crops, including bananas, mangoes and coffee, which are sold at markets in Mombasa and along the coast. The Taita are also dextrous in leatherwork, metalwork and basketry.

Central Highlands
Kikuyu
The largest of Kenya's tribes, the Kikuyu, a Bantu group, live in the area around Mount Kenya, extending southwest from Nyeri to Muranga and Kiambu. They are thought to have migrated to this area in the 16th century from Meru. Here they were

THE GREEDY HYENA – A KIKUYU FOLK TALE

as told by Beatrice Mungai and translated by George Ngure and Francis Mungai

Once, in a beautiful well-blossomed wood, there lived a greedy hyena. He was a glutton and ate everything in sight, from left-overs to carcasses. He would also steal goats from an old, hard-working man who lived nearby. In these woods there also lived a cunning, sly and tricky hare.

One day, as the hyena was walking along admiring the scenery, he met his friend, the hare, who said, 'You have been a good friend since childhood. I want you to come to my wedding feast. I want you to be my best man.' The hyena accepted gladly. The wedding was to be held at the hare's home. They separated, and when hyena arrived home he was overjoyed. His wife asked him what was happening, and he told her the good news. Then he started getting ready for the feast. His wife washed his best suit, and when it was dry, it was ironed and looked very smart.

When the day of the wedding arrived, the hyena carried a sack full of carrots for the hare. He started on his long journey to the hare's home. While still on the way, he realised he had forgotten his gift and wondered what to do. He put down the carrots and dashed back like a hare to his house. It was already nine o'clock. He took his gift and ran out of the house, his wife shouting at him that he was very lazy. He ran and ran until he could run no more. When he reached the clearing where he had left the sack of carrots, he found that it had gone. He became crazy, and started searching high and low, but could not find the precious sack. He decided to continue with his long journey and started to run again.

Suddenly he arrived at a forked path. He wondered which way to go. Then he remembered the path to the right led to the old man's home, and the left to the hare's house. He could smell goats and fat being roasted. The smell was delicious and appeared to come from both directions. It seemed the old man was having a party too. He decided that if he wanted to eat both these mouth-watering delicacies, he must go to both homes. But he wondered how …

The greedy hyena figured out a way. He stretched his right foot on to the path leading to the right, and his left foot on to the path leading to the left, and started walking. He had not even taken three footsteps when he felt pain. His legs broke and he died on the spot. Since he wanted to eat at both parties, he lost. As the old wise man said, 'Greediness leads to destruction.'

Francis Mungai is a freelance Nairobi guide and can be contacted on mobile: 0722 815226.

surrounded by Maasai pastoral lands, which resulted in conflicts and border raids but also intermarriage. Their relationship with European settlers was more strained, as large tracts of Kikuyu homeland were apportioned to white settlers in the early 20th century under the British colonial regime. Highly organised, the Kikuyu responded by forming a political association, and subsequently instigated the Mau Mau uprisings in the 1950s (see page 11). Agriculturalists by tradition, today they combine small-scale farming, keeping livestock and growing food crops like millet and bananas, supplemented by cash crops like coffee and pyrethrum. The tribal organisation of the Kikuyu clan, *Mwaki*, placed great importance on the council of elders, the witchdoctor, medicine man and blacksmith. Initiation rites were an important part of life and although clitoridectomy for girls is now rarely practised, it's normal for boys to be circumcised during elaborate rituals. Each age group belongs to a specific age-set, known as *riika*. Kikuyu houses usually have the door facing Mount Kenya. This is based on the legend that their deity, *Ngai*, was believed to live on the mountain. The Kikuyu have played a dominant role in Kenya's politics and commerce, their most famous politician being Kenya's first president, Jomo Kenyatta.

Meru

The Meru number around 1.8 million, derived from eight Bantu groups, and live on the northeastern slopes of Mount Kenya to which they migrated from the coast in the 14th century. They are mainly farmers cultivating the rich volcanic soils to grow coffee, pyrethrum, maize and potatoes. Cotton, tobacco and miraa are grown on the lower slopes. The Meru administered tribal justice through a system of elders, *njuuri*, the witchdoctor and chief, *mogwe*. One of their traditions was to bless a new-born child by spitting on it while holding it to face Mount Kenya.

Western Kenya
Maasai

The most famous of Kenya's tribal groups, with a formidable reputation as warriors and a glamorous appearance, with their red *shukas* and ornate beadwork, the Nilotic Maasai number around 380,000, most living in the Narok and Kajiado regions of western and southern Kenya, although a few clans are still to be found on the Laikipia Plateau. They comprise an association of subtribes (each has its own territory, dialect and customs), which are bound by the Maa language, their belief in a supreme deity, *Enkai*, an almost religious passion for their cattle (which are central to their folklore) and the clan system. Traditional pastoralists, they are thought to have arrived in northern Kenya around the 15th century. Conquering other tribes, they continued south and by the end of the 19th century their territory extended from northern Kenya through the Rift Valley into Tanzania. During the colonial regime land was taken from Laikipia and the Rift Valley for European settlement, and subsequently by other African agriculturalists. They still retain a strongly structured age-set system. Men pass through seven life stages, the most significant being the transition from boys to warriors, marked by circumcision, and from warriors to elderhood in the colourful *eunoto* ceremony held every seven to ten years, after which they are permitted to marry and practise polygamy. When initiated into warriorhood, *il murran*, the boys leave their home village, *enkang*, to live in a *manyatta* built for them by women relatives. At this stage, the warriors sport ostrich feather headdresses and carry spears. Traditionally they would protect their herds from stock-raiding forays, and undertake a few themselves. It was also traditional practice for them to prove their prowess by killing a lion. At puberty, the girls undergo clitoridectomy. Items of beadwork jewellery worn by women also have a cultural significance. The women were responsible for building houses, low, rectangular huts made from saplings plastered in mud and dung and surrounded by a thorn enclosure. A proud people, the Maasai have clung fiercely to their traditions, but their lifestyle is now in a process of transition under the influences of education, commerce, changes in land tenure and diminished pastures.

Luo

The largest of Kenya's Nilotic groups, numbering around 2.7 million, the Luo live in the Nyanza area around Lake Victoria, having migrated from southern Sudan about 500 years ago. Their traditional livelihood of cattle farming was seriously curtailed by an outbreak of rinderpest in the 1890s which forced them into fishing and subsistence farming. Traditionally, the Luo homestead is enclosed by a fence and includes separate huts for each wife and son. The tribe consists of family groups, *dhoot*, which in turn make up an extended family, *ogandi*, led by a chief, *ruoth*. The medicine man and the spirits of the ancestors were highly regarded. Circumcision is no longer practised but was replaced by a practice of extracting four or six teeth from the lower jaw. Today, this is only evident in the older generation. Prominent in the struggle for independence, famous Luo politicians included Tom Mboya, a trade unionist and politician assassinated in 1969, and Oginga Odinga, a former vice-president. The arts, festivals, music and soccer are popular recreational activities.

Luhya

The third-largest ethnic group after the Kikuyu and the Luo, the Luhya comprise 17 different Bantu groups. Agriculturalists, they occupy a relatively small area in western Kenya and have one of rural Africa's highest population densities, with around 700 people per square kilometre. Traditionally the Luhya were renowned for their metalwork, forging knives, hoes and other products which were bartered for goods, together with pottery and basketry. Today, maize, cotton and sugarcane are their most common cash crops. Many are still superstitious and retain a strong belief in witchcraft. Today, as with their neighbours the Luo, popular pastimes include music and soccer.

Kipsigis

Numbering around 2.9 million, the Kipsigis are the largest tribe within the Kalenjin group and live in the Kericho area of western Kenya. Previously known as the Lumbwa, traditionally they were cattle herders and would often launch cattle raids against their neighbours, the Abagusii, Luo and Maasai. Cattle rustling is not unknown today. Living in smallholdings, they supplement their income by growing vegetables such as potatoes, maize, cabbage, tomatoes, onions, peas, bananas and sweet potatoes. Superb runners, many of Kenya's star athletes are Kipsigis.

Nandi

The second-largest tribe within the Kalenjin group, the Nandi migrated to the Nandi Hills from Mount Elgon in the 16th and 17th centuries. Formidable warriors, employing similar tactics to those of the Zulu in South Africa, they played havoc during the building of the Ugandan railway, which only stopped when their leader, Chief Koitalel, was killed. They favoured the copper telegraph wire running along the track, cutting communications to use the wire for making bracelets, armlets and necklaces. Traditionally agriculturalists, nowadays they also grow cash crops such as tea and pyrethrum.

Pokot (Suk)

The Pokot number around 400,000 living in land stretching from Samburu in the east, across the Rift Valley floor to the northern edge of the Cherangani Hills and their western outlies, the Sekerr Massif, down to the plains of eastern Uganda. Their strong tribal identity is moulded by an intricate language and religious belief, compounded by a response to their unfortunate history over the last 200 years. Pressurised by the Turkana and Maasai they also lost grazing lands to white settlers under the colonial regime. Their traditional society was marked by the absence of a central authority, communities being organised on a micro-scale around local assemblies of elders (as custodians of laws, ritual and mystical powers), age-sets and clans. Traditional Pokot dress is more apparent among the pastoralists where women may sometimes be seen dressed in hides, wearing broad, beaded necklaces, brass bracelets, ear hoops and lip plugs, while the men adorn their hair with mudcaps and feathers and take snuff. After circumcision, young girls, paint their faces with white clay and carry long sticks, a sign of their new status. After a healing period, they wash their faces and are ready to marry. The ecological variety of present-day Pokot territory is reflected in an economic dichotomy between hill cultivators and lowland pastoralists. The hill Pokot sell bananas, mangoes, sugarcane and citrus, grown on irrigated plots, at the Lamut market and also supplement their income with goldpanning.

Marakwet

The Marakwet are a union of five Kalenjin groups who settled about 1,000 years ago along and above the Elgeyo escarpment, from the indigenous forest of the Cheranganis to the semi-arid plains of the Kerio Valley. Traditionally they lived in villages of stone-built huts which appeared to rise in neat terraces. Their dry-stone building is unique in Kenya. Over the past 60 years they have expanded their territory into the high forests, once the preserve of Ogiek hunter-gatherers.

Skilful farmers, they use a centuries-old system of irrigation channels, diverting water from Cherangani streams into a network of furrows winding down the escarpment, watering lush gardens growing bananas, mangoes, sugar cane and citrus at the base of the scarp. The network of channels is most dense north of the Arror River where about 50 furrows have a total length of about 200km. Building, maintaining and administering this irrigation network involved a thorough understanding of engineering techniques, together with a sophisticated level of social co-operation. The Marakwet, like other Kalenjin communities, had no centralised hierarchy of authority, and decision-making was the prerogative of councils of elders. By-laws for the distribution of water, labour organisation and complex variations in irrigation regulation – individual furrows may be owned by a single clan or many – involved communal decisions from age-sets, clans and territorial units.

Gusii

Numbering around 1.3 million, the Gusii are the sixth-largest Bantu group in Kenya. Successive immigration by the Luo during the 19th century forced the Gusii to migrate east to the Kisii Highlands east of Lake Victoria. Small-scale farmers with thatched homesteads, they grow bananas, millet (sometimes brewed into beer) and maize, as well as keeping a few cattle. Traditionally, initiation ceremonies were held for boys and girls. Rituals were important as the Gusii believed that death was caused by witchcraft. The medicine men, *abanyamorigo*, were highly regarded for enhancing both physical and mental health. They performed a crude hole-in-the-head brain surgery (trepanning) over the centuries, using basic implements to remove parts of the skull or spine to cure concussion and backache. Many of the Gusii are talented sculptors, working the pink soapstone from the local Tabacca quarries into attractive ornaments which can be bought in Kenya's main towns.

Il Chamus (Njemps)

A small, Nilotic group, numbering around 16,000, the Il Chamus are Maa speakers and closely related to the Samburu and Maasai. They live around Lake Baringo combining farming with fishing, grazing their cattle along the foreshore. They have small rafts, made from tambach saplings bound together, which are used for fishing and transportation across the lake. Ceremonial dance is an important tradition, used for the coming of the rains and for celebrating the different stages of life – the birth of a baby, circumcision, and on reaching a new age-grade.

Northern Kenya
Samburu
A Nilotic people, the Samburu are Maa speakers and closely related to the Maasai. They are believed to have migrated into their present area of Maralal and northern Kenya between Lake Turkana and the Ewaso Ng'iro River several centuries ago. Their name is thought to derive from the Maa word *samburimbur* which means 'butterfly'. It's an apt description, as both the men and women are remarkably glamorous with their beadwork and brass jewellery. The young warriors, *il murran*, have ornate hairdos, with ochre dreadlocks, often decorated with a red plastic rose and filigree butterfly. Like the Maasai, the Samburu have a marked age-set system and both men and women are circumcised. Nomadic pastoralists with cattle, sheep and goats, they live in traditional villages, *enkang*, moving to new pastures with the seasons. Their huts are made from saplings, mud and dung, located within a compound surrounded by thornbush fences where they keep their livestock at night. Nowadays, many settlements are more permanent.

Turkana
Numbering around 284,000, the Nilotic Turkana are camel and cattle herders, living in the arid area of northwestern Kenya between Lake Turkana and the Ugandan border, on the western shore of Turkana, catching fish to supplement their income. Similar to the Maasai and Samburu, traditionally they survived on a diet of blood and milk from their livestock. Retaining a strong traditional identity and attire, both men and women have a wooden plug through their lower lip, and wear ornate beadwork and metal ornaments, which often have a symbolic significance. The men plaster their hair with mud which is then painted blue and decorated with an ostrich feather. Tattoos are indicative of warrior prowess. For example, a tattoo on a man's right shoulder denotes he has killed a man, while if it's on his left shoulder, he's killed a woman.

El Molo
Kenya's smallest tribe, living on the southeastern shore of Lake Turkana at Loyangalani, there are few, if any, true el Molo, as they've now been assimilated into other tribes. A Cushitic group, they have strong historical links with the neighbouring Rendille, both worshiping the same god, *Wak*. Whereas the Rendille are nomadic pastoralists, the el Molo adapted their lifestyle to changing circumstances and turned to subsistence fishing from doum palm rafts, fish being their staple food, occasionally supplemented by crocodile, turtle and hippo meat. Their traditional twigloo shelters (domed huts made from sticks and grass) have largely been replaced by larger and more permanent dwellings.

The coast
Mijikenda
The Mijikenda, often referred to as the *Nyika*, consist of around one million people of Bantu origin with nine subgroups – the Giriama, Digo, Duruma, Chonyi, Jibana, Ribe, Kambe, Rabai and Kauma. Their oral history states that they were driven south and east by the invading Oromo during the late 16th and early 17th centuries, forcing them to take refuge in fortified hilltop villages. Being on the main Arab trade routes, they became astute traders, and some gradually moved back to the coast. Today, many provide fruit and vegetables for the tourist hotels in Mombasa. Giriama

villages, with square houses made from mud and rock on a mangrove pole frame, with a palm thatch, may be seen among coconut plantations along the coast road.

THE ARTS

Kenyans abound with artistic talent, from traditional and contemporary arts and crafts to the performance arts.

Arts and crafts

When travelling around, you will come across a variety of arts and crafts, many reflecting regional traditions and designs. Reference is made to these in the regional chapters. The **beadwork jewellery** of the Maasai is particularly popular, with traditional and, increasingly, a modern range of designs geared to the tourist market. It is interesting to observe the different types of tribal beadwork – for example Maasai and Samburu beadwork differs significantly from that of the Pokot or Turkana. Exquisite beadwork applies not only to jewellery, but also to belts, sandals and keyrings. Intricate **basketry** also shows regional variations, and traditional styles, from the *kiondo* sisal baskets of the Kikuyu to the flat woven baskets of the Turkana. The Kamba specialise in **wooden carvings** – people, animals, bowls, spoons and napkin rings – while the **soapstone carvers** of Kisii produce fine ornaments, some plain and others with etched designs in pinks and purples, ranging from 'snakes in a box' to chess sets, plates and ashtrays. **Other crafts** you might come across are banana fibre pictures, batiks, metalwork, malachite ornaments, jewellery, and wire toys – push-along flying ducks or motorbikes, which are readily available from curio stalls, markets and street vendors.

Contemporary art

There is an excellent selection of contemporary art in Kenya, with a number of specialist galleries listed in the regional chapters. Further details are also given in *Chapter 6*, page 107.

NATIONAL ANTHEM

Kiswahili	English
Ee Mungu nguvu yetu	O God of all creation
Ilete baraka kwetu	Bless this our land and nation
Haki iwe ngao na mlinzi	Justice be our shield and defender
Natukae na undugu	May we dwell in unity
Amani na uhuru	Peace and liberty
Raha tupate na ustawi.	Plenty be found within our borders.
Amkeni ndugu zetu	Let one and all arise
Tufanye sote bidii	With hearts both strong and true
Nasi tujitoe kwa nguvu	Service be our earnest endeavour
Nchi yetu ya Kenya	And our homeland of Kenya
Tunayoipenda	Heritage of splendour
Tuwe tayari kuilinda	Firm may we stand to defend.
Natujenge taifa letu	Let all with one accord
Ee, ndio wajibu wetu	In common bond united
Kenya istahili heshima	Build this our nation together
Tuungane mikono	And the glory of Kenya
Pamoja kazini	The fruit of our labour
Kila siku tuwe na shukrani	Fill every heart with thanksgiving.

KENYAN WRITERS
Binyavanga Wainaina

There has been an upsurge in literary activity in Kenya over the past few years. Since 1990, Kenyans have been in a heady mood, as we demanded a government that reflects our aspirations. Since independence, government in Kenya has been about Super leaders telling Kenyans what to do. One of the effects of the movement for democratic change has been the increased interest in local, popular culture. Previously, Kenyans were more interested in Congolese and American music. Now, most popular cultural icons are local. Some books to look out for are Margaret Ogolla's epic novel, *The River and the Source*, and Peter Kimani's *Before The Rooster Crows*.

In 2002, a gardener in Nairobi, Stanley Gazemba, released a novel, *The Stone Hills of Maragoli*, which broke new ground for Kenyan writers. The book was based in a small, feudal village, set in a large tea plantation. Most Kenyan novels have started in a rural area and ended in an urban one. This is the Kenyan middle-class experience. Over the past 50 years or so, educated Kenyans, born in villages in rural locations, have made their living in the towns and cities of this country.

Although the local music industry is experiencing a sales boom, the Kenyan publishing industry has been hesitant to invest in fiction, believing that Kenyans do not read enough for fiction to be economically viable. There is a movement of younger writers who believe that this is not true; that Kenyan fiction has not been made attractive to Kenyans. Many novels have been published with the idea in mind that they will become school set-books. Most do not reflect issues and trends that a new generation of readers are interested in. This coalition of writers has come together to publish their own work in a journal, *kwani?*, which has uncovered some astonishing new talents: Andia Kisia, Muthoni Garland and Yvonne Adhiambo Owuor, to name a few.

After independence, much was being written and read in Kenya. Ngugi wa Thiong'o's early novels, *A Grain of Wheat* and *The River Between*, were widely read. In the seventies, popular books like *Down River Road* by Meja Mwangi were published. *My Life in Crime*, by John Kiriamiti, is probably Kenya's most widely read and purchased work of fiction. Loosely based on the life of the writer, it has become a cult classic. Grace Ogot and Marjorie Oludhe Macgoye have also contributed significantly to Kenya's literary body of work, Macgoye as a novelist and poet, and Ogot as a short story writer.

Ngugi wa Thiong'o is Kenya's best known writer. He has been based in the US for many years. In Kenya, his novels *A Grain of Wheat*, *Petals of Blood* and *The River Between*, *Matigari* and others have influenced much of Kenyans' literary and political debates. *Decolonising the Mind*, a non-fiction book suggests that African writing needs to shed its colonial aspirations. Ngugi has been instrumental in campaigning for political change in Kenya. He has become a larger-than-life figure in Kenyan literary circles.

Binyavana Wainaina won the Caine Prize for African literature 2002 for his short story, 'Discovering Home'. He is also a founding editor of kwani? (www.kwani.org) and his novel 'Flights of My Fancy' was published in 2003.

Previous page Samburu *muran*, Laikipia (CF)

Above Mount Kenya as seen from Mountain Lodge (AZ)

Below Mount Kasigau from Rukinga Wildlife Sanctuary, southern Kenya (CF)

viper found in Kakamega Forest and on Mount Elgon. The **traditional Luo homestead** contains a number of low-lying conical thatched huts which you can enter, while a guide will explain the intricacies of Luo village life. The **aquarium** contains different freshwater fish from Lake Victoria, but is rather disappointing. Equally so are the putrid **crocodile ponds**. Within the museum compound are a number of labelled **indigenous trees**.
Open daily 08.30–18.00; entry from KSh200

Kisumu Innovation Centre
KICK House, Ramogi Rise Road, (Opposite Winam Court), PO Box 284, Kisumu; tel: 057 22498, mobile: 0722 989309; email: kick@swiftkisumu.com
This is a project promoting the work of street children, selling furniture, metalwork and paper products made from water hyacinth. It's well worth a visit.
Open daily 09.00–17.00

Kisumu Impala Sanctuary
On the road to Hippo Point, this small sanctuary was established by Kenya Wildlife Service to protect the impala antelope found around Kisumu. It is more akin to a city park, being well-used by local people who come to walk and to see the problem animals which have been captured – for most this is their only opportunity to see these wild animals. Although the leopard, hyena, baboons and monkeys are well looked after, their cages can only be described as thoroughly depressing.
Open 06.00–18.00; entry US$5.

Hippo Point and Dunga Village
At Hippo Point, about 3km out of town, you can see hippos and it's a good spot for watching sunsets. If you're interested in exploring the lakeshore, trips can be negotiated with the fishermen here, or at Dunga 2km further on. Dunga is the best place to see the traditional *sese* canoes being made, which are used to operate a local passenger service on the lake, as well as for fishing. They are painted in gaudy colours, often depicting a favourite football team. Long and narrow, the boats are about 8m long, with a large outboard engine. They are known locally as *yie*, while those with sails are known as *yie nanga*.

Kisumu Bird Sanctuary
About 8km south of Kisumu, 3km off the A1 on the road to Ahero, is the Kisumu Bird Sanctuary, an important wetland area containing the breeding grounds for various species of stork, ibis, heron and egret. In the marshland vegetation – papyrus and reedbeds – you may also spot white-winged warblers and Carruther's cisticola. Unless you are an avid birdwatcher, there's little else to draw you here.

Bondo
This small town lies about 60km west from Kisumu on the C27 road to **Usengi**, on the northern side of the lake. Formerly an administrative outpost during the colonial era, the land round about is densely populated. Its main draw is the **Migwena festival** (see page 134) which takes place at the end of December each year, while at **Seme** near **Kombewa** about midway between Kisumu and Bondo you can see the balancing boulders of **Kit Mikaye**. According to Luo legend, the boulders were once the home of a powerful man who mistreated his wife. On her death she wrought her revenge, returning and casting him and his property to stone.

FROM KISUMU TO KORU

This route necessitates having your own transport. Take the C34 from Kisumu to the roundabout at Muhorini, and follow the signs to the Homa Lime Company, passing through sugarcane fields and a small labour settlement to Koru, which lies adjacent to the railway line, on the foothills of Mount Tindoret (2,600m), overlooking the eastern shoreline of Lake Victoria. It's about an hour's drive from Kisumu.

Where to stay

Kweissos House (5 rooms, self-catering or full service options; swimming pool) Homa Lime Company, Private Bag, Koru; tel: 057 51064; fax: 057 51419; email: homalime@africaonline.co.ke

On a private farm in the Tindoret foothills, Kweissos House, a wooden bungalow, was built in the 1920s. There are magnificent views of the Victoria Lake basin and surrounding parkland and hills from the house. It's an ideal base for day trips to the attractions of the region, but there's also plenty to do on the 1,200ha estate. **On offer:** walking, birdwatching, fishing on small dams for tilapia and catfish, tennis and horseriding. Activities are included, apart from riding at KSh500 an hour. For experienced riders, there's a cross-country course. The cooks provide excellent meals if you choose the catered option.
Rates: self-catering per person per day (minimum 4) KSh1,000; full board per person per day KSh3,000

FROM KISUMU TO KENDU BAY, HOMA BAY AND MBITA POINT

From Kisumu, take the A1 south for about 50km before turning west on to the C19. This dirt road is atrocious in parts, so unless you're travelling in a vehicle with good suspension, expect to be thoroughly rattled around. It takes between four and seven hours from Kisumu to Mbita Point and 4WD is advisable. Although the road runs parallel to the lake, visibility is limited and the surrounding scenery is fairly mundane, dry and flat with small *shambas* and shacks. After about 20km, the turning to **Kendu Bay** is on the right. About 50km further on from Kendu Bay, **Homa Bay** is a bustling market town with exceptionally friendly people. Ribbon development extends along the two main roads (this is the junction with the C20 to Rongo, which links to the A1 between Migori and Kisii). There's a cluster of kiosks and *hotelis*, and a large covered market. Continuing on from Homa Bay on the C19, **Mbita Point** is, quite literally, 'at the end of the road'. It's a collection point for the fishing industry, lorries coming to purchase fish, particularly the sprats (known as *omena*), for distribution to markets inland. It's a small village with a few wooden kiosks, but little else. There's a causeway to Rusinga Island and it's a public transport stop for lake traffic, with *ssese* canoes ferrying people to the islands and other lakeside destinations.

If wishing to visit the Ruma National Park you will need to have your own transport or go on an organised excursion (these can be arranged from Rusinga Island Lodge, page 329). Similarly, you will need your own transport to visit Thimlich Ohinga.

Getting there and around
By bus

From the main Kisumu–Kericho road (A1), *matatus* are fairly frequent from the main road along the C19. In **Homa Bay**, the *matatu* and bus stage is near the market on the main street going east to Kendu Bay, with booking offices on the opposite side of the road. The Akamba Bus office is opposite the petrol station. Kenya Bus has several buses a day to Nairobi, and Akamba Bus a 07.00 service, both on the C20 road via Rongo and Kisii. For Mbita Point you will need to take a *matatu*.

Getting organised

In the Homa Bay town centre there's a Barclays **bank** by the **post office** and a **petrol station** at the junction of the C20 to Rongo and the C19 to Mbita Point. Kendu Bay and Mbita Point have little in the way of accommodation or facilities. In an emergency, the **tourist helpline** is 020 604767.

Where to stay and eat
Homa Bay
There's only basic lodging in town, the best being:

Summer Bay Hotel Opposite Barclays Bank, PO Box 856, Homa Bay
It has simple accommodation with quiet rooms.
Rates: from KSh450 B&B per person
Bay Lodge Kendu Rd, PO Box 96, Homa Bay; tel: 0359 21436
A reasonably quiet establishment with s/c rooms.
Rates: from KSh300 per person

There are plenty of places for cheap snacks – **Akinas Café** opposite the market is recommended, or try **Neem Shade Restaurant** near the bus station, which serves good ethnic dishes.

What to see and do
Lake Simbi
Located about a 4km walk west of the village of Kendu Bay, Simbi is a small crater lake which attracts flocks of flamingos at certain times of year – normally during the months of June and July. If travelling by public transport, take a *matatu* to Kendu Bay.

Thimlich Ohinga
Forty-six kilometres from Migori town (at the junction of the A1 and C13) is the prehistoric site of Thimlich Ohinga. These drystone enclosures are similar in construction to those seen at Great Zimbabwe (in Zimbabwe), and are among the finest example of late Iron Age stone-work to be found in East Africa. The walls rise to 2.5–3.5m and there are around 140 similar sites within the Lake Victoria region. They were built by early Bantu settlers around 500 years ago as a means to protect their homes and livestock. *Thimlich* means 'thick forest' in the Luo language, while *Ohinga* refers to the enclosures. There are still remnants of fine stands of *Euphorbia candelabra* around the site. The main compound is about 150m wide, inside which are five smaller enclosures and hollows of former house-sites.
Open daily 08.30–18.00; entry KSh200; you'll need your own transport to get here.

Ruma National Park
PO Box 420, Homa Bay; tel: 059 22544
Open daily 06.00–18.00; Park entry fees US$15; vehicle entry KSh200. You'll need your own transport to get here.
Located 140km from Kisumu, signposted off the C19 road from Kisumu to Mbita point, this 120km² park lies in the Lambwe Valley. It has a unique **flora and fauna**. A mixture of rolling savanna, woodlands, hills and rivers is home to Jackson's hartebeest and oribi, more commonly seen in the Ugandan parks, and it's the only park in Kenya with roan antelope. There's also a small population of the

THE NILE PERCH – Lates niloticus

The Nile perch, endemic in Africa, was first introduced into Lake Victoria in the 1950s. A fine specimen for sports fishing, with the added bonus of being good eating, it has tasty, white flesh. Yet, its presence has been a blessing and a curse. It has successfully bred in the lake, providing an important catch for the local fishermen, as well as international anglers seeking the challenge of a trophy fish, there being three fishing camps on the lake at Rusinga, Takawiri and Mfangano islands. It's not unusual to catch a 15kg fish, and Nile perch of up to 230kg have been recorded. In Lake Victoria Nile perch at around 95kg – a fish the size of a man – are not uncommon and have been caught by local fishermen.

As the Nile perch became more prolific, it became a mainstay of the local fishing industry alongside catches of tilapia and the tiny sprats known as omena. But as the industry became increasingly commercialised, the local fishermen have been at the mercy of the fish brokers who buy the fish for the national and international markets. While the fisherman are lucky to get KSh50 for a kilo of Nile perch, in Nairobi a kilo will sell for around KSh500 and KSh1,000 for the international export market.

But the Nile perch is also considered to have wreaked havoc on the lake's ecology as it preys on the small cichlids which are endemic to the lake, wiping out many of the species. These brightly coloured cichlids are prized for aquariums around the world. (It's thought that in earlier geological times Lake Victoria comprised several smaller lakes, which led to the cichlids evolving differently, giving rise to over 200 different species found in the lake.) Subsequently research has suggested that other reasons, such as over-fishing with fine mesh nets, may partially be to blame for this ecological disaster, as in areas where fishing was banned, the cichlids were present.

rare Rothschild's giraffe and large leopard are often seen. Birdlife is interesting too, this being one of the few places to see the endangered blue swallow. Nowadays tsetse flies are rarely a problem, possibly due to the tsetse research and eradication programme which operates near by.

For accommodation there is **camping**. Book through the warden, PO Box 420, Homa Bay; tel: 059 22544 or KWS head office, page 91. The park has several campsites but no formal camping facilities, so you will need to be fully self-sufficient. *Rates: camping US$8, plus park and vehicle entry fees*

LAKE VICTORIA AND THE ISLANDS

The second largest freshwater lake in the world, covering 69,485km², the Equator lake of Victoria is divided between Tanzania, Uganda and Kenya. It played a pivotal role in the explorations of the 19th century, with the avid quest for the source of the River Nile by explorers Richard Burton and John Hanning Speke. The Kenyan section of the lake is small, covering only 3,785km², dominated by the Winam Gulf together with a scattering of islands. **Ndere Island** is a national park, located in the Winam Gulf, while **Rusinga Island** lies off Mbita Point. **Takawiri Island** is to the south of Rusinga, while west of Takawiri is **Mfangano Island**, the largest island. Most people come to Lake Victoria for the Nile perch fishing, staying in the smart fishing camps, but there are also rock paintings on Mfangano, fossils on Rusinga and prolific birdlife.

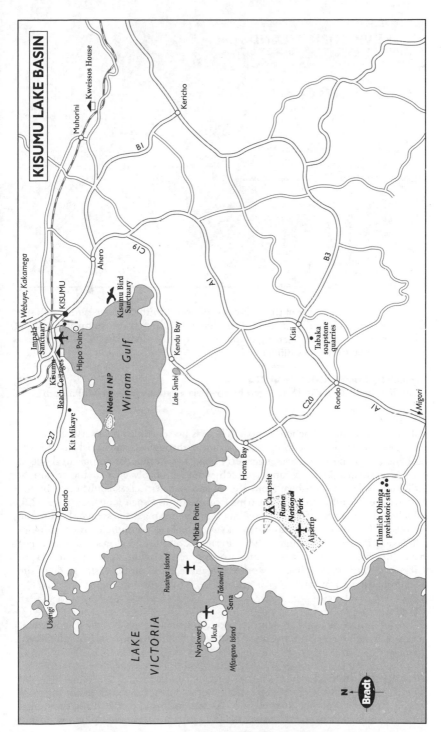

KISUMU LAKE BASIN

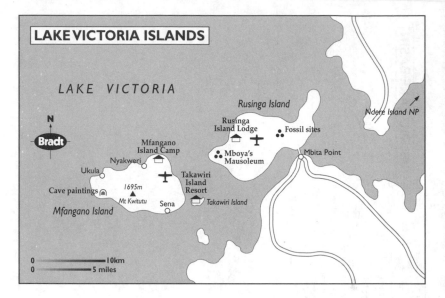

There is no accommodation on **Ndere Island**. On the other islands, the only formal accommodation is in the fishing lodges. There are no campsites on the islands, so it's a case of negotiating to camp or stay with a local family. In either case you need to be fully self-sufficient.

Getting there and around
Only Rusinga Island can be reached by road via a causeway from Mbita Point.

By boat
All the islands can be reached by boat. There is no scheduled boat service, so it's a case of chartering a speedboat from Kisumu through Takawiri Island Resorts (expensive), taking a local passenger ferry boat, a *ssese* canoe, or doing a deal with a local fisherman (also *ssese* canoe) which would probably cost in the region of KSh3,000 a day. A speedboat from Kisumu to Takawiri takes about three hours. For **Ndere Island** there are boat trips from Kisumu Beach Cottages (page 322), which cost around KSh500. From Mbita Point you can get a passenger boat to the islands of **Takawiri** and **Mfangano**. It's preferable to go in the early morning as the lake gets extremely rough in the afternoon, and the local *ssese* canoes do not have life jackets. It's a 45-minute crossing to Takawiri and 90 minutes to Mfangano. The main public jetty on Mfangano is **Sena** on the eastern side of the island opposite Takawiri.

By air
There are private airstrips on Rusinga and Mfangano islands, but no scheduled air services. If coming by air, most people come on fishing excursions from the Masai Mara.

Mfangano Island
The largest of Kenya's islands in Lake Victoria, Mfangano's dark green hills rise steeply from the shoreline, fringed by a few settlements of thatched and tin-roofed huts. Its population stands at around 18,000, a mixture of people from the Luo and

Suba tribes, whose main occupation is fishing or boat-building. Earlier inhabitants were the Twa pygmies (forest peoples also found in Uganda, Rwanda and DR Congo today) who left a legacy of fine rock paintings, around 18,000 years old, some up to 50cm across, in the hillside caves. They frequently painted a symbol of the sun on the rockface. The main villages are Sena, Nyakweri and Ukula (the closest to the rock paintings). Although covering 80km², there's no transport on the island; villages are linked by a network of footpaths.

Where to stay and eat

Mfangano Island Camp (6 rooms; swimming pool) Book through Governor's Camps, page 91

The camp nestles at the foot of the hills, on a narrow strip of land along the shoreline. The spacious cottages, with en-suite facilities, face on to the lake and are sited to make use of the shade from the mature fig trees. Their design in clay and thatch emulates the traditional Luo houses. There's a central lounge, with a good book collection, and a dining-room which enjoy views across the lake. The majority of visitors come on day trips from the Mara. **On offer:** fishing for Nile perch, climbing Mount Kwitutu (1,695m), walks to the caves to see the rock art, birdwatching and boat excursions.

Rates: from US$260 full board per person sharing.

What to see and do

Ask for a guide from one of the villages to take you to the rock paintings. Around the island, numerous birds, vervet monkeys, giant monitor lizards and otters are commonly seen. Crocodiles and hippos have been kept at bay by the fishermen, although it's possible to see crocodiles on the uninhabited Sacred Island nearby.

Rusinga Island

Rusinga is a small island dominated by high cliffs, inhabited by fishermen and subsistence farmers.

Where to stay and eat

Rusinga Island Lodge (6 cottages; swimming pool) Book through Private Wilderness, PO Box 6648, 00100 GPO, Nairobi; tel: 020 605349; fax: 020 605391; email: info@privatewilderness.com; web: www.privatewilderness.com

Formerly the home of the Roberts family, this is a delightful lodge with a collection of charming en-suite cottages made from stone, wood and grass thatch, decorated in African fabrics, each with a private veranda. The gardens contain enormous fig trees (including one where Mary Leakey had her camp at the time she discovered *Proconsul heseloni*).

Hammerkops on the sweeping lawns, and the rare double-toothed barbet are among the 100 bird species seen here. There's also an established organic garden producing all manner of vegetables and herbs to accompany the catch of the day. **On offer:** fishing for Nile perch (the current record is around 95kg) and tilapia, birdwatching, visits to the fossil sites, Tom Mboya's mausoleum, a women's project (making paper, soap and baskets to raise funds for orphan children), boat trips to Mfangano to see the rock art, watersports, though bilharzia, see page 149, is a risk, and visits to Ruma National Park (on the mainland), shop supporting local craftsmen.

Rates: from US$350 full board per person sharing, inclusive of fishing and tackle

What to see and do

From Hippo Bay you can watch nesting fish eagles and there's a chance of seeing rare spotted-necked otters. There's a footpath from the causeway which crosses the island.

Tom Mboya's mausoleum

Located not far from Rusinga Island Lodge, Tom Mboya was a human rights activist assassinated in 1969 during political unrest. Born on the island, he is buried on his family plot in Kasawanga on the northern side of Rusinga. His epitaph reads:

THOMAS JOSEPH MBOYA
'August 15th 1930–July 5th 1969
Go and fight like this man
Who fought for mankind's cause
Who died because he fought
Whose battles are still unwon.'

Adjacent to the grave is the silver, bullet-shaped mausoleum erected by the Kenya government in 1971. Inside there's an eclectic collection of memorabilia, including photographs of Mboya receiving honorary citizenship from Kansas City in 1966 and the briefcase he was carrying when he died. The mausoleum is maintained by the Mboya family who live next door.
Entry free, but donations are appropriate

Fossil sites

Fossils from the Miocene period, dating back to between 18 and 20 million years ago, may be found all over Rusinga Island, although there are three main sites. The most famous discovery was the skull of *Proconsul heseloni* (formerly known as *Proconsul africanus*), a five-million-year-old anthropoid ape, the last common ancestor of the great apes and man, found by Dr Mary Leakey in 1947. It was so small it could be held in the palm of the hand. However, other finds included ancestral elephants, rhinos, pigs and a giant, horse-sized hyrax, as well as a myriad of rodents, reptiles, gastropods and plants, giving a fossilized microcosm of life from the Miocene era. Guides to the fossil sites may be arranged through Rusinga Island Lodge.

Takawiri Island

This small, hilly island is not far from Rusinga, and about half an hour's boat-crossing away from Mfangano Camp. It's home to a couple of fishing communities, who combine small-scale agriculture – livestock and crops of maize – to supplement their fishing.

Where to stay and eat

Takawiri Island Resort (8 rooms) PO Box 188, Kisumu; tel: 057 40924, fax: 057 41030; email: takawiri@net2000ke.com or book through Let's Go Travel (page 101) or Base Camp Travel (page 102)

This is a delightful, family-owned fishing camp, not as lavish as Rusinga and Mfangano, but with its own special charm. The rooms overlook a sandy beach, complete with palm trees and sunloungers. Twin-bedded, they are comfortable with en-suite shower rooms. There's a dining-room and a thatched, open-air barbecue area. The barbecues are particularly recommended, the owner being an excellent chef. In the evening the lake twinkles with the hurricane lamps used by the fishermen to attract *omena* into their nets.

On offer: fishing for Nile perch, birdwatching, sundowners on the hill behind the camp to see the sun setting on the Mfangano Hills; walks to a nearby fishing village, boat excursions to the other islands, watersports, though bilharzia, see page 149, is a risk.
Rates: from US$220 full board per person sharing

What to see and do

See under lodge activities above.

Ndere Island
Ndere Island National Park
Open daily 06.00–18.00; park entry US$15. 'Nile cabbage', the intrusive water hyacinth, can cause navigational difficulties at certain times of year. It's usually best to go between June and December.

Located in the Winam Gulf about 50km from Kisumu, this small island (4.5km²) was given national park status in 1986 to protect the birdlife and natural vegetation. *Ndere* means 'meeting point' in the Luo language. According to Luo legend, Kit Mikaye, mother of the tribe, stopped here on her journey south from the Nile Valley, and, on finding the island so attractive, decided to settle with her people. **Birdlife** is prolific, including magnificent fish eagles and swifts. **Wildlife** includes hippo and the less familiar spotted crocodile, both of which are commonly seen, and a small herd of introduced impala in the woodland fringing the shoreline.

KISII
A rambling market town and provincial centre, growing fast and with friendly people, there's little to merit stopping in Kisii itself. On the main bus routes it's a transit stop en route to Nakuru or Homa Bay. The area is famous for Kisii soapstone, a pale pink stone, often coloured and etched with traditional designs. However you'll find a better choice of ornaments and plates for sale at the roadside stalls in Nakuru.

Getting around
Kisii is reached on the A1 from Kisumu (about 115km on a good tarmac road) or, if coming from Kericho, via the C23 to Sotik and the B3 to Kisii (100km).

By bus
There are regular buses from Kisii to Nairobi via Narok or Kericho and Nakuru, and to Homa Bay, Kisumu and Migori. Akamba bus station (tel: 058 30137) is on Moi Highway with an 08.30 daily service to Nairobi via Kericho. The Linear Coach office is opposite, with several buses a day to Nairobi via Narok (tel: 058 31322). In addition there are numerous *matatus* and share taxis which leave from Ogemba Road if heading east and from Moi Highway near the market for destinations north, south and west.

Getting organised
For **changing money**, Barclays Bank (with ATM) is on Moi Highway, as is the **post office**, open Monday–Friday 08.00–17.00, Saturday 09.00–12.00. There's a **supermarket** off Sansora Road. In a **medical emergency** it's best to go to Nakuru; alternatively go to the Kisii General Hospital at the northern end of Hospital Road (tel: 058 20471). The **police station** is at the southern end of Hospital Road (tel: 058 20223) and the **tourist helpline** is 020 604767. There are plenty of **petrol stations** on the access roads into Kisii.

Where to stay and eat
Zonic Hotel (medium-sized hotel) PO Box 541, Kisii; tel: 058 30298
A 5-storey hotel, this is one of the best hotels in Kisii. The rooms have private facilities and some have a balcony. There's a rooftop terrace with good views and a **restaurant** serving reasonable meals. There's also a disco.
Rates: from US$20 B&B per person sharing
Marsh Park Hotel, Kisii; tel: 058 30631
On the Kisumu Rd on the outskirts of town, this is of a similar standard to the Zonic Hotel.
Rates: from US$18 B&B per person sharing

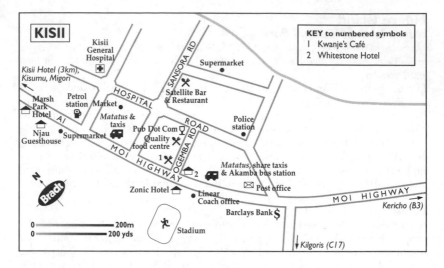

Kisii Hotel PO Box 26, Kisii; tel: 058 30134

On the outskirts of town on the Kisumu Rd, this is set in pleasant gardens. It has a jaded colonial atmosphere, and the rooms are spacious with en-suite bathrooms. There's a restaurant which has a good choice of food and a jovial bar.

Rates: from KSh800 B&B per person sharing

Njau Guest House on Moi Highway; tel: 058 30080

This is one of the best of the cheap places to stay with reasonably clean s/c rooms, but no hot water.

Rates: from KSh175 per person sharing

Whitestone Hotel on Moi Highway

This is also good value and of a similar standard to Njau, with s/c rooms and intermittent hot water.

Rates: from KSh350 per person

There are several **cheap eats** around town, the best being along Ogemba Road near the bus terminals. Try **Kwanje's Café** and the **Quality Food Centre** where basic fare, meat and *ugali*, costs around KSh150. For nightlife, **Pub Dot Com** on Ogemba Road is a popular watering hole with loud music, while there are discos at the Zonic Hotel and the Satellite Bar and Restaurant on Sansora Road.

What to see and do
Kisii Soapstone Carvers' Co-operative Society

The nearby village of Tabaka is at the centre of the soapstone quarries and carvers. Take the A1 west of Kisii for 18km to Nyachenge and take the turning on the left to Tabaka. It's about 6m along a bad dirt road to the Kisii Soapstone Carvers' Co-operative Society. Here you can see the carvers at work and take a guide to visit the quarries. There's a limited amount of work for sale as most is bought by wholesale outlets in Nairobi.

KERICHO

Lying in the heart of tea country at an altitude of 2,040m, Kericho town runs along a ridge before the hills drop down to the Victoria Lake basin to the north. It has a smattering of old colonial buildings and Asian shops in its main streets and still primarily operates as a service centre for the surrounding tea estates. Named after the British tea planter, John Kerich, the area is surrounded by bright green commercial tea plantations and smallholdings, interspersed with fast-flowing rivers. Remnants of the eastern Mau Forest may also be seen.

Getting there and away

Reached via the B1 (good tarmac road) from the Londiani turn-off from the A104 Nakuru–Eldoret road, you can continue on the B1 to Kisumu, or take the C23 road (reasonable tarmac), branching south before Sotik to Bomet, and continue to the **Masai Mara National Reserve** (page 309). Alternatively you can continue to Sotik and connect with the B3 to Kisii.

By bus

There are regular bus services to Nairobi, Kisumu, Homa Bay and Isebania (Tanzanian border), which depart from Moi Highway (Kenya Bus and Akamba have offices here), and plenty of *matatus*, which leave from the *matatu* stand near the market or along Moi Highway. The Akamba bus for Nairobi leaves at 08.00.

Getting organised

Barclays and Standard Chartered **banks** (with ATMs) are on Moi Highway, as is the **post office**, open Monday–Friday 08.00–17.00, Saturday 09.00–12.00. There's a **supermarket** on Kenyatta Road. In a **medical emergency** go to the Kericho District Hospital on Hospital Road (tel: 052 31192). The **police station** is on Moi Highway (tel: 052 20222) and the **tourist helpline** is 020 604767. There are plenty of **petrol stations** on the access roads into Kericho.

Where to stay and eat

Kericho Garden Hotel Moi Highway, PO Box 164, Kericho
This pleasant hotel has clean rooms with safe parking.
Rates: from US$10 B&B per person sharing
Kericho Lodge and Fish Resort PO Box 25, Kericho; tel: 052 20035
Ideally located for walks to the river and through tea plantations, the lodge has clean, simple, but comfortable rooms.
Rates: from US$15 per person sharing

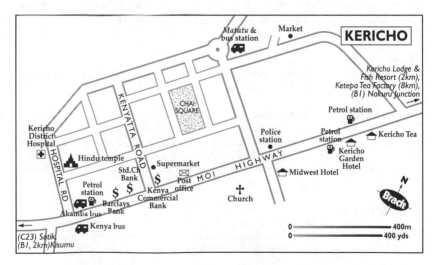

KENYA TEA

Tea, *Camellia sinensis*, was first planted in Kenya in 1903 and commercial planting started in 1924. Kenya is the world's third-largest producer of black tea and in 2001 it produced 295,000 tonnes of tea, exporting over 95% of the crop.

At altitudes between 1,500–2,700m, Kenya has ideal growing conditions for tea, where rainfall averaging 1,300mm a year combines with long periods of sunshine enabling production to continue throughout the year. The prime regions are the highland areas of Limuru, Kericho and Nandi Hills, on either side of the Rift Valley, where there are huge tea plantations.

The crop is labour intensive, with skilful tea pickers harvesting tea leaves – they pick two leaves and a bud – into large wicker baskets which they carry on their backs. Both men and women work in the tea gardens and are paid on the amount they pick. Once the basket is full, they go to weighing stations, where they deposit their crop before it is taken to the tea factory for processing. The bushes are plucked on a regular cycle, every 7–14 days, maintaining the high quality of tea for which Kenya is renowned.

The processing favoured in Kenya is the cut, tear and curl method of tea leaf manufacture, which produces strong black tea with a distinctive flavour. Most of Kenya's tea is sold through the Mombasa auction which is second in size only to the Colombo tea auction centre in Sri Lanka.

Midwest Hotel, (70 rooms) PO Box 1175, Kericho; tel: 052 20611
Situated in Kericho town within garden surroundings, it has clean and comfortable rooms. The de-luxe rooms have a TV. There's a good restaurant and snack bar. **On offer:** fitness club with sauna, beauty salon, snooker room and disco.
Rates: from KSh1,000 B&B per person sharing
Kericho Tea Hotel (medium-sized hotel; camping; swimming pool) PO Box 75, Kericho; tel: 052 30004; fax: 052 20576
An old-fashioned, but now rather jaded, country hotel, set in delightful gardens, situated just outside Kericho on the Nakuru road. Clean and comfortable rooms within the hotel and en-suite cottages in the garden. **On offer:** tennis, golf, squash and trout fishing.
Rates: from US$42 B&B per person sharing; camping from KSh200 per person

What to see and do

Birdwatching, **river walks**, **trout fishing** and **visits to tea factories** can be arranged through the Tea Hotel and Kericho Lodge and Fish Resort (page 333).

Chagaik Dam and Arboretum

Take the B1 Nakuru road past the KETEPA tea factory on the right, about 8km from Kericho. Follow signs to Chagaik from where it's a short walk to the arboretum which was planted by the tea planter, John Grumbley. Exotic tropical and subtropical trees are set in manicured gardens stretching to a lily-covered dam. It's a relaxing picnic spot.

NANDI HILLS

This is a remote hill station, surrounded by acres upon acres of commercial tea plantations. The region became famous for its Nandi warriors who clashed with the British colonial forces during the building of the Uganda railway. It is also home to the Nandi bear, an animal rather like the yeti in that it has a mythological status in local folklore, although it has actually been seen (see box below).

Getting there and away
North of Timboroa take the C36 to Kapsabet (shocking road in parts) and turn off to Nandi Hills at Lessos. Alternatively take the C37 Kapsabet road to Nandi, which joins the B1 to Kisumu at the foot of the Nandi escarpment.

By bus
Nandi is not on a main bus route, but *matatus* run along the C37 from Kapsabet.

Where to stay and eat
Nandi Bears' Club (3 self-catering cottages) PO Box 20, Nandi Hills; tel: 053 43238
A couple of kilometres out of town, the Nandi Bears' Club has 3 self-catering cottages where linen and bedding are provided, together with a stove, refrigerator and cooking

---

THE NANDI BEAR – Chemosit tugenensis
A creature with a fearsome reputation, the Nandi bear is an enigma. It attacks people, kills sheep and dogs, has a shaggy fur coat – ranging from reddish to black – can rear up on its hind legs, has the shuffling gait of a bear, large footprints and a terrifying roar. The animal has been sighted and tracked on numerous occasions, but never formally identified and the descriptions differ so much that perhaps they are describing more than one type of animal. Since the turn of the 20th century Westerners have puzzled as to its origins and various hypotheses have been put forward – a black, forest hyena, similar to the brown hyena; a primate, aardvark or honey-badger. Accounts vary, yet there has been no conclusive evidence due to its elusive nature, hiding in the western Kenya forests.

Like the yeti and the Loch Ness monster, the Nandi bear has a strong mythological status. Among the Kalenjin, which includes the Nandi and Kipsigis tribes, the Nandi bear is generally known as a *chemosit*, although it's also called a *geteit*, *kerit* and *koddoelo*. In oral tradition, the *chemosit* is described as a devil, a brain-eater which will steal babies from huts. Instilling terror into the local people, it prowls at night. As a precaution, when going out in the dark, some people would put a cooking pot over their head so that if they were attacked, the Nandi bear would make off with the pot instead of their head. Certainly there is recorded evidence of livestock being killed and only their brains being eaten. As recently as 1997, in the Uasin Gishu district a hundred sheep were slain in a month, where the beast severed lambs' heads and tore the teats off the ewes leaving the rest of the carcasses untouched. This might have been a leopard or hyena, but the animal was never tracked down and the locals believe it was a *chemosit*.

The Nandi bear remains enshrouded in an aura of mystery – is it beyond the realms of possibility that such a creature, as yet unidentified, does exist? It's difficult to say, but inevitably the myth remains to be substantiated.

There is an exhibit about the Nandi bear in the Kipsaraman Museum in the Tugen Hills. See page 304.

utensils. Two cottages sleep 2 and the third sleeps 4. Situated near the clubhouse, meals can also be taken at the club (good basic fair – bacon and eggs, fish and chips), and there's an amiable bar. It's at its liveliest on Wednesday evening's club night and at the weekend. *Rates: from KSh1,200 per person*

Alternatively, in town there are a couple of **cheap hotels** above the Maasai butchery and supermarket, where s/c rooms cost from KSh500 B&B per person.

What to see and do
There's little to see in Nandi itself, apart from visiting a tea factory (ask at the club or in town), but it's only a day trip from here to visit Kisumu or Kakamega Forest. If you play golf, Nandi's course is one of the most picturesque in Kenya. There's also an interesting water garden on a tea estate about 5km from the club. Ask at the club for directions.

KAKAMEGA
The small town of Kakamega lies in the heart of Luhya country. Agriculturalists, the Luhya are Kenya's second largest ethnic group, which is divided into a number of sub-clans, the best-known being the Tiriki and Isukha. There's little of interest to see in the town, the main reason for going there being to visit Kakamega Forest.

Getting there and away
The A1 north from Kisumu to Kakamega (a distance of about 100km) rises steadily, snaking its way through rounded, cultivated hills, with splendid views of the Nandi escarpment and outcrops of giant boulders, some precariously balanced on each other, before reaching the forest of Kakamega (1,500m). Nearing Kakamega is the linear township of Khayega. Look out for a sign on the left which reads: 'Mortuary, cold rooms available', after which is the turning to a pottery making the traditional Luhya rounded, clay, cooking pots. Alternatively, from Eldoret you can travel via the C39 through Kabsabet and turn off to the right near Chesonoi.

Getting organised
Standard Chartered and Kenya Commercial **banks** and the **post office**, open Monday–Friday 08.00–17.00, Saturday 09.00–12.00, are situated in the centre of town and Barclays is on the A1 near the petrol station. For **internet access** try the Highland Computer College on Kenyatta Avenue. There's a **supermarket** on Mumia Road. The **police** station is also in the town centre (tel: 056 20222) and the **tourist helpline** is 020 604767. There's a small **hospital** on Okwemba Road (tel: 056 30051). There are plenty of **petrol stations** on the access roads into Kakamega.

Where to stay and eat
To make the most of being there, staying in the forest is highly recommended, although there is the option of cheap lodging or the Golf Hotel in Kakamega town. For places to stay and eat in Kakamega Forest, see page 338.

Golf Hotel (62 rooms; swimming pool) Khasakhala Rd, PO Box 118, Kakamega; tel: 056 20125; fax: 056 30155. A comfortable hotel set in colourful gardens with views to Mount Elgon and the Bunyore Hills. All bedrooms have private bathrooms and balconies, and there's a reasonable restaurant. **On offer:** guests are given reciprocal membership of the Kakamega Sports Club nearby with its golf course, tennis and squash courts. *Rates: US$38 B&B per person sharing*
Bendera Hotel Sudi Rd, PO Box 423, Kakamega; tel: 056 2077. Next to the BP petrol station, this is a friendly, clean establishment and probably the best of the cheaper hotels.

The s/c rooms are spacious and there's a bar and restaurant downstairs. *Rates: rooms from KSh400 B&B*
Franka Hotel Mumias Rd, PO Box 621, Kakamega; tel: 056 20086. The s/c rooms are clean and there's a bar and restaurant below which can get noisy. *Rates: rooms from KSh400 B&B*

In addition to the hotels listed above, there are a number of cheap places to eat. Those recommended include the **Merry Eating House** (try the tilapia), **Dreamland Café** and **Pizza Hut**.

What to see and do
The Weeping Stone of Shinyalu
About 3km before the township of Kakamega, on the right-hand side of the road is the weeping stone of Shinyalu. It's a granite monolith rising to about 20m, with a boulder on top which sits in a hollow. Seemingly, when it rains, the hollow fills with water and overflows, giving the appearance of a weeping stone. It's the subject of several local legends. In one, the stone weeps for all mankind, while in another, a young girl eloped with a young man and her disapproving father turned her to stone – the stone symbolises the weeping girl. It's about a ten-minute walk to the rock through smallholdings, and if you ask, someone will take you there.

Bullfighting
See page 134 for further details.

Kakamega Forest
Open daily; national forest reserve entry US$10 (forest reserve currently free)
The eastern remnant of the equatorial Guinea-Congolian rainforest which once stretched across the continent, Kakamega Forest is an isolated pocket of forest covering 23,000ha. It's surrounded by a buffer zone of tea plantations, the aim being to protect the forest from human encroachment and logging by giving local people an income from the tea crop. The southern part of the forest forms the **Kakamega Forest Reserve**, which comes under the jurisdiction of the Forestry department and is reached from the A1 at Kakamega, or off the C39 Kabsabet road near Chesonoi. Access to the **Kakamega Forest National Reserve**, managed by Kenya Wildlife Service, is signposted off the A1 about 20km north of Kakamega. If travelling by public transport, this gives the easiest access to the forest, as you can take a *matatu* from the Total petrol station in Kakamega, and then walk the 2km into the reserve. Be aware that when wet all the forest roads are impassable without 4WD.

Flora and fauna The forest itself is fascinating and well worth the effort of getting there. Trees tower up to 60m high, 350 species being indigenous and many having a medicinal value or trailing brightly coloured orchids. The soft-wooded parasol tree, *Filisia fulva*, is ideal for making drums and is reportedly used by mother monkeys when delivering their babies. The leaves of the sandpaper tree, *Ficus exasperata*, are rough and tough, used as the name suggests. Birds are prolific (350 species), although being high in the canopy they are difficult to see. Black and white casked hornbills, tinker birds and joyful greenbuls are common, while you may be lucky and glimpse the magnificent turquoise plumage of the great blue turaco. The forest has exquisite butterflies (400 species), best seen during the breeding months between August and October. Rarely seen are the 30 different types of snake, apart from pythons which have a preference for lazing on

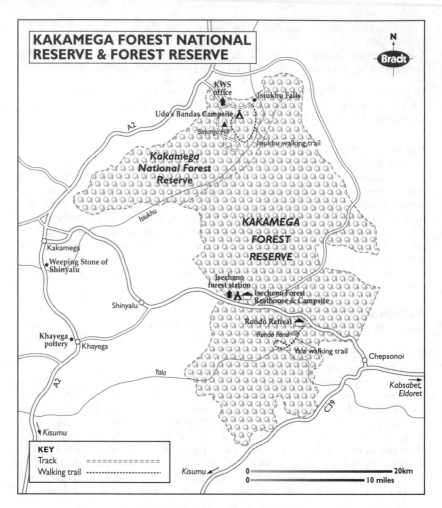

KAKAMEGA FOREST NATIONAL RESERVE & FOREST RESERVE

N

Bradt

KWS office

Isiukhu Falls

Udo's Bandas Campsite

Bayangu Hill

Isiukhu walking trail

A2

Kakamega National Forest Reserve

Isiukhu

KAKAMEGA FOREST RESERVE

Kakamega

Weeping Stone of Shinyalu

Isecheno forest station

Isecheno Forest Resthouse & Campsite

Shinyalu

Khayega pottery

Khayega

Yala

A2

Rondo Retreat

Rondo Pond

Yala walking trail

Chepsonoi

Kabsabet, Eldoret

C39

Kisumu

KEY

Track ==============

Walking trail ....

Kisumu

0 _____ 20km
0 _____ 10 miles

riverbanks. Among the mammals, primate viewing is best, with troops of black-and-white colobus, Sykes, de Brazza and red-tailed monkeys. Other forest animals include bushpigs, clawless otters, porcupines, civet, suni, ground pangolin, grey duiker and nocturnal wildlife – flying squirrels, bushbabies and potto.

There are several kilometres of marked **forest trails**, from 1km to 6km long, but the guides are extremely informative, so you'll miss out if you go alone.

Where to stay and eat

Rondo Retreat (4 rooms in main house; 3 cottages) Rondo Retreat Centre, PO Box 2153, Kakamega; tel: 056 30268; fax: 056 20145; email: tfrondo@maf.or.ke.
The Rondo Retreat is located on the forest road between the main roads of Kakamega (13.6km) and Kapsabet (9.7km). If you enjoy a little time for peace and reflection, the Rondo Retreat is recommended, but you'll need to bring your own alcohol and smoking is banned indoors. A sign on the veranda reads: 'Be still and know that I am God'. Certainly this former saw-miller's house built in the 1940s comes as a surprise in the middle of the

forest, but it does have a remarkably tranquil, old world atmosphere, with its polished floors and chintz furnishings. Now run by the Trinity Fellowship, the main house has been extended. It contains a main sitting room with an open log fire, a dining-room serving wholesome meals and 4 en-suite rooms, while in the cottages, Colobus has 3 double rooms, Turaco 5 doubles and Founders 1 double and a triple room. There's a small chapel at the foot of the garden. The gardens themselves are delightful with plentiful birdlife and butterflies and there's an enormous 500-year-old Elgon teak under which the founder of the fellowship, Howard Dawkins, is buried. **On offer:** guided forest walks for trekking and birdwatching.

Rates: KSh5,000 per person full board; forest guides can be hired for KSh300 per person. Not suitable for children.

Udo's Bandas and Campsite (7 bandas) KWS, PO Box 879, Kakamega; tel: 056 20425, or via KWS head office in Nairobi, page 91

Located in the Kakamega Forest National Reserve, about 1km from the Kenya Wildlife Service office. The self-catering bandas are simple, with a larger, thatched building for cooking and eating. Water is available from the stream and there's a bucket shower area and long-drop toilets.

Rates: KSh250 for bandas and camping

Forest Rest House and Campsite (4 rooms) Kakamega Forest Station, PO Box 2731, Kakamega

Situated not far from the main office, the wooden rest house is on stilts at the side of the campsite. Not particularly clean, the double rooms are basic, but have a separate bathroom and toilet, although water can be spasmodic. There's a small canteen nearby where you can have meals cooked by arrangement.

Rates: from KSh200 for a room; camping around KSh100

ELDORET

Formerly known as '64' as it was established at the 64th milepost on the wagon route from Londiani, Eldoret sprung up as a market town serving the agricultural community. An area settled by Afrikaners after their Great Trek from South Africa, together with European settlers, the Uasin Gishu Plateau was at one time known as the bread basket of Kenya. The town evolved to embrace industrial development, and was a major textile centre until the market collapsed at the end of the 20th century. It has grown in importance as a university town. **Moi University** is located here, and its training hospital is among the best in Kenya. An international airport opened in the 1990s but the runway is too short for large passenger planes, so it's mainly used for freight (especially by the cut-flower market) and internal flights. Eldoret's main claim to fame is as the home town of Kenya's renowned international athlete, **Kipchoge Keino**, the double-gold Olympic long-distance runner.

Getting there and away

Eldoret lies on the main trucking route to the north, on the A104 from Nairobi and Nakuru. An alternative, quieter and scenically stunning drive, through magnificent stands of natural forest and with views across the Kerio Valley, is via Eldama Ravine on the B54 and C55 (off the B4 Nakuru to Baringo road). This route also gives access to the fluorspar mine in the Kerio Valley. Shortly after Eldoret, the A104 branches west to Bungoma and the Ugandan border at Malaba.

By bus

There are regular bus services between Nairobi and Eldoret via Nakuru. Akamba Bus leaves from the corner of Oginga Odinga Street and Nandi Road, while Kenya

Bus departs from the main bus station and *matatu* stand off Uganda Road, next to the market.

By air
There are daily scheduled return flights between Eldoret International Airport and Nairobi on Flamingo Airways, with offices at Eldoret International Airport (PO Box 2323 Eldoret; tel: 053 32874 or 0733 959845) and a town office at Sirikwa Hotel, tel: 053 63433. The airport is about 16km out of town on the C39 Kisumu road. Taxis into town cost about KSh1,000.

By rail
There are no passenger services to Eldoret.

Getting organised
Barclays and Standard Chartered **banks** (with ATMs) are situated in the centre of town on Uganda Road, as is the main **post office,** open Monday–Friday 08.00–17.00, Saturday 09.00–12.00. Kenya Commercial Bank is on Kenyatta Street. For **internet access** try Klique bar and restaurant and Write Image on Oginga Odinga Street. There's a well-stocked Uchumi **supermarket** on Oloo Road. There's also a **pharmacy** in Oginga Odinga Street and plenty of others in town. In a **medical emergency** go to the Moi Referral Hospital on Nandi Road (tel: 053 33471). The **police station** is on Uganda Road (tel: 053 32222) and the **tourist helpline** is 020 604767. There are plenty of **petrol stations** on the access roads into Eldoret.

Where to stay and eat
White Castle Motel (118 rooms) Uganda Rd, PO Box 566, Eldoret; tel: 053 33095; fax: 053 62209
This is a rather featureless businessmen's hotel, but it's clean with friendly service. The rooms are good, with private facilities, and there's a reasonable restaurant.
Rates: from KSh2,500 B&B per person sharing
Sirikwa Hotel (100 rooms; swimming pool) Elgeyo Rd, PO Box 3361; tel: 053 63433; fax: 053 61018
Despite its jaded appearance, the Sirikwa Hotel has good, clean rooms with private facilities. The main attraction is the large swimming pool, and there's a good weekend barbecue (about KSh600).
Rates: from KSh3,000 B&B per person sharing
Eldoret Wagon Hotel Elgeyo Rd, PO Box 2408, Eldoret; tel: 053 62270; fax: 053 62400
This old settlers' hotel has a lively character and comfortable rooms, all with private facilities. It was the first hotel in the area, started as a private members' club for senior railway staff, and the dining-room is built like an elongated railway carriage with a hooped ceiling. There's a restaurant serving international and local cuisine, and a *nyama choma* restaurant and bar.
Rates: from KSh1,200 B&B per person sharing

For **cheap lodging** try:

Top Lodge Oginga Odinga St, Eldoret; tel: 053 32259
It has basic s/c rooms.
Rates: rooms from KSh400–800
Mahindi Hotel Uganda Rd, Eldoret; tel: 053 31520
This is convenient to the bus station, but noisy. The s/c rooms are very basic.
Rates: rooms from KSh400–600

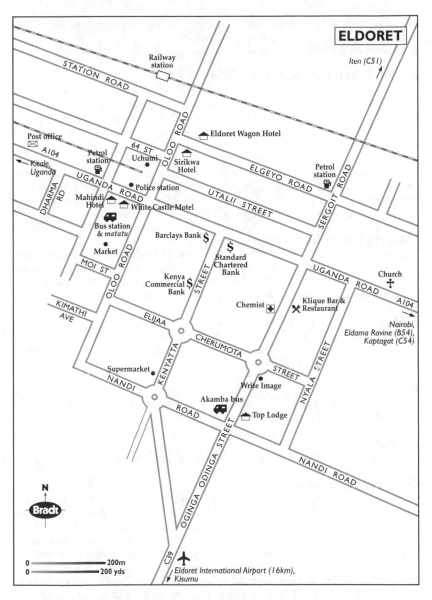

ELDORET

Iten (C51)

Railway station

STATION ROAD

Post office
A104
Kitale, Uganda

64 ST

Petrol station

Uchumi

OLOO ROAD

Eldoret Wagon Hotel

Sirikwa Hotel

ELGEYO ROAD

Petrol station

SERGOIT ROAD

UGANDA ROAD

DHARMA RD

Mahindi Hotel

Police station

White Castle Motel

UTALII STREET

Bus station & matatu

Barclays Bank $

$

Market

Standard Chartered Bank

MOI ST

OLOO ROAD

Kenya Commercial Bank $

STREET

Chemist

Klique Bar & Restaurant

UGANDA ROAD

Church

A104

KIMATHI AVE

ELIJAA

CHERUMOTA

STREET

Nairobi, Eldama Ravine (B54), Kaptagat (C54)

Supermarket

NANDI

KENYATTA STREET

STREET

Write Image

NYALA STREET

Akamba bus

Top Lodge

ROAD

NANDI ROAD

N

Bradt

OGINGA ODINGA STREET

0 ———— 200m
0 ———— 200 yds

C39

Eldoret International Airport (16km), Kisumu

Outside Eldoret on the C54 to Kaptagat

Naiberi River Campsite (camping, dormitory and self-catering bandas) PO Box 142, Eldoret; tel: 053 33029; fax: 053 62916; email: campsite@africaonline.co.ke

About 20km out of Eldoret, this is a delightful, picturesque spot on the river and a favourite with overlanders. There's a restaurant on site (plenty of Indian food and snacks) and good ablution facilities. The bandas are rustic but well equipped.

Rates: camping KSh200; bandas KSh500

Kaptagat Hotel (rooms, cottages, camping) PO Box 2900, Eldoret; tel: 053 62992

This old hotel has a river running through its attractive gardens. The hotel rooms are a

little more lavish, while the cottages are comfortable. There's a pleasant bar and the food is reasonable. Camping is by arrangement with the hotel.
Rates: rooms from KSh1,500 per person; camping around KSh200

KITALE AND MOUNT ELGON

A small, market town, Kitale is at the centre of the main maize-growing area in Kenya, but it's also famous for its apple orchards. A strong frontier spirit still prevails – it's the last town before heading on to the remote areas of northwestern Kenya or Mount Elgon. Lying on the route of the Karamoja slave trade which operated in the 18th century between Tanzania and Uganda, there are still trees in the area (see Lokitela Farm, page 344, and Kitale Club below) where the slaves were shackled when the caravans stopped on their long journey to the Indian Ocean. The area used to be teeming with game, but the last black rhino was shot in 1945. It was a settler stronghold in the colonial era when there were 900 settler families; today, four remain.

Getting there and away

Kitale lies at the junction of the B2 to Eldoret, the A1 heading north to Lodwar, and the C48 to the Cheranganis and the C45 to Endebess. To get to **Mount Elgon**, continue along the main street past the railway station, or, if going via Lokitela Farm and KWS offices, follow Moi Avenue on to the Elgon road out of town.

By bus

The bus station and *matatu* stand is on the main street by the Esso petrol station. Kenya Bus and Akamba have departures to Nairobi. The Akamba bus leaves at 09.00. For Mount Elgon and the north, you'll need to take a *matatu*.

By air

Kitale has a small airport, but there are no scheduled flights. Mount Elgon National Park has a landing strip for light aircraft.

By train

The passenger service from Nairobi is no longer in operation.

Getting organised

Barclays (ATM) and Standard Chartered banks are on the corner of Kenyatta Avenue and Bank Street and Kenya Commercial Bank is on Moi Avenue. The **post office** is on Post Office Road, between Kenyatta Street and Askari Road, open Monday–Friday 08.00–17.00, Saturday 09.00–12.00. For **internet access** try Alrood Enterprises on Moi Avenue. There are a couple of **supermarkets** on Kenyatta Street. The **Mount Elgon Hospital** is on Hospital Road (tel: 054 20025). The **police station** is off Moi Avenue (tel: 054 20895) and the **tourist helpline** is 020 604767. There are **petrol stations** on the access roads into Kitale.

Kitale
Where to stay and eat

Kitale Club (rooms and cottages; swimming pool) PO Box 30, Kitale; tel: 054 31330; fax: 054 30924
Open to non-members, who pay a nominal entrance fee, the accommodation is comfortable, the rooms all having private bathrooms. There's a congenial bar with satellite TV and a restaurant offering wholesome meals. **On offer:** golf, (18-hole course) and tennis.
Rates: from about US$25 B&B per person sharing

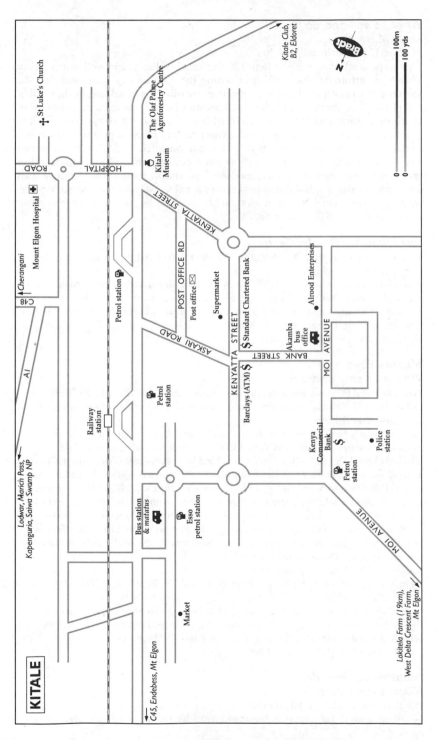

KITALE

Lodwar, Marich Pass,
Kapenguria, Saiwa Swamp NP

C45, Endebess, Mt Elgon

Cherangani
C48
A1

ROAD

St Luke's Church

Mount Elgon Hospital

HOSPITAL

The Olaf Palme
Agroforestry Centre

Kitale
Museum

KENYATTA STREET

Petrol station

POST OFFICE RD

Post office

ASKARI ROAD

Supermarket

Railway
station

Petrol
station

Bus station
& matatus

Esso
petrol station

Market

Standard Chartered Bank

KENYATTA STREET

Barclays (ATM)

BANK STREET

Akamba
bus
office

Alrood Enterprises

MOI AVENUE

Kenya
Commercial
Bank

Petrol
station

Police
station

MOI AVENUE

Lokitela Farm (19km),
West Delta Crescent Farm,
Mt Elgon

Kitale Club,
B2, Eldoret

N

Bradt

100m
100 yds

0
0

What to see and do
Kitale Museum
PO Box 1219, Kitale; tel: 054 20670
This is an excellent regional museum in the centre of Kitale, and well worth a visit.
There's an **ethnographic gallery** depicting the evolution of man, with specific
reference to East African discoveries, together with displays of wildlife, birds, reptiles,
and plants from the area, including gardens with indigenous trees. A collection of
traditional homesteads from the Luhya, Nandi, Luo and Sabaot have been built to
give an insight into their cultures, and a white settler's house is planned, which will
double up as visitor accommodation. The **snake park** has a selection of venomous
and non-venomous snakes, and there's also a **crocodile pond**. A **biogas generation
unit** demonstrates how to produce methane from animal waste. A short **nature trail**
with a **picnic site** winds through pockets of natural forest that once covered the area
where you have a good chance of spotting black-and-white colobus monkeys.
Open daily 08.00–18.00; entry KSh200

Olaf Palme Agroforestry Centre
Vi Agroforestry Project, PO Box 2006, Kitale; tel: 054 20139; email:
viafp@net2000ke.com
If you have an interest in the land-use of the area, this Swedish-run project gives a
practical demonstration of agroforestry (the combination of growing trees with
grazing for animals or crops like beans) alongside an arboretum and tree nursery.
The centre is next door to the museum.
Open daily 08.00–18.00; free entry

Mount Elgon
Where to stay and eat
Lokitela Farm (3 rooms and cottage sleeping 6) PO Box 122, Kitale; tel: 054 20695,
mobile: 0722 729726; fax: 054 20695; email: tonymills@swiftkenya.co or through Bush
Homes of East Africa, page 90
Situated 19km west of Kitale on the foothills of Mount Elgon, the farm produces milk and
maize. The owners, Adrianne and Tony Mills, are experienced safari operators and
extremely knowledgeable on the Mount Elgon and West Pokot areas. The farm itself has
350 bird species, among them Africa's largest owl – the Verreaux eagle owl – and crowned
cranes. There's a good view of Mount Elgon from the farm and it's only 15km to the park.
Rooms are comfortable and nicely furnished, the sitting room gleams with trophies from
agricultural shows and there's a roaring log fire in the evenings. During the day, meals are
taken on the veranda with all the trimmings you'd expect on a dairy farm. **On offer:** an
ideal base for walking and birdwatching on the farm, visiting the nearby parks of Elgon,
Saiwa Swamp and Kakamega and West Pokot.
Rates: US$300 full board per person sharing
Delta Crescent Farm (camping and bandas) PO Box 126, Endebess; tel: 054 31462;
mobile: 0722 261022
Located 28km from Kitale and 6km from the Chorlum gate to Mount Elgon National
Park, this is a well-run campsite in a pleasant setting with food and drink for sale. **On
offer:** horse and camel rides. Camping equipment and 4WD vehicles are available for hire.
Rates: Camping KSh200; banda KSh1,500

What to see and do
Mount Elgon Orchards
PO Box 124, Kitale; tel: 054 31458
Growing flowers for export is big business in Kenya (page 19). By arrangement,

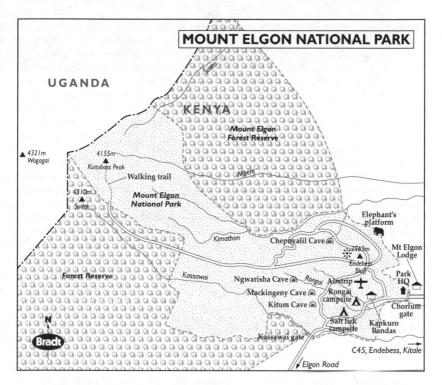

you can visit this 40ha flower farm at Suam, about 30km from Kitale, near Mount Elgon. It is remarkable how the greenhouse environment can be controlled to such a degree that roses can be nurtured to flower at a specific time – ideal for the Valentine's Day market.
Open by arrangement

Mount Elgon National Park

PO Box 753, Kitale; tel: 054 31456
Open daily 06.30–18.00; park entry fees US$15; vehicle entry KSh200.
Located 26km from Kitale, Mount Elgon is the dominant feature for miles around. A free-standing mountain, the distinctive flat top of **Koitoboss Peak** (4,155m) and the cliffs of the **Endebess Bluff** (2,563m) to the east are clearly defined. A caldera which borders Uganda, Elgon's summit, Wagagai (4,321m), is in Uganda, while Kenya's highest peak is **Sudek** (4,310m). Elgon's name comes from the Maa language *ol doinyo ilgoon*, which literally translates as 'breast-shaped mountain'. The national park has a tremendous diversity of habitats within its 169km², clearly illustrating the effects of altitude on vegetation.

Flora and fauna From the park boundary at 2,200m, open glades change to magnificent stands of forest, with podocarpus, Elgon teak and cedar – home to black-and-white colobus and de Brazza monkeys – rising up through thick bamboo forest to open moorland where there are everlasting flowers and giant heather, continuing up to the clusters of giant lobelia and groundsel nearing the rockface at the summit. **Wildflowers** are at their best between November and January. The park contains the headwaters of the Suam, Turkwel and Nzoia rivers, the importance of conserving the forest being all too evident, as beyond the park boundary forest has given way to intensive cultivation. There are a number of caves on the mountain, some being used for traditional ceremonies by the Sabaot community, while **Kitum cave**, featured in an excellent David Attenborough BBC documentary, is famous for its salt-mining pachyderms. Inside the cave opens into a 50m-wide chamber which extends back 160m, where numerous fruit bats dangle from the ceiling. There are striation marks on the rock where elephants have gouged out the salt with their tusks. It is amazing how the elephants manage to manoeuvre their giant bulk up the steep, narrow path to the entrance, all the more so as they usually visit the cave at night. In the 1980s there were about 500 elephants on Elgon, but severe poaching devastated their numbers and there are now thought to be only around 70 left. The **Mackingeny cave** nearby has a huge domed entrance and is preferred by buffalo. Other animals commonly seen are bushbuck and Defassa waterbuck. **Birdlife** is prolific (240 species), among them Hartlaub's turaco, cinnamon-chested bee-eaters and red-headed parrots. There are several **viewing circuits**, but you'll need 4WD, and **hiking trails**. The trails are marked, but you're best to take a guide from the park entrance. If available, purchase the Kitum cave guidebook at the gate, which describes the trails. The best time for trekking and climbing is between November and March. **Rock climbing** and **caving** can be arranged through specialist operators (page 113, activities chapter).

Where to stay
Kapkuro Bandas and campsites (4 bandas, 2 public and 1 special campsite) Kenya Wildlife Service, Mount Elgon National Park, PO Box 753, Kitale; tel: 054 31456 or through KWS (page 91)
The double, solid, stone-built bandas (2 in 1), each have one room with a single and double bed, a small bathroom, a kitchenette (with cooking utensils and a gas cooker) a small veranda and outside barbecue. They are set in a peaceful glade surrounded by bush and forest, where shy bushbuck may be glimpsed. The campsites are near streams and have no facilities.

HILL FARMING AND PASTORALIST POKOT
Dr David Roden
The ecological variety of present-day Pokot territory is reflected in an economic dichotomy between hill cultivators and lowland pastoralists, although distinctions between the two can be blurred.

Two-thirds of the Pokot are farmers, settled in the valleys, slopes and plateaux of the High Cheranganis and the Sekerr Hills, where rainfall is adequate for crop husbandry, and along the base of the escarpment where there is sufficient water from streams and springs for irrigation. The major concentration of settlement is at around 2,000m above sea level. Scattered family homesteads are located within territorial units, known as *Korok*, which encompass land in several ecological zones from upland sheep moors and indigenous forest above 3,000m to irrigated plots along valley flood plains at about 1,000m. Families commonly hold agricultural plots in several zones, and farm routine is carefully programmed so that there is a constant movement between plots and no intolerable workload at any one time. Much of the farm labour is shared communally and, apart from semi-permanent gardens around homesteads, most land is still tilled for only a few seasons before being left to long fallows. One household may well have four to six fields under crop and 20 others fallow, although the growing population over the last 50 years has brought a reduction in the length of fallow and continuing encroachment on virgin forest.

Rates: Bandas US$40–70 a day plus park entry and vehicle fees; camping US10 per person a day plus park entry and vehicle fees

KITALE NORTH TO THE MARICH PASS

The A1, a good tarmac road, from Kitale to Marich Pass (and on to Lodwar, see *Chapter 13*, page 351) winds through superb scenery, with magnificent panoramic views, passing through the blue, angular, Cherangani Hills and dropping to the arid regions of the north. Before the road was built in the 1970s, this was primarily a trucking route through to Sudan, and it used to take a week for the heavily loaded lorries to ascend the Marich Pass; now it takes a matter of hours. The region remained an isolated economic backwater and only began to change after the Cherangani Highway (as the A1 is known) was built. Even today, people from the region still talk of 'going south to Kenya'. As a result the Pokot still retain a strong traditional culture, although this is changing fast as the young aspire to the trappings of the Western world. If heading north to Lodwar it's well worthwhile spending a couple of days in the Marich Pass area and Cheranganis on the way.

Getting there and away
By bus
There are around half a dozen *matatus* a day from Kitale heading north down the Marich Pass to Lodwar (see *Chapter 13*). They leave from 08.00, and it's best to start early. It's feasible to get dropped off at some of the attractions which are not far off the main road (like Saiwa Swamp National Park, a 6km hike). The main transport stops along the way are the villages of **Makutano** from which you'll need to get a taxi or walk a few kilometres to Kapenguria, and **Ortum**, which centres on a small mission hospital. If heading straight through to Lodwar (a good six-hour journey), carry plenty of water, as it's scorchingly hot on the Turkana plains.

Semi-nomadic Pokot pastoralists graze goats, cattle and the occasional camel, in thick and sometimes tsetse-infested bush, on plains and low hills north of the Rift Valley wall and along the Kenya–Uganda border. As with pastoral peoples elsewhere, they have retained traditions longer than sedentary cultivators. They also frequently come into armed conflict with neighbouring Turkana, Karamajong and Marakwet over grazing rights and watering points. The dry plains are less than a day's walk from hill-farming communities, and a long-established commerce in milk and milk products, livestock, grain and tobacco flourishes at several weekly markets which have grown up along the escarpment base, the interface between herders and farmers. People walk for hours to trade and socialise. Lanut Market, held on Saturdays, is now the largest market, a kaleidoscope of the traditional and the modern. Completion of a metalled road north from Kitale in the early 1980s opened up the area to outside influences. Now petty traders from as far away as Lodwar and Kitale come here to buy the bananas, mangoes, sugar cane and citrus produced from irrigated plots. They mingle with pastoralists adorned in the old way – women are still occasionally garbed in hides and bedecked with broad, beaded necklaces, and brass bracelets and ear hoops, while young dandies stand around in self-conscious knots, snuffing tobacco powder and ogling the girls.

Dr Roden is a director of the Marich Pass Field Studies Centre which is ideally placed for seeing both the hill and pastoralist Pokot lifestyles.

By air

The Marich Pass airstrip, suitable for light aircraft, is 5km from the Marich Pass Field Studies Centre. There is no scheduled service.

Getting organised

It's best to get organised in Kitale before heading north. Limited provisions are available on the way, although there are lively **Pokot markets** at Sigor on Thursdays, Lomut (the most colourful) on Saturdays and Chesegon on Wednesdays, southeast of Marich Pass. In an emergency, the **tourist helpline** is tel: 020 604767. The last main **petrol** stop is at **Makutano**, after which services are unreliable until you reach Lodwar.

Where to stay and eat

Sirikwa Safaris – Barnley's House (rooms, tents and camping) PO Box 332, Kitale; tel: 054 20061, mobile: 0722 767055
Take the A1 north of Kitale and turn off to the right after about 24km. This is an ideal base for exploring the western side of the Cheranganis and for visits to Saiwa Swamp National Park and Mount Elgon. Barnley's House is a delightful old settler home in a rambling garden. This is a family-run operation managed by Jane with her daughter Julia; guests can stay in the house or in furnished tents in the garden. There's also a well-organised campsite providing hot showers and firewood. Jane Barnley's home-cooking and picnics are highly rated. **On offer:** birdwatching and trekking in the Cheranganis with excellent English-speaking guides available for hire (KSh600 a day); visits to Saiwa Swamp and Mount Elgon National parks; visits to Sirikwa holes.
Rates: from KSh3,600 full board per person sharing; camping KSh360
Marich Pass Field Studies Centre (camping, 19 rondavels, 4 cottages, 2 dormitories) PO Box 564, Kapenguria
This is a delightful setting at the foot of the Marich Pass on the Moruny River, where Pokot come to water their livestock. The centre is located on a 12ha site surrounded by the magnificent Cherangani Hills with views to mounts Koh and Mtelo. Primarily an educational enterprise catering for school and university groups, the centre opened in 1994 and works in close collaboration with the Pokot people. It also provides volunteers to work in the area. It established the Marich Development Fund which donates US$15 per visitor towards community projects. The campsite has showers and long-drop toilets. The simply furnished rondavels (sleep 2/3), similarly furnished cottages (sleep 6) and dormitories all share communal long-drop toilets and showers. There's an excellent, small restaurant serving a mixture of ethnic dishes and wholesome fare. **On offer:** English-speaking Pokot guides can be hired for trekking, caving, visiting Pokot homesteads and local markets and goldpanning.
Rates: camping from KSh250; rondavels from KSh950 a double; dormitories from KSh300

What to see and do

Kapenguria Museum

PO Box 383, Kapenguria; tel: 054 2050
In the small town of Kapenguria, 35km from Kitale off the A1 to Lodwar, the museum is at the top of the rise leading to the district offices. Formerly the prison where a number of Mau Mau freedom fighters were banished for seven years hard labour during colonial times, including Kenya's first president, Jomo Kenyatta, you can visit the prison cells where they were held. There's a collection of press records and photographs relating to the Mau Mau uprising (page 11). In addition there are excellent ethnic displays of the Pokot and Sengwer cultures.
Open daily 08.00–18.00; entry KSh200

Kaisagat Desert Garden

About 18km from Kitale on the A1 to Lodwar, this garden, owned by John Wilson, a renowned plant collector, contains a superb variety of indigenous and exotic succulent plants. A network of paths wind around rocky mounds, where plants from Africa and South America may be seen.

Sirikwa holes

There are a number of Sirikwa holes in the Cherangani Hills, Kaptagat and Moiben areas, with some of the best examples around Barnley's House (see opposite). The holes are depressions in the ground, either natural or excavated, which were used by the Sirikwa tribe as dwellings or stockades for containing their livestock. Little is known about the Sirikwa, but it is thought they were driven out of northern Kenya about 200 years ago by invading tribes.

Saiwa Swamp National Park

PO Box 753, Kitale; tel: 054 55022
Open daily 06.30–18.00; park entrance fee US$15; vehicle entry KSh200
Take the A1 north from Kitale, turn off at Kipsaina village and follow the dirt road for 6km to the park entrance. Tiny in size, only 3km², it's the only national park in Kenya where one may see the elegant, semi-aquatic **sitatunga** antelope. There are three **nature trails** and a rickety board walk around the swamp, with several sitatunga viewing platforms. Other species which may be seen are the endangered de Brazza monkey, otters, giant forest squirrels, black-and-white colobus monkey, bushbuck and grey duiker. **Birdwatching** is excellent and there are no vehicles in the park.

There is **camping** available in the park. There's one camping ground and a serviced campsite near the park entrance, but you'll need to be self-sufficient. It's not a particularly attractive site and better value to stay at Sirikwa Safaris Campsite near by.
Rates: US$8 plus park entrance fee US$15 and vehicle fee KSh200

Kipsaina Wetland Project

PO Box 18, Kipsaina; tel: 054 55006 (call box – ask for Maurice).
This project is situated about 20km from Kitale on the A1 to Lodwar; turn off shortly after the village of Kipsaina. It's run by Maurice Wanjala, a keen conservationist with an in-depth knowledge of the area. From here you can hire English-speaking guides and bicycles for visits to Saiwa Swamp nearby.

Kitale Nature Reserve

PO Box 1556, Kitale; tel 0325 31476
Located 5km from Kitale on the A1 to Lodwar, the turn-off is just before the bridge crossing the Koitoboss River. A 40ha reserve, it contains a variety of habitats – acacia grassland and woodland, riverine forest and seasonally flooded swamp – with nature trails bordered by wild date palms and orchids. There's also a snake collection. Light refreshments are for sale.

Kongolai Escarpment and Kacheliba Circuit

Follow the A1 north of Kitale to Makutano, and after about 5km turn off to Kongolai. The 700m descent offers panoramic vistas to Mount Kadam (3,000m) in Uganda, the angular outline of the Cherangani range and the arid lands stretching far to the distant northern horizon. The road crosses the Suam River, where Pokot watering their livestock are a familiar sight, and then branches off, rejoining the A1 again at Cheperaria.

GOLDPANNING IN THE MORUNY RIVER

The Moruny River, which rises in the Cheranganis, contains traces of alluvial gold. Not enough to merit commercial exploitation, it gives a supplementary income to the Pokot agriculturalists who farm on the terraced hillsides of the Cheranganis. This cottage industry evolved in the 1950s. Goldpanners, equipped with large metal basins (*souferias*) and a stick, will rinse through the gravel and sand in search of specs of gold. It's a thankless task under the scorching sun, but patience and persistence pay off. Minute fragments of gold are found, scarcely the size of a pinhead, and stored in a chicken-feather quill, bunged with a piece of rubber and then conveniently wedged in the hair. The gold is weighed and sold at the co-operative at Ortum, which in turn sells the gold to Asian traders from Eldoret. A day's work might earn KSh200, but often less.

You can try your hand at goldpanning at the Marich Pass Field Studies Centre (page 348) where guides and equipment cost about KSh350 for a half day.

Cherangani Hills

This is the most extensive mountain range in Kenya, rising to Nagen (3,581m), with the eastern flank running parallel to the Kerio Valley and forming one of the major escarpments in the Rift Valley, dropping abruptly from 3,000 to 1,000m in as little as 6km. The hills provide some of the finest **trekking** in the country in dramatic scenery. The foothills around 2,200m are inhabited by the Hill Pokot, farmers growing sorghum and finger millet on the terraced hillsides. Donkey trails wind up into the hills, passing the thatched huts of Pokot homesteads, where you can see ancient irrigation channels, many of which are still in use. Passing through riverine, coniferous and bamboo forest, the country finally opens up on to an extensive area of open moorland, sparsely inhabited by shepherds tending their flocks, in the High Cheranganis. The best way to explore the Cheranganis is to arrange treks through Sirikwa Safaris or Marich Pass Field Studies Centre (page 348) who have English-speaking guides. Alternatively bookings can be made through Savage Wilderness Safaris (page 102). **Caving** is another option. The Marich Pass Field Studies Centre sells a booklet by Edward Allen on *Caves around Marich Pass*, there being a couple of deep caves at Sokar, a three-hour climb above Wakor, halfway between Marich and Ortum, and rock shelters in the Wei Wei Valley. Guides can be hired from Marich, but for more serious expeditions contact the Cave Exploration Group of East Africa (page 114).

Northern Kenya

Northern Kenya covers a third of the country, for the most part arid rangelands sparsely inhabited by nomadic pastoralists – Pokot, Turkana, Samburu, Boran, Rendille and Gabbra. Remote and inaccessible, interspersed with isolated, forested mountain ranges and bisected by the northern Rift Valley lake of Turkana, the region boasts two World Heritage Sites at Sibiloi and Central Island national parks and a biosphere reserve at Mount Kulal near Loyangalani. It's also central to the discoveries of early man at Koobi Fora. This chapter covers the areas north of the Cheranganis, Maralal and Isiolo. The rugged wilderness of the north is not for the faint-hearted – it's a tough environment – but for those who seek challenge and adventure, it's irresistible.

LODWAR AND WEST TURKANA

Lodwar is essentially a one-horse town at the foot of the Ngapoi Hills, but it's the most sizeable settlement in the northwest, discounting the 'Aid City' of Lokichogio, and has a distinct frontier spirit. It's the administrative area for Turkana and its inhabitants are predominantly a mix of the feisty Turkana tribespeople and the transient trucking community. North from Lodwar the A1 continues through bleak arid scenery passing through **Kakuma** (300km), with its large refugee camps, to **Lokichogio** (250km) near the Sudanese border. The aid city of Lokichogio is in essence an oasis of affluence in the impoverished lands of Turkana. It's the base for the United Nations, Red Cross and other aid organisations for their work in southern Sudan. Consequently, it has one of the busiest airfields in Kenya flying in food aid for distribution in Sudan as well as the refugee camps. There's little reason to head this way unless you're involved in the aid business, and if you do, it's preferable to fly in on the scheduled daily service from Nairobi. Accommodation is scarce and very expensive. There's still a civil war in southern Sudan so access is inadvisable and difficult.

Getting there and away

Prior to heading north, you will need to check the security situation. Leaving the Marich Pass in the south, the A1 (tarmac, but surface variable due to damage after El Niño and the heavy haulage trucks of the World Food Programme ferrying supplies to the refugee camps at Kakuma and Lokichogio) runs parallel to the Rift Valley escarpment crossing the Pokot plains to **Kainuk** (40km), the border zone between the tribal areas of Pokot and Turkana. It's a busy transit settlement – lorries and buses stop here and vehicles congregate for the convoy running north to Lodwar (although in practise vehicles travel at their own pace). However, there are plenty of cheap hotels serving local food. From Kainuk to **Lokichar** (50km)

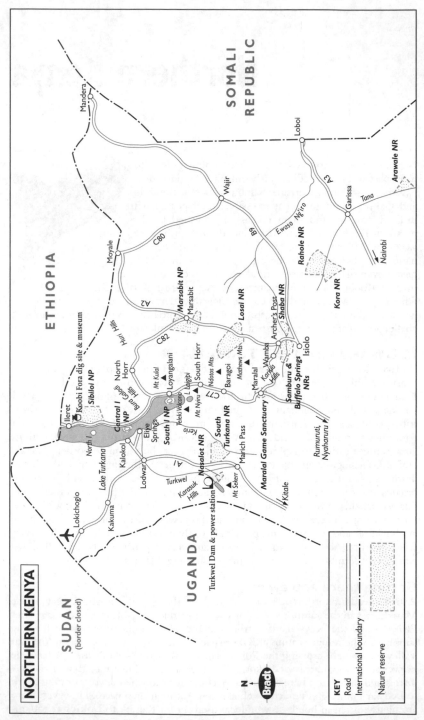

there are outcrops of volcanic hills to the east, with the scenery becoming increasingly arid. At Lokichar you can sometimes watch the graceful Turkana nomads watering their camels at the shallow wells. There's a collection of small shops and the Reformed Church Mission has a good craft shop. From Lokichar to Lodwar it's a further 100km across a dry plain interspersed by the occasional oryx and Turkana camel herders eking out a desperate existence. Be aware that the road can sometimes be closed for 48 hours due to flash floods during the rainy season, there being around 100 drifts where riverbeds cross the road. North from Lodwar the A1 continues to Lokichogio. As with the southern section of the A1, the road is subject to flash floods during the rains and you will need to drive in convoy and check the security situation before leaving due to banditry on the route.

By bus
There are regular *matatus* from Kitale to Lodwar. If going from Marich Pass, you're best to go to Ortum to connect with a *matatu* heading north. Ask at Marich Pass Field Studies Centre (see page 348) or in Ortum for details.

By air
Lodwar has an airstrip, but no scheduled services are available. There are daily scheduled flights to Lokichogio from Nairobi.

Getting organised
It's best to get organised in Kitale or Eldoret before heading north. In Lodwar, for **changing money** there's a Kenya Commercial Bank (but service can be slow and do not rely on being able to cash travellers' cheques), a **post office** (open Monday–Friday 08.00–17.00, Saturday 09.00–12.00) and a lively **market** – a good place to purchase **turkana baskets** – in the centre of town. In an emergency the **tourist helpline** is tel: 020 604767. There are also a couple of **petrol stations** but fuel is much more expensive here than in other parts of the country.

Where to stay and eat
North of Marich Pass
Mtelo View Campsite (self-catering; 2 rondavels, camping)
About 15km north of the Marich Pass in the Sekerr Mountains, this campsite is run by a Pokot family who live on site. From Marich follow the A1 for 2km and turn left along a sandy track and on to a concrete road leading up the escarpment, continuing on a track to Mareng before descending across farm plots to Mba'ara. It's an ideal base for trekking to Mount Mtelo and the Sekerr range. There are 2 rondavels, showers and pit latrines. Wood is for sale – it does get chilly, being at 2,500m – and the family kitchen is shared with self-catering visitors. Basic meals – breakfast, KSh100, lunch and dinner, KSh150 – and soft drinks are available.
Rates: rondavels from KSh400; camping KSh200

Lodwar
Nawoitorong Guest House (rooms, bandas, camping) PO Box 192, Lodwar; tel: 054 21027
About 1km south of Lodwar, the guesthouse is 2km off the main road to the east. If coming by bus, take a taxi from the stage in Lodwar which will cost about KSh200. It's run by a local women's group. The dormitory rooms in the main building are well kept and clean, with separate showers and toilets, while food varies. The bandas, sleeping 2–4, have more privacy, and some are self-catering with their own kitchen.
Rates: rooms from KSh400 B&B; bandas from KSh1,200; camping from KSh100
Turkwel Lodge PO Box 14, Lodwar; tel: 054 20166

The lodge is west of the bus stage in the centre of town. The rooms vary in quality, but most have a fan, and en-suite shower rooms, while the cottages have similar facilities but are more spacious. There's a reasonable restaurant which serves Western-style meals like steak and chips. There's often a disco at weekends, so it can be noisy.
Rates: rooms from KSh500 B&B; cottages from KSh1,000

In addition to the restaurants listed above there are several **cheap eats** in town. **Hotel Salama**, next to the bus stage and run by Somalis (open 24 hours) is probably the best. Others of a similar vein are **Africana Silent Lodge** and the **Lucky Star Hotel**.

What to see and do
The section below is structured from south to north.

Climbing Mount Mtelo and the Sekerr range
It's a day's excursion to climb Mount Mtelo (3,325m) from Mba'ara (2,133m) at the top of the Koimat escarpment. Guides can be arranged through the Mtelo Mountain View Campsite (page 353) or the Marich Pass Field Studies Centre (page 348). The mountain is revered by the Pokot as it's the resting place for their supreme being in Pokot mythology. As the altitude changes, so does the vegetation, passing through distinct zones of thornscrub and bracken to dense montane forest, with orchids, lichens and a variety of monkeys, to bamboo thickets and forest glades leading on to groves of giant lobelias and heather to open moorland.

Nasalot National Reserve
Kenya Wildlife Service, page 61
Open daily 06.30–18.30; reserve entry US$15; vehicle entry KSh200
The reserve is about 20km northwest of Marich, signposted off the main A1 highway to the left. Covering 92km², it's bordered by the Turkwel and Wei Wei rivers, creating an important ecosystem of river valleys and flood plains, with evergreen forests dominated by fig and acacia trees. Although there's plenty of game – elephant, hippo, eland, lesser kudu, bushbuck, lion, leopard and jackal – it's not easy to see, but the scenery is interesting, with views to Mount Mtelo and the Karasuk Hills on the way to the Turkwel Gorge. Around 150 bird species have been recorded in the reserve.

Turkwel Gorge and dam
Kerio Valley Development Authority, PO Box 2660, Eldoret; tel: 053 63361
Entry is via the Nasalot National Reserve north of the Marich Pass. Visits to the dam wall and the turbine house can be arranged by special permission through the Kerio Valley Development Authority and you'll require your own transport. The Turkwel dam was opened in 1993 by the former president, Daniel Arap Moi. At the time it was the largest single development project undertaken by the Kenya government and it's capable of supplying 20% of the country's electricity. Although local Pokot were compensated for their land, the long-term environmental effects on the Turkwel River downstream are yet to be fully appreciated.
Rates: free entry to the gorge, but US$15 park entry and KSh200 vehicle-entry fee applicable for Nasalot National Reserve

South Turkana National Reserve
Kenya Wildlife Service, page 61

Open daily 06.30–18.30; free entry, although this may be reviewed in the future to US$15 with vehicles KSh200

The reserve is about 50km north of the Marich Pass to the east of the A1 highway. Until 2002 it was only possible to walk in the reserve, but KWS has been busy upgrading the road network. It covers 1,000km² and has a number of permanent **rivers**, the Kerio being the most significant, fringed by thorny riverine forest, and a number of salty springs. **Birdlife** is abundant, congregating along the water courses, and there are plenty of elephant, lesser kudu and buffalo. There are views to the volcanic hills of Laiteruk and Kailongol. **Walking** with an armed ranger is currently permitted.

Camping is available. Book through KWS, page 91. There's a rangers' camp, where it would probably be possible to camp, in the reserve, but there are no facilities.

Rates: currently free, but this may change soon due to the improvements in the reserve's infrastructure, in which case payment would be US$8 plus reserve and vehicle entry fees.

LAKE TURKANA

The first Europeans who trekked through the hostile expanse of desert terrain to reach the lake were Count Samuel Teleki and Lieutenant Ludwig von Hohnel in 1888 who named the lake Rudolf, after the then crown prince of Austria. During the 1970s its name was changed to Lake Turkana, and it's also affectionately known as 'The Jade Sea' after John Hillaby's book of the same name, a reference to its ever-changing, colourful reflections. A long, narrow, Rift Valley lake, stretching 265km from the Ethiopian border to the Suguta Valley in the south and averaging 30km wide, it has three volcanic islands, Central and South islands being national parks. In addition there's the famous fossil site at Koobi Fora in Sibiloi National Park. The national parks are World Heritage Sites.

The lake itself sustains 60 species of fish, many being a huge attraction to visiting anglers – tiger, cat and puffer fish, tilapia and enormous Nile perch being common – as well as providing a subsistence living for the Turkana, El Molo and Dassenach tribespeople. The lake is fed by waters from the Omo River in the north and the Turkana and Kerio rivers in the south, but lake levels have fluctuated dramatically over the years. Of the freshwater Rift Valley lakes, Turkana is the most saline, and in parts the water is completely unpalatable.

The western shore and Central Island

From Lodwar, the main places accessible on the lake are **Kalokol**, **Lobolo Springs** and **Eliye Springs** and visits to **Central Island** from Kalokol.

Getting there and away

From Lodwar take the road northeast to **Kalokol** (about 60km) on Lake Turkana. If going to **Eliye Springs**, about 10km from Lodwar, there's a road on the right heading east (about 40km). Lobolo springs are about 25km north of Eliye Springs. If going to Eliye and Lobolo springs the tracks pass through heavy sand and you'll need 4WD.

By bus

There are plenty of *matatus* running from Lodwar to Kalokol, but no public transport to Lobolo or Eliye Springs.

By air

There's an airstrip at Eliye Springs, but no scheduled flights are available.

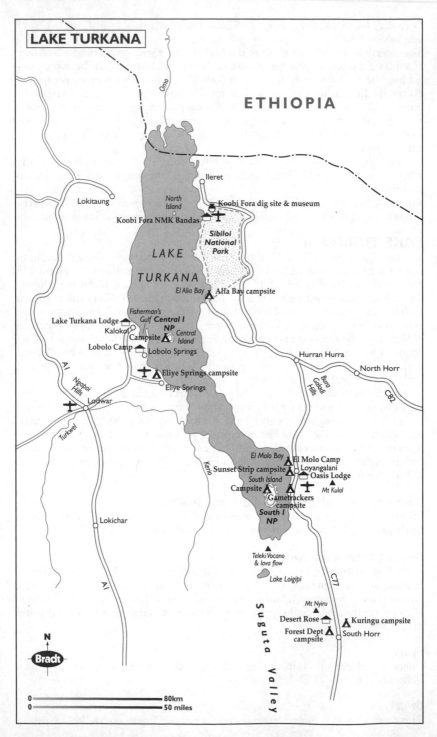

LAKE TURKANA

ETHIOPIA

Omo

Ileret

Lokitaung

North Island

Koobi Fora dig site & museum

Koobi Fora NMK Bandas

Sibiloi National Park

LAKE

TURKANA

El Alia Bay

Alia Bay campsite

Fisherman's Gulf

Lake Turkana Lodge

Central I NP

Kalokol

Central Island

Campsite

Lobolo Camp

Lobolo Springs

Hurran Hurra

North Horr

Eliye Springs campsite

Bura Galadi Hills

C82

Eliye Springs

Ngaboi Hills

Lodwar

Turkwel

Kerio

El Molo Bay

El Molo Camp

Sunset Strip campsite

Loyangalani

Oasis Lodge

South Island

Campsite

Mt Kulal

Gametrackers campsite

Lokichar

South I NP

Lokichar

A1

Teleki Vocano & lava flow

Lake Loigipi

Mt Nyiru

Desert Rose

Kuringu campsite

Forest Dept campsite

South Horr

Suguta Valley

C77

N

Bradt

0 ———— 80km
0 ———— 50 miles

By boat

There's no formal boat transport on the lake, although in theory it's possible to cross the lake with a local fishing boat for a negotiated fee. But be aware that there have been crocodile incidents at the southern end of the lake, with boats being attacked, and give due consideration to the safety aspects of the boat and weather conditions. At times Lake Turkana, with its fearsome, turbulent winds, gets as rough as the North Sea, so it can be very dangerous.

Kalokol

There's little to see here apart from an abandoned Norwegian fish factory: well-intentioned aid gone awry, it was built so that the Turkana could freeze their catch, but before long the generator packed up and, to make matters worse, the lake levels receded leaving the factory high and dry. Ironically, it's now used for drying fish, a method of preservation more suited to the environmental conditions. Kalokol's only draw is as a hop-off point for visiting Central Island, although the lake itself is about 4km from Kalokol on Ferguson's Gulf where you can watch the Turkana net-fishing. There are numerous 'plastic boys' as the touts are known, who will arrange boat trips, often at hugely inflated prices. But do be aware of the safety aspect – most of the boats are unlicensed and the lake weather is unpredictable. You're best to arrange a boat trip with Jade Sea Journeys at Lobolo Springs Camp about 25km south of Kalokol, but they're not cheap (US$250 a day for a boat), or through Lake Turkana Lodge.

Where to stay and eat

Lake Turkana Lodge (16 cabins; swimming pool) Book through USA booking office: tel: 0425 895 8585; fax: 0425 895 9599; email: turkana@hillbarrett.com; web: www.ivorynet.com/laketurkana

This was the original fishing lodge on Ferguson's Gulf and is reached by boat from the shore about 4km from Kalokol town. It has basic accommodation in wooden cabins which have en-suite shower rooms, with flush toilets, and a large veranda overlooking the lake. Simple meals can be taken at the lodge. The swimming pool is undergoing refurbishment, so may not be operational. The campsite has basic facilities. **On offer:** boat transfers, boat excursions on the lake, sport fishing with antiquated equipment from a motorised *ssese* canoe and visits to a Turkana village.

Rates: cabins from US$25 per person sharing; camping US$10

There's little to merit staying in Kalokol itself. If you do have to stay you could try **Skyways Lodge**, where rooms cost around KSh400. It is also possible to camp at the lakeshore 4km away, but it's not very peaceful due to a persistent entourage of children.

Lobolo Springs
Where to stay and eat

Lobolo Camp (6 tents) Book through Bush Homes of East Africa, page 90

This is a private fishing camp in a peaceful setting surrounded by a doum palm forest on the lakeside. The camp is owned and run by Halewijn and Joyce Sheuerman, who have an in-depth knowledge about the lake and its environs, having spent many years running expeditions to the Omo Delta. The tents, under a doum palm thatch, face on to the lake, each individually designed with small verandas, large windows and en-suite showers and short-drop toilets. **On offer:** lakeshore fishing, birdwatching, visits to Turkana villages. Boats can be hired for the day (US$250) for sport fishing offshore and visiting Central Island. Longer excursions around the lake to the Omo River Delta are also available.

Rates: from US$295 full board per person sharing. Closed April.

TURKANA NILE CROCODILES

Lake Turkana has one of the world's highest populations of Nile crocodile, estimated to be around 20,000, although today you never see thousands of crocodile at a time, as some accounts suggest. Crocodiles have inhabited the lake since prehistoric times. On the eastern shore, at the Koobi Fora fossil site, jaws over 1.5m long were found from a crocodile believed to have been over 13.5m in length. At one time there were five different species of crocodile in the lake; today one species remains. At Koobi Fora, present-day crocodiles can be seen mating between November and December, with the eggs hatching in March. On the spit, at night, you can sometimes see up to 100 crocodiles. At Lobolo on the western shore nesting females can be viewed at the lodge, while at Crocodile Lake on Central Island there are about five adult crocodile and numerous sub-adults which spend their first year in the crater before heading for the fish-rich waters of Turkana. For the most part, the crocodiles do not cause a problem, but there are man-eaters in the north and south of the lake, and boat attacks have been known. In the Suguta Valley south of the lake, on Lake Loigipi, it's possible to watch hyena preying on young crocodile on the Teleki lava flow.

Fishing and lake excursions

Jade Sea Journeys Book through Bush Homes of East Africa, page 90.

Based at Lobolo Lodge at Lobolo springs, mid-way between Eliye Springs and Kalokol, Jade Sea Journeys offers **fishing** for Nile perch and tilapia from the lodge and lake excursions north to the **Omo River Delta**, a 1,000km² delta 35km wide which has magnificent birdlife and fascinating Dassenech tribesmen, to **Koobi Fora** on the eastern lake shore and to **South Island** and the **Suguta Valley** by arrangement.

Rates: from US$1,825 per person for a 5-night expedition circumnavigating the lake, inclusive of park fees

Eliye Springs

The Eliye Springs are about 50km south of Kalokol, near the lake. A rundown, semi-abandoned angler's resort, visited by the occasional overland truck, it has a pleasant, laid-back ambience with doum palms surrounding the spring and friendly Turkana selling their trinkets. Its main attraction is that, at your own risk, you can swim in the lake here – but do keep an eye out for crocodiles. There's also a swimming pool which is usually full, fed by the springs.

Where to stay

Eliye Springs (camping; swimming pool)

The fishing resort is now closed, but you can negotiate to camp here. You'll need to be completely self-sufficient.

Rates: by negotiation

Central Island National Park

Open daily 06.30–18.30; park entry fee US$15

This small (5km²) volcanic island is about 10km offshore from Ferguson's Gulf. It has three vents, two of which have formed freshwater and soda crater lakes. The **Flamingo Crater** has superb birdlife – up to 20,000 lesser flamingos cover the lake at certain times of year while goliath and grey herons and Eurasian spoonbills can be seen nesting on the cliffs. Crocodiles inhabit **Crocodile Lake** and large water turtles may also be seen on the island, but they are severely threatened by poaching.

It is possible to **camp** on Central Island but there are no facilities available so you'll need to be self-sufficient.

Rates: US$8 in addition to park entry fee

The eastern shore

The main places to visit along Turkana's eastern shore are **Loyangalani**, at the southern end of the lake, the best place for taking excursions to **South Island National Park**, and **El Molo Bay** a few kilometres north of Loyangalani, home to Kenya's smallest tribe, the el Molo; while in the north are **Sibiloi National Park**, the fossil site of **Koobi Fora** – about 40km south of the **Omo River basin** – and the Ethiopian border.

Getting there and away

Prior to heading north, you will need to check the security situation. In addition 4WD (preferably in convoy) is a necessity together with self-sufficiency for supplies and fuel. From **Maralal** the most direct route is the C77 north through **Baragoi**, **South Horr** and the **Kibrot Pass** to **Loyangalani**. Alternatively, if coming via **Marsabit**, take the A2 from Samburu National Reserve passing the Losai National Reserve to **Marsabit**. In Marsabit, take the C82 to the northwest crossing the Chalbi Desert to **North Horr** and then head south on the C77 to **Loyangalani**.

By bus

There is no public transport to Loyangalani, and it's inadvisable to try hitching here as any local transport, which tends to be few and far between, is normally missionary vehicles which favour giving locals a lift rather than itinerant travellers. By far the best option is to take the Turkana Bus or the Gametrackers equivalent (see page 129).

By air

There are airstrips at Loyangalani and Koobi Fora, but no scheduled air services are available.

By boat

Although Loyangalani is theoretically accessible from other lakeside destinations, in practice it is used more as a base from which to take boat trips on the lake.

Where to stay and eat

Oasis Lodge (15 rooms; swimming pool) PO Box 14829, Nairobi; tel: 020 503267; fax: 020 501585; email: willtravel@swiftkenya.com

Run by an eccentric German, the lodge has superb views over the lake and is flanked by the Mount Kulal massif to the east. Primarily a fishing lodge, the rooms are in simple, rather basic, wooden chalets and all have en-suite shower rooms. The food is variable, although there's usually a cold beer to wash it down. If you're not staying at the hotel, it is possible to use its facilities for KSh300, although access is not always guaranteed. **On offer:** boat trips to South Island, hiking up Mount Kulal, lake fishing and boat hire.

Rates: from US$100 full board per person sharing. Closed mid-May to July.

LAKE TURKANA – STUDIES OF HUMAN EVOLUTION AND PREHISTORY

Dr Louise Leakey

Kenya's northernmost lake, over 200km long, Turkana has appropriately been named the 'Jade Sea' for its striking colour and size. Surrounded by wind-blown sands, arid shrubland, extinct volcanoes and lava flows, its main inflow is from the north, where rain in the Ethiopian highlands drains into the lake via the Omo River. The lake has not been a permanent feature in geological time. In the past, it was reduced to a large meandering river flowing through the basin and out to join the ocean. There is no outflow of water from the present lake, although large amounts of water are lost through evaporation.

The ancestral Omo River, lined with lush riverine forest and swamps, provided an ideal habitat for an array of mammals and reptiles. With rapid deposition and burial of skeletal remains, alongside regular volcanic activity, the Turkana basin has preserved a detailed and well-dated fossil record. Volcanic ash horizons are an integral part of the interpretation and dating of the deposits in the region.

The Turkana basin has been the focus of investigations by the **Koobi Fora Research Project** of the National Museums of Kenya (NMK). Palaeoanthropological research began in the late 1960s with a team of Kenyans led by Dr Richard and Meave Leakey. Their work concentrated on fossil deposits encompassing 1,200km² on the east side of the lake. This area is now protected within the boundaries of Sibiloi National Park, now designated a World Heritage Site in recognition of its prehistoric value. Numerous important

Mama Changa (18 rooms) on the main street near the Cold Drink Hotel
The rooms and ablution facilities are basic but good value and conveniently there's cheap food available nearby at the Cold Drink Hotel.
Rates: rooms from KSh200
El Molo Camp (camping; swimming pool)
Located next to Oasis Lodge, this is a pleasant campsite providing an open, shaded banda, showers and long-drop toilets
Rates: from KSh200 for camping; swimming KSh200
Sunset Strip Campsite (camping)
This campsite is used by the **Turkana Bus** and offers basic shade, showers and long-drop toilets. When a tour is in residence, it is not always possible to camp here
Rates: from KSh200
Gametrackers Campsite (12 bandas)
Located 7km south of Loyangalani, this is a private campsite used by Gametrackers, see page 102. The bandas are thatched with Turkana palms and there are separate showers and toilets and a kitchen area. The camp has a delightful setting among doum palms on the shore with views across the lake to South Island. If not in use, it may be possible to stay or camp here.
Rates: on application
Lokel Houseboat (4 cabins) Book through Mellifera Collection, PO Box 24397, Nairobi; tel: 020 577381; email: mellifera@swiftkenya.com. A hosted, custom-built houseboat, 46ft x 20ft, Lokel is designed to provide a safe haven from the desert winds. There's a covered deck for relaxing and eating (wholesome meals) and fishing tackle is provided. The cabins sleep 2 and there are toilets (heads) and a hot shower on board.

fossils were recovered contributing to the understanding of human evolution and its context. In the 1980s the research team worked fossil deposits on the west side of Lake Turkana making further important discoveries including a complete skeleton of *Homo erectus* (1.6 million years) and a new species of hominid, *Kenyanthropus platyops* (3.6 million years) which extended diversity in the hominid fossil record back in time.

The research team, supported by the National Geographic Society and other donors, has now moved back to the east side of the lake. The Turkana basin continues to provide new evidence to the understanding of our evolutionary past. The team of trained fossil hunters and young professionals work from the research camp at Koobi Fora, a sandy promontory on the eastern lakeshore. This multidisciplinary and international research initiative aims to continue to contribute to the understanding of our evolutionary past.

Growing numbers of livestock and people provide an increased threat to both wildlife and fossils outside the protected area of Sibiloi National Park making fossil recovery outside the park a priority. All the fossils recovered are stored and studied in the National Museum of Kenya in Nairobi.

Louise Leakey is the leader of the Koobi Fora Research Project. She is the daughter of Richard and Meave Leakey and granddaughter of the late Louis and Mary Leakey whose investigations into human origins began in 1931 in Olduvai Gorge in Tanzania.

Visitors to Sibiloi National Park can visit the NMK site at Koobi Fora. Further information on the Koobi Fora Research Project is available from www.leakey.com and www.nmk.or.ke.

The houseboat is used as a mother boat, with fishing being from a smaller craft. **On offer:** fishing and more fishing, but birdwatching and lakeside excursions can be arranged.
Rates: from US$200 full board per person sharing. No children under 10.

South Island National Park
Open daily 06.30–18.30; park entry fee US$15
A 30km round trip from Loyangalani, the park covers an area of 39km². It has excellent crocodile viewing, with enormous crocodiles sunning themselves on the volcanic sand banks, together with pods of hippo. It also has a number of venomous snakes – puff adders are the most likely to be seen, but there are also vipers and spitting cobras.

It is possible to **camp** on the island but there are no facilities and you'll need to get permission from the warden.
Rates: US$8 plus park entry fees

El Molo Bay
About 8km north of Loyangalani is El Molo Bay, where you can get a brief, if commercialised, insight into Kenya's smallest tribe – the el Molo. They live in scattered twigloos – grass shelters on a domed frame – and lead a subsistence existence dependent on fishing. It costs a few hundred shillings to visit the village, which is payment for photographs and walking around. The people are exceptionally friendly, but in fact there are few true el Molo left, as they have been assimilated into other tribes.

> ## USEFUL TIP
> When camping at Loyangalani, the wind funnels off Mount Kulal in the late afternoon, and by the evening can be a howling gale which often does not blow out until the following morning. During a storm, the wind can be even more ferocious. Ensure that your tent is well secured.

Fishing excursions

Book through Mellifera Collection (PO Box 24397, Nairobi; tel: 020 577381; email: mellifera@swiftkenya.com). Operated by the Lokel Houseboat, day trips can be arranged on their Swift catamaran, *Born Free* which has two 75hp outboard engines. The excursion includes all fishing tackle and licences and a packed lunch. They operate a 'tag and release' system unless it's a record-sized fish.
Rates: from US$480 for the boat – maximum 4 people. No children under 10.

Note Other fishing excursions can be arranged through Oasis Lodge in Loyangalani, page 359.

Sibiloi National Park

Open daily 06.30–18.00; park entrance fee US$15; vehicle entry KSh200
It's a long, hot, dusty drive north from Loyangalani to Sibiloi National Park. Follow the C77 north for about 45km, and then turn left on to a track to the park. Ask for clear directions from Loyangalani as it's easy to get lost. The road continues north through the Bura Galadi Hills to the small settlement of **Hurran Hurra** (about 40km) where there's a left turn to another small settlement, **Gajos** (about 45km), after which the road descends for another 40km to the southern end of the park at **Alia Bay,** continuing north through the park to **Koobi Fora** and **Ileret**. Alternative transport options are to fly to the Koobi Fora airstrip and then hire an old NMK Land Rover for game drives around the park, or to come by boat on an organised excursion from Lobolo Springs.

History Regarded as the 'Cradle of Mankind' due to its treasure trove of palaeontological discoveries, the Sibiloi National Park opened in 1973 following the Koobi Fora finds of hominids by Richard Leakey in the 1960s and 1970s. It became a World Heritage Site in 1997. Fossils of early man, both *Homo habilis* and *Homo erectus*, were found here, together with those of numerous mammals and Stone Age artefacts. Among the finds were the now extinct behemoth, the forebear of the elephant, which had enormous tusks, dating back some 1.5 million years, and the three-million-year-old shell of a giant tortoise. Research work is ongoing at the site, and, following in the Leakey tradition, Louise Leakey is currently based here running a research project. A visit to the museum and dig sites is fascinating.

Flora and fauna The park covers 1,570km², dominated by yellow spear grass on the plains and doum palms, with increasingly arid bush in its eastern section. There's no water inland from the lake, but the park has a surprising amount of game in its stark environment. Animals such as Grant's gazelle, Grevy's zebra, gerenuk, lesser kudu, cheetah and the rare striped hyena are found here. On the shore the crocodiles mate and nest during November and December, with the baby crocodiles hatching in March. Birdlife is varied, from ducks, pelicans and flamingos to the rare Taita falcon and black-tailed godwit.

At **Koobi Fora** there is simple but perfectly acceptable accommodation in the NMK bandas which have mesh windows and a separate ablution block with showers and toilets. At the southern end of the park there are several campsites on Alia Bay, but these only have basic facilities. Book bandas through NMK (page 183), and camping through KWS.

Rates: bandas KSh1,000, plus park and vehicle entry fees; camping US$8, plus park and vehicle entry fees

Climbing Mount Kulal

Mount Kulal (2,295m), a UNESCO Biosphere Reserve, is a tough climb in the Turkana heat, although it gets cooler as you enter the forest. There's a reasonable footpath to the summit, although it's best to take a guide from Loyangalani. Trips can be arranged through Oasis Lodge (page 359). The top of Mount Kulal has stupendous views west across Lake Turkana with its distinctive jade hue and the vast expanse of the Chalbi Desert to the east.

Rates: excursions with Oasis Lodge cost in the region of US$100 a day

The southern shore
Suguta Valley

The easiest way to reach the valley is from the southern lake shore with Jade Sea Journeys (page 358). It is possible to access the valley from the west, but security can be a problem and there are at present no organised trips. Independently, you might be able to arrange a guide from Baragoi north of Maralal. It is one of the hottest and most hostile places on earth, where temperatures can soar to over 60°C in the shade at midday. It's attraction lies in its very remoteness and barren scenery – the perfect cone of Mount Nyiru, known as the 'stomach of the elephant' and the Teleki volcano and its lava flows, extend some 20km, surrounding Lake Loigipi where around March you can see hyenas preying on the crocodile hatchlings.

MARALAL AND ENVIRONS

Another frontier town and administrative centre, Maralal has a charming Wild West atmosphere, with its wide, dusty, potholed streets lined with pepper trees and wooden houses with wide verandas. It can be a little intimidating at first due to the preponderance of the 'plastic boys', but once that impression's worn off, it's actually a friendly place with a quaint mix of services and shops, particularly for vehicle repairs. It is spread out around forested hills, a contrast to the parched plains of the Leroghi Plateau. Nearby are the Karisia Hills (also known as the Leroghi Hills) which are superb for trekking.

Getting there and away

There are several routes to Maralal. The most direct is the C77 from **Nyaharuru**, a good tarmac road to **Rumuruti** and then a good dirt road to the **Kisima junction** where it joins the C78 from **Wamba**. The road continues north as the C77, crossing the Leroghi Plateau to Maralal. If coming from **Baringo**, the dirt road east of **Loruk** to **Tangulbei** meets the C77 coming from the south. Alternatively, if coming from **Isiolo**, take the A2 north for about 140km, turning northwest at the huge domed massif of Ol Lololokwe on to the C79 to **Wamba**, and then heading west from Wamba on the C78 and C77 to **Maralal**.

By bus

There are regular buses daily leaving early morning and around midday to Nyaharuru where you can connect with buses to Nairobi, and plenty of *matatus* ply the route. If heading north, there are infrequent *matatus* heading to Baragoi.

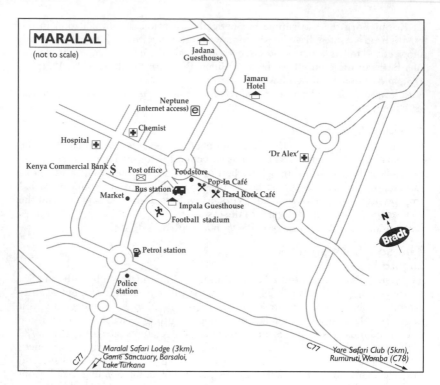

By air

There's an airstrip in Maralal and also at Kisima 16km to the south, but there are no scheduled flights.

Getting organised

Maralal is the last place with a **bank** if heading north. The Kenya Commercial Bank and **post office** (open Monday–Friday 08.00–17.00, Saturday 09.00–12.00) are situated in the centre of town near the lively **market**. For **internet access**, try Neptune, but rates are expensive and you can only send emails. There's also a **pharmacy** and '**Dr Alex'** (tel: 065 2446) has a surgery Monday–Friday from 09.00–19.00, and Saturday 09.30–18.00. In a **medical emergency** there's a hospital (tel: 065 2043). The **police station** (tel: 065 2222) is on the C77 entering town, next to the roundabout, and in an emergency the **tourist helpline** is 020 604767. There are several **petrol stations** in Maralal. Be aware that this is the last reliable petrol stop before heading north.

Where to stay

Yare Safari Club (12 bandas and camping) PO Box 281, Maralal; tel: 065 2295; email: info@yaresafaris.com; web: www.yaresafaris.com
Located about 5km south of Maralal on the C77, this is a popular overlanders campsite, run by Malcolm Gascoigne who trucked the trans-Africa trail in years past. It has a friendly, relaxed, laid-back atmosphere, with a restaurant serving both European-style and African meals – *ugali*, *sukuma wiki* and meat stew, and *nyama choma* on occasion – a bar and lounge and a games room with pool and darts. The bandas are simple but comfortable with en-suite shower rooms, and there are separate showers and long-drop toilets for campers

ARTHUR HENRY NEUMANN (1850–1907)
Peter Faull

Arthur Neumann achieved an almost legendary status in his lifetime – certainly amongst the ranks of the big-game hunters – with the publication in 1898 of his acclaimed book, *Elephant Hunting in East Equatorial Africa*. He is chiefly known for his occupation as a successful hunter of elephants in the wilds of northern Kenya, but what is not generally considered is the fact that this phase of his career only took up a relatively short period of his life. During his less-known years he fought in the Zulu and Boer wars, farmed in South Africa, spent a short time mining for gold in the Transvaal in the 1870s and operated as a transporter and trader in present-day Swaziland. He also acted as a magistrate in Zululand and hunted in the Limpopo Valley before becoming an employee of the Imperial British East Africa Company (IBEAC). Leaving his employment with the IBEAC, he became a professional ivory hunter, outfitting his first foot safari into the interior from Mombasa in 1893. Neumann purchased donkeys and hired porters for his long trek to the Seya Valley, El Bogoi, the Leroghi Mountains and the Omo River at the northern end of what was then Lake Rudolf, now Lake Turkana. Here, his cook, Shebane, was taken by a crocodile and Neumann himself was gored by a cow elephant. Miraculously, he survived thanks to three months of virtual incapacitation and careful nursing by his staff and Ndorobo girlfriend.

The accumulated ivory was then loaded on to the donkeys and the caravan proceeded back to his ivory depot base camp at El Bogoi. In Neumann's day, throughout his travels he did not see one camel between Mombasa and the Omo River – hence his use of donkeys with traditional woven panniers for the long-distance transportation of elephant tusks. He could not claim to be an explorer in the full sense, although he was, indisputably, the first white man to reach into quite a few corners of East Africa, and was the first to record the sighting of Lake Kisima south of Maralal.

In 1995, having read Neumann's book, I decided to interview the last surviving old Ndorobo (hunter-gatherer) tribesmen still living in the area around Bawa and El Bogoi with the objective of finding his almost legendary El Bogoi and his beloved camp with the 'bower tree' repeatedly referred to in his memoirs. Packing two donkeys and one mule and accompanied by my ever-present Staffordshire bull terrier, Pokk, my Ndorobo guide and I explored the montane forests of the Leroghi range and identified Neumann's haunts in the arid *Acacia* bush scrub down in the El Bogoi below. Remarkably little has changed here since this famous ivory hunter read the elephant spoor and checked the wind along many of the same trails that we tread today.

This expedition inspired Peter Faull to set up his safari company, Samburu Trails Trekking Safaris, where you can follow in Neumann's footsteps. For information contact www.samburutrails.com or see page 118.

(although they can use the flush toilets in the main lodge). The campsite is next to a camel pen. **On offer:** this is the venue for the International Camel Derby and Elite Cycle races, held in August (book accommodation well in advance). Available year round are visits to a Samburu blacksmith and *manyattas*, camel hire, camel excursions and guided walks.
Rates: bandas from KSh850 B&B per person sharing; camping Ksh200

Maralal Safari Lodge (20 rooms; swimming pool) PO Box 70, Maralal; tel: 065 2060
About 3km outside Maralal on the road to Barsaloi, this is Maralal's best accommodation.
The main building has a dining-room and lounge area, and a veranda where you can watch
wildlife – gazelle and zebra – at the waterhole. The rooms are in cottages in the garden and
are simply furnished with en-suite shower rooms and flush toilets. There's a reasonable
restaurant where meals cost in the region of KSh500. **On offer:** golf and game watching.
Rates: from US$90 full board per person sharing

There are also numerous **cheap rooms** in town, among them:

Jamaru Hotel tel: 065 2215
The s/c rooms are comfortable and it's reasonably quiet. There's also a good restaurant
serving basic meals.
Rates: room only from KSh350
Jadana Guest House tel: 065 2033
This is one of the newer guesthouses and has good, clean rooms with en-suite facilities. It
combines a bar and butchery and serves good *nyama choma*.
Rates: room only from KSh300
Impala Guest House tel: 065 2290
This is slightly out of the town centre, next to the football stadium. Rooms are reasonable
with shared bathrooms and hot showers. In addition there's secure parking.
Rates: room only from KSh150

Where to eat
In addition to the restaurants listed above, Maralal town boasts several popular
cafés. The **Hard Rock Café** has friendly service and a good selection of food, as
does the Somali-run **Pop-in Café**.

What to see and do
Maralal has its fair share of 'plastic boys' (see page 357) who can be intimidating on
arrival. Some are reasonable guides, while others are unreliable. A couple who come
recommended are Ismail and Lucas, if you want someone to show you around the
town.

International Camel Derby and Elite Cycle Races
Held annually during August by the Yare Safari Club, this is an entertaining
weekend where amateurs and professionals can take part in camel and cycling
races. See page 137 for further details.

Maralal Game Sanctuary
This small sanctuary can be viewed from Maralal Game Lodge – which overlooks
the only permanent waterhole. The zebra, buffalo, impala and warthog are readily
seen. It's a good opportunity for seeing game if you cannot get to the parks and
reserves, but rather a tame alternative.

Camel trekking
Short camel excursions can be arranged in Maralal – from afternoon treks between
Yare Safari Club and Maralal Safari Lodge, to day walks in the Maralal Game
Sanctuary. In addition Yare Safaris (page 364) can arrange longer treks from Maralal.

Karisia Hills – walking and donkey trekking
Also known as the Leroghi range, the Karisia Hills lie to the east of Maralal, rising
to 2,133m. The hills are superb for forest trekking and longer walks to the Il

Ponyeki plains and Seiya Lugga between the Karisias and Mathews ranges. It's easy to get lost in the forest, so you'll need a guide – but it's highly recommended to go on one of the Samburu Trails trekking safaris, run by Peter and Rosalie Faull who know the area intimately. They have knowledgeable Ndorobo and Samburu guides and provisions are carried by a caravan of donkeys as the mountainous terrain is unsuitable for 4WD or camels. Walks to the summit entail following narrow mountain streams and then climbing through thickly wooded and tangled undergrowth, with stinging nettles in places, beneath stands of towering podocarpus and cedar trees and on to elephant trails which traverse the ridge. Elephant and buffalo still frequent the forest and can occasionally be seen if you're in a small group. A day's walking will bring you to Tilia rock, from which there are stupendous views across the plains to the Mathews range some 50km to the east and the Ndotos Mountains to the north. This area was a favoured elephant hunting ground by Arthur Neumann over a century ago (see box, page 365).

MARALAL NORTH TO LOYANGALANI

When heading north of Maralal, check security on the route before you leave – if not with KTF in Nairobi (see page 157), at least with the Yare Safari Club in Maralal who are their local representatives. About 22km after passing through the forested hills from Maralal, on the C77 is a turning west to the village of **Poror**. Surprisingly, after all the forest and arid terrain, this is fertile wheat country. Pyrethrum and miraa are also grown in the area and there are fast-growing gum plantations for supplying poles, firewood and charcoal. From Poror it's about 6km to the crescent-shaped **Losiolo escarpment** from which there are panoramic vistas into the Suguta Valley. The C77 continues north, dropping to the Lopet Plateau and the El Barta plains. The hot, dry and rather featureless terrain passes through the small settlements of **Morijo** and **Marti** before reaching the market town of **Baragoi** (about 150km from Maralal). From Baragoi, the road starts to climb towards the mountainous area of **South Horr** (about 40km). Some 30km south of Baragoi you'll pass a track to the west signposted to Desert Rose Camel Safaris (page 368). Leaving South Horr, the road descends through the narrow Horr Valley, with dramatic scenery as the road is flanked by the mountains of Ol Doinyo Ng'iro on the west and Ol Doinyo Mara to the east, on to blisteringly hot, black lava plains with the massif of Mount Kulal in the distance. After crossing several luggas, you get the exciting first view of Lake Turkana, an inland sea of blue-green waters, and South Island with its distinctive volcanic cones. The road then descends the Kibrot Pass, a rocky, boulder-strewn stretch known as 'the staircase' before reaching the lakeshore about 40km south of **Loyangalani**.

Baragoi evolved as the main trading centre for livestock, buyers coming from as far south as Isiolo. But its urban nature, with one-storey buildings, comes as rather a surprise in this northern backwater. Interestingly, it's a reflection of UN wealth that infiltrated into the area due to the Bosnian war. Samburu warriors enlisted for the Kenyan peace-keeping forces sent to Bosnia, which paid them handsomely. The **South Horr Valley** with its cool, verdant surroundings comes as a welcome respite after the heat and dust of the El Barta plains. A small village, there's a Catholic mission and a couple of hotels. At certain times of year, a camel market takes place here. The valley grows papaya and bananas which can sometimes be purchased at the roadside.

Getting there and away
Heading north, you will need 4WD and need to be fully self-sufficient, carrying extra fuel and water as well as provisions. Being a proficient mechanic for vehicle

breakdowns and having a working knowledge of Swahili is also helpful. It's advisable to drive in a convoy of two or more vehicles, regardless of whether or not there's a regulated requirement to travel in convoy.

By bus
A 4WD *matatu* heads north from Maralal as far as Baragoi – the last outpost for public transport in the north – but its timing is erratic, so check locally for details.

By air
It's possible to helicopter in to Desert Rose Lodge, but there's no airstrip or scheduled flights.

Where to stay and eat
Poror
Poror Farmhouse (4 rooms, farm stay; camping) PO Box 40 Maralal; or book in advance through Samburu Trails, page 118
About 30km from Maralal, this is a charming, rustic farmhouse made from olive and cedar wood with ochre-coloured cement walls on the Faull's family farm. Farmstays and camping are available when they are in residence. The rooms are comfortably furnished with separate bathrooms. The campsite provides showers, long-drop toilets and security. **On offer:** walks and picnics on the farm and to the 'Roof of the World' at the top of the Losiolo escarpment, longer excursions to the Karisias east of Maralal and Bird Mountain – Loporen – in the Rift Valley to the northwest.
Rates: from US$190 full board per person sharing; camping from US$3

Baragoi
For **cheap rooms**, the best is the **Bowmen Hotel**, rooms from KSh350 with shared facilities. There are several **cheap eats** – try **Wid-Wid Inn** or **Hotel Mukhram**. The **Bosnia Bar** is aptly named for the soldiers who fought for the UN in the Bosnian war.

North of Baragoi
Baragoi Water Pump Station Campsite (camping)
About 4km north of Baragoi, there's a track on the right to the pump station (about 1km). Ask for clear directions from Baragoi as there are several tracks and it's easy to take the wrong one. The campsite has showers and long-drop toilets with Samburu askaris. It's colourful, if not very peaceful, as this is the main watering point for the local community.
Rates: KSh200
Desert Rose (5 rooms; swimming pool) Book through the Mellifera Collection, page 91
This mountain eyrie comes as a pleasant retreat after the searing heat of the desert. It nestles in high-altitude podocarpus forest on the southern slopes of Mount Nyiru (2,740m), an hour's drive north of Baragoi, overlooking the granite peak of Mowongosowan, revered by the Samburu as the home of their deity. It's the home of Emma and Yaov Chen, and has been sympathetically designed to complement the natural environment. The rooms are in individual 'houses', with hand-carved four-poster beds and en-suite open-air bathrooms and flush toilets. Food is simple but delicious, with fresh fruit and vegetables from an organic garden, with meals taken on a dining deck overlooking the Seleyan River. **On offer:** bush walks with Samburu guides, birdwatching in the riverine forest (150 species recorded), camel safaris, beauty therapy, natural rock slides, game drives and helicopter excursions.
Rates: from US$325 full board per person sharing. Closed mid-April to mid-May.

South Horr
Forest Department Campsite (camping)
About 1km south of the village is a track to the left leading to the campsite. Only long-drop toilets and an askari are provided, but the site is pleasant, next to a stream.
Rates: from KSh100
Kurungu Campsite (camping) Book through Safari Camp Services, page 102
About 6km from South Horr, the campsite is signposted to the right. This campsite is owned by Safari Camp Services. It has an idyllic setting, surrounded by forest, and good facilities – showers, long-drop toilets and firewood available – and good security. **On offer:** guides can be organised to take you trekking up Mount Nyiru and there's Samburu dancing by arrangement.
Rates: from KSh200

What to see and do
Losiolo escarpment
The view from the top of the escarpment has been dubbed the 'Roof of the World' and 'World's View'. Undoubtedly, the panoramic vista is awesome, peering down from the escarpment edge into the Suguta Valley some 2,000m below. There are a number of trails leading down into the valley, and guides can be arranged. If planning on walking down, go in the cool, early morning hours and take plenty of water as it's scorchingly hot at the bottom of the escarpment.
Rates: entry to the site KSh100; day guide down the escarpment from around KSh300

Camel trekking – the Seiya and Malgis luggas
Several operators have longer camel treks – see page 112. Among them, **Wild Frontiers** and **Desert Rose** have excursions along the Malgis and Seiya luggas between the Ndotos and Mathews ranges. The Seiya flows into the Malgis which eventually disappears into the Kaisut Desert some 50km to the east. These seasonal luggas are up to a kilometre wide, draining water off the forested mountains and even during times of drought water can be found in the brown sand. It's hot walking along the sandy riverbeds, but this remote wilderness has prolific birdlife and there are encounters with the scattered, transient settlements of the Samburu and Rendille on the way.

Mount Nyiru (2,740m)
There are forest trails (not marked) on the lower slopes of the mountain, and Samburu guides can be arranged from the Kurungu Campsite. The forest is home to varied wildlife, where you may glimpse bushbuck, the scarlet flash of a Hartlaub's turaco in flight and attractive butterflies. For those with the stamina, it's an arduous day's trek to the top of the mountain – but the effort comes well rewarded. From the top there are superb views to Lake Turkana.
Rates: guides cost from around KSh300 a day

ISIOLO AND ENVIRONS
Isiolo lies at the end of the tarmac on the A2 heading north. It marks the boundary between the fertile highlands and the arid northern frontier district. Despite its somewhat ramshackle appearance, Isiolo is the gateway to Samburu country, and the lands of the northern nomadic pastoralists – Samburu, Boran, Gabbra, Rendille and Turkana – interspersed with islands of magnificent forested mountains, as well as the Ethiopian border, although most people only venture as far as Samburu, Buffalo Springs and Shaba national reserves. There's a thriving and colourful livestock market – cattle, goats and camels are traded here – as well as an established military training post.

Getting there and away

Isiolo is reached by the A2 if coming from the south, continuing north to Moyale, while from Isiolo the B9 heads east and north to Wajir and the Ethiopian border at Mandera.

By bus

Akamba Bus operates a twice-daily service to Nairobi, leaving early morning and evening. In addition there are numerous *matatus* on the route.

By air

There's an airstrip at Samburu National Reserve with a scheduled daily service on Air Kenya to Nairobi and the Masai Mara and from Meru three times a week on Wednesdays, Fridays and Sundays. There's also an airstrip at Shaba National Reserve, but it has no scheduled flights.

Getting organised

You're best to get organised with major provisions and money in Nairobi, or failing that, Nanyuki rather than in Isiolo. For **changing money**, there's a Barclays Bank, but no ATM. Alternatively, the lodges will exchange money at a premium rate. There's a **post office** open Monday–Friday 08.00–17.00, Saturday 09.00–12.00 and a fruit and vegetable **market**. For **shopping** this is the cheapest place to buy the finely crafted bronze, copper and steel Samburu bracelets. There's a **police point** on the A2 at the northern end of town and in an emergency the **tourist helpline** is tel: 020 604767. There are plenty of **petrol stations** along the main street.

Where to stay and eat

Rangeland Hotel (camping, cottages) tel: 064 2340
About 10km south of Isiolo the Rangeland Hotel, set in extensive gardens, has a pleasant campsite, with basic facilities, although it does get crowded at weekends, and a few cottages. It has a restaurant and bar serving wholesome meals.
Rates: cottages from KSh1,000; camping from KSh200
Bowmen Hotel (40 rooms) PO Box 67, Isiolo; tel: 064 2389
A 3-storey hotel, the rooms are comfortable with en-suite shower rooms. There's a reasonable restaurant and bar and safe parking.
Rates: from KSh1,750 B&B per person sharing

Of the cheap accommodation in Isiolo, consider:

Jamhuri Guest House PO Box 88, Isiolo; tel: 064 2065
Set back from the main street, it's built around a courtyard. It's a friendly place with comfortable rooms, but shared facilities.
Rates: rooms from KSh200
Mocharo Lodge PO Box 106, Isiolo; tel: 064 2385
On the eastern side of town, this is a large establishment, but good value. Rooms are s/c with spacious facilities. In addition there's safe parking.
Rates: rooms from KSh300
Silver Bells Hotel PO Box 247, Isiolo; tel: 064 2251
Next door to the Mocharo Lodge, this hotel is of a similar standard. The rooms are s/c and there's safe parking. It has a reasonable **restaurant** serving good curries.
Rates: rooms from KSh300

In addition to the restaurants listed above there's also a good selection of **cheap eats**. Try the **Salama Restaurant** and the **Frontier Green Café** on the eastern side of the main street.

Above Il Ngwesi and room steward, Laikipia (CF)

Left Maasai men jousting, Selenkay
Conservation Area, near Amboseli (CF)

Below Maasai with cattle at sunset, Amboseli (AZ)

Right Young Luo girl gutting fish at Lake Victoria (CF)

Below Fishing village on Takawiri Island, Lake Victoria (CF)

Samburu and Buffalo Springs national reserves

Open daily 06.30–18.30; reserve entry fees US$30; vehicle entry fee KSh200.
Note *The entrance fee gives access to both reserves*
Located about 10km north of Isiolo to the west of the A2, these two small reserves share a common boundary, the Ewaso Ng'iro River; its name is Samburu for 'muddy waters'. Entry to **Buffalo Springs National Reserve** is off the A2 through the **Ngare Mara gate**, closest to Isiolo, and the **Buffalo Springs gate**, further north. From Buffalo Springs you cross the bridge to enter **Samburu National Reserve** at the **Samburu gate** (main gate and reserve headquarters) or the **Archer's post gate**, about 5km west of Archer's post on the A2. The **West gate** is rarely used as it's on minor back roads in Samburu. There are a number of **game circuits** in both reserves. Although the tracks are well graded, in parts there is heavy sand and 4WD is recommended.

History Initially established as the Samburu-Isiolo Game Reserve in 1948, which was once included in the extensive Marsabit National Reserve, their present boundaries were formed in 1985 and the reserves are managed by the Samburu and Isiolo county councils respectively. Buffalo Springs National Reserve (130km²), south of the river has rolling volcanic plains, rocky outcrops, swamp and a couple of seasonal rivers – the Isiolo and Ngare Mara which flow into the Ewaso Ng'iro. The scenery of Samburu National Reserve (105km²) is similar but more rugged with isolated inselbergs.

Flora and fauna Within both reserves, the thorn scrub and sandy, arid terrain supports **northern species of game**: the Beisa oryx, Somali ostrich – smaller than its contemporary, the Masai ostrich, and with blue legs – Grevy's zebra with their large tufted ears and pinstripes, reticulated giraffe and the gerenuk, as well as buffalo, leopard, cheetah and lion. If you're lucky, you might catch a glimpse of an aardwolf in the evening hours. The **riverine forest** has magnificent *Acacia elatior*, *Kigelia africana*, giant fig trees, Tana river poplar (*Populus ilicifolia*) and Doum palms (*Hyphaene compressa*). There's good bush cover too, with the toothbrush tree, *Salvadora persica*, (so-named because the Samburu use the twigs for cleaning their teeth) being a favourite shrub for browsing elephant. The **Ewaso Ng'iro River** has a healthy crocodile population and hippos. It's also a major draw for wildlife, especially the numerous **elephant families** which cavort and play in the shallow waters. The **birdlife** is superb with over 380 recorded species. White-headed mouse birds, African fish eagles and kingfishers are often seen around the lodges, while the rocky outcrops are the nesting sites for numerous raptors, among them the endangered lesser kestrel and Taita falcon.

Where to stay

Elephant Watch Safari Camp (5 tented rooms) PO Box 54667, Nairobi 00200; tel: 020 334868; fax: 020 243976; email: info@elephantwatchsafaris.com; web: www.elephantwatchsafaris.com
A few kilometres west of Samburu Intrepids, the camp is located on a sand bank of the Ewaso Ng'iro River, surrounded by enormous *Kigelia africana* and *Acacia elatior* trees. Built on land leased from the county council it is run by the Douglas-Hamiltons, renowned for their work in elephant conservation. Stylish and small, the camp opened in 2001 and complements the charity, Save the Elephants. Being quasi-educational, it gives visitors an insight into the fascinating work being undertaken by the research team nearby and game drives centre on meeting the elephant families (look out for the Royals headed up by Queen Victoria) and bulls which roam in the vicinity. The open-plan mess and rooms are under

thatched roofs, facing on to the seasonal river. The mess is swathed in colourful materials, furniture has been fashioned from knarled pieces of wood and rope and novel items have been sourced from Nairobi-based artisans. Meals have an Italian flair with fresh produce from the family farm in Naivasha and are often taken alfresco under the trees. The rooms have spacious square tents with mosquito netting, a private veranda, washing area, smart long-drop loos (with a view) and an open-air bucket shower. **On offer:** game drives, elephant tracking, bush and bird walks with knowledgeable Samburu guides, Samburu dancing and *manyatta* visit.

Rates: from US$475 full board per person sharing

Larsens Camp (17 tents) Book through Block Hotels, page 90

This permanent tented camp is east of the reserve headquarters set in thick riverine forest on the Ewaso Ng'iro. It has an air of exclusivity. The tents are on raised wooden platforms, comfortably furnished and have en-suite showers, flush toilets and a small veranda with leather camp chairs. Gourmet dinners by candlelight, complete with fine china, are taken in a 3-sided dining tent overlooking the river. **On offer:** game drives, bush walks, treehouse cocktails, leopard bait, crocodile feeding and swimming-pool visits at the Samburu Lodge nearby.

Rates: from US$140 full board per person sharing. No children under 5.

Samburu Intrepids Club (27 tents; swimming pool) Book through Heritage Hotels, page 91

This permanent tented camp, developed on ecotourism principles, is west of the reserve headquarters, set under enormous fig and acacia trees on the Ewaso Ng'iro River. The thatched tents are reached by boardwalks. Built on raised wooden platforms facing the river, they are comfortably furnished with four-poster beds, en-suite showers and flush toilets, and a small veranda with reclining chairs. The public areas are spacious with a large bar and dining area. There's also a small museum displaying natural fauna and flora. The buffet-style meals are of a good standard and the service excellent. For each guest, a donation is made to a community development fund which has financed a primary school, bee-keeping project and medical services in the area. **On offer:** game drives with excellent guides, bush walks, birdwatching, camel riding, Samburu dancing, *manyatta* visit, river rafting in season, cultural talks, children's Adventurer's Club, shop, resident doctor.

Rates: from US$100 full board per person sharing

Samburu Lodge (60 rooms, swimming pool) Book through Block Hotels, page 90

The lodge is next door to the reserve headquarters. The first to be built in Samburu, it is a typical old-style Kenyan lodge in a delightful setting. When you come into the reception you look on to the crocodile feeding area, and in the tree opposite a leopard is baited in the evenings. The rooms all have en-suite shower rooms with flush toilets and are in cottages or blocks of rooms facing the river. The public areas are spacious, and the food good. **On offer:** leopard bait, crocodile feeding, game drives, bush walks, Samburu dancing, shop. Petrol is available here.

Rates: from US$100 full board per person sharing. No children under 5.

Samburu Serena Lodge (62 rooms, swimming pool) Book through Serena Hotels, page 91

This is the only lodge on the southern bank of the Ewaso Ng'iro and is located outside the reserve boundary, about 5km away from the reserve headquarters. It's on a wide bend of the river and designed using natural materials, inspired by Samburu culture. All the rooms are in cottages facing on to the river and have en-suite shower rooms, flush toilets and private verandas. The buffet has a good choice of meals. Crocodiles can be seen basking on the sand spits and a leopard is baited each evening. **On offer:** game drives, bush walks, camel rides, Samburu dancing.

Rates: from US$125 full board per person sharing

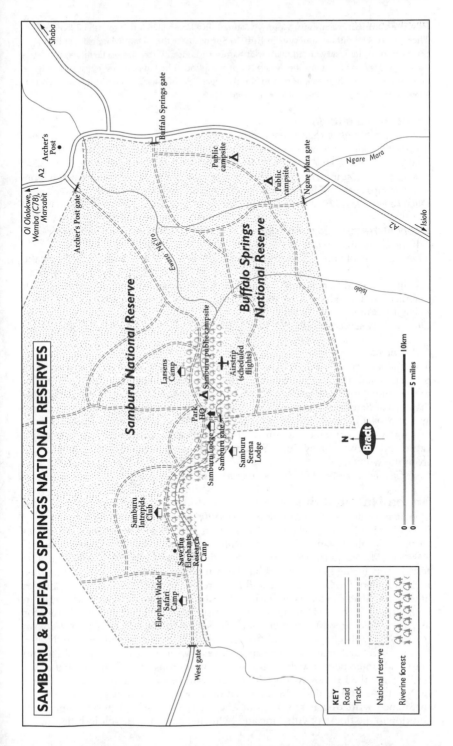

SAMBURU & BUFFALO SPRINGS NATIONAL RESERVES

Shaba

Ol Ololokwe,
Wamba (C78),
Marsabit

A2

Archer's
Post

Buffalo Springs gate

Archer's Post gate

Ngare Mara

Ngare Mara gate

A2

Isiolo

Public
campsite

Public
campsite

Ewaso Ng'iro

Samburu National Reserve

Buffalo Springs
National Reserve

Isiolo

Larsens
Camp

Samburu public campsite

Airstrip
(scheduled
flights)

Park
HQ

Samburu gate

Samburu Lodge

Samburu Serena
Lodge

N

Bradt

Samburu
Intrepids
Club

Save the
Elephants
Research
Camp

Elephant Watch
Safari Camp

West gate

0   5 miles

0   10km

KEY
Road
Track
National reserve
Riverine forest

Reserve Campsites Samburu County Council, PO Box 53, Maralal; tel: 065 2053
There are several public campsites in Buffalo Springs near the Ngare Mara gate, and in
Samburu near the reserve headquarters at Samburu Lodge. There are no facilities, and be
aware that leaving your tent unguarded is not an option. The baboons are complete thugs
here and will tear a lightweight tent to shreds, regardless of what's inside, if left unattended.
Rates: camping US$8 plus reserve and vehicle entry fees

What to see and do
Save the Elephants (STE) research camp
Advance booking is required through Save the Elephants, PO Box 54667, 00200
Nairobi ; tel: 020 891673; fax: 020 890441; email: save-eleph@africaonline.co.ke
The elephant researchers will lecture to groups in the lodges or, alternatively, for
small groups at the STE camp near Samburu Intrepids Camp.
Rates: donation to STE from US$400

Elephant-tracking day excursion
Advance booking is required through Elephant Watch Safaris, page 371
These consist of lunch and drinks at the Elephant Watch Safari Camp on the
Ewaso Ng'iro River, a game drive with elephant watching where you gain an
insight into the different family groups in Samburu and the work of the research
scientists, and a walk tracking the elephants. People can be collected from their
lodge if required.
Open daily by advance booking; 11.30–17.00; cost: US$170 plus reserve entry fees

Cultural visits
The lodges arrange excursions to Samburu *manyattas* and local community
projects where you can meet the Samburu people, although, in practice, many
of the guides are Samburu *morani*, young warriors, and the lodges regularly have
displays of Samburu dancing. The Samburu retain a strong traditional culture
and their *manyattas* are similar to those of the Maasai, low mud dwellings on a
sapling frame, contained within a thorn enclosure with goats, chickens and
cattle and a few mangey dogs. Samburu beadwork is readily available for sale
from the women.
Costs vary: in the region of US$15 per person a visit

Shaba National Reserve
Open daily 06.30–18.30; reserve entry fees US$30; vehicle entry fee KSh200.
Follow the A2 north for about 15km from the Ngare Mara gate turn-off to
Buffalo Springs National Reserve, and then turn east to Shaba National
Reserve. The entrance to the reserve is about 8km from the main road. The
reserve was formed in 1974 and has been used for a number of film locations,
including *Born Free*, *Out of Africa* and more recently, *Survivor 3*. Covering an area
of 239km², Shaba's scenery is stark and beautiful, dominated by **Shaba Hill** in
its southern section, and surrounded by steep ravines, a favourite haunt for
leopard. There are also good views to the sugarloaf mountain of Ol Ololokwe
(Ol Donyo Sabache) north of Archer's post. Bisected by the Ewaso Ng'iro
River, there are tracts of **riverine forest** with ragged doum palms and
grasslands interspersed with lava outcrops, numerous springs and marsh areas,
leading into the **Lorian swamp**. The **flora and fauna** are similar to that found
in Samburu and Buffalo Springs national reserves, although clans of the
threatened **wild dog** may sometimes be seen. The **birdlife** too is superb. In
addition to the flocks of vulturine and helmeted guineafowl, saddle-billed stork,

THE LIONESS AND THE ORYX

The old saying, 'Truth is stranger than fiction' is an apt description for a bizarre sequence of events which took place in Samburu National Reserve. Christmas 2001 saw a lioness adopting a newly born Beisa oryx calf. The unusual pair attracted much attention from visitors to the reserve, but the liaison ended in tragedy at the beginning of January 2002 when the calf was eaten by another lion. Then, surprisingly, the lioness (who by this time had been named *Kamuniak*, which means 'Blessed one' in the Samburu language) adopted another baby Beisa oryx on Valentine's Day. It was duly named Valentine. Game wardens mounted a 24-hour watch over this unlikely pair, keeping the lioness away from other lions. In the meantime, the distraught mother oryx was found a couple of kilometres away, too frightened to come any closer for fear of the lioness. The baby oryx, which had no chance of survival with the lioness, was gradually getting weaker, and so the Kenya Wildlife Service (KWS) stepped in and Valentine was taken to Nairobi animal orphanage where he can still be seen today. Undeterred, on Easter Sunday, Kamuniak adopted another baby oryx. This one, called Easter, was more sturdy than its predecessors and would suckle its mother as the lioness looked on. The Kenya Wildlife Service again mounted a vigil, and the rangers only intervened when the duo were surrounded by a pride of lion. Easter was successfully reunited with her natural mother, and instead of returning to the lioness, to the relief of the rangers, was re-integrated into the herd. Kamuniak proceeded to adopt a further two baby oryx who were reunited with their mothers.

In 2003 Kamuniak renewed her obsession with baby oryx. This animal behaviour has caused a great deal of intrigue among the scientific fraternity – while there's a plausible explanation for a young oryx imprinting on another animal that comes into its sphere at that time, there's still debate as to how to explain the lioness's misplaced maternal instinct.

red-billed hornbill, martial and bateleur eagles, this is one of the few places where you can see the rare **William's lark**.

Where to stay and eat

Shaba Sarova Lodge (85 rooms, 6 suites; swimming pool) Book through Sarova Hotels, page 91

The lodge is in the west of the reserve, next to a natural spring on the forested southern banks of the Ewaso Ng'iro River. Spring waters flow through the naturally landscaped grounds and cascade into the river. The lodge is attractively designed, the thatched roofs and natural stone and timber walls blending with the arid surroundings. Rooms are spacious with simple furnishing, small balconies, fans and en-suite shower rooms with flush toilets. There's a good choice of food and attentive service. **On offer:** game drives, 'survivor courses', guided bush walks, Samburu marriage ceremonies. Petrol is available here.
Rates: from US$80 full board per person sharing

Campsites

Theoretically there are a couple of public campsites (no facilities), but they are not always open – so you'll need to check at the gate on arrival. There are also a number of special campsites which are favoured by the upmarket mobile safari operators.

A GAME OR A WAY OF LIFE?
In 2001, the film *Survivor 3* was filmed in Shaba National Reserve. Security was extremely tight to prevent leaks of the competition reaching the outside world. National journalists hoping to report a news-breaking story were thwarted. But one enterprising reporter interviewed an old Samburu women. On explaining the challenges facing the competitors, the old women is said to have replied: 'But that's how I've lived all my life. I wish they would give me the money.'

What to see and do
Survivor challenge
Book through Sarova Hotels, page 91.
Inspired by the *Survivor* series, a gameshow where competing teams are set tasks to test their initiative and survival skills, Shaba Lodge has initiated its own 'Survivor challenge', where you can learn how to survive in the bush, track wildlife and catch and release butterflies. It includes attending traditional ceremonies, such as blood-letting, or role play at being a Samburu or Boran warrior.

ISIOLO NORTHEAST TO ETHIOPIA
The B9 (dirt road) from Isiolo leads through arid wastelands, sparsely inhabited by nomadic tribes such as the Boran, and Somali bandits, the *shifta*, to the outpost of Wajir, from which you can take the C80 northwest to Moyale or continue on to Mandera on the Ethiopian border. This route is not advisable, and if considering it, you are advised to check the safety situation with KTF in Nairobi, page 157.

ISIOLO NORTHWEST TO WAMBA
The two main features of this area, apart from the national reserves of Samburu, Buffalo Springs and Shaba already mentioned, are the distinctive sugarloaf mountain of Ol Ololokwe (also know as Ol Donyo Sabache), a landmark for miles around and the blue, forest-clad slopes of the Mathews Mountains. Ol Ololokwe is revered by the Samburu people and has played a central part in their history, the young *moranis* spending time on the mountain before becoming junior elders. On the southwestern extreme of the Mathews range, at the foot of Mount Uarge (2,680m), the highest mountain in the Mathews, is the small settlement of Wamba, dominated by a large Catholic mission and the best hospital in the north.

Getting there and away
The A2 north of Isiolo (dirt road, badly corrugated) continues to **Archer's post**, after which it's about 15km to the C79 turn-off at the foot of the huge mesa of Ol Ololokwe west to **Wamba** (about 35km).

By bus
There's only one bus service, the Babie coach, which runs between Isiolo, Wamba and Maralal, departing on alternate days at around midday.

By air
There are airstrips in Wamba, Ngelai (for Kitich Camp) and Namunyak (for Sarara Camp), but no scheduled services are available.

What to see and do
Ol Ololokwe – Samburu cultural walking safaris
Book through Let's Go Travel, page 101, or you could try pot-luck if passing.
Day walks from the *manyatta* at the foot of Ol Ololokwe are organised with the Samburu from the Namunyak group ranch, with revenue from the walks being paid into a community fund distributed through the Namunyak Wildlife Conservation Trust. The walk is not suitable if you are unfit, as it's hot and steep-going near the summit (2,000m), but it's fine for anyone of average fitness. The local English-speaking Samburu guides are excellent, enthusiastically explaining the natural flora and its medicinal uses, as well as their culture and the history of Ol Ololokwe in tribal folklore. The mountain is still used for ceremonies and dry-season grazing – at the top, a number of small holes have been carved into the rock where over the years herders watching their livestock played the ancient game of *bau*. Panoramic vistas stretch across the arid plains to Mount Kenya and the Mathews range. The path rises from *Acacia* scrub to the high-altitude mist forest on the summit, with giant cyclads and superb birdlife, including Kenya's largest nesting colony of Ruppell's vultures. For shorter walks, there's an airstrip on the summit for light aircraft and helicopters, but its presence rather jars with the cultural significance of the mountain for the Samburu.
Rates: from US$25

Wamba
Where to stay and eat
The **Saudia Lodge** is the only place to stay (rooms with shared facilities from KSh250) or you might be able to have a room or camp at the **Catholic mission**.

Mathews Mountains
The Mathews Mountains were named by Count Samuel Teleki on his expedition to Lake Turkana in 1888, in honour of General Lloyd Mathews, a British naval officer who had assisted him in Zanzibar. The mountain range rises from the flat arid plains of the northern frontier district, extending for some 250km, the hills averaging around 2,000m. The angular slopes are etched by deep gulleys, with tumbling mountain streams, and covered in thick natural forest of Cape chestnut, podocarpus and cedar trees. In the north, the range is separated from the Ndoto Mountains by the Malgis lugga. Access to the mountains is difficult and inadvisable, unless you have competent guides.

Where to stay and eat
Kitich Camp (6 tents) Book through Bush Homes of East Africa, page 90; web: www.kitichcamp.com
This is a delightful permanent tented camp at the southern end of the Mathews range. It nestles in a grove of fig trees in the Ngeng Valley, overlooking the seasonal river, frequented by wildlife, including elephant, and surrounded by thick forest and giant cyclads. Kitich means the 'Place of Happiness' in Samburu, as the valley always provided the Samburu and Soyei peoples with water and grazing for their cattle and honey for brewing beer. The tents are comfortably furnished, with hurricane lighting, and have en-suite bucket showers and smart long-drop toilets. The sitting and dining areas are simply designed using natural materials – stone and reed thatch. The camp is owned by Giulio Bertoli and the delicious meals have a distinctly northern Italian influence (the olive oil comes from his Tuscany farm). **On offer:** escorted and guided game walks, 40-minute walk to a natural swimming pool in the forest, stalking game,

birdwatching (100 species recorded), visits to Samburu families and bush picnics. **Note:** no game drives.

Rates: from US$345 full board per person sharing. Closed April, May and November.

Sarara Camp (community lodge; 6 tents; swimming pool) Ker & Downey Safaris, PO Box 86 Karen, 00502 Nairobi; tel: 020 890754; fax: 020 890725; email: info@kerdowneysafaris.co.ke; web: www.kerdowneysafaris.com

This camp has a superb location on the 30,350ha Namunyak group ranch. Located on the east of the Mathews range on the lower slopes of Uarges Mountain, it has expansive views from a natural-form swimming pool across the group ranch. The mess area overlooks the pool, and there's a waterhole nearby. The camp has recently been leased to Ker & Downey Safaris and was closed for refurbishment before re-opening in December 2003. Previously, an area rife with elephant poaching, Namunyak now boasts three large herds and over 100 wild dog, the largest concentration in East Africa. **On offer:** natural rock slides, camel treks, game drives, birdwatching, bush walks and seasonal visits to the singing wells where the Samburu water their cattle.

Rates: from around US$300 per person sharing plus a conservation fee of US$20.

NORTH TO MARSABIT

Marsabit means 'Mountain of Cold', a reference to the forested volcanic mountain – an oasis in the desert – which gives the backdrop to this administrative outpost. The town itself is hot, and is fascinating for its meeting of the clans of nomadic herdsmen in the market where Rendille, Gabbra and Boran come from afar to trade their livestock.

Getting there and away

The A2 north from Isiolo passes through **Archer's post** and **Serolevi** to the **Losai Mountains**, passing through the eastern section of the Losai National Reserve, to **Laisamis,** a small settlement on the reserve boundary, continuing across the Kaisut Desert to the forested oasis of **Marsabit** (about 280km from Isiolo). Be aware that owing to insecurity in this region, all transport must travel in convoy. Before setting out on this route, check the security situation with KTF in Nairobi, page 157. Note too that there is no petrol between Isiolo and Marsabit and it is not always guaranteed in Marsabit.

By bus

Miraj Express is the only bus service operating between Isiolo and Marsabit and normally runs three times a week – but check locally for details as the service can be spasmodic.

By air

There's an airstrip in Marsabit but there are no scheduled services.

Getting organised

For **changing money**, there's a Kenya Commercial Bank, only open in the mornings, and a **post office**, open Monday–Friday 08.00–17.00, Saturday 09.00–12.00, in the centre of town, together with a **police checkpoint** on the Isiolo road coming into town and a couple of **petrol stations**. In an emergency the **tourist helpline** is 020 604767.

Where to stay and eat

There's a limited choice of **cheap lodging**, the best being the **J J Centre** (rooms from KSh250) or the **Marsabit Highway Hotel** (self-contained rooms from KSh250) which also has a **restaurant** and **bar**, so can get quite noisy.

THE ELEPHANT – A BORAN FOLK TALE

as told by Ali Halkano, a senior ranger in Samburu National Reserve.
The Boran say the elephant was once part woman. In past Boran times, after a woman gave birth she stayed in her house for 40 days and was given many types of food, especially meat – cows and sheep. Some people say that when the woman gave birth, her husband went to look for food. She told her children to wake her when her husband returned with big meat. When the children saw their father returning, they woke their mother. She asked them, 'Which animal?' and the children replied, 'Sheep.' Furious at not being brought a bull, the woman took everything from the house and left. The gourd containers became the feet of an elephant, the large skins lining the house became the ears of an elephant, the pole that holds up the house became the elephant's trunk. And, like a woman, the elephant has breasts at the front.

What to see and do
Boran singing wells
There are several singing wells around Marsabit, the most accessible being at Ulanula, about 5km south of town off the Isiolo road. These are large, stepped wells, sometimes up to 12m deep, where the pastoralists have dug down to the water-table. As many as six people work in a chain, passing up leather buckets or calabashes of water, singing as they go, to water their livestock in the dry season.

Communications tower
Clearly visible from the centre of town is the communications tower. A hike up here through the forest is rewarded with panoramic views across the desert.

Marsabit National Park
Open daily 06.30–18.00; entry fee US$15; vehicle entry KSh200
The **main gate** to the park is readily accessed from Marsabit town. Covering an area of 1,500km² this forested mountain, often enshrouded in mist which can linger until midday, has three exquisite crater lakes, at **Gof Sokorte Dika** near Marsabit Lodge, **Gof Sokorte Guda** in the centre of the park – also known as Paradise Lake – and **Gof Bongole** on the southern boundary. These are the best places for **viewing wildlife**, where greater kudu, elephant, buffalo, leopard, caracal, bushbuck and reticulated giraffe may be seen. Large tuskers have long been associated with the area, Ahmed being the most famous. After being protected by Jomo Kenyatta's presidential decree until he died at the age of 55, a life-size fibreglass model was erected in his memory at the National Museum in Nairobi. The **birdlife** is spectacular with 370 recorded species, among them 52 types of raptor. Lammergeyer vultures nest in the 200m cliffs at Gof Bongole, while you may also see the rare masked lark. At certain times of year butterflies are abundant, while several types of **snake**, particularly cobras, are also found here, but rarely seen. There's a good network of tracks within the park.

Where to stay and eat
Marsabit Lodge (24 rooms; swimming pool) PO Box 488, Marsabit; tel: 069 2027; fax: 069 2416
Located near the main gate, the lodge is surrounded by thick forest but has a superb position overlooking the crater lake of Gof Sokorte Dika, which is often teeming with

game. The rooms are simply furnished but comfortable, with en-suite shower rooms and flush toilets and open views to the waterhole.

Rates: from US$130 full board per person sharing

Marsabit National Park Campsites

There are several public campsites within the park, the one at the main gate having long-drop toilets and showers. The nicest (special, but often available) is the Paradise Campsite on Lake Paradise, a crater lake in the centre of the park.

Rates: public campsite US$8; special campsite US$10, plus park and vehicle entry fees

MARSABIT NORTHWEST TO LOYANGALANI
Getting there and away

On the northern side of Marsabit the C82 heads northwest across the sweltering expanse of the Chalbi Desert, tinged with white soda in parts (which is liable to flooding during the rains), towards the **Huri Hills** on the Ethiopian border before heading southwest to the windswept settlement of **Kalacha** (about 150km). Just before reaching the village is a tiny oasis with doum palms where the Gabbra come to water their camels. From Kalacha, the road heads northwest to **North Horr** (about 55km), where it turns west and then due south through the **Bura Galadi Hills** to **El Molo Bay** and **Loyangalani** (about 100km) on Lake Turkana.

By air

There's an airstrip at Kalacha. Don't be too phased as you come in to land, as the only thing signifying there's an airstrip are white marker stones in the desert.

Where to stay and eat

Kalacha (4 bandas, self-catering community lodge; swimming pool) Book through Tropic Air, page 82 or Let's Go Travel, page 101

Facing on to a palm-fringed oasis where the nomadic Gabbra come to water their livestock, this small lodge is on the outskirts of Kalacha in the lee of the windswept Huri Mountains. The design is rustic and minimalist – a thatched, open sitting and dining area adjacent to a small swimming pool, centred between four bandas, each with en-suite shower rooms, flush toilets and a veranda. The bandas are run by Gabbra women from the Kalacha Camel Improvement Group, sponsored by a Community Development Trust Fund. You only need to bring food and drink, and the staff will prepare the meals. **On offer:** guided walks to Kalacha, evening performances (by request) of plays and singing about Gabbra culture by the Kalacha Poverty Rebellion Youth Group, and bird shooting in season.

Rates: from around US$10 per person sharing for self-catering

Kalacha Mission Campsite (camping)

Despite its barren surroundings, the campsite is well-run with good showers and long-drop toilets.

Rates: from KSh200

PHOTOGRAPHY IN THE NORTH

Be aware that there's a great aversion to being photographed in the far northern areas of Kenya. It's essential to seek permission first, not just for photographing people, but also for general scenic shots of a landscape with huts, a small village or town.

What to see and do
Kalacha village
A bleak, dusty, wind-blown desert settlement, Kalacha is a quaint mix of a few concrete *dukas,* a large school, a Catholic mission church (with a fine mural if you can get into the church) and numerous traditional Gabbra dwellings – large domed huts in which you can stand – made from a sapling frame over which an eclectic mix of animal skins, old maize sacks and materials have been woven. On the outskirts of town is a water point where you can watch elegant women, dressed in fine swathes of traditional *kangas,* and an irrigation project producing vegetables.

MARSABIT NORTH TO ETHIOPIA
The A2 continues north from Marsabit. Again you need to join a convoy, crossing the wastelands of the Dida Galgalu – the 'plain of darkness' before cutting east through the Ngaso and Shinil plains to the Karabamba Hills at which the road heads due north again to Moyale on the Ethiopian border.

Kenya and beyond!
Go with experts, go with Acacia
OVERLAND - ADVENTURE - LODGE
Ph +44 (0)20 7706 4700 or www.acacia-africa.com

ACACIA AFRICA

Vintage Africa's
Incredible Journeys to Africa

Luxury and classic safaris
Adventure travel
Special expeditions
Family safaris
Weddings & Parties
Beach holidays

www.vintageafrica.com

Eastern Africa Reservations : vintagenbo@vintageafrica.com Tel : [254-20] 3742450/55 Fax : [254-20] 3742465
Southern Africa Reservations : vintagesa@vintageafrica.com Tel : [27-21] 5115120 Fax : [27-21] 5103131

Vintage Africa

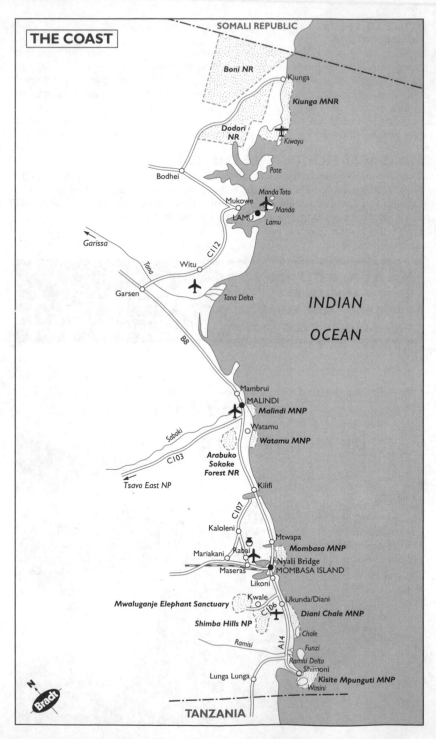

THE COAST

SOMALI REPUBLIC

Boni NR

Kiunga

Kiunga MNR

Dodori
NR

Kiwayu

Bodhei

Pate

Mukowe

Manda Toto

Manda

LAMU

Lamu

Lamu

Garissa

Tana

Witu

C112

Garsen

Tana Delta

INDIAN

OCEAN

B8

Mambrui

MALINDI

Malindi MNP

Watamu

Watamu MNP

Sabaki

C103

Arabuko
Sokoke
Forest NR

Tsavo East NP

Kilifi

C107

Kaloleni

Mtwapa

Mombasa MNP

Mariakani

Rabai

Nyali Bridge

Maseras

MOMBASA ISLAND

Likoni

Mwaluganje Elephant Sanctuary

Kwale

Ukunda/Diani

C106

Diani Chale MNP

Shimba Hills NP

Chale

Ramisi

A14

Funzi

Ramisi Delta

Shimoni

Lunga Lunga

Kisite Mpunguti MNP

Wasini

N

Bradt

TANZANIA

The Coast

Kenya has an idyllic coastline, a magnet for all who visit the country with its 480km of tropical beaches – white sands fringed with palm trees, with aquamarine and turquoise waters sheltered by coral reefs close to shore, or golden sands flanked by sand dunes. Temperatures average 28°C, tempered by the monsoon winds – the southeast monsoon, the *Kaskazi,* blows from April to October, while the northeast monsoon, the *Kazi,* blows from November to March – and there's a daily average of eight hours of sunshine. Apart from the obvious attraction of the beaches, the coast is steeped in history. From the 9th century onwards, Indian and Arab traders mingled with the indigenous inhabitants to create a Swahili culture which still thrives today, and the remains of early Swahili settlements may be found along the entire coastline, the most significant being the 15th-century Gedi ruins south of Malindi, while Lamu town has been designated a World Heritage Site due to its significance as a Swahili centre. During the 15th century, the Portuguese stamped their mark on the coast, fighting with the Omani Arabs, their main legacy being Fort Jesus in Mombasa's Old Town. The coast remained an entity in itself with little connection to the interior apart from the Arab caravans which trekked inland for ivory and slaves. At the turn of the 19th century, the British established a foothold and declared the coast, which at the time was in the hands of the Omani Arabs, a British Protectorate. Subsequently, Mombasa became pivotal in the development of Kenya as a British colony, being the starting point for the building of the Uganda railway. Today it still plays a vital role as the hub of commodity transportation inland and is a strategic port on the East African coastline. The coast also boasts unique and diverse habitats, both in maritime and terrestrial national parks and reserves. Highlights of the coast include Mombasa Old Town and Lamu, the Gedi ruins, Arabuko Sokoke Forest Reserve, Mwaluganje Elephant Sanctuary and the Shimba Hills National Park and the underwater treasures of the marine national parks and reserves.

MOMBASA

The city of Mombasa, Kenya's second most important metropolis, is spread out across Mombasa Island, covering an area of 15km². Despite being a city, it's remarkably relaxed and friendly, and noticeably less frenetic than Nairobi. The northern half of the island comprises the main dockland and industrial area, while the heart of the city revolves around Moi Avenue and Mombasa Old Town. This is the most interesting area to explore and reflects Mombasa's history since the 13th century. Enormous efforts have been made to clean up the city, both through the municipal council and a Mombasa-based NGO, the Environment Trust of

Kenya (PO Box 90193, Mombasa; tel: 041 22503; fax: 041 311789; email: etk_ke@hotmail.com) which runs a 'clean-up Mombasa' campaign annually.

Getting there and away

Mombasa Island is linked by the Makupa causeway to the A109 to Nairobi, the Nyali bridge to the B8 which heads north to Malindi (eventually linking with the A3 west of Garissa), and by the Likoni ferry to the A14 which heads south from Mombasa to the Tanzanian border.

By bus

There are numerous bus companies operating between Mombasa and Nairobi with several services a day. The Akamba Bus office is in Jomo Kenyatta Avenue (tel: 041 490269) and Coast Bus is on Mwembe Tayari Road (tel: 041 220158). Veran Safaris operate a Nairobi shuttle service; their office is in Ralli House in Mji Mpya Road off Nyerere Avenue (tel: 041 311 559, mobile: 0722 684854). Buses depart daily at 09.00.

Heading north of Mombasa, buses and *matatus* to Malindi go regularly from Abdul Nasser Road, with stops along the route from Bamburi onwards. The 08.00 bus continues through Malindi to Lamu. Do check the security situation in the route between Malindi and Lamu as it's been prone to *shifta* – Somali bandits – attacks in the past. It's preferable to spend a night in Malindi and then to take the morning bus to Lamu.

Heading south of Mombasa, you need to cross on the Likoni ferry, and then connect with buses or *matatus* on the mainland. Services run regularly throughout the day. Take a *matatu* to the ferry from the main *matatu* stage on Digo Road outside the main post office.

By air

Moi International Airport (tel: 041 433211) is located on the mainland about 10km from the centre of Mombasa (a 20-minute drive). Visas (US$50) can be purchased on arrival and the airport banks are usually open for arrivals outside normal banking hours. Taxis are readily available, costing KSh800–1,000 into town, depending on the time of day (or night), while many of the coast hotels operate an airport shuttle service. There is no public bus service, and you'll have to walk about 5km to the main road to get a *matatu* into town. The airport serves both international and domestic flights. Airport departure tax for international flights costs US$20 (normally already included in your ticket purchase). Be sure to reconfirm international flights at least 48 hours in advance with your airline office, or via a travel agent. Local departure tax is KSh300.

By rail

Mombasa Railway Station (tel: 041 312220) is located at the northern end of Haile Selassie Avenue. The night train to Nairobi departs daily at 19.00. It costs KSh3,000 per person first class, where you get a sleeping compartment for two, with sheets and blankets and a basin. Second class costs KSh2,100, where you have a shared compartment for four, with no bedding, and third-class costs KSh350, with seat only. First- and second-class passengers can have dinner on the train. You can leave luggage at the station, but it costs about KSh200 a day. It's preferable to book a couple of days in advance, either at the station or through a travel agent.

By sea

Kilindini Harbour is a major port for commercial shipping on the East African seaboard and is the base for the Kenyan Navy, but there are also a number of

cruise ships which dock in Mombasa (such as African Safari Club's MS *Royal Star*, Imperial House, 21–25 North Street, Bromley, Kent BR1 1SD; tel: 0845 345 0014; fax: 020 8466 0020; email: info@africansafariclub.com; web: www.africansafariclub.com). The **Likoni ferry** (free for foot passengers, from KSh35 for cars) links Mombasa Island to the south coast. The crossing takes about ten minutes, but there are often queues, so allow an extra 40 minutes if going to the airport. Occasionally you can see sharks in the creek.

By car

Most of the international car-hire companies have a base in Mombasa, and a number of local operators provide car hire. See *Getting organised* below and page 86 for company listings and details.

Getting organised

For **changing money**, there are several bureaux de change – try Pwani Forex opposite the Mackinnon Market on Digo Road or the Fort Jesus Forex Bureau in the old town (open 09.00–17.00). There are several Barclays, Standard and Kenya Commercial banks in the centre of town, open 09.00–15.00; some have ATMs. The large coastal hotels will exchange money, but at a premium rate. The main **post office** is on Digo Road, open Monday–Friday 08.00–17.00, Saturday 09.00–12.00 and for **internet access** try the Blue Room on Haile Selassie Avenue and Talkglobal in Moi Avenue. The **tourist information office** is on Moi Avenue near the tusks (tel: 041 311231). Friendly and helpful, but with a limited amount of information to take away, the office can assist with finding accommodation and booking safaris as well as giving general advice. It's open Monday–Friday 09.00–12.00 and 14.00–16.30 and Saturday 09.00–12.00. There's a huge Nakumatt **supermarket** (complete with snack bars, a good bookshop and internet access within the complex) off Nyerere Road on the way to Likoni. The fruit and vegetable **Mackinnon Market** is on Digo Road while the colourful **Makupa Market** is on Majengo Road. There's a **pharmacy** on Haile Selassie Avenue and plenty of others in town. In a **medical emergency** go to the Aga Khan Hospital on Vanga Road (tel: 041 312953/5). The **police station** is on Mama Ngina Drive (tel: 041 222121) and the **tourist helpline** is 020 604767. If you need to extend a visa the **immigration department** is at the Provincial Headquarters on Mama Ngina Drive (tel: 041 311745). There are plenty of **petrol stations** on the access roads into Mombasa.

There are numerous tour operators at the coast. In Mombasa, those with a good reputation include:

African Quest Safaris Palli House, Nyerere Av, PO Box 99265, Mombasa; tel: 041 227052; fax: 041 316501; mob: 0722 410362; email: info@africanquest.co.ke; web: www.africanquest.co.ke

Southern Cross Safaris Kanstan Centre, PO Box 99456, Mombasa: tel: 041 475074–6 fax: 041 47 1257; email: sales@southerncrosssafaris.com; web: www.southerncrosssafaris.com

Ketty Tours Travels and Safaris Diamond Trust House, Moi Av, PO Box 82391, Mombasa; tel: 041 315178; fax: 041 311355; email: kettytourssafaris@swiftmombasa.com; web: www.kettytours.visit-kenya.com

Where to stay

Manson Hotel (80 rooms) Kisumu Rd (off Moi Av), PO Box 83565, Mombasa; tel: 041 222356

A modern, 6-storey brick building located near the centre of town within walking distance of the Old Town, the rooms are comfortably furnished with private shower rooms, AC or

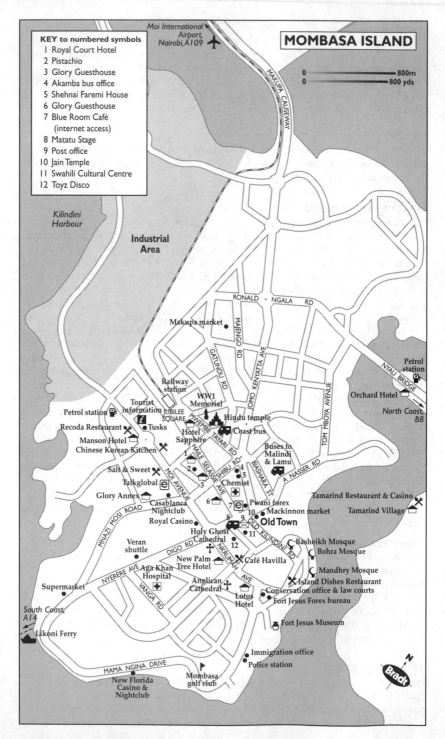

fans, telephones and a private balcony. There's friendly service and a good restaurant specialising in vegetarian dishes. **On offer:** massage.

Rates: rooms with AC US$13 B&B per person sharing; triple rooms US$11 B&B per person; rooms with fans US$11 B&B per person sharing

Royal Court Hotel Haile Selassie Av, PO Box 41247, Mombasa; tel: 041 223379; fax: 041 312398; email: royalcourt@swiftmombasa

Located near the railway station, this 6-storey hotel has rooms with AC, bathrooms and satellite TV. There's an excellent roof restaurant and bar which can be noisy at the weekend.

Rates: from US$30 B&B per person sharing

Hotel Sapphire (110 rooms; swimming pool) Mwembe Tayari Rd (near railway station) PO Box 1254, Mombasa: tel: 041 491657; fax: 041 495280; email: sapphire@ikenya.com. This modern 5–10-storey hotel has rooms with AC, bathroom and satellite TV, telephone and piped music. There are several restaurants serving snacks, continental, Chinese and a good range of Indian dishes. **On offer:** private parking, health club.

Rates: from KSh1,400 B&B per person sharing

Lotus Hotel Cathedral Lane off Nkrumah Rd, PO Box 90193; tel: 041 313207; fax: 041 220673; email: lotushotel@supercopier.com

A small hotel, this used to be a settlers' favourite and British troops were stationed here during World War I. It still retains its character and, incredibly, Africans were not served here until 1972, 9 years after independence. Run by the Nderu family, the rooms are comfortably furnished with AC, telephones and spacious bathrooms overlooking a small courtyard restaurant serving African, Western and Oriental food. It's a friendly place, often full, and ideally located for walking in the Old Town at night. **On offer:** business centre and safe parking with a night askari on duty.

Rates: from KSh1,250 B&B per person sharing; triple rooms KSh1,000 B&B per person sharing.

New Palm Tree Hotel Nkrumah Rd, PO Box 90013; tel: 041 315272

This large, whitewashed building has a faded elegance, and service in the restaurant is desperately slow. However, the rooms are clean and comfortable with fans and shower rooms. It's well-placed for exploring the Old Town and good value at the price.

Rates: from KSh750 B&B per person sharing

There are numerous **cheap lodgings** available. The Glory Guest Houses have a good reputation and helpful service.

Glory Guest House Haile Selassie Av, Mombasa; tel: 041 220265. Located in the centre of town, the rooms are clean, if small, and there's a choice of single, double and triple s/c rooms with fans or communal rooms with fans. *Rates: singles from KSh400–600 B&B; doubles from KSh350–500 B&B per person sharing; triples (s/c only) from KSh500*

Glory Guest House Kwa Shibu Rd, between Haile Selassie and Moi Av, Mombasa; tel: 041 223239. Centrally located, there's a choice of single, double and triple s/c rooms with AC or fans, or communal rooms with fans. *Rates: singles KSh600–1,000 B&B; doubles from KSh600–750 B&B per person sharing; triples from KSh550–700 B&B per person sharing*

Glory Annex Mnazi Moja Rd, Mombasa; tel: 041 220419. Located near the sports ground south of Moi Av, the annex has single, double and triple s/c rooms. *Rates: singles KSh400–600 B&B; doubles from KSh350–500 B&B per person sharing; triples (s/c only) KSh500 B&B per person sharing*

Where to eat

In addition to hotel restaurants, there are numerous **pavement cafés** and **cheap eats** in Mombasa. The following are recommended:

Chinese Korean Kitchen Moi Av. Authentic Chinese meals – good and cheap, cost around KSh330.

Café Havilla ground floor in NSSF building, Nkrumah Rd. Good chicken and beef curries at around KSh200.

Pistachio Chembe Rd. On the expensive side for what you get, but it has a lunchtime buffet (eat all you can) and good ice-cream and coffee.

Blue Room Haile Selassie Av. Conveniently sited near the bus stations, this has African and Indian fast food, as well as pizzas – it's good, but pricey.

Recoda Moi Av. Opposite Glory Car Hire, this is a pavement café with very cheap and delicious kebabs, bananas in coconut and a range of tasty Swahili snacks – cost around KSh150.

Salt n' Sweet Moi Av. A Pakistani restaurant with a good menu choice.

Casablanca Nightclub Mnazi Mmoja Rd. Also has a good restaurant and snacks.

Island Dishes Mombasa Old Town. Possibly the best for Swahili dishes at reasonable prices, and has plenty of atmosphere – costs around KSh250.

If you feel like splashing out, highly recommended are:

Tamarind Restaurant and Casino (Nyali) PO Box 99456, Mombasa; tel: 041 474600–2
A renowned seafood restaurant, the Tamarind lives up to its reputation. Much of its ambience is due to a superb location overlooking Mombasa's Old Town harbour, where at night you can watch the twinkling lights and catch the sea breezes in the terraced dining-room. The 5-course menu is superb, with a mixture of European, Eastern and Swahili dishes and the helpings are very generous.
Cost: from around KSh2,500. Open daily for lunch and dinner.

Tamarind Dhow PO Box 99456, Mombasa; tel: 041 474600
From the same stable as the Tamarind Restaurant, the dhow can seat up to 70 people on 2 decks. It cruises up and down Tudor creek with views of Mombasa's Old Town and Fort Jesus and then moors in a sheltered bay where the cooks prepare a feast of lobsters and steak on charcoal grills. At night, tables are candlelit, there's a band on board, and dancing on the upper deck.
Cost: lunch US$40; dinner US$70. Open daily. Lunch 12.30–14.30 and dinner 18.30–22.30.

Shehnai Faremi House, Mungano St; tel: 041 224801
A classic Indian restaurant, with traditional clay ovens, the Shehnai combines Mughalai and Tandoori dishes, a good selection of vegetarian meals and rich Indian desserts. It's decorated to emulate the grandeur of the Mughals, and is air conditioned.
Cost: in the region of KSh1,000. Closed Monday; open 12.00–14.00 and 19.30–22.30.

Entertainment

The **Royal Casino** on Moi Avenue has slot machines, gaming tables and pool, while for discos there's the **New Florida Casino and Nightclub** on Mama Ngina Drive (entrance around KSh150), the **Casablanca Nightclub** on Mnazi Mmoja Road (entrance around KSh200) and **Toyz Disco** on Baluchi Street off Nkrumah Road (free entry).

What to see and do
A walk around Mombasa Island

The main places of interest in Mombasa revolve around the central business area and the Old Town, which are within easy walking distance. Starting at the **tusks** on Moi Avenue, erected in honour of Princess Elizabeth's visit in 1952, head north along Aga Khan Road to Haile Selassie Avenue, and turn left. This leads you to Jubilee Square and the **railway station**, built in 1932. At the northern end of the square turn right into Mwembe Tayari Road where there's a **Hindu temple**. From here it's a few blocks north to the **Makupa Market** (it's most interesting in the morning). Returning to Mwembe Tayari Road, the bus station is on the site of Mombasa's old market place, and there's a **war memorial** in honour of Kenyans who fell in World War I. At the roundabout, take the road opposite the bus station which brings you into **Biashara Street**. This is a colourful bazaar (closed Sundays), a street full of small shops selling the traditional *kangas* and *kikois*, and swathes of other fabrics – from fine silks to cottons. Take a right turn down Biashara Street, which brings you on to Digo Road opposite the **Mackinnon Market**, with umpteen tropical fruits and vegetables for sale. Continuing right down Digo Road is the **Jain temple** built in 1963 (open daily 10.00–12.30; free entry), ornately decorated both inside and out, and cut through the old town along Old Kilindini Road, passing the **Basheikh Mosque** which leads down to the old Mombasa harbour. Here is the **Bohra Mosque**, the **fish market**, the **Old Customs House** and the **Mandhry Mosque**, considered to be the oldest mosque, dating from 1570. Occasionally you will see the large, ocean-going **dhows** in the harbour, but sadly, with the demise of the dhow trade, there are few these days. In former times the harbour was filled with dhows, as they waited for the change in the monsoon winds for their return voyages. Continuing right along the waterfront will bring you to **Fort Jesus Museum**, from where you head past the **law courts** to Nkrumah Road (from which you can see the **Anglican cathedral** to the left) which crosses Digo Road into Moi Avenue. Alternatively, from the **law courts** you can head south past the **town hall** and more law courts on to **Mama Ngina Drive**, which cuts through **Mombasa golf course**, with views out to sea, and links with Nyerere Avenue at **Likoni**, from which you can walk or get a *matatu* back to the town centre. This is popular with the Mombasa residents of an evening, where you catch the sea breezes and can snack on kebabs from pavement vendors.

Mombasa Old Town

Dating from the 13th century, it's easy to get transported back in time when wandering around the Old Town in Mombasa, which has similarities to Lamu and Stone Town in Zanzibar. The narrow winding streets are overhung by filigree, timber balconies, casting indigo shadows, and houses have intricately carved wooden doors, a symbol of status for the merchant residents who commissioned them, and arched windows. Alongside are more recent Indian and colonial styles of architecture. People still live within the Old Town, and a walk through the backstreets gives a flavour of their lifestyle. It's particularly interesting in the late afternoon and evening. Within the Old Town there are more than 20 mosques. During the 1800s slaves were shipped from the harbour, as well as spices and mangrove poles. Refer to the *Walk around Mombasa Island* above for other sites of interest. With population expansion in Mombasa, the architectural heritage of the Old Town was beginning to suffer. In recognition of this, the National Museums of Kenya initiated a **Mombasa Old Town Conservation Project** in 1985, with an aim to preserve the Old Town's salient historical features and character. As a result, in 1991, a section of the Old Town was given protected status.

An excellent booklet is available, *The Old Town Mombasa: A Historical Guide*, which can be purchased at the Fort Jesus Museum shop; the Mombasa Old Town Conservation office is in the old law courts opposite the museum, tel: 041 312246.

Fort Jesus Museum

PO Box 82412, Mombasa; tel: 041 312839; email: nmkfortj@swiftmombasa.com
This Portuguese fort, built in 1593, is a huge bastion with a key position overlooking the old port of Mombasa. One of the oldest European buildings in Africa, it's surrounded by a deep moat. Designed by Joao Batisto Cairato, to protect Portuguese interests in East Africa, it is considered one of the finest examples of 16th-century

Portuguese military architecture. During the ferocious battles between the Portuguese and the Omani Arabs, between the 16th and 18th centuries, the fort changed hands nine times. Subsequently, when Kenya became a British protectorate in 1895, the fort was turned into a prison and remained so until 1958. Thereafter it was declared a national monument and made into a museum in 1962. The museum houses artefacts from other coastal historical sites, and the shipwreck of the San Antonio de Tana which sank off Fort Jesus in 1697. In addition there's a major exhibit about the Swahili peoples depicting the culture and history of the Kenya coast. In the evening there's a *son et lumière* show within the fort. Men bearing fire torches mark the entrance to the fort, as visitors are given a presentation about the fort and the coast's turbulent history. This is followed by a dinner served by waiters dressed in Portuguese attire. There's a gift shop and café on site.

Open daily 08.30–18.00; entry KSh200; guided tours are available; the evening presentations are organised by Jahazi Marine (tel: 041 472213) daily except Tues and Sun, starting at 19.30, costing about US$40, with a cruise option US$70

Swahili Cultural Centre
PO Box 42042 Mombasa; tel: 041 222947; email: scc@swiftmombasa.com
Based in buildings to the rear of the main post office, this is an offshoot of the Mombasa Old Town Conservation Project; the Swahili Cultural Centre was initiated in 1992 to teach and retain the skills of Swahili craftsmanship, to revitalise a dying tradition. Woodcraft and textile skills are taught and a few items are available for sale.

NORTH TO KILIFI
Leaving Mombasa Island, Mombasa town merges with the suburbs of Nyali and Bamburi, which gradually diminish on reaching Mtwapa, after which the road passes through sisal plantations and dairy farming around Vipingo, and a mixture of cashew nut and mango trees near Kilifi. Heading inland from Kilifi on the back road to Kaloleni, the road passes through magnificent stretches of indigenous forest along undulating hills, before opening up on to small settlements among scattered palm trees and subsistence farming towards Maseras and Mariakani.

Getting there and away
By road
Heading north from Mombasa Island, the B8 crosses Nyali bridge, after which there's a turn-off to the right to Nyali town and beach. Continuing north, there are further turn-offs to the right to Kenyatta, Bamburi and Shanzu beaches, before the road crosses Mtwapa bridge about 15km from Mombasa. The B8 continues north to Kilifi bridge (a further 40km), passing turn-offs to Kikambala, Vipingo and Takaungu. About 5km south of Kilifi is the turn-off to the C107 (4WD when wet) which heads southwest to Kaloleni and Mariakani to join the A109 Mombasa–Nairobi Highway. At Kaloleni, the C111 heads south to Rabai and Mazeras, from which it's a tarmac road, before it too joins the A109.

By sea
Mtwapa and Kilifi creeks are popular anchorages. Be aware that there is a very strong tidal rip in Mtwapa.

Getting organised
Nyali and Kilifi have **banks**, a **post office** and **supermarkets**, while the larger hotels have **internet access** and can change money. In an emergency the **tourist helpline** is 020 604767. There are plenty of **petrol stations** en route.

Where to stay and eat
Nyali and Nyali beach

Orchid Bay Hotel (42 rooms; swimming pool) PO Box 81915, Mombasa; tel: 041 473238; fax: 041 471263; email:orcdbay@africaonline.co.ke; web: www.visit-kenya.com
Located in a peaceful setting on the Kisauni Creek, near the new Nyali bridge, a few minutes from the centre of Mombasa, this Moorish-style hotel is well placed for the airport. All bedrooms are large and well furnished with telephones, AC, large TVs and en-suite bathrooms with separate baths and showers, together with airy balconies overlooking the sea. There are three restaurants in the hotel, continental, Lebanese and Indian. **On offer:** internet access, parking, airport shuttle.
Rates: from US$30 B&B per person sharing

Tamarind Village (40 self-catering, fully serviced apartments; swimming pool) PO Box 95805, Mombasa; tel: 041 474600; fax: 041 473073; email: village@tamarindsma.co.ke; web: www.tamarind.co.ke
Located on the creek overlooking Mombasa's Old Town and harbour, the village was built in 1990 and combines Arab architecture with cool, spacious, smart, modern apartments with AC, fans, a kitchen, dining and sitting room area, with 1–3 bedrooms and large bathrooms with separate baths and showers, together with small verandas. There's a restaurant next to the pool serving good meals and snacks (and which also offers room service), while next door is the renowned Tamarind Restaurant – staying at the village gives a 20% discount; highly recommended. It's ideally placed for the airport. **On offer:** squash, fitness centre, therapy room, casino, email facilities and watersports, Tamarind dhow.
Rates: apartments from KSh7,000–13,000 a night, depending on number of rooms

Mombasa Beach Hotel (150 rooms; 2 swimming pools) Kenya Safari Lodges and Hotels, PO Box 90414, Mombasa; tel: 041 471861; fax: 041 472970; email: mombasabeachhotel@kenya-safari.co.ke
Located just north of Mombasa, this large hotel is perched on a clifftop overlooking the beach, set in tropical gardens. The reception areas appear rather dated, but the rooms are spacious, light and airy with single and double beds, en-suite bathrooms, AC, telephones, balconies and sea views. There are 4 restaurants with buffet-style service, a couple of bars and a beach bar. **On offer:** chauffeur-driven and self-drive car hire, 24hr taxi service, tennis, mini-golf, table tennis, pool table and a watersports centre.
Rates: from US$60 full board per person sharing

Nyali Beach Hotel (175 rooms; 2 swimming pools) Book through Block Hotels, page 90. On Nyali beach, 9km north of Mombasa set in 8ha of tropical gardens this was the first of Kenya's beach hotels. The palm wing rooms facing the beach are the nicest, while the others overlook the gardens. All the rooms have comfortable furnishings, AC, minibars and en-suite bathrooms. There are 5 restaurants, from gourmet seafood to pizza, a couple of bars (where you can down a pint of draught at Harry's Bar), a couple of shopping arcades and entertainment each evening. **On offer:** free windsurfing and mini-sailing, scuba diving, deep-sea fishing, snorkelling, tennis, aerobics and golf at Nyali Golf Club.
Rates: from US$115 half board per person sharing

Voyager Beach Resort (233 rooms; 2 swimming pools) Book through Heritage Hotels, page 91, or contact the resort on tel: 041 475114; fax: 041 472544; email: info@voyagerResorts.co.ke
On Nyali beachfront, 10km north of Mombasa, the resort is set in tropical gardens, with typical coastal architecture – whitewashed walls and palm-thatched roofs. The rooms are bright and spacious, with fans, AC, telephone, private balconies, and en-suite bathrooms. Several of the rooms interconnect, making them ideal for families, and there's plenty of entertainment here for children of all ages and an evening babysitting service. There are 3 restaurants, the Smuggler's Cove having delicious seafood, 3 bars, one open 24 hours. **On offer:** Adventurer's Club for children, a shopping arcade, watersports centre with sailing,

snorkelling, glass-bottomed boat trips, scuba diving, deep-sea fishing, health centre, volleyball, golf, dhow safaris and local excursions.
Rates: from US$135 full board per person sharing. Child friendly.
Reef Hotel (165 rooms; swimming pool) PO Box 82234, Mombasa: tel: 041 47177; fax: 041 471349; email: reef@africaonline.co.ke
Located on Nyali beachfront, the hotel is set in tropical gardens. The rooms, spread out in double-storey blocks, have AC, telephone, en-suite bathrooms and a balcony or terrace. There are 3 restaurants serving international cuisine, and regular evening entertainment with dancing troupes, discos, karaoke and live bands. **On offer:** scuba-diving school, windsurfing, tennis, beauty salon, shops, business centre and courtesy shuttle.
Rates: from US$35 B&B per person sharing

Kenyatta and Bamburi beaches

Bamburi Beach Hotel (150 rooms; 2 swimming pools) PO Box 83966, Mombasa; tel: 041 485611; fax: 041 485900; email: saleem@africaonline.co.ke
Located 12km north of Mombasa on Bamburi beach, this large hotel complex has a friendly atmosphere. The rooms have single and double beds, AC, en-suite bathrooms and a balcony. The main restaurant has buffet-style European and Indian cuisine, and there's also a Chinese restaurant, 3 bars, nightly entertainment and a disco. **On offer:** children's adventure centre for 4–12-year-olds, health club, watersports centre with scuba diving, snorkelling and windsurfing, deep-sea fishing by arrangement, squash court and golf at the Nyali course nearby.
Rates: from US$45 half board per person sharing. Child friendly.
Neptune Beach Resort (78 rooms; swimming pool) PO Box 83125, Mombasa; tel: 040 483620; fax: 040 483019; email: neptune@africaonline.co.ke; web: www.neptunehotels.com
Located on Bamburi beach, the resort is set in palm-fringed gardens. The hotel is a mixture of brightly-decorated spacious rooms, with AC, en-suite bathrooms and balconies, and a large, circular pool, together with rather dated public areas. The restaurant has buffet-style service with local and international dishes. There are a couple of bars, evening entertainment and a disco. **On offer:** watersports centre with windsurfing, jet-skiing, scuba diving and snorkelling, floodlit tennis and deep-sea fishing by arrangement.
Rates: from KSh2,700 full board per person sharing
Severin Sea Lodge (201 rooms; 2 swimming pools) PO Box 82169, Mombasa; tel: 041 485001; fax: 041 485212; email: severin@severin-sea-lodge.com; web: www.servin-sea-lodge.com
Located on Kenyatta beach north of Mombasa, the lodge consists of thatched bungalows and 2–3-storey main buildings. The rooms are bright and simply furnished, with noiseless AC, mosquito nets, additional roof ventilation, telephone, en-suite bathrooms and a balcony. The 'Comfort class' rooms have Lamu-style furniture, fruit and a minibar and are more expensive. There's evidence of the German–Swiss management in the restaurant with its international cuisine and gourmet dinners, while the Imani dhow restaurant is built on an authentic Arab sailing dhow. There are several bars, one open 24 hours, the Johari roof terrace being popular in the evenings. **On offer:** tennis centre, scuba-diving school, watersports centre, glass-bottomed boat excursions and golf nearby.
Rates: from US$83 B&B per person sharing
Whitesands (346 rooms; 3 swimming pools) PO Box 90173, Mombasa; tel: 041 485926; fax: 041 485652; email: reservations@whitesands.sarova.co.ke; web: www.sarovahotels.com
Located on Bamburi beach, 12km north of Mombasa, this is a large, impersonal hotel, but it has one of the best swimming pools on the coast with a waterslide which is popular with children. There's a range of rooms, from standard to suites, all with sea or pool views in

3-storey blocks. All rooms, comfortably furnished, have AC, mosquito nets, telephones, en-suite bathrooms with a shower and a balcony. There are several restaurants and bars, and an open-air amphitheatre for discos, live bands and traditional dancing. **On offer:** health club, windsurfing, snorkelling, scuba diving, deep-sea fishing, waterslide, tennis and a cultural village.
Rates: from US$80 half board per person sharing. Child friendly.

Shanzu beach
Mombasa Serena Beach Hotel (166 rooms; swimming pool) PO Box 90352, Mombasa; tel: 041 48721; fax: 041 485453; email: mombasa@serena.co.ke
Located 18km north of Mombasa on the small, exclusive Shanzu beach, the Mombasa Serena is considered one of Kenya's best beach hotels and is a member of the Leading Hotels of the World. Emulating Lamu's Arabesque architecture, with dark, carved wooden doors and whitewashed walls, with complementing Lamu furniture in the spacious public areas, the rooms are in 2–3-storey blocks set in delightful tropical gardens thick with the scent of frangipani. The rooms, on the small side, are comfortably furnished with AC, telephone, TV, minibar, en-suite bathrooms with a separate shower and private balcony, while a couple of suites include a sitting room. There are several restaurants serving continental and Indian cuisine; the Jahazi Grill, specialising in seafood, is highly recommended and there's an ice-cream parlour. There are several bars and a roof terrace and evening entertainment varies from dance troupes to discos. **On offer:** watersports centre offering scuba diving, mini-sailing and deep-sea fishing, a business centre, massage, floodlit tennis, squash, dhow cruises, glass-bottomed boat trips for snorkelling and excursions into Mombasa.
Rates: from US$120 B&B per person sharing

What to see and do
Mombasa Marine National Park and Reserve
Open daily 06.00–18.00; entry US$8
Extending north from Mombasa Island, the park and reserve cover an area of 200km². The Nyali, Bamburi and Shanzu beaches all have access on to the park which has a variety of corals and reef fishes, although the **snorkelling** is not as spectacular as the marine national parks at Kisite, Watamu and Kiungu. There are also some good **dive sites** within the area.

Bombolulu Workshops and Cultural Centre
PO Box 83988, Mombasa; tel: 041 471704; fax: 041 475325
The Bombolulu workshops started in 1969 as a project for training and employing physically disabled Kenyans in handicraft production. Since then it has developed to produce sophisticated hand-printed textiles, jewellery, carvings, beadwork and basketry which are available for sale at reasonable prices in the showroom. In 1994, a cultural centre was added, which displays aspects of traditional Kenyan culture, with examples of homesteads, traditional dance, music and theatre.
Cultural centre open Mon–Sat 08.00–17.00; workshops open Mon–Fri 08.00–12.45 and 14.00–17.00; showroom open Mon–Sat 08.00–18.00

Nyali Golf and Country Club
PO Box 95678, Mombasa; tel: 041 471589
An 18-hole competition golf course, with caddies available for hire; a round costs about KSh2,000.
Daily membership available

The Baobab Adventure
Baobab Farm, PO Box 819995, Mombasa; tel: 041 485901–4; fax: 041 486459; email: info@baobabfarm.com; web: www.baobabadventures.com
About 8km from Nyali Bridge, the Baobab Adventure consists of three sites. *Open daily 09.00–17.00*

Haller Park
A magnificent example of land reclamation by the Bamburi Cement Company, this was the original Bamburi Quarry nature trail which has been renamed in honour of René Haller who instigated the projects over the past 30 years. Derelict limestone wasteland has been transformed into a wonderful nature park, where casuarina pines and millipedes were used to create soil, after which trees were planted, and now the area is a leafy oasis containing a small game sanctuary and commercial fish farm. Within the park is a nature trail where you see a variety of wildlife including antelope, hippo, giant tortoises and Rothschild's giraffe, together with crocodile and fish ponds, a snake park and palmetum. The **Whistling Pine Restaurant** serves 'homegrown' meals from the farm.
Entry KSh450/225

Bamburi Forest Trails
About 4km north of Haller Park, there are cycling, jogging and walking trails around another area of reclaimed wasteland. The Dorly fitness trail has instructions and 15 exercise points, and there are also picnicking and barbecue areas. There's a **Butterfly Pavilion** displaying indigenous butterflies, and a **Sunset terrace** overlooking a lake.
Entry KSh200/100; bicycles are available for hire from KSh150 an hour

Nguuni Wildlife Sanctuary
Located in the Nguu Tatu area about 5km from Haller Park, this is another reclaimed area, now a sanctuary-cum-game-farm with Masai ostriches, eland and oryx and a rich birdlife (260 species recorded) among the acacia trees and long grasses. Nearby is **Baobab Rock Craft**, where fossils found in the limestone during quarrying operations have been processed into artefacts for sale.
Entry KSh450/225

Mamba Village
PO Box 85723, Mombasa; tel: 041 472281, mobile: 0722 415778
Located in Nyali, opposite the golf club, this is a large **crocodile farm** with over 10,000 crocodiles, where you can see them ranging in size from hatchlings to the man eater, 'Big Daddy'. In addition, there are camel rides and horseriding on the beach. There's also an inexpensive **restaurant** and a large **nightclub**.
Open daily, with feeding time at 17.00. Entry KSh450/250; camel rides KSh50; horseriding from KSh950 an hour

Ngomongo villages
PO Box 88478, Shanzu; tel: 041 486425; web: www.ngomongo.com
Located in Shanzu, about 1km off the main road and signposted, the Ngomongo villages are an attempt to represent ten of Kenya's tribes, illustrating their traditional homesteads, dress and activities. So, you can join the Maasai *moranis* in a jumping competition, go hook-line fishing with the Luo, pound maize Kikuyu and Kalenjin style, or get intoxicated on Akamba honey brew and have a go at archery. It's genuinely entertaining 'canned culture', but its authenticity is highly dubious.
Open daily 09.00–17.00; entry KSh500/250; wear tough shoes

Jumba la Mtwana

About 2km north of Mtwapa creek, there's a sign on the right, from which it's about 3km down a track to the ruins on the beach. The remains of a **13th- century Swahili settlement**, abandoned after a century's habitation, *Jumba la Mtwana* means, 'Large House of the Slave', but there is no historical or archaeological evidence to support this. However, there are remains of domestic houses, mosques and tombs. The domestic houses have carved niches and arched doorways with decorative motifs. The settlement would have been home to Swahili fisherman, craftsmen and merchants who traded commodities with India and Arabia. Excavations on the site in 1991 revealed decorated local pottery and shell beads, imported Chinese and Islamic ceramics and glass beads. Surrounded by baobab trees, Jumba beach in itself is a pleasant attraction.

Open daily 08.00–18.00; entry KSh200 and a guidebook or guide is available at the office

Kilifi

Where to stay and eat

Takaungu (3 rooms; swimming pool) Book through Bush Homes of East Africa, page 90 Takaungu lies to the south of Kilifi and the house overlooks a sandy beach. The home of Charlotte and Philip Mason, the rooms, all painted white, are airy and spacious. There's a master bedroom with four-poster bed with mosquito net and en-suite bathroom, and a couple of other rooms, also en suite, in a separate cottage. **On offer:** sailing on a 40ft ketch, scuba diving, snorkelling, birdwatching and visits to local reserves and historical sites.

Rates: from US$200 full board per person sharing. Closed April and May.

Kilifi Bay Beach Resort (58 rooms; 2 swimming pools) PO Box 537, Kilifi; tel: 041 22264; fax: 041 22258; email: sales@madahotels.com; web: www.madahotels.com Set in tropical gardens with palms and cashew nut trees, the hotel has 130m of sandy beachfrontage and is the only hotel on this stretch of the beach. The rooms are simply furnished with AC or fans, mosquito nets, a private terrace or balcony and en-suite bathrooms (including bidets). Forty-nine are in 14 cottages while the remaining 9 are junior suites, suitable for families. There are 3 bars and 2 restaurants serving international cuisine with a weekly barbecue, snack and à la carte options. **On offer:** windsurfing, snorkelling excursions, volleyball, table tennis, TV, video, darts, billiards and bicycles for hire. Diving and big-game fishing can be arranged.

Rates: from US$80 half board per person sharing

Mnarani Club (84 rooms; swimming pool) PO Box 1008, Kilifi; tel: 041 22318; fax: 041 22200; email: mnarani@africaonline.co.ke; web: www.mnarani.com This all-inclusive club is perched on a cliff above Kilifi creek, with a small, private beach in 16ha of tropical gardens. The public areas are decorated in traditional Swahili style, with bright colours and natural wood finishes, and there are live bands 3 nights a week. The rooms all have AC, telephones, mosquito nets and spacious bathrooms with a shower. The restaurant has buffet-style meals, while there's also an à la carte menu (costs extra) and service is excellent. The resort specialises in weddings and honeymoons. **On offer:** sailing Lasers, Optimists and catamarans (with instruction), snorkelling and kayaking, deep-sea fishing, scuba-diving, squash, beginners' windsurfing, cycling and creek excursions to go birdwatching.

Rates: from US$150 all inclusive per person sharing. No children under 16; dress for dinner.

What to see and do

Mnarani ruins

Signposted from the main road on the south side of Kilifi creek, these are the remains of a **15th-century Swahili settlement**. Among the ruins is a magnificent

pillar tomb, which has been carefully reconstructed. Also present are the remains of a large **Friday mosque**, several tombs and wells. Even if not interested in old ruins, there's a superb view of the creek.
Open daily 08.00–18.00; entry KSh200

Kilifi creek
The creek is a popular anchorage with the international yachting fraternity, who tend to congregate at **Swynford's Boatyard** (tel: 041 25067), which has an informal **restaurant** and **bar**, serving fresh seafood, and you can go **waterskiing** with Tony Stubbs (tel: 041 22047). Other watersports, deep-sea fishing and creek excursions are offered by the hotels.

Rabai Museum
Kraph Museum, PO Box 82, Rabai
On the C11 Kaloleni to Maseras road (good tarmac) in the forested hinterland at **Rabai**, the museum is located in the St Paul's Church complex. This was the site of the **first Christian Mission of Kenya**, founded by the German missionary Dr Ludwig Krapf in 1846 among the Mijikenda (coastal peoples). Krapf set off on an exploratory expedition inland in 1849, when he was the first European to see and document Mount Kenya. A few months before, his fellow missionary and assistant, Johannes Rebmann, had seen Mount Kilimanjaro. Due to ill health, Krapf left Kenya, but returned between 1862 and 1864 to found another mission at Ribe, about 6km from Rabai. An extraordinary man, he wrote a book on Swahili grammar and a dictionary of six languages, and translated parts of the Bible into the Akamba language. Within the church complex are Krapf's and Rebmann's houses, and the original whitewashed church. Perhaps the most interesting display is the exhibit 'From the *Kaya* to the Cross' which shows the traditional Mijikenda *kaya* culture, with its emphasis on holy sites, in parallel to the development of Christianity in the village.
Open daily 09.30–18.00; entry KSh200

NORTH TO MALINDI
The road from Kilifi heads north in a direct line, with a few coconut plantations along the way, but is primarily dominated by the Arabuko Sokoke Forest. There are a few clusters of kiosks at the roadside before reaching the Watamu turning. **Watamu** itself is a small village with a pristine white sandy beach, where private houses and hotels line the beachfront. The beach itself has been voted one of the world's top ten beaches. It's about 8km long, and a main advantage is that you can swim in the sea at high and low tide – and there are no beach boys. The disadvantage is that, between June and October, there can be quantities of leafy seaweed and murky water which disappear with the change in the monsoon winds. A 20-minute drive from Watamu is **Malindi**, the last major centre on the north coast until you reach Lamu. One of the oldest coastal settlements, it's a quaint mix of Swahili, Asian traders, old settler colonials, Italian (rumour has it that at one time Mafia magnates laundered money here) and a few Germans. The shopping centres around town are very much geared towards the European fraternity, and the town's income is predominantly dependent on the tourist trade. Yet, despite its hotchpotch of nationalities, Malindi is all-embracing (perhaps part of its heritage) and still retains a strong Swahili identity, with easy-going, friendly people. It's been voted the cleanest town in Kenya and has an active 'Malindi Green Town Movement', where the local community organises regular clean ups and tree planting.

Getting there and away

Heading north from Kilifi on the B8, it's about 50km to the **Watamu** turn-off (signposted), from where it's about 3km from the turn-off to the junction. Turn left to go to Watamu village. Access to the beach is via the hotels which are to both sides of the junction. Mida creek is at the far end of the beach road if you turn right. From the Watamu turn-off, the B8 continues to **Malindi** (about 15km). Local taxis are available in Malindi and now operate a fixed tariff. From Malindi the C103, a good dirt road, heads west to Tsavo East National Park.

By bus

The bus station in Kilifi is on the north side of the creek at the southern end of the village and there's regular daily transport between Mombasa and Malindi. Buses and *matatus* can drop you at the Watamu turn-off, from where you can catch a *matatu* to the village. In Malindi, there's a new bus station at the southern end of town, from where it's a ten-minute walk to the town centre.

By air

Malindi airport (tel: 042 31201) is 3km to the south of town and there are daily flights to Nairobi, Mombasa and Lamu. Taxis into town cost about KSh600.

Watamu

Getting organised

For **changing money** in Watamu, there's a tour operator with an informal forex bureau at the village square (at the end of the tarmac), but there are no banks. There's a **post office** open Monday–Friday 08.00–17.00, Saturday 09.00–12.00 and a couple of **supermarkets**, curio shops and tourist boutiques. The **tourist helpline** is 020 604767. There are several **tour operators**, including Eco-Resorts (see page 102) in the supermarket complex and a couple of Italian **restaurants**. Several **petrol stations** are located along the Watamu road.

Where to stay

Barracuda Inn (64 rooms; swimming pool) tel: 042 32509; fax: 042 32304; email: barracudainn@swiftmalindi.com; web: www.barracudainn.com
Located on Blue Bay Lagoon north of Watamu beach, the rooms have en-suite facilities and are in cottages in the garden. **On offer:** watersports centre, snorkelling.
Rates: from US$30 full board per person sharing
Kikapu Cottages (4 cottages; small swimming pool) Book through Acacia Trails, PO Box 30907, Nairobi; tel/fax: 020 446261; email: acacia@swiftkenya.com
Located on Blue Bay Lagoon off the northern end of Watamu beach, the cottages are in a leafy, peaceful setting perched above the lagoon. Cleverly positioned to maximise privacy, each cottage is on a raised platform, made from mangrove poles and palm-matting giving an interesting ecostyle of architecture, with a veranda and sunbathing deck. The rooms, with palm-matting walls, are brightly furnished and comfortable with mosquito nets and large shower rooms to the rear. There's a small thatched lounge and dining area, where you can watch fishermen netting their catch at low tide, while in the evening, a fire is lit on the patio, perfect for stargazing. **On offer:** scuba diving, snorkelling, game fishing and dhow excursions can be arranged through the hotels on Watamu beach.
Rates: from US$150 full board per person sharing
Ocean Sports (29 rooms; camping; swimming pool) PO Box 100, Watamu; tel: 042 32008; fax: 042 32266; email: oceansps@africaonline.co.ke; web: www.oceansports.net
Located next to Hemingways on Watamu beach, Ocean Sports has long been a favourite with Kenya residents and the British fraternity. Run by the Darnborough family, the hotel

is noted for its friendliness, informality, deep-sea fishing and diving school. The rooms are in comfortable cottages in the garden with en-suite bathrooms and showers and sea views. The bar, decorated with mounted heads of different game fish, has snack meals, while the restaurant specialises in seafood (lobsters) and curry lunches (eat all you can) on Sundays which cost about KSh800. The campsite is to the rear of the rooms and has ablution facilities. **On offer:** deep-sea fishing, creek fishing, windsurfing, scuba-diving courses, tennis, squash and snorkelling in the marine park.

Rates: from US$100 half board per person sharing; camping from KSh500

Hemingways Resort (78 rooms; 2 swimming pools) PO Box 267, Watamu; tel: 042 32624; fax: 042 32256; email: hemingways@swiftmalindi.com; web: www.hemingways.co.ke
Located at the northern end of Watamu beach, Hemingways is a privately owned hotel and a member of the Small Luxury Hotels of the World. Internationally renowned for its big-game fishing (with its own fleet of boats), the hotel is well designed with views out to sea from the rooms and terrace, while service is friendly and efficient. There's a bar, famous for its 'bitings' – nibbles with drinks – while the restaurant has a selective menu. All rooms have AC, fans, mosquito nets, good quality furnishings and en-suite bathrooms – the standard rooms are by the beach, while the superior and de-luxe rooms are more spacious with balconies, and the suites include a sitting room. **On offer:** fishing, fitness centre, windsurfing, sailing, scuba diving and snorkelling in Watamu Marine National Park, dhow excursions to Mida creek for picnics, bird watching and sundowner cruises, weddings.

Rates: from US$60 per person sharing

Turtle Bay Beach Club (150 rooms; swimming pool and children's pool) PO Box 457, Malindi; tel: 042 32003; fax: 042 32268; email: manager@turtlebay.co.ke; web: www.turtlebay.co.ke
Located on Watamu beach, the child-friendly Turtle Bay Beach Club is on the seafront and is popular with families. The sunbathing garden is rather crowded, but the hotel itself is well spread out and the service is friendly and efficient. Plenty of activities are organised for those who are not cut out for sunbathing. The rooms are comfortably furnished with AC fans, bathrooms with a shower, balconies or terraces. There's a choice of rooms from standard to ocean front, some being quite noisy with the nightly entertainment – bands and discos; ask for a room away from the centre of the hotel. Meals are buffet-style and there's a pizzeria and cocktail bar. **On offer:** children's club for 4–12 year olds and babysitting service, organised activities such as volleyball and beach soccer, horseriding, watersports centre with windsurfers, Toppers, sailboards and canoes, scuba diving, tennis, bicycles, Swahili lessons; complimentary email service; community and conservation centre, birdwatching and village visits.

Rates: from US$80–120 fully inclusive per person sharing; some activities, like scuba diving, cost extra

Baraka House (3 rooms; serviced or self-catering) tel: 042 32250; email: tarawood@wildfitness.com web: www.wildfitness.com
Located on Watamu beach, Baraka House is the base for Wildfitness (see page 402) but is also available for guests not participating in the programme who can stay on a full board or self-catering basis. Set in natural forest and gardens, this 2-storey Arab-style house has panoramic views from the rooftops and is 100m from the beach. Each room has its own Bohemian character, with mosquito nets, en-suite bathrooms and balconies looking out to sea, while the African staff are friendly and helpful. If self-catering, you just need to bring food and drink. **On offer:** Wildfitness programme, yoga, massage, dhow trips to Mida Creek, snorkelling, diving and fishing excursions.

Rates: from US$115 per person full board, or self-catering from US$280 for the whole house

Self-catering, houses and cottages for rent

Plot no 3 Blue Lagoon On main Watamu bay (3 rooms; self-catering serviced house, sleeps 6) Book through Steve Curtis, PO Box 275, Watamu; tel: 042 3240; mob: 0733 897661; email: aquav@africaonline.co.ke

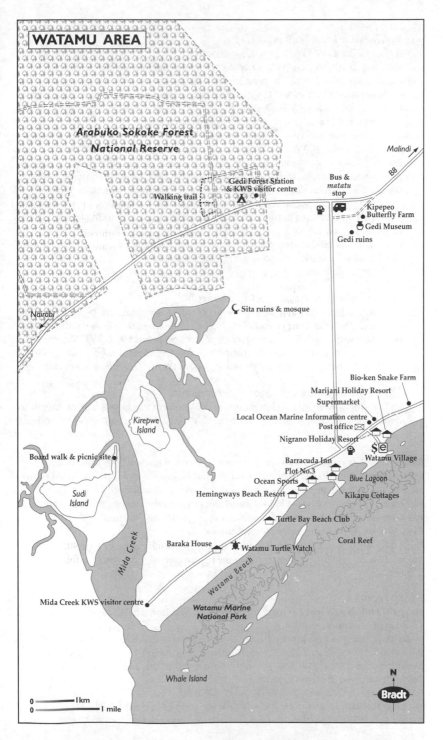

WATAMU AREA

Arabuko Sokoke Forest
National Reserve

Malindi

B8

Gedi Forest Station
& KWS visitor centre

Bus &
matatu
stop

Walking trail

Kipepeo
Butterfly Farm

Gedi Museum

Gedi ruins

Nairobi

Sita ruins & mosque

Bio-ken Snake Farm

Marijani Holiday Resort

Supermarket

Local Ocean Marine Information centre

Post office ⊠

Kirepwe
Island

Nigrano Holiday Resort

Watamu Village

Board walk & picnic site

Barracuda Inn

Plot No.3

Ocean Sports

Blue Lagoon

Sudi
Island

Hemingways Beach Resort

Kikapu Cottages

Turtle Bay Beach Club

Coral Reef

Baraka House

Watamu Turtle Watch

Mida Creek

Watamu Beach

Mida Creek KWS visitor centre

Watamu Marine
National Park

Whale Island

N

0 ———— 1 km
0 ———— 1 mile

Bradt

WATAMU TURTLE WATCH

Richard Zanre, WTW Project Co-ordinator

Watamu Turtle Watch (WTW) was initiated by the late Barbara Simpson. It's a community-based marine conservation organisation for the protection of endangered sea turtles and the marine environment in the Watamu/Malindi area. It works with Kenya Wildlife Service (KWS), Kenya Sea Turtle Conservation Committee (KESCOM) and the Fisheries department. Major funding comes from the International Fund for Animal Welfare (IFAW) and the East African Wildlife Society (EAWLS). The marine parks and reserves of Watamu and Malindi have important habitats for fish and coral, with five species of endangered sea turtle found in the local waters, three of which nest on Watamu beaches. However, the area is threatened by damaging resource exploitation.

WTW relies on public support for its conservation programmes. It offers the chance of participating in turtle conservation in Watamu/Malindi by adopting sea turtle nests laid on Watamu beach, or adopting turtles caught in fishermen's nets. Tourists to the area can learn more about turtle conservation by visiting the Turtle Information Centre at Plot 19, Watamu.

WTW's work involves:

Turtle nest protection and research

All nests laid on Watamu beach are protected from poachers by local people, who are paid for their efforts. In Malindi marine park WTW works in co-operation with Malindi KWS rangers to protect nests laid there. WTW carries out research on nest success and nesting females, including a tagging study. Since 1997, 140 nests have been protected and more than 150,000 hatchlings released.

Turtle fishing net release and research

WTW works with local fishermen around Watamu to release turtles caught in their fishing nets. Fishermen contact WTW on turtle capture, WTW collects

An airy bungalow on the beachfront at the northern end of the beach near Ocean Sports. Rooms have fans and mosquito nets, 2 with en-suite bathrooms and there's a shared family bathroom. The living areas are spacious and there's an excellent seafood cook and house servant. You need only to provide food and drink and groceries can be delivered. There's also a separate cottage which sleeps 4.

Rates: main house from US$90 a day plus staff gratuities

Let's Go Travel (page 101) is the booking agent for a number of self-catering houses at Watamu, costing from around US$60–80 a day.

Cheap rooms

Marijani Holiday Resort (10 rooms) PO Box 282, Watamu; tel: 042 32448; email: marijani@swifmalindi.com

In Watamu village (not on the beach), this is a German-owned, characterful house with a somewhat shabby appearance and a resident African grey parrot. The rooms, not particularly clean, are a reasonable size with showers and toilets, and guests have the use of a fridge. Lunch and dinner is by request.

Rates: single rooms KSh1,000 B&B; double KSh1,400 B&B

Nigrano Holiday Resort (5 rooms, self-catering; swimming pool) tel: 042 32119

A small villa in Watamu village, this is a pleasant, low-key, quiet establishment with clean

biometric data and the turtle is tagged before release, with a compensatory payment made to the fishermen. Since 1998 WTW has rescued 320 turtles from fishermen's nets.

Education and awareness
Education is vital to changing attitudes and the importance of marine environment and sea turtle conservation is stressed. The programme targets eight local schools, where WTW has set up Turtle Clubs, 13 fish landing sites, 11 villages and Watamu hotels. Educational materials are distributed at workshops and events.

National campaigning
WTW campaigns nationally against the poaching of turtles, illegal and destructive fishing activities (including commercial trawlers) and damage to the coastal environment by development. It also co-operates with fishermen and other conservation minded groups, creating awareness and advising on turtle conservation issues.

Community development
WTW assists communities in a range of local development issues and explores alternative, non-destructive sources of income with them. Examples include the mobilisation of fishermen into groups, the provision of technical advice to assist with improved management of fish resources and encouraging local handicraft production.

For advice on turtle adoption schemes and information, contact: Watamu Turtle Watch, Plot 19, PO Box 125, Watamu; tel: 042 32118; fax: 042 32280; email: wtwkenya@swiftmalindi.com

rooms, a shared kitchen with basic cooking facilities and a fridge, while rooms have a fan and mosquito nets, some with private bathrooms. There's a large veranda and small pool with sunloungers.
Rates: from KSh1,500 for a double room

Where to eat
Most of the hotels listed above have restaurants, and there's an Italian pizza garden in Watamu village.

What to see and do
Turtle watching
The **Local Ocean Marine Information Centre** next to Watamu supermarket represents the Local Ocean Trust and includes Watamu Turtle Watch. It's open Monday–Saturday 10.00–12.30 and 14.30–17.30 and is a good source of local information and will advise on turtle nest hatchings.

Watamu Turtle Watch itself is at Plot no 19 on Watamu beach, about half-way along the Mida creek road from Watamu village. At the office, there are displays about the different turtles found in Kenyan waters – green, olive ridley, hawksbill, loggerhead and leatherback – and information about the turtle watch project. They monitor turtle nests on the beach, and, when they hatch, it's possible to watch the tiny turtles, about 10cm long, burrowing their way out of the nest and then scurrying down the beach to the sea. Only the green, hawksbill and olive ridley turtles nest on Kenyan beaches. See box (page 401) for more details on the project. *Open 08.30–17.00; free entry*

Deep-sea fishing
Ocean Sports (page 397) and Hemingways (page 398) are the main hotels specialising in deep-sea fishing at Watamu.

Fitness and yoga courses
Wildfitness Baraka House, PO Box 406, Watamu; tel: 042 32250; email: tarawood@wildfitness.com; web: www.wildfitness.com
Based at Baraka House on Watamu beach, Wildfitness runs a variety of fitness and holistic programmes (massage, yoga) throughout the year with qualified trainers. The courses cater for all levels of fitness, and all that's required is a desire to increase your fitness levels and well-being.
Rates: courses and costs vary. A 9-day 'kick-start' or 10-day yoga course cost from around US$2,460, full board

Bio-Ken laboratory and snake farm
PO Box 3, Watamu; mob: 0733 290324; email: corncon@africaonline.co.ke
Not to be confused with the snake farm next to Gedi, this research station owned and run by snake expert James Ashe is about 3km north of Watamu village. It houses the largest snake collection in East Africa totalling some 200, with around 30 snake varieties, including 80 green mambas which are milked for their venom. They operate a service providing anti-venom to hospitals and can advise on snakebites. The guides are extremely informative.
Open daily 09.00–12.00 and 14.00–17.00; entry KSh300

Watamu Marine National Park
PO Box 333, Watamu; tel: 042 32393
Open daily 06.00–18.00; park entry fee US$8
Located off Watamu beach, the Watamu Marine National Park stretches from Blue Lagoon to Whale Island and is an exclusion zone for fishing. It has **coral gardens** with over 140 species of hard and soft corals, the most recognisable being mushroom, brain and staghorn. The colours have diminished with the effects of el Niño (the change in sea temperature caused the coral to die back but they are gradually growing again). In addition there are shoals of **fish** – angel, trigger, parrot, sturgeon, domino and butterfly fish – giving a dizzy array of colour, while starfish, sea urchins, clams, squid and moray eels are sometimes seen. The **outer reef** is only a ten-minute boat ride from shore, with excellent scuba diving, and over 1,000 identified fish species, including **whale sharks** in season. The lagoon also has **blacktip** and **whitetip reef sharks** – you can watch the blacktips (up to 1.5m long) swimming in the shallows on the rising tide from the southern end of Watamu beach during October.

Mida Creek and Whale Island
PO Box 333, Watamu; tel: 042 32393
Open daily 06.00–18.00; the marine park fee also applies to Mida creek, cost US$8
From the Malindi–Mombasa road take the turn-off to Watamu, and then turn right at the junction. Follow the road to the end, which brings you to the KWS office on **Mida creek**. Part of the Malindi–Watamu marine reserve and

SCUBA DIVING OFF WATAMU
Steve Curtis of Aquaventures

The seas around Watamu were designated as a marine park and reserve in 1963 – the first marine park to be established in eastern Africa. The dive sites are within the marine reserve and all have been buoyed for years to prevent anchor damage on the reefs. We have approximately 13 different dive sites and have a policy of only one boat per dive site, so there's no overcrowding.

The outer fringing reef, where the diving takes place, lies 1.5km off, and parallel to, the beautiful, unspoiled white beaches. The top of the reef lies between 7m and 14m, dropping down to a sandy bottom at 22–30m. The Indian Ocean is well known for its vast numbers and different species of fish. Watamu is no exception and with no spear fishing, the fish ignore the divers and carry on their daily lives as normal which is great for observing natural fish behaviour. Dives here offer up anything from the small, but beautiful, nudibranches and leaf fish to the amazing critters such as frog fish, octopus and crocodile fish, not forgetting the reef fish such as angel, butterfly fish and groupers. Last, but definitely not least, there is always the chance of seeing the larger critters such as turtles, barracuda, whitetip reef sharks, manta rays, whale sharks and dolphins.

As the dive sites are only 10–20 minutes' boat ride away, operators mainly offer one-tank dives, thus leaving the schedule flexible to cater for both the keen diver and the diver with other commitments in the day.

Scuba diving in Watamu is available from Ocean Sports (page 397, for Aquaventures) and Turtle Bay Beach Club, page 398. For details of dive operators in Kenya, see page 127.

covering an area of 32km², the creek has superb **snorkelling** and excellent **birdwatching** in the mangrove forests. It has a couple of islands, **Sudi**, where there's a boardwalk and picnic site, and opposite is **Kirepwe**, which has the ruins of an **old mosque**. There are some other ruins and a mosque at **Sita** at the head of the creek. A number of **boat trips** are offered to the creek by the main hotels in Watamu, and it's also possible to negotiate a **canoe ride** (about KSh200) with one of the local fishermen. Time **snorkelling** to catch the tides, as it's a long swim from the beach out to **the caves**, where you can see groupers – giant rock cod – so it's worth catching the ebb and flow or alternatively you can take a goggle boat. The tidal rip is not as strong here as at Mtwapa, but even so, it's important to pay attention to the tides. There's good snorkelling on the way, and if you are an accomplished snorkeller it's possible to swim through the caves. Alternatively you can dive down, hold on to the lip of a cave and peer in and sometimes see a monster grouper. The best **birdwatching** is at the head of the creek on the mud flats which attract yellow-billed and woolly necked storks, greater flamingos, herons, sanderlings and whimbrels, while pied and malachite kingfishers perch on the mangroves and fish eagles fly overhead. Opposite the mouth of the creek is **Whale Island**, where often you can see roseate and bridled terns nesting between June and October. The creek contains six different types of **mangrove** and numerous **crabs** – with large colonies of fiddler crabs on the mudflats.

Gedi

Gedi ruins

Founded in the late 13th or early 14th century, the town of Gedi – located about 4km north of Watamu, signposted off the main Malindi road – was a flourishing settlement in the mid-15th century, yet had been completely abandoned by the 17th century. Quite why it was established remains a mystery, yet it was probably due to a feud in Malindi, which formed a breakaway settlement. Despite the fact that it is not mentioned in Portuguese, Arab or Swahili sources, the rich quantity of Chinese and Islamic porcelain and the size of the houses suggests that the inhabitants must have been prosperous. By the 17th century the Galla tribe were invading from the north, and it's thought that Gedi, which means 'precious' in the Galla language, was either named for a Galla leader who camped there, or alternatively was their name for the town.

The ruins are spread over several acres, surrounded by natural forest (keep a look out for elephant shrews while walking round) and it's likely that the town covered 18ha in its time. Excavations of the site in the 1940s–1950s revealed domestic, religious and commercial structures, including a palace with sunken courts, a Friday mosque, elaborately decorated pillar tombs, wells, and an inner and outer town wall. Finds from the site included glass and shell beads, gold and silver jewellery and coins and porcelain and local pottery, some of which are displayed in the museum.

Central to the site is the **great mosque** and a **pillar tomb**, with the **palace** and **houses** to the west and several **mosques** around the **inner wall**.

Within the inner and outer wall is a **nature trail**, a shaded walk under the tree canopy, where some 30 indigenous trees are labelled, including baobab and tamarind. It typifies the coastal dry forest which grew on the raised coral reef prior to human settlement. At the entry to the ruins, there are a few craft sellers. Among the items for sale are ingenious rat traps made from baobab pods – ask for a demonstration.

Open daily 07.00–18.00; entry KSh200; excellent guidebook (KSh300) and guides (KSh150) are available from the office.

Gedi Museum

PO Box 5067, Malindi

The Gedi Museum, on the same site as the ruins, opened in the millennium, and has a display of pottery and bronze, together with an interpretation centre and a photographic exhibition about the Kenya coast. There's also a restaurant.

Kipepeo butterfly farm

PO Box 58, Gedi; tel: 042 32380; email: kipepeo@africaonline.co.ke

Located next to Gedi ruins is a butterfly farm (*kipepeo* being the Swahili for 'butterfly'). This is the base for a community project linked with the Arabuko Sokoke Forest. Initially funded by a UNDP global environment grant of US$50,000 in 1993, it aims to benefit the rural community around the forest by providing them with an income from rearing butterfly pupae which are then sold to butterfly projects worldwide. This gives the farmers an incentive to protect the forest which is home to over 260 butterfly species. On site there is a butterfly house and a visitor centre with a display showing the process of butterfly rearing, and a fundraising shop selling mangrove honey and local handicrafts.

Open daily 08.30–17.00; entry KSh100

THE KIPEPEO PROJECT
Sally Crook

In 1993 Dr Ian Gordon, a British lecturer at Nairobi University, came up with a scheme to help conserve the unique Arabuko-Sokoke Forest. This forest, near to the Gede Ruins on coastal Kenya, is the last remaining piece of dry coastal forest in East Africa and home to several endangered birds and mammals.

He knew that butterfly farms in Europe and America pay good money for live tropical butterflies among which paying visitors can roam. If the profits from producing butterflies for export to these live displays could be secured for the farmers living around the forest, these local people would have a vested interest in conserving the forest themselves, and in protecting it from others' depredations.

Dr Gordon obtained a grant to begin breeding butterflies in the grounds of the Gede Ruins. With a Master of Science student, Washington Ayiemba, he also began training people around the forest to produce butterflies on their farms. There are a couple of rare butterflies in the forest, such as *Charaxes blanda*, but only common species are bred for export, to minimise impact on the forest. These include the beautiful *Charaxes cithaeron*, the blue-spotted charaxes that resembles Blanda's charaxes, but like all of this genus spends much of its time on the roof of the cage with the wings closed. The favourite of most butterfly houses, is *Papilio dardanus*, the mocker swallowtail, whose black and white females, mimicking the poisonous friar, *Amauris niavius*, differ from the yellow and black male. Swallowtails are not only good-looking, but they 'behave' better than the fruit-eating *Charaxes* species as they land or hover to feed on nectar from flowers in full view of visitors.

Live female butterflies, which mate almost immediately on reaching adulthood, are caught in the forest reserve by licensed butterfly farmers. The female is caged with the appropriate food plant for the species and the caterpillars that hatch from the eggs laid are fed and protected from predators until they pupate. New pupae are bought by the Kipepeo (Butterfly) Project in Gede for export to various live butterfly displays – notably at Stratford–upon-Avon, UK, and at Branson, Missouri. They are sent by courier service (such as FedEx) to arrive before the adult butterflies emerge from the pupal cases. Displays of live butterflies in all stages, and the Kipepeo Project story, are also on display to visitors at the project headquarters just inside the gates of the Gede Ruins.

Profits for the butterfly farmers of over US$4,000 in 1994 rose to well over US$1 million by 2001, when the events of 9/11 caused some problems owing to the imposition of more stringent import restrictions to the US. However, the Kipepeo Project, which won a 1998 Dubai International Award for Best Practices to Improve the Living Environment, is still thriving with virtually no cost to the Arabuko-Sokoke Forest. It has become almost self-supporting, though still under the protection of the National Museums of Kenya, and is now headed by Washington Ayiemba. Therefore, a good idea, daringly implemented, has benefited the environment and the local human population.

For more information on the Kipepeo Project, visit www.watamu.net, www.Naturekenya.org and www.kipepeo.org.

Arabuko Sokoke Forest Reserve

PO Box 1, Gedi; tel: 042 32462; email: sokoke@africaonline.co.ke
Open daily 06.30–18.00; entry fee US$10. The visitor centre is open 08.00–16.00.
Guides cost KSh400 for two hours or KSh600 for six hours. Specialist bird guides can be
hired at the visitor centre or booked a week in advance by email: sokoke@africaonline.co.ke
Located a few kilometres inland from the coast, near Watamu, south of Malindi,
the forest stretches for several kilometres to the west of the main Kilifi–Malindi
road, off which there are several entrances, the main ones being **Kararacha** in the
south and **Gedi forest station** further north. The other main access point is
through **Jilore forest station** in the northwest (4WD essential) which links to the
C103 Malindi road to Tsavo East National Park. There's a KWS **visitor centre** at
Gedi which has displays on the forest and excellent guides for hire. It also has an
informative visitor's guide (KSh120) which has details of the walking and driving
trails.

History Covering an area of 417km², the Arabuko Sokoke Forest Reserve is the
largest remaining fragment of a dry coastal forest which once stretched along much
of the East African coastline. It was gazetted as a forest reserve in 1943 and in 1991
the Kenya Wildlife Service became a partner with the Forest Department in
recognition of the forest's rich biodiversity. Surrounded by agriculturalists, the
forest has been prone to illegal hunting of small mammals and logging – some trees
like the *Brachylaena huillensis* have been virtually logged out as they are favoured for
wood carving. Efforts have been made to bring an income to the local people from
the forest – hence the development of the butterfly centre – so that they have a
reason to preserve its habitat. There's an active support group, **Friends of
Arabuko Sokoke Forest**, PO Box 383, Gedi; web: www.watamu.net.

Flora and fauna The forest contains **three forest types**, with mixed forest,
Brachystegia woodland and *Cynometra* forest giving rise to a surprisingly high
number of endemic species – six types of butterfly (it boasts 260 butterfly
species in total), Ader's duiker, the golden-rumped elephant shrew, the Sokoke
bushy-tailed mongoose and nine globally threatened birds – the Sokoke scops
owl, the Sokoke pipit, the east coast akalat, spotted ground thrush, Amani
sunbird, Fischer's turaco, plain-backed sunbird, the southern banded snake
eagle and Clarke's weaver. Among the 230 recorded bird species, more
commonly seen are palaearctic migrants like the Eurasian bee-eater, Eurasian
golden oriole and spotted flycatcher. In addition there's a herd of 'thin'
elephants, which are rarely seen, preferring the dense thickets, and buffalo,
while golden cat and brown hyena are occasionally spotted. With a number of
forest ponds there's rich reptile life, including Bunty's dwarf toad which is
endemic to the coast. If walking, watch out for the columns of safari ants, *siafu*,
which often cross the footpaths.

Within the forest, there are a number of **4WD tracks** with deep sand. Make sure
you get clear directions as it is easy to get lost. Along the **main driving track**,
highlights are the whistling duck pools, the viewpoint, Kararacha pools and Spinetail
way. There's also a **jogging track** and several **walking trails**. The most accessible
are those starting at Gedi forest station, from which there's a 4km nature trail weaving
between the bushes, where guinea fowl are common and you have an excellent
chance of seeing elephant shrews. It links on to the 3km sand quarry and treehouse
trail, which leads to an open glade, and there's also a 14km elephant trail, part of the
4WD track.

On the first Saturday of each month, organised by the Arabuko Sokoke Forest

Guides Association, there's a **guided birdwatch** in the forest. It meets at the visitor centre, Gedi, and costs KSh100 per person.

Camping (PO Box 1, Gedi; tel: 042 32462) is permitted in the reserve at Sokoke Pipit campsite near the visitor centre at Gedi (it has water and a toilet) and at Kararacha campsite and other parts of the reserve with permission. You will need to be self-sufficient and take water.
Rates: camping KSh200 per person plus reserve entry fee

Malindi
Getting organised
There's a Barclays Bank with an ATM on Harambee Road, and Standard Chartered and Kenya Commercial banks have branches in the centre of town. The **post office**, open Monday–Friday 08.00–17.00, Saturday 09.00–12.00, is at the corner of Uhuru Street and for **internet access** try Malindi Connections in the Malindi complex or Oasis Communications next to the gelatti parlour in the shopping complex at the northern end of Silversands beach, where there's also a good **travel agent**, Scorpio Enterprises (tel: 042 31390). There are other travel agents, **car-hire** companies and a **tourist information office** (open Monday–Friday 08.00–4.30, tel: 042 20747) on Harambee Road, as well as several **supermarkets**, **pharmacies** and **newsagents**. The fruit and vegetable **market** is on Mama Ngina Street and there's another market next to the bus station. In a **medical emergency** go to the Galana Hospital on Lamu Road (tel: 042 30574). The **police station** is off Harambee Road (tel: 042 31555) and the **tourist helpline** is 020 604767. There are plenty of **petrol stations** on the access roads into Malindi.

Where to stay
Coral Key Beach Resort (120 rooms; 7 swimming pools) PO Box 556, Malindi; tel: 042 30717; fax: 042 30715; email: coralkey@africaonline.co.ke; web: www.coralkeymalindi.com
Located on Silversands beach, the resort is designed in Swahili style, with palm-thatched *makuti* roofs and white-washed walls. Spread out around the swimming pools, all the rooms have AC, fans, en-suite bathrooms, balconies or terraces. There's an excellent Italian poolside restaurant, several bars and evening entertainment. **On offer:** health club, beauty salon, deep-sea fishing, scuba diving, tennis court, watersports centre.
Rates: from KSh2,500 B&B per person sharing
Driftwood Beach Club (20 rooms, luxury cottages, self-catering villas; swimming pool) PO Box 63, Malindi; tel: 042 20155; fax: 042 30712; email: driftwood@swiftmalindi.com; web: www.driftwoodclub.com
On Silversands beach in Malindi overlooking the bay and close to the marine park at Casuarina Point, this family hotel is popular with local residents and prides itself on 'informality at its best'. It centres around a bar and thatched, open lounge area and the swimming pool. Rooms are spaced out on either side of the main building in cottages in the garden. In addition there are 2 luxury cottages (each sleep 4) with private swimming pools and 3 self-catering villas (2 en-suite rooms, kitchen, living room, veranda and use of private swimming pool). The rooms are comfortably furnished with AC, fans, mosquito nets, en-suite bathrooms and small verandas. The north beach rooms are the nicest, having sea views. The staff are exceptionally helpful, and the restaurant serves excellent meals, seafood being a speciality. There's often a weekly disco on a Saturday. **On offer:** big-game fishing, snorkelling in the marine park, scuba-diving school, boutique, local excursions.
Rates: from US$40 B&B per person sharing; cottages from US$170 B&B per night; self-catering villa from US$135 per night

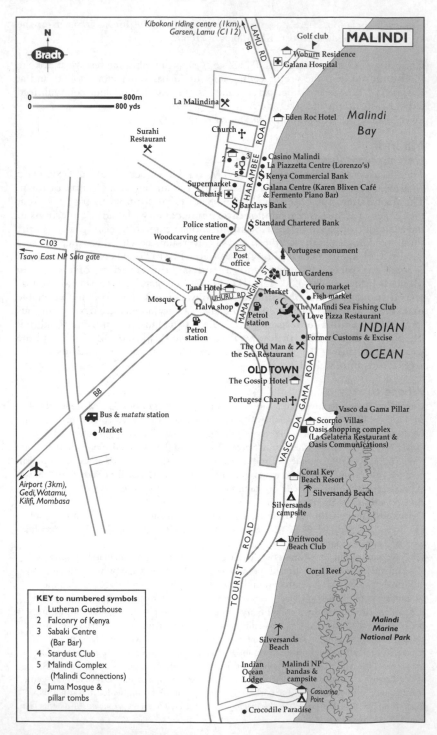

Kibokoni riding centre (1km),
Garsen, Lamu (C112)

MALINDI

Golf club

Woburn Residence

Galana Hospital

LAMU RD B8

La Malindina

Church

Eden Roc Hotel

Malindi Bay

Surahi Restaurant

HARAMBEE ROAD

1
2 3
4
5

Casino Malindi
La Piazzetta Centre (Lorenzo's)
Kenya Commercial Bank
Galana Centre (Karen Blixen Café & Fermento Piano Bar)

Supermarket
Chemist

Barclays Bank

Standard Chartered Bank

Police station
Woodcarving centre

C103
Tsavo East NP Sala gate

Post office

Portugese monument

Uhuru Gardens

Mosque

Tana Hotel
UHURU RD
Halva shop

Market

MAMA NGINA ST

Curio market
Fish market
The Malindi Sea Fishing Club
I Love Pizza Restaurant

Petrol station

Petrol station

6

INDIAN

The Old Man & the Sea Restaurant

Former Customs & Excise

OCEAN

B8

OLD TOWN

The Gossip Hotel

Portugese Chapel

VASCO DA GAMA ROAD

Vasco da Gama Pillar
Scorpio Villas
Oasis shopping complex
(La Gelateria Restaurant & Oasis Communications)

Bus & *matatu* station

Market

Coral Key
Beach Resort

Silversands Beach

Silversands campsite

Airport (3km),
Gedi, Watamu,
Kilifi, Mombasa

Driftwood
Beach Club

Coral Reef

TOURIST ROAD

Malindi Marine National Park

Silversands Beach

Indian Ocean Lodge

Malindi NP bandas & campsite

Casuarina Point

Crocodile Paradise

KEY to numbered symbols
1 Lutheran Guesthouse
2 Falconry of Kenya
3 Sabaki Centre
   (Bar Bar)
4 Stardust Club
5 Malindi Complex
   (Malindi Connections)
6 Juma Mosque &
   pillar tombs

N

Bradt

0 ———— 800m
0 ———— 800 yds

Eden Roc Hotel (150 rooms; 3 swimming pools) PO Box 350, Malindi; tel: 042 20480; fax: 042 20333; email: edenroc@africaonline.co.ke; web: www.edenrockenya.com
A 5-minute walk from Malindi town, the hotel is on the beach, but a long walk from the sea. One of the original hotels in Malindi, it retains facets of a faded elegance and most guests are German. The rooms have a mix of AC or fans, en-suite bathrooms and sea views. There are several restaurants – serving European, African, Indian and Arab cuisine – and bars, while nightly entertainment includes an open-air disco and tribal dancing. **On offer:** tennis, squash, deep-sea fishing, snorkelling trips, watersports, while golf and horseriding are available nearby.
Rates: from US$35 half board per person sharing
Woburn Residence (14 suites and 3-roomed apartments; swimming pool) PO Box 33, Malindi; tel: 042 31085; fax: 042 31183; email: woburn@swiftmalindi.com; web: www.woburnresidenceclub.com
Located in Malindi, this is a modern villa complex set in tropical gardens around a 3-tier swimming pool (with a jacuzzi). The rooms and apartments are spacious, bright and airy with smart furnishings. All rooms are large, with AC and en-suite bathrooms. There's a good restaurant specialising in seafood and a veranda bar. **On offer:** local excursions and a nature walk.
Rates: rooms from US$40 B&B per person sharing; suites from US$160 B&B per person sharing
Indian Ocean Lodge (8 rooms; swimming pool) PO Box 171, Malindi; tel: 042 20394. Book through Savannah Camps and Lodges, page 91
Located on Casuarina Point about 10 minutes' drive south of Malindi, this is a delightful, Arab-style lodge built on a coral promontory within 1.5ha of walled garden. More like a homestay, it is managed by Tina and Charlie Harris. An historical Swahili theme is maintained throughout, with heavy, carved Arab chests, Persian rugs and brass ornaments. Two rooms are in the main house, while the remainder are in a couple of buildings in the garden. Each room has Lamu four-poster beds and 2 single beds, louvred shutters, fans and mosquito nets (no AC), en-suite bathrooms and private verandas. Seafood is a speciality in the restaurant which also offers an à la carte menu. There's also access to a small, private cove at the southern end of Silversands beach. **On offer:** use of a private boat for snorkelling in the reserve, guided excursions to Arabuko Sokoke Forest, and tennis, golf, squash, windsurfing, scuba diving and deep-sea fishing by arrangement.
Rates: from US$240 full board per person sharing
Scorpio Villas (40 rooms; self-catering villas; 3 swimming pools) PO Box 368, Malindi; tel: 042 20194; fax: 042 21250; email: scorpio@swiftmalindi.com; web: www.scorpiovillas.com
Located at the northern end of Silversands beach, this Italian villa complex consists of 17 cottages set out in a hectare of landscaped tropical gardens. Furnished in Lamu style with 7ft beds, the rooms have AC, fans, en-suite bathrooms and verandas. Some have kitchens and are available for self-catering with staff provided. There's an excellent restaurant, specialising in seafood, Italian and Swahili dishes. **On offer:** on-site travel agency and tennis; golf, watersports, marine excursions and safaris can be arranged. *Rates: from US$35 B&B per person sharing*

Cheap rooms and camping

The Gossip Hotel Vasco da Gama Rd (next to the Sea Fishing Club) tel: 042 20307
Pleasantly located in an old house on the seafront, the staff are friendly and the rooms, with showers, are reasonable. There's a veranda restaurant and bar downstairs serving inexpensive meals (around KSh400 for a main course). It has a colourful atmosphere and locals often stop by for a chat.
Rates: from KSh400

Tana Hotel Uhuru Rd, tel: 042 20116
Conveniently located for catching buses to Malindi and Lamu, the rooms, some s/c, are
basic, but have fans and mosquito nets.
Rates: from KSh300
Lutheran Guest House Set back from the Lamu Rd, tel: 042 21098
A quiet location with rooms set around a garden courtyard. Rooms, some s/c, are clean
with fans and mosquito nets. No alcohol is permitted on the premises.
Rates: from KSh300 B&B per person sharing
Malindi Marine Park Bandas and Campsite (7 bandas; camping) Book through KWS
warden, Malindi Marine National Park, PO Box 109, Malindi; tel: 042 20845 or via KWS
in Nairobi, page 91
Located on Casuarina Point south of Malindi, next to the Marine Resource Centre, a
modern block contains the bandas which have one room with a fan and en-suite bathroom,
with a dining area and well equipped kitchen with a gas cooker but no fridge. Towels, linen
and mosquito nets are provided. You only need to bring food and drinks (including
drinking water). The campsite has basic facilities – water and long-drop toilets – and good
security. For details of the park, see page 412.
Rates: bandas KSh500 and camping US$2 per person
Silversands Campsite (bandas and camping) PO Box 422, Malindi; mobile: 0733 802926.
Located next door to the Driftwood Club on Silversands beach, this small campsite is right
on the beach and has a few basic bandas to rent, although your own tent is preferable, and
there's a functional ablution block – if water is a problem, the daily membership at the
Driftwood Club, KSh200, enables you to use their facilities. You can buy sodas on site,
cheap meals are available at the café next door and it's a short walk to the Italian
supermarket (expensive) in the Oasis Centre. **On offer:** bicycles for hire (KSh200 a day).
Rates: bandas from KSh390–590; camping KSh150

Where to eat
In addition to the beach hotels of Watamu and Malindi, Malindi town has a variety
of restaurants, bars, cafés and entertainment.

Cafés
Bar Bar Sabaki Centre, Lamu Rd. A good cappuccino café serving delicious Italian pastries
during the day, and drinks and snacks in the evening when it's popular with card-playing
Italians.
Karen Blixen Café the Galana Centre, Lamu Rd. A good place for fresh fruit juices and
oven-baked pizzas.
La Gelateria in the Oasis complex, Vasco da Gama Rd. A corner known as 'Little Italy',
there's a choice of about 30 different flavours of Italian ice-cream – mango recommended –
together with a snack bar.

Restaurants
Lorenzo's La Piazzetta Centre, Lamu Rd; tel: 042 31758. One of the best Italian
restaurants in town, it has a pleasant ambience, and being upstairs catches the sea breezes.
Meals, with a drink cost around KSh1,500.
 La Malindina Set back from Lamu Rd. A well-established Italian restaurant with a good
reputation, it has a set menu, with a multi-course dinner (with plenty of seafood) at the
poolside. Expect to pay about KSh1,500 inclusive of drinks.
Malindi Sea Fishing Club Vasco da Gama Rd. A residents' fishing club on the
beachfront, daily membership is available (about KSh200). Drinks and simple seafood
(good prawns) are excellent value (around KSh400), and you can book a fishing trip or
watch satellite TV.

Surahi One block back from Lamu Rd, near Barclays Bank.
Considered Malindi's best Indian restaurant, it has a range of meat and vegetarian curries, in a cool, air-conditioned environment.
The Old Man and the Sea Vasco da Gama Rd; tel: 042 31106. An excellent seafood restaurant where everything is char-grilled. It has a limited vegetarian choice and does not serve beer – only wine, juices and sodas. Meals cost from around KSh1,500 with drinks.

Entertainment
Stardust Club Harambee Rd. A lively disco with AC and seating, but it's also a hang-out for twilight ladies, so preferable to go in a group to avoid harassment. *Entry from KSh400 for men and KSh100 for women. Opens around 23.00 until late*
Fermento Piano Bar Galana Centre. On the top floor of the centre, this smart cocktail bar has an air-conditioned disco, but the Italian karaoke has limited appeal. Entry from KSh500. *Open 20.00 until late*
Casino Malindi Lamu Rd. For light-hearted entertainment as well as serious gamblers, roulette, blackjack, pontoon, Indian Ocean stud poker, punto banco and a range of slot machines can be played. There's a pleasant cocktail bar with a piano player in the evenings, when you'll need to dress smartly. *Entry free. Open 12.00–05.00 daily*

What to see and do
A walk around Malindi
It's best to go in the early morning or late afternoon to avoid the heat. Starting at **Uhuru gardens**, there's a **Portuguese monument** to **Prince Henry the Navigator**, built in 1959. Head south along the main road along the foreshore. Immediately on the right are the **Juma mosque** and **pillar tombs**. Continuing on, you pass the **curio market** (which has a mixed range of carvings, kiondos and jewellery for sale, some of excellent quality) on the left, followed by the **fish market** where you can see some huge game fish. On the right is the former customs and excise house which is being made into a **museum**. Continuing south, the road curves round to the **Portuguese chapel** dating from the 17th century, from which you can see **Vasco da Gama Pillar** on the promontory to the right, which marks the spot where the Portuguese landed in 1499. From the Portuguese chapel, turn right into the winding streets of the old town. Bearing right you will pass another **mosque** and join the southern end of Mama Ngina Street. A turn right, passing the fruit and vegetable **market** on your left, will bring you back to **Uhuru gardens** past a halva shop and numerous shops selling kikois and kangas and beaded sandals. Often you will be approached by people wanting to show you around. They are genuinely friendly, and it'll cost you about KSh50, depending on how long you take. This walk does not include the main tourist areas along Harambee and Lamu roads.

Falconry
Just off the Lamu road, opposite the casino, Falconry of Kenya has a display on the art of falconry, with free-flying demonstrations, together with educational exhibits. It operates a breeding programme and has a rehabilitation centre for rescued birds. There's a gift and coffee shop and hawking safaris can be arranged.
Open daily 09.00–17.30; entry from KSh300

Reptile Park
Crocodile Paradise Casuarina Point; tel: 042 20121
This reptile display includes about 1,500 crocodiles and 60 snakes.
Open daily 09.00–17.30; Entry KSh300/150

Horseriding

Kibokoni riding centre Lamu Road; tel: 042 21273
Horseriding around the area (more akin to pony trekking) is available for different
standards, and includes beach and bush rides.
Rates from about KSh800 an hour

Golf

A couple of kilometres north of town, Malindi Golf and Country Club is a nine-
hole golf course and daily membership is available while golf clubs and caddies can
be hired.
Rates: expect to pay about KSh1,000 in total

Windsurfing

This is available at Roland's windsurfing school on Silversands beach near the
Driftwood Club.

Deep-sea fishing

Malindi Fishing Club (page 410) and Kingfishers (page 118) are the deep-sea
fishing specialists at Malindi.

Scuba diving

The Driftwood Club (page 407) has the main scuba-diving school in Malindi with
Frank Scheller. In the Malindi Marine Reserve, the dive sites are very different and
average 15–20m. Stork Passage has a good current which brings large shoals of
barracuda, white tip and reef sharks, together with turtles, mackerels, schools of
grouper, various coral fish, moray eels and lobsters.

Malindi Marine National Park

Casuarina Point, PO Box 109, Malindi; tel: 042 20845
Open daily 06.00–18.00; park entry fee US$8
Access to the marine park is by glass-bottomed boat from Silversands beach or
from the park headquarters at Casuarina Point. The national park covers an area of
6km², with superb coral gardens, and is part of the greater Malindi and Watamu
Marine Reserve. For details on the snorkelling, see the Watamu section, page 402,
as similar corals and fish may be seen.

From Malindi, expect to pay around KSh1,000 for a glass-bottomed boat trip in
addition to park fees.

NORTH TO LAMU

Heading north from Malindi, the road crosses the **Sabaki River**, the southern
section of the Galana which flows through Tsavo East. During the rainy season,
the Sabaki is red with silt flowing into Malindi bay. In the prolific El Niño
flooding, a hippo was washed out to sea, causing quite a sensation at the time;
it's more normal to see birdlife on the mudflats. A little further on is the turn-
off to **Che-Shale**, the only place in Kenya where you can go kite-surfing, and
the extensive, rectangular salt mines near **Mambrui**. Inland is the Marafu
Depression, a small canyon, known locally as Hell's Kitchen. Continuing north,
the scenery is fairly bland until you cross the Tana River at **Garsen**. It used to
be possible to take a boat, African Queen-style, through the marshlands nearing
the **Tana Delta**, where numerous crocodile nested in the sandbanks, but
changes in the delta channels stopped access to the sea. Now to explore the
delta, it's best to go to the Tana River Delta Camp. Security permitting, the road

THE BEACH BOYS

Nothing to do with, 'We're all going on a summer holiday...,' in Kenya, the beach boys are the touts on the beach, who sell everything, from carvings to sex, as I was to discover:

'My name's Edward,' said a tall African as he fell into step beside me, walking on the beach near the hotel. 'You may call me King Edward, but I'm not a potato.' I had to admit, it was a novel chat-up line. Naively, the previous day I had fallen for the, 'Don't you remember me, Mama, you saw me last time you came from Nairobi,' and said that he must have mistaken me for someone else – but of course, it was all part of the game. King Edward then suggested we go for a walk to which I replied I was leaving and going to another beach. 'What is the name of your hotel and your room number?' he asked. Gobsmacked, I replied angrily, 'I beg your pardon,' to which he sheepishly said, 'I'll come and visit you.' Certainly there's a fine line between sense of humour failure and harassment, but I did feel a tinge of pity for King Edward – after all, he was only trying to earn his keep, and sadly there are still plenty of European sea, sun and sex tourists who come to Kenya, despite the prevalence of AIDS. If sex tourism did not exist, King Edward would have a different occupation.

Tourists may also come in for harassment when shopping at the little stalls selling curios. People can descend on you like a swarm, badgering you to visit their stall and buy. Emotional blackmail is not uncommon, 'Please buy this, or this or this – it will be my first sale today, and then I can feed my children tonight.' The sales pitch obviously works, but it becomes wearing. Again, it's worth bearing in mind that tourists are rich pickings and fair game for those living in comparative poverty, where making a living is genuinely tough (and they often do have lots of kids to feed), even if it does make you feel a little uncomfortable.

Recognising a problem with the beach boys, the tourism industry has tried to regulate them to certain areas, so that tourists are not subject to a constant barrage of harassment. A relocation scheme has been implemented in Malindi, and along other parts of the coast, which appears to be working well.

from Garsen to **Garissa** is a long but interesting journey along a reasonable dirt road following the Tana River. Heading up to **Lamu**, it's a fairly mundane drive, where you can take a detour to the town of **Witu**, another old settlement, before continuing on past the Kenyatta settlement scheme, where Kenyans ousted from Tanzania following the break-up of the East African Community in 1977 (the East African Community has subsequently been revived) were given land to farm. Nearing **Makowe**, you begin to get glimpses of the **Lamu Archipelago** – rich, midnight blue waters tinged with the bright green of mangrove forest, and dhows sailing on the narrow channel between the mainland and **Lamu Island**.

Getting there and away

Prior to heading north from Malindi, do check out the security situation first as there have been incidents on the route in recent years due to *Shifta* and tribal skirmishes between the Orma and Pokomo. The B8 continues north (4WD recommended from Garsen), crossing the Sabaki River to the small village of

Mambrui, with huge areas being mined for salt. Turn left to Marafa, about 25km, to get to Hell's Kitchen. Continuing north from Mambrui, there's a turn-off to the right for Che-Shale. It's several kilometres down to the beach and you'll need 4WD. The B8 continues north. If heading to the Tana River Delta Camp get explicit directions; the turn-off is to the south of Garsen. At Garsen (about 115km from Malindi), a small, linear village, the B8 heads north to Garissa (a further 240km). This is the easiest way to reach the Tana River Primate National Reserve (about 50km). If heading to Lamu, at Garsen the C112 heads to Witu (about 50km) and on to Mokowe (another 50km) where you have to leave your vehicle.

By bus
From Malindi it's a six-hour journey to Lamu. The route has been subject to hold-ups by *Shifta* – Somali bandits – in the past, but at the time of writing was considered reasonably safe, but not without risk. Buses run daily between Malindi and Mokowe via Garsen. There is currently no bus service operating between Malindi and Garissa.

By air
There's an airstrip at Tana River Delta Camp and daily scheduled services to Manda Island (for Lamu) from Nairobi, Malindi and Mombasa.

Getting organised
In **Garsen**, there are limited facilities and no banks although **petrol** is available.

Where to stay and eat
Che-Shale
Che-Shale (5 rooms) PO Box 1434, Malindi; mob: 0722 426752; email: che-shale@africaonline.co.ke; web: www.che-shale.com
Located about 25km north of Malindi (4WD required), this small club on the beachfront, with 10km of beach, is informal and a perfect place to relax. Run by Marzia (a jewellery designer) and Justin Aniere (who can also organise bird shooting and safaris on the Galana River) the club is artistically decorated with local materials. The rooms are in sea-facing bandas, each with en-suite facilities and a private veranda. There's a restaurant with an Italian emphasis and a bar, while beach barbecues are organised at the weekends, Fri–Sun. **On offer:** camel rides to Giriama villages, *ngalawa* (traditional outrigger canoe) trips, kite-surfing school, scuba diving, snorkelling and safaris to Tsavo East can be arranged.
Rates: from US$90 full board per person inclusive of transfer from Malindi

Tana Delta
Tana River Delta Camp (4 cottages, 3 forest tents; swimming pool) Book through Bush Homes of East Africa, page 90
Located about 2 hours' drive north of Malindi to a point on the Tana River, after which it's a 15-minute boat ride to the camp which nestles in the sand dunes at the mouth of the delta. This is a perfect combination of 'beaching about the bush'. Reached by a series of steps and timber decking, the open-air, thatched rooms look on to the creek, or out to sea, and are individually designed with driftwood-style beds, with mosquito nets, en-suite showers with flush toilets and a small veranda area. The tents (also en suite) are near the river, but get rather hot and airless. There's a bar-cum-dining area (with plenty of fresh crab and prawns) near the jetty, while the pool and day house are at the top of the dunes to catch the sea breezes. A short walk through the dunes brings you to miles of empty beach littered with sand dollars and old flip flops. **On offer:** bush walks in the dunes tracking buffalo and

bushbuck, bird (over 200 species) and crocodile-watching boat trips upriver, sand yachting, dune jumping and natural mud baths.
Rates: from US$330 full board per person sharing

LAMU ISLAND

The most famous island in the Lamu archipelago, measuring about 16km by 7km, Lamu resembles a miniature version of Zanzibar, but here transport is by foot, donkey or dhow. The magnificent Swahili settlement of Lamu Town, a World Heritage Site, (similar to Zanzibar's Stone Town, with its maze of narrow winding streets and intricately carved doorways) dominates the north east of the island. The fishing village of **Shela** lies to the south, with a 12km beach, while opposite the mainland **Matondoni** is the centre for dhow-building and **Kipungani** for palm-mat weaving.

Getting there and away

There's a boat stage on **Manda Island** and transfers to Lamu Island take about ten minutes. Be prepared for bustling touts pitching cheap accommodation. The more expensive hotels will arrange transfers which are often included in the price of stay. The touts are remarkably persistent, so select accommodation before you go, and if once there you don't like it, then move on. It will avoid a lot of hassle.

As there are no vehicles on Lamu Island, bar the police Land Rover, vehicles need to be left on the mainland at **Mokowe**. It's a 20-minute crossing by motorboat to Lamu (costs about KSh40). Lamu is still an important centre for seafaring dhows, but private passages by dhow are difficult to arrange nowadays.

Getting organised

In **Lamu**, there's a Kenya Commercial Bank on the waterfront for changing money.. It's reasonable for cashing travellers' cheques, but can charge exorbitant commissions on credit card advances (Visa only), so check first. Otherwise hotels will exchange money, but at a premium rate. The **post office**, also on the waterfront, opens Monday–Friday 08.00–17.00, Saturday 09.00–12.00 and for **internet access** try Lamu Internet Spider in the New Maharus Guest House off the main square. There are a couple of **supermarkets** on Harambee Avenue. The **tourist information office** (tel: 042 633132) is on the waterfront. The fruit and vegetable **market** is next to the fort. In a **medical emergency** you are best to go to Malindi. There's a health centre near Lamu Palace Hotel on the waterfront. The **police station** (tel: 042 633120) is at the southern end of town and the **tourist helpline** is 020 604767. The **immigration department** is near the Manda jetty on the waterfront.

Where to stay and eat
Lamu town

Baytil Ajaib (2 apartments, 2 suites, sleeps 8) PO Box 328, Lamu; tel: 042 32033; email: b.ajaiblamu@swiftmalindi.com; web: www.baytilajaib.com
A beautifully restored palatial town house, this is a fine example of Swahili architecture, with exquisitely carved wooden doors and ceilings, rooms opening out on to courtyards and capacious verandas with views across the higgledy-piggledy rooftops of Lamu town. *Baytil Ajaib* means 'House of Wonder' and it typifies the opulence which surrounded wealthy Arab traders who sailed the Indian Ocean, trading in spices, ivory, mangrove poles (and slaves), and lent their patronage to Swahili culture over the centuries. The ambience of luxury and history are emphasised by authentic Lamu furniture – hand-carved beds and tables inlaid with pottery. Spacious and airy, the rooms have en-suite bathrooms. There is a dining hall and numerous sitting areas around the house. **On offer:** local excursions can be arranged.
Rates: from US$90–120 B&B per person sharing or US$5,000 a week for 8 people

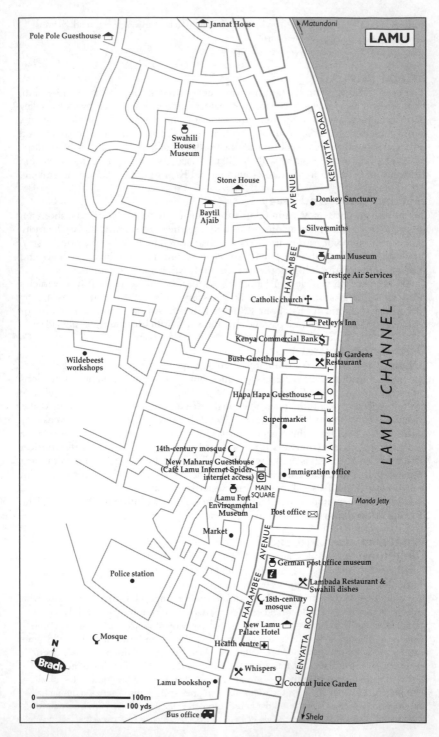

LAMU

Pole Pole Guesthouse

Jannat House

◄ Matundoni

KENYATTA ROAD

Swahili House Museum

Stone House

AVENUE

Baytil Ajaib

Donkey Sanctuary

Silversmiths

HARAMBEE

Lamu Museum

Prestige Air Services

Catholic church ✝

Petley's Inn

Kenya Commercial Bank $

Bush Guesthouse

Bush Gardens Restaurant

Wildebeest workshops

WATERFRONT

Hapa/Hapa Guesthouse

Supermarket

14th-century mosque

New Maharus Guesthouse (Café Lamu Internet Spider internet access)

Immigration office

MAIN SQUARE

Lamu Fort Environmental Museum

Post office ✉

Manda Jetty

Market

German post office museum

ℹ

Police station

Lambada Restaurant & Swahili dishes

18th-century mosque

HARAMBEE AVENUE

KENYATTA ROAD

New Lamu Palace Hotel

N

Mosque

Health centre ✚

Bradt

Whispers

Lamu bookshop

Coconut Juice Garden

0   100m
0   100 yds

Bus office

▼ Shela

LAMU CHANNEL

Jannat House (16 rooms; swimming pool) PO Box 195; tel: 042 33414 or book through Base Camp Travel in Nairobi, page 102
Built in the 18th century, this former Arab merchant's house has been restored and furnished in traditional Lamu style. Owned by a Swedish family, there's a leafy courtyard, a swimming pool in the garden and a rooftop terrace with views across town to Manda Island.
Rates: from US$24 half board per person sharing
Stone House (13 rooms) PO Box 193, Lamu; tel: 042 33544 or book through Kisiwani in Nairobi, page 91
An 18th-century house, the rooms are large and comfortable with en-suite bathrooms. There's an excellent rooftop restaurant (no alcohol) catching the sea breezes, with panoramic views across town.
Rates: from KSh1,200 B&B per person sharing
New Lamu Palace Hotel (22 rooms) PO Box 421, Lamu; tel: 042 33272; fax: 042 33104; email: islands@africaonline.co.ke
Located on the waterfront of Lamu town, the hotel has been refurbished. It has a choice of an awning-covered terrace at street level for watching the world go by, or an airy rooftop restaurant for meals, seafood being a speciality. The rooms are comfortable with AC, mosquito nets and en-suite bathrooms.
Rates: from US$60 full board per person sharing
Petley's Inn (11 rooms; swimming pool) PO Box 421, Lamu; tel: 042 33272; fax: 042 33104; email: islands@africaonline.co.ke
Also on the waterfront, next to the museum, Petley's is one of the oldest hotels in Kenya – a typical 19th-century colonial building, square in shape, with balconies and palm-thatched roof. The rooms have AC, mosquito nets, en-suite bathrooms and sea views. There's a rooftop bar, one of the few places in Lamu town selling cold beer, and swimming pool.
Rates: from US$45 B&B per person sharing

There are numerous **cheap lodgings** in Lamu, in the old houses, where often you can sleep on mattresses under mosquito nets on the rooftop. Among guesthouses to consider are:

Pole Pole Guest House (15 rooms) PO Box 195, Lamu; tel: 042 33344
One of the tallest buildings in Lamu, it has good rooms with fans and mosquito nets. Most are s/c.
Rates: KSh400 a double
Hapa Hapa Guest House PO Box 213 Lamu; tel: 042 33145
Reasonable rooms, but not all have fans. Aim for rooms on the top floor which catch the sea breezes. Some rooms are s/c.
Rates: rooms from KSh250
Bush Guest House (8 rooms) PO Box 22, Lamu; no telephone
Few of the rooms are s/c, but they are clean with mosquito nets and fans. There's a pleasant lounge with sea views and a roof terrace.
Rates: from KSh500 B&B

In addition to the **restaurants** mentioned under accommodation, Lamu town has a good selection of **cheap eats** – yoghurt and fruit bars, small cafés with Arab-style, strong, stand-up-your-spoon coffee, and home cooking in people's homes. They are much of a muchness, but recommended are:

Bush Gardens On the waterfront. A good ambience and has excellent fruit juices and seafood kebabs. Meals cost from KSh200–800. *Open daily 07.00–19.00*
Whispers on Harambee Av. This has delicious espresso coffee and pastries, as well as meals from around KSh300. It's open during Ramadan. *Open daily 09.00–20.30 and opening times vary in the off season*

Ali Hippy This is a family affair. Ali is one of a number of locals offering traditional cooking in their homes. The food is quite good – perhaps not to everyone's taste – but part of the fun is the novel experience. It costs KSh300–500 depending on the choice of food. Just ask locally for Ali Hippy.

Shela

Peponi Hotel (24 rooms; swimming pool) PO Box 24, Lamu; tel: 042 33154; fax: 042 33029; email: peponi@africaonline.co.ke; web: www.peponi-lamu.com
This is Lamu's *classic* hotel, located in Shela village, at the end of the beach, with views over the Lamu channel with the sea lapping at the walls at high tide. It was built in 1967 by the Korschen family who still run it today. The rooms, all individual in style with Swahili furnishings, are in a collection of small buildings in the colourful garden. Mealtimes are flexible – you can dine on the terrace or at the poolside grill, while the restaurant provides sumptuous dinners of fresh crab, lobster, squid and giant prawns cooked in ginger, lime and garlic. Alternatively you can opt for a Swahili feast and eat in the traditional manner, seated on the floor around a huge brass platter. The bar is open to everyone and is the only place to buy alcoholic drinks in Shela. **On offer:** watersports centre with scuba diving (PADI), waterskiing and windsurfing instruction, snorkelling and dhow excursions, deep-sea fishing. *Rates: from US$100 B&B per person sharing. Closed from mid-April–June.*

Island Hotel (13 rooms) PO Box 179, Lamu; tel: 042 33290; fax: 042 33568; email: island@net2000ke.com or book through Kisiwani in Nairobi, page 91
Located on the edge of Shela village and a 5-minute walk to the beach, this is a delightful, understated hotel, decorated in Lamu style, where Chris Hawley and his staff give a friendly, knowledgeable and helpful service. The rooms (not large) have mosquito nets, fans and en-suite shower rooms, and there's a spacious penthouse which is well worth the extra cost. There's an excellent rooftop restaurant, the Barracuda (where in season you can watch carmine bee-eaters while having breakfast), or dine by candlelight on delicious Swahili cuisine with plenty of fresh seafood and vegetarian options. You need to order in advance as it can take half an hour to prepare the food – but no alcohol is available. **On offer:** guided tours of Lamu town and dhow excursions and watersports can be arranged; air packages from Nairobi are available.
Rates: rooms from US$36 B&B per person sharing inclusive of boat transfer; penthouse from US$47 B&B per person sharing inclusive of boat transfer. Usually closed in May.

Kijani House (10 rooms; swimming pool) PO Box 266, Lamu; tel: 042 3325–7; fax: 042 33374; email: kijani@africaonline.co.ke; web: www.kijani-house.com
A traditional Lamu house in Shela village, this small hotel is set in 3 former private houses within colourful tropical gardens overlooking the dhow harbour. The rooms are spacious and airy, furnished in traditional Lamu style with four-poster beds, mosquito nets, fans, en-suite bathrooms and private balconies. The restaurant has an excellent chef specialising in seafood, Italian and African dishes. It's about 15 minutes' walk to the beach. **On offer:** dhow excursions and watersports can be arranged.
Rates: from US$90 B&B per person sharing

Bahari Guest House (5 rooms) PO Box 59, Lamu; tel: 042 32046
A small, yellow 3-storied house on the pier at Shela, where you catch a dhow taxi to Lamu town. The owner is friendly and helpful, while the rooms have mosquito nets and en-suite bathrooms, the top room being the best.
Rates: from US$15 B&B per person sharing

Shela Royal House (10 rooms) PO Box 305, Lamu; tel: 042 33091; fax: 042 33542; email: shela@africaonline.co.ke
A large house in Shela village, the top storey rooms are best, and the cook produces excellent meals. Not all rooms are en suite.
Rates: from US$65 B&B per person

Above Aerial view of Gabbra settlement in Chalbi Desert, northern Kenya (CF)

Left Gabbra girl (AZ)

Below Gabbra homestead, Kalacha (AZ)

Above Kikuyu girl (AZ)

Above right Market day, Sigor (CF)

Below Turkana girl building hut at Loyangalani (AZ)

Shela White House (5 rooms) PO Box 305, Lamu; tel: 042 33091; fax: 042 33542; email: shela@africaonline.co.ke
Located behind Peponi Hotel, being modern this lacks the atmosphere of the traditional houses, but it has a pleasant roof terrace and friendly management. Not all rooms have en-suite facilities.
Rates: from US$50 B&B per person
Shela Rest House (8 rooms) PO Box 305, Lamu; tel: 042 33091; fax: 042 33542; email: shela@africaonline.co.ke
In Shela village, set back from the beach near Island Hotel, most rooms have shared facilities.
Rates: from US$45 B&B per person
Mnarani House (6 rooms, self-catering) Book through Kisiwani in Nairobi, page 91
A delightful, spacious house in Shela with sea views, 3 en-suite doubles and 2 single rooms. There's a full-time cook, who will also organise the shopping for provisions, and resident house staff.
Rates: from US$220 a day for the house
Jasmine House (3 rooms, self-catering) Book through Kisiwani in Nairobi, page 91
A similar arrangement to Mnarani above, with resident staff.
Rates: from US$210 a night for the house
Beach House (5 rooms, self-catering; swimming pool) Book through Shela House Management, PO Box 39486, Nairobi; tel: 020 4442171; fax: 020 4445010; email: shela@africaonline.co.ke; web: www.lamu-shela.com
Located on the beachfront with immediate access to Shela beach, the house is owned by Princess Caroline of Monaco. Spacious and airy, it's on three floors with panoramic views of the Lamu channel. There's a large dining and sitting room opening on to a terrace, while the bedrooms are all en suite, some with a private terrace. The resident cook and staff assist with household duties and can arrange excursions.
Rates: from US$7,000 a week
Shela House (5 rooms, self-catering) Book through Shela House Management, PO Box 39486, Nairobi; tel: 020 4442171; fax: 020 4445010; email: shela@africaonline.co.ke; web: www.lamu-shela.com
Located in Shela village, this spacious, 3-storey house is built around an open courtyard. Rooms are all en suite and nicely furnished, and the rooftop's ideal for relaxing. A resident manager assists with menu planning or arranging excursions, and there's a full complement of house staff.
Rates: from US$3,500 a week
Palm House (4 rooms, self-catering) Book through Shela House Management, PO Box 39486, Nairobi; tel: 020 4442171; fax: 020 4445010; email: shela@africaonline.co.ke; web: www.lamu-shela.com
On the edge of Shela village next to the sand dunes, the house is built around an open courtyard, off which are the main living and dining areas. The rooms are on two floors, all with private facilities, while the rooftop has a bar with sunbeds. The house staff assist with catering and arranging excursions.
Rates: from US$3,500 a week

Kipungani

— Stayed at Feb 2005. Very relaxing.

Kipungani Explorer (14 rooms; swimming pool) Book through Heritage Hotels, page 91.
A half-hour boat trip from Lamu town, Kipungani is a secluded, Robinson Crusoe-style, informal beach hotel where you can perfect the art of 'chilling out'. It's on the southwestern tip of Lamu Island where you can watch sunsets and dhows sailing past. There's a central, open-sided restaurant – good seafood menu – with bar, deck with moon beds (huge hammocks) and pool area, while the bandas, linked by sandy paths, are spread out in a coconut plantation. Palm-thatched with spacious verandas, rooms have king-size

beds, fans and mosquito nets with large shower rooms attached. Some are on stilts, but the best face on to the mangrove-lined beachfront. Near by you can walk on to the southern end of Shela beach. **On offer:** trips to Lamu town, Matondoni and the coastal hinterland, the village school, dhow trips for snorkelling (with the chance of seeing dolphins) and sundowners.
Rates: from US$150 full board per person sharing

Lamu town

Designated a World Heritage Site in 2001, Lamu's Old Town is the oldest and best-preserved Swahili settlement in East Africa and it's become a significant centre for the study of Swahili culture. The majority of buildings date from the 18th century although the town originated in the 13th century and was an active port during the 1500s. Rather than following a set trail, it's more fascinating to wander around the maze of narrow, winding alleys, which are surprisingly cool, and to savour the town's historical intrigue and observe present-day Swahili culture. There's a distinctly Arab flavour with strong traditions. Kohl-eyed women wear black *bui buis* which cover them from head to toe, while men wear embroidered *kofias*, the traditional hat. The majority of the population are Muslim and the day is punctuated with the muezzin calling men to prayer at the 23 mosques around town. Lamu has hosted important Muslim festivals since the 19th century, it's most important today being the Maulidi (see page 134). In the evening, men sit on the steps outside their houses, sipping coffee and philosophising, while children peer out from doorways and the small restaurants run brisk business.

What to see and do
Lamu Museum
On the waterfront next to the town jetty, PO Box 48, Lamu; tel: 042 33073; fax: 042 33402; email: lamuse@africaonline.co.ke
If you visit only one museum in Lamu, this is the one to go to as it gives a wonderful introduction to the region, both past and present. Set in a two-storey house, typical of 18th-century Swahili architecture, the building was the governor's residence during the British colonial period before being transformed into a museum. It contains exhibits on the **Lamu Archipelago** and the islands of **Manda** and **Pate**, **Lamu town** and a reconstruction of a **Swahili house**, together with plans and maps, a model display of **traditional dhows** and artefacts include **Swahili furniture**, **musical instruments** and **jewellery**. It also has a fascinating **ethnological collection** about the Swahili, together with the hinterland tribal groups – the Orma, Pokomo and Boni. There's also an interesting slide show.

The museum has a small shop which sells copies of *Lamu: a study of a Swahili town*, a good reference book, and a detailed map of Lamu town.
Open daily 08.00–18.00; entry KSh200

Lamu Fort Environment Museum
PO Box 48, Lamu; tel: 042 33073; fax: 042 33402; email: lamuse@africaonline.co.ke
Located off the main square, the fort, when it was built in 1809, would have occupied a position on the seafront, but subsequently buildings were erected in front of it. A large, solid building, it was the town prison from 1910 until 1984. It now houses an excellent exhibit illustrating the local environment and Kenya's unique biodiversity. It also contains the Lamu Old Town Conservation office and town library.
Open daily 08.00–18.00; entry KSh200

German Post Office Museum

PO Box 48, Lamu; tel: 042 33073; fax: 042 33402; email: lamuse@africaonline.co.ke

Built at the turn of the 19th century as a private residence, the house was transformed into a post office by the Germans between 1888–1891 when Witu, on the mainland south of Lamu, was a German protectorate. It opened as a museum in 1996, restored with assistance from the German embassy. It illustrates a period in Kenya's history which is poorly documented. During that time Lamu's maritime trade extended as far as Europe and the connection with Germany revealed the early development of postal communications in Kenya. The exhibits contain a selection of **photographs** and **artefacts** of the period.

Open daily 08.00–18.00; entry KSh200

Swahili House Museum

PO Box 48, Lamu; tel: 042 33073; fax: 042 33402; email: lamuse@africaonline.co.ke

Located in the northern part of the town, this museum has been authentically restored and furnished to illustrate a period Swahili home.

Open daily 08.00–18.00; entry KSh200

Donkey sanctuary

Located at the northern end of the waterfront, the sanctuary is affiliated to the International Donkey Protection Trust based in the UK. It looks after the beasts of burden who have gone into retirement. With over 3,000 donkeys in the Lamu region, the sanctuary gives respite to donkeys that would otherwise meet an untimely end.

Open daily 09.00–13.00; free entry, but donations welcome

Wildebeeste workshops

PO Box 175, Lamu; tel: 042 32261; email: wildebeeste@africaonline.co.ke

Situated in a house northwest of the main square, the workshops are part of a project supporting unemployed people and teaching them creative skills. Many of the women design and embroider delightful wall-hangings, known as *mkonokono*, which means, 'handmade'. The workshops are also open to artists and students, where you can learn about print and papermaking, traditional bookbinding or

---

THE AFRICAN STORY SNAKE

In 1992 the Lamu branch of Wildebeeste Environmental Workshops International (WEWI), a group encouraging creative work among unemployed people while stressing the importance of the environment, was asked for a contribution to take to the Earth Summit in Rio de Janeiro. Over one hundred women from Lamu were asked to design and embroider an image in nature which they would most miss if it were gone for ever. They each embroidered black squares, using multi-coloured threads, sequins, beads and patches. The squares were then sewn together in a 150ft-long banner that was paraded through the streets of Rio in the street festival at the end of the summit. An exquisite and original piece of embroidery, the banner has since toured around the world.

For information contact Wildebeeste Workshops, PO Box 175, Lamu; tel: 042 32261; email: wildebeeste@africaonline.co.ke.

THE SWAHILI HOUSE

The winding alleys of Lamu contain some fine examples of Swahili houses, most of which date from the 18th century.

Constructed from coral rag (broken up pieces of hard coral resembling building blocks) bonded with coral lime or soil, walls were around half a metre thick, while roofs were generally made from mangrove poles covered by coral rag to a depth of about 60cm and then plastered, giving a beamed effect. (Roofs today are mostly rusted corrugated iron sheeting, with the occasional thatched *makuti* roof.) The plasterwork varied. Normally, dressed coral was only used around prayer niches and lintels, carved with symbolic motifs.

The design of the Swahili house was quite specific – an inward-looking complex arranged around a central courtyard, with a careful balance of indoor and outdoor spaces. The intricate plasterwork, with ceiling friezes, architraves and central niches, became more elaborate within the rooms furthest away from the courtyard. The innermost room was normally used as the master bedroom and women's quarters, where often half the wall would be covered in an array of niches. The sleeping quarters were usually separated by curtains draped across the end of the room.

The front door of the house was normally rectangular in shape – later buildings sometimes had an arched doorway. The heavy wooden doors were intricately carved and the size of the door and its decoration reflected the prestige of the family home. At the top of the doorway was an insignia of the family who lived within (rather like a family crest), while the carved motifs – rosettes, dolphins and the like – had a specific symbolic reference. Many of the doors had brass bosses, a design feature thought to have originated in India or Persia to keep out war elephants.

For detailed information on Swahili houses, visit the Lamu and Swahili House museums.

tapestry and weaving (you need to arrange this through the workshops). They also have some accommodation for visiting students.
Visitors are usually welcome but it's best to ring in advance

Excursions from Lamu town
Dhow trips, watersports and fishing
Dhow trips are very much part of the attraction of visiting Lamu, with short and day excursions being available. A dhow ride to Shela costs around KSh50–100, while a day trip snorkelling (which includes swimming, fishing and a beach barbecue lunch, with the chance of seeing dolphins) costs in the region of KSh500–750 per person. Dhow captains abound, and Ali Kupi who skippers *Asali* is recommended. Excursions to Manda Island to see the Takwa Ruins (see page 425), Matondoni to see dhows being built and longer trips to Pate Island (see page 425) can be arranged. Be aware that most dhows do not have any shade so take full precautions against the sun and plenty of drinking water.

Tusitiri (sleeps 7) Book through Borana Lodge, page 258
A traditional 20m *Jahazi* dhow, hosted by Richenda and Mark Eddy (a CASA yacht master)

the dhow sails the archipelago. **On offer:** scuba diving and windsurfing, with options for waterskiing and big-game fishing.

Rates: from US$325–650, full board for 2–7 people
Utamaduni (sleeps 7) Book through Blue Safari Club, PO Box 15026, 00509 Langata, Nairobi; tel: 020 890184; fax: 020 890096; email: info@bluesafariclub.com; web: www.bluesafariclub.com
Another traditional 20m *Jahazi* dhow, with 3 berths, a head (toilet) and outdoor shower.
On offer: scuba diving with a compressor on board, windsurfing and options for fishing.
Rates: from US$325–650, full board for 2–7 people

Shela village

Located about 3km south of Lamu town is the peaceful fishing village of Shela. It can be reached by dhow taxi or via a footpath from Lamu town. A sizeable village, it has an almost biblical feel to it, with little boys in Wee Willy Winky nightshirts (*jallabiyas*) and *kofias* herding fat-tailed sheep and donkeys through the backstreets. The Friday mosque (1829) in Shela is unusual for its distinctive, rocket-shaped minaret. Most people come here for **Shela beach**, 12km of golden sand flanked by sand dunes and devoid of shade, where occasionally you can see dolphins playing in the shallows. Several years ago there were a couple of rapes on the empty sections of this beach, so be vigilant. A privately owned fortress has recently been built at the northern end of the beach around the corner from Peponi Hotel. **Dhow excursions** can be arranged near the jetty at Peponi, which also has a **watersports centre**. **Dhow racing** is organised through Peponi Hotel – see page 135 for details – and the hotel is also the office for the **Lamu Marine Conservation Project**, see page 426.

Matondoni village

Located on the western side of Lamu, this is a pleasant boat ride (about half an hour by motorboat, or a little longer by dhow, depending on the wind), with the chance to birdwatch in the mangroves along the way. Alternatively it's quite a long walk across the island, and, as it's easy to take the wrong path, it's best to get directions locally. Matondoni, a small village with a few thatched houses, is the centre for traditional dhow making, a craft which is fortuitously being kept alive by the demand for tourist dhows. Half-built dhows can be seen on the beach, and it is interesting to see the amount of skill that goes into making these seafaring vessels.

Kipungani village

A little further on is Kipungani, a sizeable village where people make the traditional woven palm-matting – *djambe* matting – which has multiple uses as illustrated by Kipungani Sea Breezes Hotel where it's used for walls and flooring. Continuing on past the hotel, you eventually reach the southern end of Shela beach.

ISLANDS OF THE LAMU ARCHIPELAGO

The Lamu Archipelago consists of numerous islands which extend for about 100km north of Lamu Island, after which the most significant islands are **Manda**, opposite Lamu, with the smaller **Manda Toto** off its northern shore, **Pate** and **Kiwayu**. Apart from the Swahili ruins dating back to the 14th century, there's also a rich marine life, while inland from Kiwayu, remote, and virtually inaccessible, are the reserves of **Dodori** and **Boni**.

Getting there and away
By air
The main airport for Lamu is on Manda (see page 414) and there's an airstrip on Kiwayu which has a scheduled daily service.

By sea
Boat transport is the main link with all the islands. There's the option of a local dhow or a motorised launch. For **Manda**, half-day dhow trips are the norm which cost in the region of KSh1,000. For **Pate** you can arrange a local dhow and negotiate a fee per day (usually in the region of US$50) or take the local passenger ferry service on a motorised launch which runs from Lamu to Mtangawanda (about two hours) and Faza (about four hours), costing around KSh200. These normally run three times a week on Mondays, Wednesdays and Friday. For **Kiwayu** you can opt to take a local dhow (up to two days, depending on conditions) or a speedboat (about an hour) which is expensive. In all cases, be prepared to be flexible with timing, especially on dhow trips, as journey times will be dependent upon tides and weather conditions.

Manda Island
Where to stay and eat
Blue Safari Club (10 bandas) Book through central office, PO Box 15026, 00509 Langata, Nairobi; tel: 020 890184; fax: 020 890096; email: info@bluesafariclub.com; web: www.bluesafariclub.com or on Manda Island, tel: 042 33470
Accessed by boat, this is an exclusive, informal hideaway run by Bruno Brughetti and his son Marco. Located on a stretch of empty beach on Manda Island, the cottages are well

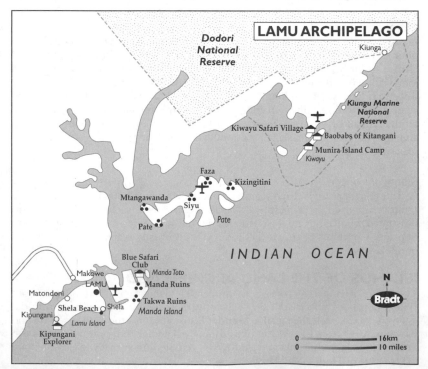

spaced for privacy, designed in traditional style with spacious en-suite rooms decorated in African fabrics and large verandas. There's a good restaurant which specialises in sea food with an Italian influence. **On offer:** a range of watersports – lasers, windsurfing, canoeing, waterskiing, snorkelling – fishing excursions and boat rides to nearby islands, underwater photography, scuba diving.

Rates: from US$300 full board per person sharing inclusive of most activities

Takwa Ruins (banda and camping) Book at the office on the island

There's a communal banda at the ruins, and camping is permitted. The facilities are basic and you'll need to be fully self-sufficient, but it's an attractive setting.

Rates: banda around KSh1,000; camping about KSh300

What to see and do
Takwa Ruins

The remains of a thriving 16th-century Swahili trading post, the Takwa Ruins are a 90-minute boat ride from Lamu. Visiting times are dependent on the tide, as the last section of the boat trip is through the mangrove channels, fascinating in itself. The ruins are similar to those at Gedi, but the site is much smaller. The main feature is the unique Friday mosque with a large pillar on top of the wall. It's thought that the pillar may signify a previous burial site. Guides are available.

Open daily 08.00–18.00; entry KSh200

Manda Toto

Located off Manda is the smaller island of Manda Toto, (*toto* meaning 'child' in Swahili). It has superb snorkelling on its coral reefs and coves on the island are used for beach barbecues.

Pate Island

If you are interested in travelling to Pate, a round trip will take around five days. It's best to speak to the curator at Lamu Museum (page 420) who will advise on accommodation and transport, together with local guides. The main reason to visit Pate is to see the ruins of Swahili settlements, around the fishing communities of Pate, Mtangawanda, Siyu, Faza and Kizingitini, although its appeal also lies in being well off the beaten track. The main attraction is the village of **Siyu** which dates from the 15th century. It has an established leathercraft industry where they make sandals, belts and stools. The town rose to prominence during the 19th century – it's thought that the fort was built by the Omani Arabs in an effort to quell the rebellious Siyu residents. The fort is an impressive building and open to the public (entry KSh200). Around Siyu there are some superb ruins of tombs and mosques.

There is no formal **accommodation** on Pate, but rooms are available to rent in private homes costing around KSh200.

Kiwayu
Where to stay and eat

Kiwayu Safari Village (18 bandas) Book through Cheli & Peacock, page 90

Situated on a sheltered lagoon within the Kiunga Marine National Reserve, on an empty beach overlooking the northern end of Kiwayu Island, this retreat will appeal to those seeking barefoot luxury and informality. The long, narrow dining-room, bar and lounge areas are open with palm-thatched roofs, palm-matting half-walls and floors, decorated with colourful cushions and Swahili furniture. The bandas are similarly constructed, spaced out along the beachfront, with open, spacious rooms with mosquito nets, large verandas

LAMU MARINE CONSERVATION PROJECT

Working in collaboration with KWS, the fisheries department and WWF, with support from Tusk Trust, the Lamu Marine Conservation Project is primarily involved with turtle conservation and community education about the marine environment. Its work covers the coral reefs around Lamu, Manda and Manda Toto islands, the beaches of Lamu and Manda and the local communities in Shela, Lamu, Kipungani and Matondoni on Lamu Island.

Turtles

Similar to Turtle Watch Watamu (see page 400), it monitors **turtle nests** on Manda and Lamu islands. Patrol teams collect data on false crawls (when a female turtle leaves tracks up the beach, but does not nest; this behaviour is usually indicative of an imminent nesting); the number of eggs laid, the date of laying and whether the nests have been translocated and, if so, the reasons why. The nests are then observed and the hatching date recorded. Once a nest hatches the nest is excavated and the hatched and unhatched eggs are recorded. Another aspect of the project is the **turtle tagging** of female turtles once they have laid their eggs. Turtle tag and release has proved an effective monitoring tool and local fishermen eagerly co-operate by bringing in caught turtles for a small reward.

Community education

An **information banda** has been built at Takwa ruins on Manda Island to distribute information both to the local people and tourists, and marine clubs have been started at the island's schools.

If you would like to support the project, contact Carol Korschen at Peponi Hotel, PO Box 24, Lamu; tel: 042 33154; fax: 042 33029; email: peponi@africaonline.co.ke

with day-beds and hammocks, and en-suite showers and flush toilets. The restaurant specialises in mouth-watering seafood dishes with a Swahili emphasis. **On offer:** windsurfing, snorkelling, waterskiing, dhow trips around the islands for picnics in far-off coves, fishing in the mangrove channels; game fishing is available at extra cost.

Rates: from US$318 full board per person sharing inclusive of most activities. Closed May to August.

Baobabs of Kitangani (1 room) Book through Cheli & Peacock, page 90

A 3km boat ride from Kiwayu, this is a romantic hideaway nestling at the foot of two baobab trees on the beach opposite Kiwayu Safari Village. There's a spacious open sitting room leading on to a large bedroom with en-suite facilities and a private 1km beach. **On offer:** activities as per the Safari Village above.

Rates: from US$550 full board per person sharing (no singles!). Closed May to August.

Munira Island Camp (7 bandas, ecocamp) Book through Munira Island Camp Kiwayu Ltd, PO Box 40088, Nairobi; tel: 020 512213; fax: 020 512543; email: paradiseisland@kiwayuisland.com

This is a charming, homely camp, built by Caroline and Mike Kennedy, where all the buildings are made from mangrove poles with palm-matting walls and floors and thatched roofs. The main mess has comfortable sitting areas with large scatter cushions, where you can gorge yourself on fresh crab and lobsters cooked in coconut milk and spices. The bandas are open plan with attached shower rooms (safari shower and flush toilet), where both the rooms (large beds with mosquito nets) and the loo have a view. Water is transported by donkey from half a mile away while all power is by wind and solar. **On offer:** dhow, *ssese* canoe and big-game fishing excursions, birdwatching in the creeks and excellent snorkelling.

Rates: from US$150 full board per person sharing. Closed May and June.

Kiunga Marine National Reserve
KWS PO Box 82, Lamu
Open daily 06.00–18.00; entry US$8
Located north of Pate Island, Kiunga is an International Biosphere Reserve as well as being a national marine reserve. It extends from the southern tip of Kiwayu Island to just north of Kiunga south of the Somali border. Access to the reserve is from the beach at Kiwayu, or by boat excursions to the reef where there's excellent **snorkelling**. A 250km² marine reserve, it lies at the confluence of the north- flowing East African coastal current, and the southern-flowing, nutrient-rich, Somali current. Extending about 60km along the coastline, it includes coral reefs interspersed with around 50 islands which are important **nesting grounds for birds**, with a colony of over 10,000 roseate terns, the largest breeding population in the world. The seagrass beds are an important habitat for the rare **dugong** which resembles an enormous seal, but has a tail like a mermaid and is thought to have been the origin of the mermaid legend. Your chances of seeing a dugong are minimal. Five types of **turtle** are found in Kiunga's waters, with the green, olive Ridley and hawksbill turtles nesting on the beaches. The **mangrove forests** along the coast have not been exploited and contain seven of the nine mangrove species found in Kenya. Since 1996, KWS has been working in partnership with WWF on a management strategy to combine conservation and development. Being a reserve, the local people have access to its resources. A **Kiunga marine ecofriendly handicraft** industry has been started with the women, who collect washed-up flip-flops from the beach (of which there are many) and fashion them into mobiles and keyrings.

MOMBASA SOUTH TO UKUNDA AND DIANI BEACH
Leaving Likoni ferry, with its hawkers selling cashew nuts (at vastly inflated prices for tourists, so negotiate hard) and the bustling township of **Likoni** with its roadside stalls, the road heads south through acres of coconut plantations. The road runs parallel to the coastline but you cannot see the sea. Passing roadside villages, there are Asian-style stores with covered verandas, where it's not unusual to see a tailor working a treadle sewing machine, and square huts made from coral and mud on a mangrove pole frame, with a palm thatch or corrugated iron roof. About 12km south of Likoni, the road heads west on the C106, climbing steeply through coconut and cashew-nut plantations to the tree-shaded town of **Kwale**, a provincial centre for the coast. It's remarkably cool here after the sweltering tropical heat. There's little to see apart from the shell of a cashew-nut factory and a few dilapidated colonial houses before heading on to the Shimba Hills and Mwaluganje, where there are superb stretches of tropical forest at the roadside. Continuing along the coast road is the sizeable ramshackle village of **Ukunda** and the turning to **Diani** where the beach road has become the main service centre for the residents and visitors. Diani is the epitome of the south-coast beaches: white and sandy, with the coral reef exposed at low tide, it's ideal for exploring rock pools and it extends for about 12km. It has numerous hotels and beach-based activities, and plenty of beach boys touting to take you on goggleboat trips, and beachside kiosks selling carvings and kangas. They've been allocated a set spot, so are not too intrusive.

Tiwi lies a few kilometres to the north on a quieter stretch of beach, while **Galu** is the southern extension of Diani beach.

Getting there and away

The A14 heads south from Mombasa (good tarmac road) running parallel to the coastal as far as the Tanzanian border at Lunga Lunga. About 20km south of Mombasa is the turn-off to the right to Kwale on the C106 which climbs up to the Shimba Hills.

By bus

There are regular buses from Mombasa along the south coast. If stopping off at the Tiwi junction, do *not* walk the 3km to the beach, as many people have been mugged on this road. Instead, take a local taxi or hitch a lift. Stopping at the Ukunda turn-off, there are plenty of *matatus* going to Diani, about 2km – this stretch is safe to walk. There are also KBS buses between Likoni and Diani.

By air

There's a regional airport at Ukunda with daily scheduled services to Nairobi and Mombasa.

Getting organised

Tiwi and **Shimoni** are small villages with a few basic shops. The main shopping centre is at **Diani** along Diani Beach Road. Here, for **changing money**, there's a Barclays Bank near the junction to the main road, and Diani forex bureau is about 5km south next to the KFI supermarket. Otherwise, the hotels will exchange money, but mostly at a premium rate. There's a **tourist information point** (tel: 040 2234) in the Barclays bank shopping centre which is helpful and gives good general advice. The **post office**, open Monday–Friday 08.00–17.00, Saturday 09.00–12.00, and MICS cybercafé for **internet access** are in the Diani shopping complex north of the junction, where there's also a **supermarket** and **pharmacy**. In a **medical emergency** you are best to go to Diani Hospital (tel: 040 2435), next to the shopping complex. The **police station** is in Ukunda (tel: 040 2229) and the **tourist helpline** is 020 604767. There are several **petrol stations** along the main Mombasa Road and on Diani Beach Road.

Likoni and Shelly beach
Where to stay and eat

Shelly Beach Hotel (68 rooms; swimming pool) Book through Rhino Safaris, tel: 020 720611

Located on a sandy beach 3 miles south of Mombasa Island, this is a friendly, informal hotel set in tropical gardens on the beachfront. The rooms are in one-storey blocks (facing the ocean US$10 supplement) or in garden cottages. All are comfortably furnished with AC, en-suite bathrooms and a private terrace or balcony. There is a central restaurant, lounge and bar under thatched roofing. **On offer:** tennis, windsurfing, scuba diving and visits to the coral gardens by glass-bottomed boat.
Rates: from US$45 full board per person sharing

Shimba Hills
Where to stay and eat

Mukurumuji Tented Camp (4 tents) Book through Diani House, PO Box 5002, Diani Beach; tel: 040 3487; fax: 040 2412; email: info@ dianihouse.com; web: www.dianihouse.com

KWALE DISTRICT EYE CENTRE

The Kwale District Eye Centre (KDEC) opened in 1993, and provides an important community eye-care service. Run by Helen Roberts, a qualified eye surgeon, it has over 14,000 patients on its records, and in 2000 alone performed 695 operations. Of these, 265 people were blind and can now see; 18 were children. The majority of operations involved the removal of cataracts. Apart from performing operations, the KDEC operates an outreach programme to educate people about eye health, whether through schools, religious centres, or local meetings. Community volunteers seek out people with visual disability and encourage them to come for treatment.

Located 11km south of Likoni off the main C14 road, the centre is open to the public and welcomes visitors. By arrangement, transport can be organised from Diani. Entry is free, but donations are welcome – US$15 will pay for a cataract operation.

For further information or donations: Kwale District Eye Centre, PO Box 90142, Mombasa: tel: 040 51409; fax: 040 51050; email: eyskwale@africonline.co.ke.

Located on a forested hill in the privately owned Sable Valley Game Sanctuary overlooking the Shimba Hills National Park, this is a small, permanent, tented camp, where tents are under thatched roofs and have en-suite safari showers and flush toilets. **On offer:** guided walking safaris in the sanctuary, and excursions to Shimba Hills National Park and Mwaluganje Community Elephant Sanctuary (page 431).
Rates: from US$200 fully inclusive per person sharing
Shimba Rainforest Lodge (28 rooms; tree hotel) Book through Block Hotels, page 90
Located in rainforest on the edge of Shimba Hills National Park, the lodge is constructed largely from timber and designed to blend with the luxuriant forest vegetation. The rooms overlook a floodlit waterhole where elephant, buffalo, leopard, civet, serval and genet cats are frequent visitors. The rooms are comfortable but there are no private bathrooms. A walkway built at treetop level leads to a viewing platform in a nearby glade. **On offer:** game drives, walking to Sheldrick's falls, visits to cyclad forest and Marere dam for birdwatching, bush weddings.
Rates: from US$150 full board per person sharing. No children under 7.
Travellers Mwaluganje Elephant Camp (20 tents) PO Box 87649, Mombasa; tel: 041 485121–6; email: travhtls@africaonline.co.ke
Located in the 2,400ha Mwaluganje Community Elephant Sanctuary (page 431), this permanent tented camp is sited on an elephant trail. The main buildings are rustic, built from wood with thatched roofs, while the tents, on a raised timber deck also under thatch and sited closely together, are simply furnished with en-suite showers, flush toilets and small verandas. **On offer:** game drives around the sanctuary.
Rates: from US$80 per person sharing

Shimba Hills National Park

PO Box 30, Kwale; tel: 040 4159
Open daily 06.30–18.00; entry fee US$23; vehicle entry fee KSh200
About 16km south of Likoni, take the C106 turn-off to Kwale (tarmac road) at Kombani junction. The road climbs up into the Shimba Hills from the coast, passing through the town of Kwale (16km), shortly after which is the entrance to

SABLE ANTELOPES
Dr Karen Ross

Sable and roan antelopes are the only living species of the antelope genus *Hippotragus*. The bluebuck (*Hippotragus leucophaeus*) of the Cape Province of South Africa became extinct in the early 1800s, having the dubious distinction of being the first large mammal to become extinct in Africa at the hand of man.

Sables are large antelopes, horse-like in appearance, with an upstanding mane along their short necks, long and narrow ears, slender legs and rounded chest and haunches. Unlike most antelopes, both sexes carry long, scythe-shaped horns that rise parallel from a narrow forehead, sweeping back in a pronounced curve. Sables have striking facial markings, except for the dun-coloured calves. From afar the pattern is mask-like – a white face divided by a broad, dark blaze from forehead to nose, with dark stripes from the eye to muzzle that emphasise the sweep of the horns. Sable antelope change their coat colour with age. Adult males become a glossy, jet black (hence the name) while the females' colouration varies according to sub-species. There are several sub-species of sable. The northernmost race of sable, the sub-species *Hippotragus niger roosvelti*, only occurs in Kenya, in the Shimba Hills National Park, and in northern Tanzania, including Mkomazi Game Reserve. The females are golden chestnut, their colour darkening with age, and their body size and horn lengths are smaller than in other races.

The sub-species *Hippotragus niger niger* occurs south of the Zambezi River in Zimbabwe, Botswana, Namibia, Mozambique and the Transvaal, and the females are almost as dark as the males. In *Hippotragus niger kirkii* the females are chocolate brown and occur north of Zambezi River into Zambia, Malawi and northern Mozambique. The legendary giant sable, *Hippotragus niger variani*, occurs in Angola, and was thought to be extinct following the prolonged civil war. However, Richard Estes found evidence of their survival in a trip into Angola in 2002. Although giant sable were thought to be a separate sub-species, recent genetic studies are questioning this. In all races of sable the herds comprise females and their young, led by an alpha female. They roam widely through large home ranges that will include many territories of sable bulls. The males have mating access only to receptive females passing through their territories and do not really have control over the movements of the female herds.

The sable antelopes in the Shimba Hills are essentially an island population, surrounded by a sea of humans and agriculture. Ideas on ecological islands have shown that the rate of extinction is higher than in larger areas. In the Shimba Hills National Park the number of sable has declined from over 200 in 1980, which is the number I calculated while living there from 1980–82, down to approximately 109. Lions have also become extinct in the Shimba Hills National Park, and care needs to be taken to ensure that Kenya's only sable population does not also become extinct as human pressure – logging and illegal hunting – continues.

Dr Karen Ross is an ecologist with Conservation International (www.conservation.org). She was brought up on a Kenyan farm and did her PhD on the ecology of the sable antelope in the Shimba Hills National Park, although she is more renowned for her work on the Okavango Delta in Botswana.

the park. It's advisable to have 4WD in the park, where tracks can be quite muddy. Covering an area of 320km² the park has lush forest and grassland, supporting elephant, buffalo, bush buck, monkeys, serval cat and Kenya's only population of sable antelope. Within the forest are **rare orchids** and varied **birdlife**, from African crowned eagles to the tiny Zanzibar red bishop. The best area for game viewing is on the grasslands near **Sheldrick's falls**, and on the Lango plains near **Giriama Point**. There are superb views from the escarpment to the coastline about 20km away.

Mwalugange Elephant Sanctuary

PO Box 167, Kwale; tel: 040 4121
Open daily 06.30–18.00; entry US$15; vehicle entry fee KSh200
Follow the same directions to Kwale as for the Shimba Hills National Park, above. From Kwale, take the Kwale-Kinango road for 13km to the Kibaoni junction. Turn right and it's about 2.5km to Mwaluganje Elephant Sanctuary's **main gate**. A 4WD is advisable. There's a shorter route from Kwale via **Golini gate**, but it's difficult to find and once in the park there's an atrocious descent even by 4WD standards. Linked to Shimba Hills National Park by a fenced elephant corridor the sanctuary is owned and run by the local Duruma community. Covering 24,000ha, it opened in 1995 as a solution to the severe conflict between elephants and the Duruma people, whose smallholdings were regularly subjected to elephant raids. Three-quarters of the sanctuary boundary is fenced, enabling the Duruma to pursue their agricultural activities without a threat from elephants. The Mwaluganje River runs through the sanctuary, with a backdrop of the Golini escarpment, where you can regularly see large herds of elephant cavorting in the shallows, while the vegetation is dominated by silver-trunked baobabs, wild gardenia and ancient cyclads. Plains game like zebra and gazelle may also be seen.

Tiwi beach – 20km south of Mombasa
Where to stay and eat

Capricho Beach Cottages (10 cottages, self-catering; swimming pool) PO Box 5177, Diani; tel: 040 51231; email: capricho@tiwibeach.com
The cottages are in a peaceful setting on Tiwi beach, sited to catch the sea breezes and views, with direct access to the sandy beach. There are 1–3-bedroomed cottages, each with a lounge/dining-room, equipped kitchen, bathroom and veranda. Linen, towels, mosquito nets and kitchen towels can be provided at extra cost. Use of the swimming pool is KSh200 a day. *Rates: from US$28–60 a day per cottage, depending on size. Closed May.*

Coral Cove Cottages (7 cottages, self-catering) PO Box 200, Ukunda; tel: 040 51062, mobile: 0733 577708 or 0722 732797; email: coralcove@tiwibeach.com; web: www.tiwibeach.com
This is a homely and friendly set-up run by Kerstin and Michael Handelman, with plenty of dogs and helpful advice on hand. The cottages are spread out in the garden, and are fully equipped with simple furnishings, mosquito nets and a small veranda. In addition you can pay an extra KSh400 for a cook, who will also clean and do the laundry, while shopping trips can be arranged and fresh fish and crab can be bought direct from the fishermen. *Rates: from KSh3,200–4,500 for 2–4 people*

Beehive Cottages (3 cottages, sleep 4–6, self-catering) PO Box 5123, Diani; tel: 040 51234, mobile: 0733 665544 or 0722 781162; email: beehive@tiwibeach.com; web: www.tiwibeach.com
The cottages are owned by 'Aussie Mike', an intrepid traveller who's crossed the Sahara seven times and is the inspiration behind Funzi furniture. The main cottage is in a renovated colonial house set back from the beachfront. Bohemian in style, it's comfortably and uniquely

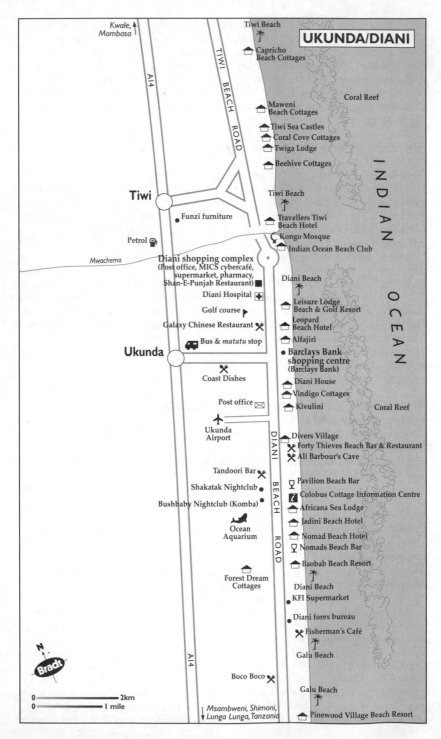

Kwale,
Mombasa

A14

TIWI BEACH ROAD

Tiwi Beach

UKUNDA/DIANI

Capricho
Beach Cottages

Coral Reef

Maweni
Beach Cottages

Tiwi Sea Castles
Coral Cove Cottages
Twiga Lodge
Beehive Cottages

INDIAN

Tiwi

Tiwi Beach

Funzi furniture

Travellers Tiwi
Beach Hotel

Petrol

Kongo Mosque
Indian Ocean Beach Club

OCEAN

Mwachema

Diani shopping complex
(Post office, MICS cybercafé,
supermarket, pharmacy,
Shan-E-Punjab Restaurant)

Diani Beach

Diani Hospital

Leisure Lodge
Beach & Golf Resort

Golf course

Leopard
Beach Hotel

Galaxy Chinese Restaurant

Alfajiri

Ukunda

Bus & matatu stop

Barclays Bank
shopping centre
(Barclays Bank)

Coast Dishes

Diani House
Vindigo Cottages
Kivulini

Coral Reef

Post office

Ukunda
Airport

DIANI BEACH ROAD

Divers Village
Forty Thieves Beach Bar & Restaurant
Ali Barbour's Cave

Tandoori Bar

Pavilion Beach Bar

Shakatak Nightclub

Colobus Cottage Information Centre

Bushbaby Nightclub (Komba)

Africana Sea Lodge

Ocean
Aquarium

Jadini Beach Hotel
Nomad Beach Hotel
Nomads Beach Bar
Baobab Beach Resort

Forest Dream
Cottages

Diani Beach
KFI Supermarket

Diani forex bureau

Fisherman's Café

Galu Beach

N

Bract

0   2km
0   1 mile

Boco Boco

Galu Beach

A14

Msambweni, Shimoni,
Lunga Lunga, Tanzania

Pinewood Village Beach Resort

furnished – much of the furniture having been made on site, and furnishings designed by Mike's partner, Sabine, a former professional windsurfer. All have a living/dining-room, well-equipped kitchen and bathroom. Excellent cooks can be hired for US$10 a day.
Rates: from US$150 a night

Maweni Beach Cottages (15 cottages, sleep 2–8, self-catering) PO Box 96024, Likoni; tel: 040 51008; mob: 0722 755721; email: julianestephan@kenyasouthcoast.com
Located on Tiwi beach, some cottages overlook the sea, while others are set out in 9ha of tropical garden. The cottages, of varying size, are spacious and well equipped with mosquito nets in the rooms, a dining/sitting room, kitchen, shower, toilet and private veranda. Extra beds, linen and mosquito nets can be hired, and help can be provided on request.
Rates: from KSh1,7400–3,850 a day depending on cottage size

Tiwi Sea Castles (9 villas, 13 apartments; swimming pool) Book through Let's Go Travel, page 101
Set in tropical gardens with sea views, the villas sleep 4 and have a living room, bathroom and terrace, while the apartments have a bedroom and bathroom. There's also a restaurant.
On offer: scuba-diving school, snorkelling, windsurfing.
Rates: from KSh1,800 full board per person sharing

Twiga Lodge (10 rooms, cottage (sleeps 4), camping) PO Box 80820, Mombasa; tel: 040 51267
An old favourite amongst the backpacking fraternity, the lodge has seen better days and there have been reported incidents of theft from rooms when staying there. That aside, it's got a superb location on the beach and is very cheap. Rooms are basic, while the campsite provides showers, toilets and security. There's a restaurant and bar providing simple fare.
Rates: rooms from KSh600 per person; cottage KSh1,200; camping KSh160

Travellers Tiwi Beach Hotel (210 rooms; 3 swimming pools) PO Box 87649, Mombasa; tel: 040 51202–6 or 041 485121–6; email: travhtls@africaonline.co.ke
This large hotel is grandiose in scale, with spacious public areas designed in traditional style. Set in 4ha of tropical gardens, the rooms are in 2-storey blocks, large and comfortably furnished with AC, TV, telephone, parquet floors, en-suite bathrooms and private balconies. There are 3 restaurants – the Shere-e-Punjab Indian restaurant is considered one of the finest in Kenya – together with 5 bars and a coffee shop. **On offer:** health centre, waterskiing, windsurfing, snorkelling and scuba diving. Deep-sea fishing and excursions to Mwaluganje Elephant Sanctuary can be arranged.
Rates: from US$80 full board per person sharing

What to see and do
Funzi furniture
Located at the Tiwi turn-off, on the seaward side of the road, there's a small showroom displaying Funzi furniture. Each piece is individually designed and carved. For example a table might be crafted from wood and carved with elephants. Each piece is unique and original.
Open daily

Diani beach
Where to stay
Leisure Lodge Beach and Golf Resort (140 rooms in hotel; 113 rooms in club; swimming pools)
Located on Diani beach, the lodge particularly appeals to golfers as the resort includes a championship 18-hole golf course. A large, modern hotel, it's somewhat impersonal and regimented. Nevertheless, the 'club' rooms (nothing to do with the golf club) are of especially good value, with poolside views among landscaped gardens. These are spacious

and have double and single beds, AC, minibars, en-suite bathrooms and separate toilet, a sitting area with TV and a private veranda or balcony. Meals are buffet style while there's a seafood restaurant, the Fisherman's Cove which is excellent. There's a seaview terrace with evening entertainment, a disco and casino. Although the lodge is raised above the beachfront, access to the beach is through a gate. **On offer:** golf, casino, shopping arcade, tennis, windsurfing and scuba-diving school and local excursions.
Rates: from US$55 full board per person

Alfajiri (4 rooms; swimming pool) PO Box 454, Ukunda; tel: 040 2630: fax: 040 2218; email: molinaro@africaonline.co.ke; web: www.alfajirivillas.com
On Diani beach, perched on a coral cliff above the beachfront, Alfajiri, which means 'sunrise' in Swahili, is an exclusive retreat catering for individual groups and families. The home of Fabrizio and Marika Molinaro, it is exquisitely designed, with a superb collection of African and Eastern artefacts. The guest rooms are in a 2-storey, tiered, hexagonal tower with sweeping ocean views through large, plate-glass windows. Sumptuously furnished, with four-poster beds and mosquito nets, the bedrooms have AC and en-suite bathrooms, and on the ground floor a dining-room, kitchen and lounge open on to a veranda next to the cliff-hanging swimming pool. The food, with fresh fish and garden salads, has a strong Mediterranean influence. **On offer:** reflexology and massage, trained African nannies for looking after children and a vehicle for local excursions. Watersports, golf, tennis and deep-sea fishing can be arranged.
Rates: from US$375 full board per person sharing. Closed April to July.

Baobab Beach Resort (30 rooms; swimming pool) PO Box 32 Ukunda; tel: 040 2623; fax: 040 3032; email: r.baobab@africaonline.co.ke
Set in 2ha of tropical gardens, the resort has a predominantly German clientele. Access to the beach is through the Kilifi Beach Club, an old colonial clubhouse, close by. The rooms are in rondavels or in a block attached to the main hotel building. All have AC, with en-suite bathrooms and have a balcony or terrace. There's a good restaurant with a weekly barbecue, a couple of bars, a lounge with TV and evening entertainment and a disco. **On offer:** plenty of beach activities – volleyball, football – watersports centre with scuba diving, windsurfing, snorkelling and tennis. *Rates: from US$50 half board per person sharing*

Diani House (4 rooms) PO Box 5002, Diani Beach; tel: 040 3487; fax: 040 2412; email: info@dianihouse.com; web: www.dianihouse.com
Located on Diani beach, this is an archetypal colonial beach property – a sprawling bungalow and cottage set in a forested garden (with monkeys, antelopes and a variety of birds) which slopes down to the beach, where you can swim straight out to the reef and go snorkelling. All bedrooms have Lamu-style beds with mosquito nets and fans with en-suite bathrooms. There's a small, informal sitting room where you can help yourself to drinks and delve into a good selection of books, and a capacious veranda which also serves as a dining-room. Fresh seafood is a speciality. Guests are hosted by Joff Minns, an affable Kenyan. **On offer:** excursions to Mukurumuji private camp in the Shimba Hills, snorkelling in the cave pools at Tiwi, windsurfing and deep-sea fishing.
Rates: from US$215 full board per person sharing

Divers Village (10 rooms) Diani Marine Ltd, PO Box 340, Ukunda; tel: 040 320 2367; fax: 040 320 3452; email: dimarine@africaonline.co.ke; web: www.dimarine.com
The village is set back about 50m from the beach, which is accessed along a concrete path next to Forty Thieves, a popular beach bar and restaurant. Primarily used by divers (there's an excellent diving school attached), there's an easy-going atmosphere. The rooms are a good size and simply furnished, with comfortable beds, fans, mosquito nets and en-suite shower rooms, built around a small, covered landscaped courtyard which is pleasantly cool during the heat of the day. Breakfast is fruit, eggs and toast, taken alfresco on the terrace by a small swimming pool where there's also a bar. **On offer:** scuba diving, snorkelling and dolphin-watching excursions to Shimoni.
Rates: from US$30 B&B per person sharing

Above Gabbra women collecting water, Kalacha, northern Kenya (CF)
Below left Knife grinder, Nandi Hills, western Kenya (CF)
Below right Pokot woman grinding corn, Marich, northwest Kenya (CF)
Bottom right Pokot man panning for gold in the Moruny River, Marich (CF)

Above Diani Beach, on the south coast (CF)

Right Early morning net fishing from Galu Beach, south coast (CF)

Below Dhow sailing past Lamu town (AZ)

Vindigo Cottages (7 self-catering cottages; camping) PO Box 77, Ukunda; tel: 040 2192; email: vindigo@hotgossip.co.ke
The cottages are simple and set in woodland by the beach. Rooms are self-contained with fans and the kitchens well equipped. The campsite has basic facilities.
Rates: cottages from KSh800 per person; camping KSh150
Kivulini (self-catering, serviced house sleeps 8, and cottage sleeps 2) PO Box 843, Ukunda; tel: 040 320 2130; email: dianibeach@dianilink.com (attn Mackenzie)
A delightful, private, rambling family house and cottage set in forested gardens (with colobus monkeys) leading down to Diani beach, next door to the now derelict Trade Winds hotel. Airy and spacious, built from traditional materials with whitewashed, arched walls and palm-thatched roof, there's a large sitting room, an inner and upper veranda and an open-air shaded sitting area outside. Decorated with an artistic flair, furniture and fabrics have been purchased locally. The bedrooms all have AC and mosquito nets, 2 are en suite, and there's a family bathroom. The cottage has a sitting room, small kitchen, bedroom, bathroom and shower. There are 3 permanent staff, helpful and friendly, who do all the cooking, laundry and cleaning and who can assist with shopping, although fruit and fish vendors come to the door. You only need to bring food and drinks.
Rates: from US$150 a day for the house and KSh1,000 a day for the cottage and staff gratuities
Forest Dream Cottages (7 self-catering cottages with 2–6 rooms, with catered option; swimming pool) PO Box 787, Ukunda; tel: 040 320 3517; fax: 040 320 3223; email: recycle@africaonline.co.ke; web: www.forestdreamcottages.com
Located in the forest reserve with colobus monkeys and turacos, this is an interesting luxury cottage and villa complex with an environmental leaning. Designed by the owner, Kees van Velzen, who helped found the Colobus Trust (see page 438), each cottage has a peaceful setting in an acre of garden among indigenous trees. Individual in design, they have a sitting room with satellite TV, large verandas, a kitchen, and rooms with large beds, overhead fans, mosquito nets and en-suite bathrooms, while the villas include AC and jacuzzis. The resident staff are available to do the cooking if you wish. The swimming pool has novel features – underwater bar stools with a poolside bar, massage pumps for muscle relaxation, underwater speakers and a water slide, while the sea is a short walk away across the main Diani Beach Road. **On offer:** tennis, open-water and advanced diving courses, cruising on a 20m catamaran.
Rates: self-catering from KSh8,000–19,600 a day depending on size of cottage; rooms from KSh2,200 B&B per person sharing; suites from KSh5,100 B&B per person sharing
Indian Ocean Beach Club (100 rooms; swimming pool) PO Box 73, Ukunda; tel: 040 3203730; fax: 040 320 3557; email: iobc@afriaonline.co.ke or book through Block Hotels, page 90
Designed in the style of a Swahili village, the club is at the northern end of Diani Beach, near the mouth of the Tiwi River and the 16th-century Kongo mosque. The central buildings have Moorish-style arches and the rooms are in adjacent whitewashed individual cottages and double-storey buildings. All rooms have a sea view, with AC, ceiling fans, luxurious Arab-style hand-carved furnishings and hand-woven rugs, en-suite bathrooms and a terrace or balcony. There's an excellent seafood restaurant and several bars. **On offer:** tennis, golf, watersports centre with windsurfing, sailing and boogie boards, deep-sea fishing and scuba diving.
Rates: from US$175 half board per person sharing inclusive of most activities
Leopard Beach Hotel (114 rooms; 46 suites) PO Box 34, Ukunda; tel: 040 3202721; fax: 040 320 3424; email: leopardb@africaonline.co.ke; web: www.leopardbeachhotel.com
Located on a promontory on Diani beach, where the sea laps at the coral cliffs at high tide, Leopard Beach is considered one of the best beach hotels. It's undergone extensive refurbishment since the millennium, and the rooms, built in 2-storey blocks, are spacious

with AC, minibar, satellite TV, telephone and en-suite bathrooms (with bidet) and good views. The suites include a sitting room and veranda; a couple have a jacuzzi. The hotel is well spread out in landscaped gardens. Mario's bar is the main meeting place – with AC and rather like a pub – while the Chui Grill is an excellent award-winning restaurant specialising in seafood. Other bars and restaurants abound – with a choice of pizza, barbecues and tutti-frutti ice-cream parlour. There's plenty of evening entertainment from cultural displays to a poolside disco. **On offer:** watersports centre with scuba-diving and windsurfing schools, internet café, nature trail, beauty salon, Wasini Island booking office for snorkelling trips, diving and dhow excursions, babysitting, shuttle service and other excursions and big-game fishing by arrangement.
Rates: rooms from US$70 half board per person sharing; suites from US$135 half board per person sharing

Jadini Beach Hotel (160 rooms; swimming pool) PO Box 84616, Mombasa; tel: 040 2021/5; fax: 040 2269 or book through Alliance Hotels, page 90
A popular family hotel, it's located on Diani beach, and has a mix of informality, plenty of action and friendly service. The rooms are in 3-storey blocks or spacious garden cottages. All have AC, telephone, radio, minibar, en-suite bathrooms and a balcony or terrace. There are several restaurants (and you can interchange with the sister hotel, the adjoining Africana Sea Lodge) and bars, and regular evening entertainment, often with live bands. **On offer:** shopping arcade, watersports centre with windsurfing and diving schools, tennis, squash and snorkelling excursions, kids' club, chapel, shuttle bus.
Rates: from US$50 B&B per person sharing. Child friendly.

Africana Sea Lodge (rondavels; swimming pool) PO Box 84616, Mombasa; tel: 040 2021/5; fax: 040 2269 or book through Alliance Hotels, page 90. Adjoining Jardini Beach Hotel, facilities are comparative, the main difference being that rooms are in double rondavels, some with connecting doors for families, and there's a greater choice of restaurants. **On offer:** as with Jardini Beach Hotel, above.

Nomad Beach Hotel (21 bandas and cottages) PO Box 1, Ukunda; tel: 040 2155; fax: 040 2391; email: nomad@swiftmombasa.com.
Located at the southern end of Diani beach, the rooms are in comfortable bandas and cottages (en suite with fans) set among the palm trees on the beachfront. An informal setting, it's conveniently located next door to Dive the Crab for scuba diving, has a popular beach bar and there are regular live bands. The treetop restaurant has an emphasis on fresh seafood. **On offer:** scuba-diving school and snorkelling, with tennis and squash nearby.
Rates: from US$38 B&B per person sharing

Where to eat and drink
Restaurants
There are plenty of pizzeria-type places in the Diani shopping complexes and many of the hotels listed above have excellent restaurants. When going out in the evenings, take a taxi or make use of the free transport service offered by some restaurants. Other places to consider are:

Ali Barbour's Cave Tel: 040 2033. Set in a naturally formed coral cave, the restaurant specialises in seafood. There's a good ambience and service and a meal with drinks costs in the region of KSh2,500. *Open daily from 19.00; provides transport locally.*
Galaxy Chinese Restaurant Tel: 040 2529. An authentic Chinese kitchen with a good selection of seafood and Oriental cuisine at reasonable prices. *Open daily for lunch and dinner.*
Boco Boco Tel: 040 2344. In a pleasant garden setting, this is an inexpensive (around KSh500 a main course) Seychellois restaurant with spicy Creole and seafood dishes. It offers a transport service in Diani.

Fisherman's Café Tel: 040 2063, mobile: 0733 822870. Also known locally as Kathy's Restaurant, this has excellent Italian cuisine where all the pasta is freshly made daily. Small and intimate it has an elegant setting on a spacious veranda in a private house, so it's advisable to book in advance. It costs about KSh2,000 for a 3-course meal, and there's a free transport service in Diani. *Open for lunch and dinner; closed Tuesdays.*

Shan-E-Punjab Diani shopping complex; tel: 040 3092. This offers traditional Indian cuisine at reasonable rates (around KSh800) with a selection of vegetarian dishes. It offers a free transport service in Diani. *Open daily 10.00–24.00.*

Tandoori Bar A good local Kenyan pub for cheap beer and pool situated on the Diani Beach Road. It has good *nyama choma*. For other food, service is slow and quality questionable.

Coast Dishes About halfway along the link road from the main highway to Diani beach. Serves excellent local Swahili dishes – the *biriani* and *pilau* are recommended, but there's no alcohol. Costs about KSh300.

Beach bars

Forty Thieves Beach Bar and Restaurant A friendly place on the beach, with all day snacks, bar food and a daily special menu. It has discos on Wednesdays, Fridays and Saturdays and informal evenings with fun on the beach. It's popular with the locals for curry lunches (about KSh600) on Sundays and has live entertainment.

Nomads Beach Bar Another popular meeting place serving snacks and Sunday curry lunches.

Pavilion Beach Bar On the beach, it has a friendly atmosphere, bar snacks and a beer garden. Its speciality is a Sunday afternoon coffee-and-cake buffet. *Closed evenings.*

Entertainment

Apart from hotel floor shows and discos, there's a **casino** at Leisure Lodge Hotel, and for **discos**, there's the **Shakatak Nightclub** (entrance about KSh200 – go midnight onwards, and best to go in a group to avoid hassle from twilight persons) and **Bushbaby Nightclub** (Komba) (entrance about KSh200) is an outdoor club with a beer garden and traditional dance shows.

What to see and do

Kaya Kindondo

PO Box 86, Ukunda; tel: 040 2518; mob: 0722 446916; email: cfcu.kwale@swiftmombasa.com

Located a few kilometres south of Diani (ask locally for specific directions and opening times) Kaya Kindondo is regarded as a sacred site by the local Digo people. It was gazetted in 1992 due to an appeal from the Kaya elders as the forest was threatened by agricultural encroachment. Kayas are sacred places, and this community-run excursion gives a potted history of Digo culture and takes you on a walk through the forest where the guide explains some of the medicinal uses of the plants.

Open daily; cost around KSh300

Ocean Aquarium

Tel: 040 3163

Located off Diani Beach Road, take the turn opposite Two Fishes Hotel past Bush Baby and then take a left and a right. If you are hydrophobic but would like to see the coral fishes, this small aquarium has a variety of ornamental marine fish, invertebrates and plants.

Open Mon–Sat 09.00–17.00; entry KSh250

Dhow and boat excursions

There are a number of choices of dhow and boat excursions offered from Diani to Shimoni. They vary slightly in what's offered, but a typical day trip might be with Charlie Claw's Wasini Island Tours to combine a few hours **snorkelling**, with the option to have a **fun dive** (no experience required, but you put on all the gear and qualified instructors take you down to about 5m, so you get the gist of the diving experience) at Kisite Marine National Park with a **Swahili seafood feast** (whole crab steamed in ginger, barbecued fish with coconut rice and a Swahili sauce) at Wasini Island Restaurant. Guests can be collected from hotels along the coast and transported to Shimoni. It's about a 40-minute drive from Diani to Shimoni, where the motorised dhow collects passengers at the jetty. Alternatively you can

THE COLOBUS TRUST

The Colobus Trust was established in 1997 in response to the number of colobus monkeys getting killed on the road in Diani. It is a conservation project working towards the protection of the rare Angolan colobus monkey (*Colobus angolensis ssp palliatus*) and its coastal forest habitat in southern Kenya. The Diani Forest is becoming increasingly fragmented and has reduced by 75% in the last 20 years, but it's an important habitat for 65 troops comprising around 400 Angolan colobus. A census along the south coast suggests there are only 2,000 of this sub-species in total. The Angolan colobus is a sub-species of the black-and-white colobus monkey. In Kenya it is only found in the coastal forests south of Mombasa. The forest also has yellow baboons, Sykes and vervet monkey and the nocturnal thick-tailed and lesser bushbaby.

Driving along the Diani beach road, you may be intrigued to see black rope ladders crossing the road. These are 'colobridges', built by the Colobus Trust so that colobus and other primates can safely cross the road. The trust has developed significantly and is now involved with a variety of projects concerning wildlife and people, including animal welfare, biological and ecological research, community development and education, forest protection and enrichment and ecotourism awareness.

Colobus Cottage Information Centre

Visitors are welcome to visit Colobus Cottage which lies between the Africana and Two Fishes hotels along the Diani beach road. It's an office, research base and information centre. A 5ha site of coastal forest, it has a habituated troop of colobus monkeys and a nature trail. A visit will give you a tour of the site, a talk about the trust's work and information on the colobus. As an active conservation centre visitors are likely to see volunteers and staff at work, building bridges, caring for injured monkeys, or doing research.

- Open 08.00–17.00 Monday–Saturday; alternate times and night walks need to be booked in advance; entry KSh300.
- independent research projects are welcomed from volunteers and students with behavioural, biology, psychology, zoology and ecology backgrounds.

For further information contact: Wakazulu, Friends of the Colobus Trust, PO Box 5380, Diani; tel: 040 3519; email: wkazulu@colobustrust.org.

take a motor boat, with Diani Marine to Shimoni, which takes about half an hour, go snorkelling and then go to Wasini Island Restaurant for lunch. Other trips go to Chale, Funzi and the Ramisi Delta.

Day excursions cost from US$80–100 inclusive of transport; fun dives US$30

There are a number of operators running dhow excursions. Among those with a good reputation are:

Charlie Claw's Wasini Island Restaurant and Kisite Dhow Tours PO Box 281, Ukunda; tel: 040 2331; fax: 040 3154; email: diving@wasini-island.com; web: www.wasini-island.com

Pilli Pipa Dolphin Safari PO Box 5185, Diani; tel: 040 2401; fax: 040 3559; email: ppipa@africonline.co.ke

Diani Marine Diani Marine Ltd, PO Box 340, Ukunda; tel: 040 320 2367; fax: 040 320 3452; email: dimarine@africaonline.co.ke; web: www.dimarine.com

Kinazini Funzi Dhow Safaris PO Box 37, Msambweni; tel: 040 3221; fax: 040 3182

Scuba diving

There are some superb dive sites – around 20 different sites - on the south coast with a choice of reef, wall and drift dives, and wrecks. Part of the attraction is that they are not far away, the closest being a ten-minute boat ride with most of the sites within a 45-minute boat trip. Visibility averages around 15m. The different sites each have their own speciality – superb coral formations, fields of sea anemones, unusual fish such as guitar sharks, frog, leaf and ghost-pipe fish and sea horses, large schools of barracuda, whale sharks and pelagics species.

There are a number of diving schools along the south coast. Among those with a good reputation are:

Diani Marine Diani Marine Ltd, PO Box 340, Ukunda; tel: 040 320 2367; fax: 040 320 3452; email: dimarine@africaonline.co.ke; web: www.dimarine.com

Diving the Crab PO Box 5011, Diani; tel: 040 2003; fax: 040 2372; email: info@divingthecrab.com; web: www.divingthecrab.com

Dream Diving PO Box 787, Ukunda; tel: 040 3517; fax: 040 3223; email: kaskazi444@yahoo.com; web: www.kazkazi.com

Charlie Claw's Wasini Island Restaurant and Kisite Dhow Tours PO Box 281, Ukunda; tel: 040 2331; fax: 040 3154; email: diving@wasini-island.com; web: www.wasini-island.com

Big-game fishing

For information on deep-sea fishing, see page 117. There are a number of operators on the south coast offering deep-sea fishing. Recommended operators are:

Hemphills Sea Adventures PO Box 348, Ukunda; tel: 040 52220; email: hemphill@bigame.com; web: www.bigame.com

Pemba Channel Fishing Club (at Shimoni) PO Box 86952, Mombasa; tel: 041 313749; fax: 041 316675; mobile: 0722 205020; email: pembachannel@africaonline.co.ke

Galu beach
Where to stay

Pinewood Village Beach Resort (20 self-catering villas; swimming pool) PO Box 190, Ukunda; tel. 040 3720; fax: 040 3131; email: pinewood@africaonline.co.ke; web: www.pinewood-village.com

Named after the casuarina pines, this modern villa complex is well designed and is located on Galu beach (the southern continuation of Diani beach) where fishermen net

their catch. It's about 12km from Diani along a dirt track, so best if you have your own transport, although there's a shop on site. Set in bougainvillea gardens, the 2–3-room villas are bright and spacious with typical Swahili architecture. Each has a sitting/dining-room, veranda, kitchen, and bedrooms are en suite with AC and mosquito nets. The staff are well trained and friendly and villas include a personal chef and room attendant. There's also a central area with a restaurant, a poolside snack bar and full-board options. **On offer:** tennis, squash, shop, beauty salon, excellent birdwatching, boat excursions to the mangroves and Kisite Marine National Reserve, scuba diving, weddings.
Rates: from US$65 self-catering per person; US$95 half-board per person; US$115 all inclusive per person

Chale Island
Where to stay
Chale Paradise Island (55 rooms; swimming pool) PO Box 4, Ukunda; tel: 040 3235; fax: 040 3319; email: romantic@africaonline.co.ke
Located on Chale Island 600m off the mainland about 12km south of Diani beach, Chale Paradise Island has been dubbed the 'budget Funzi'. It consists of 35 tents, spacious rooms under palm-thatched roofs, and 18 apartments. All have comfortable Lamu-style beds and sitting areas furnished with Swahili-style antiques, en-suite shower rooms, a private balcony or terrace and the tents have a private beach area with views across the Chale channel or out to sea. In addition there's a penthouse and a couple of villas. One restaurant has international cuisine and caters for vegetarians, while the Japanese tepanyaki is the only one of its kind at the coast. There's also a beach bar and small library. **On offer:** scuba diving, snorkelling, boating, canoeing, deep-sea fishing, nature walks, natural sulphur mud baths and massage.
Rates: from US$100 full board per person sharing

SOUTH TO SHIMONI AND THE TANZANIAN BORDER
Leaving Diani, the road continues through more coconut plantations, passing the Msambweni turn-off, to Ramisi, once a dominant sugar-growing area, on the Ramisi River which flows into a substantial mangrove delta before reaching Funzi bay. Offshore lie the islands of Chale and Funzi. Shortly after Ramisi is the turning to Shimoni, a small village which is the jumping-off point for dhow excursions for snorkelling and diving in the Kisite Mpungati Marine National Park and Reserve, and for big-game fishing in the Pemba channel. Opposite is Wasini Island with its Swahili ruins and fishing villages. Continuing south on the coast road, the village of Lunga Lunga is the last Kenyan settlement before reaching the Tanzanian border 5km further on. Having crossed the Kenyan border, which can be slow, it's a further 6km to Horohoro on the Tanzanian side where you can connect with transport to Tanga.

Getting there and away
Continue south along the C14; Msambweni and Shimoni, both down several kilometres of dirt track, are signposted.

By bus
To get to Msambweni or Shimoni, you'll need to take a bus for Lunga Lunga and get dropped off at the respective turn-off. Alternatively you can take a *matatu* direct from Ukunda. If going on a snorkelling excursion to Shimoni, transport is included from the beach hotels.

By sea
Dhows from Pemba come into the jetty at Shimoni (see page 443).

Getting organised

You're best to get organised in Mombasa or Diani before going to the fishing villages of Msambweni or Shimoni as facilities here are limited and you can buy basic provisions only. In an emergency the **tourist helpline** is 020 604767.

Msambweni
Where to stay and eat

Samawati House (4 rooms, self-catering, serviced house, sleeps 8) Book through Safaris Unlimited, PO Box 24181, Nairobi; tel 020 891168; fax: 020 891113; email: info@safarisunlimited.com; web: www.safarisunlimited.com

A delightful Lamu-style house overlooking the Indian Ocean at Msambweni, Samawati, which means 'A Heavenly Place' in Swahili, is set in 3.6ha of garden with views to the sea through the coconut palms. Two rooms are en suite, and the house is comfortably furnished. The house staff do the cooking and cleaning, and there's mains electricity for lighting, and solar heating for water. Fresh fruit, vegetables and fish are available locally, but you'll need to bring other provisions and drinks – the nearest place for supplies being Diani, 24km away. **On offer:** tranquil beach and snorkelling, but swimming is limited at low tide.
Rates: from US$100–200 a day, depending on numbers, and staff gratuities

Mkunguni Beach House (4 rooms; self-catering, serviced house, sleeps 8) Tel: 020 3762411; fax: 020 3762178; email: mepsom@wananchi.com. Located near the fishing village of Msambweni on the uncommercialised Mkunguni beach, the house faces on to a sandy foreshore where at low tide the reef is exposed to reveal numerous rock pools. Comfortably furnished, the house is cool with ceiling fans in each room. One room has an en-suite bathroom, 1 a private shower and the other 2 a shared bathroom. Facing the sea, all have twin beds and mosquito nets. There is a part-shaded sun terrace, a sitting room, dining-room and fully-equipped kitchen with a fridge and deep freeze. The 3 staff speak good English and do the cooking, laundry and cleaning and will help with shopping if required, and fruit and fish vendors come to the house. **On offer:** tranquil beach and snorkelling, but swimming is limited at low tide.
Rates: from KSh6,000 a day plus staff gratuities

Funzi Island
Where to stay and eat

The Funzi Keys (9 rooms; swimming pool) PO Box 92062, Mombasa; sat tel: 00 871 762 955; fax: 00 871 762 203 956; email: funzikeys@aboutafrica.co.uk; web: www.thefunzikeys.com

Located on the southern end of Funzi Island at the mouth of the Ramisi Delta, the hotel is surrounded by mangrove forest and faces on to a small beach. One of the most exclusive hideaways at the coast, attracting the rich and famous, the owners, Alessandro Torriani (a former coffee trader) and his wife Claudia are charming hosts. The rooms, with a bottle of champagne on ice to set the tone, are like cottages, well spread out for maximum privacy. Open air, with mosquito screening on the windows, blinds as well as curtains, the rooms have comfortable four-poster beds with fine linen and mosquito nets, stone floors, high, thatched roofs, jacuzzis, a sitting area, 24hr electricity, en-suite shower rooms, and individual camp-fire areas. The main building is 2-storey – a downstairs lounge area with Lamu sofas and a bar and an upstairs restaurant. There's a novel approach to dining here – you choose what you like – from seafood to Japanese or Indian cuisine, pizza or succulent steaks. You can also dine where you like; the beach banquets, sitting under the stars on bean bags around low tables are excellent. **On offer:** swimming off a sand spit, dhow sundowner cruises, boat excursions into the Ramisi delta, a range of water sports – sailing, snorkelling, canoeing, creek fishing and scuba diving and deep-sea fishing by arrangement.
Rates: from US$500 full board per person sharing. Closed April to August.

Funzi Island Club (5 tents) PO Box 90246, Mombasa; tel: 040 2044; email:
funzicamp@africaonline.co.ke
A 15-minute boat ride from Bodo village on the mainland brings you to this idyllic
permanent tented camp. The tents are under thatch and have en-suite facilities, while
there's an open, thatched dining and sitting area and a bar on a floating pontoon. **On offer:**
deep-sea fishing, snorkelling, waterskiing and windsurfing.
Rates: from US$160 fully inclusive per person

Ramisi Delta

Accessible by boat from Mwazaro and Bodo, opposite Funzi Island, or from
Funzi itself, boat trips depend on the tide. The Ramisi Delta consists of 36km² of
mangrove forest containing nine types of mangrove – five saltwater species,
which use feeder roots to collect oxygen, together with two stilt and two knee-
root species. It's been dubbed Kenya's answer to the Everglades – but that is
somewhat far-fetched. The boat trip is fascinating, navigating labyrinthine
channels among the mangroves which are an important breeding reservoir for
prawns, and **five types of crab**, with fiddler crabs being the most common.
Birdlife is intriguing too – palm nut vultures, nesting colonies of pied
kingfishers and fisheagles may be seen. The tide goes inland for up to 12km,
where there are clusters of royal palm trees, and upstream inland you have the
chance of seeing **crocodiles**.
*Some operators at Bodo offer inexpensive boat trips, but do check out boat safety before
selecting an operator, as some boats you see in the delta look grossly overladen – and there are
crocodiles. Expect to pay in the region of Ksh1,000 for a trip.*

Where to stay and eat

Mwazaro (11 bandas; camping) PO Box 14, Shimoni; mob: 0722 711476
The sign, about 10km from Shimoni (ask locally for directions) reads, 'Mwazaro, where
God makes holidays'. It's at the mouth of the Ramisi Delta on a stretch of beach looking
across to Funzi Island (where Funzi Keys lights up like a Christmas tree at night). A
wonderful, low-key set-up; not every day do you meet a man who's been run over by a
lorry and survived to tell the tale, but Hans von Loesch, the owner, is the living proof.
Mwazaro means 'Place of Prayer' and it's a kaya site sacred to the Digo people. Given
time, Hans will expand on this, and also tell you about the mangrove forests and ecology
of the Ramisi Delta. The rooms (sleep 2–3) are in simple, thatched bandas with sand
floors, beds with mosquito nets and all lighting is by hurricane lamp. Each has a small
veranda with a basin made from a giant clam shell. The showers and flush toilets are in
separate bandas. Some bandas with en-suite facilities are planned. The main building is
sited to catch the sea breeze and view. Open plan and under thatch, it has plenty of sitting
areas, with comfortable sofas and lemon-grass tea available throughout the day. The
restaurant is superb. Hans is a Zanzibari chef, and gourmet, mouth-watering dishes appear
one after another in rich, spicy sauces. The campsite is right on the beach. **On offer:** visits
to sacred kaya sites and boat excursions up the Ramisi River and to Funzi Island. *Rates:
from US$30 full board per person; camping KSh100 for a tent and KSh150 per person, or inclusive
of full board KSh1,200 per person*

Shimoni
Where to stay and eat

Pemba Channel Fishing Club (10 rooms; swimming pool) PO Box 86952, Mombasa;
tel: 040 52016/7; fax: 040 52416; email: pembachannel@africaonline.co.ke
Located in Shimoni overlooking the channel, the club is renowned for big-game fishing.
Run by Peter Ruysenaars, a passionate fisherman, and his wife Sandra, the lodge has nicely

furnished rooms with mosquito nets, en-suite bathrooms and private verandas in garden cottages, while the cosy, open, thatched lounge is adorned with marlin trophies. The bar resonates with fishing stories in the evening, and the restaurant serves excellent meals. **On offer:** deep-sea fishing with first-class boats and experienced crews; local excursions for non-fishermen.

Rates: from US$125 full board per person sharing. Fishing season August to March.

Betty's Camp (2 tents, 4 rooms; swimming pool) PO Box 55, Ukunda; tel: 040 52027; email: kisitenp@africaonline.co.ke; web: www.bettys-camp.com

Opened in 2003, Swiss-owned Betty's Camp is near the jetty and overlooks the Shimoni channel. The buildings are well designed, in natural stone and palm-thatch, creating an intimate atmosphere. There's a poolside terrace restaurant and bar (open to the public) and an open, shaded dining-room where seafood is a speciality. The rooms and tents are comfortably furnished, with ceiling fans and en-suite bathrooms. **On offer:** diving, fishing and excursions to local attractions can be arranged.

Rates: from US$75 per person sharing; non-resident use of pool KSh750

Shimoni Reef Lodge (10 rooms; swimming pool) PO Box 82234, Mombasa: tel: 040 52015

In Shimoni, sited on top of coral cliffs overlooking the channel, the lodge is somewhat rundown, but the rooms, in garden cottages, are clean and comfortable with mosquito nets and en-suite bathrooms. The restaurant serves good meals at reasonable prices. **On offer:** scuba-diving school, deep-sea fishing and dhow excursions.

Rates: from US$30 per person sharing

Camp Eden Bandas (bandas and camping) Book through KWS, PO Box 55, Ukunda; tel: 040 52027

The simple, thatched bandas sleep 2–3 and provide mosquito nets. There's a central, covered cooking area, showers and pit latrines. The campsite shares the facilities.

Rates: bandas from US$10 per person; camping US$2

What to see and do
Slave Cave, Shimoni

Shimoni means the 'Place of the Cave' in Swahili, and a village community project has developed a guided tour to the caves. Initially the caves were used as **kayas**, holy places, and for refuge by the local Digo community when they were being attacked by the Galla tribe from the north. Even today there is a small shrine with offerings. During the 18th and 19th centuries, the caves were used as holding pens for **slaves** being shipped to Zanzibar, and there are still rings in the caves where the slaves were shackled which gives credibility to local legend. The Kenyan lyricist Roger Whittaker wrote a song, *Shimoni*, about the gruesome history which he recorded inside the caves. It's thought that up to 1,000 slaves were cooped up here before being transported by dhow to Zanzibar. Within the caves are a number of **stalactites** and **six species of bat**, including the rare long-eared bat. Revenue from your visit goes towards the community dispensary and village school.

Open daily 08.30–10.30 and 13.30–18.30; entry KSh100

Dhows to Pemba

A number of trading dhows sailing to Pemba come to Shimoni pier. You may be able to negotiate a passage for around KSh500 (or more if the boat requires fuel). The journey takes about three to five hours depending on conditions. Do be aware of the safety aspects before taking a passage, as dhows are often overloaded, and note that there are no immigration facilities at Shimoni, the closest being Mombasa. On arrival in Pemba you would need to proceed with immigration facilities for Tanzania.

Wasini Island

To get to Wasini, boats cross the channel from Shimoni pier several times a day, while dhow excursions with Charlie Claw's Wasini Island Tours and Pilli Pipa include lunch on the island after snorkelling in the coral gardens. Located between Shimoni and the coral gardens, Wasini is a low-lying island with distinctive baobab trees and is home to fishing communities at Wasini and Mkwiro. The island has a number of **Swahili ruins**, with mosques and tombs, the most accessible being those near Wasini village. Some of the ruins are around 400 years old and there's evidence of Chinese pottery, which possibly gave the island its name – *Sin* means 'Chinese' in Arabic – hence the *Wa* ('people of') *Sin – Wa-sin-i*. Several of the ruins were destroyed by German warships shelling the island during World War I. At the end of Wasini village, there's a fascinating coral maze, where the tide seeps in through the mangroves on a spring tide. The **Kokoni bridge boardwalk**, 350m long, has been constructed to assist the local community and it gives a good close-up view of the mangrove forest. If you are on an organised excursion, generally entry to the boardwalk is free as the organisers contribute funds direct; otherwise entry costs around KSh150.

Where to stay and eat

Charlie Claw's Wasini Island Restaurant
Celebrating 25 years of operation with a name change to 'Charlie Claw's' in 2003, this is the original Wasini Island restaurant and it provides excellent crab and Swahili seafood dishes. Meals are normally included as part of a tour (see page 439) and the restaurant supports local community projects.
Mpunguti Lodge – Masood's (rooms and camping) PO Box 19, Shimoni; tel: 040 52288. The rooms are clean and comfortable and there are separate showers and flush toilets. Masood is a good source on island history and cooks delicious Swahili meals.
Rates: rooms from KSh1,000 full board; camping from KSh200

Kisite-Mpunguti Marine National Park and Reserve

PO Box 55, Shimoni; tel: 040 52027
Open daily 06.00–18.00; entry US$8
Boat – motor or dhow – is the only way to get out to the marine park which lies about 8km offshore, and most people go on an organised snorkelling excursion from either Shimoni or Diani (see page 439 for operators). The **coral gardens** extend for 28km^2 and have some of the finest **snorkelling** in Kenya, with numerous types of coral and around **250 types of fish**. The waters are shallow, and visibility is generally good. The reserve includes the Mpunguti and Kisite islands and around 4km of coral reef. Most snorkelling is off the tiny coral islet of Kisite where, at low tide, you can rest on the beach. Some excursions include a visit to the KWS rangers' camp at **Mpunguti ya Chini** where you can see the rare **coconut crabs** – huge crabs that can crack a coconut with their pincers. It is not unusual to see **dolphins** and around October the occasional school of **humpback whales**.

As You Like It (Safaris) Ltd.
Photographic Wildlife Safaris & Specialty Safaris in Kenya.
Email: aylis@africaonline.co.ke for more details.

Appendix 1

WILDLIFE GUIDE
Adapted from material written by Philip Briggs

This wildlife guide gives a 'snapshot' description of the most widespread and common mammal species that may be seen in Kenya. On an organised safari a qualified guide will be able to identify the animals and give information on their behaviour. For detailed information on the wildlife, a good field guide is invaluable (see *Further reading* page 467), best purchased before arrival. The wildlife reference chart on page 38 gives some of the best places to view the most common species. Interestingly, Kenya covers two major wildlife zones, so certain species are only found in the northern and arid areas. Due to having two rainy seasons, Kenya is able to support higher densities of game than in southern Africa, making for excellent game-viewing opportunities.

Cats, dogs and hyenas

Lion (*Panthera leo*) Shoulder height 100–120cm. Weight 150–220kg. Swahili: *simba*
Africa's largest predator, the lion is a sociable creature, living in prides of five to ten animals and defending a territory of between 20 and 200km². Lions hunt at night and in the early morning, their favoured prey being large or medium antelope such as wildebeest and impala. Most of the hunting is done by lionesses, but dominant males normally feed first after a kill. Rivalry between males is intense and takeover battles are frequently fought to the death, so two or more males often form a coalition. Young males are forced out of their home pride at three years of age, and male cubs are usually killed after a successful takeover. When not feeding or fighting, lions are remarkably indolent – they spend up to 23 hours of any given day at rest. At night and the early hours of the morning, a lion's roar and steady grunting can often be heard. Lions naturally occur in any habitat but desert and rainforest but these days are largely restricted to conservation areas and national parks. One of the best places to see lion is in the Masai Mara National Reserve, the location for the BBC series *Big Cat Diary*, while Tsavo is famous for its maneless lions. A lion predator research project is underway in Laikipia. Other parks with good opportunities to see lion are Nairobi, Meru and Amboseli national parks and Samburu National Reserve.

Leopard (*Panthera pardus*) Shoulder height 70cm. Weight 60–80kg. Swahili: *chui*

Leopard

The leopard is the most solitary and secretive of Africa's large cats. It hunts using stealth and power, often getting to within 5m of its intended prey before pouncing, and it habitually stores its kill in a tree to keep it from hyenas and lions. It is distinguished from the cheetah by its rosette-like spots, lack of black 'tearmarks' and more compact build. It makes a distinctive 'sawing' sound, sometimes heard at night. Leopards occur in all habitats, favouring areas with plenty of cover such as riverine woodland and rocky outcrops. There are many records of individuals living for years undetected in close proximity to humans. Although the most common of Africa's large cats, it is still rare to get a good sighting. The Masai Mara National Reserve and Lake Nakuru National Park are among the best places to see leopard, while some lodges rig up a leopard bait which gives the opportunity to observe these beautiful animals at close quarters.

Cheetah (*Acynonix jubatus*) Shoulder height 70–80cm. Weight 50–60kg. Swahili: *duma*

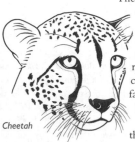
Cheetah

The cheetah is not strictly speaking a cat, belonging to a family of its own, and only having a sharp dewclaw as opposed to retractible claws. With a greyhound-like build, it is capable of running at 70km/h in bursts, making it the world's fastest land animal. It is often seen pacing the plains restlessly, either on its own or in a small family group consisting of a mother and her offspring. A diurnal hunter, favouring the cooler hours of the day, the cheetah's hunting habits correlate with peak game-viewing hours for tourists. This has impacted adversely on cheetah populations where there are high tourist concentrations and off-road driving is permitted. In Kenya, some efforts are being made to limit the number of vehicles around cheetah and their kills, to ensure that they are not completely surrounded, and a cheetah research project is underway in the Masai Mara. The males are territorial, and generally solitary. A cheetah has simple spots (as opposed to a leopard's rosettes), a disproportionately, rather dog-like, small head, and distinctive black tearmarks which absorb the glare of the sun when hunting. They

purr like a moggy, but you're only likely to get close enough to hear this from a domesticated cheetah. Cheetahs prefer open savanna and arid habitats, with good opportunities for sightings in Nairobi National Park and the Masai Mara National Reserve.

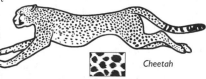
Cheetah

Serval (*Felis serval*) Shoulder height 55cm. Weight: 10–18kg. Swahili: *mondo*

Serval

Lightly built with long legs, a short tail and big ears, the serval cat has a yellow coat with large, black spots giving way to longitudinal stripes near the head. Nocturnal, but occasionally seen during the day, it is widespread and quite common in moist grassland, reedbeds and riverine habitats. It feeds on small mammals and birds up to the size of a guinea fowl. It is most likely to be seen on night game drives.

Caracal (*Felis caracal*) Shoulder height 40cm. Weight 15–20kg. Swahili: *paka mwitu*

The caracal resembles the European lynx with its uniform tan coat and tufted ears. It is a solitary hunter, feeding on birds, small antelope and livestock, and ranges throughout the region favouring relatively arid savanna habitats. It is nocturnal and rarely seen. Other similar species, also nocturnal, are the **golden**

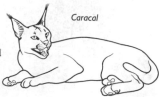
Caracal

cat (*Felis aurata*), a West African species that occurs sparsely in western and central Kenya which resembles a caracal but lacks the ear tufts and has a spotted underbelly; and the smaller **African wild cat** (*Felis sylvestris*), which is more common and similar in appearance to the domestic tabby cat.

African civet (*Civettictis civetta*) Shoulder height
40cm. Weight 10–15kg. Swahili: *fungo*

African civet

A nocturnal animal, its coat is densely
blotched with large, black-on-tan spots on
its body behind the shoulders and with
stripes nearing its head, together with a long,
black-tipped tail and dark coloured legs. It is
primarily carnivorous, feeding on small animals and
carrion, but will also eat fruit.

Large-spotted genet (*Genetta tigrina*) Shoulder height 40–50cm. Weight 1–2–3kg. Swahili: *paka mzuri*
A small, nocturnal carnivore in a similar family to the civet and mongoose, it has exquisite markings, with dark stripes and large spots on a light coat, a long, banded, bushy, black-tipped tail and short legs. The **small-spotted genet** (*Genetta genetta*) is, as its name suggests, smaller, with small spots and a pale-tipped tail. Both species are semi-arboreal and they often forage near lodges, where they are often semi-tame, and fed nightly on scraps of raw meat.

Banded mongoose (*Mungos mungo*) Shoulder height 20cm. Weight around 1kg. Swahili: *kicheche or kitete*
The banded mongoose is among the most common of the mongoose family which numbers about 20 in total. Small, terrestrial carnivores, they are uniformly dark brown except for a

Banded mongoose

dozen black stripes across the back. They are mostly seen in family groups around termite mounds, which they inhabit, and are commonly seen in savanna and woodland. Other mongooses which may be seen in Kenya are the **marsh mongoose** (*Atilax paludinosus*), a large, normally solitary mongoose with a scruffy brown coat, often seen in the vicinity of water; the **white-tailed ichneumon** (*Ichneumia albicauda*), a nocturnal, solitary, large grey-to-black mongoose, easily identified by its long, bushy, white tail; and the **dwarf mongoose** (*Helogate parvula*) (shoulder height 7cm), a highly sociable light brown mongoose.

Wild dog (*Lycaon pictus*) Shoulder height 70cm. Weight 25kg. Swahili: *mbwa mwitu*
Also known as the African wild dog or Cape hunting dog, the wild dog is distinguished from other African dogs by its large size and black, brown and
cream coat. Highly sociable, living in packs of up to 20
animals, they are ferocious hunters which can literally
tear apart their prey on the run. An endangered species
threatened with extinction as a result of its susceptibility
to diseases spread by domestic dogs, in Kenya it is seeing a
comeback in areas where it was previously wiped out.
Namunyak has one of the largest packs of wild dog. Still very
rare, there's a chance of seeing wild dog in northern and
southeastern Kenya. A wild dog research project is underway
in Laikipia.

Wild dog

Black-backed jackal

Black-backed jackal (*Canis mesomelas*) Shoulder height 35–45cm. Weight 8–12kg. Swahili: *mbweha*
The black-backed jackal, also known as the silver-backed jackal, resembles a small fox. An opportunistic feeder, it's capable of adapting to most habitats. Most often seen singly or in pairs at dusk or dawn, or waiting in the wings on a kill, it is tan in colour with a prominent black saddle flecked by varying amounts of white or gold, and a bushy tail. It's readily seen in the Masai Mara National Reserve and Amboseli National Park on the savanna plains.

Common jackal (*Canis aureus*) Shoulder height 38–50cm. Weight 7–15kg. Swahili: *mbweha*
Slightly larger and similar in appearance to the black-backed jackal, the common jackal is also known as the golden jackal. A North African species, it has a relatively pale coat and a black tail tip. Its range extends across the Kenyan savanna and arid regions.

Bat-eared fox (*Otocyon megalotis*) Shoulder height 30–35cm. Weight 3–5kg.

Bat-eared fox

This silver-grey insectivore is unmistakable with its huge ears, alertly tuned to insects underground, and black eye-mask. Most often seen in pairs or small family groups during the cooler hours of the day, it's associated with dry open country and is often seen around termite mounds.

Spotted hyena (*Crocuta crocuta*) Shoulder height 85cm. Weight 70kg. Swahili: *fisi*
Hyenas are characterised by their bulky build, short hind legs, brownish coat, powerful jaws

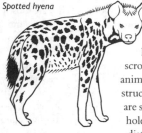
Spotted hyena

and dog-like expression. Contrary to popular myth, hyenas are not exclusively scavengers: the spotted hyena in particular is an adept hunter capable of killing an animal as large as a wildebeest. Nor are they hermaphrodites. This misconception stems from the false scrotum and penis covering the female hyena's vagina. Sociable animals, and fascinating to observe, hyenas live in loosely structured clans of about ten animals or more, led by females who are stronger and larger than males. Hyena dens consist of shallow holes in the ground. The spotted hyena is the largest hyena, distinguished by its blotchily spotted coat. At night it's common to hear the manic cackles of a hyena, guaranteed to send a shiver up your spine. It's seen in most of Kenya's parks and reserves. Amboseli National Park and the Masai Mara National Reserve have particularly good sightings.

Striped hyena (*Hyaena hyaena*) Shoulder height 65–80cm. Weight 25–45kg. Swahili: *fisi*
Quite rare and only found in Kenya's dry country, the striped hyena has a slimmer build than the common hyena, with long legs, a long mane and a pale brown coat with several distinctive dark vertical stripes. Its range overlaps with the more dominant spotted hyena, hence its preference for savanna habitat is restricted

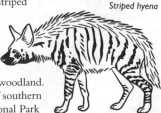
Striped hyena

and it's more likely to be seen in thornbush and woodland. Occasionally it may be seen in the Shompole region of southern Kenya, near the Tanzanian border, and in Sibiloi National Park on Lake Turkana.

Aardwolf (*Proteles cristatus*) Shoulder height 40–50cm. Weight 8–12kg. Swahili: *fisi mwitu*
An insectivorous member of the hyena family, it's a lightweight version of the striped hyena and is mostly seen at dusk or at night in arid regions like Samburu. Night game drives give the best chances of viewing it.

Aardwolf

Primates

Common baboon (*Papio cynocaphalus*) Shoulder height 50–75cm. Weight 25–45kg. Swahili: *nyani*

This powerful terrestrial primate, distinguished from any other monkey by its much larger size, inverted 'U'-shaped tail and distinctive dog-like head, is fascinating to watch from a behavioural perspective. It lives in large troops which boast a complex, rigid social structure characterised by matriarchal lineages and plenty of intertroop movement by males seeking social dominance. Omnivorous and at home in almost any habitat, the baboon is widespread and frequently seen in most game reserves. When in danger they communicate with a distinctive bark. Subspecies seen in Kenya are the **yellow baboon** (*P. c. cynocephalus*), a yellow-brown race found in eastern Kenya, which has a distinctive kink in its tail, and the **olive baboon** (*P. c. anubis*), a large, hairy baboon with a greenish-brown coat which is common in the main parks.

Common baboon

Vervet monkey (*Cercopithecus aethiops*) Length (excluding tail) 40–55cm. Weight 4–6kg. Swahili: *tumbili*
Common and widespread, it inhabits savanna and woodland rather than true forest, spending a high proportion of its time on the ground. Frequently seen around park campsites, this endearing little monkey often becomes a pest. It has a light grey coat, black face and white forehead while the males have powder blue genitals.

Vervet monkey

Sykes monkey (*Cercopithecus mitis*) Length (excluding tail) 50–60cm. Weight 5–8kg. Swahili: *kima*
Also known as the blue monkey, this variable monkey is divided by some authorities into several species. Members of the *Cercopithecus* family (24 different species) are known as guenons and this is the most common forest guenon in Kenya. Unlikely to be confused with any other species through most of its range, the Sykes monkey has a uniformly dark blue-grey coat with a white throat which in some races extends all down the chest and in others around the collar. It lives in troops of up to ten animals and associates with other primates where their ranges overlap, such as the black-and-white colobus monkey. Other guenons found in Kenya include the **red-tailed monkey** (*Cercopithecus ascanius*), a small brown guenon with white whiskers, a red tail and a distinctive white heart on its nose, found in the Kakamega Forest of western Kenya. The **De Brazza's monkey** (*Cercopithecus neglectus*), is a thickset guenon with a shortish tail, rusty forehead patch and long, white beard. An endangered species with a patchy distribution in Kenya, it is most likely to be seen in western Kenya and in the Tana Delta Primate Reserve. **L'Hoest's monkey** (*Cercopithecus lhoesti*) is black, except for the backward projecting white whiskers that partially cover its ears, and easily recognised as it carries its tail in an upright position. It can

be seen in Kakamega Forest. The **crested mangabey** (*Cercocebus galeritus*) is a rare yellow guenon which can be seen in the Tana Delta Primate Reserve.

Black-and-white colobus (*Colobus guereza*) Length (excluding tail) 65cm. Weight 12kg. Swahili: *mbega mweupe*

This beautiful, jet-black monkey has bold white facial markings and a long white tail, while baby colobus are born completely white. Almost exclusively arboreal, colobus are capable of jumping up to 30m, a spectacular sight with its white tail streaming behind. The black-and-white colobus is relatively common in Kenya's indigenous forests. They have a guttural, muttering call which resonates through the canopy if they are disturbed. In the past the Kikuyu tribe used colobus monkey skins for ceremonial occasions. The **Angolan colobus** (*Colobus angolensis ssp palliatus)* is a sub-species found in the coastal forests south of Mombasa, commonly seen around Diani.

Black-and-white colobus

Red colobus (*Procolobus badius*) Length (excluding tail) 60cm. Weight 10kg.

The status of this monkey is debatable, with between one and ten species recognised. A small monkey, most have black on the upper back, red on the lower back, a pale tufted crown and a long-limbed appearance unlike that of any guenon or mangabey. In Kenya it can be seen along the Tana River in the Tana Delta Primate Reserve.

Greater bushbaby (*Galago crassicaudatus*) Length (without tail) 25cm. Weight 1.4kg. Swahili: *komba*

The size of a domestic cat, the greater bushbaby has a long bushy, black-tipped tail (about 35cm) and a woolly light grey coat with pale underparts, and a small, pointed face, with rounded ears and a pointed snout. A nocturnal primate, it prefers evergreen forest although it is not averse to manmade habitats. Fruiting and gum-producing trees are a favourite haunt. It has a distinctive, almost human, high-pitched scream while mothers will cluck to their babies.

Lesser bushbaby

Lesser bushbaby (*Galago senegalensis*) Length (without tail) 17cm. Weight 150g. Swahili: *komba*

The lesser bushbaby is widespread and more common than the greater bushbaby. Also nocturnal, it is found in woodland outside the rainforest and may also be seen in domestic gardens. It's about the same size as a squirrel, has a bushy tail, and can leap through the canopy. Often heard rather than seen, the lesser bushbaby can sometimes be picked out by tracing a cry to a tree and shining a torch which lights upon its large, round eyes.

Antelopes

Roan antelope (*Hippotragus equinus*) Shoulder height 120–150cm. Weight 250–300kg. Swahili: *korongo*

This handsome, horse-like antelope is uniform fawn-grey with a pale belly, short horns which curve backwards, a light mane and distinctive black-and-white facial markings. Rare in Kenya, the roan is only found in the Ruma National Park of western Kenya.

Roan antelope

Sable antelope (*Hippotragus niger*) Shoulder height 135cm. Weight 230kg. Swahili: *pala hala*
The striking male sable is jet black with a distinct white face, underbelly and rump, and long horns which curve backwards. The female is chestnut brown and has shorter horns. In Kenya sable are only found in the Shimba Hills National Park in the coastal hinterland.

Sable antelope

Oryx (*Oryx gazella*) Shoulder height 120cm. Weight 230kg. Swahili: *choroa*
This regal dry-country antelope is unmistakable with its grey-tan coat, bold black facial marks and

Oryx

flank strip, and rapier horns. Subspecies found in Kenya are the **fringe-eared oryx** (*O. g. callotis*) which is smaller and more tan-coloured with less distinctive markings, found in Amboseli and Tsavo national parks, and the **Beisa oryx** (*O. g. beisa*) a northern species of oryx, commonly seen in the Samburu and Shaba national reserves.

Common waterbuck (*Kobus ellipsiprymnus*) Shoulder height 130cm. Weight 250–270kg. Swahili: *kuro*
The waterbuck is easily recognised by its shaggy grey/brown coat and the male's large lyre-shaped horns. The females do not have horns. It has a distinctive white ring around its rump. The waterbuck is frequently seen in small family groups grazing near water in all but the most arid national parks. The **Defassa waterbuck** is a separate race seen in the Rift Valley and areas further west, distinguished by a full white rump and darker legs. It is commonly seen in Lake Nakuru National Park.

Common and Defassa waterbuck

Common wildebeest (*Connochaetes taurinus*) Shoulder height 130–150cm. Weight 180–250kg. Swahili: *nyumbu*
This ungainly antelope, also called the gnu and blue wildebeest, is easily identified by its dark coat and bovine appearance. It has a large head, shaggy mane and beard, and big shoulders sloping down to the flank. Huge herds of wildebeest migrate annually from their breeding grounds in Tanzania's Serengeti National Park, forging north into Kenya's lush pastures of the savanna plains in the Masai Mara National Reserve, where many fall prey to crocodiles in the frenetic crossings of the Mara River. The two white-bearded subspecies, the **eastern white-bearded wildebeest** (*C. t. albojubatus*) and **western white-bearded wildebeest** (*C. mearnsi*) are both found in Kenya.

Hartebeest

Hartebeest (*Alcelaphus buselaphus*) Shoulder height 125cm. Weight 120–150kg. Swahili: *kongoni*
Hartebeests are ungainly antelopes, readily identified by the combination of large shoulders, a sloping back, red-brown coat and small curved horns in both sexes. **Coke's hartebeest** (*A. b. cokii*), a subspecies, is most common in Kenya. Small family groups are often seen in open country, particularly in the Masai Mara National Reserve and Nairobi National Park. Another subspecies,

Jackson's hartebeest (*A. b. jacksoni*), more common in Uganda, is also found on the Laikipia Plateau and Ruma National Park.

Also related to the hartebeest family are the **Hirola antelope** (*D. hunteri*) also known as Hunter's antelope, one of the world's most endangered antelopes. Currently endemic to Kenya, it is found in the Tana River and Lamu districts. A National Hirola Task Force was established in 1996 and 35 Hirola were translocated to Tsavo East National Park.

Topi (*Damaliscus lunatus*) Shoulder height 115cm. Weight 130kg.
Similar to the hartebeest, but more streamlined, the topi is distinguished by a darker coat with a blue-grey sheen and striking yellow stockings. A plains antelope, it is often seen in the Masai Mara National Reserve, a favourite haunt being on top of an anthill.

Common eland (*Taurotragus oryx*) Shoulder height 150–175cm. Weight 450–900kg. Swahili: *pofu*
Africa's largest antelope, the eland is light tan in colour, and its somewhat bovine appearance is accentuated by relatively short, spiral horns and a large dewlap. It can jump several metres from a virtual standstill. Listen out for the 'clicking' of its hind legs as it walks along. Widely distributed, small herds may be seen almost anywhere in grassland or light woodland. It is often seen in the Masai Mara National Reserve.

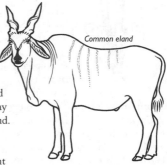

Common eland

Greater kudu (*Tragelaphus strepsiceros*) Shoulder height 140–155cm. Weight 180–250kg. Swahili: *tandala*
The greater kudu is the second largest antelope, with a grey-brown coat and up to ten stripes on each side. The male has magnificent double-spiralled horns. It is most often seen in mixed or single-sex herds of up to ten animals but is rare in Kenya where its lowland habitat has diminished. There are now only isolated populations on some mountains and in Lake Bogoria National Reserve.

Greater kudu

Lesser kudu (*Tragelaphus imberbis*) Shoulder height 120cm. Weight 90–105kg.
Smaller than the the greater kudu, it has more side stripes, a white throat patch and a short, white, bushy tail with a black tip. It can easily jump over fences 2.5m high. Its preferred habitat is *commiphora* woodland and it is commonly seen in Tsavo National Park. Other good places to see it are the Samburu and Shaba national reserves and Meru National Park.

Bongo (*Tragelaphus euryceros*) Shoulder height 110–130cm. Weight 240–400kg.
A West African rainforest species, this is a secretive antelope found in isolated populations in the bamboo zone of some of Kenya's montane forests. In days past it used to be a rare visitor to the Ark, a tree hotel in the Aberdares National Park. It has exquisite markings – a distinctive dark brown coat with white side stripes.

Sitatunga (*Tragelaphus spekei*) Shoulder height 125cm. Weight 125kg.
This semi-aquatic antelope may be seen in Saiwa Swamp National Park, in western Kenya, and in Lewa Wildlife Conservancy, where a small herd was translocated as a conservation measure (although strictly speaking this is not within the normal range for the sitatunga). The male, with a shaggy fawn coat, is easily recognised. The smaller female might be mistaken for a bushbuck but it has far more defined stripes.

Bushbuck (*Tragelaphus scriptus*) Shoulder height 70–80cm. Weight 30–45kg. This attractive antelope, a member of the same genus as the kudus, shows great regional variation in colouring. The male is dark chestnut-brown while the smaller female is generally a pale reddish brown. The male has relatively small, straight horns. Both sexes have similar throat patches to the lesser kudu, and are marked with white spots and sometimes stripes, athough the latter are not as clear as the vertical white stripes on the otherwise similar-looking female sitatunga. It occurs in forest and riverine woodland, where it is often seen in woodland glades, either singly or in pairs. One of the best places to see bushbuck is at the Ark in the Aberdares, where it's not uncommon to see half a dozen or more at the waterhole.

Bushbuck

Thomson's gazelle (*Gazella thomsonii*) Shoulder height 60cm. Weight 20–25kg. Swahili: *swala tomi*
The Thomson's gazelle are characteristic of the East African plains, with large herds in the Masai Mara National Reserve. It has a tan coat with white underparts. It is sometimes confused with Grant's gazelle, but it is smaller, has a white fluffy tail and a distinctive black, horizontal side stripe. When threatened, they often begin stotting, jumping upwards on all four legs, an action designed to convey that they are bigger than their size suggests.

Grant's gazelle (*Gazella granti*) Height 85–90cm. Weight 65kg. Swahili: *swala granti*
The elegant Grant's gazelle is similar in size to an impala, but is often confused with Thomson's gazelle which often occur in the same habitat. It is easily differentiated by its lack of a black side-stripe, pale fawn coat, thin, wiry tail and comparatively large horns, particularly the subspecies G. g. raineyi which occurs in Kenya's Samburu National Reserve. The subspecies G. g. robertsi is found west of the Rift Valley and is distinguished by the bent-down tips to its horns. The females have smaller horns. It is widespread and commonly seen in the Masai Mara, Samburu and Shaba national reserves and Tsavo, Amboseli, Nairobi, Sibiloi and Meru national parks.

Gerenuk (*Litocranius walleri*) Height 90–105cm. Weight 45kg. Swahili: *swala twiga*
A northern species of antelope, it is readily identified by its

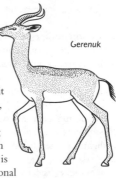

Gerenuk

long neck and singular habit of browsing on trees standing on its hind legs. Similar in colour to the impala, with a reddish tan coat, it has white underparts, a white eye-ring, throat patch and blaze. It is often called the 'giraffe antelope' due to its long neck. Only the males have horns, which are short, curved and thick. It is commonly seen in Tsavo and Meru national parks, and Samburu National Reserve.

Impala

Impala (*Aepeceros melampus*) Shoulder height 90cm. Weight 45kg. Swahili: *swala pala*
This slender, handsome antelope is superficially similar to some gazelles, but in fact belongs to a separate family. Chestnut in colour, the impala has black and white stripes running down its rump and tail, and the male has

large lyre-shaped horns. One of the most widespread antelope species in Kenya, the impala is normally seen in large herds in wooded savanna habitats.

Bohor reedbuck (*Redunca redunca*) Shoulder height 80–90cm. Weight 55kg. Swahili: *tohe*
An East African species, it is yellow-brown in colour with a white throat-patch and distinctive horns with the tips curving forwards. It occupies high grasslands, often on savanna floodplains. Good places to see them are the Masai Mara National Reserve, Lake Nakuru and Meru national parks.

Mountain reedbuck (*Redunca fulvorufula*) Shoulder height 65cm. Weight 38kg.
The smallest reedbuck, it has distinctive markings, with a clear white belly, tiny horns, and an overall grey appearance. It has a broken distribution, occurring in mountainous parts of Kenya, where it is best seen in the Aberdares National Park.

Klipspringer

Klipspringer (*Oreotragus oreotragus*) Shoulder height 60cm. Weight 13kg. Swahili: *mbuze mawe*
The klipspringer is a goat-like antelope, normally seen in pairs, and easily identified by its dark, bristly grey-yellow coat and slightly speckled appearance. It is aptly named: in Afrikaans *klipspringer* means 'rockjumper', and its favoured habitat is on rocky outcrops. It is often seen at Hell's Gate National Park and the *kopjes* of Tsavo.

Steenbok (*Raphicerus cempestris*) Shoulder height 50cm. Weight 11kg. Swahili: *dondoro*
This rather nondescript small antelope has a red-brown coat and clear white underparts. The male has short straight horns. Like most other antelopes of its size, the steenbok is normally seen singly or in pairs and tends to 'freeze' when disturbed. Within Kenya, it is more-or-less restricted to the Tanzania border area and coastal belt.

Steenbok

Common duiker (*Sylvicapra grimmia*) Shoulder height 50cm. Weight 20kg. Swahili: *nysa*
This anomalous duiker holds itself more like a steenbok or grysbok and is the only member of its family to occur outside forests. Generally grey in colour, the common duiker is easily recognised from other small antelopes due to the black tuft of hair between its horns. The **red duiker** (*Cephalophus natalensis*) is the most common forest duiker and is slightly smaller. It is deep chestnut in colour with a white tail and, in the case of the East African race *C. n. harveyi* (sometimes considered to be a separate species), a black face. Another very localised forest species is **Ader's duiker** (*Cephalophus adersi*), endemic to the Arabuko Sokoke Forest National Reserve.

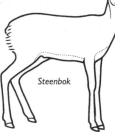

Common
duiker

Kirk's dik-dik (*Madoqua kirki*) Shoulder height 43cm. Weight 5kg. Swahili: *diki diki*
A dwarf antelope, the dik dik is the most common small antelope in Kenya. They are nearly always seen in pairs in thornbush country. Grey in colour, with a long snout, large white eye

circle, pale underparts and short, straight horns about 8cm long, it is replaced by the outwardly very similar **Guenther's dik-dik** (*Madoqua guentheri*) in northern Kenya. Evidence of dik dik is easy to find, as they defecate in the same place, producing large middens, and have a scent gland near the eye which secretes a black dollop, known as 'dik dik pearls', which are often found on long grass. The **suni** (*Neotragus moschatus*) is the smallest of the dwarf antelopes to be seen in Kenya. It has a plain red-brown coat and a black and white tail and is often seen in coastal forest areas.

Other mammals

African elephant (*Loxodonta africana*) Shoulder height 2.3–3.4m. Weight up to 6,000kg. Swahili: *ndovu* or *tembo*

The African elephant is easily differentiated from the Indian elephant by its large ears. It is a fascinating animal, highly intelligent with a complex social structure. Cow elephants live in closely knit clans lead by a matriarch, usually the eldest female. The females are very protective of their young and have teats between their forelegs. Calves under three months old can fit beneath their mother's bellies. Elephants may be distinguished by their profiles. Bulls have a rounded profile while that of a cow is knuckle-shaped; mature males have an hour-glass-shaped head if viewed from the front. Males generally leave the family group at around 12 years to roam singly or joining bachelor herds. Apart from their distinctive tummy rumbles, heard when they are feeding peacefully, and their trumpeting screams, they can also communicate over long distances through infrasound. Versatile feeders, they can consume 150kg a day. Although an endangered species and badly poached, they are seen in most parks and reserves apart from Nairobi and Lake Nakuru national parks.

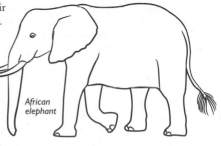

African elephant

Rock hyrax (*Procavia capensis*) Shoulder height 35–30cm. Weight 4kg.

Resembling a giant guinea pig in appearance, hyraxes are more closely related to elephants and although not clearly visible they have tusks. They are often seen scuttling around on rock faces, and are common at Hell's Gate and Mount Kenya national parks and at Menengai Crater. The less common **tree hyrax** (*Dendrohyrax arboreus*) is a nocturnal forest creature which often announces its presence with an unforgettable shrieking call.

Rock hyrax

Black rhinoceros (*Diceros bicornis*) Shoulder height 160cm. Weight 1,000kg. Swahili: *faru* or *kifaru*

Endemic in Kenya, the black rhino is found in woodland habitat where it browses on the branches of bushes and trees. It has a distinctive hook-shaped lip. Badly poached, rhino-breeding programmes in Kenya have been successful. A southern African species, the **white rhinoceros** (*Ceratotherium simum*), which is larger than the black rhino (typically weighing between 1,500 and 2,000kg) was introduced to Kenya from South Africa as part of a species conservation programme. It is no paler in colour than the black rhino – the 'white' derives from the Afrikaans *weit* (wide) and refers to its distinctive

Black rhino

White rhino

flattened mouth, which is suited to cropping grass. Both species are commonly seen in Lake Nakuru National Park and Laikipia Wildlife Conservancy.

Hippopotamus (*Hippopotamus amphibius*) Shoulder height 150cm. Weight 2,000kg. Swahili: *kiboko*
A large, amphibious mammal, the hippo has a brownish-grey, rotund body, with pink underparts, short legs, a huge head, broad muzzle, small, rounded ears and a stumpy tail. Its canine teeth are enlarged, resembling tusks. They live in 'pods', often up to 100 in size, dominated by a territorial bull. By day they congregate, submerged in water, surfacing every few minutes to breathe, dispersing at night to graze on land. They are characteristically noisy in the water, with muffled chortles, belligerent snorts and explosions of water as they exhale. Hippos eat around 40kg of grass a night, grazing for five hours, sometimes covering 6km in a nightly forage. Although large, hippos move surprisingly fast – 30km/h in an emergency. Their jaws are strong enough to sever a 2m crocodile. Accounting for many human deaths in Africa, it's advisable not to get between a hippo and water. They are readily seen in lakes and rivers within and outside parks and reserves. The Tsavo national parks, the Masai Mara National Reserve, and Lakes Naivasha, Nakuru and Baringo have excellent viewing.

Cape buffalo (*Syncerus caffer*) Shoulder height 140cm. Weight 700kg. Swahili: *nyati* or *mbogo*
Frequently and erroneously referred to as a water buffalo (a docile Asian species), the Cape buffalo, also known as the African buffalo, is a distinctive ox-like animal that lives in large herds on the savanna and occurs in smaller herds in forested areas. Dark brown in colour, they have distinctive horns which meet in a boss across their head – those in the male are larger and they thicken with age. Once past their breeding prime, males leave the herd, often staying in bachelor herds or alone. They can be extremely aggressive, and can attack unprovoked.

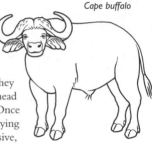

Cape buffalo

Giraffe (*Giraffa camelopardis*) Shoulder height 250–350cm. Weight 1,000–1,400kg. Swahili: *twiga*
The world's tallest and longest-necked land animal, a fully grown giraffe can measure up to 5.5m high. They live in loosely structured herds of up to 15 head and are often seen singly or in smaller groups. Both males and females have distinctive, stumpy horns – on the females these have tufts. Other characteristics are a short mane, high shoulders sloping down to their haunches and a thin tail with a tufted end. They have an ungainly run, and their docile appearance is deceptive. A giraffe's kick can kill a man. They browse on trees and bushes. There are three subspecies of giraffe found in Kenya – Commonly seen is the **Masai giraffe** (*G. c. tippelskirchi*) recognised from other giraffe species due to its irregular pattern of tan and yellow coloured markings. The **reticulated giraffe** (*G. c. reticulata*) is found in northern Kenya, and has distinctive crazy-paving markings of chocolate brown on white, while the **Rothschild's giraffe** (*G. c. rothschildi*) is sometimes mistaken for a Masai giraffe, but it has paler markings, with no spots below the knee, and on

Reticulated and Masai giraffe

the male there's a pronounced forehead, sometimes giving the impression of three horns. It is seen in Lake Nakuru National Park and Kigio Wildlife Conservancy.

Common zebra (*Equus burchelli*) Shoulder height 130cm. Weight 300–340kg. Swahili: *punda milia*

Common or Burchell's zebra is like a striped, stocky horse. It has broad stripes and is seen in herds consisting of a stallion and several mares. They are common and widespread on the Kenyan savanna, often seen alongside wildebeest. Their stripe patterns are distinctive to each individual, and it's thought that these help to confuse predators when they are in a large group, as the stripes blur, making it difficult to single out individual animals.

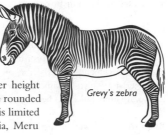

Grevy's zebra

The **Grevy's zebra** (*Equus grevyi*) is larger (shoulder height 140–160cm) and heavier (weight 430kg) and has large rounded ears and pin-stripes. An endangered species, its range is limited to northern Kenya, where it is best seen in Laikipia, Meru National Park and Samburu National Reserve.

Warthog

Warthog (*Phacochoerus africanus*) Shoulder height 60–70cm. Weight up to 100kg. Swahili: *ngiri*

This widespread and often conspicuously abundant resident of the African savanna is grey in colour with a thin covering of hairs, wart-like bumps on its face, and large upward-curving tusks. It's often seen in family groups, with parents and piglets trotting briskly in a straight line with tails erect. If alarmed, they rush for cover, going backwards down their holes. Similar in appearance, the **bushpig** (*Potomochoerus larvatus*) has a heavier build and is more hairy. It too is widespread, but it's infrequently seen due to its nocturnal habits and preference for dense vegetation.

Giant forest hog (*Hylochoerus meinertzhageni*) Shoulder height 85–100cm. Weight 130–200kg. Primarily a species of the West African rainforest, the giant forest hog is more robust in shape than the bushpig, and has long, black hair. It's commonly seen in the Aberdares and Mount Kenya national parks.

Aardvark (*Orycteropus afer*) Shoulder height 60cm. Weight up to 70kg. Swahili: *muhanga*

Also known as an antbear, this nocturnal insectivore is unmistakable with its long snout and huge ears, which give it a pig-like appearance. It is common throughout Kenya but sightings are extremely rare. You are more likely to come across their large holes in the ground.

Aardvark

Cape clawless otter (*Aonyx capensis*) Length to tail 90cm. Weight 18–28kg.

A large, chocolate-brown otter, with white throat and cheek markings, it has hand-like paws with unwebbed fingers and nails instead of claws. Its diet is varied and includes fish, frogs, snakes, turtles, molluscs and waterfowl. Living in fresh water, it is commonly seen on Lake Naivasha among the reedbeds in the early morning or late afternoon.

Cape clawless otter

Spotted-necked otter (*Lutra maculicollis*) Length including tail 100cm. Weight 4.5kg. The smallest of the African otters, it is dark in colour with light, spotted markings on its throat. It has webbed paws with claws. It spends most of the time in the water and lives on fish. In Kenya it is most commonly seen off the islands of Lake Victoria.

Scrub hare (*Lepus saxatilis*) This is the largest and most common African hare or rabbit. In some areas a short walk at dusk or after nightfall might reveal three or four scrub hares. They tend to freeze when disturbed.

Ground squirrel

Unstriped ground squirrel (*Xerus rutilus*) An endearing terrestrial animal of arid savanna, the unstriped ground squirrel is grey to grey-brown with a prominent white eye-ring and silvery black tail. It spends much time on its hind legs, and has the characteristic squirrel mannerism of holding food in its forepaws. In Kenya, it is most likely to be seen in Samburu and surrounds.

Bush squirrel (*Paraxerus cepapi*) This is the typical squirrel of the eastern and southern savanna, rusty brown in colour with a silvery black back and white eye-rings. A great many other arboreal or semi-arboreal squirrels occur in the region, but most are difficult to tell apart in the field. One exception is the strikingly colourful red-bellied **coast squirrel** (*P. palliatus*), which is easily observed scampering around the wooden walkways of Shimba Hills Lodge in the Shimba Hills National Park.

Africa Geographic
and
Africa – Birds & Birding

Award-winning magazines about a continent worth saving

For subscription details contact:
Africa Geographic/Africa – Birds & Birding
P O Box 44223, Claremont 7735,
Cape Town, South Africa.
Tel: (+27-21) 686 9001. Fax: (+27-21) 686 4500.
E-mail: wildmags@blackeaglemedia.co.za
Website: www.africa-geographic.com

Appendix

LANGUAGE

With so many tribal groups in Kenya, there are numerous languages, each tribal group having its own tongue. It is not unusual for African Kenyans to speak several languages – a couple of tribal languages, Swahili and English – while at the coast especially you'll find many speaking Italian, German and French too. In the large cities, a street slang, 'sheng', is spoken by some.

Kiswahili

Kiswahili, more often referred to in the abbreviated form, Swahili, is the national language of Kenya. It is a Bantu language which developed on the East African coast about 1,000 years ago and has since assimilated words from Arabic, Portuguese, Indian, German and English. It spread into the Kenyan interior along with the 19th-century slave caravans and is now the *lingua franca* in both Kenya and Tanzania. It is also spoken in parts of Uganda, Malawi, Rwanda, Burundi, DR Congo, Zambia and Mozambique. There are variations in Swahili – a purer form of Swahili is spoken at the coast (akin to that spoken in Tanzania, sometimes called 'sanifu' or 'cha Bwani' Swahili, which means 'very fine'). Inland it's more colloquial, sometimes being referred to as 'cha bara' Swahili which translates as 'street language' (implying that it is corrupted by vernacular), or, in the colonial days of the *memsahibs*, 'kitchen' Swahili. It's not difficult to learn the basics, and attempts at speaking the language are always encouraged and appreciated, often amidst great hilarity.

In the main towns and cities – Nairobi, Mombasa, Nakuru, Kisumu, Eldoret – English is readily spoken. If you travel in remote parts of the country, it is useful to understand some Swahili.

Before leaving, you could try the internet on www.unforgettableswahili.com which claims to teach you Swahili in three hours. In addition there are numerous Swahili phrase and grammar books and Swahili–English dictionaries on the market. A useful dictionary for travellers is Baba Malaika's *Friendly Modern Swahili–English Dictionary* (MSO Training Centre for Development Co-operation, PO Box 254, Mombasa, second edition 1994), which costs around US$25. Better still is the *TUKI English–Swahili Dictionary* (University of Dar es Salaam, 1996; ISBN 9976 91129 7), which costs around US$16. Peter Wilson's *Simplified Swahili* (Longman) was regarded as the best book for teaching yourself Swahili, but has been superseded by Joan Russell's *Teach Yourself Swahili* (Hodder and Stoughton, 1996; ISBN 0340 62094 3), which comes complete with a cassette and costs around US$15. Of the phrasebooks, the Lonely Planet or Rough Guide's *Swahili* are both good. It is best to buy a Swahili book before you arrive in Kenya as they are difficult to get hold of once you are there.

The following introduction to Swahili aims to assist communication with Swahili-speakers and is not a substitute for a dictionary or phrasebook.

Pronunciation

Vowel sounds are pronounced as follows:

a   like the a in *father*
e   like the e in *wet*

i   like the ee in *free*, but less drawn-out
o   somewhere between the o in *no* and the word *awe*
u   similar to the oo in *food*

The double vowel in words like *choo* or *saa* is pronounced like the single vowel, but drawn out longer. Consonants are in general pronounced as they are in English. *L* and *r* are often interchangeable, so that *Swala* is just as often spelt or pronounced *Swara*. The same is true of *b* and *v*.

It is best to speak slowly, avoiding the common English-speaking habit of clipping vowel sounds; listen to how Swahili-speakers pronounce their vowels. In most Swahili words there is a slight emphasis on the second-last syllable.

Basic grammar

Swahili is a simple language in so far as most words are built from a root word using prefixes. To go into all of the prefixes is confusing for people new to Swahili. They are covered in depth by Swahili grammar books and dictionaries. The following are some of the most important:

Pronouns

me	*ni*	they	*wa*
you	*u*	he or she	*a*
us	*tu*		

Tenses

present	*na*
future	*ta*
past	*li*
infinitive	*ku*

Tenses (negative)

present	*si*
future	*sita*
past	*siku*
negative, infinitive	*kuto*

From a root verb such as *taka* (to want) you might build the following phrases:

Unataka soda	You want a soda
Tutataka soda	We will want a soda
Alitaka soda	He/she wanted a soda
Sitaki soda	I do not want a soda

In practice, *ni* and *tu* are often dropped from simple statements. It is more common to say *nataka soda* than *ninataka soda*.

Singular and plural

The prefix '*m*' is used in the singular and '*wa*' in the plural. So, for example, *toto* , means child. For one child you'd say *mtoto*, for several children *watoto*.

Questions

In many situations there is no interrogative mode in Swahili; the difference between a question and a statement lies in the intonation.

Greetings

There are several common greetings in Swahili. The first greeting you will hear is *Jambo*. The most widely-used greeting is *Habari?*, which more-or-less means 'What news?' The usual reply is *Nzuri sana* ('very good'). *Habari* is rarely used on its own; you might well be asked *Habari ya safari?*, *Habari yako?* or *Habari gani?* (very loosely, 'How is your journey?', 'How are you?' and 'How are things?'). *Nzuri* ('good') is the polite response.

A more fashionable greeting among younger people is *Mambo*, especially on the coast and in large towns. Few tourists recognise this greeting; reply *Safi* or *Poa* and you've made a friend.

Another word often used in greeting is *Salama*, which means 'peace'. When you enter a shop or hotel reception, you will often be greeted by a friendly *Karibu*, which means 'Welcome'. *Asante sana* ('Thank you very much') is an appropriate response.

If you wish to enter someone's house, shout *Hodi!* It basically means 'Can I come in?' but would be used in the same situation as 'Anyone at home?' in English. The answer, *Karibu*, loosely means 'Come in'.

It is respectful to address an old man as *Mzee*. *Bwana*, which means 'Mister', is a polite form of address to a male who is equal or senior to you in age or rank, but who is not a *Mzee*. Older women may be addressed as *Mama*.

Useful phrases

Where have you come from?	*(U)natoka wapi?*
I have come from Nairobi	*(Ni)natoka Nairobi*
Where are you going?	*(U)nakwenda wapi?*
We are going to Mombasa	*(Tu)nakwenda Mombasa*
What is your name?	*Jina lako nani?*
My name is Claire	*Jina langu ni Claire*
Do you speak English?	*Unasema KiIngereza?*
I speak very little Swahili	*Ninasema KiSwahili kidigo sana*
Sleep well	*Lala salama*
Bye for now	*Kwaheri sasa*
Have a safe journey	*Safari njema*
Come again (welcome again)	*Karibu tena*
I don't understand	*Sielewi*
Say that again	*Sema tena*
Sorry	*pole*
Please	*tafadhali*
I would like…	*Ninapenda...*
How much?	*Bei gani; shillingi ngapi*
	(literally how many shillings)
Good luck!	*Maisha marefu*
	(used when drinking, like cheers!)
Very good	*Nzuri sana*
Wait a little	*Ngoja kidogo*
Let's go	*Tuende*
Thank you	*Asante*
Goodbye	*Kwaheri*
Where's the toilet?	*Wapi choo?*

Numbers

1	*moja*		30	*thelathini*
2	*mbili*		40	*arobaini*
3	*tatu*		50	*hamsini*
4	*nne*		60	*sitini*
5	*tano*		70	*sabini*
6	*sita*		80	*themanini*
7	*saba*		90	*tisini*
8	*nane*		100	*mia moja*
9	*tisa*		150	*mia moja na hamsini*
10	*kumi*		155	*mia moja hamsini na tano*
11	*kumi na moja*		200	*mia mbili*
20	*ishirini*		1,000	*elfu (moja)* or *mia kumi*

Swahili time

Many travellers to Kenya fail to come to grips with Swahili time. It is essential to be aware of it, especially if you are catching buses in remote areas. The Swahili clock starts at the equivalent of 06.00, so that *saa moja asubuhi* ('hour one in the morning') is 07.00, *saa mbili jioni* ('hour two in the evening') is 20.00, and so on. To ask the time in Swahili, say *Saa ngapi?*

Always check whether times are standard or Swahili. If you are told a bus leaves at nine, ask whether the person means *saa tatu* or *saa tisa*. This does not apply so much where people are used to tourists, but it's advisable to get in the habit of checking.

Day-to-day queries

The following covers such activities as shopping, finding a room, etc. It's worth remembering that most Swahili words for modern objects, or things for which there would not have been a pre-colonial word, are often similar to the English. Examples are *resiti* (receipt), *gari* (car), *polisi* (police), *posta* (post office), *stesheni masta* (station master) or *kiplefti* (roundabout). In desperation, it's always worth trying the English word with an *ee* sound on the end.

Shopping

The normal way of asking for something is *ipo* which roughly means 'is there?', so if you want a cold drink you would ask *ipo soda baridi?* The response will normally be *ndio* – 'yes' - or *hakuna* ('there isn't'). Once you've established the shop has what you want, you might say *nataka koka mbili* ('I want two cokes'). To check the price, ask *shillingi ngapi?* It may be simpler to ask for a brand name: *Omo* (washing powder) or *Blue Band* (margarine), for instance.

Accommodation

The Swahili for guesthouse is *nyumba ya wageni*. Also in common use is *gesti*. If you are looking for something a bit more upmarket, bear in mind *hoteli* means restaurant. A *chumba self-contendi* is a self-contained room. To find out whether there is a vacant room, ask *nafasi ipo?*

Getting around

The following words and phrases are useful for getting around:

Where is there a guesthouse?		*Gesti ipo wapi?*	
Is there a bus to Nairobi?		*Ipo basi kwenda Nairobi?*	
When does the bus go?		*Basi itaenda saa ngapi?*	
When will the vehicle come?		*Gari litakuja saa ngapi?*	
How far is it? How many kilometres?		*Mbale gani?* or *kilometa ngapi?*	
I want to pay now		*Ninataka kulipa sasa*	
passenger	*abiria*	far away	*mbale sana*
station	*stesheni*	near	*karibu*
bus	*basi*	stop	*simama*
boat	*meli*	danger!	*hatari!*
dhow	*jahazi*	left	*kushoto*
outrigger canoe	*ngalawa*	right	*kulia*
aeroplane/bird	*ndege*	today	*leo*
minibus	*matatu*	tomorrow	*kesho*
vehicle	*gari*	day	*siku*
road/street	*bara bara*	daytime/afternoon	*mchana*
slowly	*pole pole*	the whole day	*mchana kutwa*
fast	*upesi upesi*	night	*usiku*
soon (a little later)	*bado kidogo*	morning	*asabuhi*
later	*badaye*	evening	*jioni*
straight or direct	*moja kwa moja*	sun	*jua*

Foodstuffs

avocado	*parachichi*	meat	*nyama*
bananas	*ndizi*	milk	*maziwa*
bananas (cooked)	*matoke or ndizi zo kupika*	onions	*vitungu*
beer, local	*pombe*	orange	*chungwa*
bread (loaf)	*mkate*	pawpaw	*papai*
bread (slice)	*tosti*	pepper	*pili pili*
beef	*(Nyama ya) ngombe*	pineapple	*nanasi*
chicken	*kuku*	potatoes	*viazi*
coconuts	*nazi*	rice (cooked plain)	*wali*
coffee	*kahawa*	rice (uncooked)	*mchele*
doughnut	*mandazi*	salt	*chumvi*
egg	*yai*	soda	*soda*
fish	*samaki*	solid maize porridge	*ugali*
food	*chakula*	sugar	*sukari*
fruit	*matunda*	tea	*chai*
goat	*mbuzi*	vegetable	*mboga*
mangoes	*embe*	water	*maji*

Wildlife

antelope	*swala*	hippo	*kiboko*
baboon	*nyani*	hyena	*fisi*
buffalo	*nyati*	leopard	*chui*
cheetah	*duma*	lion	*simba*
crocodile	*mamba*	rhino	*kifaro or faro*
elephant	*ndovu*	warthog	*ngiri*
giraffe	*twiga*	zebra	*punda milia*

Other vocabulary

again	*tena*	no problem	*hakuna matata* or
and	*na*		*hakuna shida*
big	*kubwa*	now	*sasa*
bring here	*lete hapa*	OK, fine	*sawa sawa*
brother	*kaka*	pay	*lipa*
cat	*paka*	the people	*wananchi*
child (children)	*mtoto (watoto)*	person (people)	*mtu (watu)*
cold	*baridi*	pretty, decorative	*maridadi*
come here	*njoo hapa*	restaurant (local)	*hoteli*
do	*fanya*	sea	*bahari*
dog	*mbwa*	shop, kiosk	*duka*
eat	*kula*	sister	*dada*
European(s)	*mzungu (wazungu)*	sleep	*lala*
father	*baba*	small	*kidogo*
fierce	*kali*	there is	*iko or kuna*
fire	*moto*	there is not	*hakuna*
friend	*rafiki*	thief (thieves)	*mwizi (wawizi)*
go away	*kwenda or toka*	time	*saa*
good	*mzuri*	toilet	*choo*
here	*hapa*	traditional enclosure/	
horse	*ferasi*	homestead	*boma*
hot	*joto*	very much, a lot	*sana*
I	*mimi*	want	*taka*

like	*penda*	when	*lini*
matches	*kiboriti*	where	*wapi*
medicine	*dawa* (also a Kenyan cocktail)	why	*kwa nini*
		wood	*kuni*
money	*pesa/shillingi*	yes	*ndio*
more	*nyingine*	yesterday	*jana*
mother	*mama*	you	*wewe*
no	*hapana*		

Useful conjunctions include *ya* (of) and *kwa* (to or by). Many expressions are created using these; for instance *stesheni ya basi* is 'bus station' and *bara bara kwa Nakuru* is the 'road to Nakuru'.

Days of the week

Monday	*Juma tatu*	Friday	*Ijumaa*
Tuesday	*Juma nne*	Saturday	*Juma mosi*
Wednesday	*Juma tano*	Sunday	*Juma pili*
Thursday	*Alhamisi*		

African English

Although many Kenyans speak a little English, not all speak it fluently. Africans who speak English tend to structure their sentences in a similar way as to how they would in their own language: they speak English with Bantu grammar.

For a traveller, knowing how to communicate in African English is just as important as speaking a bit of Swahili, if not more so. It is noticeable that travellers who speak English as a second language often communicate with Africans more easily than first language English-speakers.

The following ground rules should prove useful when you speak English to Africans:

- **Unasema KiIngereza?** *Do you speak English?*
- **Greet in Swahili, then ask in English**.
  It is polite to proffer a Swahili greeting (even *Jambo* will do) before asking a question.
- **Speak slowly and clearly**.
- **Phrase questions simply and with Swahili inflections**.
  'This bus goes to Nanyuki?' is simpler than 'Could you tell me if this bus is going to Nanyuki?'; 'You have a room?' is simpler than 'Is there a vacant room?' If you are not understood, don't keep repeating the same question; find a different way of phrasing it.
- **Listen to how people talk to you, and not only for their inflections**.
  Some English words are in wide use; others are not. For instance, 'lodging' is more likely to be understood than 'accommodation'.
- **Make sure the person you are talking to understands you**.
  Try to avoid asking questions that can be answered with a yes or no. People may well agree with you simply to be polite.
- **Keep calm**.
  No-one is at their best when they arrive at a crowded bus station after an all-day bus ride; it is easy to be short tempered when someone cannot understand you. Be patient and polite; it's you who doesn't speak the language.

Appendix 3

GLOSSARY

acacia woodland	type of woodland dominated by thorny, thin-leafed trees of the genus *acacia*
banda	a hut, often used to refer to hutted accommodation at hotels and lodges
bau	a traditional board game
boma	a traditional homestead within a thorn enclosure
bui-bui	full length black garment and headdress worn by Swahili women mainly in Islamic parts of the coast
chai	the Swahili for tea, but also means a bribe (tea money!)
cichlid	family of colourful fish found in the Rift Valley lakes
closed canopy forest	true forest in which the trees have an interlocking canopy
dhow	traditional wooden seafaring vessel
duka	kiosk, local shop
endemic	unique to a specific country or biome
enkang	a traditional Maasai village (often mistakenly referred to as a *manyatta*)
exotic	not indigenous, for instance plantation trees such as pines and eucalyptus
forex bureau	bureau de change
fly-camping	temporary private camp set up remotely from a permanent base
group ranch	a ranch held in communal ownership, such as by a tribal clan
guesthouse	cheap local hotel
hoteli	local restaurant
indigenous	naturally occurring
irio	traditional dish of potato mixed with beans and maize
kanga	colourful wraparound printed cloth with Swahili proverbs, similar to a sarong , mostly worn by women
kitenge (pl *vitenge*)	similar to kanga
kikoi	traditional woven cloth mostly worn by men at the coast
kikapu	traditional woven basket
kiondo	traditional sisal basket
kopje	an Afrikaans word used to refer to a small hill, such as those seen in Tsavo
lugga	a dry river bed
mandazi	traditional deep-fried doughnut
manyatta	a specially built Maasai homestead for young warriors (*morani*) or for tourists to visit – such as a Maasai cultural manyatta
matatu	light vehicle, especially minibus, serving as public transport
matoke	traditional savoury staple made from bananas
mbwa kali	fierce dog
mishkaki	meat (usually beef) kebab

mitumba	secondhand markets, mostly selling items of clothing
morani	Maasai warriors
mzungu (pl *wazungu*)	white person
murram	red, lateritic soil, often used to describe dirt roads
ngalawa	traditional outrigger canoe
NGO	non-governmental organisation
ngoma	dance or party
nyama choma	roast meat – usually goat
panga	machete
rondavel	a round hut, often used to describe tourist accommodation
savanna	grassland studded with trees
shamba	traditional agricultural smallholding or garden
shifta	Somali bandits
self-contained room	room with en-suite shower and toilet (not necessarily salubrious)
sukuma wiki	cooked greens like spinach
ssese canoe	traditional long, narrow, wooden, open boats with engines and/or sails on Lake Victoria
ugali	stodgy porridge-like staple made from *posho*, ground maize meal
woodland	area of trees lacking a closed canopy

www.tourismconcern.org.uk

TOURISM CONCERNED?

There is a need to be...

We have nearly all travelled and seen the negative effects of tourism. For many people who live in tourist destinations around the globe their culture and homes are being destroyed through a lack of consideration of their interests and rights.

Tourism Concern campaigns to raise awareness of the many abuses that take place and encourage change to eradicate these negative effects on the indigenous population. Through our educational work, campaigning and challenging the tourism industry we aim improve the quality of life in the host locations.

You can help by becoming a Tourism Concern supporter, member or donor and help us change tourism for the better.

For more info, visit our website or call or E-mail us below.

E-mail: info@tourismconcern.org.uk
Call: 020 7753 3330

TourismConcern
Transforming the negatives into positives

Appendix 4

FURTHER READING

Numerous books have been written on Kenya and only a selection are listed here. The Text Book Centre in the Sarit Centre in Westlands, Nairobi, probably has the best selection of *Africana*.

Field guides
Mammals

The Field Guide to African Mammals Jonathan Kingdon (Academic Press 1997). A detailed and comprehensive illustrated guide with photographs and distribution maps.

Field Guide to the Larger Mammals of Africa Chris and Tilde Stuart (Struik 1997). Less detail than Kingdon's guide, but still good for the average safari-goer.

The Safari Companion Richard D Estes (Chelsea Green and Russel Friedman Books, 1993). Excellent guide on mammal behaviour. It only has outline drawings, but is fascinating reading.

Field Guide to the Larger Mammals of Africa Jean Dorst and Pierre Dandelot (Harper Collins). Well-established standard guide, with good illustrations, but some of the information is now dated.

Mammals of Africa T Haltenorth and H Diller (Harper Collins). Another standard guide comparing with Dorst and Dandelot's guide, but with more detailed information.

Birds

A Field Guide to the Birds of Kenya and Northern Tanzania Zimmerman, Turner and Pearson (Adlard Coles Nautical). This is the serious birdwatcher's bible, and a long-standing classic, with excellent colour plates. Available in hard and soft back.

Field Guide to the Birds of East Africa Terry Stevenson and John Fanshawe, (T & A D Poyser 2001). This compares well to the Zimmerman guide and is more user-friendly, with plates, maps and text on the same page.

Reptiles

A Field Guide to the Reptiles of East Africa Stephen Spawls, Kim Howell, Robert Drewes and James Ashe (Academic Press, 2001). A comprehensive illustrated guide which is particularly good on snakes.

Fish

Coral Fishes of the Indian Ocean and West Pacific Oceans R H Carcasson (HarperCollins). A well-illustrated guide to the marine species you are likely to encounter when snorkelling and diving.

Dive Sites of Kenya and Tanzania Anton Kornhott (New Holland, 1997). An excellent guide which covers diving and snorkelling sites and the marine life.

Trees and plants

Kenya Trees, Shrubs and Lianas H J Beentj (National Museums of Kenya). An authoritative, comprehensive and detailed description of 1,850 trees, shrubs and lianas found in Kenya with illustrations and distribution maps.

Field Guide to Common Trees & Shrubs of East Africa Najma Dharani (Struik Publishers, 2002). A selective field guide to more than 330 trees, shrubs, palms and mangroves (indigenous and exotic) found in the region. It describes social, economic and religious importance and uses in traditional medicine and is fully illustrated.

The Wildflowers of East Africa Michael Blundell (Collins pocket guides, 1987). A useful general guide to wildflowers.

History and travelogues

Nine Faces of Kenya Elspeth Huxley (Harvill 1997 ISBN 0002721732). An anthology of Kenya's history from AD100.

Empires of the Monsoon: a History of the Indian Ocean and its Invaders Richard Hall (Harper Collins 1996 ISBN 0006380832). Sets the stage for the past 1,000 years along the East African coast.

Let Freedom Come: Africa in Modern History Basil Davidson (Penguin). A comprehensive account of the 19th and 20th centuries.

Africa – a Biography of the Continent John Reader (Penguin 1997 ISBN 0140266755). A pan-African account from the geological formation of the continent to early man and modern times.

Through Maasailand: to the Central African Lakes and Back Joseph Thomson (2 vols, Frank Cass 1968). A compelling account of Thomson's pioneering journey across the Rift Valley to Lake Victoria.

The Man-Eaters of Tsavo J H Patterson (Fontana 1974 ISBN 0006132995). An eyewitness description of the lions which wreaked havoc on the building of the Uganda railway.

The Lunatic Express Charles Miller (Macdonald ISBN 356038548). Good on East African history.

The Iron Snake Ronald Hardy (Collins 1965). A history of building the Uganda railway.

Safari – Chronicle of Adventure Bartle Bull (Viking and Penguin 1992). A history of the big-game hunters of Africa

Pioneers Scrapbook – reminiscences of Kenya – 1890–1968 ed: Elspeth Huxley and Arnold Curtis (Evans Brothers ISBN 0237505606). An insight into Kenya's colonial history.

Silence Will Speak Errol Trzebinski (Grafton Books 1977) A study of the life of Denys Finch Hatton and his relationship with Karen Blixen.

White Mischief James Fox (Penguin 1984). An accurate investigative account about the Lord Erroll murder and a sharp portrayal of the Happy Valley set.

The Life and Death of Lord Erroll: The Truth Behind the Happy Valley Murder Errol Trzebinski (Fourth Estate 2000 ISBN 1857028945). Another excellent account of the intrigue surrounding the Lord Erroll murder.

The Charging Buffalo – a history of the Kenya Regiment 1937–1963 Guy Campbell (Leo Cooper 1996 ISBN 043608290X). An interesting account of military history in Kenya during World War I and World War II.

Mau Mau and the Kikuyu and *Defeating Mau Mau* L S B Leakey (Methuen 1952). Interesting insights into the Kikuyu tribe and the origins of Mau Mau.

Where Giants Trod: The Saga of Kenya's Desert Lake Monty Brown (Quiller Press ISBN 1870948254). An account of 14 early expeditions.

Journey to the Jade Sea John Hillaby (Constable 1993). A camel trek through the northern frontier district to Lake Turkana in the 1960s.

Autobiographies and biographies

Out of Africa Karen Blixen (Isak Dineson) (Penguin 1999). Evocative descriptions of Kenya and the life of the privileged early settlers, immortalised in the film, *Out of Africa*.

West with the Night Beryl Markham (Penguin 1988) Autobiography of an aviatrix – the first woman to be granted a pilot's licence in Africa and to fly the Atlantic solo from east to west.

Straight on til Morning – the Life of Beryl Markham Mary Sewell (Arena 1987). A vivid portrait of the pioneer aviatrix, top racehorse trainer and her controversial affairs with Bror Blixen and Denys Finch Hatton.

Flame Trees of Thika Elspeth Huxley (Pimlico 1998). A vivid portrayal of life as a coffee planter's daughter in the early 20th century. The sequel is *The Mottled Lizard*, equally evocative and amusing.

Child of Happy Valley: A Memoir Juanita Carberry (Arrow 2000 ISBN 0099281392). A rather grim insight into the debauched Happy Valley set.

Elephants at Sundown – the story of Bill Woodley Dennis Holman (WH Allen 1978). Bill Woodley was legendery in Africa, a conservationist and a warden of Mount Kenya National Park.

Lost Lion of Empire: The Life of Ewart Grogan DSO (1876–1976) Edward Paice (Harper Collins 2002 ISBN 0006530737). An interesting account of Grogan of Cape-to-Cairo fame and the settler years in Kenya.

I Dreamed of Africa Kuki Gallmann (Penguin 1992 ISBN 0140144595). An autobiography of the tragic family bereavements which led to the setting up of a conservation organisation – the Gallmann Foundation. Other books by the same author: *Night of the Lions* and *African Nights*.

Nomad – Journeys from Samburu Mary Lee Fitzgerald (Sinclair-Stevenson 1992). A journalist's story of events in Kenya, dipping into mysticism, tribalism and current affairs.

Bill Bryson's African Diary Bill Bryson (Doubleday 2002 ISBN 0385605145). Bryson travels in Kenya as a guest of CARE International. His sharp observations bring wit and empathy to the charity's work which is supported by royalties and profits from the sale of book.

Fiction

Rules of the Wild Francesca Marciano (Jonathan Cape 1998 ISBN 022405256). Contemporary novel with a tongue-in-cheek depiction of safari guides and white Kenyan society.

Green City in the Sun Barbara Wood (Pan 1989 ISBN 0330307231). A *Thorn Tree*-style saga of life in Kenya covering the days of the early settlers through to the Mau Mau rebellion.

My Enemy: My Friend David Lovatt Smith (order through web: www.mau-mau.net). A well-received novel set during the Mau Mau emergency which gives a balanced view on the contrasting factions in Mau Mau.

A Primate's Memoir: Love, Death and Baboons in East Africa Robert Sapolsky (Vintage 2000 ISBN 0099285770). An extremely entertaining and sometimes sad account about a 'green' research student coming to study baboons in Kenya in the 1970s.

The Constant Gardener John le Carré (Coronet Books 2001). A gripping thriller set in Kenya.

Kenyan fiction

See box page 34

A Grain of Wheat Ngugi wa Thiong'o (Penguin 2002). A novel about the eve of independence. Other books by the same author (also published by Heinemann): *Petals of Blood*, a detective story, *The River Between* about old Kikuyu society and the coming of the white settlers and *Decolonising the Mind*, a non-fiction book which suggests that African writing needs to shed its colonial aspirations. Thiongo'o is Kenya's most eminent established writer.

Before the Rooster Crows Peter Kimani (East African Educational Publishers 2003 ISBN 9966251553)

Going Down River Road Meja Mwangi (Heinemann 1976 ISBN: 0435901761) A vivid
   portrayal of River Road in Nairobi.
The River and the Source Margaret Ogolla.
The Stone Hills of Maragoli Stanley Gazemba.
My Life in Crime John Kiriamiti.
Discovering Home Binyavana Wainaina (Jacana Media, 2003). Also by the same author: *Flights
   of My Fancy.*

Photographic and coffee-table books

Kenya from the Air Anne Arthus-Bertrand, Anne Spoerry and Yann Arthus-Bertrand
   (Thames and Hudson 1994 ISBN 0500541892). Superb aerial photographs of Kenya.
Safari Style by Beddow and Burns (Thames and Hudson 2002 ISBN 9966 848 95 9).
   Photographic account and description of fancy lodges and camps in Africa.
Longing for Darkness – Kamante's Tales from Out of Africa Peter Beard (Chronicle Books 1988).
   An interesting collection of photographs from the Blixen era.
Vanishing Africa Mirella Ricciardi (Collins 1972) Still one of the best photographic books on
   the different tribes, if you can get hold of it. Also by the same author: *African Visions.*
Maasai Tepilit Ole Saitoi and Carol Beckwith (Harvill 1991). Powerful portraits of the
   Maasai and an interesting introduction to their culture.
Railway across the Equator Mohammed Amin, Duncan Willetts and Alastair Matheson
   (Bodley Head 1986 ISBN 0370307747). Features the late Mohammed Amin`s superb
   photographs of the modern scene in East Africa.

Environment and wildlife

Elephant Memories: Thirteen Years in the Life of an Elephant Family Cynthia Moss (Chicago
   Press 2000 ISBN 0226542378). A fascinating insight into elephant society gleaned
   from over 27 years spent researching Amboseli's elephants. Also by the same author:
   Portraits in the Wild (Elm Tree Books 1989), a behavioural study of East African
   animals.
The Tsavo Story Daphne Sheldrick (Collins and Harvill Press 1973 ISBN 0002628015). A
   tribute to her husband David Sheldrick, a warden in Tsavo. Covers the period 1948–73.
   Also by the same author: *Orphans of Tsavo,* about her work rescuing orphan elephants.
In the Dust of Kilimanjaro David Western (Shearwater Books 2002 ISBN 1559635347).
   Western was a researcher in Amboseli and this book describes how he learned to look
   through the eyes of a Maasai cow. An insight into the intricacies of pastoralism and
   wildlife conservation central to present-day conservation measures. Western was a past
   director of the Kenya Wildlife Service.
Born Free Trilogy – Born Free, Living Free and *Forever Free* Joy Adamson (Pan 2000 ISBN
   0330391909). The conservation story of Elsa the lioness and her cubs.
My Pride and Joy George Adamson (Harvill Press 1986). Autobiograhpy about his life with
   Joy and their work with lions. Also by the same author: *Bwana Game* (Fontana 1972).
The Big Cat Diary: A Year in the Masai Mara Brian Jackson and Jonathon Scott (Collins 2002
   ISBN: 0007146663). An insight into the life of lions, cheetahs and leopards in the Masai
   Mara National Reserve. Other books by Jonathon Scott include *The Marsh Lions* (with
   Brian Jackman) and *Big Cat Diary: Lion.*
The Sixth Extinction: Biodiversity and its Survival Richard Leakey and Roger Lewin (Phoenix
   1996 ISBN 1857994736). Are we on the verge of a sixth extinction? A thought-
   provoking read on biodiversity.
Wildlife Wars: My Battle to Save Kenya's Elephants Richard Leakey (Macmillan 2001 ISBN
   0333745663). A fascinating autobiography, charting Leakey's remarkable career from
   palaeontologist to head of the National Museums of Kenya, director of the Kenya
   Wildlife Service, erstwhile conservationist and politician.

Walking and mountaineering

Trekking in East Africa David Else (Lonely Planet 1998). Excellent for hiking in Kenya, and especially good for Mount Kenya.
Guide Book to Mount Kenya and Kilimanjaro (Mountain Club of Kenya 1991). A thorough guide filled with useful, practical information and recommended if you're climbing Mount Kenya.

Health

Bugs, Bites & Bowels Jane Wilson-Howarth. The Cadogan guide to healthy travel (1999).
Your Child's Health Abroad: A manual for travelling parents Jane Wilson-Howarth and Matthew Ellis (Bradt 1998, updated on www.bradt-travelguides.com).

WEBSITES

Kenya Tourist Board www.magicalkenya.com
Kenyan government www.statehousekenya.go.ke
Kenya Association of Tour Operators (KATO) www.katokenya.org
Kenya Wildlife Service www.kws.org
East African Wildlife Society www.eawildlife.org
National Museums of Kenya www.museums.or.ke
Nature Kenya www.naturekenya.org

Bradt Travel Guides is a partner to the 'know before you go' campaign, masterminded by the UK Foreign and Commonwealth Office to promote the importance of finding out about a destination before you travel. By combining the up-to-date advice of the FCO with the in-depth knowledge of Bradt authors, you'll ensure that your trip will be as trouble-free as possible.

www.fco.gov.uk/knowbeforeyougo

THE ULTIMATE TRAVEL MAGAZINE

Launched in 1993, *Wanderlust* is an inspirational magazine dedicated to free-spirited travel. It has become the essential companion for independent-minded travellers of all ages and interests, with readers in over 100 countries.

A one-year, 6-issue subscription carries a money-back guarantee – for further details:

Tel.+44 (0)1753 620426
Fax. +44 (0)1753 620474

or check the *Wanderlust* website, which has details of the latest issue, and where you can subscribe on-line:

www.wanderlust.co.uk

CLAIM YOUR HALF-PRICE BRADT GUIDE!

Order Form

To order your half-price copy of a Bradt guide, and to enter our prize draw to win £100 (see overleaf), please fill in the order form below, complete the questionnaire overleaf, and send it to Bradt Travel Guides by post, fax or email. Post and packing is free to UK addresses.

Please send me one copy of the following guide at half the UK retail price

Title	*Retail price*	*Half price*

Please send the following additional guides at full UK retail price

No	*Title*	*Retail price*	*Total*
...	....	......	......
...	....	......	......
...	....	......	......

	Sub total	......
Post & packing outside UK		......
(£2 per book Europe; £3 per book rest of world)		
	Total	......

Name . . . .

Address . . . .

Tel. . . . .   Email . . . .

☐ I enclose a cheque for £ . . . . made payable to Bradt Travel Guides Ltd

☐ I would like to pay by VISA or MasterCard

Number . . . .   Expiry date . . . .

☐ Please add my name to your catalogue mailing list.

Send your order on this form, with the completed questionnaire, to:

Bradt Travel Guides/KEN
19 High Street, Chalfont St Peter, Bucks SL9 9QE
Tel: +44 1753 893444 Fax: +44 1753 892333
Email: info@bradt-travelguides.com
www.bradt-travelguides.com

WIN £100 CASH!
READER QUESTIONNAIRE

**Win a cash prize of £100 for the first completed questionnaire
drawn after May 31 2004.**

All respondents may order a Bradt guide at half the UK retail price – please
complete the order form overleaf.

(Entries may be posted or faxed to us, or scanned and emailed.)

We are interested in getting feedback from our readers to help us plan future Bradt
guides. Please complete this quick questionnaire and return it to us to enter into
our draw.

Have you used any other Bradt guides? If so, which titles?. . . . .
. . . .

What other publishers' travel guides do you use regularly? . . . .
. . . .

Where did you buy this guidebook? . . . .

What was the main purpose of your trip to Kenya (or for what other reason did you
read our guide)? eg: holiday/business/charity etc. . . . .
. . . .

What other destinations would you like to see covered by a Bradt guide?
. . . .

Would you like to receive our catalogue/newsletters?

YES / NO (If yes, please complete details on reverse)

If yes – by post or email?. . . . .

Age (circle relevant category) 16–25   26–45   46–60   60+

Male/Female (delete as appropriate)

Home country. . . . .

Please send us any comments about our guide to Kenya or other Bradt Travel
Guides. . . . .
. . . .
. . . .
. . . .

Bradt Travel Guides
19 High Street, Chalfont St Peter, Bucks SL9 9QE, UK
Telephone: +44 1753 893444 Fax: +44 1753 892333
Email: info@bradt-travelguides.com
www.bradt-travelguides.com

Bradt Travel Guides

Africa by Road	£13.95	London: In the Footsteps of	
Amazon	£14.95	the Famous	£10.95
Antarctica: A Guide to the Wildlife	£14.95	Madagascar	£13.95
The Arctic: A Guide to Coastal		Madagascar Wildlife: A Visitor's	
Wildlife	£14.95	Guide	£14.95
Azores	£12.95	Malawi	£12.95
Baltic Capitals: Tallinn, Riga,		Maldives	£12.95
Vilnius, Kaliningrad	£11.95	Mali	£13.95
Botswana: Okavango Delta,		Mauritius	£12.95
Chobe, Northern Kalahari	£14.95	Montenegro	£12.95
British Isles: Wildlife of Coastal		Mozambique	£12.95
Waters	£14.95	Namibia	£14.95
Cambodia	£11.95	North Canada: Yukon, Northwest	
Cape Verde Islands	£12.95	Territories, Nunavut	£13.95
Cayman Islands	£12.95	North Cyprus	£11.95
Chile & Argentina: Trekking		North Korea	£13.95
Guide	£12.95	Palestine with Jerusalem	£12.95
China: Yunnan Province	£13.95	Paris – Lille – Brussels: The Bradt	
Croatia	£12.95	Guide to Eurostar Cities	£11.95
East & Southern Africa:		Peru & Bolivia: Trekking Guide	£12.95
Backpacker's Manual	£14.95	River Thames: In the	
Eccentric America	£12.95	Footsteps of the Famous	£10.95
Eccentric Britain	£11.95	Rwanda	£13.95
Eccentric France	£12.95	Seychelles	£12.95
Eccentric London	£12.95	Singapore	£11.95
Ecuador, Peru & Bolivia:		South Africa: The Bradt	
Backpacker's Manual	£13.95	Budget Travel Guide	£11.95
Eritrea	£12.95	Southern African Wildlife	£18.95
Estonia	£12.95	Sri Lanka	£12.95
Ethiopia	£13.95	St Helena, Ascension &	
Falkland Islands	£13.95	Tristan da Cunha	£14.95
Gabon, São Tomé & Príncipe	£13.95	Switzerland: Rai, Road, Lake	£12.95
Galápagos Wildlife	£14.95	Tanzania	£14.95
The Gambia	£12.95	Tasmania	£12.95
Georgia	£13.95	Tibet	£12.95
Ghana	£12.95	Uganda	£11.95
Iran	£12.95	USA by Rail	£12.95
Iraq	£13.95	Venezuela	£14.95
Kabul: Mini Guide	£9.95	Your Child's Health Abroad	£8.95
Latvia	£12.95	Zambia	£12.95
Lithuania	£12.95	Zanzibar	£12.95

Index

Previous page Elephant bull, *Loxodonta africana*, Samburu National Reserve (CF)

Above Hippopotamus, *Hippopotamus amphibius* (NG)

Right White rhino, *Ceratotherium simum*, and calf, Lewa Wildlife Conservancy (CF)

Below Buffalo and zebra at waterhole, Kilaguni Lodge, Tsavo West National Park (CF)

Writing

Literature on Kenya abounds, including the novels of Elspeth Huxley such as *The Mottled Lizard* and *The Flame Trees of Thika* and her historical account of the country, *Nine Faces of Kenya*, Isak Dinesen's classic, *Out of Africa*, Beryl Markham's autobiography *West with the Night*, Monty Brown's *Where Giants Trod*, an historical account of Turkana, and the controversial *No Man's Land* by George Monbiot. There's a plethora of coffee-table books, with superb photography, on wildlife, tribal cultures and safaris which can be readily purchased in Nairobi. A reading list is given on page 467.

In comparison with West Africa, Kenyan African writing has been less prolific. There's been a steady and growing trickle of eminent writers like Ngugi wa Thiong'o, Meja Mwangi, John Kiriamiti and Binyavanga Wainaina, who recently won the Caine prize for African literature. He describes the present writing scene in Kenya in the box piece opposite.

Music

Traditionally, music in Kenya centred on drumming and dance, often accompanied by humming, chanting and singing. Apart from the drums, other musical instruments included variations on flutes, lyres and guitars, which may be seen in the National Museums of Kenya among their ethnic exhibits. Since then, music in Kenya has evolved through early Afro-jazz to African hip-hop, rap and dance music. Recent years have seen an increase in FM radio stations throughout urban Kenya, and now Kenyan artists are at the forefront of the Kenyan music scene. Mr Googs and Vinnie Banton had a runaway hit, *Wazee*, about life in a Nairobi suburb which scooped a nomination at the South African Kora Awards (the African equivalent to the Grammy awards) in 2002 for the most promising new talent in Africa. Other young stars to seek out are the Deux Vultures, Nameless and Redsan. Alongside, traditional music is still important. The Kayamba Africa group and Suzanne Owiyo were both nominated for Kora awards in 2002. Within Nairobi, live bands perform regularly and venues are listed on page 179 in chapter 9.

Film

Unlike West Africa, as yet, Kenyan African productions have not featured on the film scene, which has been dominated by Hollywood blockbusters. Films like *Where Eagles Dare*, filmed in Amboseli, *Born Free* about Elsa the lioness, the award-winning epic *Out of Africa* starring Meryl Streep and Robert Redford, *I Dreamed of Africa* starring Kim Basinger, based upon Kuki Gallmann's book of the same name, *Kitchen Toto*, an endearing story set in the times of the Mau Mau and *To Walk with Lions*, the biopic of George Adamson starring Richard Harris, were all filmed in Kenya. In recent years, the excellent award-winning German film *Nowhere in Africa*, set during World War II, *Survivor: Africa*, part of the *Survivor Challenge* series, *Tomb Raider 2: The Cradle of Life*, depicting Lara Croft's latest adventure and the superb IMAX film on elephants have shown a revived interest in Kenya as a popular film location.

THE SPECIALIST IN WESTERN KENYA

tours to western and northern kenya; tanzania and uganda • safaris -
camping and lodge; walking and horseback; flying and balloon; botanical;
golfing; fishing; water sports • mountain trekking • agro- and eco-toursim

www.kwakilahalisafaris.com • PO Box 6793, Eldoret, Kenya

KENYAN TRAVEL SPECIALISTS

'Distinctive African Travel'

+44 (0) 1273 623 790

www.journeysbydesign.co.uk

'Will Jones and Journeys by Design show you the outre and the exotic
with a style and adventure that most of you thought had dispaappeared
with the Empire.' AA Gill

Journeys
by Design

KENYA

—— *Specialists since 1980* ——
**Holidays, Flights, Safaris,
Honeymoons & Anniversaries**

AFRICA TRAVEL CENTRE

Call our experienced staff
0845 450 1520
africatravel.co.uk

ATOL 3384

Gane & Marshall

Tailormade & small group
Itineraries throughout Kenya
Tanzania & Zanzibar
Safaris, Climbs & the Coast

Tel: 020 8441 9592
Email: holidays@ganeandmarshall.co.uk
WWW.ganeandmarshall.co.uk ATOL 3145

Natural Environment and Ecotourism

CLIMATE AND TOPOGRAPHY
Climate
The climatic variations are primarily determined by altitude, which gives significant changes in temperature, humidity and rainfall throughout the country. But in essence, Kenya is a dry country: 75% of its area is classed as arid or semi-arid. There are two rainy seasons throughout the Central Highlands, Rift Valley and the northern and eastern areas, with the long rains from March to May and the short rains from October to December. However, since El Niño in 1998, rainfall has been erratic and rain can occur at any time. Concern arises over the future impact of deforestation and global warming on weather patterns, but over the past century the country has been subject to extremes of weather conditions – both floods and droughts. The Central Highlands and Rift Valley have an idyllic climate, averaging around 20°C, akin to a hot summer's day in Britain, and it's cool at night, while the annual rainfall ranges from 800mm to 2,400mm. Around Lake Turkana, in the north, average temperatures rise to 34°C, with rainfall less than 500mm a year. The coast is hot and humid throughout the year, with average daytime temperatures ranging from 26°C to 32°C, with 70% humidity. But here the heat is pleasantly tempered by the monsoon winds. Most rain falls during the southeasterly monsoon, between April and July. In western Kenya, the weather pattern is influenced by the Lake Victoria basin, and rainfall regularly occurs from March to November.

Topography
Kenya has been aptly dubbed, 'All of Africa in one country'. Certainly, the Kenyan landscape is among the most scenically diverse and dramatic in Africa. It ranges from the equatorial snows of Mount Kenya, 5,200m (17,000ft), to the expansive deserts of the north and east, the Great Rift Valley with its soda and freshwater lakes, ancient forests, the golden savanna of the Maasai rangelands and the coral gardens of the Indian Ocean. The country may be broadly divided into four zones – the coastal plains, an inland plateau rising to the Central Highlands bisected by the Rift Valley, the Victoria Lake basin and the northern deserts.

NATIONAL PARKS AND RESERVES
Kenya has some 54 national parks and reserves, together with private conservancies and sanctuaries, covering over 10% of the land area, as well as seven marine national parks and reserves. The responsibility for managing the national parks and the country's protected wildlife species comes under the jurisdiction of the **Kenya Wildlife Service** (KWS). Obtusely, **county councils** are responsible for the management of national reserves in their administrative area. Other conservancies and sanctuaries are managed privately and often work in close association with KWS.

WILDLIFE VIEWING

This table is a guide to specific wildlife species you are most likely to see in the most visited parks. It is not a definitive list of either the game-viewing areas or the other wildlife you may see, nor does lack of a dot indicate that a species does not occur in that park.

	SE Kenya					Central Highlands					The Rift Valley				Western Kenya		Northern Kenya		Coast	
	Nairobi National Park	Amboseli NP	Tsavo East NP	Tsavo West NP	Chyulu Hills NP	Aberdares NP	Mt Kenya NP	Lewa Wildlife Conservancy	Laikipia	Meru NP	Hell's Gate NP	Lake Nakuru NP	Lake Bogoria NR	Kigio Wildlife Conservancy	Masai Mara NR	Mount Elgon NP	Samburu/Buffalo Springs NR	Shaba NR	Shimba Hills NP	Mwalunganje Eleph't Sanct'y
Lion	•	•	•	•		•			•	•					•		•	•		
Leopard								•			•				•		•	•		
Cheetah	•														•		•	•		
Elephant		•	•	•		•	•	•	•	•					•		•	•	•	•
Cape buffalo	•	•	•	•		•	•		•						•			•	•	
Black rhino	•	•				•		•		•		•			•					
White rhino								•	•			•			•					
Hippo		•	•	•				•							•					
Giraffe: Masai	•	•	•	•					•						•					
reticulated								•	•	•							•	•		
Rothschild's												•		•		•				
Wildebeest	•														•					
Zebra: Burchill's	•	•	•								•	•			•					
Grevy's								•	•	•							•	•		
Oryx: Beisa																	•	•		
fringe-eared		•	•												•					
Thomson's gazelle	•	•	•									•			•					
Grant's gazelle	•	•	•	•				•	•	•					•		•	•		
Waterbuck									•						•	•	•			
Bushbuck						•	•									•				
Eland	•			•	•										•					
Kudu			•	•									•							
Impala	•	•	•	•				•	•			•			•		•	•		
Dik dik			•	•													•	•		
Gerenuk			•	•						•							•	•		
Topi															•					
Coke's hartebeest (Kongoni)	•																			
Sable antelope																				•
Warthog	•		•	•											•					
Spotted hyena		•													•					
Black/silver-backed jackal		•													•					
Vervet monkey			•								•									
Baboon (various species)	•	•	•	•							•				•		•	•		
B&W colobus monkey					•													•		
Crocodile		•	•	•											•		•			
Flamingo												•	•							
Ostrich: Masai	•	•									•				•					
Somali								•	•	•							•	•		

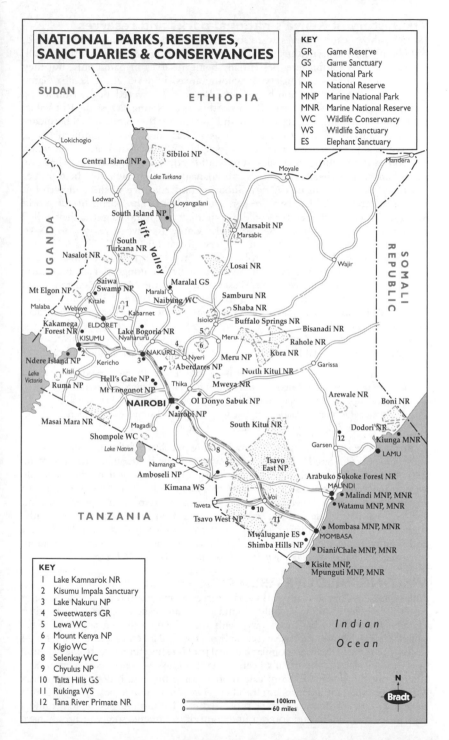

NATIONAL PARKS, RESERVES, SANCTUARIES & CONSERVANCIES

KEY

GR	Game Reserve
GS	Game Sanctuary
NP	National Park
NR	National Reserve
MNP	Marine National Park
MNR	Marine National Reserve
WC	Wildlife Conservancy
WS	Wildlife Sanctuary
ES	Elephant Sanctuary

SUDAN

ETHIOPIA

Lokichogio

Central Island NP

Sibiloi NP

Moyale

Mandera

Lake Turkana

Lodwar

Loyangalani

South Island NP

Marsabit NP
Marsabit

UGANDA

South Turkana NR

Nasalot NR

Losai NR

Wajir

SOMALI REPUBLIC

Mt Elgon NP

Saiwa Swamp NP

Maralal GS

Malaba

Webuye

Kitale

Maralal

Naibung WC

Samburu NR

Kakamega Forest NR

ELDORET

Kabarnet

Shaba NR

Isiolo

Buffalo Springs NR

Bisanadi NR

KISUMU

Lake Bogoria NR

Nyaharuru

Meru

Rahole NR

Ndere Island NP

Kisii

Kericho

NAKURU

Nyeri

Meru NP

Kora NR

Garissa

Lake Victoria

Ruma NP

Hell's Gate NP

Aberdares NP

North Kitui NR

Mt Longonot NP

Thika

Mweya NR

Arewale NR

Boni NR

NAIROBI

Ol Donyo Sabuk NP

Masai Mara NR

Nairobi NP

Magadi

South Kitui NR

Dodori NR

Shompole WC

Garsen

Kiunga MNR

Lake Natron

LAMU

Namanga

Tsavo East NP

Amboseli NP

Arabuko Sokoke Forest NR

Kimana WS

MALINDI

Malindi MNP, MNR

Taveta

Voi

Watamu MNP, MNR

TANZANIA

Tsavo West NP

Mombasa MNP, MNR

Mwaluganje ES

MOMBASA

Shimba Hills NP

Diani/Chale MNP, MNR

Kisite MNP, Mpunguti MNP, MNR

Indian Ocean

KEY

1. Lake Kamnarok NR
2. Kisumu Impala Sanctuary
3. Lake Nakuru NP
4. Sweetwaters GR
5. Lewa WC
6. Mount Kenya NP
7. Kigio WC
8. Selenkay WC
9. Chyulus NP
10. Taita Hills GS
11. Rukinga WS
12. Tana River Primate NR

0 — 100km
0 — 60 miles

N

Bradt

The history of Kenya's national parks and reserves

In 1900, three game reserves were formed – Sugota, 34,500km², and Jubaland, 65,000km², in northern Kenya, and Ukamba covering 28,000km² in the south. These were not administered, essentially being reserves in name only, but they marked the first step in conserving wildlife areas. In 1906, the Ukamba Game Reserve was renamed the Southern Game Reserve. It covered all the land to the south of the railway, from Tsavo River northwest to Ngong, across the Rift Valley from Longonot south to Lake Natron and back along the international boundary with Tanzania (or German East Africa as it was then.) The Southern Game Reserve was subject to game regulations issued by Whitehall and, amazingly when one considers the numbers employed in wildlife conservation today, only had one game ranger responsible for its entire management. It was the first proper sanctuary for wildlife in East Africa. Shooting under licence was not allowed but the Maasai and the Wakamba were permitted to hunt. The skirmishes of World War I took a toll on the reserve's wildlife: giraffe were shot on sight as they pulled down telegraph wires. Later the Southern Game Reserve gave way to Tsavo National Park and Amboseli National Reserve formed in 1948.

The first national park was Nairobi, formed in 1946, a foresight remarkable to this day when you see the Nairobi city skyline etched along the park boundary. Other early reserves were Marsabit, West Chyulu and the Mara (the current Mara Triangle area now known as the Mara Conservancy), formed in 1948, and Ngong in 1949, while Mount Kenya National Park was gazetted in 1949 and the Aberdare National Park in 1950.

The difference between national park and national reserve status can be confusing. The National Park Trustee's report of 1951 describes the difference:

> A National Reserve ... is a local term denoting an area for preservation where the reasonable needs of the human inhabitants living within the area must take preference. It is in the nature of a compromise between a National Park and a Game Reserve, where the establishment of a National Park – although eminently desirable – is not easily possible.

At the time the needs of nomadic pastoralists were not clearly defined; being transient, they were not considered to be an issue. However, by the 1970s other forces had come into play – wildlife tourism was a big money-spinner and the welfare of local people was no longer a priority as the government sought to fill its coffers from tourism revenue. Some reserves, such as Amboseli, were upgraded to national park status, and the local Maasai people lost out, giving rise to a deep resentment. Subsequently, there's been a dramatic turnaround in government policy over the last decade, and community involvement is now considered a vital element in wildlife conservation. (see page 56, *Human–Wildlife Conflict*, and *Community Tourism*, Chapter 4)

VISITING WILDLIFE AREAS

Although Kenya has so many parks and reserves, many are in remote areas and not easily accessible, resulting in only around ten being visited regularly on tourism circuits. Accordingly, park fees vary, with there being a sliding scale, the most popular being the most expensive (see table opposite). Park entry fees are valid for 24 hours. For some of the most popular national parks, a **smartcard** electronic ticketing system is in place. Although it's been extremely effective since its inception, and filtered out the corruption from gate money going missing, it does require some forward planning for independent travellers. The other thing to bear in mind is that it can take time for smartcards to be processed – early morning, itching to get into a park to see the wildlife, and you can find yourself in a queue, so if you already have

NATIONAL PARK AND RESERVE FEES (in US$)

Park entry fees Non-residents	Adult	Child/ student	Smartcard required
Category A			
Aberdares	30	10	Yes
Amboseli	30	10	Yes
Lake Nakuru	30	10	Yes
Category B			
Tsavo East	27	10	Yes
Tsavo West	27	10	Yes
Meru	27	10	
Category C			
Nairobi	23	10	Yes
Shimba Hills	23	10	
Category D			
Arabuko-Sokoke Forest	10	5	
Kakamega Forest	10	5	
Mt Kenya	15	8	
Nairobi Animal Orphanage	8	5	
Nairobi Safari Walk	8	5	
Marine	8	5	
Impala	5	2	
All other parks	15	5	
NATIONAL RESERVES			
Masai Mara	30	10	
Samburu	30	10	
Shaba	30	10	
Vehicle entry per day	KSh200		

a smartcard it's best to avoid the main gates to the most popular parks where possible. Entry for vehicles is also charged. National reserves also have a tiered pricing system – the main three, Masai Mara, Samburu and Shaba cost US$30. Private game sanctuaries and conservancies also vary in price, but the conservancy fee is normally included with the cost of accommodation. For example on Lewa Wildlife Conservancy fees are US$45 for Wilderness Trails and US$35 for Lewa Safari Camp, while for Shompole Conservancy it's only US$20. Details of prices for parks, reserves and conservancies are given in the respective regional section.

Throughout the guide, prices have been given for non-residents. Park opening times are from dawn to dusk, 06.30–18.30. It is forbidden to stay in the parks overnight unless accommodation (lodge or camping) is provided and, with the odd exception, night game-driving is not permitted.

Smartcards

Essentially, smartcards are the only means of paying park entry and vehicle fees for parks currently covered by the system: the Aberdares, Amboseli, Lake Nakuru,

SMARTCARDS

	Point of issue	Point of sale
Nairobi NP, Main Gate	•	•
Lake Nakuru NP, Main Gate	•	•
Tsavo East NP, Main Gate Voi	•	•
Aberdares NP		•
Mombasa KWS Offices	•	•
Malindi Marine NP offices		•
Amboseli NP, Meshanani Gate		•
Tsavo West, Mtito Andei Gate		•

Nairobi, Tsavo East and Tsavo West national parks. They are also applicable to flights entering the respective parks. Boring, but very important – overseas travellers need to remember the following:

- **Point of issue** (POI) These are located at Nairobi National Park Main Gate, Lake Nakuru National Park Main Gate, Tsavo East National Park Main Gate (Voi) and Mombasa KWS offices. Everyone over the age of 18 must have a smartcard. Alternatively, groups travelling together can go on one card.
- **Point of sale** (POS) This is where you load money on to your card. You must have enough money on your card to access the park – if you are short of money on your card at the gate, you must return to a POS to load more money on to your card. Don't forget to include vehicle entry. Also be aware that all money loaded on to your card is *not* refundable. When there is no money left on the card, it will be retained, so if visiting several parks, load your card with enough money for all of them, to avoid the hassle of having to go to a POI to get a new card. The POSs are located at Nairobi National Park Main Gate, Lake Nakuru National Park Main Gate, Tsavo East National Park Main Gate (Voi), the park headquarters of Aberdares National Park, the Mombasa KWS offices, Malindi Marine National Park offices, Amboseli National Park Meshanani Gate and Tsavo West Mtito Andei Gate.
- **Point of entry** (POE) These are the different park gate entrances. Your card will be debited for the required amount. Be careful to check your receipt – sometimes teenagers look adult and may be charged as an adult. This can be a nuisance if you've loaded your card with a precise amount, resulting in your then having to take a detour to go to a POS. Your card will then be checked out when leaving, and 'empty' cards retained.
- **Flying in** If you are flying into a national park within the smartcard system, smartcards *must* be obtained and loaded in advance, as there are no POIs or POSs at the airstrips.

WILDLIFE AND AVIFAUNA
What is special about Kenya's wildlife?
Kenya is home to most of Africa's large animals, the only significant gap being the major primates – no gorillas or chimpanzees are endemic (although a chimpanzee sanctuary for rescued chimps has been established on a private ranch at Sweetwaters near Nanyuki). The majority of other mammal species may be seen, and these are listed in the *Wildlife Guide* (page 445).

In comparison with southern African countries, Kenya ranks high in the numbers game. It differs from its neighbours for the sheer variety and concentration of wildlife which is easily seen on the savanna grasslands – particularly in the Masai Mara, which is a wildlife Mecca. This phenomenon is due to having two rainy seasons, which provide increased pasture, which in turn supports greater densities of wildlife than may be found in the countries with only one rainy season. In addition, Kenya is also unique for its endemic northern species

THE WILDLIFE CODE

The Kenya Wildlife Service has regulations applicable to national parks and reserves, based upon protecting the wildlife and environment, ensuring your personal safety and enhancing your enjoyment and that of other visitors.

The following 'dos and don'ts' apply:

- **Do not harass the wildlife**. Making a noise, flashing lights and sudden movements can frighten the animals and makes them aggressive towards humans. Especially when game viewing, keep quiet.
- **Do not drive off the road** where there is an existing road system. Vehicles leaving the road damage the habitat and can alter drainage patterns.
- **Do not discard litter**, food or cigarette butts – fire can cause enormous damage to vegetation and kills the wildlife which cannot escape.
- **Do show consideration** for the animals you are watching, and to other wildlife enthusiasts. Ensure that animals are not completely surrounded by vehicles.
- **Do keep to the 40km/h speed limit** and drive carefully.
- **Do not leave your car**. For your own safety, only get out of your car at designated picnic sites and nature trails. In case of a breakdown, it is best to wait for help, so always carry water and extra food.
- **Do not feed the animals** – remember they are wild. Monkeys and baboons can be a nuisance searching for food.
- **Do remember wild animals can be dangerous**. Unless you have adequate protection and are supervised by a professional guide, do not stand up in your vehicle.
- **Do not remove flora or fauna**.
- **Do not enter or leave a park except through the authorised park gates**.

At the coast

- **Do not touch the coral or remove it**. Coral is a fragile living organism which takes years to grow, and it's also host to many rare and endangered marine species.
- **Do not remove shells**, starfish or sea flora and fauna.
- **Do not buy sea shells** or any other marine animal products as souvenirs. Reefs outside the reserves are threatened by excessive shell collection.
- **Do not feed the fish** as this disrupts natural feeding patterns.
- **Do not use spearguns** in the parks or reserves, and remember hook and line fishing only is permitted in the reserves.

of game, such as the reticulated giraffe, Somali ostrich and Beisa oryx.

Even now, there is still a tendency for tour operators to promote the **Big Five** – elephant, lion, buffalo, rhino and leopard – a hangover from the major trophy animals of the early hunting days. While these prime species are readily seen (see *Wildlife viewing chart*, page 38), only leopard being difficult, there's a great deal more to Kenya's wildlife heritage. A more challenging quest is to seek out the **Little Five** – the elephant shrew, ant-lion, buffalo-weaver, rhino-horned viper and leopard tortoise.

Birdlife

Kenya has one of the richest avifauna in Africa, boasting a bird list of 1,083, about 12% of the world's bird species. This variety reflects the diversity of habitats supporting both endemic and migratory species. There are six distinct avian areas, the most significant being the Somali-Masai where Kenya has 90 of the 130 bird species. The others are the East African coast, afro-tropical highlands, Lake Victoria basin, the Guinea-Congo Forest and the Sudan and Guinea savanna. Among the prime birding areas are the Rift Valley lakes of Naivasha, Nakuru and Baringo, the forests of Kakamega, Taita Hills and Arabuko Sokoke and the arid lands of Samburu.

Birds range in size from the flightless ostrich (both species are found in Kenya, the Somali ostrich being seen only in the north) to tiny sunbirds and finches. Even common birds, like the African starling and lilac-breasted roller, have an exotic

---

ENDEMIC AND NEAR-ENDEMIC BIRDS IN KENYA
Philip Briggs

The following bird species are either endemic to Kenya, or have an extremely limited range extending into a small part of one neighbouring country:

Sokoke scops owl *Otus ireneae* A small owl thought to be unique to Kenya's Arabuko Sokoke Forest until recently discovered on Tanzania's Usambara Mountains.

William's lark *Mirafra williamsi* A nondescript terrestrial bird of lava deserts of northern Kenya, most common north of Marsabit. Kenya endemic.

Malindi pipit *Anthus melindae* A typically drab pipit confined to dry coastal belt of Kenya north of Malindi through to Somalia.

Sokoke pipit *Anthus sokokensis* A small, clearly marked pipit endemic to a handful of coastal forests in Tanzania, as well as within Kenya's Arabuko Sokoke Forest. Listed as vulnerable.

Sharpe's longclaw *Macronyx sharpei* A small, globally-threatened longclaw of montane grasslands between mounts Kenya and Elgon. Kenya endemic.

Hinde's babbler *Turdiodes hypolecus* A striking, but scarce, range-restricted pied babbler of cultivated highland valleys in Mount Kenya and surrounds. Kenya endemic.

Taita thrush *Turdus helleri* A boldly marked thrush known only from the few remaining forests on the Taita Hills. Sometimes regarded to be a race of the widespread olive thrush. Either way, its conservation status is listed as critical, with only a few elusive pairs remaining. Kenya endemic.

plumage, while others, such as the secretary bird, marabou stork and double-toothed barbet, have a bizarre and somewhat comical appearance. There are numerous raptors, nine species of eagle alone. Other birds perform quaint antics, such as the numerous colonies of weaver birds building their hanging nests. Waterbirds are plentiful, attracted to both the freshwater and soda lakes of the Rift Valley – at certain times of year, Lake Nakuru is host to two million lesser flamingos – and the coastal creeks, reefs and beaches are a major flyway for Palaearctic migrants. Wherever you visit in Kenya, you are assured of seeing varied birdlife. But birds are threatened too: Sharpe's longclaw, Aberdare cisticola and the Taita white-eye are all on the endangered list. Their habitats are being destroyed by the march of the chainsaw and agricultural expansion.

Reptiles

There are a number of reptiles, the most common being the Nile crocodile and varying species of lizard. **Crocodiles** are found in the freshwater lakes and major rivers and are readily seen basking on sandbanks looking like the proverbial log. Of the common lizards, the most exotic is the rock agama – about 100cm long, the male has a distinctive orange head and blue body. At the coast, translucent geckos, easily confused as anaemic small lizards, venture out from behind hiding places (such as pictures hanging on the walls) in the evening to catch moths and flies. Monitor lizards, harmless (although they look like small crocodiles, and can grow to 2m) may be seen rustling around in bushes at the coast. Chameleons, which

Aberdare cisticola *Cisticola aberdare* A dark, but otherwise nondescript, warbler of montane grassland in Aberdare National Park and the Mau Escarpment. Kenya endemic.

Tana River cisticola *Cistocola restrictus* A poorly documented warbler known from only seven specimens collected in the eastern Tana River basin between 1932 and 1972. Presumed Kenya endemic.

Taita apalis *Apalis (thoracica) fuscigularis* A distinctive and critically endangered warbler of the Taita Hills, sometimes designated as a full species but more often as a race of the widespread bar-throated apalis. Kenya endemic.

Grey-rested helmetshrike *Priniops poliolophus* A range-restricted Serengeti-Mara endemic, usually seen in small, active flocks in the vicinity of whistling thorn trees.

Abbott's starling *Cinnyricinclus femoralis* Striking blue and white starling whose range is restricted to fewer than ten montane forests in Kenya and northern Tanzania, most commonly on Mount Kenya.

Amani sunbird *Anthreptes pallidigaster* A small sunbird of coastal woodland, known only from Kenya's Arabuko Sokoke Forest and a handful of sites in Tanzania.

Taveta golden weaver *Ploceus castaneiceps* Bright yellow weaver endemic to swampy areas in the lowlands of Kenya and Tanzania around the base of Mount Kilimanjaro, such as Lake Jipe and the marshes of Amboseli NP.

Clarke's weaver *Ploceus golandi* Boldly marked forest weaver confined to Arabuko Sokoke Forest and similar habitats around Malindi. Kenya endemic.

resemble miniature dinosaurs, are less easily seen, possibly due to their superb camouflage and the fear they instil in many Africans due to their changing colour and unnerving, rolling eyes which can look in opposite directions at the same time.

Although there are 119 snake species in Kenya, snakes are rarely seen, unless being carried off by birds. A relatively common non-poisonous snake is the rock python, often found in branches overhanging rivers, which makes for interesting navigation. Of the poisonous snakes, black and green mambas, the spitting cobra and the puff adder are the most dangerous. Unlike other snakes which usually slither away when they hear footsteps, it's common for puff adders to stay still. With their excellent camouflage, it's easy to tread on them, with inevitable consequences (see box *Kenyan snakes*, page 152). Tortoises are most easily seen on roads in national parks and in dry bush country.

Watching wildlife

The best time to see wildlife is the early morning and late afternoon, when the animals are at their most active. Serious game viewers will be up at dawn, returning mid-morning to rest during the middle of the day (like the animals) before setting off again from around 16.00 until dusk. It's an exciting experience, as no two days are the same on safari. There's always an element of surprise: watching an elephant family silhouetted against the sunrise as the mist is rising, finding a leopard with an impala kill skilfully wedged in a tree, or watching a baby giraffe stagger to its feet while scavengers look on.

A good pair of binoculars will greatly enhance your appreciation of the animals and birds as you can zoom in on the detail: check out the length of a giraffe's eyelashes or the exquisite plumage of a yellow-throated sandgrouse – buy the best that you can afford. If scanning the horizon, keep your binoculars still, look through the frame, and then pan round. Monitoring the movements of the herbivores will often lead you to the predators. Normally, a good guide will know where to find the animals. As a rule of thumb, those who are members of the **Kenya Professional Guides Association** (page 96) are generally of a good standard. At many of the lodges, drivers are in radio contact and will inform each other of the location of the animals. Hence you will see vehicles homing in on the hot favourites like lion and cheetah. You can ask your driver to switch off the radio and take pot luck – you might miss out, but there again you might have a pride of lion to yourself.

Field guides

There are plenty of field guides available in Kenya, from the serious to a variety of small pocket guides with photographic illustrations. A good selection of the latter is readily available in hotel shops and the main bookstores. These are listed in *Further reading*, page 467.

WILDLIFE CONSERVATION
International status

Kenya is signatory to a number of international conventions. Among these are the **Ramsar Convention** for the conservation and sustainable use of wetlands. There are **Ramsar Sites** at lakes Nakuru, Naivasha and Bogoria. The **World Heritage Convention** is for conserving areas with an outstanding cultural or natural value. Kenya's **World Heritage Sites** are Sibiloi and Central Island national parks, Mount Kenya and Lamu. **UNESCO's Man and Biosphere programme** aims to conserve and develop the rational use of resources in the biosphere. **Biosphere Reserve** status has been given to the national parks of mounts Kenya and Kulal,

CITES – THE AFRICAN ELEPHANT DILEMMA

At the 2002 CITES convention held in Chile, Kenya put forward a strong case for retaining the African elephant on CITES Appendix I, opposing any form of renewed trade in ivory as advocated by the southern African countries. The elephant debate has been a long-running contentious issue, dividing conservationists. After the ivory wars of the 1970s and '80s that decimated Africa's elephant populations – in Kenya, numbers plummeted from 170,000 in 1963 to 16,000 by 1989 – CITES placed a complete moratorium on the ivory trade in 1989. At that time Kenya's former president, Daniel Arap Moi, lit a colossal bonfire of ivory that had been confiscated from poachers, making a poignant international statement. Since then, there has been a significant downturn in the illicit ivory trade, and elephant numbers have slowly begun to increase. In some southern African countries, there is an overcrowding problem in national parks like the Kruger, where elephants are culled so that they do not completely destroy their habitat. A number of conservationists in southern African countries now favour a controlled ivory trade, so that they can plough back the revenue from ivory sales into conservation. Opposing them are those who believe a resumption of the ivory trade will give the green light to illegal poaching gangs with the subsequent increase in resources that will be required to beef up anti-poaching efforts. At the crux of the matter is control. There are vast areas of Africa where it is difficult to implement the law. While countries selling the ivory might be in a position to curtail any upsurge of poaching, other African countries may well be adversely affected by the decision. Kenya has maintained a robust stance against the resumption of the ivory trade in any form. At the CITES convention South Africa, Namibia and Botswana were given permission to have a one-off sale of ivory as opposed to an annual sale which was originally proposed, but Zimbabwe and Zambia were refused requests to trade ivory. The sale will take place in 2004 subject to certain conditions being met. Despite this, there are concerns that even this proposed one-off sale in southern African will trigger an upsurge in elephant poaching elsewhere in Africa.

Amboseli and the Malindi/Watamu Marine national parks and Kiungu Marine National Reserve. Kenya has played a significant role in the **Convention on International Trade in Endangered Species** (CITES), particularly with regard to elephant.

Biodiversity

Kenya is rich in biodiversity, recording around 25,000 animal species, 7,000 plants and 2,000 fungi and bacteria. In the past, the prime reason for the formation of national parks and reserves was not to conserve biodiversity. Parks were formed because they had concentrations of big game, or for environmental reasons – to protect water catchments or tropical hardwoods. At the time, biodiversity was not a factor. Now, with a greater understanding about the intricacies of ecosystems, together with an international recognition of the global significance of biodiversity, it forms a major part of present-day conservation. Many areas are under serious threat, but national efforts are being assisted by international partnerships, such as the European Union's **Biodiversity Conservation Programme** and Birdlife

RHINO CONSERVATION
Hassan Sachedina

The rhinoceros (rhino) is an ancient and versatile species and in the past was found over a wide variety of habitats, from afro-montane forests to savanna and desert ecosystems in Africa. In Kenya, black rhino are endemic to the region, while white rhino were introduced from South Africa as part of a genetic exchange programme around the 1960s. The two species are easily distinguished by the shape of their mouths. The black rhino's upper lip is like a hook, used for breaking off twiggy branches, while the white rhino has a wide mouth (white being derived from the *Afrikaans* word *weit*, meaning wide) used for grazing.

The black rhino has experienced a massive population decline of 96% in Africa. Since 1970, the population has fallen from 65,000 to an estimated 2,700 rhino in Africa, of which 470 are in Kenya. This decline is due almost exclusively to poaching for rhino horn where it is used for dagger handles in Yemen and traditional medicine in Asia. Black rhino are currently on Appendix I of CITES, considered critically endangered and protected by a global ban on rhino horn products.

The conservation strategy of African range states (areas or countries with rhino in Africa as opposed to elsewhere) aims to increase black and white rhino to sustainable population levels by the year 2018 using a metapopulation management approach. This involves darting and translocating individual rhinos from population to population to keep the genetic diversity going.

Translocations of rhino into sanctuaries and conservancies have proved the best strategy for the survival of black rhino in many areas. There are places in Africa where notable populations of rhino still free-range under wild conditions, among them Tsavo National Park in Kenya. However, attempting to protect rhino on an ecosystem level is extremely difficult, even in relatively well-funded, protected areas.

The **sanctuary approach** has been adopted in Kenya. Remnant rhino populations were moved into small ring-fenced sanctuaries during the 1970s and 1980s in Laikipia district and several national parks such as Nakuru, Nairobi, Tsavo and the Aberdares. The sanctuary strategy and the determined efforts of the Kenya Wildlife Service have been successful in stabilising the decline and increasing rhino numbers in Kenya. Encouragingly, some sanctuaries have recorded an 11% population growth rate a year. Nairobi and Nakuru national parks and Lewa Wildlife Conservancy have excellent rhino viewing.

As of 2001, the populations of African white rhino stood at 11,670 (10,405 in 1999) while black rhinos numbered 3,290 (2,704 in 1999).

The threat of rhino extinction posed by a continued demand for rhino horn remains very real. There is no room for complacency, but the dedicated action of park services and conservation agencies is contributing to steady improvements in the status of Africa's rhino populations.

Hassan Sachedina has worked on rhino projects in Kenya and Tanzania and is now working with the African Wildlife Foundation. Further details are available on www.awf.org.

International's **Important Bird Areas Programme**, where birds, being good indicators of biodiversity, are being monitored across the country as a means of assessing conservation priorities.

Conservation and research

Research continues to play a vital role in conservation, and Kenya supports many eminent ecologists, field biologists, zoologists and botanists involved in a variety of disciplines, from individual species research to ecological monitoring. They work in close collaboration with the Kenya Wildlife Service. The most established is the **Amboseli Elephant Research Project** which has been running since 1972, during which time a wealth of data has been collected on elephant behaviour, their reproductive patterns, intelligence, family life and communications. Initiated by Dr Cynthia Moss and continued by Dr Joyce Poole, fascinating discoveries into the social structure of elephant families have been observed. The **Samburu Elephant Research Programme** is run by Dr Iain Douglas-Hamilton, another renowned elephant field-scientist and campaigner, who also heads up the charity, **Save the Elephants**. **Rhino research** has given rise to increased protection for rhino. Lake Nakuru, Tsavo, the Aberdares and Nairobi national parks together with the Ngare Sergoi Sanctuary in the Lewa Wildlife Conservancy, have created a stronghold for rhino (see box opposite). Mpala Research Station has initiated a **Laikipia Predator Project** across the Laikipia Plateau, collecting data on lion (see box page 262), as well as wild dog and striped hyena. In addition they are investigating disease transmission from the smaller carnivores such as bat-eared foxes and jackals, which may be carriers of canine distemper and rabies, which can impact badly on lion and wild dog populations, together with the Feline Immunodeficiency Virus (FIV), the equivalent of HIV in hyenas and the wild cats. In the **Masai Mara National Reserve** there are research projects on hyena, cheetah, olive baboons and rhino, together with ecological monitoring. Not all the projects are high profile. **Meru National Park** is the venue for research on naked mole rats, and there are a number of projects researching the conflict between humans and wildlife and the uses of medicinal plants.

Rare and endangered animals

Kenya has a number of endangered species, the best-known being elephant, rhino, Hirola antelope, wild dog, turtles, Grevy's zebra, Rothschild's giraffe and de Brazza's monkey, and a number of endemic species like Ader's duiker and the golden-rumped elephant shrew found in the Arabuko Sokoke Forest Reserve. In addition, some animals more common elsewhere in Africa have a limited distribution within Kenya. The roan antelope is only seen in Ruma National Park and sable antelope in the Shimba Hills National Park. Where animals are threatened, or where they need to be moved to enable them to establish a viable gene pool to maintain a healthy population, the Kenya Wildlife Service has a translocation policy. This also applies to restocking areas where wildlife populations were virtually wiped out by poaching, such as Meru National Park. Rhinos, both black and white, and elephants have been successfully translocated to different parks and reserves. Several aquatic sitatunga antelope, only protected in the small Saiwa Swamp National Park, have been translocated to Lewa Wildlife Conservancy. This gives rise to another protected population, aiding their conservation, although they would not naturally be found in the area. A number of the extremely rare Rothschild's giraffe were successfully moved from Lake Nakuru National Park in 2002 to the new Kigio Wildlife Conservancy.

THE RHINO HORN TRADE
Lucy Vigne

No other large mammal has been so systematically wiped out in recent decades as the rhino. During the 1970s poaching swept through sub-Saharan Africa eliminating rhinos from many countries by the 1980s. Kenya's rhino population fell from 18,000 in 1970 to under 400 in the late 1980s.

Across Africa, civil wars and a breakdown in law and order enabled gangs of poachers armed with modern automatic weapons – sent by developed nations to equip new armies – to comb through parks and reserves killing the rhinos.

The rhino horn trade suddenly expanded in North Yemen on the Arabian peninsula. Until 1970 only rich men could afford a *jambiya* (traditional curved dagger) with a valuable rhino horn handle. Then, over a million Yemenis worked in neighbouring countries during the oil boom. Their per capita income increased six-fold. Many could now afford *jambiyas* with prestigious rhino horn handles. In the 1970s North Yemen imported three tonnes of rhino horn annually, from over 1,000 rhinos, to make into about 6,000 *jambiyas*. In a decade the price of rhino horn rocketed from US$30 to US$600 a kilo in Sanaa – the capital and still the main *jambiya* producing centre. Since the 1970s, Yemen has been the largest importer of rhino horn in the world. Today's price of rhino horn in Sanaa is $1,300 a kilo.

By the mid-1980s oil prices were declining but an economic boom was starting in eastern Asia, enabling previously poor people to buy rhino horn to

Poaching and the bushmeat trade

While elephant and rhino remain under global threat for their ivory and horn respectively, an equally insidious danger to wildlife comes from the bushmeat trade. Initially associated with West Africa, according to a report by TRAFFIC, the wildlife trade monitoring arm of the World Wide Fund for Nature (WWF) and the International Union for the Conservation of Nature (IUCN) in 2000, the bushmeat trade is now well established within East and southern Africa. Primarily poverty related, around 80% of bushmeat is used to feed the families of subsistence hunters. Yet, there is a sinister commercial element creeping into the trade, where any surplus meat is sold, mainly to the local market, bushmeat being substantially cheaper than domestic meat. Difficult to monitor, there appears to be a direct link between declining populations of animals like buffalo, impala and kudu and the bushmeat trade. Hunting, normally using wire snares, has moved into protected areas, where it is now the main illegal activity. As numbers of the larger animals decline, increasingly small animals are threatened. The problem is a bigger issue than it might at first appear. Within Kenya, the Kenya Wildlife Service has been mapping out the problem areas and then looking at the poverty indicators causing them. They aim to resolve the problem through fighting poverty at the local level while containing the poaching.

NATURAL HABITATS

Kenya's scenery is beautiful and exotic, ranging from magnificent stands of tropical forest to the carpets of dainty wildflowers which blossom after the rains. It has 19 distinct biotic zones, which may broadly be divided into the following categories:

Afro-alpine moorland

In many ways reminiscent of rugged Scottish moors with giant species of heather – *Ericas* – and tufted grasses, Afro-alpine moorland occurs from above 3,000m. At

treat sickness – a long revered traditional Chinese medicine. Rhino horn was never used in eastern Asia as an aphrodisiac as is still often mistakenly believed in the West.

In 1985 the Worldwide Fund for Nature (WWF) initiated campaigns to close down the international trade in rhino products. The five major trading countries at that time – South Korea, Taiwan, Macao, Hong Kong and Singapore – all banned the trade. By 1990, however, smuggling of rhino horn from South Africa to Taiwan was rife. A United Nations (UN) special envoy for rhino conservation, Dr Esmond Martin, was sent for discussions. Taiwan then enforced their ban on rhino horn.

Meanwhile, efforts to clamp down on the continuing, albeit much smaller, rhino horn trade to Yemen continue. When North and South Yemen unified in 1990 the long land and sea boundaries helped smuggling of all consumer goods, including rhino horn. Since 2000, black and white rhinos have been killed in the Democratic Republic of Congo (DRC), Kenya and Tanzania, the last three countries with known wild rhino populations in eastern Africa. Almost all the horn will end up in Yemen where it is smuggled via Somalia to Djibouti or put in sacks of foodstuffs and taken by boat from Mombasa to Djibouti. From there it is shipped across the Red Sea to the Yemeni coast and transported by road to Sanaa. The 1991 Gulf War and a civil war in 1994 has kept Yemen in economic recession, reducing demand for rhino horn, but even a small trade is a huge threat to the remaining rhinos.

3,800m, the vegetation becomes sparse, dominated by species such as *Senecio* (giant groundsel) and *lobelia*, while in sheltered areas, stands of *Hagenia abyssinica* are often found. Mounts Kenya and Elgon, the Cheranganis and Aberdares have a clearly defined Afro-alpine zone.

Highland grassland

One of the most endangered habitats in Kenya, as they are not in a protected area, these rare tussocked grasslands are only found in the Kinangop and Mau Narok/Molo areas above 2,400m on either side of the Rift Valley. Other important grasslands include the **fire-induced grasslands** covering parts of the Masai Mara, and **seasonal floodplain** and **delta grassland**, as seen on the Tana River delta.

Highland moist forests

Occurring from between 1,500m and 3,000m, in areas receiving over 1,200mm of rain annually, this forest type varies enormously according to rainfall. Typical forest trees are *Podocarpus, Olea* (Olive), *Juniperus procera* (East African Cedar) and *Newtonia*. On the higher elevations, bamboo, *Arundinaria alpina* is often present. Highland moist forests occur on Mount Elgon, the Mau, the Aberdares and Mount Kenya.

Guineo-Congolian rainforest

The Kakamega Forest in western Kenya is on the eastern boundary of a great tract of tropical rainforest which once stretched across equatorial Africa, where annual rainfall averages more than 1,900mm. Tree species include: *Celtis, Croton, Fagara* and *Manilkara*. The Nandi forests lie in the transitional zone between the Guineo-Congolian rainforest and montane forest.

FIG TREES
Will Knocker

Wild fig trees (*Ficus* species) are some of the most obvious trees you will come across in Kenya. Different species grow in the various ecological zones, reflecting the differing flora which occur according to altitude.

The coast, which boasts the most diverse flora in the country, contains more *Ficus* species than elsewhere. From the exotic pipal tree (*Ficus religiosa*) which grows outside the Hindu crematorium on Mombasa Island to the huge *F. bussei* which you might observe at the Gedi ruins on the north coast, fig trees are common and obvious. In the indigenous forests rarer species occur such as the beautiful *F. bubu*, with its white trunk and exotic, heart-shaped green leaves.

Wild figs provide a favoured food for the arboreal inhabitants of forests such as fruitbats, bushbabies and primates. Fructivorous birds such as casqued hornbills, barbets and turacos also depend on the fruit above all others. As providers of food, through their ability to provide tonnes of fruit, fig trees become a micro-ecology themselves. Each species depends for its pollination on a particular species of fig-wasp which has evolved parallel to it. Fig flowers thus become fruit which are also homes for fig-wasp larvae in a bizarre but effective symbiosis.

Powerful organisms, with massive spreading crowns and an invasive root system which can compromise the foundations of nearby buildings or the survival of a host tree, wild figs tend to dominate their surroundings. Many species start as stranglers – as seeds germinating in a crevice of a host tree having passed through a carrier such as a bird or a bat. In Nairobi, some magnificent wild figs can be seen in the city parks. (Look out for the splendid specimen of *F. lutea* in the Westlands Shopping Centre!) Otherwise old *mugumo* trees (*F. thonningii*) can be seen throughout central province, where they were once sacred to the Kikuyu people living there.

Further afield, 'rock figs' such as *F. ingens* and *F. vasta* dominate hills and *kopjes* in the gamelands, where they are often favourite roosts for baboons. The presence of water will often guarantee the sighting of a wild fig. On riverbanks grow the beautiful, yellow-barked *F. sycamorus* (the sycamore of the Bible), groves of which are usually full of birds, especially if they are fruiting.

Some species of birds such as green pigeons and the superb plum-coloured violet-backed starlings depend to a large extent on fruiting fig trees, flocks of each migrating from one area to another according to availability.

On the ground, bushbuck, porcupine, bushpig and forest antelope such as duiker and suni all love to eat fallen figs and are often associated with troops of feeding primates in the canopy above.

For human beings also, fig trees are a source of inspiration. They are venerated as sacred by the Kikuyu, Maasai and Boran peoples, amongst others. As additions to gardens, arboretums and public recreation areas, wild figs are the perfect choice, growing easily from stakes and quickly establishing themselves. Look out for these fascinating trees while on safari.

Will Knocker is a director of the environmental consultancy Porini Resources (web: www.poriniresources.com).

Coastal forests

There are several types of coastal forest which vary according to soil type and rainfall. Among typical species found here are *Cynometra, Afzelia, Brachylaena and Brachystegia*. There are also rare pockets of coastal palms found on the Ramisi and Tana rivers. The Arabuko Sokoke Forest Reserve is one of the largest remaining areas of coastal forest.

Highland dry forests

The highland dry forests, sometimes called cloud forests, are dependent upon attracting mist, such as mounts Marsabit and Kasigau and the Taita and Chyulu hills. In addition there are **riverine forests**, as typified along the Mara River and **groundwater forests**, such as Kitovu.

Woodland and thornbush-land

This is the dominant vegetation type by far, covering some 42% of the land area and is dominated by *Acacia, Commiphora* and *Combretum* species (there are over 40 species of *Acacia* alone), together with grasses such as *Themeda* and *Digitaria*. The area stretches from Amboseli in the south through to the Tsavo parks, northeastern and northwestern Kenya in land favoured by pastoralists and ranchers. In the drier areas, the vegetation changes to **semi-arid wooded and bushed grassland.**

Desert and semi-desert

Occurring in the north of the country, the semi-desert areas are dominated by *Acacia* thornbush, while some of the deserts are vast barren areas, such as the **Dida Galgalu** and **Chalbi**, together with areas around Turkana.

Wetlands

With its lakes, both freshwater and alkaline, rivers and coastal areas, Kenya has a superb range of wetland habitats.

The **alkaline lakes** of the Rift Valley have large blooms of microscopic plants, such as the cyanophytes *Spirulina,* and the presence of hot springs, while **papyrus swamps**, dominated by *Cyperus papyrus,* are found around lakes Victoria, Naivasha and Jipe. The **mangrove swamps** are found at the coast along creeks and estuaries, with eight different types of mangrove, the most common being *Rhizophora mucronata*. Excellent examples may be seen in Lamu and on the Ramisi and Tana river deltas.

Manmade habitats

Although not strictly speaking a vegetation type, mention should be made of the man-modified areas found in Kenya, where natural vegetation has given way to cultivated or desiccated land. Some 18% of the land, much of it well managed, produces a variety of commercial crops, from tea and coffee to wheat and sisal, and plantations of fast-growing exotic trees. In contrast are areas of grassland denuded by overgrazing or natural forests decimated for charcoal.

Kenya's forests

The depletion of Kenya's natural forests has accelerated alarmingly. Some 5,000ha of forest are lost each year to logging, cultivation, settlement and charcoal-making, and forest cover now stands at about 3%. The forests are rich in plant and birdlife, containing tropical hardwoods and medicinal plants, half of Kenya's threatened bird species, rare animals like the bongo antelope and the endangered crested mangabey and de Brassa monkeys, as well as being home to small remnants of the Ogiek and Boni hunter-gatherer tribes.

THE OGIEK
Virginia Luling

The Ogiek (or Okiek) people have lived since time immemorial in the mountains of the Mau Forest. Other groups inhabit Mount Elgon, Kapenguria, Nandi and Samburu. There are reckoned to be about 20,000 Ogiek in all. They have always lived by gathering wild plants and hunting, but most of all they are famous as collectors of wild honey from beehives in the high branches of the forest trees. As well as eating this honey themselves, they trade it with neighbouring peoples living outside the forest. They are experts in medicinal forest herbs: for instance they use the bark and twigs of Lemeyuet (*Ozoroa reticulata*) which are boiled and drunk to treat diarrhoea and stomach pains, and they use the juice of Leblebondet (*Commelina benghalensis*) which is squeezed on sore eyes.

The Ogiek used to dress in the hide of the animals they hunted and in their chilly mountain climate were glad of fur cloaks made from hyrax skins. Nowadays, the cloaks are worn for public occasions as a form of national dress. Some Ogiek living deep in the forest still live by hunting and gathering; others now have small vegetable plots and livestock. Few now live in the traditional oval-shaped hut woven out of branches by the women. But for all Ogiek, bee-keeping and collecting honey remains central to their way of life.

As a hunter-gatherer people they are looked down on by their cattle-herding neighbours. (They are also known as *Dorobo*, from the Maasai word 'Iltorobo' meaning 'without cattle', with the inference that they are therefore poor.) When the British carved areas of Kenya into tribal reserves, the Ogiek were excluded as they lived in small scattered groups over large areas and did not appear to have any property. Ever since, governments have

The Kenyan government proposed the excision of 65,750ha of forest reserves for private use in 2001, (thought by some to be a political move to canvas favour prior to the election in 2002) resulting in an outcry from environmentalists. In retaliation, a hard-hitting advertising campaign ran in the national press, showing the snow-less craggy peaks of Mount Kenya surrounded by desert – a stark reminder to Kenyans that water is the source of life, and that the forests are vital water catchment areas. The environmental impact of deforestation is potentially devastating. For example the headwaters of the Mara River are in the Mau Forest.

The **Kenya Forests Working Group**, an umbrella body for individual organisations and non-governmental groups (NGOs), has worked to promote sustainable use of forests through sound conservation and management and lobbies the government. Encouragingly, there are a number of tree-planting projects throughout the country, together with sustainable charcoal-making from fast-growing plantations. Water catchment schemes at community level are putting forward practical means of conserving water so that those downstream do not suffer unduly. It remains to be seen whether this is enough to combat the pace of deforestation.

ECOTOURISM
What is ecotourism?

The term ecotourism is bandied about – but what does it actually mean? A variety of definitions seem to be made: some consider it to be nature tourism, others green tourism, yet others a marketing jargon for being politically correct and caring about the environment – the token gesture of the notice in the hotel room asking you not

tried to evict them from the forest, under the pretext of 'protecting the environment' from these people, who have, in fact, always occupied it sustainably. So far the Ogiek have always made their way back.

The Ogiek today are still being thrown out of their forests. Much of the forest is 'gazetted', ie: theoretically forbidden for human occupation. Other schemes would open it for settlement, but those who benefit are mostly not the Ogiek, but developers such as tea planters and logging companies, along with settlers from elsewhere in the country. Much of the forest has been cut down, with the loss of wildlife and medicinal herbs. It also threatens Kenya's environment, as the Mau Forest is a vital water catchment area. The Ogiek are determined to defend their right to live in their forests. They have formed themselves into a number of groups under the umbrella organisation, the **Ogiek Peoples National Assembly** (PO Box 12069, Nakuru; email: ogieknet@cratornet.com).

As one elder said: 'We the Ogiek do not like the forest to be opened. It was our hospital where the herbs were. When we wanted an animal, we took just one, not all at once. We did not kill a lot of animals; the time we hunted was also when we were harvesting honey. The ancestors left the forest to us – we are their children. We ask the government to stay in harmony and peace with us and give us our rights.'

Note Encouragingly, the new NARC government included representatives from the Ogiek community in discussions on the new constitution held during 2003.

Further information is available from Survival International on www.survival-international.org.

to leave your towel on the floor unless it needs washing, or the tour operator's brochure printed on recycled paper. These terms can all be included under the ecotourism banner, but ecotourism is more embracing: it's the big picture of tourism playing its part in helping to conserve the environment and bringing financial benefits to local communities. It also integrates you, the tourist, into the equation, placing an emphasis on respecting the local people and their cultural differences, the wildlife and the environment.

The International Ecotourism Society (TIES) defines ecotourism as, 'Responsible travel to natural areas that conserves the environment and sustains the well-being of local people.' It's a broad and challenging concept and is now recognised as a means to enhance and maintain biodiversity and to bring sustainable development to local communities, protecting the natural and cultural heritage for future generations. These are vital issues in Kenya, where tourism is particularly dependent upon continuing to draw international visitors to see the wildlife. As a result the forward-thinking players in the Kenyan tourism industry have rallied to form the **Ecotourism Society of Kenya** (ESOK), recognising the role that ecotourism can play, and also that for it to be successful it must be managed in a businesslike manner. It's an ethos that can be applied across the travel industry, looking at a whole range of issues, such as waste-management techniques, using fuel efficiently and from a sustainable source, boosting the local economy through buying produce, and providing employment. Importantly too, it is not limited to the size of property. Hotel groups such as Serena Hotels and Heritage have a strong ecotourism element in their operation – and many of the larger operators are playing their part in funding community projects, such as schools, in their region.

At the same time, wildlife conservation organisations have recognised the role tourism and local communities can play in conserving wildlife areas beyond the parks and reserves. The **African Wildlife Foundation** (AWF), **African Conservation Centre** (ACC), **Worldwide Fund for Nature** (WWF) and the **East African Wildlife Society** (EAWS) are brokering agreements between local communities, international donors such as the USAID's Conservation of Resources through Enterprise (CORE) and the European Union's Biodiversity Conservation Programme (BCP) and the Kenya government to develop exciting new community projects across the country. Kenya is now considered to be at the forefront of ecotourism developments in Africa.

Ecotourism Society of Kenya

Founded in 1996, the Ecotourism Society of Kenya (ESOK, PO Box 10146, 00100 Nairobi; tel: 020 331286; fax: 020 218402; email: info@esok.org; web: www.esok.org) gives a forum for defining policies and standards for Kenya's tourist industry. Its formation was prompted by concerns about the official tourism policy at the time which continued to focus on the principles of mass tourism, paying more attention to visitor numbers rather than the quality of their visit and their impact on the environment.

The society has laudable objectives, among them: promoting tourism practices which conserve the natural environment and improve the lives of local communities; providing a Members' Code of Conduct; increasing environmental awareness and putting strategies in place to mitigate the negative impacts of tourism; selecting areas suitable for ecotourism development; supporting training programmes and developing professional standards. It has linked with other like-minded professional organisations, tour operators and NGOs to host workshops, such as the Regional Conference on Ecotourism in East Africa which reported to the United Nations International Conference on Ecotourism held in Quebec in 2002.

Perhaps its most important initiative is the **ESOK Eco-rating Scheme** launched at the end of 2002, a voluntary scheme for promoting sustainable tourism development. Currently only open to accommodation establishments, there are plans to extend the scheme to include tour operators and travel agents and, finally, destinations. The rating will essentially give an industry stamp of approval for quality assurance and a benchmark for regulating ecotourism.

HUMAN–WILDLIFE CONFLICT

While tourists flock to Kenya to see the wildlife, spare a thought for the people whose livelihoods can be affected by elephants trampling their crops or lions killing their livestock. For them, wildlife is a menace. After all, what compensation do they get for flattened crops or a dead cow – and it doesn't always stop there, for people run the risk of being killed by elephant or mauled by lion when protecting their property. This does not bode well for the wildlife either, as elephants get speared, and predators poisoned.

The main reason for the increase in conflict between people and wildlife is the population growth over the past 40 years (it stood at 8 million in 1963 and is now over 30 million). At the same time, changes in land use designation from national reserves to national parks impacted badly on the local people. The situation in Amboseli was a classic example, where land was accessible to the Maasai pastoralists when it was made a national reserve in 1948, but when it was gazetted as a national park in 1974, legislation dictated that neither people nor their animals were permitted in the park. This resulted in the Maasai being exempted from their main source of water in the dry season, and understandably initiated a burning resentment towards wildlife and the government. Promises of compensation were not forthcoming, and money from the park gates went direct to government coffers. It appeared that the government cared more about the wildlife than the people. This resulted in the Maasai venting their fury on the animals and they speared 75% of Amboseli's rhino during a bleak period in the 1980s and early 1990s. Their logic ran, if there was no wildlife, then there would be no tourism, and they would be able to use the land that they believed rightly belonged to them.

In recent years changes in lifestyle have taken place: nomadic pastoralists have become less transient. Some now live in semi-permanent settlements in areas which were previously a free range for wildlife, turning to small-scale cultivation, growing crops to supplement their income. In many places this has proved too tempting for elephants who have developed a penchant for onions. There is a flourishing bushmeat trade, catching animals in wire snares and selling the meat predominantly to the local market. And there are changes in ownership from communal land to individual tenure, with the inevitable threat of more land being fenced. For the wildlife, the squeeze is on. Following the traditionally safe migration routes in the game dispersal areas linking the parks and reserves is increasingly becoming a hazard as they compete against human encroachment.

On the ecological scale, these migratory routes play an important role in maintaining the viability of ecosystems and their biodiversity. Unless the migration corridors are kept open, the areas protected for wildlife will become isolated islands, the equivalent of mega-zoos, and the entirety of ecosystems will be destroyed. While the national parks receive protected status under the Kenya Wildlife Service (KWS), other means had to be found to maintain the viability of the game dispersal areas.

Community tourism

The answer lay in community tourism, involving local communities in the conservation of their natural heritage. The development of community tourism in Kenya came about via a dramatic turnaround in attitude by the government and conservationists at the end of the 1980s. Following a continental trend that had its inception in the **Communal Areas Management Programmes for Indigenous Resources (CAMPFIRE)** movement which started in Zimbabwe, it was recognised that local communities needed a reason to value wildlife. The former preservationist attitude prevalent among conservationists took on a pragmatic approach to work with local people as allies – after all, if local people benefited from wildlife, it was then in their own interests to look after it, which in turn would preserve the wildlife habitat. Government policy stepped into line with ecotourism objectives and local communities which were previously sidelined became included in the wildlife and tourism equation. The **Kenya Wildlife Service** (KWS) formed a special department, the **Community Wildlife Service** (CWS), with a remit to work with local communities living adjacent to the parks. It aims to harmonise development and conservation, with neither being at the expense of the other. Given the resentment that had built up with local communities, their work was not easy. Today, over 80% of their time is spent dealing with issues relating to wildlife conflict and winning back people's trust. Perseverance has paid off, although it's sometimes taken years of meetings with local communities to win them round.

By the mid-1990s a cluster of ecolodges were beginning to get off the ground – most were joint-venture agreements between local communities and the private sector. However in 1996, the Il Ngwesi group ranch broke ranks with the first community-owned and -run lodge. At the same time, the Kimana Community Wildlife Sanctuary opened near Amboseli, the first sanctuary owned and managed by a local community. Although some projects like Il Ngwesi have been hugely successful since they started, largely due to the support they have received from their neighbours on the Lewa Wildlife Conservancy, others like Kimana were faced with problems such as a lack of funding to keep the project going and limitations on management due to lack of training. This ultimately resulted in the Kimana Maasai community joining forces with a private operator (African Safari Club) which has an exclusive concession on the sanctuary. The community has not lost out financially, but the case illustrates some of the teething problems that came about as pastoralists were confronted with tourism management. Other problems in community tourism projects have been caused by a lack of transparency in financial transactions, with the money not always going to all members of a community.

In 2002, Shompole marked another milestone in community lodges, not only with its sophisticated style, but importantly, the joint partnership between Art of Ventures and the local Maasai community was the first to broker a deal which will ultimately transfer full ownership of a lodge to a community. At the start of the project, Art of Ventures gave the Shompole group ranch a 30% stake in the lodge, which will increase to an 80% share over nine years and to full ownership by the end of the 15-year lease.

Increasingly, there's a great emphasis in working on community tourism projects from the grass-roots level up, so that local communities are involved from the very beginning, giving them a greater sense of ownership and involvement. The four C's are commonly cited: community, conservation, capacity building (development-speak for teaching local people new skills) and commerce. A formula is evolving for developing successful community projects. This is typified by the AWF's **Conservation Service Centre** (CSC) in Nairobi, which provides a tool-kit of proven methods to guide communities through the process of creating conservation-linked business ventures. It's also recognised that ecotourism is a viable form of land use, particularly in the arid and semi-arid areas, where it can produce more than four times the income than that from domestic livestock. However, international tourism can be a fickle industry, so the CSC remit is not restricted to tourism. Other enterprises are encouraged, such as developing new markets for handicrafts, so that communities do not become totally reliant on an income from tourism.

Ecolodges and wildlife conservancies

There are over 20 community-related tourism developments in Kenya, ranging from simple self-catering *bandas* to star beds (see page 87) and the latest in 'Safari chic' ecolodges, campsites and wildlife sanctuaries. It is an interesting phenomenon that in lands where local communities traditionally lived in harmony with the wildlife, the symbiosis is again being actively encouraged. These initiatives are innovative and evolving, offering a new cultural dimension to the traditional safari and the opportunity to experience wilderness areas where there are few other tourists. Importantly, local communities have received a considerable boost from tourism which has helped to provide funding for schools, university bursaries, clinics, dams and cattle dips in areas where previously their economy was based on pastoralism or subsistence agriculture. This has seen a significant shift in attitude towards wildlife, and gradually the previous animosity is being dissipated. Wildlife numbers have increased in these new 'safe' zones and there's been a reduction in poaching, while wildlife habitats previously denuded by overgrazing are beginning

WORKING WONDERS WITH WILDLIFE

While the theory of ecotourism sounds good, with benefits for people, wildlife and the environment, getting the first community projects off the ground has involved phenomenal patience and perseverance. James Munyugi, community development officer with Lewa Wildlife Conservancy, was a game warden at Samburu National Reserve before being seconded as a community liaison officer with the Kenya Wildlife Service in 1991. As he explains, 'I had the worst time. My biggest challenge when I started this job was being sent back to Samburu. The people said, "He used to be a game warden – he's a liar, he's a chameleon, he's just changing colour." The people still remembered the establishment of game parks where they were forcefully evicted.' He had a similar experience when he held the first meeting with the Il Ngwesi community to explain about diversifying into wildlife tourism: 'One elder said, "I have a question: why are you lying to us, because we know that you want to change our group ranch into a national park? There's no way wildlife can become people's property."' The breakthrough came by spending time with the community, explaining how this development could be to their advantage.

In 2000 the Il Ngwesi Lodge brought an income of KSh1.5 million to the Il Ngwesi community, providing employment at the lodge, nursery schools, bursaries for university students, cattle dips and medical centres. The lodge has been such a financial success for the Il Ngwesi that they now value wildlife as a tourism earner. Previously livestock was regular prey to leopard, causing a considerable conflict of interests between the people's welfare and wildlife. Now, with a no-grazing zone around the lodge, wildlife has increased, the land is recovering from overgrazing, and elephant, leopard and lion are regularly seen. Munyugi beams with enthusiasm and delight when he tells me of the transition amongst the Il Ngwesi. 'At a strategic planning meeting, they said: "Is there any way we can find alternative land where we can translocate our families and leave Il Ngwesi to wildlife and tourism?" I could not believe it, as they said this without anybody's incitement.'

to recover. As a visitor, the main attraction in staying in these areas (apart from the feelgood factor from supporting a community – but let's face it, tourism, wherever it is in Kenya, provides much needed employment) is getting away from the crowds and being able to appreciate vast areas of wilderness and its wildlife, while interacting with the local people and gaining a genuine, unadulterated insight into their culture.

Ecolodges

Among the ecolodges, **Il Ngwesi** in Laikipia has been at the forefront of community tourism, being owned and managed by the Il Ngwesi Maasai, bringing them a significant income and increasing wildlife in the conservation area. It has won a cluster of awards, including an *Equator Initiative Award* at the World Summit on Sustainable Development in 2002 and a *British Airways Tourism For Tomorrow (BATTA) Award* in 1998. **Tassia Lodge,** a sister project to Il Ngwesi, opened in 2001 on the neighbouring Lekurruki group ranch. Further north, the **Sarara Tented Camp** in the Mathews Mountains is on the Namunyak group ranch and owned by the Namunyak Wildlife Conservation Trust, while **Kalacha**

Bandas in the remote and arid settlement of Kalacha are run by Gabbra women from the Kalacha Camel Improvement Group, sponsored by a Community Development Trust Fund.

In the Masai Mara, **Base Camp Masai Mara**, which opened in 1998, follows the most stringent of ecotourism principles. Operated by a Swedish company, in association with the Koyiaki group ranch, it's located next to the settlement of Talek. **Tortilis Tented Camp**, a winner of a *BATTA award* in 1996, lies dwarfed in the lee of Mount Kilimanjaro, on a group ranch concession leased to Cheli and Peacock, bordering Amboseli National Park. In the Chyulu Hills, **Ol Donyo Wuas**, a winner of a *BATTA award* in 2001, lies in the Mbirikani group ranch, overlooking Mount Kilimanjaro. Richard Bonham Safaris has a concession on the ranch, and they've formed the **Maasailand Preservation Trust** which supports a range of community projects, while plans are afoot to build a community ecolodge on another part of the ranch. In Samburu National Reserve, the **Elephant Watch Safari Camp** opened in 2001, on the western edge of the reserve on land leased from the Samburu County Council. Stealing the glory for the most chic design among ecolodges, **Shompole Lodge** won a *Worldaware Business Award* in 2003 for combining the entrepreneurial realities of the tourism industry with a genuine community-business partnership.

Full details of the ecolodges are given in the respective regional chapters under the *Where to stay* section.

Wildlife conservancies

There are several community wildlife sanctuaries and conservancies, some of which also provide accommodation. One of the first community wildlife sanctuaries was **Mwaluganje Elephant Sanctuary** which opened in 1995 near Kwale on the south coast. Here, there was a severe human–wildlife conflict between the Duruma people and migrating elephants. After several years of negotiation the Duruma community agreed to set aside 24,000ha between the Shimba Hills and Mwaluganje Forest national reserves, a regular migration corridor for elephants. The area was fenced off, preventing the elephants from crop-raiding and the community has benefited from employment and income generated by the sanctuary and the Mwaluganje Elephant Camp. Near Amboseli, the **Kimana Community Wildlife Sanctuary** opened in 1996. At the time it was the first sanctuary to be owned and run a local community – in this case, the Maasai of the Kimana Tikondo group ranch. Covering an area of 40km^2 in an important game dispersal area linking the Amboseli and Tsavo ecosystem, it took two years of discussion with the sceptical 800 group ranch members, to set aside the land for wildlife. Subsequently it's been renamed the Kilimanjaro-Kimana Game Sanctuary, after the group ranch went into partnership with the African Safari Club. The **Selenkay Conservation Area** was formed in 1997 on the Eselenkei Maasai group ranch lying to the north of Amboseli National Park in an important game dispersal area where elephant migrate through from Tsavo to Amboseli. It's a joint venture between the community and Porini Ecotourism who have leased 6,000ha of the 81,000ha group ranch to form a conservation area. Their emphasis lies in wildlife management, combined with a small, private tented camp which provides employment and additional income through a bed-night levy, a percentage of the nightly rate, which is given to the community. An access road, 50km of viewing tracks and three waterholes are now established. Porini has assisted the community through repairing their wind pump, deepening a waterhole for livestock, donating funds to the nursery and primary school and providing uniforms for the Community Game Scouts. Now there is no longer snaring or spearing of animals on the group ranch land, and for the first time in many years, elephants are safe traversing the lands of Eselenkai. In the Rift Valley, the **Kigio Wildlife Conservancy** was founded in 1998 on a community-owned 1,500ha dairy farm near Naivasha and now has a small herd of Rothschild's giraffe. It too has an ecolodge – the Malewa River Lodge. On the Laikipia Plateau, the **Lewa Wildlife Conservancy,** covering an area of 18,000ha, is a refuge for black and white rhino, Grevy's zebra and sitatunga antelope. It is a major force in northern Kenya for conserving wildlife and involving local communities in tourism. In southern Kenya, on the Tanzanian border, **Shompole Conservancy** (part of the partnership as outlined above with Shompole Lodge) is a 14,000ha area set aside for wildlife within the 56,700ha owned by the Shompole group ranch.

A new precedent has been set in the Masai Mara National Reserve, where the Transmara County Council has employed a private company, the **Mara Conservancy**, to manage the Mara Triangle section of the reserve. This has made a dramatic impact since its inception in 2001 through improved management and infrastructure, combating poaching and increasing revenue.

On a larger scale, the **Tsavo-Kasigau Wildlife Corridor** is a joint venture between private, government and community landowners covering 154,000ha, made up of some 50 ranches. The area stretches from Tsavo East National Park, through the Taru Desert to Tsavo West National Park, along a migration corridor used by elephant and lion. In Laikipia, the **Naibung Conservancy** is a joint venture between nine community group ranches covering an area of 8,000ha where it's planned to develop ecotourism activities.

Full details of the community sanctuaries and conservancies are given in the respective regional chapters under the *What to see and do* sections.

Wildlife organisations

Kenya has a plethora of organisations working to conserve wildlife and the environment. Among these are:

Kenya Wildlife Service (KWS) PO Box 40241, Nairobi; tel: 020 602345, email: info@kws.org; web: www.kws.org

African Conservation Centre (ACC) Langata Rd, Box 15289, Nairobi; tel: 020 891360; fax: 020 891751, email: info@acc.or.ke

African Wildlife Foundation (AWF) British American Centre, Mara Ragati Rd, PO Box 48177, 00100, Nairobi; tel: 020 710367; fax: 020 710372; email: awfnrb@awfke.org; web: www.awf.org

Born Free Foundation 3 Grove House, Foundry Lane, Horsham, West Sussex RH13 5PL, UK; tel: 01403 240170; fax: 01403 327838; email: info@bornfree.org.uk; web: www.bornfree.co.uk

The David Sheldrick Wildlife Trust 1 Hunterfield Park, Gorebridge, Midlothian EH23 4AY, UK; tel: 01875 821957; email: cath_mills@hotmail.com; web: www.sheldrickwildlifetrust.org

East African Wildlife Society (EAWS) PO Box 20110, 00200 Nairobi; tel: 020 574145; fax: 020 570335; email: eawls@kenyaweb.com; web: www.eawildlife.org

Elsamere Conservation Centre PO Box 4, Naivasha; tel: 050 2655; fax: 050 21074; email: elsa@africaonline.co.ke

Friends of Conservation (FOC) PO Box 74901, Nairobi; email: foc@nbnet.co.ke; web: www.foc-uk.com

The Gallmann Memorial Foundation PO Box 63704, Nairobi; tel: 020 521220/520799; fax: 020 521220; email: info@gallmannkenya.org; web: www.gallmannkenya.org

International Fund for Animal Welfare (IFAW) PO Box 25499, Nairobi; tel: 020 570540; fax: 020 574506; email: info@ifaw.org; web: www.ifaw.org

The Kenya Forests Working Group c/o EAWS, PO Box 20110, 00200 Nairobi; tel: 020 574145; fax: 020 570335; email: eawls@kenyaweb.com; web: www.eawildlife.org

Laikipia Wildlife Forum PO Box 764, Nanyuki; tel: 062 31600; fax: 062 31600; email: info@laikipia.org; web: www.laikipia.org

Lewa Wildlife Conservancy PO Box 10607, 00100, Nairobi; tel: 020 607893; fax: 020 607197; email: info@lewa.org; web: www.lewa.org

Mpala Research Centre PO Box 555, Nanyuki; fax: 0176 32750; email: info@mpala.org; web: www.nasm.si.edu/mpala

Nature Kenya PO Box 44486, GPO 00100, Nairobi; tel: 020 749957; fax: 020 741049; email: office@naturekenya.org; web: www.naturekenya.org

Save the Elephants PO Box 54667, 00200 Nairobi; tel: 020 891673; fax: 020 890441; email: save-eleph@africonline.co.ke; web: www.save-the-elephants.org

Taita Discovery Centre Savannah Camps and Lodges, PO Box 48019, Nairobi; tel: 020 222075; fax: 020 330698; email: eaos@africaonline.co.ke; web: www.TaitaDiscovery.com

Tusk Trust 116 Battersea Business Centre, 103 Lavender Hill, London SW11 5QL, UK; tel: 020 7978 7100; fax: 020 7223 2517; email: tim@tusk.org; web: www.tusk.org

The World Conservation Union (IUCN) PO Box 68200, Nairobi; tel: 020 890605; fax: 020 890615; email: mail@iucnearo.org; web: www.iucn.org/ourwork/earo.htm

World Wide Fund for Nature (WWF) ACS Plaza, Lenana Rd, PO Box 62440, Nairobi; tel: 020 577355; fax: 020 577389; email: eafrica@wwfearpo.org; web: www.panda.org

ℛ RAINBOW TOURS

Specialists in tailor-made travel to **KENYA**, we offer guided small group safaris and an imaginative choice of private trips for the independent-minded traveller.

- **Fantastic game viewing:** Amboseli, Meru, the Laikipia Plateau, the Masai Mara
- **Spectacular birding:** Sokoke Forest, Hells Gate & the Rift Valley Lakes
- **Amazing beaches:** Lamu, Watamu, Mombasa
- **Family Holidays:** memorable safari & beach holidays

Call 020 7226 1004
www.rainbowtours.co.uk
305 Upper Street, London N1 2TU
Email: info@rainbowtours.co.uk

ATOL 4563 PROTECTED

AiTO THE ASSOCIATION OF INDEPENDENT TOUR OPERATORS

We also feature: Tanzania, Uganda, Rwanda, Ethiopia, South Africa, Botswana, Namibia, Madagascar, Seychelles and Reunion.

Planning and Preparation

This chapter covers general practical information on Kenya, from where to get tourist information to travel requirements, travelling to and around the country, and accommodation. Information on safaris and special interests and activities is given in *Chapters 5* and *6* respectively, while aspects relating to health and safety issues are covered in *Chapter 7*.

TOURIST INFORMATION

The **Kenya Tourist Board** offices overseas are well provided with tourist literature and a comprehensive map which is more than adequate for people visiting the country on an organised tour. At the time of writing these are restricted to Europe and North America. Elsewhere, the respective **Kenya embassies** and **high commissions** can supply tourist information. The Kenya Tourist Board has an excellent website: **www.magicalkenya.com**.

Surprisingly, within Kenya, there's limited tourism information available. The Kenya Tourist Board in Nairobi is not in a mainstream location, while the tourist information centres at Mombasa, Diani and Malindi at the coast, although helpful, have limited information to take away. The Ministry of Tourism and Information is more concerned with tourism policy, and information is routed through the Kenya Tourist Board.

Kenya Tourist Board offices
Overseas
Canada 1599 Hurontario St, Suite 100, Mississauga, Ontario L5G 4S1; tel: +1 905 891 3909; email: contact@kenyatourism.ca
Germany c/o The Mangum Group, Herzogspitalstrasse 5, D-80331 Munich; tel: +49 08923 662194; email: think@mangum.de
Italy Adam & Partner Italia, Via Salaino 12, 20144 Milano; tel: +39 02 481 02361; fax: +39 02 433 18385; email: kenya@adams.it
Netherlands Travel Marketing Company (TMC), Leliegracht 20, 1015 DG Amsterdam; tel: +31 020 4212668; fax: +31 020 670 5357; email: kenia@travelmc.com
Spain CS Développement, c/Tuset 10- 3°4ª – 08006 Barcelona; tel: +34 093 292 0655; fax: +34 093 415 4577; email: kenya@ketal.com
UK Hills Balfour, Notcutt House, 36 Southwark Bridge Rd, London SE1 9EU; tel: +44 020 7922 1100; email: kenyatouristboard@hillsbalfour.com
USA Carlson Destination Marketing Services, PO Box 59159, Minneapolis, MN 55459-8257; tel: +1 866 44 KENYA; fax: +1 763 212 2533; email: infousa@MagicalKenya.com

In Kenya
Kenya Tourist Board KenyaRe Towers, Ragati Rd, Upper Hill, PO Box 30630, Nairobi; tel: 020 724044; fax: 020 724169; info@kenyatourism.org; web: www.magicalkenya.com

Ministry of Tourism and Information Utalii House, Off Uhuru Highway, PO Box 30027, Nairobi; tel: 020 333555

Kenyan embassies and high commissions overseas

Australia 6th Floor, QBE Bldg, 33–35 Ainslie Av, PO Box 1990 Canberra, ACT 2601; tel: +61 2 474788/474722; telex: 071 62050 TRAVELEX; email: kenrep@dynamlte.com.au

Belgium 1–5 Av de la Joyeuse Entrée, Brussels 1040; tel: +32 2 3401040; fax: +32 2 3401051; telex: 046 62568 KENYAB; email: mission.kenya@itu.ch

Canada 415 Laurier Av East, Ottawa, Ontario K1N 6R4; tel: +1 613 563 1773; fax: +1 613 233 6599; telex: 053-4873; email: kenrep@on.aibn.com

China 4 Sanlitun Xiliujie, Beijing; tel: +86 10 6532 3381; fax: +86 10 6532 1770; email: koenyla@luol.cn.net

Democratic Republic of Congo 5002 Av Ouganda, Kinshasa; tel: +243 12 33205

Egypt 20 Boulos Hanna St, Dokki, PO Box 362, Cairo; tel: +20 2 345 3907/ 3628; telex: 091 92021; email: embaci@hotmail.com

Ethiopia Fikre Mariam Rd, PO Box 3301, Addis Ababa; tel: +251 610033; telex: (Q980) 21103-KENYAREP ADDIS ABABA; email: kenya.embassy@telecom.net

France 3 rue Freycinet, Paris 75116; tel: +33 1 45533500; fax: +33 1 45539532; email: kenparis@wanadoo.fr

Germany Villichgasse 17, Bonn 5300; tel: +49 228 935800 fax: +49 228 9358050; telex: 041 885570 KENIA D; email: amb@embassy-kenya.bn.uu

India 66 Vasant Marg, Vassant Vihar, New Delhi 11507; tel: +91 11 614 6537; fax: +91 11 6146550; telex: 081 312797; email: kenredel@ndf.vsnl.net.in

Iran Golshar Street, off African Av, Tehran 46; tel: +98 21 2057479; fax: +98 21 2053372; telex: 213752; email: kenemteh@irtp.com

Japan 3-24-3 Yakumo, Meguro-ku, Tokyo 152; tel: +81 3 4794006; fax: +81 3 723 4488; telex: 072 02422378; email: kenrepj@ma.kcom.ne.jp

Namibia 134 Leutwein St, PO Box 2889, Windhoek; tel: +264 61 226836; fax: +264 61 908823; telex: 823 WK; email: keny-net@iwwn.com.na

Netherlands Nieuwe Parklaan 21, Den Haag 2597 LA; tel: +31 70 3504215; fax: +31 70 3553594; email: kenre@dataweb.nl

Nigeria 52 Yinkan Abayomi Dr, PO Box 6464, Lagos; tel: +234 1 682768/685531; fax: +234 1 685532; email: kenya@alpha.linkserve.com

Pakistan H No10, St No 9, F 7/3, Islamabad; tel: +92 51 2279540; fax: +92 51 2279541; email: kenreppk@apollo.net.pk

Russian Federation Bolshaya Ordinka, Dom 70, Moscow; tel: +7 095 2373462; telex: 064 413495

Rwanda PO Box 1215, Kigali; tel: +250 82774; fax: +250 86234; telex: 0909 598

Saudi Arabia PO Box 94358, Riyadh; tel: +966 1 4882484/4881238; telex: 0495 401751; email: kenya@shaheer.net.sa

Somalia PO Box 618, Mogadishu; tel: +252 1 80857; telex: +0900 610

South Africa 302 Brooks St, Melo Park, Pretoria 0081; tel: +27 12 362 2249; fax: +27 12 362 2252; email: kenep@pta.lia.net

Sudan Opposite Dolly Hotel, PO Box 8242, Khartoum; tel: +249 11 940386; fax: +249 11 43758; telex: 0894 22436

Sweden BigerJarlsgatan 37 2tr, Stockholm; tel: +46 8 218300; telex: 051 17811; email: kenya.touristoffice@swipnet.se

Tanzania 14th Floor, NIC Investment House, Samora Avenue, PO Box 5231, Dar es Salaam; tel: +255 51 2112958; telex: 41700 KENREP TZ; email: khc@raha.com

Uganda Plot 60, Kira Rd, Kampala; tel: +256 41 31861

United Arab Emirates PO Box 3854, Abu Dhabi; tel: +971 2 666300; fax: 971 2 652827; telex: 24244 KENREP EM; email: kenyarep@emirates.net.ae

UK 45 Portland Pl, London WIN 4AS; tel: +44 20 7636 2371-5; fax: +44 20 7323 6717; telex: 051 262551; email: kcomm45@aol.com
USA 2249 R St NW, Washington DC 20008; tel: +1 202 387 6101; fax: +1 202 462 3829; telex: 197376; email: klqy53@prodigy.com
Zambia 5207 United Nations Av, PO Box 50298, Lusaka; tel: +260 1 250722; fax: +260 1 25389; email: kenhigh@zamnet.zm
Zimbabwe 95 Park Lane, PO Box 4069, Harare; tel: +263 4 790847; telex: 0907 4266; email: kenhicom@africaonline.co.zw

RED TAPE
Passport
A valid passport with a minimum of six months left to run is required for entering the country.

Visas
Visas are not required by citizens of the Republic of Ireland and Commonwealth countries *with the exception of* Antigua, Bermuda, Guyana, India, South Africa (for visitors staying more than 30 days), Sri Lanka and the United Kingdom. All nationals of other countries require a visa. The fee for a single-entry visa is US$50, valid for three months (and extendable for another three) which can be obtained prior to departure, at the airport as you arrive, or at border crossings. If arriving by air, this may entail a long wait and is not recommended if your flight arrives late at night, although personally I've never experienced long queues. A multiple-entry visa costs US$100 for a year, and a transit visa US$20. If you plan to get a **visa on arrival**, proceed to the visa desk first. Forms are available, and it's preferable to have US$50 in cash. It is possible to pay in sterling, but this complicates matters with change, so can slow down the procedure. At the time of writing, payment in euros was not acceptable, but this may well be revised. Your immigration can be processed at the same time as the visa, so you do not need to queue again at the immigration desk. **Visas in advance** – both multiple and single entry – can be obtained at some Kenyan high commissions. Approach them directly for a form, or alternatively you may download a form from the Kenya Airways website, www.kenya-airways.com or the Kenya Association of Tour Operators website, www.katokenya.org. You will need to send a couple of passport photographs and allow six weeks minimum for processing. If wishing to visit other countries in East Africa – Uganda, Tanzania (includes Zanzibar) – within the three-month period, ask for a **visitor's pass** so that you can re-enter Kenya without having to get a new visa. But be aware visa requirements can change, so it is always best to check with your local Kenyan embassy, high commission or consulate, or with your travel agent, prior to travel. Visa extensions can be given at immigration offices in Nairobi, Mombasa, Kisumu and Lamu but some waiting may be involved.

Health certificates
A yellow fever vaccination certificate is required if arriving in Kenya from an infected area, but no other vaccinations or immunisations are required by law in Kenya, although some are advisable. For further details see *Chapter 7, page 139*.

Imports and exports
Used personal effects and unexposed films are permitted. There is a duty-free allowance of a one-litre bottle of alcohol, 200 cigarettes, 50 cigars, half a litre of perfume, still and video cameras.

Cameras and video equipment for *commercial* use require a Customs Bond or a cash deposit equivalent to their value for the period items are in the country.

Refundable deposits are sometimes required for the temporary import of radios, tape recorders and similar equipment, including musical instruments. Before travelling, seek clarification from your local Kenyan embassy or consulate.

The international CITES convention prohibits the movement of certain wildlife items (such as ivory) across international borders. Do consider the ethics involved in buying animal and shell products. Also, be aware that while you might be able to carry items like sealed meat packages and fruit from Kenya, they may be refused entry at your destination.

If you are planning to go bird shooting and want to bring a gun to Kenya, check out the firearms certificate procedure with the organisers of the safari (see page 110).

Departure taxes

On **international flights** there's a departure tax of US$20, payable in convertible currency or the equivalent in Kenyan shillings. This is often already included in the cost of a return ticket. On **internal flights** a departure tax of KSh300 applies.

GETTING THERE
By air

Nairobi is at the hub of East African air transport, with connections to many African, European and Asia-Pacific cities. In addition there are international flights to Mombasa.

From Europe

The flight to Kenya is about eight hours, depending on the departure point. Mombasa and Nairobi are served by scheduled services and some charter flights. Prices vary. British Airways economy fares from London to Nairobi range from around £460–860.

From the Americas

There are daily connections via Johannesburg, London, Amsterdam or Addis Ababa with South African Airways (SAA), British Airways (BA), KLM/Kenya Airways and Ethiopian Airways. A flight from New York via London with BA takes about 16 hours, while with SAA via Johannesburg the journey time is around 21 hours. British Airways economy fares from New York JFK range from US$1,184–3,530; or with SAA from US$1,470–3,300.

From elsewhere

Kenya Airways and Emirates operate daily direct services to Dubai while Gulf Air and Oman Air fly twice weekly to Abu Dhabi, Bahrain and Muscat. Kenya Airways and Air India fly direct to Mumbai. All these centres provide onward connections to Asia. Kenya Airways, SAA (daily) and BA (five times a week) all fly to Johannesburg, from where there are connections to other South African cities and Australasia. For example, from Sydney to Nairobi with SAA the total journey time is 21 hours. Flights with SAA from Sydney to Nairobi cost from US$2,400–2,700.

Multi-country itineraries

In addition, there are regular scheduled flights from Kenya to Uganda, Tanzania (including Zanzibar), Ethiopia, Seychelles and southern Africa making multi-country itineraries feasible.

DIRECT INTERNATIONAL FLIGHTS TO KENYA

Nairobi

	To	From	Airline (Code)
Abu Dhabi	WFSa	FSu	Gulfair (GF)
Addis Ababa	Daily	Daily	
		2x on MThFSa	Ethiopian Airways (ET)
		TuWThFSu	Kenya Airways (KQ)
Amsterdam	Daily	Daily	Kenya Airways (KQ)
	Daily	Daily	KLM (KL)
Brussels	Daily ex Thu	Daily ex Thu	SN Brussels (SN)
Dar es Salaam	W	MW	Ethiopian Airways (ET)
	Daily	Daily	Air Tanzania (KQ/TC)
	WFSaSu	WFSaSu	Gulfair (GF)
Dubai	Daily	Daily	Kenya Airways (KQ/KL)
	Daily	Daily	Emirates (EK)
Entebbe	4 per day	4 per day	Kenya Airways (KQ)
	MWThFSu	MWThFSu	East African Airlines (QU)
	MWF	MWF	Emirates (EK)
	TuThSa	TuThSa	Ethiopian Airways (ET)
	TuWSa	TuWSaSu	Africa One (Y2)
Harare	MWFSa	MWFSa	Kenya Airways (KQ)
	MWFSa	MWFSa	British Airways (BA)
	WSa	Wsa	Air Malawi (QM)
	ThSa	ThSu	Air Zimbabwe (UM)
Johannesburg	Daily	Daily	Kenya Airways (KQ)
	Daily	Daily	South African Airways (SA)
	MWFSaSu	MWFSaSu	British Airways (BA)
Kilimanjaro	Twice daily	Twice daily	Alliance Express Rwanda (PW)
	Twice Daily	Twice daily	Regional Air (from Wilson) (QP)
London	Daily	Daily	British Airways (BA)
	Daily	Daily	Kenya Airways (KQ)
Mumbai		Daily	Kenya Airways (KQ)
		MF	Air India (AI)
Paris	Tu	W	Corsair International (SS)
Seychelles (Mahe)	ThSu	ThSu	Kenya Airways (KQ)
Zanzibar	Daily	Daily ex F	Kenya Airways (KQ)
	Daily ex Tu	Daily ex Tu	Regional Air (from Wilson) (QP)
Zurich	MWFSa	TuThSaSu	Swiss International (LX)

Mombasa

	To	From	Airline (Code)
Dar es Salaam	Daily	Daily	Precision Air (PW)
	Daily ex Su	Daily	Air Tanzania (TC)
Frankfurt	F	Su	Condor Flugdienst (DE)
Zanzibar	MWFSaSu	MWFSaSu	Regional Air (QP)
	Daily	Daily	Alliance (PW)
	Daily	Daily	Kenya Airways (KQ)
	Daily	Daily	Air Tanzania (TC)

Airline listings

The following gives contact details for airline offices within Kenya and overseas:

Air India
Kenya PO Box 43006, Nairobi; tel: 020 334662; fax: 020 340582
India Air India Bldg, 218 Backbay Reclamation, Nariman Point, Mumbai 400021; tel: +91 22 202 4142; fax: +91 22 202 4897; web: www.airindia.com

Air Tanzania
Kenya PO Box 20077, Nairobi; tel: 020 214936
Tanzania PO Box 543, ATC House, Ohio St, Dar-es-Salaam; tel: +255 22 211 0245; fax: +255 22 211 3114; web: www.airtanzania.com

Air Zimbabwe
Kenya Chester House, Koinage St, PO Box 41127, Nairobi; tel: 020 339522; fax: 020 331983
South Africa Finance House, Ernest Oppenheimer Dr, Bruma Lake Office Pk, Bruma Pk, Johannesburg 2000; tel: +27 11 615 7017; fax: +27 11 615 5635
UK Colette House, 52–55 Piccadilly, London W1V 5AA; tel: +44 20 7491 0009; fax: +44 20 7491 3164; web: www.airzimbabwe.com
Zimbabwe Head Office, PO Box AP1, Harare Airport, Harare; tel: +263 4 575111; fax: +263 4 575068

British Airways
Kenya International House, 11th Floor, Mama Ngina St, Nairobi; tel: 020 334440, 020 244430; fax: 020 217437 or Trade Bank House, PO Box 90045, Mombasa; tel: 041 312427
UK Waterside, PO Box 365, Harmondsworth, West Drayton UB7 0GB; tel: +44 20 8738 5000; reservations: 0845 7733377; other queries: 0845 7799977; web: www.britishairways.com
United States 1-800-AIRWAYS (toll free)

East African Safari Air
Kenya Wilson Airport, PO Box 28321-00200, Nairobi; tel: 020 600992; email: easaxhq@easal.intranets.com
UK Highbridge House, Bath Rd, Longford, Middx UB7 0EH; tel: 0870 774 5466; email: info@eastafrican.co.uk

Emirates
Kenya View Park Towers, 20th Floor, Monrovia St, PO Box 40993, Nairobi; tel: 020 211900
South Africa Sandton Office Tower, 5th Floor Sandton City, c/o 5th Av and Rivoria Rd, Johannesburg; tel: +27 11 3031900
UAE EK Headquarters, Deira, PO Box 686, Dubai; tel: +971 4 2951111; fax: +971 4 295 4826; web: www.emirates.com
UK 1st Floor, Gloucester Pk, 95 Cromwell Rd, London SW7 4DL; tel: +44 870 2432222

Ethiopian Airlines
Kenya PO Box 42901, Nairobi; tel 020 330837; fax: 020 219007; email: nboet@nbi.ispkenya.com
Ethiopia Churchill Rd, PO Box 1755, Addis Ababa; tel: +251 01 517000; fax: +251 01 611474; web: www.ethiopianairlines.com
UK 1 Dukes Gate, Acton Lane, London W4 5DX; tel: +44 20 8987 7000; web: www.flyethiopian.com

Gulf Air
Kenya PO Box 44417, Nairobi; tel: 020 241123-8, 020 219809; fax: 020 214447 or Ambalal House, Nkrumah Rd, Mombasa; tel: 041 312820
UAE Abu Dhabi; tel: +971 2 6332600; fax: +971 2 631547
UK Heathrow Airport, London; tel: +44 870 777 1717; fax: +44 20 7411 4221; web: www.gulfairco.com

Kenya Airways
Kenya Barclays Plaza, PO Box 41010, Nairobi; tel: 020 328 22000 or 020 822171; fax: 020 336252; Mombasa tel: 041 223552; fax: 041 313815; Malindi tel: 042 20237; Kisumu tel: 057 20081; web: www.kenya-airways.com
UK Bedfont Rd, Heathrow Airport, Staines, Middx TW19 7NL; tel: 017 8488 8233; fax: 017 8488 8299; email: info@kenyaairways.co.uk; web: www.kenyaairways.co.uk

KLM
Kenya Barclays Plaza, Loita St, Nairobi; tel: 020 320 74747; fax: 020 32074777; fax: 332788; web: www.klm.co.ke
Netherlands PO Box 7700 Schipol Airport, Amsterdam 1117ZL; tel: +31 20 649 9123, +31 20 648 2392; fax: +31 20 648 8391; web: www.klm.nl
UK London; tel: 08705 074074; web: www.klm.com
USA Central Airline Terminal, 100 East 42nd St (at 125 Park Av), 2nd Floor, New York, NY10017; tel: +1 800 447 4747 or 1721 K St NW, Washington DC 20006; tel: +1 800 447 4747; web: www.nwa.com

Regional Air
Kenya PO Box 30357, Wilson Airport, Nairobi; tel: 020 605150; fax: 020 605373; web: www.regionalair.net

SN Brussels Airlines
Kenya 5th Floor, Bandari Plaza, Woodvale Grove, Westlands, PO Box 43708, Nairobi 00100; tel: 020 4440735; fax: 020 4441147; email: brussels-airlines@karibunet.com
Belgium 2 Av E Mounierlaan, 2 ISO 5, Brussels 1200; tel: +32 2 723 2323; tel: +32 2 7232345; web: www.brusselsairlines.com
UK 2nd Floor, Gemini House, 10–18 Putney Hill, London SW15 6AA; tel: +44 20 8394 6000; reservations: 0870 7352345; fax: +44 20 8394 6001

South African Airlines
Kenya Lonrho House, Standard St, Mezzanine One, Jomo Kenyatta International Airport; tel: 020 227 486; fax: 020 227 488
Australia 7th Floor, 68 St George's Ter, Perth WA 6000; tel: +61 8 9216 2200; fax: +61 8 3924 1724 or 9th Floor, 5 Elizabeth St, Sydney, NSW 2000; tel: +61 2 8226 3300; fax: +61 2 8226 3342
South Africa PO Box 7778, South African Airways Towers, Johannesburg, Gauteng, SA 2000; tel: +27 11 28 1728; fax: +27 11 733 8988; web: www.flysaa.com
UK St George's House, 61 Conduit St, London W1S 2NE; tel: +44 20 7312 5000 or 0870 747 1111; fax: +44 20 7312 5009
USA 515 East Las Olas Bd, Fort Lauderdale, Florida 33301; tel: +1 954 769 5000; fax: +1 954 769 5079

Swiss International
Kenya 1st Floor, Caltex Plaza, Limuru Rd, Nairobi; tel: 020 374 6663; fax: 020 374 6663
Switzerland Bahnhofstrasse 25; tel: +41 1 564 6060; fax: +41 1 564 6640
UK Heathrow Airport, London; tel: 0845 6010956; web: www.swiss.com

By road

Entering Kenya by road is currently possible from Ethiopia, Uganda and Tanzania but *not* from Sudan or Somalia. The main road crossings are at Malaba and Busia for Uganda, Namanga, Taveta, Lunga Lunga and Isebania for Tanzania and at Moyale for Ethiopia. If bringing your own vehicle to Kenya a free three-month permit should be issued at the border provided you have a valid *carnet de passage*.

By train

There is no longer a train service from Kenya to Uganda and Tanzania.

By sea and lake

Cruise ships dock in Mombasa and there are **yacht anchorages** along the coast from Lamu to Shimoni. There are no longer **ferries** running between Mombasa and Zanzibar, and on Lake Victoria there are no scheduled ferry services with Uganda or Tanzania, although there is talk of these being revived. There are **dhows** sailing from Shimoni to Pemba in Tanzania.

Crossing borders

Provided you have all the correct documentation immigration procedure is straightforward, and you can usually get a visa at the border (see page 65 on visas). If travelling in your own vehicle you will require a carnet de passage and, when leaving the country, customs clearance, which needs to be done in advance at Customs Headquarters House in Nairobi (PO Box 40160, Nairobi; tel: 020 310900) or Mombasa (PO Box 90601, Mombasa; tel: 041 314044).

PRACTICAL INFORMATION
Public holidays

January 1	New Year's Day	October 10	Moi Day
February/March	Idd il Fitr ★	October 20	Kenyatta Day
March/April	Good Friday★★	December 12	Jamhuri Day
March/April	Easter Monday★★	December 25	Christmas Day
May 1	Labour Day	December 26	Boxing Day
June 1	Madaraka Day		

★ The Muslim Festival of *Idd il Fitr* celebrates the end of Ramadan. The date varies each year depending on the sighting of the new moon in Mecca.
★★ Dates for the Christian festival of Easter vary annually.

Note If a public holiday falls on a Sunday, the following Monday is observed as a holiday. If planning on travelling over public or school holidays, book accommodation and car hire well in advance.

Climate

For details on climate, see page 37.

Shopping and business hours

Standard shopping and business hours in Kenya are from 08.30–12.30 and 14.00–17.30 Monday to Saturday, although the majority of shops, travel agents and supermarkets remain open during the lunch hour. Most offices are open from Monday to Friday, although some government offices close early on a Friday afternoon. Many businesses work on Saturday mornings.

Electricity

The **standard voltage** throughout the country is 220–240V, with standard 13-amp three square pin plugs (same as in UK). There may be slight variations in places which have their own generator. A **travel adaptor** should accommodate a power supply of 240V running at 50Hz. For **video cameras** bring adaptor plugs for their rechargers. Most hotels, lodges and camps have charging facilities. (If going on safari in the wilds, check what facilities are available before you go.)

Time
GMT + 3 hours. As Kenya is on the Equator, daybreak is around 06.00 and dusk 18.30.

Communications
Country telephone code
The international telephone code for Kenya is +254, followed by the national telephone number, omitting the first 0.

Telephone services
Telcom Kenya provides a comprehensive **telephone service**, and new telephone codes, with some local number changes, were introduced in April 2003. (These have been incorporated in the guide as far as possible, but there may have been some refinements since then.) **Public payphones**, mostly painted yellow, are found in the major towns, with a choice of card or coin phones. Local calls cost KSh4 minimum, so have plenty of change to hand. They are usually located near the post office, which also sells phone cards. Phone calls from hotels are expensive – charges are often 100% more. Landlines in Kenya have been notoriously poor in the past, with the result that **mobile telephones** have proved to be enormously popular. There are two GSM mobile service providers – Kencell and Safaricom. Both networks are expanding, but at the time of writing had similar coverage around the main towns. If travelling independently, mobile telephones are extremely useful from a security point of view if you are driving (so long as you are within the network coverage area). Some packages include a **911 service**, which will come to your assistance in an emergency. Locally, it's possible to purchase a mobile phone with a call package from around US$80. 'Pay as you go' cards are readily available from supermarkets and mobile phone shops. Alternatively, if you have a mobile phone with a roaming connection, you can make use of Kenya's cellular networks. In remote areas, some lodges and safari operators have **satellite phones** where calls are charged in the region of US$5 a minute.

Radio services
Many camps and vehicles communicate by radio on set frequencies. Guides on game drives often converse by two-way radio alerting each other to game. On walking safaris many operators carry a two-way radio linked to camp.

Internet services
Kenya has a number of service providers, and internet services are available in most towns. Internet cafés abound and charges for surfing and sending emails are generally reasonable (from KSh1–4 a minute on average). The lines do get cut off frequently when surfing, and if planning on spending a lot of time online, it's worth asking around for a café which has a dedicated line; otherwise you could resort to using a mobile phone connection (expensive). Sending and receiving emails is straightforward, but *hotmail* accounts can be difficult to access; Yahoo is more readily accessible. In wilderness areas, a number of camps and lodges now have **bushmail**, similar to email, which can send and receive written messages only; it's useful for guests in an emergency.

Post

Posta Kenya has a good postal service for both local and international post. There are post offices and post boxes (red) in most towns, some with separate boxes for airmail. Many shops in tourist lodges and hotels sell stamps. Rates vary for letters by weight and postcards by size. Parcel services are available from larger post offices and there are poste restante services in Nairobi and Mombasa.

Media
Broadcasting

The Kenyan Broadcasting Corporation (KBC) has radio transmission in English, Swahili, Hindi and African languages.

The BBC World Service, Voice of America and Deutsche Welle all transmit into Kenya on shortwave frequencies. There are several commercial radio stations, like Capital FM.

There are locally produced television channels in English and Swahili. The news channels give a good insight into current affairs around the country, but programme choice is limited. South African based digital satellite TV with its selection of channels has become widespread throughout Kenya with many hotels providing this service and bars having big screens for the main sporting events.

The press

There are two daily English-language **newspapers**: the *Daily Nation* (web: www.nation.co.ke) and the *East African Standard* (web: www.eastandard.net), while the weekly *East African* is available in Kenya, Tanzania and Uganda. There are two Swahili newspapers, *Taifa Leo* and *Kenya Leo*. In addition to the newspapers, information on **local events** is available in **magazines** like *What's on*, *Go Places* and *Going out*, which can be picked up at the airport and hotels, and the monthly *Travel News and Lifestyle* magazine. International newspapers and magazines are readily available. *African Business* and *New African* are good for African **current affairs** and regularly cover Kenya. If you are interested in **wildlife and conservation**, two excellent quarterly magazines are the East African Wildlife Society's *Swara*, and the Environment Liaison Centre International's *Ecoforum*. Overseas, the quarterly magazine *Travel Africa* covers Africa's safari destinations.

Smartcards

The most popular **national parks** now have a smartcard system for paying entry fees. If travelling independently, take time to come to grips with this procedure; see page 41 for details. Park entry fees are charged in US dollars, payable in US dollars or the Kenya shilling equivalent. Park fees are sometimes included in the cost of a tour.

Money
Currency

The official currency is the Kenya shilling (KSh), also known as *bob*, written KSh10 or 10/-. One hundred cents make one shilling. There are 50ct, KSh1, KSh5, KSh10 and KSh20 coins, while bank notes are in denominations of KSh50, KSh100, KSh200, KSh500 and KSh1,000.

Exchange rates

In April 2003, the following exchange rates applied: US$1 = KSh76; UK£ = KSh119; euro1 = KSh81

Foreign currency

There are no restrictions on the amount of foreign currency that can be brought into Kenya and visitors can take it out again when they leave. Foreign money – cash, traveller's cheques and credit cards – can be exchanged at banks, bureaux de change (forex bureaux) and authorised hotels. The easiest currencies to exchange are US dollars, pounds sterling and deutschmarks, and, increasingly, the euro. Travellers' cheques are widely accepted, and many hotels, travel agencies, safari companies and restaurants accept credit card payment. Generally bureaux de change have better rates than the banks, while most hotels charge premium rates. You'll get a better rate for cash than for travellers' cheques. When exchanging currency, sound out not only the exchange rate, but also the commission rate. Banks can charge exorbitant commission rates, while most forex bureaux charge no commission. *Do not* exchange money on the black market. Apart from the fact that it is illegal, there have been scams in the past involving the black marketeers being in cahoots with the police (although with the clampdown on crime and corruption by the new government this may no longer be so prevalent).

It is possible to wire money to Kenya, but this is expensive. Western Union can arrange this (web: www.westernunion.com; UK: tel: 0800 833833; Ireland: tel: 1800 395395; USA and Canada: tel: 1-800 3256000; Australia: tel: 1800 649565; New Zealand: tel: 09 270 0050). These transactions normally take five days to clear, provided all the necessary bank codes are given. Alternatively, you can arrange a banker's draft, but these can take six weeks to process after leaving your account, with funds sitting in cyberspace (no doubt via a high-interest account en route) before finally arriving. It's useful to carry a credit card for instant emergency funding.

Before departure, it's best to convert any excess Kenya shillings into foreign currency as this is not so easy when you return to your home country.

Banks

There are branches of Barclays, Standard Chartered and Kenya Commercial Bank throughout the country. Official opening hours are from 09.00–15.00 Monday to Friday. Some branches open on Saturdays from 09.00–11.00. Many banks now have 24-hour ATM machines, but be vigilant when using them. The banks at Jomo Kenyatta International airport (Nairobi) and Moi International Airport (Mombasa) both run 24-hour forex services and have ATMs.

Credit cards

Visa and American Express are widely used for payments, together with Mastercard and Diner's Card. When paying by credit card, ensure that you have filled in the full amount, and the currency in which you are paying – so that Kenya shillings cannot to be amended to other currencies. Credit cards can be used for cash advances in banks, and ATM machines will accept Visa, Mastercard, Plus and Cirrus cards. Don't forget your PIN number. The rates are comparable with the commissions you would pay on travellers' cheques.

How to take your money

Common sense prevails: it's risky carrying around large amounts of money in cash, in case you are unfortunate and it gets stolen. It's sensible to take some cash in US dollars and to take the remainder in travellers' cheques, using a credit card as an emergency back up. Sometimes, you may be requested to pay in dollars, such as for park entrance fees, where the exchange rates from Kenya shillings to dollars are not always favourable. If backpacking, make sure that your moneybelt is not in evidence, and consider keeping a daily allowance separate from the bulk of your cash. Bum-bags and wallets hanging around your neck are an invitation for trouble.

Budgeting

This will, of course, depend on what you are planning to do. It's suggested that you familiarise yourself with the range of options available as outlined in *Chapters 6* and 7 which also list tour operators. If you are prepared to stay in **cheap** accommodation or camp, take local transport and eat simply; you can get by comfortably on around US$20 a day. If you are wanting to visit **game parks**, you'll need to cost in going on an organised tour (the cheapest work out at around US$90 a day all in, although you might find a cheap flying package into the park) or hiring a car (daily rate from around US$60 for 2WD and US$80 for 4WD Suzuki). Remember to factor in the expense of travel insurance, inoculations and anti-malarial prophylactics, park fees and tipping. If you wish to splash out on an expensive safari, these average out at around US$400 a day and there are plenty of options in between.

Tipping

Although tipping is not mandatory, it is customary. The amount is entirely at your discretion, but as a general rule tip KSh50 to porters, about US$3 a day for a driver-guide and US$5 a day for a safari (which gets divided between all the staff). Camps and lodges often have a staff tip-box. If in doubt about the amount to give, ask, as the going rate seems to vary. In hotels and restaurants, a service charge of 10% is often included in the bill, otherwise a 10% tip is standard.

Food and drink

Being an agricultural nation, fresh produce is readily available, with sumptuous tropical fruits and vegetables, quality meats and a variety of cuisine (see page 121). Most hotels and lodges provide European-style meals, but ethnic African food, from the staple *ugali* (thick maize meal, like solid porridge) and *nyama* (meat), accompanied by *sukuma wiki* (greens similar to chopped spinach) to the *Swahili* delicacies at the coast, with subtle spices and rich coconut sauces, is also available. If you are uncertain about the preparation of food when eating out, it's best to stick with cooked food and to avoid salads. Follow the maxim, 'boil it, peel it, cook it or forget it'. Having said that, in general, most hotels and restaurants have a reasonable standard of food preparation and hygiene. In the cheap *hotelis* (restaurants) eat cooked foods. Roast meat is a favourite among Kenyans, especially goat, and at many *nyama choma* joints you can select your meat before it is cooked, so if it's humming high, avoid it. Use your own judgement and bear in mind that typhoid and dysentery are conveyed by poor standards of hygiene. Hotels in Nairobi and Mombasa are generally safe for **drinking water**, but if in doubt, drink bottled water which is readily available. Elsewhere, unless water has been boiled and filtered, use bottled water for drinking *and* brushing your teeth. If drinking **fruit juices** get assurance that the water comes from a reputable source, and in most cases avoid having ice in your drinks. Fruit juice cartons are stocked by supermarkets. Brucellosis is present in Kenya, so drink pasteurised **milk**. **Sodas**, Coke, Sprite, Tangawizzy (ginger beer) Fanta orange, bitter lemon or straight soda are available even in remote areas (witness to the Coca-Cola-isation of the world). In Kenya *Coca-Cola* has provided quaint giant plastic Coke bottle kiosks which dispense sodas in rural areas; Pepsi is rarely seen. Kenya grows export quality **coffee** and **tea** (although to get a good cuppa in hotels, which seem to supply only insipid tea-bags, is rare). African-style tea, made from tea leaves boiled up in milk, sometimes with masala and sugar, is available from *hotelis*. Of the alcoholic drinks, Kenya breweries has won international gold awards for its Tusker lager **beer**; the other locally produced lager is Whitecap. South African beers, like Castle lager, and Guinness, are also popular. Local traditional brews are *pombe* (beer) brewed from whatever is available – millet, honey, bananas – and *changaa*, a lethal spirit-like rough brandy. Avoid the latter at all costs, as sometimes it's adulterated with other substances and has been known to kill people and cause blindness. Kenya also produces a fine **coffee liqueur**, Kenya Gold, and the white rum Kenya Cane. A fashionable cocktail is the *dawa* (medicine), a mixture of vodka, Kenya Cane, honey and lime juice. South African **wines** are ever present and particularly good value, although other wines from around the world are also available.

Security
The majority of large hotels have safety deposit boxes in the bedrooms. Others normally have a hotel safe where you can store money and valuables. Otherwise, keep money and valuables locked away. See page 156 for general information on security.

Maps
The **Kenya Tourist Board** has a comprehensive *Kenya Tourist Guide Map* of the country (see above) at 1:2,400,000 which includes large-scale maps of Nairobi, Mombasa Island, Lamu Island and the Kenya coast. For a general small-scale map of central and southern Africa, including Kenya, **Michelin** does a scale 1:4,000,000 map. For general maps, driving around the country, **Macmillan's** *Kenya Traveller's Map*, scale 1:1,750,000, is one of the best, although it has limited detail for minor roads. It combines well with the **Survey of Kenya's** *Kenya and Northern Tanzania Route Map*, scale 1:1,000,000, which is excellent for minor roads and topographic details, although some of the roads are now out of date. The **Globetrotter** series, published by New Holland, has a *Road Atlas of Kenya* which also includes plans of the main national parks. For national parks and reserves, the **Kenya Wildlife Service** (KWS) has maps for *Nairobi, Amboseli, Lake Nakuru, Mount Elgon* and *Meru National Parks*, and **Macmillan** has a *Tsavo East and West National Parks Map*. Mount Kenya Sundries publishes a glossy tourist map of the Masai Mara National Reserve, scale 1:100,000. For detailed maps of the parks and other remote areas, the Survey of Kenya has maps of scale 1:50,000. In addition, **Kenway publications** produces an *A–Z of Nairobi*. The KWS park maps are available from the shop at the park headquarters in Nairobi, and can usually be purchased at the park gates (but don't count on it; purchase before you go if possible). The Survey of Kenya office (PO Box 30046, Nairobi) is on the left on the dual carriageway shortly after the Muthaiga roundabout, on the A2 Thika road. Other maps are generally available at bookshops within Kenya, or specialist travel bookshops overseas, such as Stanfords in London (12 Long Acre, London WC2; tel: 020 7836 1321).

GETTING AROUND
While Kenya has a good basic infrastructure for travelling around, much of it is rundown, particularly the road and rail network. This has resulted in an upsurge in the provision of internal flights over the last decade.

PHOTOGRAPHY

Light is the essence of good photography. The quality and variety of light conditions in Kenya are superb, attracting amateur and professional photographers alike.

What to take

Camera and lenses There are numerous different cameras on the market for still photography. An **instamatic** will give good snapshots, and for wildlife you'll need one with a zoom lens. Increasingly popular are **digital cameras**. These are a great bonus when photographing people as you can immediately show them your pictures. (Make sure you bring enough memory, spare batteries and a charger.) As Kenya's scenery is on a grand scale, it's also fun to take a **disposable panoramic camera**, and similarly, at the coast to take a **disposable underwater camera** for snorkelling or diving. **Video cameras** are also popular (remember to bring a battery charger).

SLR cameras Serious amateurs and professional photographers are most likely to opt for an SLR camera – either manual or autofocus; some autofocus cameras have a manual option. These vary, and for the best results it's important to spend some time familiarising yourself with the camera before you travel and to carry the manual for reference in the field. Most SLRs have an inbuilt light meter; these can be sophisticated in the autofocus cameras which may have spot, centre-weighted and matrix metering. Many have a variety of exposure modes, such as shutter or aperture priority, and some also include a fill-in flash. The selection of **lenses** is a matter of personal preference – a standard 50mm, wide-angle 2.8mm and telephoto 200mm give a basic foundation, but carrying numerous lenses can be cumbersome. This can be combated by including one-zoom lenses. The 2.8mm–200mm is good for landscapes and wildlife, a 70mm–300mm for wildlife, and 35mm–70mm for people. For wildlife photography, a minimum of a 200mm lens is essential. For serious bird photography you'll need a 500mm lens. A 2 x converter is useful – a 200mm lens will then become 400mm – but the disadvantage is that it looses two light stops.

Film The choice of film is also a matter of preference – print or slide film. In Kenya, a good all-round film is 100 ISO, with some 200 ISO or 400 ISO for low light conditions. For slides, Fuji Velvia (50 ISO), Provia (100 ISO) or Sensia (100 ISO) give excellent quality. Film in Kenya costs about the same as in the UK, but it's best to bring film with you, especially if using professional film. Carry all film as hand luggage (the x-ray is less harmful). When travelling around ensure that the camera and film are kept out of direct sunlight. A small cooler bag is ideal for storing film. Bring at least twice as much film than you think you'll need. It's also vital to **protect your equipment** as dust and jolts can play havoc. Fit all lenses with a skylight filter for protection; keep them in plastic bags to keep out dust; regularly clean your camera and lenses – a

Hitching

While hitching was common in the 1970s and 1980s, it's unusual to see people hitchhiking in Kenya nowadays, probably due to the fact that local transport is so cheap. On mainstream routes it's still a practical option, but forget about trying to

compressed air canister, puffer brush and lens wipes are useful; carry all your equipment in a robust and protective bag and *do not* put it on the floor of a vehicle where it's subjected to bumps and heat. In the event of your **camera going wrong**, check the batteries first, and always carry spare batteries. If the fault is not obvious, Expo cameras in Nairobi (Central Nairobi and Westlands), provides a good service.

Taking pictures

Light As Kenya is on the Equator, the sunlight at midday is harsh, giving washed-out colours and a flat light. If you have an SLR camera, this effect can be combated to some degree by the use of a polariser filter. Even so, this does not compensate for the best natural light conditions between daybreak and ten o'clock and from four o'clock in the afternoon until dusk. This gives photographs a rich, soft, glowing light. When taking people, to get details in dark faces you'll need to open up the camera a couple of stops or use fill-in flash. For wildlife, try and catch the 'light in the eye' which will make the photograph come alive. For sunsets and sunrises you'll need a tripod or alternative support.

Camera shake This is one of the most common problems in SLR and video cameras. There are several ways to avoid camera shake. First, if you are in a vehicle, ensure that the engine is switched off. In SLR cameras when using a long lens, your camera will need support. A tripod is impractical in a vehicle, but a monopod is useful. Alternatively, support your camera on a bean bag (this can easily be made on arrival by filling an old sock with beans or rice purchased from the market.) As a rule of thumb, ensure that the shutter speed is greater than the focal length of the lens. For example, a 300mm lens will need a shutter speed of more tham 300 to ensure there's no camera shake, although lower shutter speeds can be used if you use a bean bag.

Composing a picture The 'rule of thirds' is a recognised guide to getting a good composition. Essentially, this means dividing the frame into thirds on the horizontal and upright planes, placing subjects on an upright and the horizon on a respective third. For wildlife, unless specifically taking an animal in its surroundings, you'll get best results by zooming in close. Also, check the frame of the photograph and ensure that you've not inadvertantly cut off legs, heads and so on.

Etiquette

Always ask for permission first before taking any picture involving people – market scenes and individuals. Also *do not* take photos of airports or military installations and be aware that in northern Kenya even scenes containing people's property can be an issue. In some instances you may be asked to pay for a photograph – in the Pokot area of western Kenya, this is the norm – so negotiate a fee (anything upwards of KSh50); if you are not prepared to do this, put your camera away.

hitch to Lake Turkana, as traffic is scarce, and local people are given preference. When flagging down a vehicle, gesture to slow down with the palm of your hand; 'thumbing' is considered impolite. Be aware that you may be asked to pay for a lift, and that driving standards vary enormously, so you take pot luck on safety.

By road
Countrywide buses
Buses are the cheapest form of public transport but are often overcrowded and many have a poor safety record. Akamba, Kenya Bus and Coast Bus, listed in the guide, generally have a fair safety record; ask local advice for the reputation of other bus companies. Between them, they have a network covering the main towns in Kenya, and on long journeys it's preferable to reserve seats in advance. For more localised services, you'll need to take country buses. Not all bus companies have set fares, and prices hike over school and public holidays. For more specific bus information see the respective regional chapters and the box below.

The following listing gives contact details for bus companies:

Nairobi
Akamba Public Road Services Ltd, Kitui Rd, Off Kampala Rd, 40322 Nairobi; tel: 020 221779; fax: 020 559885
Coastline Safaris Duruma Rd, Nairobi; tel: 020 245840

KENYA BUS SERVICE (KBS) TIMETABLE

		From	To	Dep am	Arr pm	Fare KSh
	1	Nairobi	Kitale	08.30	16.00	400
		Kitale	Nairobi	08.00	15.40	400
	2	Nairobi	Kapenguria	08.00	16.30	450
		Kapenguria	Nairobi	08.00	16.40	450
	3	Nairobi	Eldoret	09.00	15.00	350
		Eldoret	Nairobi	09.00	15.00	350
	4	Nairobi	Bungoma	08.00	17.30	400
		Bungoma	Nairobi	07.30	15.00	400
Eldoret	5	Nairobi	Malaba	07.00	15.45	420
route		Malaba	Nairobi	07.30	16.35	420
	6	Nairobi	Kakamega	08.00	15.30	400
		Kakamega	Nairobi	08.00	15.35	400
	7	Nairobi	Kapsabet	09.00	15.30	380
		Kapsabet	Nairobi	07.30	15.35	380
	8	Nairobi	Luanda	07.00	14.45	400
		Luanda	Nairobi	07.00	02.10	400
	9	Nairobi	Kimilili	07.30	14.00	420
		Kimilili	Nairobi	08.00	05.10	420
	1	Nairobi	Migori	08.00	15.05	400
		Migori	Nairobi	07.00	15.40	400
	2	Nairobi	Sori	06.30	15.30	420
Kisii		Sori	Nairobi	07.30	17.25	420
route	3	Nairobi	Kilgoris	07.30	16.35	400
		Kilgoris	Nairobi	08.00	16.15	400
	4	Nairobi	Homa Bay	08.30	16.50	420
		Homa Bay	Nairobi	08.00	16.35	420

Goldline Ltd Cross Rd, Nairobi; tel: 020 225279
Gusii Deluxe Ltd Opp OTC, Temple Rd, Nairobi; tel: 020 220059
Kensilver Enterprises Ltd (for Meru), PO Box 34003, Nairobi; tel: 0164 30659
Kenya Bus Services General Waruinge St, 1st Av Eastleigh, PO Box 30563, Nairobi; tel: 020 229707, hot line: 020 229605; fax: 020 240939; email: info@kenyabus.com; web: www.kenybus.com
Kisumu Express Vacational Tours & Travel, Hilton Arcade, Nairobi; tel: 020 220256
Malindi Bus Services Kumasi Rd, Nairobi; tel: 020 229662
Tawfiq Bus Services PO Box 55612, Duruma Rd, Nairobi; tel: 020 338920 (*not* recommended; poor safety record)

Mombasa
Akamba Public Road Services Kenyatta Av, 99020 Mombasa; tel: 041 316771; fax: 041 311427
Coast Bus Company Mombasa; tel: 041 90789
Coastline Safaris Mwembe Tayari Rd, PO Box 82414, Mombasa; tel: 041 220158

			Dep	Arr	Fare
		From	To	am	pm	KSh
	1	Naironi	Mumias	08.00	15.35	430
		Mumias	Nairobi	07.30	17.05	430
	2	Nairobi	Nambale	07.00	17.05	450
		Nambale	Nairobi	07.30	17.25	450
	3	Nalrobi	Oyugis	08.00	15.30	400
		Oyugis	Nairobi	08.00	15.20	400
	4	Nairobi	Bondo	09.00	15.45	430
		Bondo	Nairobi	08.00	16.00	430
	5	Nairobi	Usenge	08.00	16.45	450
		Usenge	Nairobi	08.00	17.05	450
	6	Nairobi	Bumala	06.30	14.25	430
		Bumala	Nairobi	07.30	15.35	430
	7	Nairobi	Kisumu	06.00	11:30	400
		Kisumu	Nairobi	06.30	12.30	400
Kisumu	8	Nairobi	Kisumu	10.00	15.35	400
route		Kisumu	Nairobi	09.00	15.35	400
	9	Nairobi	Kisumu	11.00	17.00	400
		Kisumu	Nairobi	12.00	18.00	400
	10	Nairobi	Busia	07.00	15.55	450
		Busia	Nairobi	07.30	16.50	450
	11	Nairobi	Siaya	08.30	16.20	430
		Siaya	Nairobi	08.30	16.45	430
	12	Nairobi	Siaya	07.00	14.50	430
		Siaya	Nairobi	07.30	15.45	430
	13	Nairobi	Ugunja	07.30	15.50	430
		Ugunja	Nairobi	07.30	16.15	430
	14	Nairobi	Sondu	07.30	14.10	400
		Sondu	Nairobi	08.00	14.45	400
	15	Naivasha	Busia	08.00	16.55	400
		Busia	Naivasha	09.00	16.20	400

Malindi
Tana Express Tana Bldg, Uhuru Rd, 181 Malindi; tel: 042 20095

City buses
City buses operate on set routes in Nairobi and Mombasa, with fares payable on board. The Nairobi Shuttle is an excellent service (see page 170). It operates a set route, is more expensive as you have a guaranteed seat, but is comfortable and clean.

Minibuses (matatus)
The cheapest form of transport are the minibuses, known as *matatus*, but be warned – they) have daredevil drivers and an appalling accident record. With names like *Trust in God*, *Scud Missile*, *Plodigal Son* and *King Diana*, and loud music blaring forth, the *matatus* – although a national icon – are a last resort. If you do travel by *matatu*, opt for a seat in the middle. Avoid the front seat (which will often be offered to you out of courtesy) as seat belts are a rarity, and – as one local advised – 'Don't panic until you hit'.

Share taxis
Also known as 'happy taxis' and 'speed taxis', these are normally Peugeot 504s where you are guaranteed a seat. They are about twice the price of the buses, but faster and more comfortable. If there are several of you, another option is to pay for the extra seats, and then you can request stops en route (within reason), which costs considerably less than if travelling by ordinary taxi. **Cross Road Travellers** and **Daily Peugeot Service** (DPS) operate reliable services.

DOMESTIC/INTERNAL SCHEDULED FLIGHTS
Kindly compiled by Angela Robertson

From	To	Frequency	Fare US$ (mid-season) Single	Return
Air Kenya				
Nairobi W	Amboseli	Daily	88	150
Nairobi W	Kiwayu	Daily	156	312
Nairobi W	Lamu	Daily	135	270
Nairobi W	Masai Mara	2 x daily	107	188
Nairobi W via	Samburu Nanyuki & Lewa Downs	Daily	120 (63 to Nanyuki)	210 (136 to Nanyuki)
Nairobi W	Samburu direct	Daily	100	210
Nairobi W	Meru/Samburu	WFSu	150 Meru, 190 Samburu, 60 Meru–Samburu	300 Meru or Samburu,
Nanyuki	Masai Mara	Daily	173	
Samburu	Masai Mara	Daily	220	
Lamu	Kiwayu	Daily	65	130

Taxis

All the main towns have taxis, but agree a fare before getting into a taxi as the meters rarely work. Take local advice on the correct rates. The state-controlled fleet of Kenatco taxis operate on a fixed tariff as do the black London taxi cabs, charging per kilometre. Other taxi services vary, from smart cars to old bangers. Check that they are insured. Taxis are widely available and often parked in the street around tourist areas, and can be ordered by hotels and restaurants. Many of the large hotels operate a minibus shuttle service to the airport and around town, and some restaurants operate a pick-up service from hotels in the evening.

Shuttlebuses

There are several shuttlebus companies operating services from Nairobi via Namanga to Arusha and Moshi (for climbing Kilimanjaro) in Tanzania, offering a twice daily service. In addition, there's a daily shuttle service between Nairobi and Mombasa (see *Nairobi* chapter, page 166, for details).

By air

Kenya has a well-developed domestic air network, Wilson Airport in Nairobi being one of the busiest airports for light aircraft in Africa with some 450 flights a day. There's the option of scheduled services or private air charters. There are **scheduled services** from Nairobi to Kisumu, Eldoret, Masai Mara, Nanyuki, Lewa Downs, Samburu, Meru, Amboseli, Mombasa, Ukunda (Diani Beach), Malindi, Lamu (Manda Island), Kiwayu and Lokichogio. With around 520 airfields, many in remote corners of the country not easily accessible by road, flying is an attractive alternative, and cuts out long journeys by road. Domestic air charter operations abound, offering

			Fare US$ (mid-season)	
From	To	Frequency	Single	Return
Blue Sky				
Nairobi W	Mara	2 x daily	105	186
Nairobi W	Nanyuki	Daily	63	n/a
Nanyuki	Samburu	Daily	44	n/a
Samburu	Mara	Daily	220	n/a
Nairobi W	Amboseli	FSu	87	150
Mombasa	Ukunda	Daily		
Ukunda	Mara	Daily		
Mombasa	Malindi	Daily		
Malindi	Mara	Daily	225	308
Malindi	Ukunda	Daily		
Flamingo				
Nairobi JK	Eldoret	Daily (2 x M–F)	54–70	108–140
Nairobi JK	Kisumu	4 x daily	40–70	80–140
Nairobi JK	Malindi	Daily	40–80	80–160
Malindi	Lamu	Daily	105–150	210–300
Nairobi W	Lokichogio	Daily	200	400
Queensway				
Nairobi W	Mara	2 x daily	104	174

Key W = Wilson Airport; JK = Jomo Kenyatta International

individual or group charters in a range of aircraft. Most charter companies charge a set rate for a flight, regardless of the number of passengers. For internal flights there is an **airport tax** of KSh300 for each journey, which is usually included in the ticket or charter costs. All travellers on internal flights will be required to carry their passport, or, in the case of Kenyan residents, their identification card.

Domestic airlines
Air Kenya
Lamu Baraka House, PO Box 376; tel: 042 33445; fax: 042 33063
Malindi Galana Complex, PO Box 548; tel: 042 30808; fax: 042 21229
Mombasa TSS Towers, Nkurumah Rd; tel: 041 229777; fax: 041 224063; and Moi International Airport, PO Box 84700, Mombasa; tel: 041 433982; fax: 041 435235
Nairobi Airkenya Aviation, Wilson Airport, PO Box 30357; tel: 020 605745; fax: 020 602951; email: info@airkenya.com; web: www.airkenya.com

Blue Sky Aviation
Mombasa Moi International Airport, PO Box 86686; tel: 041 432774/432775; fax: 041 434783; email: harunany@africaonline.co.ke
Nairobi Wilson Airport, PO Box 18518; tel: 020 601753; fax: 020 607238; email: blueskiavi@nbi.ispkenya.com; web: www.blue-sky-aviation.com

Other airlines
Eagle Aviation Wilson Airport, Langata Rd, Nairobi; tel: 020 606015
Equator Airlines Wilson Airport, Langata Rd, Nairobi; tel: 020 501360
Flamingo PO Box 19279, 00501, Nairobi; tel: 020 74340; fax: 020 74744; email: nbo@flamingoairlines.com; web: www.flamingoairlines.com
Ibis Aviation Wilson Airport, Langata Rd, Nairobi; tel: 020 602257
Queensway Air Services PO Box 42627, 0100 Nairobi; tel: 020 608622/020 502182; fax: 020 608619; email: queensway@iconnect.co.ke

Charter companies
Boskovic Air Charters Wilson Airport, PO Box 45646, 00100 Nairobi; tel: 020 501210; fax: 020 609619; email: boskyops@swiftkenya.com; web: www.boskovicaircharters.com
Tropic Air PO Box 161, Nanyuki; tel: 0176 32890; fax: 0176 32787; email: info@tropicair-travel.com; web: www.tropicair-travel.com
Yellow Wings Wilson Airport, PO Box 4714, Nairobi 00506; tel: 020 606313; fax: 020 605725; email: yellowwings@swiftkenya.com; web: www.yellowwings.com

By rail
Kenya Railways operates the rolling stock in the country, much of it in a dilapidated condition, although an upgrade is planned. The main passenger service is the night train between Nairobi and Mombasa, an enjoyable journey on a railway line steeped in history (it played a pivotal role in the development of Kenya as a British colony, with numerous dramas along the way), although most people now fly to the coast from Nairobi. Passenger train schedules are given on the opposite page, but bear in mind that other than the Nairobi–Mombasa service, trains on the other routes can be spasmodic, so check locally prior to travel. Book in advance for the Nairobi–Mombasa service, either through a local travel agent or at the station. There are now **Steam Specials** operated by a private company, who have renovated one of the old steam locomotives which originally ran on the *Lunatic Line*. See page 129 for details.

Left Male lion, *Panthera leo*, Masai Mara National Reserve (AZ)

Below Lioness drinking, Masai Mara National Reserve (AZ)

Above Young male leopard, *Panthera pardus*, resting in long grass (NG)

Above right Adult male serval, *Felis serval*, stalking prey (NG)

Below Cheetah, *Acinonyx jubatus*, on wildebeest kill, Masai Mara National Reserve (CF)

PASSENGER TRAINS
Schedules

From	To		Day	Dep	Arr
Butere	Kisumu		TuThSa	13.00	16.00
Kisumu	Butere		MWF	09.00	12.00
Nairobi	Nakuru	Kisumu	MWF	18.00	07.15
Kisumu	Nakuru	Nairobi	TuThSa	18.00	06.30
Mombasa	Voi	Nairobi	Daily	19.00	08.33
Voi	Taveta		TuWFSa	05.00	10.00

Fares (KSH)

From	To		First	Second	Economy
Nairobi	Mombasa	Adult	3,000	2,100	350
Nairobi	Voi	Adult	2,100	1,475	245
Nairobi	Taveta	Adult	–	–	325
Nairobi	Kisumu	Adult	955	525	200
Nairobi	Nakuru	Adult	485	265	105
Voi	Taveta	Adult	–	–	80
Kisumu	Butere	Adult	–	–	70

By boat

At the **coast**, the Likoni ferry for vehicles and passengers links Mombasa Island with the south coast. Yacht and dhow charters and excursions are available (see page 126), while sailing boats can be hired from beach hotels. A few commercial dhows still sail between Lamu and Mombasa. There are regular passenger ferry boats among the islands of the Lamu Archipelago. **Inland**, there are informal passenger ferry boats – *ssese* canoes – on Lake Victoria and boat trips are available on lakes Naivasha, Baringo and Turkana.

By bicycle

Cycling is an excellent way to travel around the country and to interact with local people. The only downside is the appalling driving you will encounter on the way, so avoid busy roads where possible. It can be a problem leaving your bike unattended, but usually it's possible to find somewhere safe to leave it. Take a strong padlock and chain. The other hazard is the sun. With cooling breezes at the high altitude it's easy to forget you are on the Equator, so take full precautions (gloves for hands, suncream, hat). For serious independent expeditions come well prepared with spare parts and a repair kit. There are plenty of bicycle *fundis* (mechanics) in most towns. Bikes can also be hired in tourist areas and there are a number of cycling safaris. See page 117.

Self-drive

Once you've overcome the initial impression that 'anything goes' on Kenyan roads, driving becomes an adventure, and gives the independence of being able to travel when and where you like. If coming from overseas a current **driving licence** is acceptable for three month's stay. Alternatively an **international driving licence** is valid. You'll also need to carry another means of identification. **Driving** is on the left-hand side of the road (when not avoiding potholes and corrugations) and most cars are right-hand drive. Distances are in kilometres, but due to variable road conditions, journey times can vary considerably. **Fuel** is sold by the litre and a few

DISTANCE/TIME CHART

Distances in kilometres between principal town centres.
Journey times in hours, to use as a guide only.
Eg: Nairobi–Mombasa is 487km, journey time about 6 hours;
Nairobi–Naivasha is 86km, journey time about 1½ hours.
(With thanks to Alan Dixson at Let's Go Travel)

Distance/time chart (each cell shows **kilometres** and, in italic, *journey time in hours*).

Busia
- Eldoret 168 / *2*, Embu 610 / *8*, Muranga 563 / *8*, Garissa 853 / *6.5*, Gilgil 364 / *4.5*, Isiolo 569 / *9.5*, Kakamega 95 / *2*, Kericho 218 / *3*, Kisii 258 / *3*, Kisumu 138 / *2*, Kitale 154 / *2*, Malindi 1087 / *14*, Mau Summit 275 / *3*, Meru 565 / *10.5*, Mombasa 909 / *12.5*, Nairobi 482 / *6.5*, Naivasha 396 / *5*, Nakuru 325 / *3.5*, Namanga 646 / *9*, Nanyuki 487 / *7.5*, Nyeri 508 / *6.5*, Taveta 923 / *12*, Thika 523 / *7*, Nyahururu 393 / *5*, Voi 811 / *11.5*

Eldoret
- Embu 442 / *6.5*, Muranga 394 / *6.5*, Garissa 685 / *5.5*, Gilgil 196 / *4*, Isiolo 398 / *8*, Kakamega 92 / *2.5*, Kericho 161 / *2.5*, Kisii 265 / *4*, Kisumu 122 / *2*, Kitale 69 / *1.5*, Malindi 916 / *12.5*, Mau Summit 104 / *1.5*, Meru 394 / *9*, Mombasa 798 / *11*, Nairobi 311 / *5*, Naivasha 225 / *3.5*, Nakuru 154 / *2*, Namanga 475 / *7.5*, Nanyuki 310 / *9*, Nyeri 337 / *4.5*, Taveta 752 / *10.5*, Thika 352 / *5.5*, Nyahururu 222 / *3.5*, Voi 640 / *9.5*

Embu
- Muranga 47 / *1*, Garissa 376 / *5.5*, Gilgil 337 / *5.5*, Isiolo 246 / *4*, Kakamega 521 / *9*, Kericho 478 / *7.5*, Kisii 525 / *7.5*, Kisumu 428 / *7*, Kitale 499 / *6.5*, Malindi 657 / *7.5*, Mau Summit 348 / *5*, Meru 128 / *1.5*, Mombasa 571 / *7.5*, Nairobi 131 / *2*, Naivasha 217 / *3*, Nakuru 288 / *4.5*, Namanga 295 / *4*, Nanyuki 131 / *2*, Nyeri 90 / *1*, Taveta 572 / *7*, Thika 90 / *1*, Nyahururu 203 / *2.5*, Voi 460 / *6*

Muranga
- Garissa 489 / *7*, Gilgil 253 / *5*, Isiolo 229 / *3.5*, Kakamega 465 / *8.5*, Kericho 374 / *7.5*, Kisii 602 / *8*, Kisumu 466 / *8*, Kitale 571 / *11.5*, Malindi 718 / *10.5*, Mau Summit 348 / *5*, Meru 170 / *3*, Mombasa 581 / *8.5*, Nairobi 84 / *1.5*, Naivasha 170 / *3*, Nakuru 241 / *3*, Namanga 248 / *4*, Nanyuki 106 / *2*, Nyeri 63 / *1.5*, Taveta 524 / *7*, Thika 43 / *1*, Nyahururu 178 / *2.5*, Voi 412 / *6*

Garissa
- Gilgil 481 / *9*, Isiolo 279 / *5*, Kakamega 768 / *11*, Kericho 638 / *9.5*, Kisii 742 / *10*, Kisumu 718 / *10.5*, Kitale 754 / *11*, Malindi 602 / *8*, Mau Summit 690 / *9.5*, Meru 374 / *5*, Mombasa 605 / *7.5*, Nairobi 380 / *5.5*, Naivasha 466 / *7.5*, Nakuru 437 / *6.5*, Namanga 544 / *8*, Nanyuki 423 / *5.5*, Nyeri 388 / *5*, Taveta 646 / *8*, Thika 339 / *4.5*, Nyahururu 528 / *7.5*, Voi 588 / *8.5*

Gilgil
- Isiolo 351 / *7.5*, Kakamega 253 / *5*, Kericho 229 / *3.5*, Kisii 265 / *8.5*, Kisumu 229 / *3.5*, Kitale 291 / *5*, Malindi 869 / *11.5*, Mau Summit 56 / *1.5*, Meru 294 / *6.5*, Mombasa 691 / *9*, Nairobi 115 / *2*, Naivasha 29 / *0.5*, Nakuru 42 / *1*, Namanga 279 / *5*, Nanyuki 154 / *4*, Nyeri 156 / *7.5*, Taveta 540 / *4.5*, Thika 156 / *7.5*, Nyahururu 70 / *2*, Voi 444 / *6.5*

Isiolo
- Kakamega 481 / *9*, Kericho 455 / *7.5*, Kisii 467 / *9*, Kisumu 431 / *8.5*, Kitale 348 / *5*, Malindi 877 / *12.5*, Mau Summit 294 / *6.5*, Meru 56 / *1.5*, Mombasa 644 / *10.5*, Nairobi 283 / *5.5*, Naivasha 250 / *4*, Nakuru 321 / *5.5*, Namanga 354 / *5.5*, Nanyuki 58 / *1.5*, Nyeri 109 / *2.5*, Taveta 644 / *10.5*, Thika 275 / *3.5*, Nyahururu 162 / *5.5*, Voi 573 / *7.5*

Kakamega
- Kericho 130 / *1.5*, Kisii 170 / *1.5*, Kisumu 50 / *0.5*, Kitale 109 / *2.5*, Malindi 999 / *13.5*, Mau Summit 178 / *2.5*, Meru 308 / *4.5*, Mombasa 877 / *12.5*, Nairobi 394 / *6*, Naivasha 308 / *5*, Nakuru 275 / *3.5*, Namanga 558 / *6.5*, Nanyuki 436 / *7.5*, Nyeri 420 / *5.5*, Taveta 835 / *11.5*, Thika 425 / *6.5*, Nyahururu 333 / *4.5*, Voi 736 / *10.5*

Kericho
- Kisii 104 / *1*, Kisumu 80 / *0.5*, Kitale 170 / *1.5*, Malindi 869 / *11.5*, Mau Summit 57 / *1*, Meru 282 / *3.5*, Mombasa 751 / *10.5*, Nairobi 264 / *4*, Naivasha 178 / *2.5*, Nakuru 107 / *1.5*, Namanga 428 / *6.5*, Nanyuki 269 / *5.5*, Nyeri 290 / *3.5*, Taveta 705 / *9.5*, Thika 305 / *4.5*, Nyahururu 175 / *3*, Voi 593 / *8.5*

Kisii
- Kisumu 113 / *1*, Kitale 237 / *3.5*, Malindi 973 / *12.5*, Mau Summit 161 / *1.5*, Meru 368 / *6*, Mombasa 855 / *11*, Nairobi 368 / *5*, Naivasha 282 / *3.5*, Nakuru 211 / *2.5*, Namanga 532 / *7.5*, Nanyuki 373 / *6*, Nyeri 394 / *4.5*, Taveta 809 / *10.5*, Thika 409 / *5.5*, Nyahururu 279 / *3.5*, Voi 597 / *9.5*

Kisumu
- Kitale 158 / *2.5*, Malindi 949 / *13*, Mau Summit 137 / *2*, Meru 258 / *4*, Mombasa 831 / *11.5*, Nairobi 344 / *5.5*, Naivasha 258 / *4*, Nakuru 187 / *2.5*, Namanga 508 / *8*, Nanyuki 349 / *6.5*, Nyeri 370 / *4.5*, Taveta 785 / *11*, Thika 385 / *6*, Nyahururu 255 / *4.5*, Voi 673 / *10*

Kitale
- Malindi 985 / *13.5*, Mau Summit 173 / *2.5*, Meru 294 / *4*, Mombasa 867 / *10*, Nairobi 380 / *7*, Naivasha 294 / *4*, Nakuru 223 / *2.5*, Namanga 544 / *8*, Nanyuki 385 / *8.5*, Nyeri 406 / *6.5*, Taveta 821 / *11.5*, Thika 421 / *6.5*, Nyahururu 291 / *4.5*, Voi 709 / *10.5*

Malindi
- Mau Summit 812 / *10.5*, Meru 864 / *11.5*, Mombasa 118 / *1.5*, Nairobi 605 / *7.5*, Naivasha 691 / *10.5*, Nakuru 752 / *10.5*, Namanga 719 / *10*, Nanyuki 795 / *10.5*, Nyeri 752 / *9.5*, Taveta 388 / *5*, Thika 646 / *8.5*, Nyahururu 790 / *4.5*, Voi 536 / *7.5*

Mau Summit
- Meru 290 / *7.5*, Mombasa 746 / *10*, Nairobi 259 / *3*, Naivasha 121 / *1.5*, Nakuru 50 / *0.5*, Namanga 371 / *5.5*, Nanyuki 212 / *4.5*, Nyeri 233 / *3*, Taveta 648 / *8.5*, Thika 248 / *3.5*, Nyahururu 118 / *2.5*, Voi 536 / *7.5*

Meru
- Mombasa 746 / *10*, Nairobi 259 / *3*, Naivasha 283 / *5.5*, Nakuru 240 / *0.5*, Namanga 423 / *5.5*, Nanyuki 78 / *1.5*, Nyeri 136 / *3*, Taveta 700 / *9.5*, Thika 218 / *3.5*, Nyahururu 172 / *2.5*, Voi 588 / *8.5*

Mombasa
- Nairobi 487 / *6*, Naivasha 573 / *7.5*, Nakuru 644 / *10.5*, Namanga 601 / *8.5*, Nanyuki 677 / *9*, Nyeri 634 / *8*, Taveta 271 / *3*, Thika 528 / *7.5*, Nyahururu 672 / *9*, Voi 158 / *1.5*

Nairobi
- Naivasha 86 / *1.5*, Nakuru 157 / *3*, Namanga 164 / *3*, Nanyuki 190 / *3*, Nyeri 147 / *2*, Taveta 441 / *5.5*, Thika 41 / *0.5*, Nyahururu 185 / *3*, Voi 329 / *4.5*

Naivasha
- Nakuru 71 / *1.5*, Namanga 250 / *4*, Nanyuki 193 / *4*, Nyeri 214 / *3*, Taveta 527 / *7*, Thika 127 / *2*, Nyahururu 99 / *2*, Voi 415 / *6*

Nakuru
- Namanga 321 / *5.5*, Nanyuki 162 / *5.5*, Nyeri 183 / *2.5*, Taveta 598 / *8.5*, Thika 205 / *3.5*, Nyahururu 68 / *1.5*, Voi 486 / *7.5*

Namanga
- Nanyuki 354 / *5.5*, Nyeri 311 / *5*, Taveta 555 / *7.5*, Thika 149 / *2.5*, Nyahururu 115 / *1.5*, Voi 443 / *7*

Nanyuki
- Nyeri 58 / *1.5*, Taveta 631 / *7.5*, Thika 106 / *1.5*, Nyahururu 94 / *1.5*, Voi 519 / *7.5*

Nyeri
- Taveta 588 / *7.5*, Thika 106 / *1.5*, Nyahururu 149 / *2.5*, Voi 476 / *6.5*

Taveta
- Thika 482 / *6*, Nyahururu 628 / *8.5*, Voi 112 / *1.5*

Thika
- Nyahururu 221 / *3*, Voi 370 / *5*

Nyahururu
- Voi 514 / *7.5*

petrol stations accept credit cards – but most require cash payment. When driving, give way to traffic on the right and it's strongly recommended that you *do not* drive at night, as many vehicles have no lights, street lighting is poor, people are difficult to see and there are security risks. If the **presidential motorcade** passes – outriders with flashing lights and a fleet of Mercedes flying the Kenya flag – by law you must pull off the road and stop. **Road maps** are best purchased before you arrive or in Nairobi (see page 75). Be aware that roads are poorly signed, and in rural areas it's helpful to have a smattering of Swahili so that you can ask and understand directions. Driving near and around towns there are often **sleeping policemen** with speed bumps varying from rumble strips to enormous bumps, usually unmarked, where you only see them before take-off; so avoid driving too fast. The little town of Gilgil has over 30 bumps. **Police road checks** are common while driving around the country, marked by ominous-looking metal spikes across the road, and certainly intimidating. Go slowly and stop if flagged down by the police who will check your licence, insurance, road tax and tyres. Generally they are friendly and courteous, and I have never been witness to them seeking bribes, although stories abound. In the event of **breakdown**, pull off to the side of the road if possible and put broken branches on the road to alert other drivers to slow down. Leave someone with the vehicle if you have to go for help. Most towns have a mechanic. If a member of the AA in UK, the Kenya AA reciprocates membership. Always ensure you have plenty of water and emergency snacks if travelling in remote areas, and carry spares, a vehicle manual, tow rope, tools, shovel, *panga* (machete), ties and tarpaulin for a roof rack, water and extra fuel. If you get a puncture, get it fixed as soon as you can (very cheap to do – usually less than KSh100). You may like to consider taking out Africa Air Rescue (AAR) membership in case you are involved in an accident. Be aware that at the time of writing certain areas in northern Kenya require you to travel in police convoy. Check with the **Safety and Communications Centre** in Nairobi before leaving (see page 157). If you break down in a game park, *do not* leave your vehicle in the first instance. Wait for help to come to you; at the same time realise that in large parks, if travelling independently, you may not be missed. When driving in **wildlife areas**, respect the speed limit and the animals, and avoid off-road driving which damages the environment.

Choosing self-drive itineraries

Deciding upon an itinerary will be dependent on whether you have a 2WD or 4WD vehicle. Whichever you choose, it's worthwhile sounding out your proposed route locally to check that it's realistic. Most of Kenya's main towns are accessible with 2WD. With a 2WD vehicle a three-to-four-day itinerary might include driving from Nairobi down the Rift Valley escarpment to Lake Naivasha on the Moi South Lake Road, visiting Hell's Gate National Park, continuing on to Nakuru and including a visit to Lake Nakuru National Park. From Nakuru it's a good day trip (or you could spend a night or two) to Lake Bogoria National Reserve and Lake Baringo. Another two-day trip might be to visit the tree hotels in the Aberdares and Nanyuki, as you can leave your vehicle at the Aberdare Country Club or the Outspan Hotel which provide transport, to the Ark and Treetops respectively. It is possible to venture as far as the Marich Pass in western Kenya with 2WD, and from Nairobi to the coast, so long as you stick to the main road. If wanting to venture further afield 4WD is preferable.

Hiring a car

The obvious advantage of hiring a car is that it gives you freedom to travel at your own pace, but it is not necessarily cheaper than travelling on an organised tour to the parks. Many of the international car-hire companies operate from Nairobi and/or Mombasa, and car hire can be arranged in advance. You can pick the car up in one place and leave it at another; car firms vary on this, and it's likely you will have to pay extra for the privilege. However, if price is an issue, you are probably better to shop around the numerous local firms for the best deal. Most companies require you to be over 23 years of age and under 70 and to have held a licence for two years.

2WD or 4WD?

This will depend on where you wish to travel. Although it's feasible to visit some of the national parks in 2WD, many car-hire companies will not permit this, and for some national parks and reserves 4WD is essential. Some car-hire companies, like Roving Rovers, will hire out a 4WD vehicle complete with camping equipment, which is another option. If inexperienced in 4WD driving, get some instruction first.

The small print

Before deciding on a company and hiring a car, it's worth scrutinising the small print. Always compare the inclusive costs of hire and insurance, and check whether VAT (18%) is included. Insurance will include **Collision Damage Waiver** (CDW), which is worth taking, as even a minor accident can be costly; nevertheless, this does not exempt the first KSh70,000 damage, for which you can pay an **Excess Liability Waiver** (ELW) premium which is worth considering. There's also a **Theft Protection Waiver** (TPW) (not an insurance cover) which is also worth paying as otherwise you are liable to pay for the parts (or the whole car) if stolen. **Personal accident insurance** is also worth considering, but may already be covered by your travel insurance. There is usually a choice of paying an **unlimited mileage** rate or by kilometre. It normally works out cheaper to have unlimited mileage, and it may also work out cheaper to hire a vehicle by the week, rather than the day. Before finalising the paperwork, and signing the appropriate contracts and waivers, check over the vehicle. Make sure there are tools, a spare tyre (or two), and ask to be shown the basics (like lights and indicators, how to open the bonnet, where to check the oil, what type of fuel/oil it takes, where the jack and wheel brace are kept) and check the fuel tank for any obvious leaks, and the fuel gauge in the vehicle. Also ask what the procedure is if you have a breakdown and for advice on itineraries.

Car-hire companies

Avenue Car Hire Kipande House, PO Box 14073, Nairobi; tel: 020 332166; fax: 020 216923

Avis Rent-a-Car College House, PO Box 49795, Nairobi; tel: 020 336703; fax: 020 339111; email: avis@form-net.com

Budget Rent-a-Car Kijabe House, PO Box 49713, Nairobi; tel: 020 212904; fax: 020 223584; email: info@budgetrentacar.com; web: www.budgetrentacar.com

Car Hire Company Standard St, New Stanley Hotel, PO Box 56707, Nairobi; tel: 020 225255; fax: 020 216553

Central Rent a Car 680 Hotel, Muindi Mbingu St, PO Box 49439, Nairobi; tel: 020 222888; fax: 020 339666; email: cars@carhirekenya.com; web: www.carhirekenya.com

County Car Hire PO Box 55650, Nairobi; tel: 020 241754, 241755; fax: 020 241756

Crossways Car Hire & Tours PO Box 10228, Nairobi; tel: 020 223949; fax: 020 214372

Dallago Tours & Safaris Mercantile House, Koinange St, Nairobi; tel: 020 212936; fax: 020 212936

Europcar has offices in Nairobi: Bruce House, Standard St, PO Box 40433; tel: 020 334722; fax: 020 218910; email: webmaster@mail.europcar.com; web: www.europcar.com; and Mombasa: Express House, Nkrumah Rd; tel: 041 312461; fax; 041 314408; email: webmaster@mail.europcar.com; web: www.europcar.com
Glory Car Hire Tours & Safaris PO Box 66969, Nairobi; tel: 020 222910; fax: 020 331533; email: glorycarhire@bidii.com. Also has offices in Mombasa, Diani and Malindi
Habibs Cars Agip House, PO Box 48095, Nairobi; tel: 020 220463; fax: 020 220985
Hertz Rent-a-Car Travel House, PO Box 42196, Nairobi, tel: 020 331974; fax: 020 216871; email: info@hertz.utc.co.ke; web: www2.hertz.com. Also has offices in Mombasa (tel: 041 316333) and Malindi (tel: 042 20069)
Let's Go Travel ABC Place, Westlands, PO Box 60342; Nairobi; tel: 020 4447151; fax: 020 4447270; email: info@letsgosafari.com; web: www.letsgosafari.com
Rasuls Car Hire & Tours Industrial Area, PO Box 18172, Nairobi; tel: 020 558234; fax: 020 540341
Roving Rovers PO Box 23, Njoro; tel: 051 343206; mob: 0722 734816; email: rrovers@wananchi.com; web: www.roving-rovers.com

ACCOMMODATION
Kenya has a **hotel star-grading scheme** which is essentially a similar system to that used by tourist boards overseas, based on the facilities provided – not on ambience. Kenya has five-star establishments, although four five-star properties are rare outside the main centres. In addition, an **eco-rating scheme** was introduced at the end of 2002 by the Ecotourism Society of Kenya (see page 56) which grades different types of properties on an environmental audit. **Prices** for accommodation are given in Kenya shillings for the budget hotels and in US dollar rates for non-Kenya residents elsewhere, based upon the high-season rate (where applicable). Be aware that prices can change and the rates quoted are for guidance only. Low-season rates are considerably less, and children's rates vary according to age, usually around 50% of the adult price. Sometimes family rooms are available. If travelling alone, check out the single supplements which can be horrendously high. Christmas and New Year usually have an additional premium to the high-season rate. The walk-in rates, particularly at the large coastal hotels, can be significantly less than quoted. The regional chapters have accommodation listings.

Types of accommodation
Tourist hotels
In the main centres, hotels of an **international standard** may be found, while in regional areas there is less choice. Standards vary, but Kenya has its share of exclusive safari hotels, such as the Mount Kenya Safari Club in Nanyuki, which oozes old-world charm and luxury, and the Norfolk Hotel in Nairobi. There are also **tree hotels** built on stilts in forest glades overlooking waterholes and salt licks which attract wildlife.

Budget hotels and hostels
Cheap hotels, often called board and lodgings (not to be confused with *hotelis* which are restaurants) are found in all the large towns. Rooms are generally basic, some are self-contained (s/c) with a shower and usually have the Asian squat-style toilet. Cleanliness varies, and only some provide mosquito nets. They often have a small restaurant serving African-style food and a bar. The hostels provide dorm beds with shared facilities. Water supply is sometimes erratic and not all offer hot showers.

Lodges

Lodges vary enormously in size and style, with the older lodges like Keekorok and Kilaguni catering for around 170 people. They are often located near a waterhole, where there is ample opportunity to see game, and many have viewing hides. The past decade has seen the growth of **ecolodges**, with smaller, more intimate lodges sympathetically built from natural materials, catering for between eight and 30 people. Initially these were rustic in appearance, but have since developed to include sophisticated design, emulating the trend for safari style. They overlap with **community lodges** (which are also ecolodges) which support (or are run by) local communities. In both cases, the rooms are generally open plan (no glass) although some combine tents within the rooms, or have mosquito net screening. Bathroom provisions are surprisingly imaginative, ranging from open-air to waterspout showers, open-air free-form baths set into the rocks or Victorian twin tubs in bush bathrooms, and a variety of flush, long-drop and compost (see page 104) toilets. A novel development has been **star beds** – beds which can be wheeled out on to a platform for stargazing. Along similar lines, as an alternative to fly-camping, are **sky beds**, built on platforms in the bush, like treehouses, and **bush beds**.

Tented camps

Tented camps, like the lodges, vary enormously in size, from 6–60 people, and in what they have to offer. Some are so sophisticated that you'd be forgiven for wondering where the tent or camp element appears in the equation. The terminology varies: a **permanent tented camp**, as the name suggests, has permanent fixtures. Canvas tents are erected on concrete platforms, often covered with a thatched roof to keep them cool. The tents are usually comfortably furnished with private verandas, en-suite showers and flush toilets. The tents vary enormously from fairly rustic to lavish luxury, complete with plush furnishings and gold-tapped baths. There's normally a central area, known as the mess, where meals are taken, and a bar. Some camps have a swimming pool and many are more akin to staying in a lodge or hotel. The more sophisticated camps tend to have more staff to pamper your needs, with meals of a gourmet standard. Most permanent camps have a generator (which can be noisy) for power, although some now operate on solar. **Seasonal camps** are based along classic camping safari lines, with camps erected for the safari season. Again, they vary enormously, but most cater for a maximum of 16 people (some fewer). There's usually a mess tent, or you can dine al fresco, and food is prepared on a traditional safari oven. The tents vary in size and style, as do ablution facilities. Some tents have en-suite showers with flush toilets, while others are more traditional, with short-drop or compost toilets, and bucket showers, or bush baths with a canvas bath. **Mobile camps** also vary. Many are like the seasonal camps, classic in style, but only put up for the duration of the safari, often in secluded private concession areas. The budget safari mobile camps are more simple, normally with domed tents and basic meals, and a communal short-drop toilet and bucket shower. Many budget safari operators have their own permanent campsites.

Campsites

There are campsites around the country ranging from **private campsites** with good ablution facilities – hot showers and flush toilets – wood provided and a shaded site, with possibly a restaurant too and a variety of activities laid on, to **park campsites**, some of which have basic facilities – long-drop toilet and showers – to no facilities at all where you have to be fully self-sufficient, bringing everything including water. The parks have public campsites, or private campsites where you pay extra to have the campsite to yourself. The latter are normally used by mobile camping safaris. The park campsites are considerably more expensive than the private campsites, from around US$8 for camping per person, with the additional cost of park and vehicle entry fees. For non-residents in Kenya, the private campsites are better value for money. Sometimes tents can be hired in private campsites. If bringing your own tent, make sure it has a sewn-in groundsheet and can zip up securely to keep out insects, especially mosquitoes and ants.

Homestays

Homestays are an attractive alternative to hotels and lodges where you are welcomed into the homes of Kenyan (usually settler) families and sometimes retired hunters who are knowledgeable about bush lore and wildlife. These are mostly situated on private farms and ranches. Although staying with a family, guests generally have a high degree of privacy with en-suite accommodation, either in the house or in cottages in the garden. Meals are communal and give an opportunity to learn at first hand about the country from people who live and work there. Much of the food is home-grown, and there are often cottage industries such as rug weaving on the go, or conservation projects to be visited. Depending

THE SAFARI OVEN

Vivien Prince

Traditional camp cooking on ashes is one of the tastiest ways to cook. Beneath a tarpaulin shelter (high enough to prevent smoke damage, with three open sides, a 3ft backdrop of solid PVC to prevent too much wind getting to the 'oven' and blowing ashes around, and some windows to stop the kitchen getting too hot) is an oblong oven, 5ft long and 3ft wide, built up to about 1ft with natural stone.

A collection of ashes from used coal makes a solid bed and a wire grate sits with its edges on the stones, leaving a space between the ashes and the grate. To fry or boil any food in pots, burning embers collected from a slow-burning log to the side of the kitchen are placed under the grate where the pot is sitting. Once food is cooked or boiling and just needs to be kept warm, the pot can be moved aside to sit over an area of the grate where there are no burning coals, only ashes.

To bake bread, cakes, casseroles and roasts a tin box is used. This sits on top of the grate in the same way, but if a high all-round oven temperature is needed more hot coals are put on the lid of the box. If the top of a casserole or cake is cooking too quickly, the coals can be removed from the lid. When you are ready to brown off, say, an eggplant parmigian, to have bubbly brown cheese on top, the hot coals on top can be replaced (akin to switching on a grill).

When baking, especially with cakes and bread, it is helpful to place a narrow, empty cake tin upside down in the box, placing the actual cake being baked on that, and in such a way lifting the cake from the bottom of the tin. This prevents the base of a cake (and the same applies to bread) from burning.

Furthermore, just as you do in a normal oven, a fruitcake, or other item which requires a long cooking time, can be further prevented from burning at the base by a small pan of water being placed inside the oven, under the grate.

It's as simple as that – *bon appétit!*

on where you stay, a range of activities is on offer, from walking and riding to game drives by day and night, and visiting local community projects.

Farmstays

Surprisingly, there are very few farmstays, most farms and ranches presenting themselves as upmarket homestays. Farmstays are more economical, and more akin to the farm bed and breakfasts that you might find in UK.

Self-catering options

There is a variety of self-catering options around the country. The national parks have some excellent **houses, cottages** and *bandas* (thatched huts, with basic furnishings) for rent. Equally there are private *bandas*, cottages and houses for hire. They vary in what they offer – beds, mattresses, cutlery, crockery and cooking facilities are usually provided – but you need to bring your own provisions and bedding. Sometimes linen is included and many provide a cook and house staff. If there are a few of you, self-catering, serviced houses, particularly at the coast, are an economical option. They are usually rented out by the day.

On the water

There are a few options available, from a **houseboat** on Lake Turkana, mainly used for fishing, to **sailing yachts**, **catamarans**, **dhows** and **liveaboard diving vessels**. They generally include skippers and catering.

Central booking

The following are hotel chains or agents with central booking or representation for an assortment of properties. It is not necessarily cheaper to book with them direct, and you may find it more convenient to deal with one travel agent or tour operator. A tour operator listing is given in the following chapter. Further detail on accommodation is given in the regional chapters.

Alliance Hotels PO Box 49839, Nairobi; tel: 020 337501; fax: 020 21912; email: alliance@africaonline.co.ke; web: www.alliancehotels.com. Naro Moru River Lodge; Africana Sea Lodge; Jadini Beach Hotel; Safari Beach Hotel.
Block Hotels Block House, Lusaka Rd, PO Box 40075, Nairobi; tel: 020 540780; fax: 020 545948; email: blockreservations@africaonline.co.ke; web: www.blockhotelske.com. Keekorok Lodge; Lake Baringo Club; Lake Naivasha Country Club; Outspan Club; Treetops; Larsen's Camp; Samburu Lodge; Shimba Hills Lodge; Nyali Beach Hotel; Indian Ocean Beach Club.
Bush Homes of East Africa PO Box 56923, 00200 City Sq, Nairobi; tel: 020 600457; 020 605008; email: bushhome@africaonline.co.ke; web: www.bush-homes.co.ke. Takaungu; Ol Kanjau; Rekero; Rekero Traditional Tented Camp; Lewa Safari Camp; Wilderness Trails; Mundui Estate; Sirata Siruwa; Lokitela Farm; Ol Malo; Kitich; Lobolo Camp; Tana Delta Camp.
Cheli & Peacock Safaris PO Box 39806, 00623a Parklands, Nairobi; tel: 020 604053; fax: 020 604050; email: safaris@chelipeacock.co.ke; web: www.chelipeacock.com. Tortilis; Elsa's Kopje; Sabuk Lodge; Mara Camp; Kiwayu Safari Village.
The Explorer Collection PO Box 74888, Nairobi 00200; tel: 020 4449115; fax: 020 4446600; email: info@explorer-collection.com; web: www.explorer-collection.com representing: Mutamaiyu – Mugie; Ol Malo; Elephant Watch Camp; Il Ngwesi; Tassia; Sarara; Wilderness Trails; Lewa Safari Camp; Borana; Desert Rose; Mara Explorer; Rusinga Island Lodge; Shompole; Ol Donyo Wuas; Campi ya Kanzi; Porini Camp; Kilalinda; Galdessa; Kipungani; Alfajiri; Diani House.

Governors' Camps Musiara Ltd, PO Box 48217, Nairobi; tel: 020 331871; fax: 020 726427; email: reservations@governorscamp.com; web: www.governorscamp.com. Governors' Camp; Little Governors' Camp; Governors' Ilmoran Camp; Governors' Private Camp; Loldia House; Mfangano Island Camp.

Heritage Hotels PO Box 74888, Nairobi; tel: 020 716628; fax: 020 716457; email: heritagehotels@form-net.com; web: www.heritagehotels.co.ke. Mara Explorer; Kipungani Explorer; Great Rift Valley Lodge and Golf Resort; Mara Intrepids; Siana Intrepids; Samburu Intrepids; Voyager Safari Lodge; Voyager Safari Camp; Voyager Beach Resort.

The Kenyan Portfolio www.kenyanportfolio.com representing: Borana; Diani House; Il Ngwesi; Loisaba; Laragai; Lewa Safari Camp; Ol Donyo Wuas; Tassia; Wilderness Trails; Cottar's 1920s Camp.

Kisiwani PO Box 70940, Nairobi; tel: 020 446384; fax: 020 446384; email: kisiwani@swiftkenya.com. The Island Hotel, Mnarani House, Jasmine House.

Lonrho Hotels PO Box 58581, 00200 Nairobi; tel: 020 216940; fax: 020 216796; email: sales@lonrhohotels.co.ke; web: www.lonrhohotels.com. Norfolk Hotel; Aberdare Country Club; The Ark; Mount Kenya Safari Club; Sweetwaters Game Reserve; Mara Safari Club.

Mellifera Collection PO Box 24397, Karen 00502, Nairobi; tel: 020 574689; fax: 020 577381; email: mellifera@swiftkenya.com representing: Bushtops; Cottars 1920s Camp; Desert Rose; Loisaba Wilderness; Hippo Point; Turkana Houseboat

Private Wilderness PO Box 6648, 00100 Nairobi; tel: 020 605349; fax: 020 605391; email: info@privatewilderness.com; web: www.privatewilderness.com. Kampi ya Kanzi; Kilalinda; Rusinga Island Camp; Saruni.

Sarova Hotels PO Box 72493, Nairobi; tel: 020 713333; fax: 020 715566; email: info@sarova.co.ke; web: www.sarovahotels.com. The Stanley; Sarova Shaba; Sarova Mara; Sarova Lion Hill; Whitesands.

Savannah Camps and Lodges PO Box 48019, Nairobi; tel: 020 331191; fax: 020 330698; email: eaos@africaonline.co.ke; web: www.savannahcamps.com. Mara River Camp; Taita Discovery Centre; Galla Camp; Indian Ocean Lodge.

Serena Hotels PO Box 48690, Nairobi; tel: 020 711077; fax: 020 718103; email: cro@serena.co.ke; web: www.serenahotels.com. Nairobi Serena Hotel; Mombasa Serena Beach Hotel; Mara Serena Safari Lodge; Amboseli Serena Safari Lodge; Kilaguni Serena Safari Lodge; Samburu Serena Safari Lodge; Serena Mountain Lodge.

Self-catering

Home From Home (at Langata Link) Langata South Rd, PO Box 15097, Nairobi; tel: 020 891314; fax: 020 891307; email: info@kenyasafarihomes.com; web: www.kenyasafarihomes.com. This has a range of self-catering accommodation (mostly serviced with cook and house staff), from cottages to houses both upcountry and at the coast.

Kenya Wildlife Service (KWS) Tourism & Business Development, PO Box 40241, Nairobi; tel: 020 602345; email: tourism@kws.org. For bandas, cottages and houses in the national parks.

Let's Go Travel (page 101) also offers self-catering in community lodges, cottages and houses around the country and at the coast.

National Museums of Kenya (NMK) PO Box 40658, Nairobi; tel 020 742141; fax: 020 741424; email: nmk@africaonline.co.ke; web: www.museums.or.ke. For bandas near museum sites.

92

A point or two about us

We offer-
- Guaranteed safari departures
- Tailor made itineraries
- Flying safaris
- Balloon flights

We've been in the Safari business for over 30 years - plenty of time to iron out the wrinkles!

So get in touch with us and we'll let you know how we can make your trip to Kenya a safari to remember.

rhino safaris

Nairobi Office: Rhino Safaris Building, Ngong Road, PO Box 48023 Nairobi
Tel: +254 20 2 720610 / 611 Email: rhinosafarisnbo@kenyaweb.com
United Kingdom office: 9 Galena Road, London W6 OLT
Tel: +44 20 8741 5333 Email: safaris.uk@rexsafaris.com

KIBO SLOPES SAFARIS

SAFARIS OF A LIFETIME

- TREK SAFARIS • 4x4 SAFARIS • BEACH SAFARIS
- ADVENTURE SAFARIS • WILDLIFE SAFARIS

EAST AFRICAN WILDLIFE ADVENTURE | TREKS NORTH OF THE EQUATOR | BEACH HOLIDAYS | TREKS SOUTH OF THE EQUATOR

W> www.kiboslopessafaris.com | E> info@kiboslopessafaris.com
PO Box 58064, Nairobi, Kenya | T> 254-2-2717373 / 2725435 | F> 254-2-2716028

WILDLIFE WORLDWIDE

AFRICA ASIA AUSTRALASIA AMERICAS EUROPE EXPEDITION VOYAGES

Classic tailor-made & small group wildlife holidays worldwide - from African safaris & expedition voyages to Tiger -viewing & bear-watching

For our brochure please call us on
020 8667 9158
sales@wildlifeworldwide.com
www.wildlifeworldwide.com

Safaris

The Swahili word for 'journey' is *safari*. The first safaris were the early Arab caravans, with their numerous porters, who trekked inland from the coast, slaughtering elephants for their ivory and capturing slaves en route to conveniently transport their booty back to the coast. Indeed, in the 1850s, at the time of the legendary Scots explorer and missionary Dr David Livingstone's travels, it is estimated that 30,000 elephants were being killed a year in Kenya, Uganda and Tanzania, and that by the 1880s this had risen to between sixty and seventy thousand, not to mention the cost in human life. The era of Victorian explorers paved the way for legendary big-game hunters like Sir Frederick Courtenay Selous, Ernest Hemingway and Arthur Neumann.

Selous' first hunting expedition to East Africa was in 1902, followed in 1909 by a hunting safari for his friend, the American President, Teddy Roosevelt. This safari, collecting specimens for the Smithsonian and American Museum of Natural History in New York, took on epic proportions, lasting nine months and covering four countries, including Kenya. It was widely reported and started the business of **commercial hunting safaris**.

The **classic African tented safari** was founded on the camps of these early hunters, where camping in the bush certainly did not mean stinting on luxury. Denys Finch Hatton was remembered for taking his wind-up gramophone on safari while a piano was considered essential when Sir Winston Churchill's father went on safari at the end of the 19th century.

As more people became aware of Africa's big game, the appeal of game watching attracted a wider audience, giving rise to **photographic safaris**, replacing the gun with the camera and attracting an increasing number of tourists on different budgets. The term *safari* has become widely used, with an increasing number of safari styles and an ever-widening variety of activities and how to experience them, as outlined in *Chapter 6*, page 107.

SAFARI PLANNING

Safaris captivate the imagination and awaken the spirit of adventure. We all have perceptions of Africa gleaned from tales of the dark continent by early explorers: sweaty jungles, bleak deserts, miles of open savanna and azure seas; dangerous animals and daring pursuits; exotic tribes living amidst the last wildlife herds of Eden or early man in the Cradle of Mankind.

Feature films like *Born Free* and *Out of Africa* have reinforced this romantic nostalgia. Television wildlife programmes like *Big Cat Diary* have heightened our desire to see wildlife in its natural environment. But in essence we have only glimpsed the reality, boosted by unrealistic expectations of seeing wildlife in action after a few hours' game viewing, when it's often taken months of patience to get the film footage captured in documentaries. More often than not, we harbour images of an African past and possess a superficial grasp of the issues relating to the conservation of Africa's natural heritage.

In Kenya, wildlife is not restricted to within the boundaries of national parks and reserves. The adjacent areas often have excellent game-viewing opportunities, and there are also private wildlife conservancies, and farms or community ranches where wildlife mingles with cattle ranching.

Selecting a safari

So, how does this relate to choosing a safari? Essentially through researching options, so that the safari you choose is the most suited to what you want to see and do. The secret of a successful safari is to plan it thoroughly. Not only is this fun to do – it will probably throw up options you did not even know existed – but if you particularly want to climb Mount Kenya, see the wildebeest migration, walk with elephants, meet colourful tribespeople, watch flocks of flamingo or snorkel in coral gardens, you will end up visiting the right place at the right time of year.

What do you want to see and do?

Kenya has a huge spectrum of safaris on offer and the range of activities and how to experience them continues to grow. Indeed, with the vogue for 'safari style', for some visitors the choice of accommodation has become as important as the wildlife. A description of activities, special interests and events is given in *Chapter 6*, page 107. This will help you to narrow down your options.

When to go

The best time to travel to Kenya depends on the seasons, the type of activities you wish to pursue and where they take place. Kenya's climate is as varied as its physical landscape, from the tropical humidity of the coast, to the dry heat of the hinterland and northern plains, and on to the cool air of the highland plateau and mountains. Wildlife safaris tend to be at an altitude of 900–1,500m, in a temperate to hot climate. The heat is dry, which is comfortable for travelling, and the nights cool. In the northern desert regions, the heat is again dry, but temperatures extreme – very hot during the day and cold at night. In contrast, the coast and the Lake Victoria region can be extremely humid, although the humidity at the coast is tempered by sea breezes blowing off the Indian Ocean.

Seasonal variations are caused by rainfall rather than changes of temperature, with most parts of the country having two rainy seasons. The long rains fall between April and June, and the short rains between October and December. Average annual rainfall varies from 127mm a year in the most arid regions of the northern plains to 1,778mm a year near Lake Victoria, while the coast and highland areas have an average of 1,000mm per year.

The **main tourist seasons** are from July to October, and January to March, avoiding the rainy seasons. Yet there are advantages to travelling in **low season**: it does not rain all the time and you can still have an enjoyable safari, with fewer tourists and cheaper accommodation. Certain activities such as whitewater rafting or botany are best just after the rains when there's often some superb light conditions for photography. If travelling during **high season**, some of the most popular attractions create 'honey pots', so consider visiting some of the less popular areas, and remember that a few overcrowded areas do not mean that the entire country is heaving with tourists.

If you have to travel at a specific time of year, be sure to check that this does not clash with the worst time to pursue the activity you have in mind.

SAFARI VEHICLES
The main types of safari vehicle are:

Overland trucks or unimogs
Varying in size, some have the capacity to take up to 18 people. These vehicles are mostly used for long, overland journeys and budget camping trips. Their advantage is a high elevation, giving you an excellent view, and some have a viewing platform above the cab. But check out the seat combinations: some face sideways, or inwards, while others face outwards giving the best option for game viewing.

Minibuses
These are the most common safari vehicles for the average-priced safari and are also used by some budget trips. They have pop-up viewing hatches, but not everyone can 'pop-up' at the same time. The buses seat nine, or seven if a guaranteed window seat is offered. Opt for the latter, as it seems a pity to go all that way on safari and then not be able to see the animals clearly. Many companies offer padded seats, and on long, often bumpy journeys, these are a godsend. They are usually driven by an African driver/guide, and sometimes accompanied by a tour leader. Vehicles *usually* carry guidebooks on the flora and fauna and some binoculars, but it's better to bring your own.

Land Rovers and Land Cruisers
These are usually used by the more expensive safaris, and being 4WD they can traverse difficult terrain. Associated with authentic safari kudos, they are more comfortable and spacious than the minibuses, and many have been modified for comfort on safari, with heightened roofs giving greater visibility from the windows, and better suspension. Most of the safari companies have enclosed vehicles with viewing hatches, but some camps have open vehicles for game drives. On private mobile safaris, the vehicles may be driven by an African or European white hunter-type guide. Guidebooks and binoculars are usually provided, together with cool boxes for cold drinks on game drives.

How to travel around
The **choice of transport** can greatly affect your enjoyment of a safari. The main things to consider when selecting a **vehicle** are the distances you will be covering, who will be doing the driving, the standard of the roads on which you will be driving, the degree of comfort provided, and how easy it is to see out of the vehicle. **Roads** in Kenya rarely equate to the standard you find in the first world. Some are tarmac, but unless new, are often in need of repair; others are graded dirt roads. These are comfortable, if dusty, but become corrugated if they have not been graded for a while. Those on black cotton soil can become a quagmire when wet. All the national parks have dirt roads and sandy tracks. The road conditions determine the time taken travelling between safari destinations. (Refer to *Distance/Time* chart, page 84.) Opt for an itinerary in which you do not spend most of your time on the road. Going at a sensible pace will be more relaxing, and give you time to appreciate the environment. The combined effects of jet lag, changes in altitude, climate and food can be exhausting, and exacerbated by a whistle-stop tour of the safari circuits. An alternative to travelling by road is **flying**, with internal flights being reasonably priced – for example from Nairobi to the Masai

Mara costs US$110 for a 40-minute flight, which cuts out a five-hour road journey. The planes used vary in size from 60-seaters to small bush planes like Cessnas with four to six seats, which are more prone to turbulence. There are scheduled flights to the most popular parks and reserves, with flying safaris or combined flying and road safaris an option. If you are on a tight schedule it's worth considering combining travel by road with internal flights or rail journeys.

Alternatively, **other modes of transport** might include more environmentally friendly ways of travelling, such as by oxwagon, horse, camel, boat, canoe, bicycle or your own two feet. (For further details, see under *Activities* in *Chapter 6*.)

Types of accommodation

The choice of accommodation ranges from camping to self-catering houses, lodges and hotels to private home and farmstays or even boats, as outlined in *Chapter 4*, page 87. It is feasible to mix and match your accommodation, combining camping with hotels or lodges. It's worth considering whether rooms are open (as with some of the ecolodges), the standard of tented accommodation and what type of ablution facilities are provided. If you're going to be fazed by spiders in the shower and hurricane lighting you might prefer to stay in a lodge. However, on safari, camping is highly recommended, as it magnifies the wilderness experience. Nothing compares to sitting around a crackling campfire in the evening under a sparkling night sky, listening to the cacophony of chirping cicadas, or awakening in the night to the steady grunts of a lion or the doleful whoop of a hyena. Only then are you truly initiated into 'Africa on Safari'.

Guides

A knowledgeable safari guide makes an enormous difference to appreciating the wildlife and its habitat, as well as giving an insight into the culture of the country. Standards of guiding vary between tour operators. Not all guides are qualified, but have spent many years in the bush and know it well. In an effort to regulate the standard of guiding in the industry, the **Kenya Professional Safari Guides Association** (KPSGA, PO Box 24397, Nairobi; tel: 020 609355; fax: 020 609355; email: info@safariguides.org; web: www.safariguides.org) was formed in 1996. It operates in association with the Kenya Wildlife Service (KWS). So far, there are bronze- and silver-level guides, and the gold level will be introduced in 2004. The KPSGA guides have a broad knowledge of wildlife, conservation, tourism, flora and fauna. If you have a particular interest, such as ornithology or botany, specialist guides are available. Some tour operators offer special safaris with a tour leader who is an expert in his field.

Costs

Safari costs will obviously depend on the type of safari you have chosen and whether you are travelling in high season. Prices vary depending on the destination and the activities and accommodation chosen. Budget camping safaris cost from US$80 a day, from US$175 for a mid-range camping safari with 4WD, a driver/guide and basic camping, to US$400 a day for upmarket mobile safaris with 4WD, driver guides and stylish camping. As a rule of thumb, the more exclusive a safari the more expensive it will be. But you do not need to go on a top of the range safari to enjoy the wonders Kenya has to offer.

Insurance extras

Many companies will ask you to sign a waiver of responsibility on activity safaris – walking, cycling, whitewater rafting – and you may incur an additional insurance premium for high-risk pursuits.

Comparing options

When finalising a safari itinerary, check what is included in the price. It is very easy to overlook additional costs, such as an extra meal here or there, drinks or tipping. Some prices only cover ground arrangements, and you must organise your own international and internal flights. If you are planning on hiring a vehicle and taking your own independent safari, there will be additional costs such as park and camp fees, as well as the costs of car hire and running the vehicle. If considering value for money, hiring a vehicle will probably work out more expensive than an organised safari, unless there are more than two of you.

Take time to assess the hidden costs in the itinerary as you are not necessarily comparing like with like – tipping is obviously an extra, but are drinks, laundry, park fees, transfers from the airstrip to camp, bush walks, bush picnics, village visits and game drives (how many?) included in the price, and if not what are the additional costs? A guided bush walk can cost from US$7–70, depending upon the company and guide.

Also, there is often an overlap of the term 'full board' and 'fully inclusive' between different companies. Full board can mean just meals – breakfast, lunch and dinner – but may also include drinks, laundry and activities. Fully inclusive, on the other hand, may include full board with most activities and drinks – but champagne, spirits and park fees may be extra. Ascertain what the price includes *before* you go and budget for any extras; then you will not have any unpleasant surprises at the end of your trip. And do not forget to include the costs which are extra to your safari, like arranging visas, medication, airport tax and insurance.

CHOOSING A SAFARI
Here is a suggested checklist for selecting a safari:

- Is there anything you especially want to see – wildlife, people, scenic attractions?
- Where are they found?
- Is there anything you especially want to do – be energetic or seated, adventurous or passive?
- Would you like to combine activities, such as a wildlife safari with a few days relaxing at the coast?
- Do you have children?
- If travelling alone, do single supplements apply?
- What is the best time of year to visit?
- Do you have any time constraints on when you travel?
- How much do you want to spend?
- What sort of accommodation do you require?
- Are you frightened of creepy crawlies?
- Do you want to have access to a swimming pool?
- What mode of transport do you prefer?
- What is the standard of guides?
- How long are you going for?
- What is included in the price of the itinerary?
- What are the additional costs?
- Does the tour operator have an ecotourism policy and contribute towards local communities and conservation?
- Do you have any special food requirements?

BOOKING A SAFARI

It is helpful to prepare a checklist which is useful when discussing the choice of safari options with a tour operator or travel agent.

Booking in Kenya or from overseas

There's a choice of booking through a travel agent or tour operator in your own country, or booking direct with a tour operator in Kenya. Tour operators can advise you on itineraries, as well as giving factual information on what you will need to take with you, medical requirements and security.

In the UK, African safaris are the domain of specialist tour operators. Some concentrate entirely on Africa, whereas others are established long-haul operators or experts in certain activities such as overland or walking safaris. These specialist companies are often run by experienced and enthusiastic Africaphiles. The advantage in using these companies is that you can combine your research with their knowledge. (Bear in mind that some companies have a leaning towards southern Africa, whereas others might prefer East Africa.) The high-street travel agents stock the brochures of the major tour operators, but generally the knowledge of the assistants is limited to the information given in the brochures. They mostly sell 'off-the-peg' safaris which are well researched, but do not necessarily offer you the safari most suited to your requirements.

Many companies offer a **package safari**, with a set itinerary, while some offer **flexitours**, where you can mix and match modules from set itineraries to make up your own safari, or take additional options to your core safari; alternatively others will **tailor-make** a safari suited to your specific interests and budget.

The advantage of booking your holiday with a UK company is that since the EC directive on package holidays was implemented in 1994, all companies now have to be bonded, which means that if the company goes into liquidation your money is safe. Companies can be bonded through ABTA, AITO or a trust fund. If you end up having complaints about your holiday which leads to the law courts, UK law (usually English) will apply. A few specialist UK tour operators have their own company in Africa, whereas others will use ground handlers known to them.

If **booking direct** with a tour operator in Kenya, you need to make your own flight arrangements. Check that you are booking a flight through an ATOL licensed company, so that your money is protected if the airline goes bust. (The Africa Travel Centre, Somak Holidays and Trailfinders are good for flights only.) If making your own arrangements on arrival with a tour operator in Kenya, unless specifically recommended to one, look out for membership of the Kenya Association of Tour Operators (KATO, Longonot Road – off Kilimanjaro Avenue – Upper Hill, Nairobi; tel: 020 713348/713386; email: info@katokenya.org; web: www.katokenya.org) which gives a degree of quality assurance. Remember that it can take time to finalise your itinerary, and if possible avoid travelling in high season and during school or public holidays, when accommodation can be at a premium and last-minute arrangements difficult. Specialised trips, such as elephant-watch safaris and camel treks are often booked up well in advance. The advantage of booking direct is flexibility as itineraries can be adapted at the last moment, for example to incorporate any seasonal variations in game movements. Also, more of your money remains in the country. However, booking direct *does not* necessarily mean that safaris cost less, as overseas tour operators receive a commission on the safaris they sell. Many overseas tour operators also make significant contributions to wildlife conservation in Kenya and you may prefer the convenience and security of booking on home ground.

At the end of the day, it's a case of personal preference. Provided you are aware of the range of safaris on offer, it does not matter whether you opt for an 'off-the-peg' or a 'tailor-made' safari, or whether you use a travel agent or a tour operator, so long as you are happy with the choice you have made and know exactly what to expect for your money. If you know what you are getting, the risk of disappointment is significantly reduced, and an African safari can live up to your expectations.

Tour operators
Overseas tour operators
In UK
A to B Tours & Travel Services 205 Winchester Rd, Basingstoke, Hants RG21 8YH; tel: 01256 351979; fax: 01256 351979; email: atob.tours@btinternet.com
Abercrombie & Kent Sloane Square House, Holbein Pl; London SW1W 8NS; tel: 020 7730 9600; fax: 020 7730 9376; email: info@abercrombiekent.co.uk; web: www.abercrombiekent.co.uk
Absolute Africa 41 Swanscombe Rd, Chiswick, London W4 2HR; tel: 020 8742 0226; fax 020 8995 6155; email: absaf@absoluteafrica.co.uk; web: www.absoluteafrica.com
Acacia Adventure Holidays 23a Craven Terrace, London W2 3QH; tel: 020 7706 4700; fax: 020 7706 4686; email: info@acacia.africa.com; web: www.acacia-africa.com
Africa-in-Focus Northay, Blagdon Hill, Taunton TA3 7SF; tel: 01823 421303; fax: 01823 421756; email: africainfocus@yahoo.co.uk; web: www.africa-in-focus.com
Africa Travel Centre 21 Leigh St, London WC1H 9EW; tel: 020 7387 1211; fax: 020 7383 7512; email: sales@africatravel.co.uk; web: www.africatravel.co.uk
Cara Spencer Independent Travel Consultant, 3 King's Apartments, Gordon Crescent, Camberley, Surrey GU15 2DX; tel: 01276 683868; fax: 01276 683868; email: caraspencer@boltblue.com
Cazenove and Loyd 9 Imperial Studios, 3–11 Imperial Rd, London SW6 2AG; tel: 020 7384 2332; fax: 020 7384 2399; email: info@caz-loyd.com; web: www.caz-loyd.com
Crusader Travel 57 Church St, Twickenham TW1 3NR; tel: 020 8892 7606; fax: 020 8744 0574; email: info@crusader-travel.com; web: www.crusader-travel.com
Discovery Initiatives The Travel House, 51 Castle St, Cirencester, Glos GL7 1QD; tel: 01285 643333; email: enquiry@discoveryinitiatives.com; web: www.discoveryinitiatives.com
Elite Vacations 98 Bessborough Rd, Harrow, Middx HA1 3DT; tel: 020 8864 9818; fax: 020 8426 9178; email: elite@alphauk.co.uk; web: www.elite-vacations.co.uk
Exodus Grange Mills, Weir Rd, London SW12 0NE; tel: 020 8675 5550; fax: 020 8673 0779; email: info@exodus.co.uk; web: www.exodus.co.uk
Explore Worldwide 1 Frederick St, Aldershot, Hants GU11 1LQ; tel: 01252 319448; fax: 01252 343170; email: info@explore.co.uk; web: www.exploreworldwide.com
Footloose Adventure Travel Services 3 Springs Pavement, Ilkley, W Yorks LS29 8HD; tel: 01943 604030; fax: 01943 604070; email: info@footlooseadventure.co.uk; web: www.footlooseadventure.co.uk
Gane & Marshall 98 Crescent Road, New Barnet, Herts EN4 9RJ. UK; tel: 020 8441 9592; fax: 020 8441 7376; email: holidays@ganeandmarshall.co.uk; web: www.ganeandmarshall.co.uk
Guerba Adventure and Discovery Holidays Wessex House, 40 Station Rd, Westbury, Wilts BA13 3JN; tel: 01373 826611; fax: 01373 858351; email: info@guerba.co.uk; web: www.guerba.co.uk
Hartley's Safaris UK The Old Chapel, Chapel Lane, Hackthorn, Lincs LN2 3PN; tel: 01673 861600; fax: 01673 861666; email: info@hartleys-safaris.co.uk
Hoopoe Safaris *UK:* PO Box 278, Watford, Herts WD19 4WH; tel; 01923 255462; fax: 01923 255452; email: hoopoeuk@aol.com; *Tanzania:* India St, PO Box 2047, Arusha; tel:

027 2507011/2507541; fax: 027 2548226; email: hoopoesafari@africaonline.co.tz; web: www.hoopoe.com

Journeys by Design 36 Park Crescent, Brighton BN2 5AA; tel: 01273 623790; fax: 01273 621766; email: info@journeysbydesign.co.uk; web: www.journeysbydesign.co.uk

Kuoni Travel Kuoni House, Dorking RH5 4AZ; tel: 01306 744672; fax: 01306 741099; email: info@kuoni.co.uk

Okavango Tours and Safaris Marlborough House, 298 Regents Park Rd, London N3 2TJ; tel: 020 8343 3283; fax: 020 8343 3287; email: info@okavango.com; web: www.okavango.com

Rainbow Tours 305 Upper St, London N1 2TU; tel: 020 7226 1004; fax: 020 7226 2621; email. info@rainbowtours.co.uk; web: www.rainbowtours.co.uk

Rhino Safaris *UK:* 9 Galena Rd, London W6 0LT; tel: 020 8741 5333; email: safaris.uk@rexsafaris.com *Kenya:* Rhino Safaris Building, Ngong Rd, PO Box 48023, Nairobi; tel: +254 20 2 720610; email: rhinosafarisnbo@kenyaweb.com

Safari Consultants Orchard House, Upper Rd, Little Cornard, Suffolk CO10 0NZ; tel: 01787 228494; fax: 01787 228096; email: info@safariconsultantuk.com; web: www.safari-consultants.co.uk

Safari Drive The Trainers Office, Windy Hollow, Sheepdrove, Lambourn, Berks RG17 7XA; tel: 0870 2406305; fax: 01488 71311; email: Safari_Drive@compuserve.com; web: www.safaridrive.com

Somak Holidays Somak House, Harrovian Business Village, Bessborough Rd, Harrow HA1 3EX; tel: 020 8423 3000; fax: 020 8423 7700; email: info@somak.co.uk; web: www.somak.co.uk

Steppes Africa 51 Castle St, Cirencester, Glos GL7 1QD; tel: 01285 650011; fax: 01285 885888; email: safari@steppesafrica.co.uk; web: www.steppesafrica.co.uk

Tim Best Travel 68 Old Brompton Rd, London SW7 3LQ; tel: 020 7591 0300; fax: 020 7591 0301; email: info@timbesttravel.com; web: www.timbesttravel.com

Time For Africa Beacon Cottage, Meonstoke, Hants SO32 3NN; tel: 014 8987 8593; fax: 014 8987 8504; email: info@timeforafrica.com; web: www.timeforafrica.com

Trailfinders 194 Kensington High St, London W8 7RG; tel: 020 7938 3939; web: www.trailfinders.com

Tribes Travel 12 The Business Centre, Earl Soham, Woodbridge, Suffolk IP13 7SA; tel: 01728 685971; fax: 01728 685973; email: info@tribes.co.uk; web: www.tribes.co.uk

Tropical Places Sussex House, London Rd, East Grinstead RH19 1HJ; tel: 01342 330746; fax: 01342 330771; email: info@shglonghaul.co.uk; web: www.tropicalplaces.co.uk

Wilderness Kenya The Clocktower, 72 Newhaven Rd, Edinburgh EH6 5QG; tel: 0131 625 6635; fax: 0131 625 6636; email: neil@wildernesskenya.com; web: www.wildernesskenya.com

Wildlife Worldwide Chameleon House, 162 Selsdon Rd, South Croydon, Surrey CR2 6PJ; tel: 020 8667 9158; fax: 020 8667 1960; email: sales@wildlifeworldwide.com; web: www.wildlifeworldwide.com

The **Africa Travel and Tourism Association** (ATTA) PO Box 60, Ryde, Isle of Wight; tel: 01983 872216; fax: 01983 875452; web: www.atta.co.uk and **Safarilink**, web: www.safarilink.com also have operator listings.

In USA/Canada

African Safari Travel Tulip Travel LLC, 828 Prospect St, Suite D, La Jolla, California 92037; tel: +1 858 551 0065; fax: +1 858 551 0054; email: safari@tulipweb.com; web; www.tulipweb.com

Eco-resorts 1535 Chatham Colony Ct, Reston, Virginia 20190 USA; tel: 1-703-437-3671; fax: +1 801 991 7410; email: anne@eco-resorts.com; web: www.eco-resorts.com

International Ventures 65 Old Ridgefield Rd, Suite 2, Wilton, CT 06897-3018; tel: 203 761 1110 or 0800 727 5475; fax: 203 762 7104; email: Jambo65@aol.com; web: www.internationalventures.com
Pulse Africa 29 Riverview Av, Swansea, MA 02777; postal address: Box 49, Boat Basin, New York, NY 10024; tel: +1 508 676 0376; email: deltaw@erols.com; web: www.africansafari.co.za
Real Traveller 116 Spadina Av, Unit 201, Toronto, Ontario M5V 2K6; tel: 1 (416) 977 0043; fax: (416) 977 0053; email: info@realtraveller.com

In Australia
Africa Travel Centre Level 12, 456 Kent St, Sydney 2000
Bench International Level 10, 36–38 Clarence St, Sydney 2000; tel: 02 9290 2877; fax: 02 9290 2665; email: bench@ozemail.com.au; web: www.benchinternational.com.au
Natural Focus Safaris 10/191 Clarence St, Sydney 2000; tel: 02 9290 1666; fax: 02 9290 1551; email: dennisj@wr.com.au
Peregrine Travel Centre 5th Floor, 38 York St, Sydney NSW 2000; tel: 02 9290 2770; fax: 02 9290 2155; email: info@peregrineadventures.com; web: www.peregrineadventures.com
Sundowner Travel 151 Dorcas St, S Melbourne 3205; tel: 03 9690 2499; fax: 03 9696 1261; email: sundownr@ozemail.com.au
Trailfinders 8 Spring St, Sydney, NSW 2000; tel: 02 9247 7666; fax: 02 9247 6566; web: www.trailfinders.com

Kenyan travel agents and tour operators
General agents
The following also offer safaris:

Bunson Travel Service PO Box 45456, Nairobi; tel: 020 221992; fax: 020 214120; email: info@bunsontravel.co.ke; web: www.bunson.co.ke
Express Travel Group Middle East Bank Bldg, Milimani Rd, PO Box 40433, Nairobi; tel: 020 334722; fax: 020 218910; email: rmarkham@africaonline.co.ke; web: www.etg-safaris.com
Let's Go Travel ABC Place, Westlands, PO Box 60342; Nairobi; tel: 020 4447151; fax: 020 4447270; email: info@letsgosafari.com; web: www.letsgosafari.com. Also has offices in the city centre and at Karen Dukas above Karen Provision Stores (tel: 020 882505; fax: 020 882171).
Muthaiga Travel Muthaiga Shopping Centre, Limuru Rd, PO Box 63220, Nairobi; tel: 020 3750034; fax: 020 3750035; email: info@supersafari.com; web: www.supersafari.com

Safari operators
Abercrombie & Kent Mombasa Rd, PO Box 59749, Nairobi; tel: 6905 0000; fax: 020 215752; email info@abercrombiekent.co.ke; web: www.abercrombiekent.com
Acacia Trails PO Box 30907, Nairobi; tel: 020 608487; fax: 020 608487; acacia@swiftkenya.com; web: www.africantravelreview.com
African Horizons Travel & Safari PO Box 54998, 00200, City Square, Nairobi; tel: 020 4443500; fax: 020 4443501; email: safari@african-horizons.com; web: www.african-horizons.com
African Quest Safaris Nyerere Av, Palli House, PO Box 99265, Mombasa; tel: 041 227052; fax: 041 316501; email: info@africanquest.co.ke; web: www.africanquest.co.ke
Archers Tours & Travel Peponi Plaza, Peponi Rd, PO Box 437, 00600 Nairobi; tel: 020 3752472; fax: 020 3752476; email: archers@archersafrica.com; web: www.archersafrica.com

As You Like It Safaris PO Box 4051, Nairobi; tel: 020 891353; email: aylis@africaonline.co.ke

Basecamp Travel Ole Odume Rd, PO Box 43369, Nairobi; tel: 020 572139; fax: 020 577489; email: mail@basecampexplorer.co.ke; web: www.basecampexplorer.com

Bateleur Safaris Ndorobo Rd, Langata, PO Box 42562, Nairobi; tel: 020 890458; fax: 020 891007; email: bateleursafaris@swiftkenya.com

Chameleon Tours PO Box 15243, Nairobi; tel: 020 890541; fax: 890541; email: info@safari-selection.com; web: www.safari-selection.com

Cheli and Peacock Safaris PO Box 39806, 00623a Parklands, Nairobi; tel: 020 604053; fax: 020 604050; email: safaris@chelipeacock.co.ke; web: www.chelipeacock.com

Chronicle Tours I & M Bank Tower, Kenyatta Ave, PO Box 49722, Nairobi; tel: 020 311787; fax: 020 246112; email: chronicle@insightkenya.com; web: chronicletours.com

East Africa Ornithological Safaris Fedha Towers, Standard St, PO Box 48019, Nairobi; tel: 020 331684; fax: 020 216528; email: eaos@africaonline.co.ke; web: www.savannacamps.com

Eco-resorts PO Box 120, Watamu; tel: 042 32191; fax: +1 801 991 7410; email: info@eco-resorts.com; web: www.eco-resorts.com

Gametrackers Nginyo Towers, Koinange St, PO Box 62042, Nairobi; tel: 020 212830; fax: 020 330903; email: game@africaonline.co.ke; web: www.gametrackers.com

Gamewatchers Safaris PO Box 388, Village Market 00621, Nairobi; tel: 020 523129; fax: 020 520864; email: jake@wananchi.com; web: www.porini.com

Geo Safaris PO Box 24696, Karen, Nairobi; tel: 020 884258; fax: 020 884445; email: geosafaris@iconnect.co.ke

Grant and Cameron Safaris PO Box 60, Rongai 20108; tel: 051 32004; fax: 051 32048; email: info@classicafricansafaris.com; web: www.classicafricansafaris.com

Hoopoe Safaris (Kenya) Wilson Airport, PO Box 60155, Nairobi; tel: 020 604303; fax: 020 604304; email: hoopoe@wananchi.com; web: www.hoopoe.com

Ker & Downey Safaris Langata South Rd, PO Box 41822, Nairobi; tel: 020 890754; fax: 020 890725; email: enquiries@kerdowneysafaris.co.ke

Kibo Slopes Safaris PO Box 58064, Nairobi; tel: 02 2717373; email: info@kiboslopessafaris.com; web: www.kiboslopessafaris.com

Kwa Kila Hali Safaris PO Box 6793, Eldoret; tel: 053 22154; email: kkhs@multitechweb.com; web: www.kwakilahalisafaris.com

Partners of Adventure Travel Highview Estate, Mbagathi Way, PO Box 5242, Nairobi; tel: 020 712997; fax: 020 712996; email: partners@form-net.com

Richard Bonham Safaris PO Box 24133, 00502, Nairobi, Karen; tel: 020 600457, mobile: 0733 347189 or 0721 464477; fax: 020 605008; email: bonham.luke@swiftkenya.com; web: www.richardbonhamsafaris.com

Robin Hurt Safaris 76 Dagoretti Rd, PO Box 24988, Karen, Nairobi; tel: 020 882826; fax: 020 882939; email: rhsk@swiftkenya.com; web: www.robinhurtphotosafaris.com

Roving Rovers Safaris PO Box 23, Njoro, Kenya; tel: 051 343206; mobile: 254 722 734816; email: mm@africaonline.co.ke/rrovers@wananchi.com; web: www.roving-rovers.com

Safari Camp Services PO Box 44801, Nairobi; tel: 020 891348; fax; 020 212160; email: safaricamp@form-net.com; web: www.safaricampserv.com

Savage Wilderness Safaris PO Box 44827, Nairobi; tel/fax: 020 521590; email: whitewater@alphanet.co.ke

Savuka Tours and Safaris PO Box 20433, Nairobi; tel: 020 215256; fax: 020 215016; email: savuka@nbnet.co.ke; web: www.savukatravels.com

Somak Travel Somak House, Mombasa Rd, PO Box 48495, Nairobi; tel: 020 535500; fax: 020 535172; email: admin@somak-nairobi.com; web: www.somak-nairobi.com

Southern Cross Safaris Symbion House, Karen Rd, PO Box 24584, 00502 Nairobi ; tel: 020 884712; fax: 020 884723; email: safaris@southerncrosskenya.com; web: www.southerncrosssafaris.com

Tony Mills Safaris PO Box 122, Kitale; tel: 054 20695; fax: 054 20695; mobile: 0722 729726; email: tonymills@swiftkenya.co.ke
Vintage Africa Makson Plaza, The Crescent, Westlands, PO Box 59470, 00200 Nairobi; tel: 020 3742450; fax: 020 3742465; email: vintagenbo@vintageafrica.com; web: www.vintageafrica.com

A detailed listing of tour operators in Kenya is given on the KATO website, www.katokenya.org, while other **special interest and activity safari tour operators** are listed under the activity or special interest in *Chapter 6*.

SAFARI PREPARATION
What to take
Clothing
- wide-brimmed hat
- sunglasses
- trousers
- socks
- shorts
- T-shirts
- swimming costume
- long-sleeved shirts
- kikoi/kanga/sarong
- spare prescription glasses
- warm clothing (fleece or light jacket) for early morning and evening game drives

Other
- field guides
- reading material/diary for afternoon siestas
- binoculars (it's well worth having your own pair)
- camera (with plenty of film and spare batteries, plastic bags and an air canister or puffer brush to keep dust off the lenses)
- medical kit including insect repellent and antihistamine
- sunblock
- torch
- nailbrush
- baby wipes
- alarm clock
- penknife
- compass and GPS if travelling in remote areas
- string and a few clothes pegs
- travel wash (laundry service often does not include underwear items)
- tape (for sticking over holes in mosquito nets)

In addition, if travelling around on a low budget, you might like to include a lightweight tent, a sleeping-bag sheet, mosquito net, Doom spray which you can purchase locally for killing insects and bed bugs, medicated soap and a universal plug.

Luggage
Lockable suitcases – squashy; if going on small planes there's a limited baggage allowance of around 15kg.

Safari attitude
- sense of adventure
- sense of humour

- respect for the wildlife and local people
- reasonable expectations – Kenya does not share the Western world's preoccupation with time: Africa time runs at a slower pace and wildlife viewing, although excellent, will not necessarily compare to documentaries on TV.

WHAT TO EXPECT
The journey
A safari will vary with the style chosen and the different activities. On a road safari, be prepared for long distances, often on bumpy roads, with heat and dust, which all adds to the experience, while light aircraft can be affected by turbulence.

Game viewing
The best times for watching wildlife are the early morning and late afternoon when the animals are most active. Some companies offer three game drives a day, but the midday game drive usually has limited viewing and it's hot which can be exhausting. Night game drives, with spotlights, take place any time after dusk.

Safari routine
A typical safari day is to be up at daybreak, with a cup of tea and biscuits before heading off on a game drive, returning to the lodge or camp around mid-morning for brunch (or you might have a bush breakfast), followed by a siesta and afternoon tea, setting out on another game drive around 16.30 (sometimes stopping for sundowners in the bush) and returning at dusk for showers and dinner. Some operators also provide bush dinners.

Safari ablutions
It's likely that at some stage on a camping safari you will come across the **bucket shower**, also known as the safari shower. There are variations on the theme, but essentially this is a canvas bucket or metal container which is filled with water heated on the camp fire. They have a rose like a watering can, with a chain to open and close the shower. As limited water is available, the technique is to get wet, turn off the shower, soap up, and then turn the shower on again to rinse off. **Safari toilets** vary from normal flush loos in some camps and lodges; to short drops – a hole about a foot deep, over which variations on the loo seat are placed (stool or box), where a shovel of soil equates to a 'flush'; to long drops – a deep hole several metres in the ground – where the box loo seats are known as thunderboxes; and compost toilets (which can be a bit smelly but it's for a good cause), where a handful of dried bark is a 'flush'.

Pests
Although solitary Cape buffalo and hippo are renowned for being dangerous, you're more likely to come across safari ants (*siafu*), baboons, monkeys, scorpions and tsetse flies which can be a nuisance.

SUGGESTED ITINERARIES
Kenya has developed a number of **safari circuits** over the years which are well tried and tested, giving a flavour of the people, wildlife and scenery for which the country is renowned, which combine well with a few days relaxing at the coast. They tend to cover large distances by road, so it's preferable to include a few internal flights or to be selective on how many places you visit on the circuit. Typically, the **northern circuit** from Nairobi goes via the tree hotels of the Aberdares or Mount Kenya, skirting west past the Mount Kenya massif to the arid regions of Samburu National Reserve, where you can see the northern species of

game – reticulated giraffe, Beisa oryx, Somali ostrich and Grevy's zebra. In recent years, the options on the northern circuit have expanded to include Lewa Wildlife Conservancy, the Laikipia ranches and Meru National Park. The **southern circuit** from Nairobi embraces Amboseli, the Chyulus and Tsavo East and West national parks. It too has expanded to include Selenkay and the Rukinga Wildlife Conservancies and other Maasai group ranches in the region. The **Rift Valley circuit** from Nairobi heads down the escarpment into the Rift Valley to Lake Naivasha and Hell's Gate National Park, on to Lake Nakuru National Park, Lake Bogoria National Reserve and Lake Baringo. The **Mara circuit** from Nairobi heads down the escarpment, turning west just south of Naivasha. These circuits are often linked together in different combinations – for example an eight-day itinerary might start in Nairobi, head north to a tree hotel and Samburu, and then continue to Lake Baringo, stopping off at Nakuru, Elmentaita or Naivasha on the way to the Masai Mara, before returning back to Nairobi. Another popular combination is Amboseli National Park with a tree hotel and Samburu National Reserve. The **western circuit** is yet to become firmly established on the safari calendar, being considerably longer with fewer spectacular game-viewing opportunities, but the scenery is superb. Leaving from Nairobi it goes down the escarpment, across the Rift Valley to Nakuru, and then branches west through the tea country of Kericho before dropping down to the humid plains around Lake Victoria at Kisumu, heading north to Kakamega Forest National Reserve, continuing to Kitale for Mount Elgon and Saiwa Swamp national parks, and then heading southeast to the Elgeyo escarpment, crossing the Kerio Valley and the Tugen Hills to Lake Baringo and Lake Bogoria National Reserve before returning to Nairobi via Nakuru. Sections of the western circuit can link in well with the Masai Mara and Rift Valley circuits. For example a week's itinerary might start from Nairobi, going down the escarpment and through Naivasha to Nakuru, visiting Lake Nakuru National Park, and then heading west through Kericho and Bomet to the Masai Mara, and back to Nairobi via Naivasha. The Mara also combines well with flying excursions to the Lake Victoria islands and on flying safaris is often linked with Samburu National Park and the coast. The **coastal circuit** may be divided between the south coast, with the marine parks and reserves of Kisite, the Shimba Hills National Park and Mwaluganje Elephant Sanctuary, the north coast with its marine parks and the Arabuko-Sokoke Forest National Reserve and the Lamu Archipelago with its marine parks and reserves. The coastal circuit combines well with the southern circuit, safari excursions often being arranged to Tsavo West and East and Amboseli national parks, or with flying packages to the Masai Mara, as well as from Nairobi.

...for simple breaks or specialist safaris from Victoria Falls, the lower Zambezi, Luangwa Valley, Chobe, Okavango and further south....

The Zambezi Safari & Travel Company

contact

www.zambezi.com

Call +44 (0)1548 830059 (UK)
or +263 61 3351 (Africa)

Hot on Africa!

Just some of our destinations for serious explorers...

*Bradt Guides are available from all good bookshops,
or by post, fax, phone or internet direct from*

Bradt Travel Guides Ltd
19 High Street, Chalfont St Peter, Bucks SL9 9QE, UK
Tel: 01753 893444   Fax: 01753 892333
Email: info@bradt-travelguides.com
Web: www.bradt-travelguides.com

Special Interests and Activities

This chapter is designed to give a flavour of the enormous range of options on offer in Kenya, many of which might not immediately spring to mind when planning a visit. Generally, perceptions of what you can do in Kenya are still limited to safaris by vehicle and a sandy beach at the coast. Many a time I've heard people say wistfully, 'I'd no idea you could do this in Kenya; if only I'd known before I came!'

If interested in wildlife, there are opportunities to participate in voluntary research, go animal tracking and meet the tribal peoples who live alongside the wildlife. Trekking with camels or donkeys into the remote wilderness of the northern deserts and mountains or cycling off the beaten track will appeal to the adventurous. At the coast, a beach holiday is more than a dip in the Indian Ocean: consider watching turtle hatchlings, sharks, whales and dolphins; scuba diving, fun diving and snorkelling in the coral gardens; sailing in a traditional dhow and experiencing Swahili culture. Sporting opportunities abound: incorporate a couple of rounds of golf on championship courses into a wildlife safari, or time a holiday to include a few days at international rugby sevens, cricket or skydiving competitions. Culture vultures will be drawn to the lively contemporary arts' scene, fascinating archaeological and historical sites, excellent museums and vibrant festivals. Shopaholics will be surprised by the range of designer fashion, jewellery and furniture alongside more traditional arts and crafts. And for those who enjoy a challenge, how about participating in the Lewa Marathon or Rhino Charge fund-raising events or climbing Mount Kenya?

For ease of reference, activities and special interests, together with festivals and events are presented below in alphabetical order. The listings are *not* definitive, but for guidance only. These give a brief description together with informaton on the best time of year to visit, a guideline on costs involved, useful tips and specialist tour operators.

Quick reference tables

If you already have a specific interest, such as wildlife, turn first to the quick reference *Wildlife Safaris and Related Activities* table on page 109, which lists the different options with a page reference. Other quick reference tables are *Active Sports and Sporting Events* on page 114, *Culture, History, Lifestyle and Special Interests* on page 128 and *Special Interests, Festivals and Events* on page 132. Often many of these options can be incorporated as part of a safari itinerary.

A TO Z OF SPECIAL INTERESTS AND ACTIVITIES
Agriculture

Agriculture has long been a backbone of the Kenyan economy, and it's possible to include visits to tea, coffee, sugarcane and sisal estates, cattle ranches, wheat, maize and flower farms, as part of a general safari, while some working ranches offer homestays.

Where Western Kenya, the Rift Valley, Laikipia, Central Highlands.
Best time to go During the dry season.
Cost Upwards from US$220 per person a day.
Contact
General itineraries
Let's Go Travel page 101
Homestays on ranches and farms
Bush Homes of East Africa page 90
Mellifera Collection page 91

Animal tracking

If you are interested in learning about animal tracking and bush skills, you'll get the gist of this going for bush walks with a local or professional guide. If you are keen to fine hone your skills, the Taita Discovery Centre offers courses, which can be tailor made for your specific interests, Governors' Camp runs an excellent five-day Field Guide Training Course for a maximum of eight people and Shaba Sarova Lodge runs 'Survivor courses' which include animal tracking. On camel treks and walking safaris you'll get the opportunity to read animal spoor.
Useful tip For the Governors' Camp course it is advisable to book in advance as spaces are limited.
Where On any guided bush walks, courses in Taita, Masai Mara and Samburu.
Best time to go During the dry season.
Cost From around US$65 a day at Taita Discovery Centre, to US$1,500 for the Governors' Camp Field Guide Training Course.
Contact
Governors' Camp page 91
Sarova Shaba Lodge page 375
Taita Discovery Centre Savannah Camps and Lodges, PO Box 48019, Nairobi; tel: 020 222075; fax: 020 330698; email: eaos@africaonline.co.ke; web: www.TaitaDiscovery.com

Art

Attracting artisans from all walks of life, Kenya's artistic community is gaining a reputation worldwide for its contemporary African art. Work ranges from traditional jewellery, basketry, carving and batik work, to wildlife, tribal portrait, botanical and abstract artists, sculptors and designers. Arriving at Jomo Kenyatta International Airport you will see the elephant sculptures on the roundabout by Kioko Mwitiki. Traditional artefacts can be found for sale around the country or under one roof at African Heritage, while a good starting point for modern art is the National Museum in Nairobi, which houses a gallery of contemporary East African Art (with workshops and work for sale) and Joy Adamson's paintings. Other Nairobi galleries include the Ramona Gallery, Gallery Watatu, the Paa ya Paa Gallery, Pimbi Gallery, Legend House and Matbronze, while at grass roots level there's a fine eclectic mix at the *Jua Kali* roadside stalls along Ngong Road. Some companies arrange Art Safaris, where you can practise and improve your own art skills under the guidance of a tutor.
Useful tip Deforestation is a serious problem in Kenya, so if purchasing wooden carvings try to ensure the wood is from a sustainable source.
Where Nairobi's the main centre for contemporary art.
Cost Variable.
Contact See Nairobi chapter listings for museums and galleries, and craft shops, page 183
Art safaris
Eco Resorts page 102

WILDLIFE SAFARIS AND RELATED ACTIVITIES – AND WHERE THEY TAKE PLACE

	Nairobi	South and Eastern Kenya	Central Highlands	The Rift Valley	Western Kenya	Northern Kenya	Coast	page
On land								
Animal tracking		•			•	•		108
Bird shooting		•	•			•		110
Birdwatching	•	•	•	•	•	•	•	110
Butterflies	•				•		•	111
Camping	•	•	•	•	•	•	•	112
Elephant watching		•	•	•	•	•	•	118
Flamingos		•		•	•	•	•	119
Horse-riding	•	•	•	•	•		•	123
Night drives		•	•	•	•			125
Snakes	•				•		•	127
Walking safaris		•	•		•	•		130
Wildebeest migration					•			132
Wildlife safaris	•	•	•	•	•	•	•	133
Airborne								
Ballooning					•			110
Flying safaris	•	•	•	•	•	•	•	120
Helicopter rides			•					122
Water-related								
Deep-sea fishing							•	117
Dolphin/whale watching							•	118
Freshwater fishing			•	•		•		120
Scuba diving							•	126
Snorkelling							•	127
Turtle watching							•	129
Events								
Lewa Marathon			•					136
Rhino Charge *varies*								137
Other interests								
Children on safari	•	•	•	•	•	•	•	114
Conservation and voluntary work	•	•	•	•	•		•	115
Cultural	•	•	•	•	•	•	•	116
Health spas			•		•		•	122
Photography	•	•	•	•	•	•	•	125
Turkana bus						•		129
World birdwatch	•	•	•	•	•	•	•	138

Ballooning

Early morning, floating across the Mara plains in a balloon gives a wonderful bird's eye view of the surroundings, and an idea of the scale of this vast savanna ecosystem that stretches south to the Serengeti in Tanzania. In the Mara, it's a somewhat commercialised operation: large, brightly coloured balloons, where on a morning it's not uncommon to see half a dozen or more on the horizon. But this is not to belittle the experience. After a dawn start, the balloon ride lasts for about an hour, before descending for a balloonists' traditional champagne breakfast in the bush. The environmental impact of balloons is questionable – some animals are frightened by the noise and shadow, yet others remain unperturbed.

Where Masai Mara Game Reserve. Flights can be booked at the time through hotels and lodges, but during the high season it's best to book in advance.

Best time to go During the wildebeest migration in the Mara, from July to October, or during the dry season.

Cost From around US$385.

Contact There are several balloon operators all offering a similar experience. Consider:

Adventures Aloft (fly from Fig Tree Camp) Mada Hotels, PO Box 40683, Nairobi; tel: 020 221439; fax: 020 332170; email: sales@madahotels.com; web: www.madahotels.com

Balloon Safaris (fly from Keekorok Lodge and Siana Springs Intrepids) Wilson Airport, PO Box 43747, Nairobi; tel: 020 605003; fax: 020 604313; email: balloons@africaonline.co.ke

Mara Balloon Safaris (fly from Governors' Camps) Book through Governors' Camps, PO Box 48217, Nairobi; tel: 020 331871; fax: 020 726427; email: reservations@governorscamp.com; web: www.governorscamp.com

Transworld Kenya Ltd (fly from Mara Serena Lodge) PO Box 44690, 00100 GPO, Nairobi; tel: 020 229570; fax: 020 333488; email: transworld@form-net.com

Bird shooting

Although big-game hunting was banned in Kenya in 1977 bird shooting is permitted and brings in a useful income to communities living in marginal areas, whatever one's personal views might be on the matter. Game birds include species like sandgrouse, guinea fowl, pigeon and francolin.

Where In various parts of the country. Popular areas include the Chyulu Hills in southwestern Kenya, Laikipia, and Kalacha in the far north.

Best time to go The bird shooting season runs from September 1 to October 31 and February 1 to March 31.

Cost Gun hire from US$75 a week; cost varies per area from US$200–500 a day for a gun (inclusive of accommodation and beaters), US$30–70 for a bird levy, together with US$100 for a bird licence.

Contact

Richard Bonham Safaris Ltd PO Box 24133, 00502, Nairobi; tel: 020 600457, mobile: 0733 347189 or 0721 464477; fax: 020 605008; email: bonham.luke@swiftkenya.com; web: www.richardbonhamsafaris.com

Safaris Unlimited PO Box 24181, 00502, Nairobi; tel: 020 891113; fax: 020 891976; email: info@safarisunlimited.com; web: www.safarisunlimited.com

Birdwatching

It's not necessary to be an ardent twitcher to appreciate the superb and exotic birdlife found in Kenya, which boasts a birdlist of 1,083, about 12% of the world's bird species. The variety of birds reflects the rich diversity of habitats which attract both resident and migratory species. Indeed, the bird areas of Kenya are now being used as biodiversity indicators. For those interested in birdwatching, there are ornithological safaris, while there are organised birdwalks in Nairobi, and Mombasa and Watamu at the coast.

Useful tip Take a good pair of binoculars, a field guide and sensible shoes.

Where Countrywide.

Best time to go Year round.

Cost A two-week Birdventure Safari with East African Ornithological Safaris costs from US$3,600. There are cheaper alternatives.

Contact Recommended tour operators include:

East Africa Ornithological Safaris page 102

Let's Go Travel page 101

Bird walk excursions

Arabuko Sokoke Forest page 406

Nature Kenya page 184

Ngong Forest page 190

Bungee-jumping

The first bungee-jumping in Kenya started in 2002, from a 60m tower over the Tana River near Sagana. Providing there are three or more people, jumps can take place at any time. Weight limits are restricted to a minimum of 40kg and a maximum of 110kg, with a combined weight for tandem jumps of 100kg. You have to climb the tower yourself, tied to a safety rope, and then have the option of being dunked in the water when you dive.

Useful tip You will have to sign a disclaimer, so check before booking that you are covered by your insurance.

Where On Tana River at the Savage Wilderness Safaris base at Sagana, about 95km northeast of Nairobi on the A2 to Nyeri.

Best time to go Year round.

Cost US$50 for a single jump.

Contact

Bungeewalla Ltd PO Box 1032, The Village Market, Nairobi; tel: 020 523094; email: reblin@mitsuminet.com. Bookings need to be made via the Nairobi office, but you could try pot-luck if passing through Sagana.

Butterflies

Clouds of butterflies appear after the rains, especially in the dry areas, but the most varieties are found in the forests. Kakamega Forest in western Kenya has 400 species recorded while in Arabuko Sokoke Forest at the coast there are around 250 species, with four endemic. If you do not have time to visit the forests, there are excellent butterfly centres in the Karen suburb of Nairobi and at Watamu on the north coast.

Where Western Kenya, Nairobi, the coast.

Best time to go August and September, mid-morning and late afternoon, when the butterflies are more active.

Cost Park entrance fee US$10; butterfly centres from around $5.

Contact

Kenya Wildlife Service for Kakamega and Arabuko Sokoke Forests, page 61

The African Butterfly Research Institute PO Box 14308, Nairobi; tel: 020 884672; fax: 020 884554; email: collinsabri@iconnect.co.ke

Kipepeo Butterfly Farm PO Box 58, Gedi; tel: 042 32380; email: kipepeo@africaonline.co.ke

Camel treks

Camel treks operate in northern Kenya and Laikipia. Although one can ride these 'ships of the desert', it's more common to walk alongside the camels through arid terrain and some of Kenya's most spectacular wilderness, accompanied by Samburu tribesmen. Birdwatching is excellent, but game viewing limited. One can learn about bushlore and play the desert detective under the supervision of knowledgeable guides. Essentially it's a walk in the bush with time to absorb the sights, the sounds and smells. Options range from a morning's walk from a lodge to several days on a camel safari, walking during the cooler hours, resting in the heat of the day and camping out under a sky studded with stars at night – the style of which all depends on the operation. There are options of organised trips, or arranging one's own safari.

Where Northern Kenya and Laikipia.

Best time to go Year round, but it's more comfortable during the cooler months of June, July and August.

Cost The most basic trips start from around US$35 a day and there are fully serviced and self-catering options.

Contact

African Frontiers PO Box 1411, Nanyuki; mob: 0722 329493; email: wreford@wananchi.com; web: www.geocities.com/african_frontiers

Bobong PO Box 5, Rumuruti; tel: 062 32718; fax: 062 32719; email: olmaisor@africaonline.co.ke

Desert Rose Book through Safari Camp Services, PO Box 44801, Nairobi; tel: 020 228936; fax: 020 212160; email: safaricamp@form-net.com; web: www.safaricampserv.com

North Kenya Ventures c/o Lewa Wildlife Conservancy, P Bag, Isiolo; mob: 0722 501241; email: 4wheeler@bushmail.net

Sabuk Book through Cheli & Peacock, PO Box 39806, Nairobi; email: safaris@chelipeacock.co.ke; web: www.chelipeacock.com

Wild Frontiers PO Box 15165, Nairobi; tel: 020 884258/9, fax: 020 884445; email: wildfrontiers@pyramide.net; web: www.pyramide.net/safari

Yare Safaris PO Box 281, Maralal; tel: 065 2295; email: camelsafaris@yaresafaris.com; web: www.yaresafaris.com

Camping and bandas

There's an old saying that goes: 'If you've never slept under canvas, then you've not been on safari'. Certainly the grunts of a lion or the unearthly howl of a hyena near one's tent magnify the excitement of being in the bush. With its dry climate, Kenya's a country that lends itself to camping out, and there's a full spectrum of choice in the camping field, from do-it-yourself through to no frills and pampered luxury, all of which are reflected in the price. For more details on organised camping trips see under the *Tour operators* section on page 99.

For independent travellers, there's a range of private and park campsites – the best provide hot showers, toilets (flush or long-drops) and security, and occasionally there's a restaurant on site. Some campsites also provide bandas (small huts with a bed, some with basic facilities) where you need to bring all your bedding and equipment, and some also have tents to hire.

Useful tip In the park campsites the main hazard are baboons, which can tear a lightweight tent to shreds. This problem can be pre-empted by checking with the park on entry, and if needs be, arranging for someone to guard your tent while you're out, which will cost about KSh200 a day.

Where Countrywide. Recommended private campsites include Kembu, Malewa, Roberts Campsite, El Karama Ranch, Sirikwa Campsite, Marich Pass Field Studies

Centre and Bobong Campsite, together with the Kenya Wildlife Service (KWS) park campsites and bandas.
Best time to go Year round, but best to avoid the rainy season.
Cost From around US$4 for independent camping, to US$500 a day for the most luxurious.
Contact There are a number of operators in all categories. See page 99 and **KWS** on page 91.

Canoeing, boating, river tubing and sea kayaking
Kenya does not have the river-canoeing safaris of southern Africa, although there is talk of starting canoe trips on the Kerio River. But there is canoeing and boating on Lake Naivasha, superb for birdwatching, with the chance of seeing hippos and the Cape clawless otter. Lakes Baringo and Victoria (beware bilharzia in Victoria – see *Health and safety*, page 149) have the large, motorised *ssese* canoes, again ideal for bird and game watching. Kayaking is now available on the Tana, while on the Ewaso Ng'iro River (Ngurumans) there are plans for river tubing and canoeing. Other boating options are on Lake Turkana and at the coast.
Useful tip Safety check: on boat trips not all operators provide lifejackets so do check in advance of booking and make sure that you're covered by your travel insurance. You may be asked to sign an insurance waiver.
Where Lakes Naivasha, Baringo, Victoria, Turkana, the Tana, Athi and Ewaso Ng'iro rivers and the coast.
Best time to go Year round, but check local conditions for wind and river levels.
Cost Variable. For guidance: a boat trip on Lake Baringo costs from around US$25. A two-hour boat trip on Naivasha costs from around KSh2,000.
Contact Local contacts are listed under regional chapters. For general information and booking:
Gametrackers page 102
Kilalinda page 222
Let's Go Travel page 101
Savage Wilderness Safaris page 102

Caving
Many of Kenya's hills and mountains have caves, some of which are suited to caving proper. Of these, Leviathan in the Chyulu Hills has the world's fourth longest **lava tube system**, with passages covering 12.5km, which can be traversed in a day, although some sections are slippery and demanding and require ladder and climbing experience. Mount Suswa, an extinct Rift Valley volcano, has a major system of braided lava tubes, segmented into 40 different caves with some 8km of passages, the longest being 3km long. Generally the caving is easy, but some caves require ladder descents. **Limestone caves** occur in the Tiva area of Tsavo East and inland from the coast. **Volcanic tuff and rift caves** occur on Mount Elgon (among them those mined by elephants, Kitum being the most famous) and the Kericho area. Proper Kenyan caving requires a knowledge of the cave locations and conditions and suitable equipment – helmets, headlamps, overalls (with arm and knee pads for crawling over sharp lava) and suitable footwear. Some caving equipment is locally available for hire. Elsewhere, there are caves in the Cherangani and Tugen Hills, and the slave caves of Shimoni at the coast.
Useful tip Take a professional guide to maximise your enjoyment and safety.
Where Chyulus, Tsavo East, Mount Suswa, Mount Elgon, Cherangani and Tugen Hills, south coast.
Best time to go Avoid the rainy season.

ACTIVE SPORTS AND SPORTING EVENTS – AND WHERE THEY TAKE PLACE

	Nairobi	South and Eastern Kenya	Central Highlands	The Rift Valley	Western Kenya	Northern Kenya	Coast	page
On land								
Bird shooting	•		•	•		•		110
Camel treks			•			•	•	112
Caving		•	•			•	•	113
Cycling and mountain biking		•	•	•	•		•	117
Donkey treks						•		118
Fitness training					•		•	119
Health spas			•		•		•	122
Horse-riding	•	•	•	•	•		•	123
Mountaineering and rock climbing		•	•	•	•			124
Walking safaris		•	•		•	•		130
Airborne								
Ballooning					•			110
Bungee-jumping			•					111
Flying safaris	•	•	•	•	•	•	•	120
Gliding			•	•				121
Helicopter rides			•					122
Microlighting		•						124
Skydiving	•						•	138

Cost Cave excursions from Umani Springs Camp cost in the region of US$55 per person (minimum of four people).

Contact

Let's Go Travel page 101

Cave Exploration Group of East Africa PO Box 47583, 00100 Nairobi; tel: 020 520883; email: fajo@kenyaweb.com

Children

Kenya is an ideal family holiday, with plenty on offer to keep children entertained. Companies like Heritage Hotels have an adventure club for children, which organises activities, and also teaches them a little about the Kenyan environment and wildlife when on safari. Many companies offer reduced rates for children, and children pay less than half price in the national parks and reserves up to the age of 18. Baby-sitting services are often available for a small fee. At the same time, some camps are not child friendly, and will not take children under 12.

Useful tip Bring favourite food for toddlers, and toys or books to occupy youngsters on long journeys. Select accommodation with swimming pools, ideal for cooling off and for entertaining children in between game drives.

	Nairobi	South and Eastern Kenya	Central Highlands	The Rift Valley	Western Kenya	Northern Kenya	Coast	page
Water-related								
Canoeing, boating, river tubing and sea kayaking	•			•	•	•	•	113
Deep-sea fishing							•	117
Freshwater fishing			•	•	•	•		120
Kite surfing							•	124
Scuba diving							•	126
Snorkelling							•	127
Whitewater rafting			•					131
Sporting events								
Bullfighting					•			134
Cricket	•							135
Dhow racing							•	135
Kenya Open Golf Tournament	•							136
Lewa Marathon				•				136
Maralal Camel Derby and Elite Cycle races						•		136
Migwena Festival					•			134
Rhino Charge *varies*								137
Safari Rally *varies*								137
Safari Sevens (rugby)	•							137
Skydiving	•						•	138

Where Countrywide.
Best time to go Avoid the rainy season.
Cost Variable.
Contact
Heritage Hotels page 91
Let's Go Travel page 101

Conservation and voluntary work

Apart from international organisations such as the Earthwatch International and gap-year programmes, there are a number of Field Studies Centres in Kenya, among them: Taita Discovery Centre near Voi, Elsamere Field Study Centre on Lake Naivasha, the Gallmann Memorial Foundation on Ol Ari Ng'iro ranch in Laikipia and Marich Pass Field Studies Centre in western Kenya, which offer various programmes for scientific study, conservation and voluntary work. The Taita Discovery Centre and Marich Pass Field Studies Centre both offer flexible programmes for voluntary workers, while the tour operator Eco Resorts offers a safari itinerary which includes helping out at a children's home on the coast. In addition, Serena Hotels runs a tree-planting scheme for visitors. At the time of writing Earthwatch had voluntary programmes monitoring Grevy's zebra in Laikipia and Samburu, Tsavo lions, black rhino, rare plants, mangroves at the coast and Rift Valley lakes.

Where Northwestern Kenya, Naivasha, Rift Valley, Samburu, Laikipia, Taita, the coast.

Best time to go Year round.

Cost Variable; Earthwatch programmes cost from US$2,195 for two weeks; Taita Discovery Centre from US$180 a week (four weeks minimum) exclusive of travel arrangements.

Contact

Field studies centres and voluntary work

Elsamere Conservation Centre page 278

The Gallman Memorial Foundation PO Box 455930, Nairobi; email: info@mukutan.com; web: www.mukutan.com

Kigio Wildlife Conservancy page 286

Marich Pass Field Studies Centre page 348

Taita Discovery Centre page 223

Operators with participatory programmes

Eco-resorts page 102

Serena Hotels page 91

International

Earthwatch International 3 Clock Tower Place, Suite 100, Box 75 Maynard, MA 01754, USA; tel: (978) 461 0081; fax: (978) 461 2332; email: info@earthwatch.org; web: www.earthwatch.org

Cultural

If you're interested in learning something about Kenya's rich tribal cultures, the ethnicity exhibits at the national and regional museums provide an excellent start. With over 40 different tribes (some sources say as many as 74), when travelling around the country you're likely to come across a variety of tribal groups and a few, like the Maasai, Samburu, Gabbra and Pokot pastoralists, still retain a strong traditional lifestyle. There are displays of tribal dancing at the **Bomas of Kenya** in Nairobi, while the **Riuki Cultural Centre** in Kiambu gives an introduction to the history of Kenya's indigenous people and explains Kikuyu culture. At the coast, there's a cultural display of different Kenyan tribes at **Ngomongo** and visits to the sacred **Kaya shrines**. There are cultural **Maasai manyattas** (homesteads) around the Mara and Amboseli. The latter vary in quality and authenticity – some offer packaged culture geared to the tourist. Excursions from the **community lodges** (see page 57) give a genuine and valuable insight into respective tribal cultures, as do visits to Pokot homesteads from **Marich Pass Field Studies Centre**.

Useful tip In the past, many tribal peoples have been viewed as an exotic exhibit alongside the wildlife – another photo opportunity. Their way of life is different to that of Western developed countries, but *not* inferior – it's important to respect cultural differences, and when taking photographs or entering homesteads, remember to ask first.

Where Countrywide.

Best time to go Year round.

Cost Variable. For guidance only, an afternoon's cultural visit to the Riuki Cultural Centre costs from $30.

Contact Among companies who offer cultural experiences, consider:

Bomas of Kenya page 188

Chronicle Tours page 102
Eco-resorts page 102
Let's Go Travel page 101
Marich Pass Field Studies Centre page 348
Riuki Cultural Centre page 194
Kaya Shrines Coastal Forest Conservation Unit, PO Box 86, Ukunda; tel: 040 2518 or
0722 446916; email: cfcu.kwale@swifmombasa.com
Ngomongo Villages PO Box Shanzu, Mombasa; tel: 041 486425; fax: 041 222393; email:
rafiki@ngomongo.com; web: www.ngomongo.com

Cycling and mountain biking

This is a great way to experience rural Africa, but don't underestimate the
effects of altitude – often around 1,525m. Several companies specialise in
cycling safaris, and it's best to contact them for details if you wish to bring your
own bike. The bikes provided vary from excellent to basic, depending on the
operation, and this is generally reflected in the cost. At the coast and Lake
Naivasha, it's also possible to hire bikes for the day – terrific for short
explorative journeys.
Useful tip It's worthwhile ensuring that you get a comfortable saddle, are
prepared for plenty of punctures if independent (bring extra inner tubes), carry a
water bottle and have adequate sun protection (particularly behind the knees). The
enjoyment is that much greater if you're reasonably fit.
Where Laikipia, Loita Hills, Kajiado, Narok, Cheranganis, Naivasha, coast.
Best time to go During the cooler months from June to September. Avoid the
rainy season.
Cost Variable. For guidance: no-frills cycling with camping from US$285 for a
three-day trip; upmarket around US$230 a day.
Contact Various companies offer cycling safaris, including:
Cheli & Peacock page 102
Let's Go Travel page 101
Activity Safaris PO Box 10190, Bamburi, Mombasa; tel: 041 471308; email:
actsafari@africaonline.co.ke
Bike Treks PO Box 14237, Nairobi; tel: 020 446371; fax: 020 442439; email:
info@biketreks.com; web: www.biketreks.com
Black Mamba Safaris PO Box 119, Timau; mob: 0722 790107; email:
horsey@africaonline.co.ke; web: www.bicycleafrica.com

Deep-sea fishing

East Africa is a Mecca for deep-sea fishermen, many world and all-Africa records
being held in Kenya. Slams, grand slams and fantasy slams are the fisherman's
dream, with six types of billfish in Kenyan waters, striped, blue and black marlin
being the main species, together with sailfish, swordfish, sharks, wahoo, yellowfin
tuna and dorado. Kenya operates a 'tag and release' system. Several places specialise
in fishing. Boats depart in the early morning, troll for bait and then head out to the
deep water, where there's quite a swell in the afternoon, to wait for the big catch.
A peaceful lull contrasts with frenetic activity, reeling in a fish, some leaping clear
of the water with all the grace of a dancer.
Useful tip Take precautions against sunburn, glare from the water and
seasickness.
Where Along the coast, key areas being Shimoni, Watamu, Malindi and Kilifi.
Best time to go Fishing season is August to March, with the billfish season from
November to March.

Cost From US$350 a day.
Contact There are numerous operators at the coast. Those with an excellent reputation include:
Hemphills Sea Adventures PO Box 348, Ukunda; tel: 040 52220; email: hemphill@bigame.com; web: www.bigame.com
Pemba Channel Fishing Club (at Shimoni), PO Box 86952, Mombasa; tel: 041 313749; mobile: 0722 0502; fax: 041 316675; email: pembachannel@africaonline.co.ke
Hemingways PO Box 267, Watamu; tel: 042 32624; fax: 042 32256; email: hemingways@swiftmalindi.com; web: www.hemingways.co.ke
Howard Lawrence-Brown PO Box 10202, Mombasa; tel: 041 486394; email: hook-up@swiftmombasa.com; web: www.kenyadeepseafishing.com
Kingfishers Malindi; tel: 042 20123; email: kingfisher@swiftmombasa.com

Dolphin and whale watching

Few are not captivated by the effervescent playfulness of dolphins, as they come alongside a boat, surfing the wake. There are excellent dolphin trips at Shimoni and Lamu. Some offer trips swimming with the dolphins, but this can be dangerous and causes friction with guests from the other viewing boats. In season, during the month of October, there's also the possibility of seeing humpback whales, or even the occasional whale shark, known as the 'Kenya-bus' fish due to its size. From Diani you can take a motorboat excursion on *Maisha* to Shimoni, operated by Diani Marine, which cuts out the road journey.
Where Diani, Shimoni on the south coast, Lamu.
Best time to go Year round for dolphins, October for whales.
Cost From US$55 for a day trip from Shimoni with Kisite Dhow Tours and US$95 with Diani Marine on *Maisha*
Contact Recommended operators include:
South coast
Pilli Pipa page 439
Diani Marine PO Box 340, Ukunda; tel: 040 2367; fax: 040 3452; email: dimarine@africaonline.co.ke; web: www.dianimarine.com
Charlie Claw's Wasini Island Restaurant and Kisite Dhow Tours PO Box 281, Ukunda; tel: 040 2331; fax: 040 3154; email: diving@wasini-island.com; web: www.wasini-island.com
Lamu
Kipungani Explorer (Heritage Hotels), page 419

Donkey treks

As with the camel treks, the donkeys are pack animals for serious walking expeditions. More versatile than camels, they can traverse most terrain, and are especially adept in steep forested areas. Some companies provide a couple of mules for those who like to take to the saddle occasionally.
Where The Karisia hills east of Maralal.
Best time to go During the dry season months, but check local conditions.
Cost From US$590 for a three-day inclusive camping trip.
Contact
Samburu Trails PO Box 40, Maralal; fax: 0365 32379; email: info@samburutrails.com; web: www.samburutrails.com

Elephant watching

Despite the fact that Kenya's elephants were decimated during the poaching wars of the 1970s and 1980s – diving from a population of 170,000 in 1963 to 16,000 by

1989 – Kenya has a healthy elephant population and is renowned for the work of its eminent elephant researchers, Cynthia Moss and Joyce Poole in Amboseli, and Iain Douglas-Hamilton in Samburu. There are excellent opportunities to view elephants in most of Kenya's national parks and reserves (but not Nairobi or Lake Nakuru national parks), as well as community conservancies like Mwalugange Elephant Sanctuary and the community ranches of Il Ngwesi, Lekerruki and Namunyak. In addition are the tree hotels – the Ark in the Aberdares and Mountain Lodge on Mount Kenya. For those interested in elephant conservation, safaris operated by Elephant Watch Safaris in Samburu and Ol Kanjau near Amboseli give guests an introduction to the elephant families which have been studied by elephant researchers, while at the Taita Discovery Centre, volunteers are attached to the Earthwatch Elephant Monitoring Project and participate in active research.

Where Good places to see elephant are: Amboseli, Samburu, Masai Mara, Tsavo East and West, Aberdares and Mount Kenya, Laikipia, Mathews Mountains, Mwaluganje Elephant Sanctuary, Taita Hills, Mount Elgon (for the elephant caves – not so easy to see the elephant) and Nasalot Reserve.

Best time to go Year round.

Cost From US$170 for an elephant-watch excursion, or from US$475 a day staying at the camp, with Elephant Watch Safaris and from US$345 a day with Ol Kanjau.

Contact For special-interest elephant safaris and participatory research:

Elephant Watch Safaris page 371

Ol Kanjau page 211

Taita Discovery Centre page 223

Fitness training

Kenya is renowned for its long-distance runners and now has high-altitude training camps in western Kenya where serious athletes can train. At sea level in Watamu, Wildfitness runs a training programme utilising the sea, beach and nearby forests.

Where Western Kenya, north coast.

Best time to go Avoid the rainy season, and for the coast it gets very hot from January to March.

Cost A nine-day fitness course with Wildfitness costs from around US$2,460.

Contact

General fitness

Wildfitness page 402

Specialist athletics

Kenya Athletics Association Email: info@kenyaathletics.com; web: www.kenyaathletics.com

Flamingos

Kenya is famous for its concentrations of flamingos, both greater and lesser, on the soda lakes of the Rift Valley. The best places to see flamingos are Lake Nakuru National Park and Lake Bogoria National Reserve (they're both accessible by 2WD). In addition, you'll see flamingos giving pink fringes to the lakes at Elmenteita and Magadi in the Rift Valley, Amboseli, Simbi (near Lake Victoria) and Crater Lake in Turkana at certain times of year.

Where Rift Valley soda lakes, the best being Lake Nakuru National Park and Lake Bogoria National Reserve.

Best time to go The best time is generally after the rains in July when the lakes have reasonable water levels and the algae multiplies; but usually there's good viewing on lakes Nakuru and Bogoria throughout the year.

Cost Park entrance fees.
Contact General interest tour operators, page 99, or bird specialists, as above.

Flying safaris

Kenya has a strong flying tradition, and boasts famous pilots like the aviatrix Beryl Markham, the first woman to fly the Atlantic solo. Wilson Airport in Nairobi, which services small planes, is one of the busiest airports in Africa, with as many as 450 landings a day in the high season. Flying safaris have gained in popularity, as people have less time and wish to spend it in the prime game-viewing areas. Internal flights are reasonably priced and many companies offer flying packages to their camps. Kenya has 520 airfields, many in remote corners of the country not easily accessible by road, making flying an attractive alternative. Several companies provide scheduled services and private air charters are also available. There are scheduled services to Kisumu, Masai Mara, Nanyuki, Samburu, Amboseli, Mombasa, Ukunda (Diani Beach), Malindi, Lamu and Lokichogio. See page 80 for details. For qualified pilots, it is possible to validate a licence which involves taking a check-out flight and paying a small fee. To charter a plane (such as a Cessna 150) costs in the region of US$100 an hour inclusive of fuel, together with navigation and landing fees for some airports, and a parking fee if landing at one of the 12 manned airports.

Useful tip When considering a flying safari, bear in mind that turbulence is far greater in small planes, and the ride is more bumpy in the middle of the day. If prone to being queasy, get a seat near the front, keep your eye on the horizon, take a bag of boiled sweets or chewing gum, and always carry a bottle of water. You can also purchase acupressure wrist-bands or take travel sickness pills.

Where Countrywide.
Best time to go Year round.
Cost Variable.
Contact For scheduled services see page 80. For general information on chartering a plane:
Aero Club of East Africa Wilson Airport, PO Box 40813, 00100 Nairobi; tel: 020 600482/3; fax: 020 600482/3; email: aeroclub.ea@swiftkenya.com
Among companies offering flying safaris are:
Acacia Trails page 101
Borana Lodge page 258
Geosafaris Email: geosafaris@iconnect.co.ke
Ultralight Machines (K) Ltd PO Box 34304, Nairobi; tel: 020 2713591; mob: 0733 704065; email: alexpelulm@iconnect.co.ke

Freshwater fishing

There is good trout fishing (fly) in the lakes and streams of Mount Kenya and the Aberdares, or on private dams in western Kenya. Excellent Nile perch and tilapia fishing can be arranged from Mfangano, Rusinga and Takawiri islands in Lake Victoria, or from Loyangalani, Kalokol, or a houseboat on Lake Turkana. Spinning for black bass and tilapia is popular on Lake Naivasha. Equipment is usually provided. All fishermen require a fishing licence, obtainable from the Fisheries Department, next to the National Museum in Nairobi or through the fishing organisers.

Useful tip It's considered best to avoid a full moon, when fish feed at night.
Where Mount Kenya, the Aberdares, Kericho, Lakes Victoria, Turkana and Naivasha.
Best time to go Year round, but for trout avoid the rains.

Cost Variable. Staying on a houseboat on Lake Turkana costs from US$200 a day inclusive.
Contact The following companies can arrange fishing:
Bush Homes of East Africa for Lobolo Camp on Lake Turkana, page 90
Gametrackers page 102
Let's Go Travel page 101
Mellifera Collection, for Burch's Houseboat on Lake Turkana, page 91
Naro Moru River Lodge page 241

Gliding

Kenya has superb soaring conditions for gliding. Due to the strong tropical sun at the equator, the ground heats up fast providing strong thermals. The gliders are supported on the columns of rising air, climbing to great heights and with excellent views.
Where Elmentaita in the Rift Valley and Mweiga near Nyeri in the Central Highlands.
Best time to go January to March.
Cost In the region of US$20 for the launch with ten minutes' gliding time and US$20 per hour thereafter.
Contact
Cloud Chasers Rift Valley Gliding, PO Box 24540, Karen, 00502 Nairobi; tel: 020 882195; fax: 020 884561; email: cloudchasers@swiftkenya.com; web: www.yellowwings.com/gliding
Gliding Club PO Box 926, Nyeri; tel: 061 2748; fax: 061 2748; email: gliding@africaonline.co.ke

Gourmet

Haute cuisine might not be considered high on a safari agenda, but Kenya boasts a great diversity and high standard of restaurants, ranging from the internationally renowned Tamarind restaurants specialising in seafood, the Haandi Indian Restaurant and the Carnivore, which serves different types of game meat and, bizarrely, is a popular finale to a wildlife safari. Having a broad mix of cultures within Kenya, the multi-national influence is reflected by the variety of restaurants, from Japanese, Chinese, Indian, Italian and Ethiopian, to delicious Swahili food.
Where Restaurants are for the most part centred on Nairobi and the coast, although Finch Hatton's Camp in Tsavo, complete with Mozart and crystal, is reputed to have the best bush menu.
Cost Variable. For good restaurants, for guidance only, from around US$12 per person.
Contact See restaurant listings under regional sections.

The Great Rift Valley

Kenya is one of the best places in Africa to appreciate the scale of the Rift Valley, which stretches from the Red Sea in the north, to Mozambique in the south. This major geological feature not only has dramatic escarpments, but also a chain of lakes, both freshwater and soda. The most accessible place to view the Rift is north of Nairobi, where the escarpment drops from forestry and *shambas* at around 2,440m to the savanna plains at 915m, with expansive views of the extinct volcanic craters of Longonot and Suswa. On a clear day one can see the Rift wall on the far side rising some 80km away. The **Elgeyo escarpment** overlooking the Kerio Valley in western Kenya and the **Losiolo escarpment** north of Maralal are equally dramatic. Alternatively, flying in a small plane from Nairobi to the Masai Mara gives excellent views of the Rift Valley.

Best time to go Early morning or late afternoon for the clearest views.
Contact Tour operators for safaris to the Rift Valley.

Health spas

A recent addition to Kenya's safari repertoire are health spas ranging from massage and aromatherapy, sometimes using locally extracted organic oils, to mud facials, with the full works of body scrubs, pedicures and manicures, combined with yoga and meditation. These are offered by Loisaba and Mukutan in Laikipia and Alfajiri and Baraka House at the coast. In fact massage and beauty treatments are also offered by many of the large hotel groups, such as Serena and Heritage. If you'd like a 'do-it-yourself' natural mud bath, visit the Tana River Delta Camp or Chale Island.
Where Laikipia, the coast.
Best time to go Year round.
Cost From US$5,100 for an 11-day spa safari with Eco-resorts; from US$2,460 for a ten-day yoga course with Wildfitness.
Contact Holistic and natural therapies are included by the following:
Alfajiri page 434
Chale Island page 440
Cottar's 1920's Camp page 317
Eco-resorts page 102
Heritage Hotels page 91
Loisaba page 260
Mukutan page 261
Serena Hotels page 91
Tana River Delta Camp page 414
Wildfitness page 402

Helicopter rides

Exploring desert wilderness areas to the north, or following the Mukatan Gorge to the Rift Valley lakes of Baringo and Bogoria by helicopter (a Eurocopter Squirrel) are novel ways to experience remote places inaccessible by road. It's even possible to go heli-camping. Based in Loisaba on the Laikipia Plateau, helicopter excursions can be arranged for up to five passengers.
Where From Laikipia.
Best time to go Year round, but some rides are impossible during the rains in November, April and May.
Cost Charters of 1-3hr flying from US$1,500 per hour.
Contact
Lady Lori (K) Ltd PO Box 24397, Karen 00502, Nairobi, tel: 020 577381; fax: 020 577382; email: ladylori@africaonline.co.ke

Historical

Kenya has a wealth of historical sites. Most come under the auspices of the National Museums of Kenya. Among these are Koobi Fora, in Sibiloi National Park, and Olorgesailie for those of early man; the 15th-century dry-stone enclosures of the late Iron Age Bantu settlers in western Kenya; the Swahili and Portuguese ruins on the coast and relics of trenches and gun positions from World War I in the Taita Hills. Some sites are more easily accessed than others. The National Museums of Kenya have excellent exhibits at the Nairobi Museum and also at their regional museums – Karen Blixen in Nairobi, Lamu, Gedi and Fort Jesus at the coast, Kisumu, Kitale, Kabarnet, Kapenguria and Narok in western

Kenya, Hyrax Hill, Kariandusi and Olorgesailie in the Rift Valley, and Meru in the Central Highlands. Conservation efforts are being made to retain the architectural heritage of the old towns of Lamu (now a World Heritage Site) and Mombasa. There are a few community museums, such as Kipsaraman in the Tugen Hills, which exhibits Millennium Man.

Useful tip Due to the searing temperatures, it's preferable to visit the prehistoric sites and the ruins at the coast in the early morning and late afternoon.

Where Countrywide.

Best time to go Year round.

Cost Museum entry from KSh200; variable on private ranches.

Contact

Lewa Wildlife Conservancy page 264

Taita Discovery Centre page 223

Community Museums of Kenya PO Box 74689, Nairobi; tel: 020 2729496; fax: 020 2729496; email: johnmaringah@yahoo.com

National Museums of Kenya PO Box 40658, Nairobi; tel: 020 742141-4; fax: 020 741424; email: nmk@africaonline.co.ke; web: www.museums.or.ke

Horseriding

Kenya has a riding heritage from the settler days – with hunting, racing and polo still on the agenda. For visitors, there's provision for the novice and experienced rider. On private ranches you can go for game rides, which most often equate to pony-trekking – here you do not need to be experienced, and may well remain at a walk. Being on horseback you can get closer to the game – giraffe, zebra and antelope – than on foot, and you see more from a higher elevation. There's also the option of forest rides in Nairobi's suburbs. Serious, long-distance riding safaris across the Masai Mara and Laikipia Plateau are for those well-seasoned in the saddle, where a prerequisite is that you must be able to gallop out of trouble if the need arises.

Useful tip Hard hats are not always provided.

Where Nairobi, the Mara, Laikipia, Rift Valley, Chyulus, Naivasha, Njoro. Polo is played regularly in Nairobi, Gilgil and Timau, while there's a race meeting twice a month, or more, on Sundays in Nairobi at the Ngong race track.

Best time to go Avoid the rainy seasons.

Cost Normally included in the price of a homestay; a ten-day safari costs in the region of US$4,400 per person sharing a tent/room.

Contact

Short excursions

Kembu Campsite Njoro, page 291

Karen Riding School Marula Lane, Karen, Nairobi, tel: 020 884154; email: nineineke@yahoo.com

Homestays

Longonot Ranch House Naivasha, page 278

Ol Donyo Wuas Chyulus, page 212

Wilderness Trails Laikipia, page 257

Riding safaris

Safaris Unlimited PO Box 24181, 00502, Nairobi; tel: 020 891113; fax: 020 891976; email: info@safarisunlimited.com; web: www.safarisunlimited.com

Offbeat Safaris PO Box 56923, Nairobi; tel: 020 571649; fax: 020 571665; email: offbeat@africaonline.co.ke; web: www.offbeatsafaris.com

Racing

The Jockey Club of Kenya www.jockeyclubkenya.com

Kite surfing

Che-Shale is one of the best places in the world for kite surfing, with an empty beach and wind blowing from 8–25 knots (14–45km/h). It has the only kite-surfing school in Kenya where you can also hire equipment. Kite surfing uses a powerful traction-kite which you fly while standing on a small surfboard. The effect is similar to being towed by a powerful speedboat. The action of a traction-kite is not only horizontal (like waterskiing) but also vertical. Experienced kite surfers can take off from the water, similar to paragliding.

Where Che-Shale about 20km north from Malindi at the coast.
Best time to go Year round.
Cost Two-day courses from US$200.
Contact
Kite Surfing School PO Box 1434, Malindi; mob: 0722 426752; email: che-shale@africaonline.co.ke; web: www.che-shale.com

Microlighting

If you fancy learning to microlight in Africa, or taking a tandem flight which lasts for about 20 minutes, this can be arranged through Ultralight machines, a sideline for a company that specialises in wildlife surveys and aerial filming. Currently, it is not possible to get a microlight flying licence in Kenya, although foreign licence validation is scheduled for 2003. Machines are not available for individual hire.

Where Near Amboseli.
Best time to go Early morning and late afternoon.
Cost Around US$50 for a tandem flight, one-hour lessons from US$80.
Contact
Ultralight Machines (K) Ltd PO Box 34304, Nairobi; tel: 020 2713591; mob: 0733 704065; email: alexpelulm@iconnect.co.ke

Mountaineering and rock climbing

The draw of tropical ice, climbing **Mount Kenya** (5,199m; 17,056ft), Africa's second highest mountain, is the main attraction, with technical climbs on the two highest peaks, **Bation** (5,199m) and **Nelion** (5,188m). The third peak, **Point Lenana** (4,985m), is a challenging hike and can be reached by non-climbers, while there's also an interesting trek around the summit. Elsewhere there's excellent rock climbing and trekking in many parts of the country, including Tsavo West, Athi River, Hell's Gate, the Aberdares, Cheranganis and Mathews ranges. The **Mountain Club of Kenya** is an excellent source of information as is the Mount Kenya webpage.

Useful tip When planning a trip, bear in mind that it's important to acclimatise well, as pulmonary oedema, which can be fatal, can occur. (See *Health and safety*.) On the mountain take good sun protection, comfortable boots and appropriate clothing. A platypus water bottle and high energy snacks are useful.
Where Countrywide.
Best time to go For Mount Kenya, January and February are best and August fair, but avoid May and November; elsewhere check out regional climatic conditions.
Cost Variable, depending on operators, with prices ranging from US$300–1,230 for a five-day climb on Mount Kenya.
Contact For detailed information on *technical* climbs:
Mountain Club of Kenya PO Box 45741, Nairobi, tel: 020 501747 (evenings only); email: MCKenya@iname.com; web: www.mck.or.ke. The website includes a virtual clubhouse and there's a genuine clubhouse at Wilson Airport (near the Aero Club) with open meetings on Tuesdays at 20.00.
Mount Kenya homepage: www.mountkenya.org

Companies specialising in trekking and climbing
Basecamp Travel page 102
Kibo Slopes Safaris page 213
Let's Go Travel page 101
East African Mountain Guides (Savage Wilderness Safaris), PO Box 44827, Nairobi, tel: 020 521590, mobile: 0733 735508; fax: 020 521590; email: whitewater@alphanet.co.ke
Ice Rock Mountain Trekking NCM Bldg (4th Floor), Tom Mboya St, Nairobi; tel: 020 244608; email: icetrekk@kenyaweb.com; web: www.climbingafrica.com
For a full listing of Mount Kenya tour operators, see page 244.

Night drives

These are currently offered only on private conservancies and in some reserves, although the Kenya Wildlife Service was considering changing its policy in 2003 to include night drives in national parks. Driving using a powerful spotlight, the attraction of night drives is that you get the opportunity to see some of the wildlife which is nocturnal, such as civet cats, aardvark and white-tailed mongoose. Some people consider the lights disturb the animals. Note: Nightvision, the company which used infrared spotlights, is no longer operating in the Masai Mara.
Where Laikipia, Shaba, Amboseli, Tsavo, Chyulus, Shompole and Masai Mara areas.
Best time to go Avoid the rainy season.
Cost Night drives are normally included in the tour price.
Contact Among companies offering night drives are:
Gamewatchers Safaris page 102
Lewa Wildlife Conservancy page 264
Loisaba Wilderness page 260
Shompole page 203

Photography

The superb light conditions, diverse scenery, wildlife and people draw professional and amateur photographers alike to Kenya. For those who wish to improve their skills, there are photographic safaris with a professional tutor, and some companies offer the opportunity to hire lenses for the duration of the trip. Hoskins Tours and Eco-resorts both offer safaris with professional nature photographers.
Useful tip Bring a puffer brush or air canister and plenty of plastic bags so that you can protect your camera and lenses from the dust when they're not in use.
Where Countrywide.
Best time to go Year round, depending on aspirations. During the rainy seasons, the air clears after rain giving sharp landscape images, but lighting is variable at that time with overcast skies. In general, avoid the rainy seasons unless you are looking for special effects.
Cost From US$3,350 per person for a minimum of four on a ten-day camping safari.
Contact
Eco-resorts page 102
Hoskings Tours Pages Green House, Wetheringsett, Stowmarket, Suffolk IP14 5QA, UK; tel: 01728 861113; fax: 01728 860222; email: david@hosking-tours.co.uk; web: www.hosking-tours.co.uk

Radio

Kenya has a small but enthusiastic Amateur Radio Society and people from overseas are welcome to apply for a licence. As requirements change, it's best to consult the comprehensive Amateur Radio Society of Kenya website.

Useful tip As licences can take time to process it's best to apply well in advance.
Best time to go Year round.
Cost The licence costs in the region of US$40.
Contact
Amateur Radio Society of Kenya PO Box 45681, 00100 Nairobi; web: www.qsl.net/arsk

Sailing

There are a number of sailing options at the coast, which range from hiring dinghies and sailboards from the hotels or negotiating with a fisherman for a ride on an *ngalawa*, the traditional outrigger canoe, to chartering a yacht or going on a dhow safari. It used to be possible to pay one's passage on a working dhow sailing from Lamu to Mombasa, but those opportunities are rare these days. You're more likely to get a passage from Shimoni to Pemba. With the trade winds, there's always a breeze blowing, and Shimoni, Mtwapa, Kilifi and the Lamu Archipelago are popular anchorages. The yacht and dhow charters often combine to include other watersports like windsurfing, waterskiing and scuba diving. In addition, informal sand yachting takes place on the beach at Tana River Delta Camp.
Where The coast.
Best time to go Year round, although October sailing is particularly good. For longer trips, take into account the trade winds – the southeast monsoon, the Kaskazi, blows from April to October, while the northeast monsoon, the Kazi, blows from November to March.
Cost From KSh500 for half an hour for a dinghy to US$800 a day, fully inclusive, on a diving yacht.
Contact For dinghy hire see the coastal hotels; short dhow excursions are listed in *Chapter 14*, page 385.
Boat charters
Kaskazi A 20m catamaran. Book through Dream Diving, PO Box 787, Ukunda; email: kaskazi444@yahoo.com; web: www.kazkazi.com
Tusitiri A 20m dhow. Book through Borana Lodge, tel: 062 31075; email: borana1@bushmail.net
Sand-yachting
Tana River Delta Camp page 414

Scuba diving

The Kenyan coast has magnificent dive sites, with several dive centres catering for complete beginners and experienced divers. It's also possible to do fun dives, where no experience is required, and a guide takes you go down to 6m. Due to the Indo-Pacific current, the ocean boasts the same fish species as Australia: manta rays, reef, hammerhead and whale sharks, turtles and multi-coloured reef fish in coral gardens. Wall and pinnacle dives with dramatic drop-offs, together with wreck, drift and night dives are offered. The choice varies from daily excursions to staying on a 'live-aboard'. Divers must carry internationally recognised accreditation – both PADI (Professional Association of Diving Instructors) and BSAC (British Sub-Aqua Club) are acceptable.
Useful tip Before choosing a company, do check out you are satisfied with their safety procedures and professionalism.
Where Along the coast from Lamu to Shimoni.
Best time to go November to April considered best, although August to November is fair.
Cost From US$30 for a single dive and from US$100 for beginner's instruction and an assisted dive.

Contact There are numerous diving operators. Among those with a good reputation are:
Driftwood Beach Club Malindi, page 407
Peponi Hotel Lamu, page 418
Aqua Ventures PO Box 275, Watamu; tel: 042 32420; email: aquav@africaonline.co.ke; web: www.diveinkenya.com
Charlie Claw's Wasini Island Restaurant and Kisite Dhow Tours PO Box 281, Ukunda; tel: 040 2331; fax: 040 3154; email: diving@wasini-island.com; web: www.wasini-island.com
Diani Marine PO Box 340, Ukunda; tel: 040 2367; fax: 040 3452; email: dimarine@africaonline.co.ke; web: www.dianimarine.com
Diving the Crab PO Box 5011, Diani; tel: 040 2003; email: info@divingthecrab.com; web: www.divingthecrab.com
Pemba Diving Email: pembadiv@africaonline.co.ke

Shopping

While there's a wide selection of airport art available – wooden carvings, beaded jewellery, baskets and batiks, some of which is of excellent quality – there's also plenty for the sophisticated shopaholic, from haute couture design and jewellery to fine sheepskin and leatherwork, printed fabrics and contemporary works of art and furniture. In addition are the traditional *kiondo* sisal baskets, and the wraparound *kikois* and *kangas*, while it's also possible to purchase a range of Indian fabrics and beads from River Road (be vigilant about security) and the Parklands area in Nairobi.

Where Predominantly Nairobi and Mombasa.
Cost Variable.
Contact See regional chapter listings under *What to do and see*.

Snakes

The chances of seeing a snake in the wild in Kenya are fairly rare, despite the fact it has 119 species. The best place to see and learn about them is James Ashe's Bio-Ken laboratory and snake farm at Watamu on the coast, or alternatively there are a number of snake parks at the National Museums of Kenya and the regional museums, which vary in quality. Kisumu Museum has a good snake selection but you cannot help but feel rather sorry for the rabbits who hop around the python.

Useful tip See the box piece on snakes on pages 152–3.
Where Countrywide.
Best time to go Year round.
Cost Entrance from KSh200 for the museums; KSh300 entry for Bio-Ken laboratory and snake farm
Contact
National Museums of Kenya page 91
Bio-Ken laboratory and snake farm PO Box 3, Watamu; mob: 0733 290324; email: corncon@africaonline.co.ke

Snorkelling

Even those with a passive interest in marine life will not fail to be enthralled by the coral gardens and the variety of colourful fish when snorkelling off the Kenya coast. When arriving on a beach, you will soon be approached by the goggleboatmen, who take snorkelling trips in their glass-bottomed boats. It is possible to see the fish and coral through the bottom of the boat, but it's a poor second to being in the water yourself.

CULTURE, HISTORY, LIFESTYLE AND SPECIAL INTERESTS – AND WHERE THEY TAKE PLACE

	Nairobi	South and Eastern Kenya	Central Highlands	The Rift Valley	Western Kenya	Northern Kenya	Coast	page
Culture and history								
Art	•							108
Bullfighting					•			134
Cultural	•	•	•	•	•	•	•	116
Historical	•	•	•	•	•	•	•	122
Trains	•	•					•	129
Maulidi Festival							•	134
Migwena Festival					•			134
Lifestyle								
Craft fair	•							135
Gourmet	•						•	121
Health spas			•		•		•	122
Shopping – designer	•							127
Weddings and honeymoons			•			•	•	130
Weekend breaks	•	•	•	•	•		•	131
Other interests								
Agriculture		•	•	•	•		•	107
Camping	•	•	•	•	•	•	•	112
Children	•	•	•	•	•	•	•	114
Conservation and voluntary work	•	•	•	•	•		•	115
Photography	•	•	•	•	•	•	•	125
Radio (amateur)	•							125

Useful tips
- If you're planning on doing a lot of snorkelling it will pay to bring your own mask, as the equipment provided on boats varies.
- You can get very burnt floating on the surface, even with lashings of suncream – so if you have a fair skin, wear a T-shirt and leggings – or even pyjamas!
- If swimming within a marine national park, you will need to purchase a ticket – these are usually available from hotels and the warden's office – otherwise on an excursion the cost may be included in the boat trip.

Where Among the best places for snorkelling are the marine parks of Kisite, Watamu/Malindi and Kiungu (which includes Kiwayu).

Best time to go Snorkelling can be done at all times of year, but conditions are considered best from December to March. The best visibility for snorkelling is at low tide just before the tide turns – allow time for reaching the snorkelling area and about an hour for snorkelling.

Cost US$8 in the marine parks, glass-bottomed boat excursion around KSh800 for a two-hour trip: snorkelling dhow excursions from US$80.
Contact See *Chapter 14*, page 383 for operators; for general information on marine parks, contact **Kenya Wildlife Service** (page 61).

Trains

The night train from Nairobi to Mombasa is affectionately known as the *Lunatic Express*, after the book by Charles Miller (see page 468) about the building of the Ugandan railway which extended from the Kenyan coast to Kampala in Uganda. The gleaming steam engines were the delight of their Sikh drivers until they went out of service at the end of the 1970s. Today, there are bi-monthly **steam specials** on Mount Gelai, a Mountain Class Beyer Garratt 252-ton locomotive, 5918, which was in service on the line until 1979. After being exhibited in the National Railway Museum, it was overhauled by a team of specialists and restored to full working order, running again on the line in 2002. The project is organised by the Kenya Railway Corporation in association with East African Steam Safaris.
Where Nairobi to Mombasa.
Best time to go Year round for scheduled service; steam specials currently bi-monthly.
Cost Steam specials from KSh25,000, full board per person sharing a compartment.
Contact
Regular service
Kenya Railways booking offices, pages 167
Steam specials
East African Steam Safaris PO Box 64640, Mobil Plaza, Nairobi 00620; tel: 020 3761715; fax: 020 3761715; email: tannereps@iconnect.co.ke

Turkana Bus

The Turkana Bus is almost a Kenyan institution, being one of the original adventure safaris which was started by Dick Hedges of Safari Camp Services in the 1970s. A no-frills camping trip, the Turkana Bus travels from Nairobi via Samburu to the eastern side of Lake Turkana at Loyangalani. It explores the rugged and beautiful arid wilderness of the remote northern frontier district, sparsely inhabited by nomadic pastoralists, and Lake Turkana. A similar trip is organised by Gametrackers.
Where From Nairobi to Turkana in northern Kenya.
Best time to go Year round, but during the wet season you may occasionally get stuck.
Cost From US$555 per person for the nine-day Turkana bus trip with Safari Camp Services.
Contact Recommended operators include:
Gametrackers page 102
Safari Camp Services page 102

Turtle watching

Five types of turtle are found in Kenya waters, with the green, olive ridley and hawksbill turtles nesting on the beaches. There are turtle watch projects at Watamu, Lamu and Kiungu. It's sometimes possible to watch turtle nests hatching normally in the late afternoon and early evening, when numerous tiny turtles burrow out of the nest and make their way down to the beach to the open sea. Information on turtle hatchings is available locally.
Where Watamu, Lamu and Kiungu on the coast.

Best time to go Year round.
Cost Free
Contact
Kenya Wildlife Service (page 61)
WWF (page 62) for Kiungu
Peponi Hotel Carol Korschen, PO Box 24, Lamu; tel: 042 33154; fax: 042 33029; email: peponi@africaonline.co.ke
Watamu Turtle Watch Plot 19, PO Box 125, Watamu; tel: 042 32118; fax: 042 32280; email: wtwkenya@swiftmalindi.com

Walking safaris

Walking in big-game country, tracking the animals and learning about bushcraft is guaranteed to sharpen the senses and gives the opportunity to savour the grandeur of the natural wilderness. Walking gives the option to stretch one's legs and to see nature from a different perspective, getting away from the safe confines of a vehicle. A number of camps and hotels offer bush walks, going out for a couple of hours with a naturalist or local guide, often one of the pastoralists who live in the area, such as the Maasai or Samburu. There are also walking safaris which combine game drives with walking, but where the emphasis is on the walking. These are usually led by a white-hunter-type guide. In addition, staying at the community lodges provides excellent walking opportunities.

Useful tips
- Take comfortable boots and plenty of socks, a pair of binoculars, water on long trips, a good hat and adequate sun protection.
- You may be asked to sign a waiver of liability.
- Listen to your guide – most accidents occur when people have not paid attention.

Where Group ranches adjacent to the Masai Mara National Reserve, the Loita Hills, Solio, Tsavo East, Chyulus, Greater Amboseli, Laikipia, Shompole and Mount Kenya.
Best time to go During the dry season months, but check local conditions.
Cost From US$10 for a bush walk to US$2,075 for a seven-day walking safari.
Contact Several companies offer serious walking safaris, and consider also the camel and donkey safari operators above. For shorter excursions and community lodges see the respective listings in the regional chapters.
Operators offering a variety of excursions include
Basecamp Travel page 102
Bike Treks page 117
Kibo Slopes Safaris page 213
Savage Wilderness Safaris page 102
Wilderness Kenya 100

Weddings and honeymoons

Tying the knot in a tropical setting attracts many a couple, with civil wedding ceremonies being particularly popular at the coast, although they can be arranged elsewhere. Themed weddings, such as traditional Samburu or Maasai weddings, can also be arranged, but in this case tour operators generally recommend a civil marriage before you come. Honeymooners too are well catered for, many camps and lodges having special honeymoon suites.

Where The coast, in a lodge, balloon or Maasai *manyatta*.
Best time to go Year round, but best to avoid the rainy season.
Cost Variable.
Contact
Aberdare Country Club page 232

Previous page Wildebeest crossing the Mara River, Masai Mara National Reserve (AZ)

Above Reticulated giraffe, *Giraffa camelopardalis reticulata*, Meru National Park (AZ)

Right Gerenuk, *Litocranius walleri*, feeding on hindlegs, Samburu National Reserve (AZ)

Below Adult male Defassa waterbuck, *Kobus defassa*, Lake Nakuru National Park (AZ)

Mnarani page 395
Wedding arrangements are best made through a tour operator.
Camps and lodges with honeymoon suites
Borana Lodge Laikipia, page 258
Chui Lodge Naivasha, page 278
Crater Lake Camp Naivasha, page 279
Governors' Camp Masai Mara, page 312
Island Camp Baringo, page 298
Mara Explorer page 313
Ol Donyo Wuas Chyulus, page 212
Olonana Masai Mara, page 317
Shaba Sarova Lodge page 375
Wilderness Trails Laikipia, page 257

Weekend breaks
It might seem a little far-fetched, but Kenya is a long-haul trip from Europe where the time difference (GMT +3 hours) makes it realistically 'do-able' for a long-weekend. It's an eight-hour flight to Nairobi, and then a 40-minute flight in a light aircraft to a destination like the Masai Mara. With relaxing in the bush being one of the best ways to unwind, this is a popular (and stylish) option for time-strapped executives.
Where Can be tailor-made to suit, but options currently from Nairobi to Masai Mara National Reserve.
Best time to go Avoid the rainy season.
Cost From £995 per person full board for two nights in the Mara inclusive of all flights and transfers.
Contact
Steppes Africa 51 Castle St, Cirencester, Glos GL7 1QD, UK; tel: 01285 650011; fax: 01285 885888; email: safari@steppesafrica.co.uk; web: www.steppesafrica.co.uk
Worldwide Journeys and Expeditions 27 Vanston Place, London SW6 1AZ, UK; tel: 020 7386 4646; fax: 020 7381 0836; email: enquiry@worldwidejourneys.co.uk; web: www.worldwidejourneys.co.uk

Whitewater rafting
Kenya's rivers have a rare combination of whitewater up to grade V together with a rich scenic diversity and the opportunity to take in game viewing and birdwatching on the way. Trips are designed for full participation using Avon rubber dinghies, with good safety equipment and operated by qualified guides. If the adrenalin rush of whitewater does not appeal, it's possible to opt out for a scenic float. On longer trips, there are campsites along the riverbank downstream.
Useful tip Sun prevention is important – high-factor suncream, strong sunglasses with a retainer cord, a wide-brimmed hat and a long-sleeved shirt are recommended, and remember to take a change of clothes as you are guaranteed to get wet in whitewater. You may also need to sign a disclaimer, so check before booking that you are covered by your insurance.
Where Tana, Mathoya, Athi and Ewaso Ng'iro rivers.
Best time to go Mid-April to August and November to mid-January.
Cost From US$90 for a day to US$420 for a three-day trip.
Contact
Kilalinda page 222
Savage Wilderness Safaris PO Box 44827, Nairobi, tel: 020 521590; mobile: 0733 735508; fax: 020 521590; email: whitewater@alphanet.co.ke; web: www.whitewaterkenya.com

SPECIAL INTERESTS, FESTIVALS AND EVENTS – AND WHERE THEY TAKE PLACE

	Nairobi	South and Eastern Kenya	Central Highlands	The Rift Valley	Western Kenya	Northern Kenya	Coast	page
Special interests								
Agriculture		•	•	•	•		•	107
Animal tracking		•			•	•		108
Art	•							108
Birdwatching	•	•	•	•	•	•	•	110
Butterflies	•				•		•	111
Children	•	•	•	•	•	•	•	114
Conservation and voluntary work	•	•	•	•	•		•	115
Dolphin and whale watching							•	118
Elephant watching		•	•	•	•	•	•	118
Fitness training					•		•	119
Flamingos		•		•	•	•	•	119
Gold panning						•		350
Gourmet	•						•	121
Health spas			•		•		•	122
Historical	•	•	•	•	•	•	•	122
Photography	•	•	•	•	•	•	•	125
Radio (amateur)	•							125
Rift Valley				•				121
Shopping – designer	•							127
Snakes	•					•	•	127

Wildebeest migration

Heralded as the 'greatest wildlife show on earth', the annual wildebeest migration is a magnificent spectacle. In July 1.3 million wildebeest, together with some 200,000 zebra and 300,000 Thomson's gazelle, head north from their breeding grounds in Tanzania's Serengeti National Park into Kenya's Masai Mara National Reserve, drawn by the succulent grasses on the Mara plains. The Mara River crossings are at their best in August and September – a milling mass of wildebeest with a constant lowing and thundering of hooves before they plunge into the river. Frantically splashing, many fall prey to crocodiles or drown in the frenzy to reach the other side. That obstacle over, they are then easy prey for lions and this is the best time to see lion kills. Towards the end of October the wildebeest begin crossing back into Tanzania, and the annual merry-go-round begins again. Inevitably, the timing of the migration is dictated by the weather and does not always run to schedule.

Where Masai Mara National Reserve.

Best time to go In most years from July to October, but check for local variations.

Cost Varies according to accommodation selected in the Mara.

Contact General operators, page 99, and Masai Mara accommodation, page 312.

	Nairobi	South and Eastern Kenya	Central Highlands	The Rift Valley	Western Kenya	Northern Kenya	Coast	page
Trains	•	•					•	129
Turkana Bus						•		129
Turtle watching							•	129
Weddings and honeymoons			•			•	•	130
Wildebeest migration					•			132
Wildlife safaris	•	•	•	•	•	•	•	133
Festivals								
Maulidi Festival							•	134
Migwena Festival					•			134
Events								
Bullfighting					•			134
Craft fair	•							135
Cricket	•							135
Dhow racing							•	135
Kenya Open Golf Tournament	•							136
Lewa Marathon			•					136
Maralal Camel Derby and Elite Cycle Races						•		136
Rhino Charge *varies*								137
Safari Rally *varies*								137
Safari Sevens (rugby)	•							137
Skydiving	•						•	138
World Birdwatch	•	•	•	•	•	•	•	138

Wildlife safaris

Wildlife safaris are Kenya's main appeal for most people visiting the country, and there's a full spectrum of options from minibus to 4WD safaris staying at lodges, tented and mobile camps, with options to go walking and horseriding, drive or fly to different destinations. It's worthwhile spending a little time researching the different options, deciding what you want to see and how much you have to spend.

Useful tip When planning an itinerary, tempting though it may be, don't try to include everything. In the past, people used to joke: 'What safari are you on?' Reply: 'A roads of Kenya special.' Aim to spend more time in the parks game-viewing rather than on the road – it'll greatly increase your enjoyment – and opt for two or three nights in one place (or more) rather than a different bed each night.

Where Countrywide.

Best time to go Depends on the activities you choose, but it's generally best to avoid April and May. However, it rarely rains all day, there are fewer tourists and you benefit from low-season accommodation rates. The rain also clears the dust, giving stupendous views not seen at other times of year.

Cost A very broad spectrum: from US$40–400 per person a day, according to the safari selected.
Contact For operators see page 99.

FESTIVALS

There are a number of local festivals which do not have set dates. For these, a useful source of information is the **National Museums of Kenya**, page 183, the **Kenya Tourist Board** (KTB), page 63, or the Kenya press. Some of the annual festivals are listed here.

Maulidi

Established by Sheikh Habib Salih in the 1880s to celebrate the birth of Mohammed, this festival takes place soon after the Muslim holiday of *Idd il Fitr*, attracting pilgrims from the rest of Africa, Asia and the Middle East. Consequently, accommodation is at a premium. It's a spectacular event: the week-long festival includes feasting, dancing, dhow and donkey racing.
Useful tip Book accommodation early.
Where Lamu.
When After Idd il Fitr – dates change each year.
Contact
General operators, page 99
KATO page 98
KTB page 63

Arts Festival

Organised by the Kenya Museum Society, this is a general arts festival, with performing artists and works of art for sale.
Where Nairobi at the National Museum of Kenya.
When Normally the beginning of March
Cost Entry around KSh300.
Contact
Kenya Museum Society PO Box 40658, Nairobi; tel: 020 743808; email: info@knowkenya.org

Migwena Festival

This is a Luo cultural festival, similar in many ways to Scottish Highland Games. People rally from the Bondo and Siaya districts of western Kenya to participate in football, netball and boat racing in *ssese* canoes, while alongside villages compete in song and traditional dance.
Where Bondo in Western Kenya.
When Normally around the end of December.
Cost Free entry.
Contact
Chronicle Tours I & M Bank Tower, Kenyatta Av, PO Box 49722, Nairobi; tel: 020 311787; fax: 020 246112; email: chronicle@insightkenya.com web: www.chronicletours.com

EVENTS
Bullfighting

In the Luahya Ishuka clan, bullfights were originally held to honour the burial of a warrior, the fighting taking place on his grave. Nowadays, this is a competition to find the best bull raised by an individual village. Unlike European bullfights, the bulls are brought together to fight for dominance of a large field, testing their strength and prowess. The bulls are spurred on by excited onlookers blowing horns – believed to encourage the bulls to fight – while imbibing local brew. These bovine battles can last for up to half an hour, and often take place on Sundays in the markets of Shinyalu and Khayega.

Where Kakamega region of western Kenya.
When Various times of year.
Cost Free.
Contact As bullfights are not organised as a tourist attraction, it's a case of making enquiries locally to see if it's possible to go to a bullfight.

Craft Fair

Ideal for Christmas shopping, the Craft Fair is an event supporting many Kenyan charities, bringing together a number of craft specialists, mostly white Kenyan, from around the country. From leather fashion accessories to reproduction furniture, children's toys, hand-made soaps and natural oils made from endemic plants like the *leleshwa* bush, there's the opportunity to buy some unique products.

Where Ngong race course, Nairobi.
When Annually, beginning of December.
Cost Entry from around KSh500.
Contact See local press for details.

Cricket

A popular and rapidly growing sport in Kenya, international cricket now features strongly on the sporting agenda. Each year there are visits from several international touring sides, and Kenya was the venue for some of the Cricket World Cup matches in 2003.

Where Nairobi.
When Various times of year.
Cost On application.
Contact
Kenya Cricket Association PO Box 16962, Nairobi, tel: 020 744762; fax: 020 740093; email: kcricket@iconnect.co.ke; web: www.kca.cricket.org

Dhow racing

This is a speciality in Lamu, which hosts two annual dhow races, arranged through Peponi Hotel in Shela. The first, organised by the hotel, held on New Year's Day, is for local captains only. Eight captains are invited, from Lamu's main towns of Shela, Lamu, Matandoni and Kizingitini. With dhow captains having a strong seafaring heritage, much prestige, not to mention prize money, is given to the winner, making for fierce competition and a good spectator event. The **Twin Star Race** is organised by a couple of Frenchmen who spend August in Lamu. The race, held in mid-August, is an open event for visitors, who must sponsor a team, and there must be at least two visitors per boat. The boats and teams must be booked in advance.

Where Lamu.
When Annually, in August and at New Year.
Cost Entry for the Twin Star Race from KSh1,000 per person.
Contact
Peponi Hotel PO Box 24, Lamu; tel: 042 33154; fax: 042 33029; email: peponi@africaonline.co.ke; web: www.peponi-lamu.com

Kenya Open Golf Tournament

This is Kenya's major international golfing tournament, held annually in Nairobi, usually at Muthaiga Country Club. Golf is a popular game with Kenyans, there being 38 golf courses around the country (so it's easy enough to arrange a round of golf while on a safari circuit) and at the coast. The Kenya Open attracts many local and international competitors. The Kenya Golf Union (KGU) produces an annual calendar listing events, while their website gives detailed information on the country's courses.

Where Normally Muthaiga Country Club, Nairobi.
When Normally late February or early March.
Cost On application to KGU.
Contact
Kenya Golf Union PO Box 49609, GPO, Nairobi; tel: 020 3763898; fax: 020 3765118; email: info@kenyaopen.co.ke; web: www.kenyaopen.co.ke

Lewa Marathon

This is a fund-raising event for the Lewa Wildlife Conservancy, rural community development programmes, local schools, Nanyuki Cottage Hospital and Meru National Park. Organised by the UK charity Tusk Trust and sponsored by the mobile phone company, Safaricom, the marathon and half marathon are now well established on the international circuit, drawing entrants from 18 countries in 2002. The marathon is unique for being held in a game sanctuary and the course is monitored from the air to check for elephants and predators. The altitude 1,525m (5,000ft) and heat (it's near the equator) make it one of the toughest marathons in the world. It also attracts some of Kenya's legendary world-class athletes: Paul Tergat, Catherine and Anastasia Ndereba, Lameck Aguta, Peter Ndegwa, Isaac Chemombwo and Suleiman Kariuki, while Kip Keino, a double Olympic champion and world record holder, often starts the race. Travel and accommodation packages are available for competitors travelling from overseas and within Kenya, and it's a popular spectator event.

Useful tip Book early as entries are limited.
Where Lewa Wildlife Conservancy, Laikipia.
When Normally June.
Cost Entry fee about US$90; self-drive camping, from about US$55 a day inclusive of conservancy fee. Standard and luxury packages from UK cost from £985–1,395 for five days inclusive of international flights and accommodation.
Contact
Lewa Wildlife Conservancy page 264
Tusk Trust (Safari Marathon Event), 116 Battersea Business Centre, 103 Lavender Hill, London SW11 5QL; tel: 020 7978 7100; fax: 020 7223 2517; email: tim@tusk.org; web: www.tusk.org

Maralal Camel Derby and Elite Cycle races

The Maralal Camel Derby started in 1990, an event providing entertainment, supporting local charities and raising awareness for the Kenya Camel Association. Since 1998, the camel derby has been linked with the Kenya Amateur Cycling Association who run a series of cycle races, some of which give ranking points on the international amateur cycling circuit. The Derby has four main races. The **Amateur Camel Race** is over 12km around Maralal town, in which complete amateurs with a camel handler are permitted, while the **Semi-Professional Camel Race** covers 42km around Maralal and environs where you need to be a proficient camel rider. The **Amateur Cycle Race** covers 12km, while the **Elite Mountain Bike Race** is over 42km. There's open entry to all events – you can register on the day or in advance through Yare Safaris. In addition to serious racing are fancy-dress parades and the event is as popular with its local entrants as it is with competitors from further afield.

Useful tip Transport and accommodation packages are arranged from Nairobi for the event.

Where Maralal at Yare Safari Club.

When Normally second weekend in August.

Cost Entry fees for the amateur camel race KSh500 plus KSh2,500 for a camel and handler; semi-professional race KSh1,500 plus KSh3,000 for camel hire; entry fees for cycling events KSh100.

Contact

Camel Derby at Yare Safaris PO Box 281, Maralal; tel: 065 2295; email: camelsafaris@yaresafaris.com; web: www.yaresafaris.com

Rhino Charge

This is an off-road rally for 4WD vehicles which started in 1989. Open to the first 55 teams to enter, the event raises funds for Rhino Ark, money going specifically towards a fencing project in the Aberdares National Park. The competition is a bid to complete the shortest distance between 12 guard posts. Teams traverse some almost impossible terrain, guaranteeing some hair-raising (and side-splitting) adventure. A scheme introduced in 2002 offers two vehicles to overseas entrants who raise US$12,500 or more for each car.

Useful tip If interested, apply early.

Where This is a closely guarded secret – a different course each year.

When Normally June 1.

Cost The minimum sponsorship fee for participating is KSh102,000. Two cars are available for overseas entrants who raise a minimum of US$12,500.

Contact

Rhino Ark (Kenya) PO Box 181, Uhuru Gardens, Nairobi, Kenya, tel: 020 604246 or 609866; fax: 020 604246; email: rhinoark@wananchi.com; web: www.rhinoark.org

Safari rally

The safari rally started in 1953, to celebrate the coronation of Queen Elizabeth II. Since its origins as a bit of fun for amateur drivers over the Easter weekend, the event became incorporated on the World Rally Circuit. It lost its status in 2003, but there are plans to reinstate it again in the future. The three-day event starts from Nairobi, the course covering 3,000km on rough roads with billowing clouds of dust, mud and river crossings, attracting many roadside spectators, as well as the various support teams, television crews and helicopters. The country is abuzz with safari fever at this time.

Where The course varies.

When Normally July to fit in with the international rally calendar.

Contact

Safari Rally Simon Ball, tel: 020 891124; fax: 020 825123; email: sball@africaonline.co.ke; web: www.safarirally.com

Safari Sevens

Africa's premier international seven-a-side rugby tournament, the Safari Sevens hosts teams from around the world, fielding as many as 16 teams. Held at the Rugby Football Union of East Africa Ground in Nairobi, it runs over two days towards the end of June. Kenyans are enthusiastic rugby supporters and the Safari

Sevens have previously attracted international stars like Gavin Hastings, Naas Botha, Rob Leuw, Kieran Bracken, Chester Williams and Leo Williams.
Where Nairobi, the Kenya Rugby Union Football Club (KRFU) on Ngong Road.
When Normally June.
Cost On application.
Contact
Let's Go Travel page 101
Safari Sevens www.safarisevens.co.ke

Skydiving

There are usually two skydiving boogies a year at Diani, held on the beach in front of the Safari Beach Hotel on the south coast. Using a Twin Otter aircraft, activities generally include a student training course in accelerated freefall, tandem jumps and the opportunity for skydivers to take individual jumps. It's a popular event which attracts around 100 skydivers. There's also skydiving most weekends from Wilson Airport.
Where South coast, Diani and Nairobi.
When Normally March and October.
Cost Tandem: US$200; individual jumps: US$22. Packages available from Europe.
Contact
Sky-diving Web: www.skydivekenya.com and www.kenya-boogie.com

World Birdwatch

A birdwatchers' answer to the Olympics, this is a worldwide event. Held over a weekend, teams rise to the challenge of trying to have the highest bird count. The competition aims to be fun, and a number of birdwalks and talks run alongside the main event. Kenya has been the global leader in all previous competitions, with an average of around 700 bird species counted over the weekend.
Where Countrywide.
When Held biannually, normally over an October weekend. The next World Birdwatch is scheduled for 2005.
Contact
Nature Kenya PO Box 44486, Nairobi; tel: 020 749957; email: eanhs@africaonline.co.ke; web: www.naturekenya.org

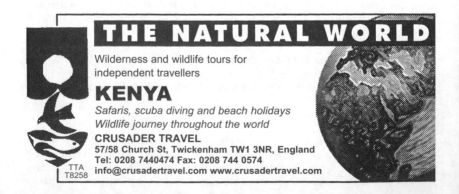

THE NATURAL WORLD

Wilderness and wildlife tours for independent travellers

KENYA

Safaris, scuba diving and beach holidays
Wildlife journey throughout the world

CRUSADER TRAVEL
57/58 Church St, Twickenham TW1 3NR, England
Tel: 0208 7440474 Fax: 0208 744 0574
TTA T8258 info@crusadertravel.com www.crusadertravel.com

Health and Safety

With Dr Felicity Nicholson

Travelling in a developing country in the tropics puts a very different slant on health and safety compared with Western countries. For the uninitiated visitor, reading about this for the first time can be rather frightening. The aim of this chapter is to point out issues relating to health and safety – forewarned is forearmed – so that you can take sensible precautions. Sometimes, with the excitement of travel, we do things that we would not contemplate doing at home. For example, many cities at home are dangerous, with areas where one would not voluntarily walk at night. The same logic applies in a foreign country. It's a case of getting the balance right between being too cautious or too casual.

BEFORE YOU GO
Travel insurance
Visitors to Kenya are advised to take out a **comprehensive medical insurance policy** to cover them for all emergencies, including evacuation. Do take the time to read the small print of the insurance policy, tedious though this may be; some policies have a cut-off time for making claims – for example you may have purchased a six-month or annual policy, but the insurance company must be advised within three months of the incident for which you are claiming. Be aware too of limits per item or claim, that you may also need to have receipts or a police statement for claims, and check that any policy excess charges are reasonable. Take several copies of your insurance documents with you (and leave one at home) and make a separate note of the contact number for claims. Within Kenya, the **Flying Doctors** provide an excellent full emergency cover for a minimal fee (from US$15). See box, page 144.

    Personal effects insurance is also a sensible precaution, but again, take note of the policy's small print regarding claim limits per item – often these do not begin to cover the cost of replacement. **Home contents insurance policies** normally give more comprehensive cover for replacement. If travelling frequently, **annual travel insurance** is an attractive option, but check out the number of days covered per trip and also make sure you are covered for all activities that you wish to do. Some policies require an **additional premium for risky sports** like white-water rafting, scuba diving, skydiving and mountaineering. Also, with certain policies, if for some reason you have to break your travel abroad and return home for a short break before resuming your travels again within the period originally covered, the policy is no longer valid once you have returned home.

Immunisations
It is recommended to visit your doctor or travel clinic 12 weeks before departure to discuss all your medical requirements, although a full course of immunisations only takes six weeks. Last-minute injections can give only partial cover for some diseases. It's useful to keep an inoculation record if you travel regularly.

Legal requirements

A yellow fever certificate is only required if you are entering Kenya from a yellow fever area. Although the number of reported cases of yellow fever is low, most experts would recommend taking this very effective vaccine for Kenya unless there are specific contra-indications. If you are planning a multi-country itinerary, you are likely to require a yellow fever certificate upon entering another country after being in Kenya, so check the requirements for ongoing destinations. For those travellers who are unable to have the yellow fever vaccine, then it is worth getting an exemption certificate. This is not an absolute guarantee for entries into other countries, though, so check with individual embassies before finalising your route.

Immunisation for cholera is no longer required anywhere in Africa, although some countries may "illegally' ask for proof of vaccination. This does not apply to Kenya.

Recommended precautions

It is sensible to be up to date with your immunisations. These are:

polio	ten-yearly	hepatitis A
tetanus	ten-yearly	rabies
diphtheria	ten-yearly	hepatitis B
yellow fever	ten-yearly	tuberculosis (TB)
typhoid	three-yearly	

Hepatitis A vaccine (eg: Havrix Monodose, Avaxim) has replaced the old-fashioned gamma globulin, which should no longer be used. It is best given two weeks or more before travel, but is still effective even if taken the day before as the incubation period of the disease is at least two weeks. One dose of vaccine provides cover for one year. A booster dose taken at least six months later will last for ten years.

For most travellers, vaccination against **rabies** (a course of three injections over a four-week period) is not necessary, but there were outbreaks in the Kerio Valley of western Kenya in 2002 with limited vaccine available, so get inoculated if you are planning to visit this area. Otherwise it's only recommended if you are travelling in remote areas where you are more than 24 hours away from medical help or if you intend to work with animals.

The newer **typhoid** vaccine (eg: Typhim Vi) is worth having unless you are travelling for a week or less and you do not receive the vaccine within four days of departure; even so, protection is not 100%. Whether or not you choose to be vaccinated against typhoid, you should still be scrupulous about hygiene.

Hepatitis B immunisation is recommended for longer trips (two months or more), for those working with children or in situations where contact with blood is likely. Three injections are needed for the best protection and can be given over a four-week period if time is short (only Engerix B is currently licensed for use over this period). Longer courses ranging over two–six months are also available and are preferred if time allows. A BCG vaccination against **tuberculosis** (TB) may also be advised for trips of two months or more. Consult your GP or a travel clinic at least six weeks before travel to see whether this applies to you.

Other medication, prescriptions and dental checks

If you are on any form of medication, remember to take enough with you to cover the length of your stay and a note of what you are taking, just in case you have to buy more.

If you wear contact lenses, take glasses too, as dust can irritate the eyes, and if you wear glasses, take a spare pair. If your one and only pair break when you need them to see the wildlife, it will be more than a little frustrating.

If going on a long trip, go for a dental check-up before you leave.

Sun protection

Skin cancer is on the increase particularly among Caucasians, who, with fair skin, are more prone to sunburn. The power of the tropical sun can be remarkably deceptive, with altitude giving rise to cooler temperatures, and sea breezes at the coast. Wear a high-factor sunscreen (20+ recommended and waterproof for swimming) and a hat with a wide brim. If sunbathing, avoid the hours between 11.00 and 15.00 when the sun is at its strongest. Beware of getting sunburnt when snorkelling (see page 127). If you have sensitive eyes wear UV sunglasses.

Medical kit

There are pharmacies in all of Kenya's major towns and cities which are well stocked, and most medicines are available although they might have different brand names. Nairobi has a 24-hour pharmacy. But it's easier to bring a basic medical kit to cover you on an organised trip. This might contain:

- eye drops
- antihistamine tablets and an antihistamine stick for applying to bites
- antiseptic such as betamine to paint on to wounds or infected bites – avoid creams
- aspirins or paracetamol
- a decongestant if you get sinusitis
- condoms and contraceptive pills
- malarial prophylaxis
- insect repellent – sprays are less messy to apply
- high-factor sunscreen (20+)
- moisturising cream
- lipsalve with a sunscreen
- diarrhoea tablets – such as Imodium
- oral rehydration sachets
- a role of sticking plaster – also useful for taping holes in mosquito nets
- hydrocolloid blister plaster
- scissors
- tweezers
- safety pins

If travelling into remote areas, you might also like to include:

- injection swabs, sutures, sterile needles and syringes
- burn dressings
- ciprofloxacin antibiotic (two 500mg tablets taken 6–12 hours apart) for bacillary dysentery (see page 149).
- anti-fungal cream – eg: Canesten
- strong painkillers – ibuprofen or codeine
- water-sterilising equipment (2% tincture of iodine)
- arnica cream to ease bruising
- clove oil and temporary fillings for emergency dentistry
- bandages and dressings
- a malaria test kit and courses for malarial treatment

Travel clinics and health information

Travel medicine is increasingly becoming a specialist area due to the increasing numbers of people travelling. The **International Society for Travel Medicine** was formed in 1991 and the **British Travel and Health Association** was launched in 1998. Consequently, travel clinics will be abreast of the latest advice for tropical medicine, and are likely to be more up to date than your doctor. A list of travel clinic websites worldwide is available on www.istm.org. For other journey preparation information, consult www.tripprep.com.

United Kingdom

If you do not have a travel clinic nearby, it's best to get a health brief from a travel clinic and to then discuss it with your doctor.

British Airways Travel Clinic and Immunisation Service There are two BA clinics in London, both on tel: 0845 600 2236; web: www.britishairways.com/travelclinics. Appointments only at 111 Cheapside, EC1V 6DT; or walk-in service Mon–Sat at 156 Regent St, W1B 5LB. Apart from providing inoculations and malaria prevention, they sell a variety of health-related goods, including malaria tablet memory cards, mosquito nets and treatment kits.
Berkeley Travel Clinic 32 Berkeley St, London WIX 5FA; tel: 020 7629 6233
Edinburgh Travel Clinic Regional Infectious Diseases Unit, Ward 41 OPD, Western General Hospital, Crewe Rd South, Edinburgh EH4 2UX; tel: 0131 537 2822. Travel helpline open 09.00–12.00 weekdays. Provides inoculations and anti-malarial prophylaxis and advises on travel-related health risks.
Fleet Street Travel Clinic 29 Fleet St, London EC4Y 1AA; tel: 020 7353 5678; email: info@fleetstreetclinic.com; web: www.fleetstreet.com. Injections, travel products and latest advice.
Hospital for Tropical Diseases Travel Clinic Mortimer Market Centre, 2nd Floor, Capper St (off Tottenham Ct Rd), London WC1E 6AU; tel: 020 7388 9600; web: www.thhtd.org. Offers consultations and advice, and is able to provide all necessary drugs and vaccines for travellers. Runs a premium-rate healthline (09061 337733) for country-specific information and health hazards; calls are charged at 50p per minute. Also stocks nets, water purification equipment and personal protection measures.
MASTA (Medical Advisory Service for Travellers Abroad), at the London School of Hygiene and Tropical Medicine, Keppel St, London WC1 7HT; tel: 09068 224100. This is a premium-line number, charged at 60p per minute. For a fee, they will provide an individually tailored health brief, with up-to-date information on how to stay healthy, inoculations and what to bring.
MASTA pre-travel clinics Tel: 01276 685040. Call for the nearest; there are currently 30 in Britain. Also sell malaria prophylaxis memory cards, treatment kits, bednets, net treatment kits.
NHS travel website, www.fitfortravel.scot.nhs.uk, provides country-by-country advice on immunisation and malaria, plus details of recent developments, and a list of health organisations.
Nomad Travel Store 3–4 Wellington Terrace, Turnpike Lane, London N8 0PX; tel: 020 8889 7014; fax: 020 8889 9528; email: sales@nomadtravel.co.uk; web: www.nomadtravel.co.uk. Also at 40 Bernard St, London WC1N 1LJ; tel: 020 7833 4114; fax: 020 7833 4470 and 43 Queens Rd, Bristol BS8 1QH; tel: 0117 922 6567; fax: 0117 922 7789. As well as dispensing health advice, Nomad stocks mosquito nets and other anti-bug devices, and an excellent range of adventure travel gear.
Thames Medical 157 Waterloo Rd, London SE1 8US; tel: 020 7902 9000. Competitively priced, one-stop travel health service. All profits go to their affiliated company, InterHealth, which provides health care for overseas workers on Christian projects.

Trailfinders Travel Clinic 194 Kensington High St, London W8 7RG; tel: 020 7938 3999. This has a resident doctor and immunisations can normally be given immediately.
Travelpharm The Travelpharm website, www.travelpharm.com, offers up-to-date guidance on travel-related health and has a range of medications available through their online mini-pharmacy.

Irish Republic
Tropical Medicine Bureau Grafton Street Medical Centre, Grafton Buildings, 34 Grafton St, Dublin 2; tel: 1 671 9200. This Irish-run organisation has a useful website specific to tropical destinations: www.tmb.le

USA
Centers for Disease Control 1600 Clifton Rd, Atlanta, GA 30333; tel: 877 FYI TRIP; 800 311 3435; web: www.cdc.gov/travel. The central source of travel information in the USA. Each summer they publish the invaluable *Health Information for International Travel*, available from the Division of Quarantine at the above address.
Connaught Laboratories PO Box 187, Swiftwater, PA 18370; tel: 800 822 2463. They will send a free list of specialist tropical-medicine physicians in your state.
IAMAT (International Association for Medical Assistance to Travellers) 417 Center St, Lewiston, NY 14092; tel: 716 754 4883; email: info@iamat.org; web: www.iamat.org. A non-profit organisation which provides health information and lists of English-speaking doctors abroad.

Canada
IAMAT (International Association for Medical Assistance to Travellers) Suite 1, 1287 St Clair Av W, Toronto, Ontario M6E 1B8; tel: 416 652 0137; web: www.iamat.org

Australia, New Zealand, Thailand
TMVC Tel: 1300 65 88 44; web: www.tmvc.com.au. Twenty-two clinics in Australia, New Zealand and Thailand, including:
Auckland Canterbury Arcade, 170 Queen St, Auckland; tel: 9 373 3531
Brisbane Dr Deborah Mills, Qantas Domestic Bldg, 6th Floor, 247 Adelaide St, Brisbane, QLD 4000; tel: 7 3221 9066; fax: 7 3321 7076
Melbourne Dr Sonny Lau, 393 Little Bourke St, 2nd Floor, Melbourne, VIC 3000; tel: 3 9602 5788; fax: 3 9670 8394
Sydney Dr Mandy Hu, Dymocks Bldg, 7th Floor, 428 George St, Sydney, NSW 2000; tel: 2 221 7133; fax: 2 221 8401
IAMAT PO Box 5049, Christchurch 5, New Zealand; web: www.iamat.org

South Africa
SAA-Netcare Travel Clinics PO Box 786692, Sandton 2146; fax: 011 883 6152; web: www.travelclinic.co.za or www.malaria.co.za. Clinics throughout South Africa.
TMVC (Travel Doctor Group) 113 DF Malan Dr, Roosevelt Pk, Johannesburg; tel: 011 888 7488; web: www.tmvc.com.au. Consult the website for details of clinics in South Africa.

Switzerland
IAMAT 57 Voirets, 1212 Grand Lancy, Geneva; web: www.iamat.org

FIT TO FLY
Deep vein thrombosis (DVT)
Evidence suggests that a small percentage of passengers on long-haul flights are at risk from developing DVT. It is estimated that around 30,000 Britons a year are

FLYING DOCTOR SERVICE

The Flying Doctor Service is part of the **African Medical and Research Foundation** (AMREF), an independent charity which started in 1957. The Flying Doctor Service operates air ambulance evacuations and specialist services to rural areas in East Africa. Internationally recognized for providing an air ambulance service for medical emergencies in East Africa, the Flying Doctors offer evacuation and repatriation to destinations worldwide, including South Africa, Europe, North America and Asia. Over six hundred patients are evacuated each year, accompanied by physicians and critical-care nurses, all of whom are trained in emergency medicine and intensive care.

AMREF's 24-hour Control Centre (Wilson Airport, Nairobi; tel: 020 315454/315455/602492/501280/506521–4; fax: 020 336886; mob: 0733 639088 or 0722 314239; satellite phone: 873 762315580; satellite fax: + 873 762315581; radio frequencies HF: 9116 kHz LSB, 5796 kHz LSB; email: emergency@flydoc.org or info@flydoc.org) is open 24 hours throughout the year and staffed by experienced medical personnel. Communication systems include telephones, satellite phones, cell phones, email, fax and VHF radio network. There's also a two-way high-frequency radio network to over 100 facilities throughout East Africa, giving direct access to lodges and tour operators. Apart from arranging and dispatching medical evacuations, the centre offers 24-hour medical advice to those in need.

The fleet

To operate this service, AMREF Flying Doctors own and maintain a fleet of regional light aircraft, crewed by experienced pilots. A partnership has been formed with Phoenix Aviation Ltd, which provides Beechcraft King Air 200 for regional flights requiring pressurisation, and a Cessna Citation Bravo Jet for long distance and international flights. These aircraft are equipped with the latest LifePort® stretcher systems. Access to helicopters is also available. In Nairobi ambulances are on hand for transfers to hospital.

The **Flying Doctors' Society of Africa** (FDSA), a separate fundraising body, was started 30 years ago to raise money for the Flying Doctor Service. The society's motto is: 'It's the people that matter'. It caters for the disadvantaged communities living in remote parts of East Africa, providing them with free health-care services and evacuation if required.

The FDSA **Membership Scheme** gives members access to free air ambulance evacuation services, using the Flying Doctor Service aircraft and medical teams, in the case of serious illness and accident. Different schemes are available, starting from US$15, and the subscription helps to finance the outreach programmes and charity evacuations. Temporary membership for visitors gives peace of mind in the knowledge that help is at hand in the event of a medical emergency.

For further information contact: Flying Doctors' Society of Africa, PO Box 30125, Nairobi; tel: 020 604651–9; fax: 020 601594; email: flyingdocs@amrefke.org; web: www.amref.org.

affected by flight-induced blood clots. Those at highest risk on flights of four hours or more are:

* people suffering from varicose veins, heart disease or cancer
* people with a history of blood clots or who have undergone recent surgery
* people with leg injuries
* people over six feet and under five feet tall
* people over 40
* women who are pregnant or taking the pill

To reduce the risk of DVT
* exercise your legs while seated
* walk around the cabin during the flight
* drink plenty of water or soft drinks
* wear compression hosiery to prevent swelling

After landing, a DVT may develop. If you have severe swelling of the ankles, a swollen or painful calf or thigh, an increase in skin temperature or local skin discolouration, seek medical advice immediately.

TROPICAL DISEASES AND KEEPING HEALTHY
Malaria
In Kenya, the chances of exposure to malaria are high. There are four types of malaria, three benign forms and *Plasmodium falciparum* malaria which is potentially fatal if not treated. It is transmitted by the female *Anopheles* mosquito, which bites from dusk until dawn. The presence of malaria is determined by temperature, as the parasite cycle is stopped when the temperature drops below 14°C. The outbreak of malaria in the Kenya highlands in 2002 was not a different strain of malaria, but an outbreak due to the unusually warm temperature conditions. Generally, areas above 2,000m are malaria-free. The asexual malarial cycle in man is completed every 24 hours, with parasites multiplying in an exponential manner. This is why *falciparum* can rapidly become fatal: on the first day, there is one parasite; by the second day, 16–32; and by the fourth from 65,536 to 1,048,576.

Avoiding malaria
In addition to anti-malarial prophylaxis, there are four main ways to reduce the risk of getting malaria:

* **Insecticide sprays** Spray under the bed and in dark corners before going to sleep. Also consider mosi-chips, an electric vaporiser, or a mosquito coil.
* **Insect repellents** Check that the repellent contains the chemical DEET, unless you are pregnant in which case a natural repellent such as Mosiguard may be recommended. Children should use a product with a lower percentage of DEET. So take advice if you are in any doubt. Mosquitoes are attracted by heat so tend to bite where the skin is thinner, and blood vessels are closer to the surface; apply repellent to exposed skin, especially the wrists, elbows, knees, ankles and neck.
* **Insect barriers** Cover up your arms and legs in the evening and wear light-coloured clothing. Sleep under a mosquito net, that has been impregnated with permethrin.
* **Vitamin B** Various reports suggest that vitamin B, particularly thiamin, discourages the mosquito as it modifies the smell of perspiration.

Anti-malarial prophylaxis

There are several different types of anti-malarial prophylaxis. These are mostly in tablet form and should be taken with food, although research trials are underway to find an inoculation against malaria. Medication recommendations can change, so do get up-to-date advice before travel. No anti-malarial drugs are 100% effective, and you may still develop malaria, so take other preventative measures too. At the time of writing, the following give the most comprehensive protection:

Chemoprophylaxis

Lariam (also known as mefloquine) is usually very effective. However, it is not suitable for everyone. If Lariam is suggested, start this two-and-a-half weeks (three doses) before departure to check that it suits you; stop it immediately if it seems to cause depression or anxiety, visual or hearing disturbances, severe headaches, fits or changes in heart rhythm. Side effects such as nightmares or dizziness are not medical reasons for stopping unless they are sufficiently debilitating or annoying. Anyone who is pregnant, who has suffered fits in the past, has been treated for depression or psychiatric problems, has diabetes controlled by oral therapy or who is epileptic or has a close blood relative who is epileptic, should avoid Lariam. It is vital not to take Lariam with other mind-altering substances, such as alcohol and other street/recreational drugs, as this can lead to severe psychotic effects.

Malarone (proguanil and atovaquone) has more recently been licensed for prophylaxis and is almost as effective as Lariam. It has several advantages over Lariam. It need only be started two days before entering a malarial area, has few side effects (such as upset stomach if not taken with food and, rarely, headaches or a cough), and needs to be continued for only one week after returning. However, it is expensive and because of this tends to be reserved for shorter trips although it can be prescribed for up to three months from the UK. Malarone may not be suitable for everybody. It has recently acquired a licence for children weighing 11–39kg (after 40kg the dose is as for an adult).

The antibiotic **doxycycline** (100mg daily) is a viable alternative when either Lariam or Malarone are not considered suitable for whatever reason. Like Malarone it can be started two days before arrival into a malaria area, but must be taken for four weeks after leaving. Unlike Lariam, it may also be used in travellers with epilepsy, although certain anti-epileptic medication may make it less effective. There is a possibility of allergic skin reactions developing in sunlight in about 3% of people; the drug should be stopped if this happens. It can also cause vaginal thrush in women, so it's worth taking Canesten with you as a precaution. Women using the oral contraceptive should use an additional method of protection for the first four weeks when using doxycycline. It is unsuitable in pregnancy or for children under 12 years.

Primaquine may also be used for treating malaria, although it is not the treatment of choice. A daily 30mg dose can also be used as a prophylactic. Start the day before and take for a week after return.

Note The combination of Paludrine (proguanil) and Avloclor (chloroquine) is no longer recommended for Kenya, due to malarial resistance.

Homoeopathic and herbal prophylaxis

While we strongly recommend chemoprophylaxis, for those seeking a homoeopathic alternative in preventing malaria, below are some of the options. Only take such alternatives after consulting your doctor.

- *Artemisia annua* A herbal medicine. Take 20 drops in the morning for seven days prior to travel, daily while travelling and for one month after return.
- **Qing Hao** A Chinese herbal medicine containing *artemesiae* and *apiaceae*. Take a teaspoon of this bitter tasting powder mixed with hot water morning and evening. Purchase from a reputable stockist, and follow directions from a qualified herbalist.
- **Demal200**: A homoeopathic treatment and prophylactic, rapidly gaining acceptance, which is sprayed under the tongue, has a reasonable taste and can be used by children, nursing mothers, pregnant women and for long-term use. It is available from www.blueturtlegroup.com.

Treating malaria

Firstly, if you are near a doctor, go for a malarial blood test. If you are in the wilds, you should consider using a self-test kit and commencing self-treatment according to the testing kit's advice. Currently, Rapimal is the testing kit most likely to be recommended. There are a variety of treatments available. At the time of writing, Malarone (four tablets per day for three days) or quinine and doxycycline are considered the most effective. There is also Riamet, which combines artemetta and lumefantrine. The three-day course involves taking a lot of tablets, but is well tolerated and highly effective.

The Chinese herbal cure Kotexen is also considered by some to be effective, but better treatments are available and it is not recommended; if you do use this, check that it comes from a sound source.

Halfan, which used to be a popular treatment, should be avoided. It is considered medically unsafe, especially if you are taking Lariam. The most suitable treatment will depend on several factors, including whether you are taking anti-malaria prophylaxis and if so, which one(s), and whether there are any medical contra-indications. It is best, therefore, to seek expert advice and to buy treatment before you go. No matter what you use, if you suspect that you have malaria you should always get medical help as soon as possible.

Getting ill on return

Malaria can mimic flu and traveller's diarrhoea or just about anything else. The one consistent feature is a temperature of 38°C or higher. The incubation period for malaria is anything from seven days into a malarial area up to one year after you leave, especially if you have taken anti-malarial prophylaxis. You should go immediately to a doctor if you have a high temperature and feel unwell. Make sure you emphasise that you could have been exposed to malaria so that you can be tested and treatment started as soon as possible.

Other insect-borne illnesses

The mosquito-borne **dengue fever** may mimic malaria, but there is no prophylactic medication available to deal with it. The mosquitoes that carry this virus bite during the daytime, so it is worth applying repellent if you see any mosquitoes around. Symptoms include strong headaches, rashes, excruciating joint and muscle pains, and high fever. Dengue fever only lasts for a week or so and is not usually fatal. Complete rest and paracetamol are the usual treatment. Plenty of fluids also help; some patients are given an intravenous drip to keep them from dehydrating. It is especially important to protect yourself if you have had dengue fever before, as a second infection with a different strain can result in the potentially fatal dengue haemorrhagic fever.

Tick typhus and **tick-borne relapsing fever** are both caught from tick bites.

PREVENTION IS BETTER THAN CURE

I met a British couple on holiday in Kenya who had been scoffed by mosquitoes. By way of conversation, I asked them what anti-malarial prophylaxis they were taking (it's a common traveller's topic of conversation – particularly Lariam) to which they proudly replied, 'Oh, we don't bother.' This attitude is foolish: malaria kills 3,000 children a day, over a million people a year; it infects between 1.5 and 3 million people annually, and nine out of ten cases are in sub-Saharan Africa. It is estimated that the UK has about 3,500 cases annually with ten to 15 preventable deaths. We all have a choice, but some tropical diseases are extremely debilitating and we are wise to take precautions to avoid getting them. Equally, they can be insidious, with vague symptoms such as lethargy and 'not feeling right'. Illnesses like amoebic dysentery, giardia and bilharzia can be difficult to diagnose. Undoubtedly, the old adage, 'prevention is better than cure', still carries weight. In the six months spent researching this guide, I was diagnosed by reputable doctors with malaria, typhoid, typhus, brucellosis, and told there was nothing wrong with me, before finally being diagnosed with bilharzia after further blood tests in UK on my return.

Did you know?

- Malaria kills more people today than it did 30 years ago due to mutations of the illness and drug resistance.
- It is second only to tuberculosis in its impact on world health.
- The World Health Organisation estimates that the provision of mosquito nets can reduce malaria transmission by 35% and the deaths of children from malaria by 25%.
- A leading malarial researcher, Professor Chris Curtis from the London School of Hygiene and Tropical Medicine, has estimated that it would cost US$0.5 billion to provide Africa's rural poor with treated mosquito nets. This is equivalent to the amount of money Americans spend on protecting their pets from fleas annually.

Neither is life-threatening. Tick typhus is similar to a mild viral infection with a red spot appearing to the side of the bite, which may then ulcerate, together with a red rash on the arms and trunk, spreading to the palms and soles of the feet. About a week after a tick bite, severe headaches, fever and aches and pains accompany tick-borne relapsing fever, with bouts of illness every five to nine days, which disappear after about six weeks. **Sleeping sickness** is caught from a tsetse fly bite. Not all tsetse flies are carriers, and the illness is extremely rare, although a couple of British tourists have been infected within the last year. Unlike mosquitoes, with a tsetse-fly bite, you know when you've been bitten, as they give a very sharp sting (very similar to the Scottish horse-fly or cleg). The first stages of the illness are a redness and swelling at the side of the bite, about 10 to 20 days afterwards. If caught at this stage, treatment is straightforward. If left, the infection then spreads to other parts of the body, and finally (and often fatally) to the brain, at which stage sleepiness sets in and treatment is difficult. **Tumbu flies** can be a problem where the climate is hot and humid. The adult fly lays eggs on the soil or on laundry drying on the grass or bushes. If the eggs come into contact with human flesh (when you put on clothes or lie on a bed) they hatch and bury themselves under the skin. Here they form a crop of 'boils' from each of which a grub hatches after about eight days; after this the inflammation will settle down. The risk from tumbu fly can be reduced by ironing clothes and laundry. **Jiggers** or **sandfleas** are another flesh-feaster. They latch on if you walk barefoot in contaminated places, and set up home under the skin of the foot, usually at the side of a toenail where they cause a painful, boil-like swelling which can be very itchy. They need to be picked out by a local expert; if the distended flea bursts during eviction the wound should be dowsed in spirit, alcohol or kerosene, otherwise more jiggers will infest you.

Parasites

There are a number of illnesses where infection is water-related, from assorted worms (hook, ring, thread, tape) and bilharzia to various types of dysentery (bacillary and amoebic) and giardia. If you find blood and mucous in your stools, the chances are that you have dysentery. The best way to avoid getting parasitic infections is to be scrupulous about hygiene and to avoid raw food and salads unless you are sure of the way they have been washed (see *Travellers' diarrhoea*, page 154), or in the case of bilharzia avoiding swimming or paddling in contaminated water.

Giardia lamblia

Giardia, also known as giardiasis, is one of the most common parasitic infections of the human intestine. Symptoms vary from greasy, yellow diarrhoea with a rancid smell alternating with constipation, abdominal bloating and cramps, to belching ('eggy burps') and chronic fatigue. The symptoms are often mistaken for irritable bowel syndrome. It is usually diagnosed from stool samples, but it is not always easy to detect, especially when the giardia colony is well established in the gut when few cysts are excreted. An antibody test from blood or the Elisa antigen detection in the faeces have been found to give a 30% more accurate diagnosis. Once diagnosed, the best treatment for giardiasis is tinidazole (Fasigyn). Four 500mg tablets are taken in one dose followed by another four, seven days later, if symptoms persist. Metronidazole (Flagyl) is also effective, but can have some unpleasant side effects and a longer course is necessary.

Amoebic dysentery

Amoebic dysentery can also be fiendishly difficult to diagnose from stool tests. Its symptoms are not dissimilar to giardia, but often there is no diarrhoea. Gut spasms and bloating are common. The lethargy and fatigue associated with the illness are often mistaken for depression. Once diagnosed, the treatment regime is usually the same as for treating giardia.

Bacillary dysentery

This is characterised by severe diarrhoea, sometimes with blood and/or slime in the stools and a fever. It needs to be treated immediately with an antibiotic like ciprofloxacin. One 500mg tablet followed by another taken 6–12 hours later usually works, but more severe cases may need a longer course. Again it is always best to consult a doctor if you can.

Bilharzia or schistosomiasis

There are six forms of the disease. The two most common in Africa are African bowel *Schistosoma mansoni* and urinary bilharzia, *Schistosoma haematobium*. Both are found in Kenya. Freshwater lakes, ponds, streams, irrigation canals and stagnant water can harbour bilharzia-transmitting snails which produce vast numbers of worms called *cercariae* which then invade human hosts. Swimming, paddling and washing in infected water exposes you to infection. The worms migrate to their favoured place in the body, and then mate, and females can produce hundreds of eggs a day. Some pass out of the body (which then hatch and find a host snail before the cycle begins again) while others get lodged in different organs. It is the eggs rather than the worms which cause the worst effects of the disease, as they become lodged in the body's organs and affect the immune system.

Symptoms
These may include itching during the first couple of days where the *cercariae* entered the skin, but more often than not there is no evidence. After four to six weeks you may develop a flu-like illness, often confused with malaria, or you might feel completely well. It is only at this stage that blood tests become positive, but it can take much longer than that to test positive, so if you have been exposed, have another blood test nine to 12 months later. Often the only symptom is a general fatigue. Once established, a longer-lasting reaction is caused by the eggs, which do not escape, causing liver or kidney damage, and on rare occasions paralysis through affecting the spinal cord.

Prevention
Avoid water contact in contaminated areas – in Kenya's freshwater lakes, Victoria has bilharzia, not only along the lakeside, but off the islands too, while to date Baringo and Naivasha do not have a bilharzia problem. If you do swim in potentially affected water, apply DEET insect repellent before and after swimming, and towel vigorously to reduce your chances of infection. If you cannot resist the temptation of swimming in the water then it is safer in the early morning than in the latter part of the day. Also try to avoid spending more than ten minutes in the water, and keep away from the edge of the lake.

Treatment
Once bilharzia is diagnosed, a three-day dose of Praziquantel is successful in killing off the worms, but this does not stop the immune reaction in the tissues which can leave long-lasting problems.

Rabies
Rabies is a viral infection, which attacks the brain and if contracted is always fatal. It's carried by many domestic and wild animals, among them, dogs, cats, monkeys, foxes, jackals, civets, mongooses and bats. A bite from a domestic rabid dog is the most common form of transmission. Scratches or licks over an open wound are also a risk. Avoid contact with animals unless they are known to you and seek medical help immediately if you think you may have been exposed to rabies. In the interim, scrub the wound with soap and clean water, and then douse it with a strong iodine or alcohol solution. Gin or whisky will suffice if no alcohol solution is available. This helps to stop the rabies virus entering the body. If you are unfortunate enough to be bitten by any animal, tell the doctor if you have received pre-exposure rabies vaccine, as this requires a different and simpler treatment regime.

Meningitis
Kenya does have outbreaks of meningitis which are generally reported in the press, but visitors are unlikely to be exposed. There are viral forms of meningitis that are usually self-limiting and rarely fatal. However, the bacterial form (caused by *Meningitis meningitides*) is much more serious. Unless it is treated promptly it can kill within hours of the first symptoms appearing – a combination of a blinding

THE TRAVEL SAFE CODE
To reduce your risk of contracting AIDS:

* Avoid unnecessary medical or dental treatment.
* Avoid having casual relationships, but if you have sex with someone new, always use a condom (see *Safe sex* below).
* Don't inject drugs or share needles, syringes or any other parts of drug paraphernalia.
* Remember that alcohol and drugs affect your judgement.
* Avoid having a tattoo, acupuncture, ear or body piercing unless sterile equipment is used.

headache (light sensitivity), a blotchy rash and a high fever. Meningitis vaccines come in various forms. Either meningitis A+C or ACWY are recommended for travellers intending to spend a month or longer in Kenya. Vaccination may also be advised if you are intending to work with children.

Hepatitis
Hepatitis A is a virus infection that attacks the liver and can be caught from contaminated food or water. It causes jaundice (yellowing of the skin) and can cause fever, vomiting and stomach pain. A full recovery can take many months, but rarely leads to death. **Hepatitis B** also affects the liver and is spread by contaminated blood, unprotected sex and bodily fluids. It can be fatal. Both diseases are preventable by safe and effective vaccines (see above). Remember though that hepatitis B is not the only blood-borne virus. **Hepatitis C** and **HIV** are also spread through blood and contaminated needles, and HIV is a particular risk from unprotected sex. That is why it is sensible to take a 'needle and syringe kit' and condoms (see *HIV/AIDS*).

HIV/AIDS
Over two million adult Kenyans are infected with HIV/AIDS and 500 Kenyans die daily from the illness. AIDS has been declared a national disaster and a National Aids Control Council (NACC) has been set up to help to mitigate the disease. It's estimated that the number of deaths from the AIDS epidemic could rise to 2.6 million by the end of 2005 if no intervention measures are put in place. It has placed an enormous strain on medical resources. In 1992 AIDS patients accounted for 15% of hospital beds. This had risen to 50% by 2000. AIDS in Kenya is no different to the illness worldwide and the same risks apply.

Safe sex
Travel liberates the mind, and, it would seem, sexual mores. The risks of contracting sexually transmitted diseases are high, regardless of whether sexual partners are local or fellow travellers. About 40% of HIV infections in British heterosexuals are acquired abroad and in 2000 the UK Public Health Laboratory Service reported a 28% increase in HIV among those under 24. Gap-year students take note. Ensure you have protected sex – use condoms or femidoms, preferably those with a BS Kitemark, purchased before you go. Spermicide pessaries can also help to reduce the risk of transmission. If you notice any genital ulcers or discharge, seek prompt treatment, as these increase the risk of acquiring HIV.

KENYAN SNAKES: RECOGNISING SNAKES AND WHAT TO DO IF YOU ARE BITTEN
Anthony Childs

There is a wide variety of snake species in Kenya, 74% of which are non-venomous to man. The chances of coming across a snake, let alone being bitten by one are very slim indeed. People who have been bitten by snakes are in the minority and more often than not have been bitten when either handling or trying to trap, catch or kill a snake.

The most dangerous snake in Kenya is probably the puff adder, solely because of the large number of recorded bites. This is a snake that is in no hurry to move and will bite readily in order to avoid a risk of being bitten; so stick to clear paths and always carry a torch when moving around at night.

A few general rules for recognising DANGEROUS SNAKES
- A snake over 2m in length is likely to be dangerous.
- A grey, greenish or brown tree snake over 1.3m long is likely to be a vine snake, boomslang or mamba.
- A snake that spreads a hood or spits is a cobra.
- A thick snake with a large triangular head is most probably an adder or viper.
- A smallish black, dark grey or brown snake, with small eyes and a tail that ends in a spike, is almost certainly a burrowing asp.

If you are unsure of a snake, treat it as a dangerous one and leave it alone. The chances are that it will move off when left. Snakes do not look for people to harm and generally strike out of self defence.

Avoid being bitten
- Leave snakes alone at all times.
- Never handle small, harmless-looking snakes.

MOUNTAIN HEALTH
Altitude sickness

The best way to avoid altitude sickness is to acclimatise properly, as even the fittest people succumb to the effects of altitude. Ironically, it is often those who are fit who tend to suffer more, as in their enthusiasm they ascend too fast. If you are fit and have a tendency to forge ahead, make a concerted effort to *slow down*.

Altitude sickness has a number of conditions, all associated with a lack of oxygen:

Acute mountain sickness (AMS)

This is characterised by a headache and mild nausea, which is common over 4,000m. Other symptoms, depending on its severity, are dizziness, a loss of appetite, vomiting and difficulty in sleeping. AMS may be mild to severe, and can lead to cerebral oedema. If the symptoms are mild, take time for the body to adapt to altitude: slow down, rest in camp and drink plenty of fluids. Mild headaches may benefit from taking paracetamol. If the symptoms have not diminished in 24 hours, descend; as little as 500m can make a huge difference. If you are travelling with an experienced guide, it is always best to tell them as soon as symptoms appear. They are in the best position to decide what to do.

* Do not touch snakes that appear to be dead.
* Wear heavy trousers and boots if walking out in the bush.
* Never walk barefoot or without a torch at night.
* Never try to kill a snake if you come across one in the wild; that is just looking for trouble.

Dealing with a snake bite
Do not waste time. Most of the following can be done in a car on the way to hospital.

* Lay the victim down and keep him/her calm; it is important to stop the victim from panicking which would cause blood to be pumped around the body faster, spreading the poison.
* Apply firm pressure to the area of the bite using your hand
* Wrap the limb firmly with a crêpe bandage, starting at the site of the bite and working towards the heart.
* DO NOT cut around the wound.
* DO NOT try to suck the venom out.
* DO NOT electrocute the victim.
* DO NOT give the victim any liquid.
* DO NOT try to kill the snake responsible; a second bite would complicate matters.

Spitting snakes
With spitting snakes (like cobras) rinse the affected area immediately, usually the eyes, with the closest liquid at hand (beer, milk, water and, in desperate circumstances, even urine). Then get the victim to a doctor for a check up as soon as possible.

Anthony Childs is a snake expert and safari guide.

High-altitude cerebral oedema
The symptoms are a severe headache, confusion, a drunken gait and abnormal behaviour which can lead to increasing degrees of coma and death. This is a medical emergency and if possible it's vital to descend before the symptoms become this severe.

High-altitude pulmonary oedema
This is also a serious form of altitude sickness that can be fatal. Typical symptoms are a shortness of breath at rest, a dry cough (sometimes with a pink, frothy spit), blue lips, audibly rattling lungs, a rapid heartbeat and an increased breathing rate. It is imperative to descend *immediately*, as rest at altitude does not help, and to seek urgent medical attention. Deterioration can be extremely fast.

Acclimatisation
At 2,500m the air holds 26% less oxygen than at sea level, the percentage increasing with altitude. The body's oxygen requirements remain the same, so the lungs and heart have to adapt. Before climbing or trekking above 3,000m, spend a couple of days at that altitude or below. Aim to sleep at an altitude of no more than 300m above the previous night's stop, and have a full rest day for each 1,000m ascended.

Avoid alcohol, reduce salt intake, eat more carbohydrates and maintain a high fluid intake (at least four litres a day).

Medication (acetazolamide: Diamox) is available to help prevent altitude sickness, but it can cause a tingling sensation. Seek medical advice before taking it.

Hypothermia

Weather at altitude can be deceptive and hypothermia can occur at 10°C. Mild symptoms are uncontrollable shivering which can be alleviated by raising the body temperature – put on dry clothes and get into a sleeping bag. Severe symptoms include disorientation, lethargy and confusion, leading to coma which can be fatal. To alleviate the risks of hypothermia, wear several thin layers of clothes and take a woolly hat, as most heat loss from the body is through the head.

Useful addresses

British Mountaineering Council 177–179 Burton Rd, Manchester, M20 2BB, UK; tel: 0161 445 4747; fax: 0161 445 4500; web: www.thebmc.co.uk. They have information sheets available for doctors, climbers and trekkers.

Mountain Club of Kenya (MCK) Also provides information specifically relevant to mounts Kenya and Kilimanjaro.

COMMON MEDICAL PROBLEMS

Many common ailments you can treat yourself. However, if in doubt, seek medical advice.

Travellers' diarrhoea

Few travellers escape getting a dose of the runs when they're abroad. The body is subjected to time changes, different types of food (and their attendant bacteria), different standards of hygiene, the effects of altitude, temperature changes and often sheer exhaustion due to long hours spent travelling. Also, many people do not drink enough and become dehydrated. All these factors can contribute towards making the body more susceptible to travellers' diarrhoea.

Avoiding diarrhoea

The way to avoid getting diarrhoea is to adhere to a strict code of hygiene. Always wash your hands before a meal and ensure that the food you eat has been prepared and cooked properly and that you drink bottled or boiled and filtered water. If you are not sure about standards of hygiene, stick to the maxim, 'Boil it, cook it, peel it or forget it'.

Avoid cold buffets which are poorly refrigerated, food covered in flies, food that has been reheated, raw vegetables, unpeeled fruits, meat that is not thoroughly cooked, ice-cream and unpasteurised dairy products, ice cubes and local drinking water or cold drinks. This will reduce your chances of succumbing to travellers' diarrhoea and 'will also reduce the risks of other illnesses like typhoid and dysentery.

Treatment

A bout of diarrhoea usually lasts from two to four days and will clear up without treatment. Avoid all fatty foods (includes milk) and maintain your fluid intake (at least three litres a day). Eat dry toast or bland carbohydrates and avoid fruit and vegetables. However, the symptoms of diarrhoea can be controlled by taking an anti-diarrhoeal like Imodium, which slows down the bowel movement and reduces fluid loss. This should be used only when it is not convenient to be rushing to the toilet every few minutes. Otherwise it is best to let the diarrhoea happen to get the bugs out of your system. Rehydration is paramount, and if you are losing a lot of fluids, take oral rehydration sachets (eg: Electrolade) as well. Alternatively, add a teaspoon of salt and six teaspoons of sugar to a litre of water. The solution should not taste more salty than tears. Another option is to add salt to a sweet soda like Fanta orange. Flat Coke can also help to settle an upset stomach. A good way of assessing whether you need to increase your fluid intake is to look at your urine – if it is dark you need to increase your fluid intake.

If these remedies do not work and you still have a bad dose of diarrhoea, you may require antibiotics. A good guide to this is if you have a fever, and/or blood and/or slime in the stool. A dose of ciprofloxacin (500mg) repeated after 12 hours should suffice, and in very severe cases continue for three days; otherwise seek medical advice.

Menstruation
Travel and changes in time zones can affect the menstrual cycle, with periods coming early or late. Tampons and sanitary towels are readily available in Kenya's main towns and cities, but you may choose to bring a preferred brand. Oral contraception can be used to suppress menstruation.

Sinusitis
The dry heat and dust can combine to irritate the sinuses. If prone to sinusitis take a decongestant, especially if you are on a flying safari.

Eye problems
Dust can also irritate the eyes, especially for those who wear contact lenses. Medicated eye drops can soothe sore eyes. Pink eye (bacterial conjunctivitis) can be a problem, particularly at the coast during the change in the monsoon winds. This will need to be treated with antibiotic ointment or drops. If sensitive to glare, be sure to have a good pair of UV sunglasses, especially if going on water or trekking on ice.

Coral infections
At the coast, try to avoid getting cuts from coral while walking on the reef, by wearing rubber-soled canvas shoes or jellies. If you cut yourself on coral, apply antiseptic immediately, as infections can be nasty.

Ear problems
Another relatively common infection at the coast is known as **coral ear** which you can catch from getting sea water in your ears. This can be quite painful, and young children are especially prone to the infection. It is easily treated with antibiotic drops.

Prickly heat
This is a reaction to heat causing a red, pimply rash, normally on the torso, which commonly affects young children at the coast, although adults are not immune. It's more uncomfortable than harmful. Aim to keep cool and to wear loose cotton clothing. Have cold showers and avoid using soap or rubbing the area. Calamine lotion dabbed on to the rash can help to cool down the patient (it's also good for taking the sting out of sunburn).

Hospitals and pharmacies
Kenya has some first class medical facilities and there are hospitals and pharmacies in the main towns. These are listed in the regional chapters. Be aware that even

with medical insurance you are likely to have to pay for consultations and treatment and to claim on your insurance later. Make sure you keep all receipts.

Further reading

Self-prescribing has its hazards so if you are going anywhere very remote consider taking a health book. Recommended are:

Bugs, Bites & Bowels The Cadogan guide to healthy travel by Dr Jane Wilson-Howarth (1999)
Your Child's Health Abroad: A manual for travelling parents by Dr Jane Wilson-Howarth and Dr Matthew Ellis, published by Bradt Travel Guides and updated on www.bradt-travelguides.com

SAFETY

The terrorism alert in May 2003 had a severe impact on Kenya's tourism industry and economy. Although the Kenyan government had already beefed up its security operations following the Mombasa bombing in 2002, this was increased substantially. Close liaison between the UK, US and Kenyan governments has further increased security. Once the US National Security Strategy to set up counter terrorist activity has been implemented, Kenya's security measures will be among the best in Africa.

Before you go

Apart from ensuring that you have a comprehensive travel insurance policy (see page 139), the following websites give the latest travel information and advice, after which you can assess the information objectively:

UK Foreign and Commonweath Office; web: www.fco.gov.uk
US Department of State Travel Warnings; web: www.travel.state.gov/travel_warnings
Canada Department of Foreign Affairs and International Trade; web: www.voyage.gc.ca/destinations
Australia Department of Foreign Affairs and Trade; web: www.dfat.gov.au/consular/advice
France Ministre des Affaires Etrangères; web:www.dfae.diplomatie.fr
Germany Federal Foreign Office; web: www.auswaertiges-amt.de/www/de
Kenya Kenya Tourist Board; web: www.magicalkenya.com; Kenyan government; web: www.statehousekenya.go.ke

International terrorism

The threat of international terrorism is not restricted to Kenya alone and is a worldwide phenomenon. New York, Bali, Saudi Arabia and Morocco bear witness to the tragic events associated with international terrorism in the 21st century. Kenya too has been the target for terrorist attacks (the American Embassy and Mombasa bombings in 1998 and 2002, respectively), together with the threat of a terrorist attack on British Airways flights to Nairobi in May 2003. This put the country on to high-security alert, and resulted in the UK government issuing a commercial flight ban, which was lifted later in the summer of 2003.

Other airlines like Kenya Airways and South African Airways maintained their flight schedule, and Kenya's Minister of Tourism, Raphael Tuju, was swift to point out that no flight ban had been imposed on Saudi Arabia or Morocco, and that the ban was having a catastrophic effect on tourism and the Kenyan economy. Certainly, there is a terrorist threat in Kenya, with a small cell of al-Qaeda sympathisers, but this should be seen in perspective. Arguably, there are terrorist risks associated with visiting any country, including the UK and US.

Kenyan government response

The Kenyan government responded quickly to the terrorist threat in 2003, placing all defence units, including an anti-terrorist police squad, airports, ports and all tourist destinations, on a high-security alert. Flight paths into international airports were under surveillance and the Kenyan government worked in close co-operation with the UK and US to meet their security concerns. Recognising the threat that terrorism poses to the country, a Suppression of Terrorism Bill was placed before parliament in June 2003.

Future security

The **US National Security Strategy** set up to counter terrorist activity in Africa has chosen Kenya as a key strategic regional partner. This is due to its proximity to the horn of Africa. Kenya is expected to receive US$15 million towards implementing this strategy, which will certainly help to improve consumer confidence.

Kenya Tourism Federation Safety and Communications Centre (KWS Complex, Langata Road, PO Box 15013, Nairobi; tel: 020 505614; fax: 020 604730; tourist helpline: 020 604767; mob: 0722 745645 or 0733 617499; email: safetour@wananchi.com) is an umbrella body representing six tourist associations in Kenya (tour operators, hotelkeepers and caterers, travel agents, budget hotels, Mombasa and the coast tourism and air operators). In response to a series of security incidents involving tourists – tourist buses being hijacked and a few highly publicised murders, such as the Julie Ward case – it set up the **Safety and Communication Centre** (SCC) in 1998, which provides the following:

- operations control room, manned 24 hours a day, seven days a week
- a countrywide safety communications high-frequency radio network
- professional assistance for tourists involved in incidents
- destination information – roads, weather, security
- links with the tourism industry, police, Kenya Wildlife Service and the Flying Doctors.

The SCC is an excellent one-stop-shop for up-to-date information relating to security. They advise on safe and risky areas and can give a direct link to the **Tourism Police Unit**, a branch of the police dedicated to dealing with tourist incidents. If you are on a self-drive safari, you are strongly advised to get an update from SCC on your proposed route prior to travel. If you are unfortunate enough to be involved in a security incident, make a point of contacting the SCC as they can help to streamline formalities and to follow up if necessary. Encouragingly, since SCC was initiated the number of incidents involving tourists has been on the decline. And remember that, statistically, you are more likely to be mugged in Miami.

Personal safety

Common sense prevails, but remember the following:

- Be streetwise and vigilant.
- Keep an eye on your belongings at all times.
- Never leave cameras and bags in unlocked vehicles.
- Do not be ostentatious with money and avoid carrying large wads of cash.
- Do not wear expensive jewellery and watches.
- Make use of hotel safety deposit boxes.
- Take local advice on what areas are best avoided (even during daytime).

- Take taxis at night.
- Do not walk on empty beaches alone (especially women, as rape is not unknown).
- Do not walk on beaches at night.
- Do not accept food from strangers (especially on buses) as it may be drugged.
- If staying in cheap lodgings, keep your valuables close to you at night (under the pillow or in your bed).
- If you think there is someone in the room, pretend you are having a nightmare and start screaming out and thrashing around – the chances are you'll scare them off.

What to do in an emergency

In the majority of incidents, opportunist robbery is the reason for attack and people get hurt when they put up a fight. For your own safety, be compliant. Hand over cameras, money and jewellery. Assess the situation for yourself – if there is only one thief and you are alone, you could try throwing all your valuables to the side and making a run for it. If it's a hijack, just do as you are told. Importantly, try and stay calm.

Women travellers

Apart from the general points on personal safety, women travelling alone are occasionally subject to sexual harassment, but it's rare. Conversations will usually revolve around 'Where is your husband?' and 'How many children do you have?' I once replied, 'I have two husbands and nine children,' which was greeted by looks of astonishment before we all burst out laughing. Sometimes, rather than explaining that you are on your own, it's easier to invent a husband and to flaunt a fake wedding ring. Being family oriented, for Kenyans it's strange for a woman to be travelling alone without a member of her family. Avoiding eye contact (sunglasses are useful) and dressing conservatively will also help to dissuade unwanted attention.

It's also advisable for women travellers to check out accommodation, especially if staying in cheap lodgings. Ask to see a room first, avoid staying on the ground floor and check door and window locks. Do not open your door to strangers and avoid staying in the red-light district – which in Nairobi means the River Road area.

Wildlife hazards

Incidents involving wildlife are few and far between, but whenever there is an interaction with wildlife there is an element of danger. It pays to have a healthy respect for wildlife, and if on a walking safari to pay attention to your guide. Remember, the animals are *wild* and their behaviour can be unpredictable. Insects like safari ants (*siafu*) and tsetse flies are more likely to be a nuisance. Do not feed animals, such as cute little monkeys – they can give a nasty bite. When camping, be sure to keep your tent closed at night.

Hippo

Hippo are said to be the most dangerous animals in Africa. Keep your distance and avoid getting between a hippo and the water.

Buffalo

Lone buffalo can be cantankerous. They often rest up in bushes during the day and may charge unprovoked. If this happens, immediately lie face-down on the ground. It is likely you will get a good buffeting, but lying down makes it difficult for the buffalo to get its horns underneath you (the horns curve upwards). It is the horns that cause the damage, as they can rip open any soft flesh.

Elephant

There have been a couple of incidents in the past decade where elephants have trampled and even killed tourists. In one such incident, a woman was jogging on the Il Ngwesi community group ranch in Laikipia, when an elephant attacked (probably in self-defence because it got a fright). This incident highlighted how sometimes management will comply to tourist whims, in this case with tragic results. The woman did have a guide, who tried to distract the elephant, but she was badly trampled and fortunate to survive. The bottom line is that it's foolhardy to go jogging in a wildlife area. Another incident was on Mount Kenya, a freak accident where a woman was trampled to death. Elephants will also occasionally charge vehicles – this is usually if they have been frightened, or if a bull is in musth. Be alert to their behaviour and approach them with care.

Lion

If you come across a lion in the bush, back off slowly. Do not run, as it will trigger the 'cat-and-mouse' instinct.

Road hazards

The state of the roads, combined with some appalling drivers and badly maintained vehicles, has accounted for Kenya's extremely high incidence of road-traffic accidents. Travel with reputable bus or tour companies, avoid travel by *matatu* and, if on a self-drive safari, keep your wits about you and do not travel at night (see page 83 for further information). The spate of car-jackings, particularly of 4WDs, in the 1980s and 1990s has diminished. They are now rare, but not unknown. If you think you are being followed and you have a mobile phone, call for help; otherwise drive to the nearest police station or garage. The mobile phone company, Safaricom, operates a 911 emergency service.

OKAVANGO TOURS & SAFARIS

for expert knowledge and individually designed holidays in **Kenya**

We also specialise in Botswana, Zambia, Malawi, Namibia, Zimbabwe, Tanzania, South Africa, Madagascar, Réunion, Mauritius, Seychelles, Uganda

Tel:020 8343 3283 Email: info@okavango.com
www.okavango.com   **ATOL 2945**
Marlborough House, 298 Regents Park Road, London N3 2TJ

Individually tailored holidays to the land of safari

KENYA

SAFARI CONSULTANTS LTD

Telephone: +44 (0)1787 228494
E-Mail: bill@safariconsultantuk.com
WEBSITE
www.safari-consultants.co.uk

Specialists in holidays to East and Southern Africa

ATOL AITO
IATA

HOOPOE SAFARIS

Hoopoe Safaris is an East African safari company, with a UK marketing office, offering a range of luxury safaris, mountain climbs, beach holidays and special interest safaris in Kenya, Tanzania, and along the Swahili Coast. We also arrange tailor-made walking safaris throughout East Africa with our dedicated sister company Tropical Trekking, and we are the marketing agents for Kirurumu Tented Camps & Lodges. We are renowned for being flexible and innovative in tailor-making personalised itineraries to accommodate individual budgets and time restrictions and also offer special set departure itineraries. In addition to the wide range of lodge accommodation available, we specialise in luxurious mobile tented classic camping safaris.

For further information on Hoopoe Safaris or Tropical Trekking and for details of your local specialist tour operator who features Hoopoe/Tropical Trekking safaris, please contact:

KENYA	TANZANIA	UK (Marketing)
Tel: +254 20 604303	Tel: +255 27 2507011	Tel: +44 1923 255462
Fax: +254 20 604304	Fax: +255 27 2548226	Tel: +44 1923 255452
Email: hoopoe@wananchi.com	Email: information@hoopoe.com	Email: hoopoeuk@aol.com

Or visit our websites at
www.hoopoe.com & www.tropicaltrekking.com & www.kirurumu.com

"A traveller without knowledge is like a bird without wings"
(Mushariff-Ud-Din, 1184-1291)

Part Two

The Guide

FROM THE SPECTACULAR MASAI MARA TO LAMU ON THE COAST AND KILIMANJARO

SCHEDULED SERVICE DESTINATIONS SERVED BY:

AIRKENYA

1. Samburu
2. Meru
3. Nanyuki
4. Nairobi
5. Masai Mara
6. Lamu
d. Kilimanjaro

REGIONAL AIR

a. Grumeti
b. Seronera
c. Manyara
d. Kilimanjaro
e. Arusha

Airkenya, with over 20 years of general aviation experience in East Africa provides a network of scheduled services throughout Kenya and operates charters within the East African region.

Destinations served by the scheduled services from Nairobi are Lamu on the Coast, Kilimanjaro in Tanzania and the game parks of Nanyuki, Meru, Samburu and the Masai Mara.

Airkenya has a sister company, Regional Air Services, based in Arusha, Tanzania, which provides scheduled services to Kilimanjaro, Manyara, Seronera, Grumeti as well as charter flights throughout the country.

THESE ARE JUST THREE OF THE EXOTIC DESTINATIONS WE FLY TO IN KENYA AND TANZANIA.

For more information contact your travel agent or Tour Operater.
Airkenya website: www.airkenya.com

Nairobi

The sprawling, cosmopolitan city of Nairobi combines the first-world glamour of reflecting-glass skyscraper buildings with abject third-world poverty. It originated in 1899 from a handful of shacks that marked the end of the railhead during the building of the Uganda railway. Subsequently it was given township status in 1900 and city status in 1950. The area was known by the Maasai as *enkare nyrobi*, a reference to the cool waters where they came to water their livestock. The name became corrupted to Nairobi, and as the city grew – and with it an increase in crime – it's become referred to wryly as 'Nai-robberi'.

Apart from being Kenya's capital and the main centre of government and commerce in the country, Nairobi is the most significant city in East Africa and an important player on the pan-African stage. It's the diplomatic base for many countries in Africa, with a broad spectrum of international embassies, together with headquarters for the United Nations, multi-national companies, non-governmental organisations (NGOs) and press correspondents for Africa. It's also the gateway for safaris. As a result it has embraced a broad range of cultures – primarily African, European and Asian – and is remarkable for its lack of racial tensions. It has also attracted a high proportion of the diverse ethnic mix of Kenya's rural population, drawn by the magnet of employment and the bright city lights.

At independence, in 1963, the city had a population of half a million and covered an area of 350km². Today its population is officially about 2.2 million, although some estimates put its informal population as high as 3 million (it's estimated 800,000 people live in the Kibera slums alone) and it's doubled in size. Inevitably, this has placed a huge strain on the city's resources and water shortages and electricity cuts are not unknown.

The city is bisected by the Mombasa road and the leafy avenue of Uhuru Highway. To the east is a vast industrial area which stretches from the city centre almost as far as Jomo Kenyatta International Airport to the south and the Thika road to the north, while to the southwest is Langata Road, with Wilson Airport, Nairobi National Park and the rusting corrugated rooftops of the shanty town, Kibera, around Nairobi dam. The remainder of the area is divided into residential suburbs – Karen, Langata, Kilimani, Upper Hill, Hurlingham, Lavington, Westlands, Parklands and Muthaiga. The traffic is at times severely congested, with vehicles belching out black fumes which comes as rather a shock after the catalytic-converter mentality of Europe. Equally so is the erratic driving. Nevertheless, senses sharpen and one soon becomes engulfed in the thrusting bustle of entrepreneurial activity, living life on the edge.

Most visitors to Kenya hive off to the safari destinations, spending little time in the city. But Nairobi has its share of highlights, including the National Museum

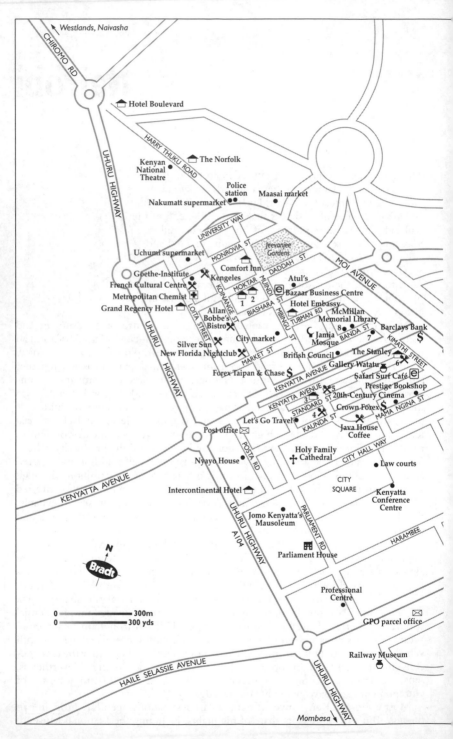

CENTRAL NAIROBI & RIVER ROAD

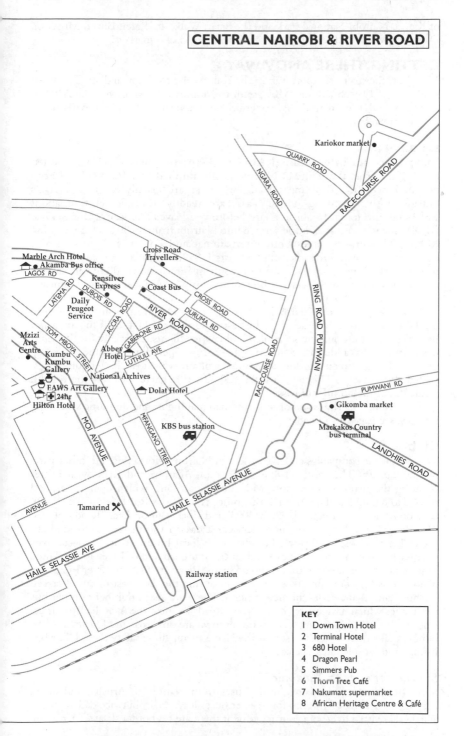

KEY
1 Down Town Hotel
2 Terminal Hotel
3 680 Hotel
4 Dragon Pearl
5 Simmers Pub
6 Thorn Tree Café
7 Nakumatt supermarket
8 African Heritage Centre & Café

of Kenya, Nairobi National Park and the Safari Walk, the Karen Blixen Museum, Daphne Sheldrick's Elephant Orphanage and the Maasai markets.

GETTING THERE AND AWAY

Nairobi is the main transport hub in the country, by road, rail and air. The main roads out of Nairobi are the A109 south to Mombasa (linking with the A104 to Namanga and Tanzania), the A2 to Thika and the northeast, and the A104 north to Nakuru and western Kenya.

By air

Jomo Kenyatta International Airport (JKIA) (tel: 020 822111) is located about 13km from the centre of Nairobi (a 30-minute drive). Visas (US$50) can be purchased on arrival and the airport banks are usually open for arrivals outside normal banking hours. Taxis are readily available, costing about KSh1,000 into town. Establish a fare before you leave. The Kenya Bus Service (KBS) operates a metro shuttle service into Nairobi from 06.00 to 00.55, costing KSh50. The airport serves both international and domestic flights. Airport departure tax for international flights costs US$20 (normally already included in your ticket purchase). Be sure to reconfirm international flights at least 48 hours in advance with your airline office, or via a travel agent. Domestic departure tax is KSh300.

Wilson Airport (tel: 020 606838) is located about 8km from Nairobi city centre on the Langata road. It's one of the busiest airports for light aircraft in Africa and the main base for domestic scheduled and charter flights, especially for the safari destinations. In addition, domestic air-charter operations abound, offering individual or group charter flights in a range of aircraft. Most charter companies, such as Boskovic Air Charters Ltd (tel: 020 501210) charge a set rate for a flight, regardless of the number of passengers.

For a listing of airlines and offices, international flights and domestic scheduled services, see pages 66 and 88.

By bus

The major bus companies all have offices in Nairobi with services to other parts of the country. The most reliable services are Akamba and KBS, with routes covering the main towns countrywide, and Coast Bus, which operates a good service to Mombasa. The Akamba Bus office is on Lagos Road (tel: 020 221779), KBS on Mfangano Street (tel: 020 246093) and Coast Bus on Accra Road (tel: 020 214819). They offer one or more services a day to the major towns, and it's preferable to book in advance. For the more local buses, go to the Machakos country bus station on Landhies Road, at the southern end of River Road. These buses tend to operate on a 'fill up and go' basis. Be aware that the River Road area is notorious for being unsafe, so be careful during the day (best to take a taxi to the bus station) and avoid the area at night. There are also a number of other bus companies which have offices in the River Road area near the Akamba Bus office. The *matatu* stands operating services out of town are on Cross and Duruma roads, but only take them as a last resort as they have an appalling safety record. For bus listings and sample fares, see page 78.

Shuttle services to Tanzania

Several companies run daily shuttle buses from Nairobi to Arusha, and on to Moshi and Marangu. Twenty-four-seater buses leave Nairobi twice daily at 08.00 and 14.00, with a five-hour journey time if there are no border delays. Departure points are city-centre hotels and seats need to be confirmed in advance. Single journeys from Nairobi to Arusha cost US$25–35. Companies include:

Davanu Shuttle Phoenix House, Kenyatta Av, 2nd Floor, Nairobi; tel: 020 316929, 020 222002; fax: 020 316931; email: davanu@nbnet.co.ke

Riverside Pan African Insurance Bldg, at East Africa Shuttles and Safaris, 3rd Floor, Kenyatta Av, PO Box 11644, GPO, Nairobi; tel: 020 241032; mob: 0722 348656; email: info@eastafricashuttles.com; web: www.safari.cc/shuttle

Impala Shuttle Services Kibo Slopes Safaris Ltd, Lenana Rd (near Egyptian Embassy), PO Box 58064, Nairobi; tel: 020 717373, 020 725435; fax: 020 716028; email: info@kiboslopessafaris.com; web: www.kiboslopessafaris.com

Shuttle services to Mombasa
Varan Safaris Ltd (tel: 020 750072) operates a daily shuttle service between Nairobi and Mombasa, departing Nairobi at 10.00, costing KSh800.

Share taxis
Cross Road Travellers on Cross Road (tel: 020 245377) and Daily Peugeot Service (DPS) on Dubois Road (tel: 020 210866) operate reliable services. See page 80 for further details.

By train
Nairobi railway station (tel: 020 221211) is at the southern end of Moi Avenue, about 15 minutes' walk from Kenyatta Avenue. The night train to **Mombasa** departs daily at 19.00 and costs KSh3,000 per person first class, for a sleeping compartment for two, with sheets and blankets and a basin. Second class costs KSh2,100, with a shared compartment for four, with no bedding, and third class costs KSh350, for a seat only. There have been incidents of theft on the train in the past, so if you can afford it, it's preferable to go first class. First- and second-class passengers can have dinner on the train, announced by a waiter playing chime bars, although some of the bars have gone missing over the years. The service has certainly seen better days, but it does not detract from the excitement of leaving the highlands to awake to new sounds and smells as you near the coast in the morning. It's preferable to book a couple of days in advance, either at the station or through a travel agent. You can leave luggage at the station, but it costs about KSh200 a day.

Steam specials run about once a month between Nairobi and Mombasa. See page 129 for details.

In addition there's a passenger service to **Kisumu** on Monday, Wednesday and Friday, departing at 18.00 and arriving around 07.15. Check that the service is running, as it can be spasmodic.

By car
Most of the international car-hire companies have bases in Nairobi, and a number of local operators provide car hire. See page 86 for company listings and details.

CENTRAL NAIROBI
This area centres on Nairobi's central business district around Kenyatta Avenue, which houses the Kenyan parliament off City Square, and extends to the residential suburbs of Langata and Karen to the south and Muthaiga to the north. Despite its urban sprawl, the city is remarkable for its tree-lined avenues, with many exotic species, and it's particularly attractive around December when the jacarandas, with their pale mauve flowers, are in flower.

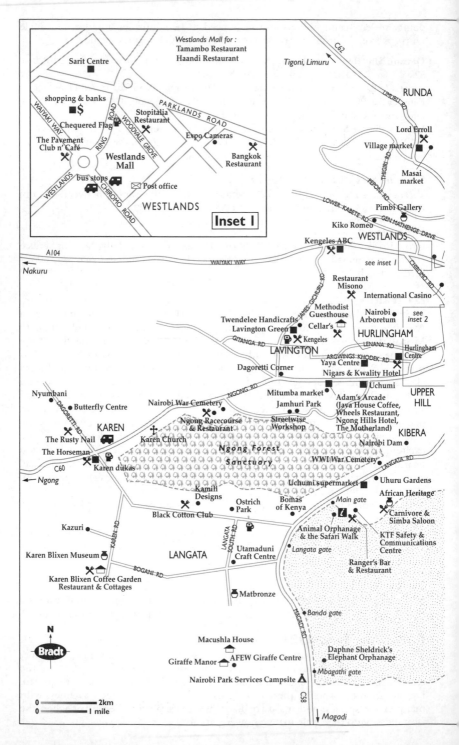

Inset I

Westlands Mall for :
Tamambo Restaurant
Haandi Restaurant

Tigoni, Limuru

C62

LIMURU RD

RUNDA

Sarit Centre

shopping & banks

PARKLANDS ROAD

Stopitalia Restaurant

Lord Erroll

Chequered Flag

WOODVALE GROVE

RING ROAD

WAIYAKI WAY

The Pavement Club n' Café

Westlands Mall

Expo Cameras

Village market

THIGIRI RD

PEPONI RD

Masai market

Bangkok Restaurant

bus stops

Post office

WESTLANDS

WESTLANDS

CHIROMO ROAD

LOWER KABETE RD

GEN MATHENGE DRIVE

Pimbi Gallery

Kiko Romeo

WESTLANDS

CHIROMO RD

Kengeles ABC

see inset I

A104

WAIYAKI WAY

Nakuru

Restaurant Misono

International Casino

JAMES GICHURU RD

Methodist Guesthouse

Nairobi Arboretum

see inset 2

Twendelee Handicrafts

Cellar's

HURLINGHAM

Lavington Green

GITANGA RD

Kengeles

LENANA RD

Hurlingham Centre

LAVINGTON

ARGWINGS KHODEK RD

Dagoretti Corner

Yaya Centre

Nigars & Kwality Hotel

UPPER HILL

NGONG RD

Mitumba market

Uchumi

Nyumbani

Butterfly Centre

Nairobi War Cemetery

Jamhuri Park

Adam's Arcade
(Java House Coffee,
Wheels Restaurant,
Ngong Hills Hotel,
The Motherland)

DAGORETTI RD

Ngong Racecourse & Restaurant

Streetwise Workshop

KIBERA

KAREN

Karen Church

Ngong Forest Sanctuary

Nairobi Dam

The Rusty Nail

WWI War Cemetery

LANGATA RD

The Horseman

C60

Karen dukas

Uchumi supermarket

Uhuru Gardens

Ngong

Kamili Designs

African Heritage

Ostrich Park

Bomas of Kenya

Main gate

Black Cotton Club

KAREN RD

Carnivore & Simba Saloon

Kazuri

Animal Orphanage & the Safari Walk

KTF Safety & Communications Centre

LANGATA SOUTH RD

Karen Blixen Museum

LANGATA

Utamaduni Craft Centre

Langata gate

Ranger's Bar & Restaurant

BOGANI RD

Karen Blixen Coffee Garden Restaurant & Cottages

Matbronze

Banda gate

MAGADI RD

N

Bradt

Macushla House

Daphne Sheldrick's Elephant Orphanage

Giraffe Manor

AFEW Giraffe Centre

Nairobi Park Services Campsite

Mbagathi gate

C58

0   2km
0   1 mile

Magadi

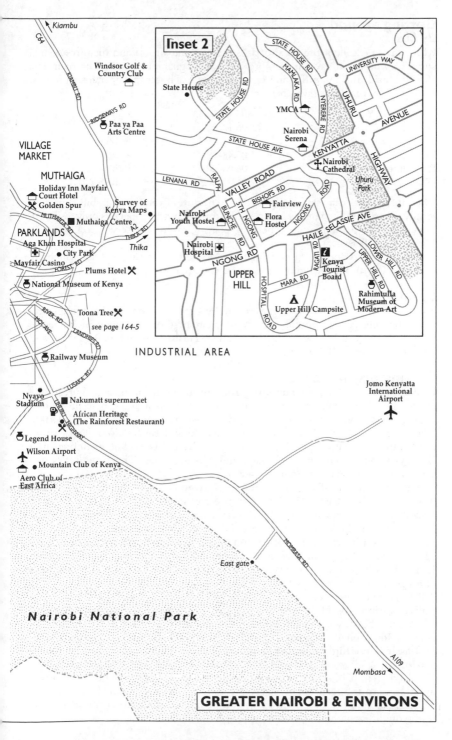

Kiambu

Inset 2

STATE HOUSE RD

Windsor Golf &
Country Club

State House

MAMLAKA RD

UNIVERSITY WAY

UHURU

STATE HOUSE RD

NYERERE RD

RIDGEWAYS RD

Paa ya Paa
Arts Centre

YMCA

AVENUE

Nairobi
Serena

KENYATTA

HIGHWAY

VILLAGE
MARKET

STATE HOUSE AVE

Nairobi
Cathedral

MUTHAIGA

LENANA RD

Uhuru
Park

Holiday Inn Mayfair
Court Hotel

Golden Spur

Survey of
Kenya Maps

VALLEY ROAD

BISHOPS RD

Fairview

NGONG

RALPH

5TH NGONG

BUNCHE

PARKLANDS

Muthaiga Centre

A2

Nairobi
Youth Hostel

Flora
Hostel

ROAD

HAILE SELASSIE AVE

THIKA RD

Aga Khan Hospital

City Park

Thika

Nairobi
Hospital

RAGATI RD

Mayfair Casino

FOREST

Plums Hotel

NGONG RD

UPPER
HILL

MARA RD

Kenya
Tourist
Board

LOWER HILL RD

UPPER HILL RD

National Museum of Kenya

RIVER RD

MOI AVE

LANDHIES RD

Toona Tree

see page 164-5

HOSPITAL

ROAD

Upper Hill Campsite

Rahimtulla
Museum of
Modern Art

INDUSTRIAL AREA

TUSAKA RD

Railway Museum

Nyayo
Stadium

Nakumatt supermarket

Jomo Kenyatta
International
Airport

UHURU HIGHWAY

African Heritage
(The Rainforest Restaurant)

Legend House

Wilson Airport

Mountain Club of Kenya

Aero Club of
East Africa

MOMBASA RD

East gate

Nairobi National Park

A109

Mombasa

GREATER NAIROBI & ENVIRONS

Getting around
By bus
KBS runs an excellent **metro shuttle** service to the airport and main residential suburbs, where you pay a little more but have a guaranteed seat. The main bus stage is outside the post office on Kenyatta Avenue. The shuttle operates set routes, Monday to Saturday, as given below:

Lavington via Yaya Centre	06.12–20.36	KSh40
Lavington via Westlands	06.12–20.00	KSh40
Karen via Ngong Rd	05.45–19.30	KSh50
Karen via Lang'ata Rd	05.48–19.00	KSh50
Buru Buru	06.08–20.00	KSh40
JKIA	06.00–00.55	KSh50

The shuttle buses run regularly, every 10–20 minutes from the main bus stops (ask locally if unsure). The Sunday service at the time of writing operates only to Karen, but check the situation locally. There are plans to extend the service to Upperhill, Ngong and Kileleshwa.

There are also normal buses, which tend to be packed, and *matatus*, which are cheaper (KSh10–30, depending on how far you are going).

By taxi
Taxis are readily available for hire, found at the airport, outside the large hotels and at the shopping centres around town. Agree a fare first. Among taxi firms operating in Nairobi are **Jambo** taxis (tel: 020 822011), **Hallo** taxis (tel: 020 825469) and **Edmar** taxis (tel: 020 827296).

Getting organised
In Nairobi city centre, for **changing money**, there are numerous bureaux de change which generally have the best rates – try Taipan and Chase in Muindi Mbingu Street and Crown Forex on Mama Ngina Street (open 09.00–17.00). There are several branches of Barclays, Standard and Kenya Commercial banks around the city centre, open 09.00–15.00; most have ATMs. The main branch of Barclays is on the corner of Kenyatta and Moi Avenues. The large hotels will exchange money, but at a premium rate.

The main **post office** is on Kenyatta Avenue, open Monday to Friday 08.00–17.00, Saturday 09.00–12.00. For **internet access** there's a good choice of places, with similar rates – try the Bazaar Business Centre on Muindi Mbingu Street and Safari Surf Café in the IPS building on Kaunda Street.

There's a **pharmacy** in the Hilton Hotel on Mama Ngina Street and a Metropolitan Chemist in Mercantile House on Loita Street and the Nyakinya Kangei building on Kenyatta Avenue, and plenty of others in town. In a **medical emergency** go to the Aga Khan Hospital on 3rd Parklands Avenue (tel: 020 740000) or Nairobi Hospital on Argwings Khodek Road (tel: 020 722160). The **police station** is on University Way (tel: 020 240000) and the **tourist helpline** is tel: 020 604767. If you need to extend a visa the **immigration department** is in Nyayo House on Posta Road (tel: 020 332110). For **airlines**, see page 68 and **embassies** and **high commissions**, see below. There are plenty of **petrol stations** in and around Nairobi. For **vehicle repairs**, the Chequered Flag in Westlands (tel: 020 441888) gives a reliable service. There are numerous **travel agents** and **tour operators** in Nairobi. In the city centre, Let's Go Travel (tel: 020 340331) has an office in Caxton House on Standard Street. For a comprehensive listing on different safari operators, see page 101.

If you're planning a mountaineering trip within Kenya or to Mount Kilimanjaro, see page 124 for details of the Mountain Club of Kenya. For details of supermarkets and other shops, see pages 179 and 186.

Overseas embassies, high commissions and consulates within Kenya

American Embassy Barclays Plaza, Loita St, PO Box 30143, Nairobi; tel: 020 537800; fax: 020 537810; email: usis@usis.africaonline.co.ke; web: www.usembassy.state.gov.nairobi

Australian High Commission Riverside Dr (400m off Chiromo Rd), PO Box 39341, Nairobi; tel: 020 445034/445039; fax: 020 444617

High Commission of Bangladesh Ole Odume Rd, PO Box 41645, Nairobi; tel: 020 562815/6; fax: 020 562 817

Belgian Consulate CMB, c/o Cotts House, Moi Av, Mombasa; tel: 041 314531; fax: 041 312617

Brazilian Embassy Eagle Court, 2nd Floor, Vuli Lane (Off Muranga Rd), PO Box 30754, Nairobi; tel: 020 337722; fax: 020 766442; email: nairobre@africaonline.co.ke

British High Commission Upper Hill Rd, PO Box 30465, 00100 Nairobi; tel: 020 714699; fax: 020 719082; email: bhcinfo@iconnect.co.ke web: www.britain.or.ke

High Commission of the Republic of Cyprus Eagle House, 5th Floor, Kimathi St, PO Box 30739, Nairobi; tel: 020 220881; fax: 020 331232

Eritrean Embassy PO Box 38651, New Waumuni House, 2nd Floor, Westlands, Nairobi; tel: 020 443164; fax: 020 443165

Embassy of the Federal Democratic Republic of Ethiopia State House Av, 45198 Nairobi; tel: 020 723035; fax: 020 723402

Finnish Embassy International House, 2nd Floor, Mama Ngina St, PO Box 30379, Nairobi; tel: 020 334777; fax: 020 33598; telex: 22010 finamb ke; email: finland@ form-net.com

French Embassy Barclays Plaza, 9th Floor, PO Box 41784, Loita St, Nairobi; tel: 020 339783

Indian Embassy Jeevan Bharati Bldg, Harambee Av, PO Box 30074, Nairobi; tel: 020 222566; fax: 020 334167; email: hcinfo@iconnect.co.ke

Indonesian Embassy Menengai Rd, Upper Hill, PO Box 48868, Nairobi; tel: 020 714196; fax: 020 713475

Irish Consulate Masai Rd, off Mombasa Rd, Dante Burba Diesel, Workshop Bldg, PO Box 30659, Nairobi; tel: 020 56647; email: irconsul@swiftkenya.com

Israeli Embassy Bishop Rd, PO Box 30354, Nairobi; tel: 020 722182; fax: 020 715966

Italian Embassy International Life House, Mama Ngina St, Nairobi; tel: 020 337356/7 /337777; fax: 020 337056; telex: 0022251 ITALDIPL; email: ambnair@swiftkenya.org

Mexican Embassy Kibagare Way, Loresho, Nairobi; tel: 020 583009; fax: 020 581500; email: mexico@embamexken.com

New Zealand Consulate Minet ICDC Insurance, 3rd Floor, Minet House, Nyerere Rd, PO Box 47383, Nairobi; tel: 020 722467; fax: 020 722556

Portuguese Embassy Taifa Rd, PO Box 34020, Nairobi; tel: 020 338990; fax: 020 214711; telex: 0987 22634

Romanian Embassy Nyari Estate, Red Hill Dr, PO Box 48412, Nairobi; tel: 020 743766; fax: 020 741696; email: roembken@africaonline.co.ke

Royal Netherlands Embassy Riverside Lane, off Riverside Dr, PO Box 41537, Nairobi; tel: 020 447412; fax 020 447416; email: nlgovnai@africaonline.co.ke

Royal Thai Embassy Rose Av, off Denis Pritt Rd, PO Box 58349, Nairobi; tel: 020 715800; fax: 020 715801

Russian Federation Embassy PO Box 30049, Lenana Rd, Nairobi; tel: 020 722462; telex: 25261

South African High Commission 17/18th Floor, Lonrho House, Standard St, PO Box 42441, Nairobi; tel: 020 215616/7; fax: 020 223687; email: sahc@africaonline.co.ke

Spanish Embassy Bruce House, Standard St, 5th Floor, PO Box 45503, Nairobi; tel: 020 226568; fax: 020 332858

Swedish Embassy International House, Mama Ngina St, PO Box 30600, Nairobi; tel: 020 229042; fax: 020 218908; email: embassy.nairobi@sida.se

Tanzania Diplomatic Mission Continental House, Harambee Av, PO Box 47790, Nairobi; tel: 020 331056; fax: 020 721874; telex: 25351; email: tanzania@users.africaonline.co.ke

Turkish Embassy Gigiri Rd (off Limuru Rd), Nairobi; tel: 020 520404; fax: 020 522778; telex: 0987 22 346 TURKEL; email: temdelhi@del2.vsnl.net.in

Where to stay
Top of the range

The Norfolk (313 rooms; 22 suites; swimming pool) Book through Lonrho Hotels, page 91

Located in central Nairobi, the Norfolk, built in 1904, is one of Kenya's oldest and most famous hotels. A member of the Leading Hotels of the World, it has historical associations with the upper crust of the early settlers: the Lord Delamere bar and Lord Delamere's Terrace Restaurant are still popular meeting points. In its early days it was often referred to as 'the House of Lords' due to its titled guest list of trophy hunters on big-game hunting safaris. The rooms have plush furnishings and en-suite bathrooms, while the suave service is more reminiscent of a smart London hotel. There are several restaurants and the terrace is good for lunch. **On offer:** health club, hair and beauty salon and shop. Local excursions may be arranged.

Rates: from US$145 per person sharing

Windsor Golf and Country Club (130 rooms; swimming pool) Ridgeways Rd, PO Box 45587, Nairobi; tel: 020 862300; fax: 020 802322; email: info@windsor.co.ke

Located off the Kiambu road, this neo-Victorian country club is a member of the small, Luxury Hotels of the World. It's set in 200 acres of grounds, surrounded by coffee estates and with views to mounts Kenya and Kilimanjaro from the end of the fairway on a clear day. It boasts a championship 18-hole golf course, considered to be one of the finest in Africa. The hotel and rooms overlook the golf course, and rooms are in blocks or cottages. All are comfortably furnished with TV and spacious bathrooms. The hotel has a choice of 3 restaurants. **On offer:** golf, tennis, squash, jogging track, gym, steam room and boutiques.

Rates: from US$160 per person sharing

The Stanley (142 rooms; swimming pool) PO Box 30680, Nairobi; tel: 020 228830; fax: 020 229388; email: reservations@thestanley.sarova.co.ke

Situated in the city centre on the corner of Kenyatta Av, the Stanley was one of Nairobi's first hotels and opened in 1902, moving to its present site in 1913. It underwent major refurbishment in 1999 and rooms are comfortably furnished with a floral décor, minibar, an email facility and en-suite bathrooms, with a non-smoking option. There are several restaurants and shops. Among the travelling fraternity, the hotel is better known for the **Thorn Tree Café**, where central to the pavement café is a thorn tree with a travellers' noticeboard. It's good for sharing lifts and leaving messages for friends, although to some degree it's been superseded by the use of emails and the noticeboards in the out-of-town shopping centres. It serves excellent coffee, good pizza and from 18.30 has evening entertainment – jazz, rock, reggae, soul and African fusion. **On offer:** health club.

Rates: from US$105 per person sharing

Boulevard Hotel (70 rooms; swimming pool) Harry Thuku Rd, PO Box 42831, Nairobi; tel: 020 337221; fax: 020 334071; email: hotelboulevard@form-net.com; web: www.kenyaweb.com/boulevard

Located near the city centre, the hotel is one street back from Kenyatta Highway and close to the National Museum of Kenya. The rooms are comfortable with en-suite bathrooms and private balconies. There's secure parking and a popular poolside café (good-size pool) together with a restaurant and snack bars. **On offer:** tennis, business centre and internet café; local excursions may be arranged.

Rates: from KSh3,340 half board per person sharing

Fairview Hotel (103 rooms; swimming pool) Bishops Rd, Nairobi Hill, PO Box 40842, Nairobi; tel: 020 710090; fax: 020 721320; email: reserv@fairviewkenya.com

Often referred to as a garden hotel, the Fairview is 2km from the city centre, set in 5 acres of tropical gardens. Built in the 1930s, the hotel is family-run and provides friendly and efficient service. The rooms are comfortably furnished with telephones, satellite TV and en-suite bathrooms. There are several restaurants, the garden terrace being popular at lunchtime. **On offer:** business centre and health club.

Rates: from KSh3,650 per person sharing

Giraffe Manor (6 rooms; homestay) PO Box 15004, Langata, Nairobi; tel: 020 891078; fax: 020 890949; email: giraffem@kenyaweb.com; web: www.giraffemanor.com

Located in 120 acres of woodland, Giraffe Manor is unique and well worth its premium price. Where else in the world can you have giraffes joining you for breakfast, or peering in through the front door to search your pockets for pony nuts? Built in 1932 by Sir David Duncan, the manor has a grand baronial staircase, a wood-panelled dining room and a bright, airy drawing room, while the bedrooms have private bathrooms, some with the original 1930s fittings. One room is furnished with original furniture from Karen Blixen's guestroom and hung with animal paintings by Kamante, her famous cook. In 1974 the house was bought by Jock and Betty Leslie-Melville who founded the African Fund for Endangered Wildlife (AFEW). They introduced rare Rothschild's giraffes which have bred well – some have been translocated to other sanctuaries. Giraffe Manor is now run by Betty's son, Rick Anderson, and his wife Bryony, who are remarkably unfazed and tolerant of their tall pets and the inevitable eulogising of their guests. **On offer:** walks in the indigenous forest where bushbuck, dik dik and 180 bird species may be seen, and visits to the Giraffe Centre next door.

Rates: from US$270 B&B per person sharing

Grand Regency Hotel (240 rooms) PO Box 57549, Nairobi; tel: 020 211199; fax: 020 217120; email: gregency@africaonline.co.ke; web: www.grandregency.co.ke

Situated on Loita St off Uhuru Highway, near the city centre, this is one of Nairobi's smartest hotels. The rooms and suites, all with plush furnishings, have satellite TV, minibars and en-suite bathrooms. The public areas are spacious, cool and opulent, with several restaurants and bars. **On offer:** health club, business centre and shopping arcade.

Rates: from US$140 per person sharing

Holiday Inn Mayfair Court Hotel (171 rooms; 2 swimming pools) Parklands Rd, PO Box 66807, Nairobi; tel: 020 3740920; fax: 020 3748823; email: Mayfair@africaonline.co.ke

Located in the residential suburb of Westlands, not far from the city centre, this double-storey, child-friendly hotel has a garden setting and is popular with tourists and businessmen. The rooms (with facilities for disabled and non-smoking options) are comfortably furnished with en-suite bathrooms and have access on to the garden or an upper veranda. The service is friendly and efficient, and there are 2 restaurants, the poolside Oasis for light snacks and the Golden Spur restaurant and cocktail terrace, a popular steakhouse (open 11.00–23.00). **On offer:** hourly shuttle service into central Nairobi, children's activities and babysitting, health club, business centre, hair salon, shops; golf and excursions may be arranged.

Rates: from US$80 B&B per person sharing

Aero Club of East Africa (12 rooms; swimming pool) Wilson Airport, PO Box 40813, Nairobi; tel: 020 600482; email: aeroclub.ea@swiftkenya.com

Located at Wilson Airport (and close to the Mountain Club of Kenya clubhouse), the child-friendly Aero Club was founded in 1927 to promote flying in Africa. It has remained

at the heart of aviation within Kenya and remains a popular meeting place for those who love flying. Memorabilia, including paintings, propellers, photographs and engine blocks, is present in the characterful clubhouse. Temporary membership is available (around KSh800 a week) and the Richmond House rooms have TV and en-suite bathrooms, while there are also single and family rooms. The club is friendly and efficient and often has evening entertainment at the weekend. The veranda restaurant, with an Italian emphasis, serves good food at reasonable prices. **On offer:** squash courts, flying school.
Rates: from KSh1,750 per person sharing
Karen Blixen Coffee Garden Restaurant and Cottages (17 cottages; swimming pool) PO Box 163, Karen 00205, Nairobi; tel: 020 882138; fax: 020 882508; email: blixen@swiftkenya.com; web: www.blixencoffeegarden.com
Located in the leafy suburb of Karen, about half a mile from the Karen Blixen Museum (set in Karen Blixen's home, Bogani House), and close to Nairobi National Park, the cottages are set in tropical gardens behind **Swedo house** which has the main restaurant. This was the original farm manager's house, built in the early 1900s, on Karen Blixen's coffee estate. Aake Sorgren, the Swedish Consul in British East Africa until 1913, and the American philanthropist Sir Northrup McMillan formed the Swedo African Coffee Company which was bought by Bror Blixen, Karen's husband, in 1913. The cottages are spacious – rooms have fresh décor, with wrought-iron beds, mazeras stone floors, a minibar, satellite TV, internet and telephone connections, en-suite bathrooms and a private veranda. There's a choice of an individual room, two bedrooms with a shared sitting room with a fireplace and the honeymoon cottage which has a large bedroom and sitting room with open fireplaces. The swimming pool is only for use by residents. In Swedo house, the restaurant, open to the public, serves excellent meals. **On offer:** honeymoon suite, 24hr room service, private garden bar, local excursions.
Rates: from US$98 B&B per person sharing
Macushla House (6 rooms; swimming pool) Nguruwe Rd, off Gogo Falls Rd, PO Box 42510; tel: 020 891987; fax: 020 981971; email: macushla@africaonline.co.ke
Located in Langata's leafy suburbs, near the Giraffe Centre, this small hotel overlooks indigenous forest and natural gardens. There are two wings, each with a sitting-room with an open fireplace, 2 double rooms, a single room and a terrace overlooking the pool. The rooms are comfortably furnished with wrought-iron four-poster beds, kilim rugs, and spacious en-suite bathrooms, while the public areas have interesting artefacts (including a Yemeni wedding dress adorned with silver and a brass jigsaw cutter from the 1930s) beamed ceilings and natural woodwork. There's a cosy bar and dining area with wholesome food.
Rates: from US$85 B&B per person sharing
Ngong House (6 rooms; swimming pool; homestay) PO Box 24963, Nairobi; tel: 020 891856; fax: 020 890674; email: NgongHouse@form-net.com; web: www.ngonghouse.com
Set in wooded gardens in Langata, Ngong House has 5 unique treehouse rooms and a private apartment in the main house. The treehouses, raised 4m off the ground on stilts, are fun for their novelty value and have delightful views across the woodland to the Ngong Hills. The bedrooms, each individual in design, have four-poster beds, interesting artefacts and a small balcony, while downstairs is a comfortable, private, sitting-room with a fireplace (where you can also dine if you wish) and there's a bathroom at the back of the house. Built by Paul Verleyson, a Belgian diplomat, and his son, Christoff, who was brought up in Africa, the house is now hosted by Christoff. Meals are communal affairs where you eat *en famille*, with delicious food presented with a Belgian flair. **On offer:** a 4WD vehicle is available for local excursions.
Rates: from US$270 half board per person sharing
Nairobi Serena (192 rooms; swimming pool) PO Box 46302, Nairobi; tel: 020 725111; fax: 020 725184; email: info@serenahotels.com; web: www.serenahotels.com

Adjacent to central park off Kenyatta Av, with views across the Nairobi skyline, this 6-storey hotel is a member of the Leading Hotels of the World and has excellent service. The rooms are comfortably furnished with TV, internet and email facilities, AC, and en-suite bathrooms. The hotel has a choice of restaurants and bars. **On offer:** courtesy shuttle bus to city centre, health club, golf, 24-hour taxi service, babysitting.
Rates: from US$165 per person sharing

Mid-range to cheap hotels

Dolat Hotel City centre: Mfangano St, PO Box 45613, Nairobi; tel: 020 222797
Also called the Orchid Hotel, it has good rooms and hot showers. It's excellent value.
Rates: rooms from KSh735 a double

Flora Hostel 5th Ngong Rd, Nairobi; tel: 020 723013; email: florah@wananchi.com
Run by the Consolata sisters, this small hostel is friendly and clean, with a choice of s/c rooms or shared bathrooms.
Rates: rooms from US$18–22 full board

Methodist Guest House Lavington Green, Oloitokitok Rd, PO Box 25086, Nairobi; tel: 020 571080; fax: 020 562385; email: info@ methodistguesthouseke.com; web: www.methodistguesthouseke.com
Located about 2km from the city centre, the guesthouse is a popular conference venue with NGOs working in Africa. The staff are pleasant and friendly, while rooms, although Spartan, are clean and comfortable. There's a veranda restaurant serving a mixture of African and European food, but no bar, and there's safe parking.
Rates: from US$25 B&B per person sharing

Down Town Hotel City centre, Moktar Daddah St; PO Box 3834, Nairobi; tel: 020 310485; fax: 020 310435; email: downtownhotel@wananchi.com
A friendly establishment where all rooms are s/c with a telephone. The hotel runs a taxi service.
Rates: from KSh600 per person sharing

Marble Arch Hotel (40 rooms) City centre: Lagos Rd, off Tom Mboya St; PO Box 12224, Nairobi; tel: 020 24090; fax: 020 245724; email: marblearchhotel@swiftkenya.com
Located in a rather seedy area, this 5-storey hotel is well maintained. All rooms are en suite with plush décor, piped music, telephone, TV and video. There's a restaurant, bar and coffee shop and secure parking.
Rates: from US$30 B&B per person sharing

Abbey Hotel City centre: Gaberone Rd, PO Box 75260, Nairobi; tel: 020 243256; fax: 020 247729
This 5-storey, red brick hotel has friendly management. The s/c rooms are clean and simply furnished, with a telephone. There's a comfortable bar and restaurant serving buffet-style meals.
Rates: from KSh750 B&B per person sharing

Hotel Embassy City centre: Tubman Rd, opp City Market, PO Box 47247, Nairobi; tel: 020 224087; fax: 020 224534; email: hotelembassy@yahoo.com
The hotel has s/c rooms and a lively, fully licensed bar and restaurant.
Rates: from KSh750 per person sharing; breakfast KSh150

Terminal Hotel City centre: Moktar Daddah St, PO Box 66814, Nairobi; tel: 020 228817; fax: 020 220075
This is a well-run, friendly establishment, despite its rather shabby appearance. The rooms are self-contained with a telephone, and there's a small café downstairs.
Rates: from KSh650 per person sharing

Comfort Inn (90 rooms) City centre: Muindi Mbingu St, PO Box 30425, 00100 Nairobi; tel: 020 316666; fax: 020 317610; email: comfortinn@kenyaweb.com

Overlooking Jeevanjee Gardens, this 7-storey hotel is family-run and is known as the 'wananchi (people's) star hotel'. It has friendly service, and rooms have clay or parquet floors, comfortable beds, telephones and en-suite bathrooms. They are decorated with paintings (available for sale) by local artists and there's a restaurant with African and international food. **On offer:** business centre, shop, travel agent and fitness centre.
Rates: from KSh1,400 B&B per person sharing
YMCA (swimming pool) State House Rd, off Uhuru Highway, PO Box 30330, Nairobi; tel: 020 713599; fax: 020 728825; email: kenyaymca@net2000ke.com
A large establishment, open to both sexes and all religious denominations, the YMCA has a choice of dorm beds and s/c rooms or shared facilities. There's a good swimming pool, free to residents and about KSh50 for non-residents. Take a taxi here at night.
Rates: s/c rooms from KSh750 B&B per person sharing
Nairobi Youth Hostel Ralph Bunche Rd, near Nairobi Hospital, PO Box 48661; tel: 020 721765
Clean and efficiently run, there are dorm beds and rooms with shared facilities.
Rates: dorm beds KSh400; rooms KSh500

Camping
Upper Hill Campsite Menengai Rd, Upper Hill, PO Box 29886, Nairobi: tel: 020 720290; fax: 020 719662; email: campsite@alphanet.co.ke.
Located about 2km from the city centre, the campsite is set in the gardens of a private house, with day and night security. There's parking on the premises, good facilities and hot showers. The restaurant is in the house, with cheap and tasty meals, with dining indoors or on the terrace. The Gimmie shelter bar is a good meeting spot for travellers and Nairobi residents.
Rates: from KSh250
Nairobi Park Services Campsite (rooms and camping) Magadi Rd, PO Box 54867, Nairobi; tel: 020 89261; fax: 020 892262; email: nps@swiftkenya.com
Located in Langata, this is a popular campsite with overland companies. The staff are friendly and helpful, and it also has dorm beds and rooms. There's a lively restaurant and bar (the Rhino Place next door sometimes has live bands) serving reasonable meals. It's not the quietest of campsites, with revelry often continuing into the early hours. **On offer:** telephone, email and internet facilities; airport transfers, tours and safaris can be arranged.
Rates: dorm bed US$6; rooms US$15; camping US$3
Ngong Road Forest Sanctuary (camping) PO Box 42281, Nairobi; tel: 020 710740; fax: 020 718737; email: ngong@rugkenya.com
Fencing of the forest is underway at the time of writing and scheduled for completion by the end of 2003, when it is proposed to offer camping facilities. Check locally for details.

Where to eat
Most of the hotels above have restaurants, as do some of the clubs on page 179. In addition, there are several independent establishments, where a three-course meal averages US$12–15 per person. Among the best are:

Karen Blixen Coffee Garden Restaurant Karen Rd, PO Box 163, Karen 00205, Nairobi; tel: 020 882138; fax: 020 882508; email: blixen@swiftkenya.com; web: www.blixencoffeegarden.com. Located near the Karen Blixen Museum, the main restaurant is in Swedo House (see page 174), with a bar and formal dining room, while during the day you can dine outside under umbrellas in the garden. There's a good choice of international-style food. The dining-room often has exhibitions by local artists and there's usually jazz on Tuesday evenings and Saturday lunchtimes and African folk songs at Sunday lunch. *Open daily 07.00–22.00*

Lord Erroll off Limuru Rd; tel: 020 521308. A smart restaurant in the Runda area of Nairobi, it has a pleasant garden setting and a varied menu with excellent barbecue, Italian, Oriental and European dishes.

Racecourse Restaurant Ngong Rd, at the Racecourse, PO Box 40373, Nairobi; tel: 020 575715, mobile: 0733 878588; email: racecourserest@wananchi.com. Overlooking the gardens of the Jockey Club of Kenya, the restaurant has a pleasant ambience, with a French-style bistro and a terrace for informal dining, with a choice of pasta, pizza and fondues. On Sundays there's a continental and Indian buffet. There's safe and secure parking.

Carnivore Langata Rd near Wilson Airport; tel: 020 501706. The Carnivore has gained international notoriety for its barbecued game meats and is a popular venue with locals and often (bizarrely) a finale to a wildlife safari – see the wildlife and then eat it. Efficiently run, with excellent service, the restaurant is in a series of terraces, with tropical plants where smiling waiters come round with hunks of roast meat, cutting off slithers of ostrich, zebra, gazelle and crocodile. There is also a popular hot-spot disco at the Simba Saloon with rock night on Wednesday and Sunday soul evenings. *Open daily for lunch and dinner*

Tamarind Restaurant National Bank Bldg, Harambee Av; tel: 020 338959. Part of the Tamarind group, this is a smart restaurant with superb seafood and excellent service.

Tamambo The Mall, Westlands; tel: 020 448064. Also in the Tamarind stable, this is upstairs in the Westland's Mall and opens on to Kenyatta Avenue. More informal than the Tamarind, and reasonably priced, it does not scrimp on quality and has excellent seafood and a choice of run-of-the-mill pastas.

The Pavement Club n' Café off the Westlands roundabout in the Westview Centre; tel: 020 749337. This is another local hot spot for entertainment. It combines a restaurant café and coffee shop (good pastries) with a buzzing bar and disco. There's a choice of Japanese, Thai and Mediterranean food and traditional grills. (It gets quite busy, so an alternative is to go to Gypsies Bar near by before moving on to the Pavement.) The disco is loud, so the outside bar is sometimes preferable for a drink. They also have theme nights – salsa is usually on Thursdays.

Dragon Pearl Chinese Restaurant City centre, Bruce House off Standard St; tel: 020 338863. This Chinese restaurant is well established and noted for its good food.

Silver Sun Chinese Restaurant City centre, Uniafric House, Loita St; tel: 020 330858 This is another popular Chinese restaurant.

Restaurant Misono Lenana Rd; tel: 020 568959. This is an excellent, authentic Japanese restaurant where you can eat in the garden under umbrellas, or indoors. The lunch boxes are good value and recommended.

Bangkok Restaurant Rank Xerox House, Parklands Rd; tel: 020 751311. This is an excellent Thai restaurant, and is probably the best for Thai food in Kenya.

Ranger's Bar and Restaurant Main gate, Nairobi National Park off Langata Rd; tel: 020 600861. Conveniently located at the national park headquarters, the restaurant is large and spacious, with a high thatched ceiling. Opt for a table on the deck, where you can dine and watch wildlife at the same time. The menu has a good selection of standard fare – steaks, salad and pizza.

Allan Bobbe's Bistro City centre, Cianda House, Koinange St; tel: 020 224945. A well-established and popular bistro, Allan Bobbe's provides delicious French cuisine in a formal atmosphere. They also provide a *free* pick-up service to and from any city-centre hotel.

Haandi Restaurant The Mall, Westlands; tel: 020 448294. Located upstairs in the Mall, this Indian restaurant has an excellent reputation and serves authentic north Indian cuisine. It's very popular with local residents, so it's best to make a reservation.

Toona Tree Restaurant Westlands Rd; tel: 020 742600. A pleasant Italian restaurant surrounding a large tree. It's a large establishment, but the food is good and there's also a salad bar.

Stopitalia Restaurant Woodvale Grove, Westlands; tel: 020 445234. This is a small, unpretentious restaurant serving excellent Italian food.

Cedars Restaurant Lenana Rd; tel: 020 710399. An excellent Lebanese restaurant not far from the city centre.

Rusty Nail on Dagoretti Rd, not far from Karen roundabout on the left; tel: 020 882461. This restaurant is in an old house and is popular with local residents. It has a pleasant, intimate ambience where you can lounge on comfortable cushions in the bar (which also has a big screen for sports events) or dine on the veranda by candlelight, overlooking the garden, in the evening. The food is generally good, with a European emphasis. *Open 10.30–22.30 Mon–Sun.*

Horseman located at Karen Dukas; tel: 020 882782. A popular spot with local residents, there's a cosy bar and a good chargrill restaurant, with a good variety of food from fish to game meats. *Open daily 11.30–23.00.*

Cellar's Restaurant and Bar opposite the Methodist Guest House on Oloitokitok Rd. Essentially a neighbourhood bar, it's located in an old house. It has a relaxed atmosphere and there's an outdoor terrace with an open fire in the evenings and a small, lively bar. There's a TV for sports events and pool tables in the garden. It has excellent lunchtime buffets Mon–Fri for around KSh500.

Nigars Restaurant and Sippers Bar Hurlingham Shopping Centre. Owned by an affable Indian, this is a small bar with a friendly atmosphere, cold beers and 2 TV screens for sporting events.

Kwality Hotel Argwings Kodhek Rd, between Hurlingham and the Yaya centres. This is a trendy bar with a novel atmosphere, and there's a small outdoor disco. It has a large screen for sporting events.

Village Market on the Limuru Rd. There are a number of fast-food outlets and cafés at the Village Market. The German Pub has good food and a jovial atmosphere, and there's also a good Chinese restaurant (don't be put off by the 'sweat and sour' on the menu). There's safe and secure parking.

Rainforest Restaurant African Heritage, Mombasa Rd; tel: 020 530056. This café has a good selection of food, with salads and sandwiches, game meats and an African buffet. It's recommended after wandering around the Heritage Gallery of African artefacts. *Open Mon–Sat 09.00–18.00; Sun 11.00–16.00.*

Wheels Restaurant Ngong Rd, next to Adam's Arcade. A large garden restaurant with small bandas and indoor seating where it's pleasantly cool. It has good *nyama choma* and a couple of TV screens for major sports events. It features **live bands** which usually play on Wed, Fri and Sun. There's safe parking in the restaurant compound.

Kengeles This is a chain of popular cafés that are generally of a good standard, with a choice of snacks, salads, burgers, stir fries and steaks at reasonable prices (around KSh480). They are based at: **Lavington Green**, off James Gichuru Rd; tel: 020 577360; **ABC** on Waiyaki Way; tel: 020 577360; **Nairobi West** on Langata Rd; tel: 020 505283 and in the **city centre** on Koinange St; tel: 020 344335.

Java House Coffee There are several Java coffee houses around Nairobi, which serve only Kenya's premium coffee, and, to accompany the cappuccino, espresso, mocha and lattes are delicious pastries, omelettes and pancakes, ice-creams and an assortment of savoury snacks. They are found on Ngong Rd at **Adam's Arcade**, tel: 020 573583 and on **Mama Ngina St**, tel: 020 313564 in the city centre.

Entertainment
Local clubs
Apart from **The Pavement** and **Simba Saloon** already mentioned, there are a number of nightclubs and local clubs, some with excellent live bands, and many with restaurants as well. A selection are:

Above Sykes monkey, *Cercopithecus mitis*, Mountain Lodge, Mount Kenya (AZ)
Above right Black-and-white colobus monkey, *Colobus guereza*, Aberdares National Park (AZ)
Below Greater bushbaby, *Galago crassicaudatus*, Shimba Hills National Park (AZ)

Above Lesser flamingos, *Phoeniconaias minor*, in Lake Nakuru National Park (NG)

Right Ruppell's griffon vulture, *Gyps rueppellii* (NG)

Below right Male red-headed weaver, *Anaplectes rubriceps*, building a nest (NG)

Bottom right Village or black-headed weaver, *Ploceus cucullatus*, Lake Baringo (AZ)

Below Adult female bateleur eagle, *Terathopius ecaudatus* (NG)

Ngong Hills Hotel Ngong Rd, next to Ngong hypermarket. This has a friendly atmosphere and good grilled meat. It normally features live bands on Wed and Fri–Sun.
The Motherland on Ngong Rd between Adam's Arcade and Ngong hypermarket. This is an Ethiopian restaurant with authentic cuisine, at reasonable prices, and they have genuine Ethiopian live entertainment.
Klub House Westlands – on Parklands Rd near the sports club. This comprises a good music and disco venue with a large aquarium in the main disco hall, together with pool tables and a 24-hour TV screen sports channel. Outdoors is Joe's Burger Bar which has cheap snacks and a bar, where you can congregate around a bonfire in the evenings.
Plums Hotel Westlands, next to the Klub House. This has good *nyama choma*, and often has live bands playing, including some of the top names in African music.
Florida 2000 and New Florida nightclubs Central Nairobi. Long established, the Florida nightclubs have good discos and live bands, and Chinese food is served all night. It's a renowned pick-up joint with plenty of twilight ladies and gents – make sure you do not leave drinks unattended.
Black Cotton Club Langata Rd, Karen. This is a nightclub with a large disco which attracts the settler community who live out of town. It's open on Fridays only, and not every Friday, so check locally for details. Entry free before 22.00, thereafter KSh250.
The Simmers Pub City centre opposite the 680 Hotel on Muindu Mbingu St
This is an excellent venue for live bands and one of the few in the city centre. It's very loud, but there's a lively bar and good food. Be sure to take a taxi after dark.

Theatres, cinemas and casinos
In addition to the **French Cultural Centre** and **Mzizi Arts Centre** (see pages 182 and 183), other venues for the performing arts are the **Goethe Institute** in Maendeleo House on Loita Street (tel: 020 224640; open Mon–Fri 10.00–17.00), the **British Council** in the ICEA building on Kenyatta Avenue (tel: 020 334855; open Tue–Fri 10.00–18.00 and Sat 10.00–13.00), the **Italian Cultural Institute** in Chiromo Court on Chiromo Rd (tel: 020 746739; open Mon–Tues 08.00–13.00 and 14.00–18.00 and Wed–Fri 08.00–14.00) and the **Japan African Culture Interchange Institute** on Kamburi Drive (tel: 020 566262).

The **Kenyan National Theatre** on Harry Thuku Road, opposite the Norfolk Hotel (tel: 020 225506), has an emphasis on the African arts and Kenyan playwrights, while the **Professional Centre** on Parliament Road, (tel: 020 225506; open Mon–Fri 10.00–17.00) is the venue for the **Phoenix Players**, who have a wide repertoire and put on excellent performances.

If you want to go to the **cinema**, the best is at the **Sarit centre** in Westlands, which screens the most recent films. In the city centre the **20th Century Cinema** is on Mama Ngina Street.

Nairobi also has its share of **casinos**. The **International Casino** is on Museum Hill (tel: 020 742600; open Mon–Fri 21.00–late and Sat–Sun 16.00–late). You need to dress smartly, and there is a range of gaming rooms and slot machines. Make sure to take a taxi from the venue. Alternatively, there's the **Mayfair Casino**, near the Holiday Inn (open 12.00–03.00 daily).

Shopping
There are several small branches of **supermarkets** in the city centre, including Uchumi on Market Street and Nakumatt at the junction of Kenyatta Avenue and Kimathi Street. For fruit, vegetables, meat and fish, **City Market** is on Muindi Mbingu Street. For further information on markets, see page 186.

For **maps**, **books** and **stationery**, the Prestige Bookshop on Mama Ngina Street and the Textbook Centre in the Sarit Centre (in Westlands) have a good

NAIROBI – TURNING THE TIDE ON URBAN DECAY
Richard Lumbe

Nairobi was known as the 'Green City in the Sun' until the early 1980s. It was a growing metropolis with a bustling Central Business District (CBD) where visitors came shopping by day and to revel at night. Then the downfall began. It started with political brinkmanship at the Nairobi City Council that rendered the City Hall ungovernable. The central government responded by throwing out elected leaders and replacing them with an appointed commission. By end of the 1980s successive commissions brought the city to its knees with poor service delivery and a deteriorating infrastructure. Business performance started to decline, causing companies to close shop or move, and the destitute, joined by opportunists up to no good, started to move in. Soon, tourists avoided the downtown hotels and the CBD in general. The city centre was dying.

In 1994, a few entrepreneurs formed the Nairobi Central Business District Association (NCBDA) as a lobby group for the private sector. In 1997, after protracted negotiations with the city council in improving service delivery, the government eventually registered the association. Guided by the motto *'Improvement through Action'*, NCBDA has initiated projects that have contributed immensely to central Nairobi's regeneration.

Some of the contributions NCBDA has made

• Installing 30 police information centres (PICs) in the CBD and its environs. The purpose of the PICs is to bring the police closer to the community.
• Providing a mobile patrol unit servicing the police information centres in the CBD. Taxi drivers, private security personnel and traders at the City Market have joined hands with the police to stamp out petty theft.

selection. For national park maps, some are available from the Kenya Wildlife Service shop at the park headquarters on Langata Road. For more detailed maps the Survey of Kenya (signposted to the left off Thika Road if driving out of town) has large-scale maps.

Shopping centres

As Nairobi city centre became more congested, satellite shopping malls with safe parking multiplied in the greater Nairobi area. In addition to the city centre, the shopping centres have a good range of services, including forex bureaux, banks, post offices, pharmacies and supermarkets.

Shopping centres in greater Nairobi include the **Sarit Centre** in Westlands, the **Hurlingham** and **Yaya centres** on Argwings Kodhek Road, **Adam's Arcade** on Ngong Road, **Muthaiga shopping centre** (esso plaza) and **Muthaiga Mini Market** on Muthaiga Road, **Village Market** on Limuru Road, **ABC** on Waiyaki Way, **Lavington Green** on James Gichuru Road and **Karen *dukas*** at the junction of Ngong and Langata roads. The dominant chains of **supermarket** are Uchumi and Nakumatt. Uchumi has branches in the Sarit Centre, on Ngong Road (before Adam's Arcade if heading out of town) and Langata Road (near the Carnivore), while Nakumatt, set back from Uhuru Highway (opposite the Nyayo stadium), is a vast emporium, selling foodstuffs, lifestyle, household and some camping items.

- Developing business improvement districts (BIDs) in the heart of the city.
- Enhancing security with the introduction of close circuit television (CCTV) in a project being developed by Kenya Police, NCBDA and the City Council.
- Working in partnership with the police and residents in promoting community policing across the city.

Policing and Community Safety Programme
Initiated by NCBDA and partly sponsored by the Ford Foundation, after two years in operation the frayed relations between residents and the police have started to mend. The police acknowledge this has been one of the contributing factors in the decline of crime in Nairobi. There is growing cooperation between citizens and the police in identifying and apprehending criminals. In 2002 NCBDA sponsored the training of more than 100 police officers in public relations and computer skills and 20 police officers in community policing. Through its membership, NCBDA has contributed communications equipment to police stations all over the city. NCBDA's example is slowly transforming advertising behaviour. The once neglected city roundabouts are now receiving floral face-lifts sponsored by the private sector.

A vision for the city
NCBDA and residents are now working towards the vision: 'Nairobi: The Choice of Africa – Clean, Secure, Vibrant – Home for All'.

Richard Lumbe is a consultant for NCBDA. For further information contact NCBDA, PO Box 10687, 00100 Nairobi; tel: 020 219412; fax: 020 340296; email: ncbda@bidii.com; web: www.ncbdakenya.org

If you're shopping to go on **safari**, you're probably best to stock up at Uchumi or Nakumatt, while Abduls in Biashara Street (city centre) sells gas and hires out camping equipment.

What to see and do
A walk around the city centre
The centre of Nairobi is relatively compact, and although bustling with hawkers and sometimes a little intimidating, west of Moi Avenue it's normally safe to walk around during daylight hours, although it goes without saying don't look too ostentatious and be vigilant. In the past there have been incidents of petty crime, bag snatching and the like, (but remember this can happen in capital cities worldwide, so keep things in perspective). Encouragingly, in recent times there has been a clampdown on crime in the city centre (see box above). A good place to start is the **Thorn Tree Café** at the **Stanley Hotel** on the corner of Kenyatta Avenue and Kimathi Street, which has been a popular meeting spot for travellers over the years (see page 172). Kenyatta Avenue was Delamere Avenue during the colonial era and formed the core of the city at that time. Some of the banks are fine buildings, their façades showing a faded elegance, and the northern side of the street is typical of colonial Asian architecture, with shops set back under wide, covered walkways. It was designed to allow a team of oxen to turn around in the street – today it roars with traffic, so cross the road carefully and

head north to Banda Street where you can visit the **McMillan Memorial Library** (open Mon–Fri 09.00–17.50, Sat 09.30–13.00) and the **African Heritage Centre** which has a collection of authentic African arts and crafts for sale and a café serving African food. Turn left along the street and take a right up Muindi Mbingu Street which will bring you to the **City Market** on the left. There's a butcher and an assorted array of fresh fruit, vegetables and cut flowers, while at the back there's a collection of kiosks with a variety of African arts and crafts for sale – the usual *kiondo* baskets, Kisii soapstone carvings, and carvings of wooden animals, Maasai beadwork and jewellery and skin-covered drums. The mamas bargain hard, all part of business, and you're expected to do the same. Opposite the market is the **Jamia Mosque**, distinctive with its decorative green and white paintwork. Keep heading north along Muindi Mbingu Street, to **Biashara Street**. This is the best place to go shopping for *kikois* and *kangas*, and the Asian shops have a good selection, together with the usual safari hats and T-shirts. Also, on the right side of the street is **Atul's**, the camping shop, where you can buy camping gas canisters and hire equipment. Continuing north along Muindi Mbingu Street, you come to **Jeevanjee Gardens**, a pleasant little park. The **Maasai Market** operates on Tuesdays and Fridays from 09.00–15.00. If a market day, cross the park diagonally to join the junction of Moi Avenue and Monrovia Street, and cross the road, where you will see an assortment of Maasai crafts for sale. (This market is far cheaper than the Maasai Market held at Village Market on the Limuru Road each Friday which also includes curios from other parts of Africa.) Otherwise, continue north and cross University Way and it's a short walk along Harry Thuku Road to the **Norfolk** (see page 172), one of Kenya's smartest hotels, where you get a bit of a culture shock after the raw energy on the streets. It was a major meeting point for the early settlers, Lord Delamere among them, but today is more of a tourist venue for those coming to and from safari. But it's worth a visit to see the snippets of history from the colonial era, including the Delamere Bar and Terrace, where you can have a drink before heading back across town. If you sneeze at the prices at the Norfolk, retrace your steps to Monrovia Street and turn right and then left down Loita Street to the **French Cultural Centre**, which has a pleasant, shady café, and is also a venue for visiting arts (open Mon–Fri 08.30–17.30). Continue south along Loita Street and then turn left along Market Street where you can see the silver mushroom of the **New Florida nightclub** (see page 179), one of Nairobi's original nightclubs often with live bands, and turn right down Koinange Street. Cross over Kenyatta Avenue and continue past the post office down to Kaunda Street, which bears right and continues south to **City Square**, with its distinctive flag poles. On Parliament Road is **Jomo Kenyatta's mausoleum** and statue on the right. At the opposite end of City Square are the impressive **law courts**, stately colonial buildings, south of which is the round tower of the **Kenyatta Conference Centre**. Wood-panelled and rather gloomy inside, the centre has numerous rooms and wide corridors. With permission, for KSh100, you may be able to go to the top floor of the tower, which was once a restaurant, from which there are expansive views across the city skyline. If you are not flagging by this stage, you can continue south along Parliament Road, and turn right at the roundabout on to Harambee Avenue, where you can visit **Parliament House**. If you are interested in watching parliament in session, ask for a visitor's permit and then you'll be ushered to the public gallery. Returning back to Parliament Road, head south from the roundabout to Haile Selassie Avenue, from which you can visit the **Railway Museum**, with its fine stock of old steam engines (see page 184), and then continue to the **railway station**, with its remnants of 1930s architecture. Opposite is the **Memorial garden** (open daily 06.00–18.00; entry KSh20) on the site of the 1998 American Embassy bombing which killed 263 people and injured 5,000. Then head north up Moi Avenue for several blocks to the **National Archives** on the corner of Luthuli Avenue (open Mon–Fri 08.30–16.30 and Sat 08.30–13.00) which have an interesting documentary photographic record of the struggle for independence, and the office of past presidents Jomo Kenyatta and Daniel Arap Moi. Then cross back to Mama Ngina Street and head into the cylindrical tower of the **Hilton Hotel**, where you can have a look at the **Kumbu Kumbu Gallery** of African art and the **East African Wildlife Society (EAWS) Art Gallery** and visit the EAWS shop in the arcade. Continue north up Moi Avenue to the **Mzizi Arts Centre** in Sonalux House, a vibrant venue for Kenyan poets and playwrights. This is a hive of creativity, and often has lively, monthly performances of new works. There are also displays of art and sculpture. Thereafter it's a short hop back to the Thorn Tree on Kamathi Street.

Museums and art galleries
National Museum of Kenya (NMK)
Museum Hill, off Uhuru Highway, PO Box 40658, Nairobi; tel: 020 742141-4; fax: 020 741424; email: nmk@africaonline.co.ke; web: www.museums.or.ke
This is a superb museum, with a collection comparable to Western museums, and it has excellent exhibits for anyone interested in the origins of man, the geomorphology of the landscape, natural history, Kenya's tribal cultures and contemporary art. For an enlightened insight about the country, a morning's visit here is well spent prior to travelling around, as it gives a valuable introduction to Kenya's rich natural and cultural heritage. Within the museum are several galleries. The **Mammal Gallery** is divided between displays of animals in their natural setting and mounted specimens so that you can get a close up of animals you might see on safari, like giraffe and elephant. The **Bird Gallery** has a collection of the birds seen in Kenya, from raptors to tiny sunbirds, while the **Fish and Reptile Gallery** contains some bizarre exhibits, like the lungfish found in Lake Turkana which can survive for up to four years in mud during a drought. Casts of snakes are exhibited for identification purposes, although the live exhibits in the **snake park** outside the museum are more interesting – with snakes, crocodiles and terrapins – although it's not as informative as the Bio-Ken snake farm at the coast, see page 402. The **Prehistory Gallery** covers the origins of man in East Africa, from palaeontological discoveries through to the Stone Age and early Iron Age. Perhaps its finest exhibit is a case containing a complete skeleton of *Homo erectus* 1.6 million years old, from western Lake Turkana, discovered by the **Koobi Fora Research Project** (see page 360) in the 1980s. The **Geology Gallery** gives a good background to Kenya's most significant geological feature, the Rift Valley (see page 302), with its faults, volcanoes and calderas, and is also of interest to those climbing Mount Kenya, which at one time may have been as high as Everest. The **Ethnography Gallery** has a collection of Joy Adamson's *Peoples of Kenya* portraits – detailed watercolours, commissioned by the government between 1949–1955 to document Kenya's traditional tribal cultures which even at that time were beginning to disappear. They provide a fine historical record of over 40 of Kenya's ethnic groups. In addition there are artefacts from different tribes around the country, with displays relating to daily life and ceremonial significance, from skin clothing, basketry and beadwork to agriculture, medicine, music and religion. The **Botanical Paintings Gallery** contains another collection of Joy Adamson's work – watercolours of indigenous plants, hung in groups reflecting the country's different habitats. The **herbarium** contains plant specimens she collected, and notes on their ethnobotanical use in medicine and rituals, food, crafts and natural insecticides. The **Swahili Gallery** illustrates the history of the coast, from the first century to the present day and the development of Swahili culture. Items on display include typical Swahili furnishings, pottery and furniture and a replica 19th century kitchen. The **Gallery of**

Contemporary East African Art exhibits a wide array of paintings, prints and sculptures for sale by contemporary African artists. There's also a **Museum Studio and Arts Centre** which encourages young talent.
Open daily 09.30–18.00; entry KSh200/KSh100

Also based at NMK are:

Kenya Museum Society PO Box 40658, Nairobi; tel: 020 743808; email: info@knowkenya.org
Both the contemporary art gallery and studio are co-ordinated by the Kenya Museum Society (KMS), a voluntary association promoting the work of the museum. It runs an annual **Arts festival**, normally in March, and an excellent **Know Kenya course** with a series of lectures, usually in October.
Office open Mon–Fri 09.00–14.00

Nature Kenya (The East African Natural History Society) PO Box 44486, 00100 Nairobi; tel: 020 374995; email: info@naturekenya.org; web: www.naturekenya.org
The oldest scientific society in Africa – it started in 1909 – the office, shop and library are located in the museum compound. The society supports a number of conservation projects ranging from succulent plants to butterflies, and often arranges natural history outings and birdwatching excursions. It organises **Wednesday morning birdwalks** at sites in and around Nairobi, meeting at the National Museum car park at 08.45, returning about 12.30. Those who are not members of Nature Kenya can get temporary membership at US$2 per birdwalk, payable on arrival at the car park. As available transport is shared, there is no guarantee of a place, but they almost always manage to take everyone. It also organises a **Sunday birdwalk** on the third Sunday of the month. An all-day outing for members, it meets at the National Museum car park in Nairobi. Membership can be obtained from the Nature Kenya office. They have also helped to set up the Ngong Forest birdwalks, see page 190.
Office open Mon–Fri 09.00–15.00

Railway Museum
Located to the west of Nairobi station and visible from Uhuru Highway, if you are a steam-train buff, the museum will keep you fascinated for several happy hours. It was established in 1971 to preserve and display the steam locomotives and rolling stock of the then East African Railways and Harbours Corporation. It has an eclectic collection of memorabilia from the history of the Uganda railway, from its infamous beginnings when numerous workers perished at the jaws of the man-eating lions of Tsavo (see page 221) until the present day, together with the Tanzanian railway. There's an area with wonderful old steam engines, together with smaller exhibits and models. Exhibits from the Kenya Uganda railway include several *Vulcan Foundry*, 2 *Beyer-Garatts* and a *Nasmyth Wilson*. An East African Railways engine, the 5918 *Mount Gelai* Beyer-Garratt has been resurrected to run steam specials (see page 129).
Open daily 08.15–16.45; entry KSh200

Karen Blixen Museum
Karen Road, PO Box 40658, Nairobi; tel: 020 882779; email: karenblixen@bidii.com
'I had a farm in Africa, at the foot of the Ngong Hills...' So began Isak Dinesen's classic love story, *Out of Africa*. With its evocative writing, immortalised by the film

of the same name, it captures the magic of Kenya. Dinesen, who came to Kenya from Denmark as the game hunter Bror Blixen's wife, is more commonly known today as Karen Blixen. She lived in the house between 1914 and 1932, struggling to run a coffee farm. Donated by the Danish government to Kenya in 1963, the house is now a museum which opened in 1986. Much of the filming for *Out of Africa* was done here, and the house is a period piece, displaying original items of furniture giving an insight into the privileged lives of the early aristocratic settlers. There are also pieces of antiquated farm machinery and plans are afoot to restore the coffee factory. There's a museum shop on site and the Karen Blixen Coffee Garden is close by.
Open daily 09.30–18.00; entry KSh200

Rahimtulla Museum of Modern Art (RAMOMA)
Rahimtulla Tower, Upper Hill Road, PO Box 1040, Sarit Centre 00606, Nairobi; tel: 020 729181; email: ramoma@africaonline.co.ke
The RAMOMA gallery, as it is more commonly known, hosts revolving **exhibitions** of Kenyan and international artists displaying mainly paintings and sculpture. **Art workshops** are also regularly held in the gallery space. RAMOMA is a charitable trust, works on display are for sale and shipping can be arranged worldwide.
Open Mon–Fri 09.30–16.30; Sat 09.30–13.00; closed Sundays. Entry free.

Paa ya Paa Arts Centre
Ridgeway Road, off the Kiambu Road (C64); tel: 020 512421
This is very much an African arts centre, run by Mr Njau, a kind, gentle character with a passion for the arts. It is delightfully refreshing after the more commercial galleries, and contains some powerful works by contemporary artists – large wooden sculptures and paintings – in a low-key, leafy compound, where there's an informal performing area among the banana trees. If you have an eye for art, you can often see the work of up-and-coming artists here before they become scooped up by the larger galleries.
Open daily – no formal opening times

Gallery Watatu
City Centre, Lonhro House, Standard Street; tel: 020 228737
In many ways, this is the antithesis of Paa ya Paa, although it too specialises in contemporary African art. It's a formal gallery with a well-lit exhibition space, and is a regular showcase for art in different media – sculpture, paintings, screen prints and etchings – with monthly exhibitions.
Open Mon–Sat 09.00–18.00; Sun 10.00–17.00

Matbronze
2 Kifaru Lane, off Langata South Rd; tel: 020 891251
Not far from the AFEW Giraffe Centre, Matbronze is a **gallery** displaying bronze sculptures, mostly of wildlife, by well-known sculptors like Terry and Denis Mathews (father and son) and Rob Glen. There's a foundry on site, where you can see the bronze-casting process from wax model to finished bronze sculpture. There are some exquisite pieces on display, from life-size crocodiles to elephants and sunbirds. Bronze is not cheap, but most pieces are limited editions and original.
Open Mon–Fri 08.00–17.00; Sat 08.00–17.30; Sun 10.00–17.30

Pimbi Gallery
General Mathenge Close, off General Mathenge Drive, Westlands; tel: 020 581124
The gallery displays sculptures made from scrap metal by Kioko Mwitiki whose

elephants may be seen on the roundabout at Jomo Kenyatta International Airport. An artist first known as the 'junk man' and then the 'elephant man' his visionary work as a sculptor is now recognised in collections in the US and Europe.

Legend House
Wilson Airport, off Langata Road; PO Box 42360, 00100 Nairobi; tel: 020 501796; fax: 020 609528; email: legends@nbi.ispkenya.com; web: www.artsncraftsafrica.com and www.safariclothinglegend.com
Located in a small wooden house on the left before entering into Wilson Airport, Legend House is set up as a 'living gallery' for a variety of artists and designers, with sculptures, paintings, engraved glass, furniture and jewellery alongside safari clothing. Cheap it is not, but it has some finely crafted pieces for sale.

Crafts and markets
In addition to the markets and shops selling local crafts, look out for the *jua kali* artisans who sell their wares at the roadside. *Jua kali*, literally translates as 'hot sun', and refers to the informal economy. Extremely versatile in what they produce, typical examples of their wares may be found along the Ngong road near the racecourse (as well as in other parts of Nairobi), where you will see wrought-ironwork, basketry and woodwork for sale amidst refurbished lawnmowers, coffins and safari furniture, while on the other side of the road is the equivalent of a pavement garden centre, with a variety of plants and pots on display.

Apart from **City Market**, **Village Market** (a shopping centre) and the **Maasai markets** mentioned above, the **Kariokor Market** on Racecourse Road is one of the best places to buy *kiondo* sisal baskets (and is also excellent for cheap eats), and there are a number of **mitumba markets**. The largest mitumba is **Gikomba** near the Machakos country bus station, and there's also a good one behind Adams Arcade on Ngong Road. These secondhand markets sell all sorts of things, from designer clothing to ritzy bathroom fittings. The clothing comes from the West in huge bundles – the end of lines from design houses. You need patience sifting through the piles, but there are bargains galore to be had, and some of the clothing is brand new. Be sure to go with small change as shirts will cost around KSh30–50, jeans KSh300. Also leave any valuables, cameras and large amounts of money behind – here the maxim 'thou shalt not tempt' is pertinent. These markets are found across the country – they have impacted on the local economy, killing off any incentive to manufacture cheap clothes – but at the same time, poor people have access to clothing which they'd normally not be able to afford.

Kazuri Mbagathi Ridge, Karen; tel: 020 884058
Kazuri, meaning 'small and beautiful' in Swahili, makes exquisite handmade ceramic beads, jewellery and pottery. Established more than 25 years ago, over the years it has given a number of near-destitute women an important livelihood. You can watch all processes of the beads being made at the workshop, a finely dextrous process, and there's also a shop. The designs are colourful and bold, reflecting Kenya's culture and wildlife.
Open Mon–Fri 09.00–16.30; Sat 08.00–17.30; Sun 11.00–16.30
Jigsaw Designs Lower ground Floor, Sarit Centre, Westlands, PO Box 14235; Nairobi; tel: 020 440330; fax: 020 444624; email: jigsaw@africaonline.co.ke
This has a range of innovative wrought-ironwork for contemporary homes – ranging from four-poster beds to zebra-screen fire guards and stylish furniture incorporating sea grass, bone, wood, glass and ceramics.
African Heritage Mombasa Road and Carnivore on Langata Road and Banda Street, PO Box 17517, Nairobi; tel: 020 333157

BUTTON MAKERS OF KIBERA

Handmade bone buttons for the fashion world are an important cottage industry in Kibera. It's hard work, but brings in a small income and reflects the remarkable tenacity of people working to survive even in the toughest of living conditions. The bones come from the meat factory at Athi River, south of Nairobi, where they are discarded on to wasteland. These are collected, cleaned and dried and then ground into buttons. As the button makers began to make a success of their business, there was an increased demand for bones. Stepping into the ring came new entrepreneurs – this time bone brokers – who collect the bones, selling them on to the button makers.

A wide range of pan-African curios, arts, crafts and jewellery is displayed. The Carnivore shop includes an **exhibition** of the African Bead, tracing the history of African peoples over the past 12,000 years through their beadwork.
Open Mon–Sat 09.00–18.00; Sun: 11.00–16.00
Banana Box Sarit Centre, PO Box 14477, Nairobi; tel: 020 440564; fax: 020 449596; email: banana@iconnect.co.ke
The shop has sourced a variety of quality crafts, often from small self-help groups, with interesting designs – ideal for presents as they're beautifully packaged.
Kamili Designs signposted off Langata Road, PO Box 42281, Nairobi; tel: 020 883640, mobile: 0733 607025
There's a range of animal designs screen-printed on to *Americani* (calico), with bedspreads, cushion covers and tea-cosies for sale.
Kiko Romeo Westlands, PO Box 76138, Nairobi; tel: 020 740254, mobile: 0733 835438; email: kikoromeo@africaonline.co.ke; web: www.kikoromeo
A leading Kenyan fashion house with well-made, locally designed, modern clothes in traditional fabrics.
Kitengela Glass Adams Arcade, Nairobi; tel: 020 561945, mobile: 0722 512699
This recycled glass in aquamarine and dark blue has been made into a range of chunky glasses, jugs, beads and stained-glass panels. If interested in the recycling process, the factory is not far from Nairobi and visits can be arranged.
Utamaduni Bogoni East Road, Karen; tel: 020 884576, mobile: 0722 511231
This is a one-stop shop for diverse, quality curios and Africana, with some 18 individual craft shops located here. There's also a good restaurant.
Le Amiche Lavington Shopping Centre, PO Box 25370, Nairobi; mob: 0733 785457
Specialises in *kiondos*, reinterpreting traditional designs to include leather and beadwork.
Spinner's Web ABC, Waiyaki Way; tel: 020 440882
This has a good collection of quality crafts, textiles and jewellery, much of it sourced from women's groups.
Twendelee Handicrafts Shop Lavington Church, Muthangari Road, PO Box 25030, Nairobi; tel: 020 571642; fax: 020 576594; email: Luc@insightkenya.com
This shop supports the Twendelee Women's Self-help Project. *Twendelee* means 'let us develop' in Swahili, and the women have focused on knitting, although they also weave, crochet, sew and do beadwork. They have exquisite jumpers and colourful mats in interesting designs for sale.

Other places of interest
Ngong Racecourse Ngong Road, The Jockey Club of Kenya, PO Box 40373, Nairobi; tel: 020 566108; fax: 020 560000

A hangover from settler days, horseracing is still a popular sport across the board, with plenty of entertainment on the racing calendar, some top quality bloodlines and excellent African jockeys. Meetings are usually held on the second Sunday of the month, but check locally for details.
Entry KSh250

Daphne Sheldrick's Elephant Orphanage Turn left off the Magadi road at the Mbagathi gate to Nairobi National Park
This is a wonderful morning's outing to see the baby elephants and rhinos which have been rescued by the David Sheldrick Wildlife Trust (it was set up by Daphne in memory of her husband who was a park warden in Tsavo East National Park). Daphne has successfully reared numerous baby elephants, and you can read about it in her book, *Orphans of Tsavo*. Once the elephants have become reasonably self-sufficient, they are translocated to Tsavo East National Park (see page 221) where they join the older orphans. Elephants can be adopted. For information look up the websites: www.sheldrickwildlifetrust.org and www.wildorphans.org.
Open daily 11.00–12.00; entry free but donations welcome

AFEW Giraffe Centre Koitobus Road, Langata; tel: 020 891658
The giraffe centre is a circular wooden building, raised on stilts, so that you can look eye to eye with a Rothschild's giraffe (unlike the Maasai and reticulated giraffe which have two horns, the Rothschild's have three.) The Rothschild's are the most rare of Kenya's giraffe, and this is an African Fund for Endangered Wildlife project to raise conservation awareness about their status. There's an exhibition by local schoolchildren about the giraffe and a visit entitles you to feed the giraffe on pony nuts. There's also a small café on site.
Open daily 09.00–17.30; entry KSh500

Butterfly Visiting Centre 256 Dagoretti Road, about 2.5km from Karen roundabout, on the right; tel: 020 882297
Operated by the African Butterfly Research Institute, the centre has an excellent live butterfly house, with some butterflies the size of small birds, and an educational exhibit, together with a gift shop and Caterpillar Café in a pleasant courtyard garden which has delicious lunches. There are often art exhibitions by local artists.
Open daily 09.00–16.30; entry KSh500

Bomas of Kenya Forest Road off Langata Road; tel: 020 891802
A cultural and entertainment centre, the Bomas of Kenya are a tourist trap for presenting African culture and dance. The Harambee dancers give lively displays of different tribal dances, illustrating the varied Kenyan tribes, and play an assortment of traditional musical instruments. There's an African theme village with around 11 different types of tribal houses. The *nyama choma* boma restaurant serves traditional fare.
Open daily; dance troupes Mon–Fri 14.30–16.00; Sat–Sun 15.30–17.00; entry KSh600

Ostrich Park Langata Road
Good for entertaining children, you can feed the ostriches, observe local craftsmen at work and there's also a children's playground.
Open daily; entry KSh200/100

Nairobi War Cemetery Set back from Ngong Road next to the racecourse
The World War II cemetery is well maintained, among plenty of trees, so it's a

NYUMBANI

The Nyumbani children's home was founded in 1992 by Father Angelo d'Agostino to provide a refuge for HIV-positive orphans and abandoned children. It is thought that over 150,000 children in Kenya are HIV positive, and the number is increasing. Many babies are abandoned at birth by their mothers due to the stigma associated with HIV disease. It's been found that although many babies admitted to Nyumbani test HIV positive to start with, in fact they are only carrying their mother's antibodies. Three out of four babies test HIV negative at around 18 months old. The home also cares for children who are HIV positive and who have lost both their parents to the illness.

In 1992 three orphans were taken into the home; there are now 75 living in family units in separate houses in the Nyumbani village compound on Dagoretti Road in Karen (near the Butterfly Centre). Here they are not only cared for, but receive an education too. The home has been so successful that it's been unable to meet the demand for placements. To counteract this, in 1998 the **Nyumbani Outreach Programme** was started, known as **Lea Toto**. This has been expanded into a fully fledged community-based programme which targets over 200 HIV-positive children living in the Nairobi slums, assisting them with medical care and providing both the children and their families with support.

Nyumbani welcomes visitors to the village on Dagoretti Road. A donation in the form of food for the children – bread or fruit – is appropriate. Four o'clock in the afternoon is a good time to visit.

The Nyumbani and Lea Toto programmes welcomes volunteers and financial support. For further information, contact Nyumbani on www.nyumbani.com or Lea Toto on www.leatoto.com.

pleasant walk even during the heat of the day. The World War I cemetery is off Langata Road.

Nairobi Arboretum Located on Arboretum Road, off State House Road and Uhuru Highway
The Arboretum covers 30ha, and has a collection of more than 350 species of indigenous and exotic plants, as well as over 100 bird species, Sykes and vervet monkeys and butterflies. There are footpaths, jogging trails and picnic spots. If you are interested in trees, Nature Kenya produces an excellent field guide, the *Arboretum guidebook* (KSh350), which gives descriptions about the trees you will see, and a **tree walk** is held on the last Monday of each month. (Times vary so check with Nature Kenya on tel: 020 374995.) The Arboretum started in 1906 as an experimental trial to test out the suitability of trees for forestry in Kenya. It was made a forest reserve in 1932 but between the 1970s and 1990s management became laissez-faire due to lack of funding. This sparked the formation of the **Friends of Nairobi Arboretum** (FONA), a local society actively working to revitalise the arboretum, with the long-term aim of promoting environmental education, recreation and scientific knowledge. FONA relies on volunteers, subscriptions and donations to carry out its activities. Contact them through Nature Kenya, page 184.

STREETWISE TRUST: HEADING FOR THE OTHER SIDE OF THE STREET

Founded in 1994 by Lesley Lodge, Streetwise is a small charity helping the street children of Nairobi. It aims to give them an informal education in the three Rs (reading, writing and arithmetic) and to equip them with practical skills so that they can become financially independent. There's been an artistic emphasis in the training, with the children making and painting a number of household and gift items, as well as decorating houses and offices. Some have attended sewing school and are now making soft furnishings. Children are also learning how to grow vegetables, teaching them another skill to help them supplement their food when they leave the centre.

Currently, there are around 20 children on the scheme, and once the centre has equipped them with skills to earn an income, they are assisted in getting employment. When someone leaves, another child is taken on to the scheme. The philosophy of the project is based on the old adage '*If you buy a man a fish you feed him for a day. If you teach him to fish you feed him for a lifetime*'.

The Streetwise workshops are based in Nairobi at Jamhuri Park and visitors are welcome to meet the children and encouraged to buy some of the items, as this gives the children a sense of achievement. Most of the fund-raising for the project (they require KSh50,000 – about US$655 – a month to feed and house the children and pay staff salaries) comes from selling items that the children have made.

In Nairobi, you can support Streetwise by buying items made by the children from:

Streetwise workshop Regina Seed premises, Jamhuri Park
Open Mon–Sat 09.00–16.30; closed Wed afternoon
Utamaduni Craft Centre Off Bogani East Rd, Langata Rd
Open daily 09.30–18.00

For further information, or if you'd like to make a donation, contact Streetwise Trust, PO Box 89, Village Market, Nairobi; mob: 0733 742 738; email: neelshah@wananchi.com

City Park Located opposite the Aga Khan Hospital, next to the Hawkers' Market with its stalls selling vegetables
The city park combines indigenous forest, where you can see Sykes and vervet monkeys and clouds of butterflies, with colourful gardens, ornamental trees and a concrete canal. It's a popular recreational park and is especially busy at the weekends with people picnicking on the grass. If going alone, be vigilant. It has a tea kiosk and restaurant. The **Friends of City Park** (also operated through Nature Kenya, see page 184) is a local society which strives to maintain the quality of park.

Ngong Road Forest Sanctuary Covering an area of 528ha, the forest, with many indigenous trees, remains relatively unspoilt despite its closeness to the city. Stretching east from Dagoretti to Kibera, it is now managed by the **Ngong Road Forest Sanctuary Trust** (PO Box 42281, Nairobi; tel: 020 710740; fax: 020 718737; email: ngong@rugkenya.com) who have sourced international funding for fencing and developing the forest. In due course they plan to have four entrances, a full-time warden and education centre, and to open the forest for recreational activities – with nature trails, walking, horse and bicycle riding, as well as giving local people access to the forest to harvest its resources in a sustainable manner, such as through honey hives. **Thirty mammal and 190 bird species** may be seen in the sanctuary, and there are plans to introduce black-and-white colobus monkeys. At the time of writing, only birdwalks are available in the forest.

Book Ngong Forest birdwalks through Wilderness Logistics (PO Box 282, Sarit Centre 00606, Nairobi; mob: 0722 360380; email: nic@wildernesslogistics.com; web: www.wildernesslogistics.com) or via central Nairobi hotels. These nature walks, for a minimum of four people, are led by qualified birding guides and accompanied by a forest ranger and security guards. They cost US$50 and take a couple of hours, ending with refreshments at the Ngong Racecourse Restaurant.

Nairobi Safari Walk and Animal Orphanage KWS park headquarters on Langata Road, PO Box 40241, Nairobi; tel: 020 500622
A cross between a zoo and an orphanage, this is an excellent educational facility and a good introduction to some of the animals you might see on safari and the issues facing their conservation. It aims to give an understanding of Kenya's wildlife and plants and to illustrate their interdependence and relationship with people. The orphanage started in 1964 as a refuge for abandoned or injured animals. Over the years it developed to include problem animals, and in 2000 the safari walk opened. It's a raised boardwalk about 6m high, which takes you through examples of wetland, savanna and forest habitats, (where each has an information plaque with a description of the flora and fauna and their conservation status) where you can see animals from the orphanage. It takes about 45 minutes to go around the orphanage and an hour for the safari walk.
Open daily 08.30–17.30; entry US$5/US$2

Nairobi National Park
KWS, PO Box 40241, Nairobi; tel: 020 500622
Open daily 06.00–19.00; park entry US$23; vehicle entry KSh200; smartcard required; main gate is a point of issue and point of sale for smartcards
There are seven entrances to Nairobi National Park. On the western side of the park, closest to the city centre, is **Main gate**, with the park headquarters, animal orphanage, safari walk and shop, where you can purchase and load a smartcard (see page 41). Still on the western boundary, and heading south on the Magadi road are **Langata gate**, followed by **Banda gate** and **Mbagathi gate** (also the entrance to Daphne Sheldrick's). On the southern boundary is **Maasai gate**, about 10km along a deeply rutted dirt track to the left off Magadi Road, while **Cheetah gate** is at the southeastern tip of the park and is accessed off the Namanga road. **East gate** (sometimes called Embakasi gate) is, as its name suggests, on the eastern boundary and is accessed off the Nairobi–Mombasa Highway, on the city side of Jomo Kenyatta International Airport. The roads inside the park are good, and, with the exception of the the Maasai gate, access by 2WD is normally fine.

Getting around
The KWS produces a free park map, which is worth having, although not all the tracks within the park are clearly marked. If unfamiliar with the park, it's best to enter at the main gate, where you can get an update on game sightings from the rangers, which will flag up the best spots to visit, or you could take a ranger. Other highlights in the park are the **hippo pools**, where there's also a **nature trail** along the Athi River, shaded by acacia trees inhabited by vervet monkeys. The **impala**

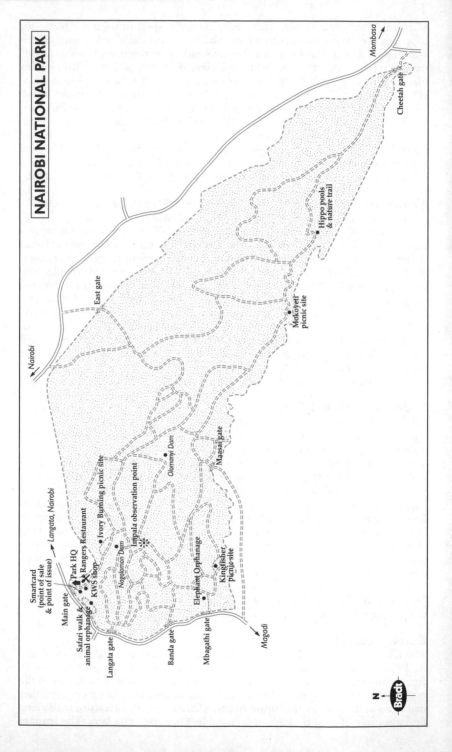

NAIROBI NATIONAL PARK

Mombasa

Cheetah gate

Hippo pools
& nature trail

Mokoyeti
picnic site

East gate

Nairobi

Maasai gate

Olomanyi Dam

Impala observation point

Ivory Burning picnic site

Langata, Nairobi

Rangers Restaurant

Park HQ

KWS Shop

Ngolomon Dam

Elephant Orphanage

Kingfisher
picnic site

Smartcard
(point of sale
& point of issue)

Main gate

Safari walk &
animal orphanage

Langata gate

Banda gate

Mbagathi gate

Magadi

N

Bradt

observation point gives views across the plains to Mount Kilimanjaro on a fine morning and the **dams** are a magnet for wildlife in the dry season. In addition there are several **picnic spots** around the park, including the ivory-burning site.

History Kenya's oldest national park, which opened in 1946, Nairobi National Park is remarkable for being a wilderness area so close to the city centre (7km). Where else in the world can you see a wild rhino silhouetted against the skyline of a capital city? In 1989, at the height of the ivory crisis, the former president, Daniel Arap Moi, lit an ivory pyre in the park, a dramatic event which at the time drew the world's attention to the crisis facing the survival of elephant and rhino. The park is also an important sanctuary for black rhino.

Flora and fauna Covering an area of 117km², it's primarily a **savanna** park, with rolling grasslands interspersed with **riverine woodland**, pockets of whistling thorn acacia, **thick bush** in the valleys, rocky gorges and **dry forest** characterised by *Croton* species. Its seasonal rivers flow into the Athi near Cheetah gate, and there are also dams and ponds. The park is fenced on three sides, enabling wildlife to migrate into the park from the Kitengela and Athi-Kapiti plains, giving an extended range of 2,000km² (although increased housing in the area is creating a conservation dilemma).

Despite its relatively small size, the park has a wide diversity of wildlife and avifauna, with **over 100 mammals**, where you can see lion, cheetah, rhino, giraffe, kongoni, Grant's gazelle, buffalo, hippo and crocodile, although there are *no* elephant in the park. Since its inception, the park has had its own **migration**, normally in July and August, when herds of around 20,000 zebra, wildebeest and eland move into the park from the Kitengela and Athi-Kapiti plains which are important wet-season grazing areas. Over **500 bird species** have been recorded in the park, more than for the whole of the British Isles. The grassland is an important breeding area for Jackson's widowbird while African crowned eagles nest in the forest.

Conservation Inevitably, being next to a large area of population there are enormous pressures on the national park. It is vital for the park and the future of its ecosystem that wildlife can continue to migrate to the plains beyond the boundary, otherwise 50% of the wildlife could be lost, and the park's habitat would change. Increasingly, the migratory area is being impinged upon by settlement and industrial development in the Kitengela area. A local conservation group, the **Friends of Nairobi National Park** (FoNNAP, PO Box 42076, Nairobi; tel: 020 500622; fax: 020 585866; web: www.fonnap.org) have developed a **wildlife conservation lease programme** as a pragmatic measure to address this problem. Essentially it involves leasing land from the Maasai who own the land in the migration corridor at an annual rate of around US$4 an acre (a rate similar to the return they would get from livestock). In return the Maasai can continue to graze their livestock and agree to keeping the land unfenced and as rangeland. Eventually it is intended to include the entirety of the migration corridor and game dispersal areas under this scheme. Initiated at the turn of the millennium, the scheme was initially successful. However, the conflict between the Maasai herdsmen and lion was exacerbated in May and June 2003 when ten lion were speared to death by the Maasai in the Kitengela area bordering the park. In some cases, the lion carcasses were subsequently mutilated. The East African Wildlife Society intervened, brokering a meeting between KWS and the Kitengela livestock owners, which has resolved the problem in the short term. Nevertheless, the long-term solution to this conflict remains a cause for concern. (For further information on lion refer to the Lion Predator Project, page 262.)

AROUND NAIROBI
The prime coffee-growing area of Kiambu and Ruiru lies to the north and east of Nairobi, while to the northwest the land rises through the tea plantations of Limuru at around 2,500m to the lip of the escarpment overlooking the Rift Valley. To the east lie the Ngong Hills, while to the south are Nairobi National Park and the Kitengela plains.

Where to stay and eat
Limuru
Kentmere Club (16 cottages) Limuru Rd, PO Box 39508, Tigoni; tel: 066 41053; fax: 066 40692; email: kenclub@net2000ke.com.

Located in Tigoni, in the tea-growing area of Limuru, about 20km from Nairobi, the club is set in terraced tropical gardens. It has a country-inn ambience with a roaring log fire in the evenings and is popular with local residents. The rooms are in cottages in the garden and have simple furnishing with en-suite bathrooms. There's a terrace restaurant for alfresco meals, with excellent French cuisine and friendly service. **On offer:** informal birdwatching.

Rates: from US$42 B&B per person sharing; if not staying at the club, there's an entry fee of around KSh200

Kiambu
Paradise Lost (camping) tel: 020 315273, mobile: 0733 812820; email: paradiselostcaves@yahoo.com.

Located 10km out of town off the Kiambu Rd (turn left after the Evergreen Centre) this is a 54-acre picnic spot where you can pitch a tent next to a coffee farm. There are cold showers and flush toilets. Wood is free and there's a *nyama choma* restaurant on site and good security.

Rates: US$20 per person – this includes all the activities offered – camel- and horseriding, exploring Stone Age caves, fishing, boating, ostrich feeding and a coffee-farm tour. You may be able to negotiate a better rate.

What to see and do
Ngong Hills
The blue, knuckle-shaped hills of the Ngongs are a distinctive landmark for miles around Nairobi. Made famous by Isak Dinesen's book, *Out of Africa*, interestingly, Denys Finch Hatton's memorial lies in the hills, now fenced by an entrepreneurial owner who charges about KSh100 to visit. The Ngong Hills, readily accessible from the Ngong village, some 8km out of Nairobi along the Ngong road from Karen *dukas* (local shops), are good for walking, with spectacular views, but it's best to go in a group as muggings have taken place in the past. Check out the security situation before you go. You may be able to take an escort from the Ngong police station (costs about KSh600).

Kiambu
Riuki Cultural Centre
PO Box 42458, 00100 Nairobi; tel: 020 765760, mobile: 0722 741921

Located 31km from Nairobi. Take the Kiambu road, C64 to Kiambu town. Continue through the town and branch right after the Ndumberi shops, and then turn right again at the Ikinu shops. The centre is about 1km along on the left.

VOLUNTEERING IN KENYA – PROJECT: RUIRU
James Foottit

In January 1999, five architecture students from Edinburgh University set out on a year-long voluntary project to build a maternity unit and adjoining counselling centre for the Kenyan charity, Wholistic Caring and Counselling, a Christian ministry assisting marginalised women and girls. One of the group, Naeem Biviji, a Kenyan national, had come across Grace Gitaka who was at that time working in Nairobi with young, pregnant and often vulnerable girls. She lived with some of her girls in Kibera, Kenya's largest slum. Grace had a vision to build a centre outside Nairobi from which to expand and continue her ministry to unaided young girls with nowhere else to turn.

A chance meeting led Naeem to Grace and subsequently to the beginning of Project: RUIRU, which was completed one year later. The group of architecture students were inexperienced in every sense of the word. However, this in no way impaired the ambitiousness of the project. The design was for four buildings arranged around a courtyard and was to be built using a method of soil-block construction previously untried in the area. Grace was able to provide the land just outside Ruiru (near Nairobi) and in April two of the team left to begin construction work. At this time only a small amount of money had been raised but over the next three months a registered charity was formed and more than £60,000 was raised by the rest of the team through lively fund-raising events – the *jenga* (Swahili for 'to build') bands were a highlight on the student social calendar – and sponsorship from individuals, charitable trusts and companies. The design proposal won the Ede & Ravenscroft Award for its strong ecological agenda, which gave great encouragement.

The design of the building remained flexible throughout its construction. This meant that the building became a collaborative product of both young designers and local builders. A dynamic shape, mosaic floors and the unusual nature of the building materials all contributed to a sense of fun that surrounded the whole building process. By the end of the year there were sometimes 50 people working on site as it raced towards completion. This led to the development of a formidable site football team.

Grace and some of her girls moved into their new home in time to see in the new millennium. Wholistic Caring and Counselling has continued to operate from Ruiru since then and always welcomes visitors who want to see their craftwork. Volunteers from the UK have worked at the centre but it is largely staffed by girls who have been treated there and never wanted to leave. It can be found next door to the Bible Translation Centre on the outskirts of Ruiru off the Kiambu road.

For further information or if you would like to support the work of Wholistic Caring and Counselling, contact: PO Box 975, Ruiru 00232; email: walthera_gitaka@yahoo.co.uk; web: www.wholisticcaring.org. The architectural students working on Project: Ruiru were: Susanna Laughton, Naeem Biviji, Mark Campbell, Calvin Ruysen and James Foottit.

There are regular buses to Ikinu from Nairobi. The Riuki cultural centre is located in Kikuyu country and aims to promote the indigenous cultures of central Kenya, in particular Kikuyu, through lectures, storytelling and theatrical presentations – much of it to local schools as well as tourists. On the afternoon tour (commences 15.00) you visit a traditional Kikuyu homestead, get an explanation about Kikuyu culture, sample traditional African food and *muratina*, a home-brew, before watching a dancing display. At the weekends, **Mumbi's kitchen** is open 10.00–18.00 for traditional meals.

Open daily; entry US$30 or US$50 with food

Lord Erroll's Grave
See box on page 10 for information on Lord Erroll.

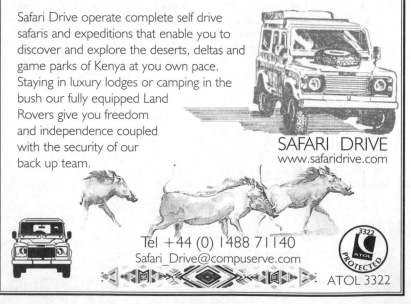

SELF DRIVE SAFARIS & EXPEDITIONS

Safari Drive operate complete self drive safaris and expeditions that enable you to discover and explore the deserts, deltas and game parks of Kenya at you own pace. Staying in luxury lodges or camping in the bush our fully equipped Land Rovers give you freedom and independence coupled with the security of our back up team.

SAFARI DRIVE
www.safaridrive.com

Tel +44 (0) 1488 71140
Safari_Drive@compuserve.com

ATOL 3322

South and Eastern Kenya

The south and eastern part of Kenya encompasses the largest part of the country where wildlife is protected. It includes two of Kenya's oldest and most famous national parks – Amboseli which lies in the lee of Africa's highest mountain, Kilimanjaro, with its sugarloaf dome rising high above the savanna plains, and Tsavo, dry thornbush country for the most part, interspersed with giant baobabs. In Tsavo the Athi and Tsavo rivers join to form the Galana which then becomes the Sabaki River, reaching the Indian Ocean to the north of Malindi. These two parks dominate the southern safari circuit from Nairobi and are also popular for coastal safari excursions, Amboseli and Tsavo West being the prime game-viewing areas. This region was a favourite hunting patch for the likes of Ernest Hemingway and elephants are still synonymous with Tsavo. On the surrounding Maasai ranches some of the Maasai are becoming involved in ecotourism ventures. These projects are helping to maintain vital wildlife migration corridors and the integrity of the greater Amboseli and Tsavo ecosystems as well as broadening the choice of game-viewing options and activities. Other highlights within the region are Lake Magadi and the Nguruman escarpment at the southern extreme of Kenya's Rift Valley, the Chyulu and Taita Hills which border Tsavo West National Park and the Tana River which runs through Garissa and Garsen to branch into a huge delta as it enters the sea south of Lamu.

GARISSA TO GARSEN

There's no reason to go to Garissa unless you're taking the back route to Lamu via Garsen, as the Somali/Kenyan border is closed at Liboi. It's dry, flat and featureless country, the only reprieve being the Tana River which flows through Garissa and south to Garsen. In the recent past this area's been prone to intra-tribal skirmishes between the Orma and Pokomo and attacks by the Somali *shifta* (bandits).

Getting there and away

From Nairobi take the A2 highway to Thika and then turn east on to the A3, turning south on to the B8 to Garsen, about 10km before Garissa. It's a reasonable dirt road but you'll require 4WD and will need to get an update on the security situation (and preferably drive in convoy) before taking this route.

By bus

Due to the security situation there are no major bus services operating on the route.

By air

Garissa and Garsen both have airstrips, but no scheduled services operate.

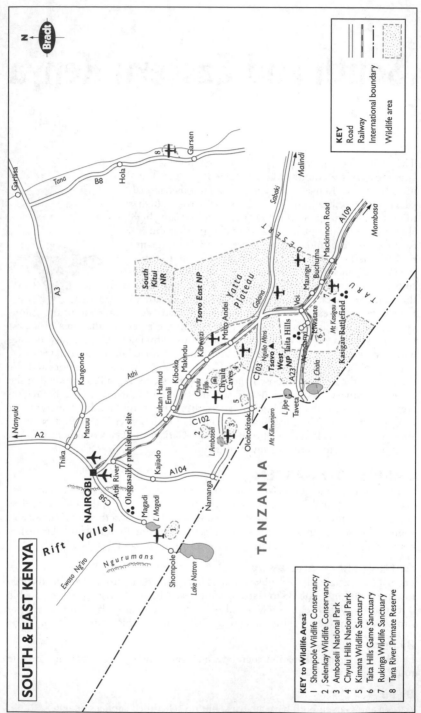

SOUTH & EAST KENYA

KEY
Road
Railway
International boundary
Wildlife area

KEY to Wildlife Areas
1 Shompole Wildlife Conservancy
2 Selenkay Wildlife Conservancy
3 Amboseli National Park
4 Chyulu Hills National Park
5 Kimana Wildlife Sanctuary
6 Taita Hills Game Sanctuary
7 Rukinga Wildlife Sanctuary
8 Tana River Primate Reserve

TANZANIA

Getting organised
It's best to get organised in Nairobi before leaving. In an emergency the **tourist helpline** is tel: 020 604767. Garissa has a **bank** and **petrol** after which the next place with fuel is Garsen.

Where to stay and eat
If you find yourself in Garissa, head for the **Garissa Government Guest House** on the outskirts of town or the **Safari Hotel**, both of which provide reasonable accommodation and food.

Tana River Primate National Reserve
Open daily; reserve entry fee US$5
The reserve lies between Hola and Garsen on the B8 to Garissa. The best access (4WD) is via the Mchelelo or Baomo tracks to the river.

Flora and fauna Covering 169km², the reserve opened in 1976 and was formed to protect two endangered species of monkey, the crested mangabey and the Tana River red colobus. Other primates found here include Sykes and vervet monkeys, yellow baboon and three types of bushbaby. The reserve has lush riverine forest, dry woodland and open savanna which are bisected by the Tana River. The forest is a relict of Central African lowland rainforest which became isolated during the seismic eruptions during the formation of the Rift Valley. Consequently, much of the flora and fauna are unusual to East Africa. The reserve includes 175 tree species, some of which are endemic, like *Cynometra lukei* and *Paveta sphaerobotrys*; over 260 bird species, including the extremely rare white-winged apalis; and 57 mammal species, including lion, elephant, buffalo, giraffe, lesser kudu, oryx and a small seasonal population of the endangered Hirola antelope (sometimes called Hunter's hartebeest). **Walking** with a guide (beware of buffalo), **boating** and **fishing** for cat-fish are available.

Conservation Although a protected area, some 54% of the surveyed Tana Forest areas were destroyed between 1994–2000, a process which ironically was accelerated by the local people cutting down the forest after a 1996 World Bank US$6.3 million project to ensure the biodiversity of the reserve was implemented. A human– wildlife/land-rights issue was heightened due to the perception by the Pokomo that their land was being taken for the monkeys and that their needs came second to conservation; the World Bank subsequently pulled the funding on the project. The situation is complex and the local people remain suspicious of change.

Where to stay and eat
Tana River Primate National Reserve (6 tents, self-catering tented camp; campsites) Book through National Museums of Kenya, PO Box 40658, Nairobi; tel 020 742141; fax: 020 741424; email: nmk@africaonline.co.ke; web: www.museums.or.ke
The self-catering tented camp has comfortable tents, each with showers and flush toilets with electricity by generator. It's available at the NMK Mchelelo primate research camp by special arrangement. You just need to bring your own provisions. Bwana mzee, the resident cook, prepares good meals and will happily cook up your catch of the day. There are also a couple of basic campsites.
Rates: from around US$10 per person self-catering; camping about US$5, plus reserve entry fee US$5

TANA RIVER RED COLOBUS AND THE CRESTED MANGABEY
Dr David N M Mbora

The Tana River red colobus and the crested mangabey are endemic to forest fragments along a narrow 100km stretch on both sides of the Tana River, between latitudes 2°15' and 1°50' south, in eastern Kenya. Their habitat is greatly threatened by forest clearing for farmland and the cutting of trees for building canoes and houses. Fewer than 1,300 individuals of each species remain in the area and there are no captive populations. Consequently, both primates are classified as critically endangered and are listed among the 25 most endangered primates taxa in the world by the International Union for Conservation of Nature (IUCN).

Tana river red colobus *(Procolobus rufomitratus)*
The Tana River red colobus is one of 14 separate species of colobus distributed across the African continent and the island of Zanzibar. The Tana red colobus is a relatively large, elusive and exclusively arboreal diurnal monkey. It appears predominantly grey, darker on its back and tail, lighter grey on limbs and underparts and paler on the front. It has a black face, conspicuous whiskers and the only red coloration on its body is a rufous tinge on the top of its head. Red colobus belong to the family *colobinae* that includes the langurs and proboscis monkeys of Asia, while the olive and black-and-white are the other forms of colobus found in Africa. All colobines are leaf eaters and have

LAKE MAGADI AND THE NGURUMANS

This is the southern section of Kenya's Rift Valley. Rarely visited, it's not on a main transport route, but it's wild, remote and beautiful country. Wildlife is not as prolific as in the main parks, but the scenery more than compensates.

Getting there and away

Take the C38 from Nairobi to Magadi. Once past the bustling outskirts of Nairobi, it's a delightful 3hr 30min drive on a good tarmac road. There's very little traffic, so you can relax and enjoy the spectacular scenery. The road descends through several vegetation zones, with mature acacia woodland giving way to dry bush scrub on the Rift Valley floor and the pink soda lake of Magadi. From Magadi, crossing over the causeway, it's a dirt road with a reasonable surface until one reaches the Ewaso Ng'iro River at the foot of the Nguruman escarpment. From here there are dusty tracks through the bush to Shompole – if you hit a pothole, you'll be enshrouded in a cloud of powder dust. A rough track climbs the escarpment to Morijo in the Loita Hills, but you'll need to seek permission to use it. Once off the Magadi road you'll require 4WD and need to know exactly where you're going as it's easy to get lost. This is a remote rural Maasai area, where few people speak English, so a knowledge of Swahili is useful. It's preferable to have your own transport if going to the Ngurumans as public transport from Magadi is spasmodic.

By bus

Akamba Bus runs a couple of buses a day to Magadi, leaving at around 13.00 and 15.00, returning early in the morning, departing from Magadi at around 06.00. There are also *matatus*. From Magadi to the Nguruman massif there's very little traffic, a few vehicles a day.

an elongated, sacculated digestive system that allows them effectively to digest large amounts of foliage unlike the other groups of old-world monkeys known as *cercopithecines*. The Tana colobus is restricted to evergreen, closed canopy, gallery forest and subsists mostly on young and sometimes mature leaves, fruit and flowers. Because the Tana colobus lives in a patchy, semi-arid environment and depends on a relatively common, but low-quality food resource, it occupies small home ranges and lives in groups averaging about ten individuals of mostly adult females and only one fully adult male.

Crested mangabey (*Cercocebus galeritus galeritus*)
The Tana River crested mangabey is one of four forms of river mangabeys found in Africa. They are known as river mangabeys because they all inhabit riverine forest. The Tana River mangabeys have a yellowish-brown back, white under parts, and dark-grey hands, feet and tail. A conspicuous crest on the forehead gives them their name. They are diurnal, arboreal, but mostly terrestrial, and spend most of their time foraging low in the forest for invertebrates, fruit and seeds that comprise the bulk of their diet. These monkeys exhibit a great deal of ecological flexibility and are known to alter their diets, social grouping and range in response to food availability and long-term habitat change. They live in large multi-male, multi-female social groups of up to 60 individuals and can be very vocal. The dominant male frequently makes a long-distance call that can be heard up to a kilometre away.

By air
Shompole Conservancy has a private airstrip for light aircraft. It's about a 35-minute flight from Nairobi, the Mara and Amboseli to Shompole, but there are no scheduled flights.

Getting organised
It's best to get organised in Nairobi before leaving. In **Magadi**, if you do need a **bank,** Barclays reportedly opens on Wednesdays only. There's a **general store** next to the petrol station which stocks basic supplies. In an emergency the **tourist helpline** is tel: 020 604767. Be aware that the **petrol station** closes over the lunch-hour. The Magadi Soda Company runs a small, private **hospital** and could be contacted in a dire emergency.

What to see and do
Olorgasailie Prehistoric Site
National Museums of Kenya, PO Box 40658, Nairobi; tel 020 742141; fax: 020 741424; email: nmk@africaonline.co.ke; web: www.museums.or.ke
Open daily; entry KSh200
About 71km from Nairobi, Olorgasailie is 1.5km from the signposted turn-off on the left. This Archeulian site has numerous hand axes and fossilised skeletons of extinct species of elephant and a hippo. Discovered in 1919 by the geologist J H Gregory, who found hand axes near Mount Olorgasailie, the site was subsequently excavated by Mary and Louis Leakey between 1942 and 1945. Excavations on the 21ha site are still ongoing, a joint project between the National Museums of Kenya and the American Smithsonian Institute. There's an excellent display of exhibits on human evolution, stone tools and information about the site in the small museum. Excursions to see the digs are best

undertaken in the early morning. A raised, wooden catwalk has been built from which you can see an impressive display of animal fossils and stone tools dating back 1.2 million years.

There is **accommodation** in the form of bandas and camping. Book through National Museums of Kenya, PO Box 40658, Nairobi; tel: 020 742141; fax: 020 741424; email: nmk@africaonline.co.ke; web: www.museums.or.ke. The campsite is next to the excavated sites, but is said not to induce nightmares of giant pigs and ancient ancestors. It gets excruciatingly hot here, 35°C is not uncommon and there's scant shade for tents. The thatched bandas are very basic with netting on the windows. You'll need to be self-sufficient, and be sure to bring plenty of water. There's a large, shaded picnic area, showers and long-drop toilets.
Rates: bandas KSh500–800; camping KSh200

Lake Magadi

The lake shimmers through a heat haze from a distance, before the road descends to a barrier where you sign in to cross the causeway. A shallow, alkaline lake on the Rift Valley floor, Magadi extends over 100km², dominated by a pink and white crust of sodium carbonate up to 30m deep in parts. Mined by the Magadi Soda Company, there's a bizarre infrastructure of railtracks and corrugated industrial buildings on the eastern side of the lake alongside the small town, a purpose-built mining settlement (with neatly ordered houses and complete with golf course and swimming pool) on a peninsula linked by causeways to the north and south, and infiltrated by Maasai from the surrounding area. It's a weird, incongruous setting which cries out to be used as a location for a sci-fi movie. There's superb **birdlife** and, at certain times of year, the lake is fringed by up to 20,000 lesser flamingos; other waterfowl include African spoonbills, chestnut-banded plovers, black-winged stilts and wintering migrants like the little stint. There are several **hot springs** which feed the lake. The easiest to reach are on the southern lakeside, but you'll need to take a guide from Magadi – ask at the store – and carry water.

Nguruman escarpment

Crossing the Magadi causeway, it's about 30km to the Nguruman escarpment which forms the western wall of the Rift Valley. Rising steeply from 900m to 2,300m, the blue hills of the Nguruman range climb steep, stepped faults from the floodplain of the Ewaso Ng'iro River, passing through *Acacia tortilis* woodland, to acacia and *Commiphora* bush on the lower slopes, thickets of *Tarchonanthus* and grassland to sub-montane forest along the ridge, to the Loita Hills. It's superb **walking** country, wild and remote, with panoramic views across the rift. A few tour operators have treks through the Loitas to the Ngurumans (see page 130). The Ewaso Ng'iro River runs along the foot of the escarpment, shaded by magnificent fig trees, where you can paddle in the shallows, walking on smooth pebbles and green quartz, or fish for catfish. The river disappears into swamp as it enters Lake Natron (in Tanzania). Game viewing in the area is improving, especially in the Shompole Conservancy.

There is camping at **Olkiramatian Campsite**. This is a very basic campsite with no facilities next to the Ewaso Ng'iro River, on the Magadi side of the bridge. It's run by the Maasai Olkiramatian group ranch.
Rates: KSh200 for camping and KSh100 for a vehicle

Shompole Conservancy

Art of Ventures, PO Box 10665, 00100 Nairobi; tel: 020 883280; fax: 020 884135; email: info@shompole.com; web: www.shompole.com

Entry fee US$20
The conservancy can be reached by turning south to Oloika from Magadi or crossing the causeway and driving 30km to the Nguruman escarpment, and then heading south to Shompole. A joint ecotourism venture between the Maasai Shompole group ranch and Art of Ventures, a 14,200ha wildlife conservancy has been formed on the 56,654ha group. Essentially the conservancy is a cattle- and people-free zone which has been set aside for wildlife. Being an area rich in biodiversity, the project has been supported by a European Union grant which has provided funding for a road network, airstrip, community buildings and ranger equipment. Opened in 2002, the conservancy is still in its infancy, but already the decrease in poaching has seen increasing numbers of wildlife – lion, buffalo, wild dog and elephant, golden jackal and honey badgers, as well as giraffe, Grant's gazelle, wildebeest and zebra. Within the conservancy the country varies from the arid salt savanna plains, ideal for bush walks, to lush swamp and riverine forest.

For accommodation, try **Shompole Lodge** (6 tented rooms, swimming pool). Book through Art of Ventures, PO Box 10665, 00100 Nairobi; tel: 020 883280; fax: 020 884135; email: info@shompole.com; web: www.shompole.com. This ecolodge sets a precedent in safari style. Set in a 14,000ha conservancy, surrounded by 56,600ha of the Shompole group ranch, it nestles on a hillside against the dramatic backdrop of the Nguruman escarpment, with views across salt and savanna plains and riverine forest to Mount Shompole. It's a scorchingly hot environment and the lodge makes clever use of shallow water channels around the buildings, providing a natural cooling system, while high pitched, thatched ceilings maximise air circulation. Local stones, pebbles and timber are integrated in the design. The open-plan dining area (good food with fresh salads) and sitting-room, furnished in minimalist style with large beds and cushions, overlook a narrow swimming pool. Each room is open plan with Bedouin-style tents under thatch, individual plunge pools and a private sitting area, while the bathrooms have waterspout showers and 'his and hers' compost toilets. Planned for the future are 'sky beds', treehouses in the bush for fly-camping. **On offer:** guided bush walks on the plains or treks into the Ngurumans, 4WD game drives, night drives, river tubing, excursions to Lake Natron with its flamingos and hot springs, Maasai *manyatta* visits and fly-camping.
Rates: from US$300 full board per person sharing; conservation fee US$20

NAMANGA

Namanga is the main border crossing between Kenya and Tanzania and the small town has developed around its *raison d'être* – government immigration offices, fuel stop, a couple of hotels and wooden kiosks, and a preponderance of Maasai traders selling trinkets to tourists (this is on the main route to Amboseli National Park).

Getting there and away

Take the A109 south of Nairobi and turn west on to the A104 at Athi River, a good tarmac road all the way to Arusha in Tanzania. It's a rather featureless, flat drive for 50km across the Athi and Kapiti plains to Kajiado, a provincial centre, where you cross the railway line and continue to Namanga (135km). The scenery changes as the road climbs the undulating Pelewa and Maparasha hills covered with numerous types of acacia, which are particularly attractive when the trees are in flower, just before the rains. There's roadside charcoal for sale and a few Maasai settlements on the way. If going to **Amboseli National Park** take the C103 from Namanga, a dirt road which is in a fair condition (about 80km), but 4WD is recommended.

By bus

Buses and *matatus* run to Namanga from Nairobi daily, and there are several shuttle services – Davanu, Riverside and Impala are recommended – between Nairobi and Arusha. (Some continue on to Moshi and Marangu for climbing Kilimanjaro.) See page 166 for details.

By air

There's an airstrip at Kajiado and Namanga, but no scheduled flights.

By train

There is no passenger service at Kajiado.

Getting organised

It's best to **change money** in Nairobi or Arusha before leaving. The **immigration post** is on the left just after the petrol station. Passport processing is normally efficient. You'll require a valid visa (US$50 for entering Tanzania) and Kenyan tourist visas usually permit re-entry from Tanzania within the three-month period. Kenyan visas (US$50) can be purchased at the border. The border is open 24 hours. If travelling independently, ensure all vehicle documents are in order – you'll need to obtain customs clearance in Nairobi prior to travel; see page 70. There's no **supermarket** and shops only have basic supplies. In an emergency the **tourist helpline** is 020 604767. There are several **petrol stations**.

Where to stay and eat
Kajiado area

Sirata Suruwa (3 tents, homestay) Book through Bush Homes of East Africa, page 90. About 20km south of Kajiado, there's a turn-off to the right (but get clear directions before leaving) to a small hideaway in the Melepo Hills on a Maasai group ranch covering 2,800ha. It's the home of Mike and Judy Rainy, ecologists, an American couple who've spent many years in Kenya. There's an ongoing ecological study on pastoral people and wildlife conservation on the ranch. It's a peaceful setting on the side of a hill, with tents comfortably furnished, well spread out along sandy paths, lit by hurricane lamps at night, with open-air safari showers and separate toilets. There's a small dining-cum-sitting-room, with beautiful views across the secluded valley. The food is interesting and delicious, a special feature being stew cooked in a *kijiko*, a round African cooking pot, and ginger tea. There's sparse game – mainly antelopes, but wild dog have been seen in the area and there's talk of running a Maasai marathon on the hills. **On offer:** day and night game drives in open 4WD, birdwatching, Maasai cultural visits.
Rates: from US$300 full board per person sharing

In Namanga

Namanga River Lodge (cabins and camping) PO Box 4, Namanga
A rather jaded lodge, which serves reasonable **snacks**, next to the tree-lined river, with wooden cabins in the garden. Rooms have en-suite facilities and camping in the grounds has reasonable security.
Rates: from KSh3,000 B&B per person sharing; camping KSh300

There are several **curio stalls** en route between Kajiado and Namanga, selling Maasai beadwork and carvings, where you can also buy **snacks** and sodas. The largest, which have good **fast food**, are near Namanga where the shuttle buses stop, but they're generally very crowded.

What to see and do
Maasai Ostrich Farm
(Swimming pool) tel: 045 22505
About 17km from the Athi turn-off, the farm is signposted to the right, about 7km. Essentially a commercial operation – they supply the local market and produce delicious ostrich paté – visitors are given a tour of the farm. There's also the added (and comical) attraction of ostrich racing, normally on Sundays.
Entry KSh100

VOI AND THE MOMBASA ROAD
The main trunk road between Nairobi and Mombasa, the A109, descends from Nairobi to the coast (6-hour drive), for the most part running parallel to the railway line. Although tarmac, in sections it's badly rutted, not helped by the heavy haulage lorries which frequent the route. Leaving Nairobi, the scenery changes from the Athi and Kapiti plains and Mua Hills to cattle-ranching country around Salama, passing through Sultan Hamud (named in honour of the Sultan of Zanzibar as the railway reached here on his birthday) to the maize farms at Emali. The rounded, volcanic Chyulu Hills lie to the south and the road bisects the thick *Commiphora* bush country of Tsavo National Park, where lesser kudu are often seen at the roadside, to sisal estates and the Taita Hills at Voi. The road continues through the scrubland of the Taru Desert to the market town of Mariakani and the palm trees of the coastal hinterland to the port of Mombasa.

Getting there and away
If doing the journey in a day, leave early, as it gets very hot, and driving is tiring due to the amount of traffic and road conditions. Make sure you have plenty of fuel and be aware that there is no petrol between Voi and Mariakani. At Voi you can turn south to Taveta, while at Mariakani if heading to the north coast the C107 to Kaloleni is a good back route to Kilifi.

By bus
Akamba, Kenya Bus and Coast Bus operate a regular service between Nairobi and Mombasa via Voi, as do *matatus*. Voi's bus stand is near the market in the centre of town. There's also an excellent shuttle service operated by Veran Safaris (page 167) which will stop off en route by request. From Voi there is a bus service to Taveta on the Tanzanian border.

By train
Nairobi to Mombasa
The train stops at Voi twice daily, departing at 04.30 and 23.15 – but check times in advance. In addition there are occasional **steam specials**, see page 129.

Voi to Taveta
There's a spasmodic passenger service on Tuesday, Wednesday, Friday and Saturday, departing at 05.00. Do check that it's operating in advance.

Getting organised
It's best to get organised in Nairobi or Mombasa before leaving. In **Voi** town centre, there's a **bank** (no ATM), a **general store** for basic provisions and a lively **market**. In an emergency the **tourist helpline** is tel: 020 604767. There are a couple of **petrol stations**, one at the north junction with the Mombasa

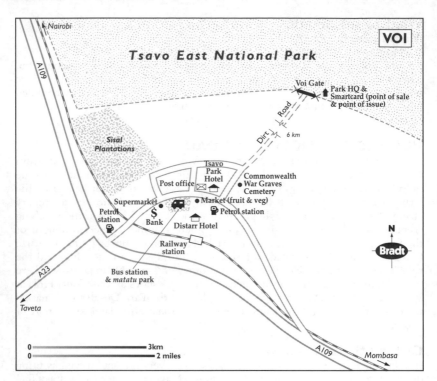

Highway and another opposite the turn-off to Tsavo East National Park's main gate.

Where to stay and eat

This section covers accommodation along the Mombasa road only, not those in the national parks and conservancies which are mentioned later in the chapter.

Kibwesi

Umani Springs Camp (8 tents) Book through Let's Go Travel, page 101

Coming from Nairobi, the turn-off is on the right just before the railway crossing at Kibwezi, from where it's a 10km drive (4WD recommended) on a rough lava track through thick bush, passing a lush, bright green swamp on the way to the camp. In the heart of the Kibwezi Forest Reserve, the camp is surrounded by a grove of newtonia and fig trees, overlooking Umani Spring which fills with water at certain times of the year. It's a particularly good area for birding with several walking trails from the camp. The tents, comfortably furnished, have en-suite showers and flush toilets. There's a central, wooden building with a rustic bar and dining area overlooking the spring. **On offer:** bird walks on 5km of trails and caving in the nearby Chyulu Hills.

Rates: from KSh6,600 full board per person sharing

Kiboko

Hunter's Lodge (20 rooms) PO Box 77, Makindu; tel: 045 22469 or book through Mada Holdings, Kimathi House, PO Box 40683, Nairobi; tel: 020 221438

Coming from Nairobi, the turn-off is on the right in a grove of yellow fever trees, just before Kiboko. Situated just off the main road, it's a good stopover point. The lodge, set in

a rundown tropical garden, has a faded colonial aura, and is rather empty of patronage. But the rooms, with en-suite bathrooms, are clean and the staff friendly.
Rates: from KSh1,500, B&B per person sharing
Tilapia Springs Restaurant (next to Hunter's Lodge)
Set in gardens with umbrella-shaded tables next to a pond, it gives a pleasant reprieve from driving. There's a reasonable menu serving good meals (KSh350) and snacks.
Open 06.30–23.00

Makindu

Sikh Temple PO Box 43, Makindu
In the centre of Makindu, the Sikh temple of the Guru Nanak faith complex is on the left if coming from Nairobi. It's a slice of little India. Drive through the entrance gates into the temple compound where there's safe parking. There is a variety of buildings – the temple, a dining hall and numerous rooms. The **dining hall** serves curries, dhal and chapatis (but no alcohol is permitted). The **rooms** are in housing blocks, and are simply furnished with en-suite bathrooms.
Rates: payment for meals and rooms is by donation

Mtito Andei

This is another good fuel stop, about halfway between Nairobi and Mombasa, with several petrol stations serving **fast food**. The best is on the left, next to the turn-off to the Tsavo Inn. Alternatively the **Tsavo Inn** has a **swimming pool** and **restaurant** in a garden setting.

Voi

Distarr Hotel Voi; tel: 043 30277
A friendly, small hotel near the bus station, with reasonable s/c rooms. There's a restaurant downstairs with basic meals from KSh200.
Rates: rooms from KSh400
Tsavo Park Hotel, PO Box 244, Voi; tel: 043 30050; email: tsavoh@africaonline.co.ke
Situated near the post office in the town centre, the en-suite rooms have fans and satellite TV. There's a restaurant serving European-style cuisine, and a disco below.
Rates: from US$22 B&B per person sharing
Ngutoni Lodge (48 rooms) Book through Kenya Game Sanctuaries, PO Box 83050, Mombasa; tel: 041 222532; email: kgs@wananchi.com
Located about 15km southeast of Voi, 5km off the main A109 highway on Ndara Ranch, the lodge is in a private 4,000ha game sanctuary which was a former sisal estate. It opened in 2002, and the rooms are comfortably furnished with en-suite shower rooms and private balconies, but there's no AC. The rooms are set in four 2-storey blocks on either side of the main lodge which has a large, airy lounge, bar and dining area overlooking a floodlit waterhole. The service and meals are good. Entry to the sanctuary is free and it has a good variety of game. **On offer:** birdwatching and escorted nature walks in the sanctuary, night drives and bush breakfasts, dinners and sundowners by arrangement.
Rates: from US$75 full board per person sharing

What to see and do

Apart from visiting the **national parks**, there's rock climbing at **Lukenya** near Athi River (contact the Mountain Club of Kenya, page 124), an interesting **Sikh temple** and the **Makindu Handicrafts Co-operative** at Makindu, a centre for the Akamba woodcarvers. The **Kibwezi Forest Reserve** (free entry) borders the road near Makindu, but the only organised trails are around Umani Springs (see page 206). There's a well-maintained **Commonwealth War Graves Cemetery** at Voi (near the turn-off to Tsavo East National Park), filled mainly with South Africans who fell during World War I. Otherwise, there's plenty of **local colour** on the way: shops and hotels en route have imaginative names which give light relief on the long journey – look out for Lady Diana's Guest House, Mount Kenya Hotel, Paris Restaurant, Soweto Complex, Wordlinks Coffin Parlour, Joyland Bar and Restaurant and Tea House of the August Moon. Three-legged Akamba stools, honey, live chickens, charcoal and fresh fruit are for sale at the roadside.

AMBOSELI, THE CHYULUS AND ENVIRONS
The greater Amboseli area includes the Amboseli and Chyulus national parks as well as large Maasai community-owned ranches, where wildlife and cattle co-exist, and wildlife sanctuaries like Kimana and Selenkay.

Amboseli
Getting there and away
The main route to Amboseli is from Nairobi via the good tarmac road to Namanga (240km) followed by the C103 to the **Meshanani gate** to **Amboseli National Park**, a dirt road which is in a fair condition, passing through thornbush country. The road continues through the park exiting at the **Kimana gate** to **Oloitokitok** (50km) at the foot of Mount Kilimanjaro, and continues on to the red soils of **Tsavo West National Park** (see page 214). The other route to Amboseli is via **Emali**, 228km from Nairobi on the A109 Mombasa road. From Emali it's about 65km on the C102, a dirt road to **Makutano** after which there's a road to the right to Amboseli National Park, entering at the **Eremito gate** (64km). Continuing on the C102, it's about 30km from Makutano to **Kimana**, but the road is atrocious when wet. It is recommended that you have 4WD.

By bus
There are infrequent *matatus* from Namanga to Oloitokitok, and from Emali, but no regular buses.

By air
There are scheduled services daily from Nairobi to Amboseli National Park. Remember to purchase a smartcard prior to flying; see page 41.

Getting organised
It's best to get organised in Nairobi or Mombasa. The lodges in Amboseli will change money, but at a poor rate, and there are limited supplies available to purchase on the way. In an emergency the **tourist helpline** is 020 604767. **Petrol** is available at the large lodges – Amboseli Serena and Ol Tukai. Be aware that a **smartcard** is required for Amboseli which *cannot* be issued at the park. For details see page 41.

Amboseli National Park
PO Box 18 Namanga; tel: 045 22251; fax: 045 22250.
Open 06.00–18.30; park entry fee US$30; smartcard required; vehicle KSh200
One of Kenya's most picturesque parks with its dominant backdrop of Mount Kilimanjaro on its southern boundary, Amboseli covers an area of 392km². It was the location for the films *Where No Vultures Fly* and *King Solomon's Mines*. Amboseli comes from the Maa word *em-posel* which means 'salty dust' and the park has swirling dust-devils during the dry season, especially in the Amboseli lake basin, a

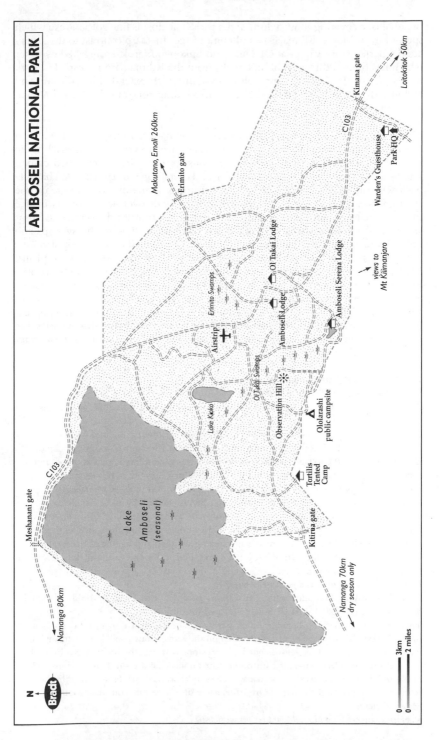

AMBOSELI NATIONAL PARK

seasonal lake covering about a third of the park. The dust is fine volcanic ash which spewed from Mount Kilimajaro a millennium ago. In sharp contrast to the aridity are the permanent swamps at Ol Tukai and Enkongo Narok, springs fed by water which has filtered through volcanic rocks from the Kilimanjaro ice cap. The park forms part of the Greater Amboseli ecosystem which extends for 3,000km² and includes the game dispersal areas in the surrounding communally owned Maasai group ranches.

Flora and fauna The park is famous for its elephant families, which have been studied by Drs Cynthia Moss and Joyce Poole for over 28 years, and superb birdlife (over 400 recorded species), including herons, egrets, bitterns, crowned cranes, kingfishers, secretary birds, plovers, African darters, Egytian geese, pale chanting goshawks and pygmy falcons. In season, flamingos sometimes congregate on the shallow lake. There's a good variety of wildlife, with over 45 mammals in five major habitats – open plains, acacia woodland, rocky thornbush country, swamps and marshland. Large herds of buffalo and elephant wallow in the swamps and often frequent the doum palm forests, while there's a resident hippo population at hippo pools and zebra, wildebeest and giraffe are commonly seen on the plains. Look out too for spotted hyena dens around Erimito. Less common are the fringe-eared oryx and gerenuk, normally found in the acacia woodland, and the spectacled elephant shrew. The park has a good network of well-maintained and signed roads, suitable for 2WD, but they can be impassable in the rains. Being small and popular it can get crowded during the high season. There are several **viewing circuits**, the best being around Observation Hill and the swamps. There's an **airstrip** about 15km from Ol Tukai Lodge.

Where to stay and eat
Within Amboseli National Park
Amboseli Serena Lodge (96 rooms; swimming pool) Book through Serena Hotels, page 91
The central part of the hotel faces on to a small waterhole where game and Maasai cattle come to water – which comes as a surprise – with Mount Kilimanjaro looming behind. Despite its aspect, the lodge is attractively designed using natural materials and does not appear as large as its room numbers might suggest. The rooms are in blocks in leafy gardens and, although on the small side, are delightful, with murals of animals. All are comfortably furnished with en-suite bathrooms. Service is friendly and efficient and the restaurant serves good-quality buffet-style meals with an excellent choice of food. A cosy bar with a veranda overlooks the waterhole where a minstrel strums his guitar in the evenings. The hotel has implemented ecotourism principles, and its tree plantation has attracted increased birdlife. **On offer:** game drives, bird walks, tree-planting, bush barbecue, Maasai dancing.
Rates: from US$125 full board per person sharing
Ol Tukai Lodge (80 rooms; cottage; swimming pool) PO Box 45403, 00100 Nairobi; tel: 020 444 5514; fax: 020 444 8493; email: oltukai@mitsuminet.com
This large lodge is set in pleasant grounds, with views of Mount Kilimanjaro, overlooking the Ol Tukai plains, where elephant are often on the move – but you'll also be treated to the minibus parade. Set in well-designed natural stone cottages, the rooms are comfortable and spacious, with large en-suite bathrooms. The public areas are similarly spacious and meals are of a good standard. New managers took over from Block Hotels in 2003 and have refurbishment plans for the lodge. **On offer:** game drives, lectures on Maasai culture, and Maasai dancing.
Rates: from around US$115 full board per person sharing

Amboseli Lodge (50 rooms, swimming pool) Book through Kilimanjaro Safari Club, PO Box 30139, Nairobi; tel: 020 338888; fax: 020 219982; email: ksc@africaonline.co.ke
Another large lodge set in pleasant gardens, very close to Ol Tukai Lodge, with views of Mount Kilimanjaro. Rooms are in bungalows and more modern bedroom blocks (preferable), with en-suite facilities. The lounge has a feature fireplace, food is fair and the staff friendly and helpful.
Rates: from US$90 full board per person sharing
Warden's Guest House (3 rooms, self-catering) tel: 045 22251 or book through KWS Tourism & Business Development, PO Box 40241; tel: 020 602345; email: tourism@kws.org
The cottage has views of mounts Kilimanjaro and Meru. Sleeping 4, there's a double and two single rooms and a bathroom. Linen, towels, cooking utensils and a gas cooker are provided, but you'll need to bring all provisions and drinks.
Rates: from KSh1,500 plus park and vehicle entrance fees

Outside the park
Ololarashi Public Campsite (camping only) Book through KWS, page 91
A basic campsite run by the Ololarashi group ranch, about 9km from Amboseli Serena Lodge, adjacent to Amboseli National Park. There's a water tap, long-drop toilets, shower and a small shop with a bar and pool table. The camping sites are well spaced out but there's limited shade. You're best to be completely self-sufficient. **On offer:** visits to a Maasai cultural boma.
Rates: from KSh300
Tortilis Tented Camp (17 tents; swimming pool) Book through Cheli & Peacock, page 90
Dwarfed in the lea of Mount Kilimanjaro, Tortilis is an ecolodge (winner of several international awards) on a group ranch bordering Amboseli National Park. A beautifully designed permanent tented camp in a natural setting, the tents are on raised concrete platforms under a thatched roof, with king-size beds, en-suite shower rooms (flush toilets) and a private veranda with day beds and views of the mountain. The open-plan bar and dining-room are on a small hill (quite steep) and Italian-influenced cuisine is a speciality. **On offer:** 4WD game drives in open vehicles (excellent driver-guides) to Amboseli National Park, authentic cultural visits to Maasai *manyattas*, massage, shop supporting Maasai beadwork project.
Rates: from US$260 full board per person sharing
Ol Kanjau (5 tents) Book through Bush Homes of East Africa, page 90
This is a delightful, private, traditional, seasonal bush camp sited among the *Acacia tortilis* trees which inspired Ernest Hemingway's book, *Snows of Kilimanjaro*. It's an area still frequented by elephants. Located on the Kisongo Maasai group ranch, the camp is adjacent to Amboseli National Park. The tents are spacious and comfortable with private showers and toilets. Lighting is by hurricane lamp and meals wholesome. In the tranquility you can 'try to count a million stars'. **On offer:** elephant watching with ecologists Mike and Judy Rainy, game drives and bush walks with Maasai guides.
Rates: from US$345 full board per person sharing
Porini Camp (6 tents) Book through Gamewatchers Safaris, PO Box 388, Village Market, 00621 Nairobi, tel: 020 523129; fax: 020 520864; email: info@gamewatchers.co.ke; web: www.porini.com/gamewatchers
Set in the private, 6,000ha Selenkay Conservancy – an ecotourism project to protect this game dispersal area and to give an alternative income to the Maasai landlords – surrounded by the 81,000ha Eselenkai group ranch and adjacent to Amboseli National Park, this is a traditional bush camp set in a shady Acacia grove, where you awake to a cacophany of francolin. The tents are spacious, simply furnished with a double and single bed, en-suite showers and flush toilets. **On offer:** 4WD game drives and excellent night game drives (with a good chance of seeing caracal and wildcat) in open-sided vehicles with an awning,

visits to Amboseli National Park, entertaining walks with the Maasai, picnic lunches in a tree platform, visits to Maasai homesteads and sundowners overlooking Kilimanjaro. The Amboseli airstrip is about an hour's drive from camp.

Rates: from US$415 for 2 nights full board inclusive of transport from Nairobi, drinks and park fees, with set departures, Mondays and Thursdays

Kimana Zebra Lodge (20 rooms) book through African Safari Club, PO Box 81443, Mombasa; tel: 041 485520; fax: 041 485994; email: info@africansafariclub.com; web: www.africansafariclub.com

Set on the banks of the Kimana River in the 40km² private Kilimanjaro-Kimana Game Sanctuary, an important game dispersal area for Amboseli, surrounded by the Maasai Kimana Tikondo group ranch, there is varied plains game, with large herds of buffalo and elephant and superb views of Mount Kilimanjaro. Rooms are in individual wooden lodges with private verandas, twin beds, en-suite shower rooms and flush toilets. There's a Hemingway Bar and barbecue meals are often taken around the camp fire. The lodge and sanctuary are exclusive to African Safari Club's guests. **On offer:** game drives. There is a private airstrip at Kimana.

Rates: a 2-night excursion from US$515 per person

Chyulu Hills National Park
Open 06.00–18.30; Park entry fee US$15; vehicle KSh200.

A volcanic mountain range, the Chyulus were given park status in 1983. Running parallel to the Mombasa highway between Kibwesi and Tsavo, they have distinctive rounded hills, and volcanic vents, interspersed by black lava flows. Access is via **Kidapo gate** near Kibwezi and **Chyulu gate** from Tsavo West National Park. Considered to be Kenya's 'youngest' hills, less than 500 years old, the road crosses the lava flow which has scant vegetation and brittle boulders full of air bubbles. You can walk on the lava, but beware of disturbing snakes. There are small herds of impala and eland among the rocky outcrops. An alternative to driving is **walking safaris,** with fly-camping, and **caving** in the park (see pages 00 and 00). The Leviathan Cave has the world's fourth longest lava tube system with 12.5km of mapped passages, some requiring rope and ladder work.

There are a couple of **campsites** in the park, but you'll need to be self-sufficient.

Rates: from US$8 plus park and vehicle entry fees

Where to stay and eat
Outside the park
Ol Donyo Wuas (7 rooms) Book through Richard Bonham Safaris, page 102

An international award-winning ecolodge perched on the rounded, volcanic, Chyulu Hills, on the 120,000ha Mbirikani group ranch, overlooking acacia woodland to open savanna, interspersed with rocky outcrops, to Mount Kilimanjaro. The stone-built lodge has a homely atmosphere with a sitting-room and dining area (food is imaginative and plentiful), a telescope for game watching on the plains, and stargazing. Rooms are spread out on the compound (watch out for elephant at night); some are open while others have plate-glass windows. All have private verandas, en-suite showers and flush 'loos with a view'. **On offer:** 4WD game drives in open vehicles, guided bush walks, picnics, sundowners on Nongiyiaa *kopje* to see the sun setting on Kilimanjaro (highly recommended), horseriding and Maasai *manyatta* and school visits. There is a private airstrip about 5km from the lodge.

Kampi ya Kanzi (6 cottages and 1 suite) PO Box 236 Mtito Adei; tel: 045 22516; email: lucasaf@africaonline.co.ke; web: www.campyakanzi.com; or book through Private Wilderness, page 91

Set in a Maasai group ranch (1,000km²) in the Chyulu Hills, this is a joint venture between the Maasai community and Luca and Antonella Belpietro. The camp, a cluster of thatched cottages, centres on Tembo House, which has an open-plan sitting- and dining-room with panoramic vistas to Mount Kilimanjaro and the Tsavo Hills. Meals have a distinctly Italian flair, conjured from an organic garden, with home-made pastas and delicious ice-cream. The rooms are spacious with Italian linen and en-suite bathrooms, 'eco' flush toilets, showers and bidets. **On offer:** game drives in open 4WD vehicles with professional guides, escorted game and forest walks, birdwatching (400 species on the ranch), bush breakfasts and dinners; visits to Maasai villages and Chyulu National Park excursions; air excursions around Mount Kilimanjaro.

Rates: rooms from US$370 full board per person sharing; suite US$450 full board per person sharing

Oloitokitok
Where to stay and eat
Kibo Slopes Cottages (5 rooms, 2 cottages; catered and self-catering options) PO Box 218, Oloitokitok; tel: 045 22091; fax: 045 22153; email: kibocot@nbnet.co.ke; or book through Kibo Slopes Safaris, PO Box 58064, Nairobi; tel: 020 717373; fax: 020 716028; email: info@kiboslopessafaris.com; web: www.kiboslopessafaris.com
Surrounded by a coffee estate, with views of Mount Kilimanjaro, the main building has 5 s/c rooms, a restaurant (wholesome food) and bar with a veranda set in a 4-acre garden. The cottages have 2 separate apartments, each with 2 bedrooms (sleep 4) with a sitting room, shower, flush toilet and electricity. The cottages are primarily used as a base for Kilimanjaro climbs. **On offer:** climbing Kilimanjaro, day walks on the lower slopes of Kilimanjaro (in Kenya) and excursions to Amboseli National Park.
Rates: from US$25 B&B per person sharing; self-catering US$60 per cottage.

What to see and do
Climbing Kilimanjaro
The **Rongai route** is the only ascent of Mount Kilimanjaro (in Tanzania) from the Kenya side. Climbs can be organised through Kibo Slopes Safaris, based at Oloitokitok, 4km from the customs post at Rongai, before proceeding with the climb in Tanzania.

Kibo Slopes Safaris PO Box 58064, Nairobi; tel: 020 717373; fax: 020 716028; email: info@kiboslopessafaris.com; web: www. kiboslopessafaris.com

Taveta
Where to stay and eat
Lake Chala Lodge Book through Let's Go Travel, page 101
A large lodge sited on the rim of the small crater lake of Chala (about 3km across) which borders Tanzania.
Rates: from US$40 half board per person sharing

What to see and do
Visits to lakes Jipe and Chala
Be aware there is no public transport to the lakes and opportunities for hitching are limited. From the A23 Voi–Taveta road, the turn-off to **Lake Chala** is to the north, about 5km before the town of Taveta, (situated on an ancient trade route and around which there were numerous skirmishes during World War I) from which it's about 5km to the lake. The crater wall is steep, but it's possible to walk down to the lake. Beware of swimming, as a person was taken by a crocodile in 2002. For **Lake Jipe**, the turn-off to the south is about 8km before Taveta, signposted to Lake Jipe Safari Lodge. Follow the track through the Jipe Sisal Estate, passing **Grogan's Castle** on the right – a 1930s house now in a dilapidated state,

built by Ewart Grogan of Cape to Cairo fame (he walked the distance) – for about 25km to the lakeshore; alternatively, the southern part of the lake is within Tsavo West National Park. The lake has a myriad of waterfowl, hippo and crocodiles, with beautiful views to the Pare Mountains and Kilimanjaro in Tanzania.

TSAVO EAST AND WEST

Tsavo East and West national parks are bisected by the A109 Mombasa Highway and account for Kenya's single largest protected area for wildlife. *Tsavo* means 'place of slaughter' in the Akamba language, a reference to early years when the Maasai, who were renowned for taking no prisoners, launched periodic cattle raids on the Akamba tribe. It's an equally apt description for the 'white gold rush', when Akamba and Waliangulu elephant hunters, traditionally armed with poisoned arrows, were joined by Somali poachers with AK47s and from 1975 to 1991 massacred Tsavo's elephant herds, reducing their population from 35,000 to 4,000. Since the CITES ban on ivory sales (see box, page 47), elephant numbers have increased in Tsavo and now stand at around 8,000.

Tsavo West
Getting there and away
The main entrance and park headquarters is at the **Mtito Andei gate** accessed directly from the A109 Mombasa Highway at Mtito Andei. If coming from Amboseli National Park on the C103, you'll need to drive in convoy or have an armed ranger escort from Kimana gate. Check departure times beforehand, as it's preferable to be in a convoy if you already have a fully laden vehicle. (This is a precautionary measure as there have not been any incidents for several years.) The C103 enters Tsavo West at the **Chyulu gate**. Other access points are **Tsavo gate**, off the Mombasa Highway, **Maktau gate** from Voi/Taita, exiting to Taveta at **Mbuyuni gate** and the rarely used **Kasigau gate** from the Taitas. A 4WD is recommended.

By bus
See under Voi section, page 205.

By air
There are no scheduled flights to Tsavo West, but there are airstrips at Kamboyo (near Mtito Andei), Kilaguni, Tsavo Gate and Maktau. However, East African Air Charters runs a scheduled service three times a week to Finch Hatton's airstrip, about 20km from the park.

Getting organised
It's best to get organised in Nairobi or Mombasa. The lodges in Tsavo will **change money**, but at a poor rate, and there are limited places to purchase supplies on the way. In an emergency the **tourist helpline** is tel: 020 604767. **Petrol** is available at the large lodges – Kilaguni and Ngulia. Tsavo West National Park requires a **smartcard**. The Tsavo East park headquarters is at Voi, the nearest point for issuing and loading smartcards. For details see page 41.

Tsavo West National Park
PO Box 71, Mtito Andei; tel: 045 22455
*Open 06.00–18.30; park entry fee US$30 – **smartcard required** (the nearest POI and POS are at Tsavo East National Park headquarters at Voi) – vehicle KSh200*
More developed than Tsavo East, Tsavo West is slightly smaller (9,000km²) and has more varied topography. It is dominated by brick-red soils and thick *Acacia*

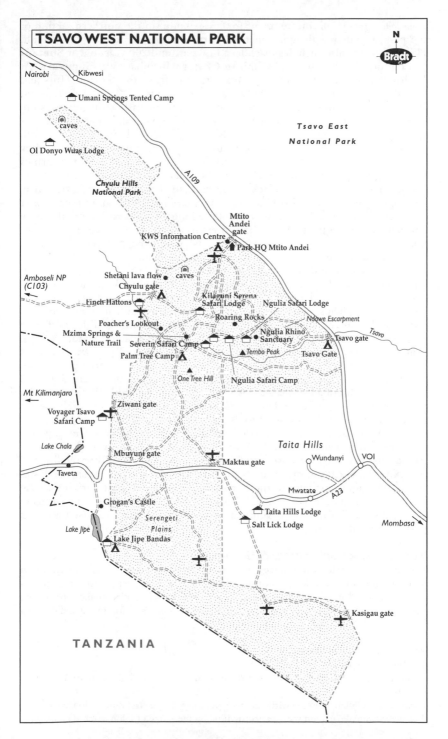

TSAVO WEST NATIONAL PARK

N

Bradt

Nairobi

Kibwesi

Umani Springs Tented Camp

caves

Ol Donyo Wuas Lodge

**Chyulu Hills
National Park**

*Tsavo East
National Park*

A109

Mtito
Andei
gate

KWS Information Centre

Park HQ Mtito Andei

Amboseli NP
(C103)

Shetani lava flow   caves

Chyulu gate

Finch Hattons

Kilaguni Serena
Safari Lodge   Ngulia Safari Lodge

Poacher's Lookout

Roaring Rocks

Ndawe Escarpment

Mzima Springs &
Nature Trail

Severin Safari Camp

Ngulia Rhino
Sanctuary

Tsavo gate

Tsavo

Palm Tree Camp

▲ Tembo Peak   Tsavo Gate

▲ One Tree Hill

Ngulia Safari Camp

Mt Kilimanjaro

Ziwani gate

Voyager Tsavo
Safari Camp

Taita Hills

Lake Chala

Mbuyuni gate

Wundanyi

VOI

Taveta

Maktau gate

Mwatate   A23

Mombasa

Grogan's Castle

*Serengeti
Plains*

Taita Hills Lodge

Salt Lick Lodge

Lake Jipe

Lake Jipe Bandas

Kasigau gate

TANZANIA

commiphora bush, a favourite haunt for lesser kudu, in the northern section of the park, together with more open thorntree country bordering the Chyulu Hills. This area also includes black lava flows around 200 years old at **Shetani** (means 'devil' in Swahili) and **Chaimu Crater** which have **walking trails**. At **Mzima Springs**, fed by underground streams from the Chyulu Hills and providing Mombasa's water supply, there are stands of *Raphia farinifera* and *Phoenix reclinata* palms. Here, there's another **nature trail**, with an interesting collection of natural trees and shrubs, with labels giving their names and uses (such as *Salvadora persica*, the 'toothbrush tree') leading down a concrete path frequented by cheeky vervet monkeys to an **underwater viewing chamber** where, if you're lucky, you'll be able to watch hippo. Not far from the springs is the **Ngulia Rhino Sanctuary,** open between 16.00 and 18.00. Covering 75km² there are around 50 black rhino contained within the electric fence, although they are not readily seen. The sanctuary has played an important part in rhino conservation; see box, page 48. Along the **Tsavo River**, the only permanent river in the park, riverine forest has large *Acacia elatior* trees, whose pods are a favourite delicacy for elephants, while the **Ngulia** Mountains, ancient metamorphic rocks, rise steeply from the plains with naked rockfaces rising to 1,800m and densely wooded lower slopes. Here you can go **trekking** with a ranger, while there's **rock climbing** on Tembo peak further along the ridge. In the west, and south of the river, open savanna – Tsavo's Serengeti – has plenty of plain's game, leading on to **Lake Jipe** with its reed beds and swamps. The park's diverse habitats give rise to prolific birdlife, with 600 species recorded, and a good variety of wildlife – buffalo, leopard, cheetah, lion, reedbuck, bushbuck and gazelle – but Tsavo (West and East) is particularly renowned for its elephant herds. Being such a large park, game viewing is at its best during the dry season, when the animals are drawn to water, although not all animals are water dependent – the dik dik, lesser kudu, gerenuk, oryx, giraffe and Grant's gazelle gain most of their water requirements from grazing and browsing.

Within the park, there are several **viewpoints** where you can have a picnic and enjoy the scenery. The best are **Poachers' Lookout** with views of Amboseli and Kilimanjaro, **Roaring Rocks**, with views over Rhino Valley and the **Ndawe Escarpment** near Ngulia Lodge, which has extensive vistas across the rhino sanctuary to the Yatta Plateau in Tsavo East. Driving in the park, the circuits are not always clearly signed, and even the map can be confusing, so if planning to venture away from the main tourist traps, it's pertinent to take a ranger.

KWS Information Centre, Mtito Andei

Located at the **Mtito Andei gate**, the visitor information centre has displays about wildlife and environmental conservation, as well as explaining the park's geological, flora and fauna attractions. Animal skulls and pickled snakes are among the exhibits. It's particularly targeted at school and conservation groups. There's a small shop selling KWS wares and sodas.

Where to stay and eat
Within the park
Kilaguni Serena Safari Lodge (51 rooms; swimming pool) Book through Serena Hotels, page 91
Located about 20km from the Mtito Andei gate, this was the first Kenyan lodge to be built in a national park and was opened in 1962 by the Duke of Gloucester. The lodge

has stood the test of time, a testimony to the estate agent's maxim, 'location, location, location'. It has superb open views to the conical Chyulu Hills and Mount Kilimanjaro, with a large waterhole which draws herds of buffalo, elephant and impala from the dry acacia bushlands. The lodge is well placed for visits to Tsavo West's main attractions. The central building has a spacious reception and dining area with lofty ceilings and there's a narrow, shaded viewing deck for watching wildlife at the waterhole. There's friendly service and good buffet meals. The rooms are in blocks on either side, most facing on to the waterhole. They underwent major refurbishment in 2002 and are comfortably furnished with en-suite shower rooms. **On offer:** game drives, bush walks with a resident naturalist, beauty therapy, shop. Fuel is available at the lodge and the airstrip is nearby.

Rates: from US$125 full board per person sharing

Ngulia Safari Camp (6 bandas, self-catering) Book through Let's Go Travel, page 101 Located 56km from Mtito Andei gate and 48km from the Tsavo River gate, the camp is situated on the northern face of Ngulia Mountain with panoramic views overlooking a waterhole and the Ngulia Valley. The bandas have one bedroom (sleeping 3) with bedding provided (bring sheets and towels), a bathroom with shower (no hot water) and flush toilet, a veranda with table and chairs and a kitchenette with a double-ring gas cooker and utensils. Lighting is by gas wall-lamps and kerosene lamps. You'll need to be self-sufficient and don't forget matches, toilet paper and a cool box.

Rates: from KSh2,500 per banda

Ngulia Safari Lodge (52 rooms, swimming pool) PO Box 42, Voi; tel: 043 3009; fax: 043 30006; email: ngulialodge@kenya-safari.co.ke Perched on the edge of the Ndawe escarpment, the lodge has sweeping views over the Tsavo plains. There are several bars and a buffet service for all meals. The rooms are in a 2-storey block to the side of the main lodge. All have en-suite bathrooms and a private balcony overlooking a floodlit waterhole. **On offer:** leopard bait each evening, floodlit waterhole, a bird-ringing project during November and December monitoring migratory birds, game drives.

Rates: from US$100 full board per person sharing

Severin Safari Camp (20 tents) Book through Jahazi Marine, PO Box 82169, Mombasa; tel: 041 487365; fax: 041 485212; email: severin@severin-sea-lodge.com; web: www.severin-sea-lodge.com Located about 49km from Mtito Andei, this permanent tented camp has a peaceful setting near the Tsavo River. The main building has a good restaurant and 'thorn-tree' bar, with a camp fire each evening. The tented rooms are under thatch, with octagonal-shaped tents, with views across a waterhole to Mount Kilimajaro. Each tent has en-suite shower rooms and flush toilets. **On offer:** game drives, sundowners at Poacher's lookout, birdwatching and visits to the rhino sanctuary. There is an airstrip nearby.

Rates: from US$120 full board per person sharing

Lake Jipe Bandas (3 bandas) Tsavo West National Park, PO Box 71, Mtito Andei; tel: 045 22455 or book through KWS in Nairobi, page 91 Very basic bandas sleeping 5 on the lake shore. The kitchen has no utensils, so you'll need to be completely kitted out for camping. Camping is normally permitted here, but ask first.

Rates: from US$8 plus park and vehicle entry fees

Tsavo West National Park campsites (camping only) Tsavo West National Park, PO Box 71, Mtito Andei; tel: 045 22455 or book through KWS in Nairobi, page 91 There are basic campsites at Mtito Andei, Chyulu and Tsavo gates and several special campsites within the park with no facilities, so you'll need to be self-sufficient. Palm Tree Camp near One Tree Hill (ask for directions at the gate) is considered to be one of the best.

Rates: from US$8 plus park and vehicle entry fees

Outside the park

Finch Hatton's (35 tents, swimming pool) Book through Future Hotels, PO Box 24423, Nairobi; tel: 020 604321; fax: 020 604323; email: finchhattons@iconnect.co.ke
Inspired by Denys Finch Hatton, the eccentric, romantic Englishman immortalised as Karen Blixen's lover in *Out of Africa*, the camp provides Mozart and crystal in the bush. It's more aptly described as a tented hotel, with 5-star luxury. The main building has a dining-room (complete with chandelier and fine china) while the sitting-room has comfortable sofas and fine prints and photographs from the Finch Hatton era. There's a small library with Mozart's clarinet concerto playing in the background (but not on a wind-up gramophone). The food (cordon bleu) and service are excellent. A terrace overlooks a hippo pool, with views to Mount Kilimanjaro. The tents, shaded by acacia trees, are under thatch, set on wooden platforms with a small veranda facing on to a spring where hippo wallow and kingfishers dive. All are comfortably furnished with en-suite shower rooms and flush toilets. In addition a minibar, electric shaver sockets and hair-dryers are provided. The camp is not suitable for children, and guests are required to dress for dinner (no shorts). **On offer:** Game drives and bush walks. There is an airstrip nearby.
Rates: from US$185 full board per person sharing. No children.
Voyager Tsavo Safari Camp (25 tents) Book through Heritage Hotels, page 91
Located just outside Tsavo West National Park in the lea of Mount Kilimanjaro, this permanent tented camp is on the edge of a small dam surrounded by yellow fever trees. The tents, situated quite close together, are comfortably furnished, with en-suite shower rooms and flush toilets with verandas overlooking the river and surrounding bush gardens. The bar and dining-room are made from natural timber and there's table d'hôte cuisine and friendly service. **On offer:** day and night game drives (where you can see hippo grazing at night), nature walks, birdwatching, Akamba and Maasai dancing, cultural and wildlife talks, excursions to Grogan's castle.
Rates: from US$125 full board per person sharing

Tsavo East
Getting there and away

The main gate and park headquarters are at **Voi**, but the park can also be accessed through **Mtito Andei**, **Manyani** and **Buchuma gates** off the A109 Mombasa Highway. Alternatively, if coming from Malindi, entry is via **Sala gate** on the C103, a good dirt road. A 4WD is recommended.

By bus
See under Voi section, page 205.

By air
There are no scheduled flights to Tsavo East, but the park has four graded airstrips.

Getting organised
It's best to get organised in Nairobi or Mombasa. The lodges in Tsavo East will **change money**, but at a poor rate, and there are limited places to purchase supplies on the way. In an emergency the **tourist helpline** is tel: 020 604767. **Petrol** is available at Voi Safari Lodge. Tsavo East National Park requires a **smartcard**. The park headquarters is at Voi, a point for issuing and loading smartcards. For details see page 41.

Tsavo East National Park
PO Box 14, Voi; tel: 043 22228; fax: 043 30034
*Open 06.00–18.30; park entry fee US$30 – **smartcard required** (the nearest POI and POS are at Tsavo East National Park headquarters at Voi) – vehicle KSh200*

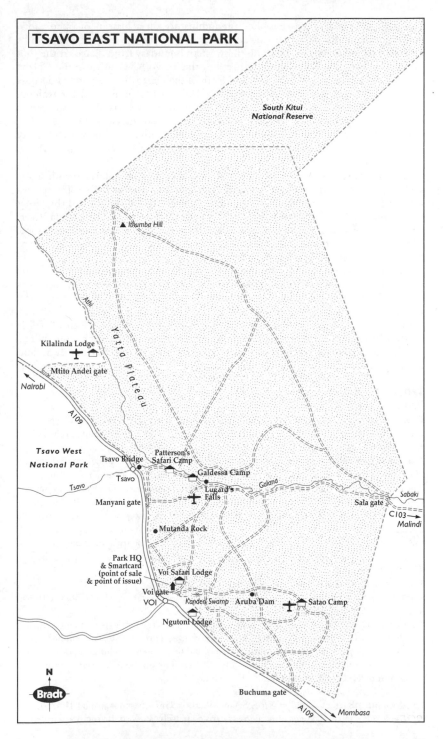

TSAVO EAST NATIONAL PARK

Covering 12,000ha, Tsavo East lies predominantly on a plateau of open thorn country with scattered rocky outcrops. The Yatta Plateau, one of the world's longest lava flows, runs north along the western boundary from Tsavo, at the foot of which is the Athi River which joins with the Tsavo River to form the Galana flowing through the park to the coast. North of the Galana is a remote wilderness area with dense *Acacia commiphora* woodland which is mainly used for walking safaris traversing the seasonal Tiva River. Closed for many years, the northern part of the park reopened to the public in 2002, but its road infrastructure is limited. The southern part of the park is the most accessible, with a good network of dusty tracks (4WD recommended) away from the C103 which follows the Galana River.

Flora and fauna Swathes of bushy grassland and open plains alternate with semi-arid acacia scrub and woodlands, giving rise to varied **birdlife** (500 species recorded) such as saddle-billed stork, martial eagle, African finfoot and the violet wood hoopoe. Among the **wildlife**, there are plenty of hippo in the Galana River, and occasionally seen are small herds of the rare and endangered Hirola antelope. More common are the 'red elephants' – not a separate species – their colour due to having dust baths in the brick-red earth.

For the most part, being flat, dry and arid, the most interesting and scenic part of the park is to follow the **Galana River**, with its smooth grey boulders and sandy banks fringed by doum palms and *Acacia elatior* trees. At **Lugard's Falls** the river plunges down a series of falls where interesting curved rock formations have been carved by water erosion over the years. North of Voi is **Mutanda rock** from where there are good views across the park, and there's usually a concentration of game and birdlife around the **Aruba dam** and **Kanderi swamp** east of Voi.

Where to stay and eat
Within the park
Galdessa (8 bandas) Book through Exclusive Classic Properties, PO Box 714, Village Market, Nairobi; tel: 020 521074; fax: 020 521099; email: galdessa@swiftkenya.com; web: www.galdessa.com
A delightful, airy bush camp on the banks of the Galana River, spread under doum palms, 15km upstream from Lugard's Falls, with expansive views of the river and Yatta Plateau. The camp is actively involved in rhino conservation within the park. The bandas are semi-tented thatched bungalows on wooden platforms, sited well apart for privacy. Rooms are spacious, and simply yet artistically furnished, with en-suite shower rooms (safari showers), flush toilets and solar heating. A couple have private sitting-rooms. There's a large thatched mess area with a pitched roof where you can relax on comfortable sofas and dine on gourmet meals. **On offer:** bush walks with professional guides, day and night game drives. There's an airstrip near the camp.
Rates: from US$340 full board per person sharing. Closed May.
Patterson's Safari Camp (20 tents) PO Box 34105, Mombasa; tel: 041 471738; fax: 041 471752; email: pattersons@iconnect.co.ke
Located 8km from the Manyani gate, on the Athi River, this is a rustic, permanent tented camp named after Colonel Patterson of *Man-eaters of Tsavo* fame. The tents are under thatch, with simple furnishings, en-suite showers and flush toilets. Lighting is powered by a generator set away from the main camp. There's a separate dining tent serving buffet-style meals. **On offer:** Game viewing and bird watching.
Rates: from US$75 full board per person sharing
Satao Camp (18 tents) Southern Cross Safaris, PO Box 95671, Mombasa; tel: 041 475074; fax: 041 471257; email: sales@southerncrosssafaris.com; web: www.southerncrosssafaris.com

THE LIONS OF TSAVO AND TAITA
Man-eaters of Tsavo
Notorious during the building of the Uganda railway were a couple of man-eating lions that caused havoc when the railway line reached the Tsavo area in 1898. Their territory was an 80-mile stretch between Voi and Kima and their prey the railway workers, mostly Indian 'coolie' labour who had been imported to construct the railway. The lions would attack at night, dragging their screaming victims into the bush. Terrified, some 500 railway workers fled to the coast, while others indignantly told the government that they had come to work on the railway, not to supply food for lions or devils. Some 28 railway workers fell victim to the lions, and it's likely that around 100 Africans died too. Lieutenant Colonel John Henry Patterson, the chief railway engineer in charge of constructing the Tsavo bridge at the time, was inveigled into dealing with the lion problem. Several nights he had a lonely vigil, almost falling prey himself when he nodded off, before he successfully shot one of the lions. It was found that the lion was in pain from a broken tooth, which might have made it impossible to hunt normally, hence resorting to soft targets. This is the most likely reason it became a man-eater, but another theory suggested that lions became used to eating human flesh after a severe famine in the Taitas between 1880–90, which only a third of the population survived. Patterson shot the second lion three weeks later, bringing an end to the man-eating incidents. His book, *The Man-eaters of Tsavo*, describes his hunting forays and the building of the railway. The two lions are exhibited at the Field Museum of Natural History in Chicago.

Tsavo's maneless lions
Today, Tsavo's lions have a reputation for being bald and belligerent. Adult males are noted for having poorly developed manes. Why this should be is not known, and it's the subject of a research project being undertaken by Dr Bruce Patterson (no relation to Lt Col Patterson). Theories abound – it may be due to the dense *Commiphora* thornbush which covers vast areas in Tsavo, where thorns tangle and tug out the mane, resulting in these lions physiologically adapting to the environment by becoming maneless; another theory suggests their scraggy manes are due to high testosterone levels leading to baldness. Photographs of Tsavo lions are being used to aid the research which is based at Taita Discovery Centre.

Located about 45km from the Bachuma and Voi gates, near the Kenyan national grid, the camp is well-spaced out among tamarind trees and has excellent game viewing at the waterhole. It's a popular excursion from the coast. The tents are comfortable with good-sized verandas and spacious en-suite shower rooms and flush toilets. There are family tents (sleeping 4) and 2 suites. Friendly staff serve buffet-style meals on a terrace built around a tree. The waterhole is floodlit, but when water levels are low the game is difficult to see, so the best viewing is from the tree platform. Lions sometimes come to drink at night, and there are plenty of elephants and impala during the day. **On offer:** Game viewing and birdwatching. There's an airstrip nearby.

Rates: from US$85 full board per person sharing
Voi Safari Lodge (53 rooms; swimming pool) PO Box 565, Voi; tel: 043 30019; fax: 043 30080; email: voilodge@kenya-safari.co.ke

Located close to the Voi gate, this is a large lodge sited on a rocky hillside with good views of waterholes and the Tsavo plains below. It's a convenient place to stay if you wish to see the orphan elephants raised by the David Sheldrick Wildlife Trust which can be visited at their *boma* nearby in the early morning and evening. There's buffet dining and rooms are comfortable with en-suite bathrooms. The swimming pool is at the edge of a cliff and there's a viewing hide for photographers and an underground tunnel for game viewing. **On offer:** visits to the orphan elephants, game drives and birdwatching.
Rates: from US$100 full board per person sharing

Outside the park
Kilalinda (6 cottages; swimming pool) Book through Private Wilderness, page 91. web: www.kilalinda.com
Kilalinda has a delightful setting on the Athi River, and is reached via Tsavo East's Mtito Andei gate (driving through dry thornbush country interspersed with huge baobab trees, about 29km, and a few tsetse flies), although the lodge is outside the park in a private conservancy. There's a central thatched split-level dining-room, sitting-room and bar, with a good book selection, overlooking a small swimming pool, well-watered gardens and the river. A wooden deck is ideal for alfresco breakfasts and sundowners. Meals are homely – delicious with fresh garden produce. The cottages are well spaced out along the riverfront. Each has four-poster beds, tiled bathrooms with showers and flush toilets and a spacious private veranda. One larger cottage, the Twiga suite, has a private jacuzzi and plunge pool. There's superb birdlife and a team of banded mongoose and genet cats come to be fed at the dining-room. A special attraction are 'star baths' – his and hers full-length Victorian-style baths in a private *boma* where you can wallow in bubbles (drink bubbles if you wish) and star-gaze through the steam. **On offer:** game viewing in open 4WD vehicles (game is shy, but dams were in the process of being built in 2002 so this will undoubtedly change), walking with a professional guide, river rafting, sundowners in a treehouse and river fishing. There is an airstrip 2km from the lodge.
Rates: from US$350 full board per person sharing (suite US$400); conservation fee US$20

TAITA HILLS AND ENVIRONS
Although off the main safari circuits focusing on Tsavo, the Taita area is interesting to visit and readily accessible from Voi.

Getting there and away
By bus
There are buses from Voi to Mwatate on the Taveta A23 road, but if going to Wundanyi, you're best taking a *matatu* from Voi. They leave morning and afternoon. If going to the Rukinga Wildlife Sanctuary, Taita Discovery Centre provides transport by arrangement from Nairobi and Voi.

By air
There are airstrips at Taita Hills Game Sanctuary, Rukinga Wildlife Sanctuary and Taita ranch, but no scheduled services.

Taita Hills
Take the A23 from Voi and turn right at the Mwatate junction on to the C104 to the district capital at Wunanyi, about 15km. The Taita Hills form the northern extreme of the Eastern Arc mountain range which stretches from the Usambaras in Tanzania. Rising from the Taita/Taveta plains, the hillsides are intensely cultivated by the Taita people, but still contain small remnants of the **cloud**

forests which once covered the mountains. The area is recognised as an important centre for **biological diversity** – Classon's aloe and the Taita white eye are endemic – and there are over 450 forest species of vascular plants. The hills also have interesting **archaeological sites**. In days past, the Taita inhabited rock shelters and there is still evidence of their burial cairns and ancestral shrines of human skulls which were stored in the caves. One cave can be visited from Wunyanyi, about 1km out of town. Ask for directions or a guide locally.

Taita Hills Game Sanctuary
Where to stay and eat
Salt Lick Safari Lodge (64 rooms, swimming pool) PO Box 30624, 00100 Nairobi; tel: 043 30270; fax: 043 30007; email: info@saltlicklodge.com; web: www.saltlicklodge.com. Book through Hilton Hotels.
Built on stilts and linked by walkways under which elephant can walk, the lodge stands out with its strange architecture resembling double-storey rondavels. Set in a private, 11,000ha sanctuary (owned by Hilton Hotels) to the southwest of Tsavo West National Park, it's surrounded by rolling savanna and rocky outcrops. Game viewing is good, with similar species to Tsavo, such as buffalo, impala and lesser kudu. All rooms have AC and en-suite bathrooms, and the facilities you'd expect of a large hotel. Accommodation in the sanctuary is also available at **Taita Hills Safari Lodge** (60 rooms, swimming pool, 9-hole golf course, tennis courts) and built like a German fortress, for the same price. **On offer:** game drives in the sanctuary, sporting facilities, health club, shop.
Rates: from US$165 full board per person sharing. No children under 5.

Rukinga Wildlife Sanctuary and Taita Discovery Centre
Turn off the A109 about 6km from Maungu at the Mombasa 122km post. There's a sign to Rukinga Ranch. Sign in at the barrier and get clear directions to Taita Discovery Centre (TDC), about 8km. Initiated as a research base where foreign visitors and local Kenyans can participate in environmental, conservation and community projects, TDC is located in the 28,300ha Rukinga Wildlife Sanctuary and also has access to the neighbouring 40,500ha Taita ranch. These two ranches are in the Tsavo Kasigau wildlife corridor, a major migratory route for elephants crossing the Taru Desert from the Galana River to Mount Kilimanjaro. The centre works in close association with conservation bodies such as Kenya Wildlife Service, African Wildlife Foundation and the Earthwatch Institute who pursue field studies research. It also caters for school and university field trips, individuals pursuing their own line of academic research, gap-year students and volunteers. The centre has a fascinating field science laboratory with displays of specimens, such as beetles and butterflies, which are sent to the National Museums of Kenya, and a couple of lecture rooms with exhibits about the area and field study work in progress – research into the maneless lions of Tsavo, archaeology in the Taitas and elephant monitoring are ongoing.

Where to stay and eat
Galla Camp (6 tents) Book through Savannah Camps and Lodges, page 91
Located on the 44,500ha Taita ranch (a working cattle station), this small, permanent tented camp has a superb elevated position at the top of Kivuko Hill, with spectacular views across the dry, flat Tsavo thornveld to Mount Kasigau and the Kizima Hills. The camp is low-key, tents being simply furnished but having en-suite showers and flush toilets, while meals are wholesome, eaten in a dining tent with equally splendid views. Below the cliffs there's a small waterhole attracting elephant, lion and leopard at certain times of the year. The camp is primarily used as a base for conservationists working on research projects monitoring

THE ASKARI APPEAL

African soldiers, *askaris*, from East and Central Africa volunteered for the African Colonial Forces during both world wars. World War II saw thousands of these loyal men fighting alongside their British and Indian army comrades in the King's African Rifles, the Northern Rhodesia Regiment and the Somaliland Scouts. They fought in Abyssinia (present-day Ethiopia), Madagascar and Burma, as well as giving invaluable support in the Mediterranean theatres of war. Many performed conspicuous acts of bravery, for which they were decorated. Others were wounded or killed. It is estimated that today there are around 12,000 of these grand veterans, many living out their years in abject poverty, with little means of support. They rely on small grants provided by the British Commonwealth ex-Services League. The Askari Appeal aims to help these old soldiers live out their remaining years with dignity. The money raised is distributed to the veterans and their immediate dependants.

For further information contact: The Askari Appeal, c/o Messrs Park Nelson, 1 Bell Yard, London WC2A 2JP

wildlife in the area. **On offer:** game drives, bird and bush walks with excellent guides. There is a private airstrip nearby.

Rates: from US$125 full board per person sharing. Not suitable for young children.

Taita Discovery Centre (4 rooms, 4 dormitories) Book through Savannah Camps and Lodges, page 91

Located in the 15,800ha Rukinga Sanctuary, the Taita Discovery Centre caters for student groups and individuals pursuing environmental education courses and field studies. Efficiently run, it resembles an African village. There's a central, open, thatched banda where meals (simple wholesome fare) are taken, around which there are 4 single-sex dormitories, each sleeping 8 and with their own ablution blocks, together with double rondavels with en-suite showers and flush toilets. There's also a small cash bar and provisions store. **On offer:** activities are dependent on interests, but game drives, bird walks, visits to community projects (such as schools) and World War I battlefield sites and climbing Mount Kasigau can be arranged.

Rates: from US$65 full board per person sharing; US$280 per person weekly (4 weeks min)

What to see and do
Battlefield of Kasigau

About 10km from Taita Discovery Centre are the Kizima Hills, the location for some fierce fighting during World War I between the German Schutztruppe, under the command of the then Colonel (later to become General) Paul von Lettow-Vorbeck, and the British colonial forces. The British troops had a large encampment at Voi, with soldiers from Kenya, Bengal, Nigeria and South Africa. These granite hills still have the German gun positions, 1m-high walls built from loose stones. The battle was also known locally as the 'Battle of Pika Pika' – *pika pika* referring to the sound of gunfire. The Germans conducted lethal raiding parties on the Uganda railway line and in 1915 succeeded in blowing up 32 trains and nine bridges.

Climbing Mount Kasigau

About 15km from TDC is the village of Kasigau, although the mountain dominates the flat landscape for miles around. By special permission (which can be arranged through TDC) it is possible to climb Mount Kasigau (1,800m) an inselberg rising from the Taita plains. It's an interesting and arduous day trip – a steep climb from the village of Kasigau, crossing expansive areas of bare rock interspersed with thorn bushes and *euphorbia*, to reach another world of thick forest with orchids and African violets and tumbling streams on the upper slopes. When clear, there are superb views from the top, but these are often restricted by the cloud which hovers around the summit.

exclusive for nature lovers

Diani Beach Road
opposite Club Baobao
PO Box 787 Ukunda

email: recycle@africaonline.co.ke
tel: 040 3203517   fax: 040 3203223

Forest Dream
C·O·T·T·A·G·E·S

The best self drive safari available in Kenya. Our Safaris can be done anywhere, and our vehicles are fully equipped with cooking and camping equipment. The 4WDs are all in good condition and back up service while on safari is a must for us.

Safaris to Uganda and Tanzania can be arranged and as an optional extra, we offer rubber dinghies for the lake trips.

We are situated at Njoro near Nakuru and have a base campsite which can be used in between safaris.

ROVING ROVERS SAFARIS LTD

PO Box 23, Njoro, Kenya
Tel: 037 61417 and 0362 43206/43294
Mobile: 254 722 734816/254 722 734877/254 722 353901
E-mail: mm@africaonline.co.ke/rrovers@wananchi.com
Web: www.roving-rovers.com

DRIVE YOUR MOUSE WILD!

Click your mouse onto www.letsgosafari.com and you can find yourself at over 400 lodges and hotels, including group ranch community lodges and over 200 different safaris'...ROOAAR!!

LETS GO TRAVEL

**Head Office Tel: Nairobi, Telephone: (254-2) 4447151 / 4441030
Fax: (254-2) 4447270 / 4441690, e-mail: info@letsgosafari.com,
Internet: www.letsgosafari.com**

Central Highlands

The rugged, snow-capped peaks of Mount Kenya, Africa's second-highest mountain (5,199m), and the Aberdares range (4,000m) are the dominant landscape features of this fertile, highly populated region. It stretches northeast of Nairobi to Meru, as far north as Isiolo and Maralal, includes the entire massif of Mount Kenya and the Aberdares, and west across the Laikipia Plateau to Nyahururu and Lake Baringo. Containing a microcosm of the country's scenic diversity, landscapes range from semi-arid savanna on the Laikipia Plateau and Meru National Park, to the fertile foothills around the Aberdares and Mount Kenya, with a tapestry of wheat farms around Nanyuki and Timau and small-scale farming by the Kikuyu and Meru tribes around the Aberdares and Mount Kenya, and the magnificent forests, moorland and sub-alpine flora in the Aberdares and Mount Kenya national parks. The most fertile land originally belonged to the Kikuyu tribe, and was parcelled out to 'white settlers' during the colonial era – the area became known as the 'White Highlands' – who pioneered cash crops like coffee and pineapples as well as mainstream wheat and livestock farming, and more recently horticulture, which are still mainstays of the agricultural economy today. It was small wonder that this area was the seat of discontent among the Kikuyu people and the stronghold of the Mau Mau rebellion (see page 11) which subsequently brought about the end of the colony and independence in 1963.

The main highlights of the region are the superb scenery and wildlife – greater Laikipia being second only to the Masai Mara for game viewing – the tree hotels in the Aberdares and Mount Kenya, the national parks of Mount Kenya, the Aberdares and Meru and the community lodges of the Laikipiak Maasai and Samburu on the northern fringes of the Laikipia Plateau. In addition, there's a surprising choice of activities in the region, with plenty of opportunities to get off the beaten track – by foot, bicycle, horse, camel or helicopter, depending on the size of your pocket.

THIKA AND ENVIRONS

Easing away from Nairobi, the road to Thika crosses grassy plains interspersed with the occasional flame tree, an association immortalised in Elspeth Huxley's book *The Flame Trees of Thika* about her early childhood on a farm. Rising to the west are the gently undulating coffee plantations of Ruiru and Kiambu, while just south of Thika is Juja, an area famous for its oranges. Thika itself is a sprawling town, with a few industries on its periphery, including a large brewery. But its main claim to fame is as the centre of vast pineapple plantations, owned by multi-national companies like Del Monte. The pimple-sized hill of Ol Donyo Sabuk is a minor landmark to the east.

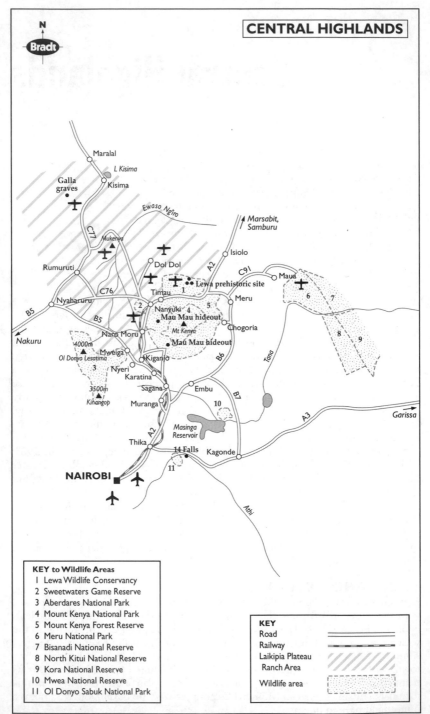

CENTRAL HIGHLANDS

KEY to Wildlife Areas
1 Lewa Wildlife Conservancy
2 Sweetwaters Game Reserve
3 Aberdares National Park
4 Mount Kenya National Park
5 Mount Kenya Forest Reserve
6 Meru National Park
7 Bisanadi National Reserve
8 North Kitui National Reserve
9 Kora National Reserve
10 Mwea National Reserve
11 Ol Donyo Sabuk National Park

KEY
Road
Railway
Laikipia Plateau
 Ranch Area
Wildlife area

Getting there and around

Take the A2 northeast from Nairobi to Thika (40km), a busy, tarmac (not too many potholes) dual carriageway, with plenty of lorries and *matatus* weaving between the traffic, bypassing the small town of Ruiru to the west. From Thika the A3 to the east passes Ol Donyo Sabuk National Park (about 27km) and continues through to Garissa (see *Chapter 9*, page 197). The C67 heads northwest from Thika passing the Kinangop at the southern end of the Aberdares National Park to join the A104 in Naivasha (about 50km).

By bus

There are local buses and frequent *matatus* to Thika from Nairobi. Similarly, there are several *matatus* a day from Thika to Ol Donyo Sabuk. The main bus stage is off Kici Road, while *matatus* for Ol Donyo Sabuk leave from Stadium Road (near the football stadium). The Garissa bus leaves from the stage on the A2.

Getting organised

For **changing money**, Barclays, Standard Chartered (ATM) and Kenya Commercial banks are situated in the centre of town. The main **post office** is on Commercial Streeet (opposite the gardens), open Monday to Friday 08.00–17.00, Saturday 09.00–12.00. For **internet access** try Thika Computer Consultants on Kici Road. There's a **supermarket** and **pharmacy** in the arcade. The **police station** is on Kenyatta Highway (tel: 067 31000) and the **tourist helpline** is 020 604767. There are plenty of **petrol stations** on the access roads into Thika.

Where to stay and eat

Blue Post Hotel off the A2 highway, PO Box 42, Thika; tel: 067 22241
This old colonial hotel has a delightful setting in gardens overlooking the Chania and Thika Falls. It's an excellent stop-off point for a snack or afternoon tea on the terrace, as well as having the best **restaurant** in town. The rooms are comfortably furnished, with en-suite shower rooms and balconies overlooking the falls.
Rates: from KSh1,200 B&B per person sharing
New Fulila Hotel Uhuru St, PO Box 1161, Thika; tel: 067 31286
This has good clean s/c rooms. There's a **restaurant** serving basic fare and a bar.
Rates: from KSh350
December Hotel Commercial St, PO Box 156, Thika; tel: 067 22140
Slightly more salubrious than the New Fulila, the s/c rooms are spacious and have a telephone.
Rates: from KSh500

There are a number of **cheap eats** in town. **Golden Plate**, **Prismos Hotel** and **David's Royal Paradise** have good standard meals at reasonable prices.

Entertainment

The **Vybestar** is a good nightclub with a disco and live bands. People are very friendly and few outsiders find their way here.

What to see and do

Chania and Thika Falls

These are in the grounds of the Blue Post Hotel adjacent to the A2 highway. They are not particularly high, but impressive nevertheless, and are only a few minutes' walk from the hotel.

Fourteen Falls

Open daily 09.00–17.00; entry KSh150, vehicle KSh200, camera KSh150
Take the A3 east out of Thika to Ol Donyo Sabuk village, from where it's a short

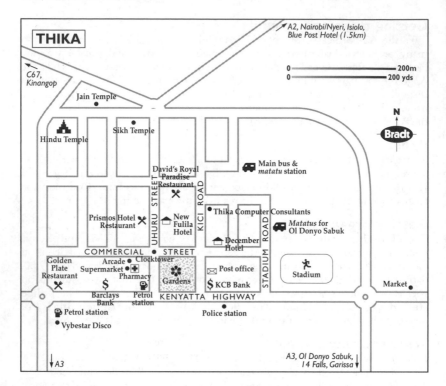

walk to the falls on the Athi River. The falls run in a series of cataracts, plunging some 30m over precipitous rocks. The whitewater is especially spectacular when the Athi is in full spate, a seething foam of water and spray.

For accommodation try **14 Falls Campsite** (camping, bandas). This is a basic campsite with limited facilities which has been prone to robbery in the past, so get an update on security first.

Rates: about KSh50 for camping and around KSh100 for a banda

Ol Donyo Sabuk National Park

PO Box 1514, Thika

Open daily 06.30–18.00; park entry fees US$15; vehicle entry fee KSh200; guides KSh300 for half a day, KSh500 for a full day

Follow the A3 to the village of Kilima Mbogo, and then take the signposted turn to the right to the main gate (about 3km). You'll require 4WD if driving in the park. Although small in size, only 20km², the park includes the entirety of Ol Donyo Sabuk Hill (2,145m), a solitary cone rising from the plains. The name means 'Big Mountain' in Maa, while the Kikuyu know it as *Kea-Njahe*, the 'Mountain of the Big Rain'. The park is superb for **walking**, and it's about 9km to the summit from where there are sweeping views to mounts Kenya and Kilimanjaro on a clear day and the Athi River nearby. You are required to take an armed escort as there are plenty of buffalo around, and you may also get sightings of colobus monkeys in the forest, bushbuck and duiker as well as prolific birdlife. Not far from the summit are the graves of early white settlers: the American, Sir William Northrup McMillan, who died in 1925, and his wife Lucy. A philanthropic couple, they were the benefactors of the McMillan Library in

Nairobi and also entertained the American president, Teddy Roosevelt, during his big-game safari in 1911.

There is **camping** available in the park. Book through KWS in Nairobi (page 91) or KWS, PO Box 1514, Thika. The campsite, near the main gate, has very basic facilities – a tap and pit latrine – so you'll need to be fully self-sufficient.
Rates: from US$2 for camping plus park and vehicle entry fees.

NORTH TO NYERI AND THE ABERDARES

From Thika, the countryside changes from pineapple and gum-tree plantations (where, passing the Kahuzi estates, you can stop and buy sustainably produced charcoal and pineapples), to the Kikuyu homelands, in the Muranga district – a highly populated area where smallholdings have the odd house cow and produce a range of vegetables – beans, tomatoes, cabbages – mingled with coffee bushes and banana trees. Crossing the Tana River, the road continues to Sagana where Savage Wilderness Safaris have their base (see page 102). The road starts to climb towards Karatina, a colourful market town, and then follows a steep valley with a tumbling mountain stream where, in season, you can see coffee beans drying on low stretcher tables just before the Nyeri bridge and the tree-clad Nyeri Hill. The forested slopes of Mount Kenya (the cloud-covered peaks usually clear in the early morning and evening) are to the north, while the distant hills of the Aberdare range lie to the west.

Getting there and around

Shortly after Thika the A2 becomes two lanes with a reasonably good surface and heads north to the **Muranga district**, bypassing Muranga town (if you wish to go there take the C71 west shortly after leaving Thika) continuing to **Sagana** and **Karatina**. About 10km south of Nyeri, the A2 branches to the right – with signboards for Naro Moru and Mountain Lodge. The road continues as the B5, crossing the river and continuing to **Nyeri** town.

By bus

From Nyeri there are several buses a day to Nairobi, Nyaharuru, Nakuru and Nanyuki. In addition there are plenty of *matatus* and Peugeot share taxis. The bus stage is on Kimathi Way.

By air

There are airstrips at Nyeri and Mweiga, but no scheduled services are available.

By rail

Although a railway passes through the area to Nanyuki, it's only used for freight.

Getting organised

Changing money, there's a Barclays Bank (with ATM) and a Kenya Commercial Bank on Kenyatta Road. The main **post office** is near the clocktower on Kanisa Road, open Monday to Friday 08.00–17.00, Saturday 09.00–12.00. For **internet access** try Niblo Stationers on Kimathi Way. There's also a **supermarket** and **pharmacy** on Kimathi Way. The **police station** is between Kenyatta Road and Market Street (tel: 0171 30555) and the **tourist helpline** is tel: 020 604767. There are plenty of **petrol stations** on the access roads into Nyeri.

Where to stay and eat
Nyeri

Outspan Golf and Country Club (45 rooms, swimming pool) Book through Block Hotels, PO Box 40075, Nairobi; tel: 020 540780; fax: 020 545948; email: blockreservations@net2000ke.com; web: www.blockhotelske.com

The Outspan Golf and Country Club is set in 12ha of delightful tropical gardens stretching down to the Chania River, with excellent opportunities for birdwatching. The hotel has an old-fashioned, 1920s ambience, with a wood-panelled dining-room and large fireplace in the lounge. The rooms are comfortably furnished with en-suite bathrooms and each has its own log fire for chilly evenings. **On offer:** birdwatching, trout fishing, squash, tennis, golf, snooker, Kikuyu dancing and excursions to the Aberdares National Park.

Rates: from US$80 full board per person sharing

Green Hills Hotel (94 rooms, 7 cottages; swimming pool) Bishop Gatimu Rd, PO Box 313, Nyeri; tel: 061 30604

This hotel has good facilities but can get rather noisy. The cottages have the best rooms, the others being in two large blocks. All have en-suite bathrooms. The restaurant serves reasonable meals for around KSh500.

Rates: from KSh1,400 B&B

Nyeri Inn (cottages) PO Box 159, Nyeri; tel: 061 31092

Situated about 1.5km from the Nyaharuru junction, the inn has a peaceful garden setting. Rooms are in simple, rustic cottages with bathrooms. There's a **restaurant** which serves reasonable meals.

Rates: from KSh800

Cheap lodgings

Kimathi Way Hotel PO Box 2188, Nyeri; tel: 061 2799

This has reasonable rooms, but only singles have bathrooms, and it can get quite noisy. The restaurant serves reasonable meals.

Rates: from KSh200

Nyeri Star Restaurant and Lodging Market St, Nyeri

More expensive, but better value than the Kimathi Way, the Nyeri Star, although large and near the *matatu* stand, is not too noisy and has good s/c rooms. There's a restaurant and bar.

Rates: from KSh 250

Ibis Hotel tel: 061 4858

Situated at the northern end of town, the hotel is built around a small courtyard. Rooms are simple but clean, with en-suite showers. The courtyard restaurant serves reasonable meals.

Rates: from KSh300

Mweiga and Solio

Aberdare Country Club (36 cottages, 10 rooms; swimming pool) PO Box 449, Nyeri: tel: 061 55620; fax: 061 55224; email: arkgm@form-net.com; web: www.lonhrohotels.com

This stone-built, creeper-clad clubhouse with a red-tiled roof nestles at the foot of Mweiga Hill in a terraced garden next to a 530ha game sanctuary, with views to the Aberdares and Mount Kenya. The cottage rooms are best and have country-house-style furnishings, fireplaces and spacious en-suite bathrooms. Service is excellent, and there's a good selection of buffet-style food – salads and home baking galore and a mixture of European, Asian and African dishes. It's very busy at lunchtime with visitors en route to the Ark. **On offer:** 9-hole golf course (complete with warthogs), jogging trail, walking in the game sanctuary and up Mweiga Hill, horseriding, sundowners and excursions to the Aberdares National Park and Solio Game Reserve.

Rates: from US$100 full board per person sharing

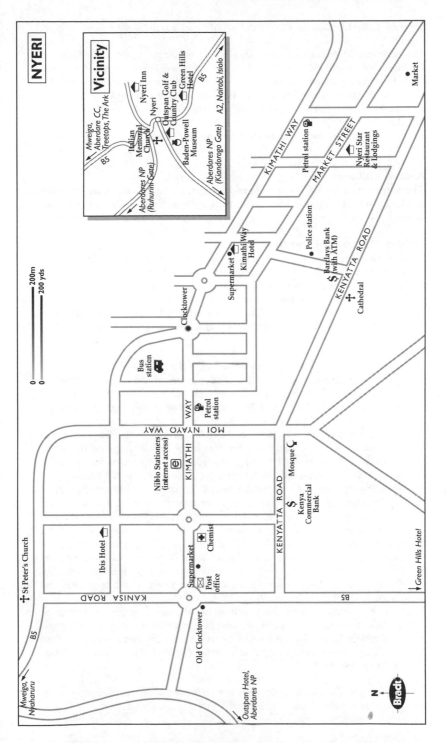

Sangare Lakeside Cottages (6 tents) Book through Savannah Camps and Lodges, page 91
This permanent tented camp is located on the 2,600ha Sangare ranch, in the Aberdare foothills. Visitors need 4WD or alternatively can be collected from the Aberdare Country Club. Overlooking a small lake, the tents are comfortably furnished with en-suite bathrooms and flush toilets, with solar lighting and electricity. **On offer:** birdwatching, escorted walks, trout fishing, game viewing and excursions to Solio ranch and the Aberdares National Park.
Rates: from US$260 full board, inclusive of activities, per person sharing

What to see and do
Kikuyu culture
The Outspan Hotel has a small, purpose-built, Kikuyu homestead, with dancing displays. An explanation is given about the dances and the traditions of the Kikuyu home.

Italian Memorial Church
Lined with cedar trees, the road to the church lies off the Nyeri–Ihururu road to the Ruhuruini Park gate to the Aberdares National Park. The church, c1955, was funded by the Italian government and the Duchess of Aosta, and was built as a memorial to Italians who died in Kenya, Tanzania and Uganda during World War II, and to house their remains. Among those buried here are Amedeo, Duke of Aosta, the Italian viceroy of Abyssinia (which became Ethiopia in 1945) who

LORD ROBERT BADEN-POWELL 1857–1941
Many pilgrims of the worldwide Scouts movement are drawn to Nyeri to pay homage to Lord Robert Baden-Powell, who founded the association in 1908. A distinguished and decorated soldier in the 13th Hussars, he fought in India, Afghanistan and South Africa and was made a major-general aged 43 after the siege of Mafeking (1899) in the Boer War. He was also an accomplished artist, but it was for his textbook on the art of Scouting, and ultimately his role in the scouting movement for which he was to be remembered. In recognition of services to his country and Scouting, he was given a peerage, taking the title, Lord Baden-Powell of Gilwell, Gilwell Park being the international training centre for Scout leaders. His wife Olave, known as the 'mother of millions', started the Girl Guides' movement. During his last years, Baden-Powell lived in Paxtu Cottage in the grounds of the Outspan Hotel. The cottage was later occupied by Jim Corbett, famous as a hunter of Indian man-eating tigers, who was the guide to the royal entourage at Treetops when HRH Elizabeth stepped up as a princess and came down as a queen after the death of her father George VI in 1952.

The **Baden-Powell Museum** is in Paxtu Cottage, a shrine of Scouting memorabilia. Baden-Powell is buried in the cemetery behind **St Peter's Church** in Nyeri. On his headstone, surmounted by the Boy Scout and Girl Guide badges, is written, 'Robert Baden-Powell, Chief Scout of the World'.

Entry to the museum is KSh50, or free to members of the scouting movement; a donation to the church is appropriate if visiting the cemetery.

commanded the defences of Amba Alagi. The church caretaker, John Baptist Mureithi, will happily show you around.
Entry free but a donation is appropriate

Gliding Club

PO Box 926, Nyeri; tel: 061 2748; fax: 061 2748; email: gliding@africaonline.co.ke
There's a gliding club at Mweiga with instruction available. *Rates: from around US$50 for 10 minutes*

Solio Game Sanctuary

Open daily; entry US$15
PO Box 2, Naro Moru; tel 0171 55271; fax: 0171 55235
Solio is about a 40-minute drive (4WD required) west from the Aberdare Country Club (who can also arrange excursions) along the B5 to Nyaharuru. This 7,300ha sanctuary is located within a 14,600ha cattle ranch. Privately run, it was initially established as a rhino breeding sanctuary for both black and white rhino. Rhino from this successful programme were translocated to Lake Nakuru National Park. In addition to the rhino, there's a variety of plains game. Among activities permitted in the sanctuary are guided bush walks, horseriding, day and night game drives and sundowners.

There is **camping** available at Solio Game Ranch (4 campsites; contact details above). The campsites are in pleasant locations but are fairly basic – they provide firewood and water – so you'll need to be entirely self sufficient.
Rates: camping KSh400 plus entry fee of US$15

Aberdares National Park

PO Box 22 Nyeri; tel: 061 55024
Open daily 06.30–18.30; park entry fee US$30; smartcard required; vehicle entry KSh200. The park headquarters near Mweiga are a point of sale for loading smartcards. For more on smartcards, see page 41.
There are several gates to the Aberdares National Park if coming from the east. From Nyeri, the easiest access is to the area known as the **salient.** Head southwest from Nyeri to the **Ruhuruini gate,** or north of Nyeri to the **Treetops gate** and the **Ark gate** west from **Mweiga.** Alternatively, directly west of Nyeri is the **Kiandongoro gate** via **Tusha.** Other access points to the park are from the north via **Rhino gate** off the Nyeri–Nyaharuru B5 road, through the **Shamata gate** if coming on the Gilgil–Nyaharuru road or via the **Matubio gate** if coming from **Naivasha.** A 4WD is recommended and essential in parts of the park.

The Aberdare range forms part of the eastern wall of Kenya's Rift Valley, running south from the Laikipia Plateau for about 200km. It has two dominant peaks – Ol Donyo Lesatima (4,000m) to the north, linked by expansive moorland reminiscent of Scotland, with its giant species of heather, to Kinangop (3,500m) in the south, while to the east is the salient, on the lower, forested land. The park is for the most part surrounded by forest reserve, fast being encroached upon due to the high regional population density. However, its conservation is essential as it's a vital water catchment area, feeding the Tana River system, the Ewaso Ng'iro River and Lake Naivasha, as well as supplying water for Nairobi. The park is also a haven for black rhino, and the fund-raising efforts of **Rhino Ark Kenya** (Uhuru Gardens, PO Box 181, 00517 Nairobi; tel: 020 604246; fax: 020 60426; email: rhinoark@wananchi.com; web: www.rhinoark.org) are helping

KWS with fencing the conservation area which includes the park. Initially the salient area was fenced to prevent poaching and also to stop animals from destroying crops on the *shambas* adjacent to the park, thereby reducing the human wildlife conflict in the region. (See details of *Rhino Charge*, page 137.) The hills are cut by steep ravines, with dramatic waterfalls – **Chania**, **Karura** and **Guru** – and several rivers, the Chania and Tharua being good for fishing. Chania falls is about 30m high, and it's a steep walk to the bottom, where you can walk behind the cascade.

Flora and fauna The vegetation is directly affected by the altitude, changing from montane rainforest on the lower slopes, with juniper and podocarpus, to the bamboo zone and the moorland which has a rich alpine flora, with giant senecios and lobelias, also found on Mount Kenya. The **wildlife** includes buffalo, elephant, lion and serval cats – some being melanistic – the shy and rare bongo antelope which inhabits the bamboo zone, and black rhino. **Birdlife** is excellent too, with some 250 species recorded – among them the Aberdare cisticola, which can be seen on grass tussocks in the moorland, a variety of mountain sunbirds – golden-winged, malachite and eastern double-collared – and the endemic Jackson's francolin.

Where to stay and eat
The Ark (60 cabins) PO Box 449, Nyeri: tel: 061 55620; fax: 061 55224; email: arkgm@form-net.com; web: www.lonhrohotels.com
A 40-minute game drive (look out for the black-and-white colobus monkeys) through the salient of the Aberdares National Park brings you to the Ark, a timber-built lodge with an arced roof overlooking a floodlit waterhole, with clear views of Mount Kenya in the early morning and evening. It's reached along a boardwalk (not quite 2 by 2) and has 3 decks, viewing balconies and a ground-level bunker. Game viewing is generally excellent, with numerous bushbuck, buffalo and elephant, and in the evening, the white-tailed mongoose and genet cats. There is a buzzer system to wake you during the night for elephant, leopard, lion, rhino or the elusive bongo, which is now rarely seen. The cabins are simple, with basic en-suite shower rooms. The lounge area has a roaring log fire – it does get cold here, being at around 2,400m – and the staff are readily on hand to talk about the wildlife. *Rates: from US$130 full board per person sharing. No children under 7 allowed.*
Treetops (50 rooms) Book through Block Hotels, page 90
Also located in the salient, this wooden lodge built on stilts, overlooking a waterhole, with views to Mount Kenya, has gained a romantic reputation for its connections with the British royal family – this is where Princess Elizabeth became queen on the death of her father George VI. There are several viewing balconies and 2 photographic hides at ground level. It's still good for game viewing, but surprisingly all the cabins, which are well furnished, have shared bathrooms. A buzzer system operates at night for the big-game.
Rates: from US$140 full board per person sharing. No children under 5 allowed.

Kenya Wildlife Service accommodation
Book the following through the park headquarters in Mweiga, PO Box 22, Nyeri; tel: 061 55024 or through KWS, Tourism & Business Development, PO Box 40241, Nairobi; tel: 020 602345; email: tourism@kws.org. Note that 4WD is essential and that it gets very cold at night.

Kiandongoro Fishing Lodge (2 bandas, self-catering)
Located near the Kiandongoro gate, the spacious bandas, each sleeping 7, are comfortable and have a large living-room with a fireplace, giving a warm atmosphere in the chilly

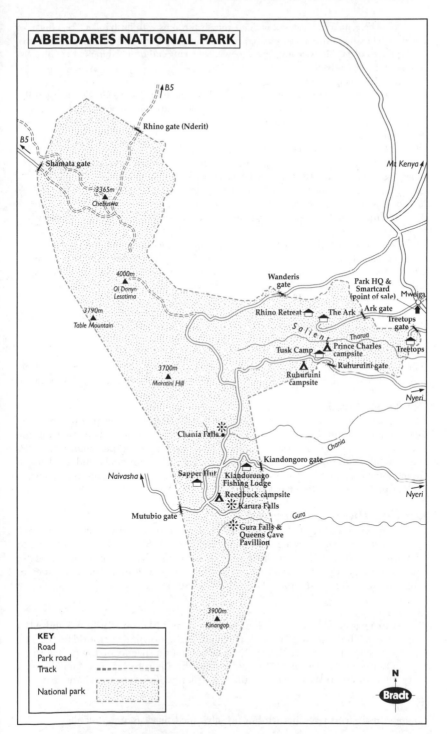

ABERDARES NATIONAL PARK

B5

Rhino gate (Nderit)

B5

Shamata gate

3365m
Chebuswa

Mt Kenya

4000m
Ol Donyn
Lesatima

3790m
Table Mountain

Wanderis
gate

Park HQ &
Smartcard
(point of sale)   Mweiga

Rhino Retreat   The Ark   Ark gate

Salient   Treetops
gate

Tharua

Tusk Camp   Prince Charles
campsite   Treetops

3700m
Maratini Hill

Ruhuruini gate

Ruhuruini
campsite

Nyeri

Chania Falls

Chania

Kiandongoro gate

Naivasha

Sapper Hut   Kiandorongo
Fishing Lodge

Nyeri

Reedbuck campsite

Karura Falls

Mutubio gate

Gura

Gura Falls &
Queens Cave
Pavillion

3900m
Kinangop

KEY
Road
Park road
Track

National park

N

Bradt

evenings. There are 3 bedrooms, 2 with en-suite bathrooms with flush toilets. Bed linen, towels, kitchen utensils, a gas cooker and paraffin lamps are provided and there's a caretaker available. **On offer:** birdwatching, game viewing, walking and trout fishing in the Guru Karuru and Chania rivers.

Rates: from US$200 per banda

Sapper Hut (banda, sleeps 2, self-catering) also booking through Let's Go Travel, page 101. On the moorland west of Chania falls, this is a simple banda with an open fireplace. A couple of beds, a shower room and toilet are provided. You'll need to bring everything else.

Rates: from KSh2,500 for the camp

Rhino Retreat (banda, sleeps 6, self-catering)
Located in the salient northwest of the Ark, the banda has 3 rooms and is fully furnished. Linen and towels are provided and the kitchen has a fridge and gas cooker, while a caretaker is available. You'll need to bring all other provisions.

Rates: from KSh10,000 for the camp

Tusk Camp (4 bandas, sleeps 8, self-catering) also booking through Let's Go Travel, page 101
Located to the west of the Ruhuruini gate, the camp is situated in a forest glade on the eastern slopes of the Aberdares (2,300m) and consists of wooden bandas, a living room with an open fire and a veranda with panoramic views across the forest to Mount Kenya. The bathroom has a shower (with hot water) and a flush toilet. The kitchen has a firewood cooker. Beds, wood for cooking and kerosene lamps are provided, but you'll need to bring everything else. **On offer:** game viewing and trout fishing.

Rates: from Ksh5,000 for the camp

Park campsites
There are several public campsites in the park, but they're not always open and have limited (if any) facilities. Prince Charles' campsite in the salient is reported to be good.

NYAHARURU
Formerly known as Thomson's Falls, or T Falls, Nyaharuru lies just north of the Equator and is Kenya's highest town (2,360m). It originally took its name from the spectacular waterfall (75m drop), named by Joseph Thomson the explorer in 1883. A sprawling settlement, it's surrounded by conifer plantations and pockets of indigenous forest, while its outskirts open on to undulating hills and maize farms, with superb views to the Aberdares.

Getting there and around
West of Nyeri, the B5 (good tarmac road) skirts northwest past the Aberdares range and the Laikipia Plateau to the north, to Nyaharuru (115km). The B5 continues to Nakuru (70km) passing through undulating farmland. If coming from the north, the C77 is a good tarmac road from Rumuruti (about 40km) and continues to Gilgil (70km), joining the main Nairobi road, the A104.

By bus
Nyaharuru has good bus connections to Nakuru and Nairobi via the B5 and A104 respectively. The buses to Nairobi leave in the early morning at around 06.00. The main bus station is off Ol Kalou Road at the southern end of town. There's a regular service to Nyeri and Nanyuki, while the Nairobi bus to Maralal passes through at about 10.00. In addition there are plenty of *matatus* and share taxis.

By air
There's an airstrip at Nyaharuru but no scheduled services are available.

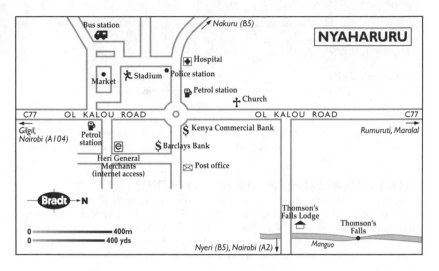

By rail
No passenger service is available.

Getting organised
For major provisions, you are best to stock up in Nakuru. For **changing money**, Barclays (with ATM) and Kenya Commercial banks and the main **post office** (open Mon–Fri 08.00–17.00, Sat 09.00–12.00) are situated in the centre of town. For **internet access** try Heri General Merchants. There's a good **market** to the south of the stadium. In a **medical emergency** you're probably better off continuing to Nakuru (page 286) though there is a hospital on the Nakuru road leaving town opposite the **police station**. In an emergency the **tourist helpline** is tel: 020 604767. There are plenty of **petrol stations** on the access roads into Nyaharuru.

Where to stay and eat
Thomson's Falls Lodge (32 rooms in cottages and chalets; camping) PO Box 38, Nyaharuru; tel: 065 22006; fax: 065 32170
The lodge is on the forested northern outskirts of town set in gardens, popular for picnicking weekenders, which look down to the river. It's a busy lunch stop on the tourist circuit between the Mara and Nyeri. The service is efficient and friendly, the main building having a bar with an open fire and large restaurant which serves excellent meals at very reasonable prices (KSh500 for lunch and dinner). The rooms are in 1930s stone-built cottages, which are rustic and simply furnished with en-suite bathrooms and open fireplaces, ideal for the chilly evenings, or in more modern chalets. The campsite is to the back of the cottages and has hot showers, toilets and free firewood. **On offer:** guides to the hippo pools and Thomson's Falls, Kikuyu witchdoctor.
Rates: Ksh 1,200 B&B per person sharing; camping from KSh300

What to see and do
Kikuyu witchdoctor
Very much a party piece for the benefit of tourists, there's a Kikuyu witchdoctor in the grounds of the Thomson's Falls' lodge, with a painted face and wearing traditional dress. For a fee, he will dance and explain (in good English) a little about

Kikuyu culture. He's genuinely entertaining, but it's difficult to gauge the authenticity of his act.
Cost: about KSh200

Thomson's Falls
There are steps down to the bottom of the falls, and walks along the leafy banks of the **Ewaso Narok River** – but check security before going as there have been isolated thieving incidents in the past. If venturing further than the falls it's advisable to take a guide from the lodge. Following the river for about 2km above the falls leads to reed-fringed **hippo pools** where you may see up to half a dozen hippo if you're lucky.

FROM NYERI NORTH TO NARO MORU
From Nyeri, the road climbs on to the shoulder of Mount Kenya, with open grassy plains to the west, while the forested slopes of Mount Kenya lie to the east. The small village of Naro Moru serves the ranches to the west, but has become important as a base for climbing Mount Kenya, the Naro Moru route being the most direct for those trekking to Mount Kenya's third-highest peak, Point Lenana.

Getting there and around
Follow the B5 south to the A2 and turn left to **Naro Moru** (about 30km), a small village with a cluster of *dukas*, and ribbon development of stalls along the main road.

By bus
There's a regular bus service along the A2 between Nairobi and Isiolo which stops at Naro Moru and a number of share taxis between Nairobi and Naro Moru. If going to Mount Kenya (about 20km to the park entrance), you can get a *matatu* from the post office in Naro Moru to Kiambuthi, 3km short of the park gate.

By rail
There is no passenger service.

Where to stay and eat
Serena Mountain Lodge (42 rooms) Book through Serena Hotels, page 91
Shortly after Kiganjo on the A2 is a turning to the right, crossing the railway line, to Mountain Lodge. A dirt road, this is the best route and far better than the access road from Karatina; even so, its surface is far from wonderful. It's about 20km to the lodge, climbing up the lower slopes of Mount Kenya, passing through the Sagana community elephant fence, trout hatchery and new tree plantations (much funded by Serena Hotels to counteract the severe deforestation in the reserve), before entering the park gate from which it's about 5km to the lodge. The lodge is on stilts, built from timber, with rooms on three levels, the top two having private balconies. It overlooks a floodlit waterhole frequented by elephant, buffalo and bushbuck. Although close to Mount Kenya, the views are impeded by the thick montane forest with trees like Cape ash and broadleaved crotons. The rooms are spacious and nicely decorated with African prints on the wooden walls, and all have en-suite shower rooms. (Be aware that the monkeys here can be a menace and are not averse to poking their heads through the louvre windows and squeezing their way in to search for food; so make sure your windows and door are firmly closed when you leave your room.) There are several viewing decks and a bunker at ground level for photography. There's a bar with a fireplace and a restaurant to the rear, with good-quality meals and service. **On offer:** bird and bush walks with excellent

guides, excursions, walking on Mount Kenya and trekking to Point Lenana, trout fishing, health spa and shop.

Rates: from US$250 full board per person sharing

Naro Moru River Lodge (31 rooms, 12 self-catering cottages, bunkhouses, camping; heated swimming pool) PO Box 18, Naro Moru; tel: 062 62622; fax: 062 662211; email: mt.keny@africaonline.co.ke; web: www.alliancehotels.com

This timber-built lodge has a delightful setting in tropical gardens running down to the Naro Moru River (which is regularly stocked with trout). It's well-organised for those wanting to climb Mount Kenya, with equipment and guides for hire. The main lodge has a small lounge and bar with a large fireplace, decorated with interesting photographs and memorabilia about Mount Kenya climbs, and the food is reasonable. The rooms, in small cottages in the garden overlooking the river, are simply furnished with en-suite shower rooms. In addition there are single-, double- and triple-roomed self-catering cottages. The campsite is about 2km from the lodge, and has basic showers and toilets and firewood is available at US$5. There are a few bunkhouses which are very grubby. **On offer:** birdwatching, trout fishing, horseriding, mountain climbing, organised walks, sauna, squash, tennis and golf.

Rates: rooms from US$65 half board per person sharing; self-catering cottages from US$80–190 depending on size and numbers of people; bunk-bed US$7; camping US$5

Mount Kenya Hostel and Campsite PO Box 274, Naro Moru: tel: 062 62414; fax: 062 62078

Located about 10km up the track towards the Naro Moru gate to Mount Kenya National Park, the hostel has basic but comfortable facilities and hot showers. It's a good meeting point for those coming to and from the mountain. Meals, by arrangement, cost around KSh250. **On offer:** There's some mountain equipment for hire at reasonable prices, and guides are available too – but check their credentials first (see page 244 for further information). Transport is available to the Met station at around KSh3,000 for 9 people.

Rates: hostel from KSh250 for a bunk-bed; camping from KSh150

What to see and do
Forest walk to Mau Mau hideouts
There are excellent guided walks into the forest from Mountain Lodge, which not only give an insight into tracking the wildlife, but take you to hideouts – holes in the ground – used by the freedom fighters during the Mau Mau rebellion, see page 11.

Mountain climbing
The **Nguniu route** up Mount Kenya to point Lenana takes three to five days and can be arranged through Serena Mountain Lodge. It has spectacular views and avoids most of the vertical bog (see opposite).

Rates: from US$550 per person for groups of 5 or more

Fishing
Fly fishing for brown and rainbow trout is also available on the Naro Moru River. Rod hire is US$5 plus a fishing permit which can be arranged through Naro Moru River Lodge. Guided fishing trips on Mount Kenya from Mountain Lodge cost from US$45 per person, while equipment hire is US$100.

MOUNT KENYA
History
As a free-standing mountain that dominates the landscape for miles around, Mount Kenya plays an important role in tribal folklore. For the Kikuyu, the mountain is the home of their god, *Ngai*, whom they called *Mwene Nyaga*, which means 'Possessor of Brightness', and they named the mountain *Kere Nyaga*

(Kirinyaga) meaning the 'Mountain of Brightness'. In Kikuyu mythology the mountain is also the location for their creation, as after *Ngai* created the Earth, he made the first humans, *Gikuyu* and *Mumbi*, on Mount Kenya. Even now, individuals are occasionally drawn to the mountain to commune with their deity. The Kamba called the mountain *Kiinyaa*, which means 'Ostrich', as from a distance the black and white of the mountain resembles the plumage of a male ostrich. The German missionary Dr Ludwig Krapf, travelling in 1849, had Akamba porters; hence he named the mountain 'Kenya' (pronounced *Keen-ia*). It became altered to the pronunciation *Ken-ya* due to the first president, Jomo Kenyatta's adopted name. In contrast, the mountain peaks Batian, Nelion and Lenana are called after Maasai *laibon* – leaders – the Maasai revering the mountain because they believed that this was where the first Maasai descended with their cattle. Krapf's sighting of the mountain was dismissed until it was verified by the Scots explorer, Joseph Thomson, in 1883. Thomson climbed part of the mountain, and attempted ascents were also made by Count Samuel Teleki and Lieutenant Richard von Hohnel in 1887 and by the geologist John Gregory in 1893. The first successful documented ascent of Bation, the highest peak, was by Sir Halford Mackinder in 1889, with a party of 170 people – five Europeans and the rest Africans. In 1929, the mountaineer Eric Shipton pioneered several routes on the mountain. The European explorers and climbers left their legacy of names on the mountain – the Teleki and Mackinder valleys and Shipton's Cave. Today, Mount Kenya attracts over 15,000 people a year. Most are not technical climbers, and will trek to Point Lenana, the third-highest peak, using a couple of well-trodden routes. This number of people does cause environmental damage in a fragile environment. You can help to minimise this by sticking to the main paths, making sure that you do not leave any litter behind and, however endearing they may be, *not* feeding the animals.

Getting organised for climbing Mount Kenya

If you are planning a mountaineering trip within Kenya or to Kilimanjaro, it makes sense to contact the **Mountain Club of Kenya** (MCK). The club is based in Nairobi at Wilson Airport, near the Aero Club, PO Box 45741; tel: 020 501747 (evenings only); email: MCKenya@iname.com; web: www.mck.or.ke. The MCK clubhouse is a good meeting point for like-minded people and also has a good library. It's open to anyone with a genuine interest in mountaineering. They have also developed a virtual clubhouse on their website if you'd like a taster before you go. Open meetings are held on Tuesdays from 20.00; entry is free.

When making preparations, before making any decisions on routes and how many days to spend on the mountain, it may help to consider the following:

Independent or organised excursions?

This is a matter of personal preference, but if you have no experience of mountains you are strongly advised to go on an organised trip. Operators are listed below. The Naro Moru route is probably the best for those climbing the mountain independently, as it's less easy to get lost. As well as arranging guides and porters, you'll also need to budget for transport to the park gates or the roadheads from the main roads.

Mountain operators

The following is a listing of recognised and recommended operators who organise excursions on Mount Kenya, or who can provide guides and porters. The list is *not* definitive.

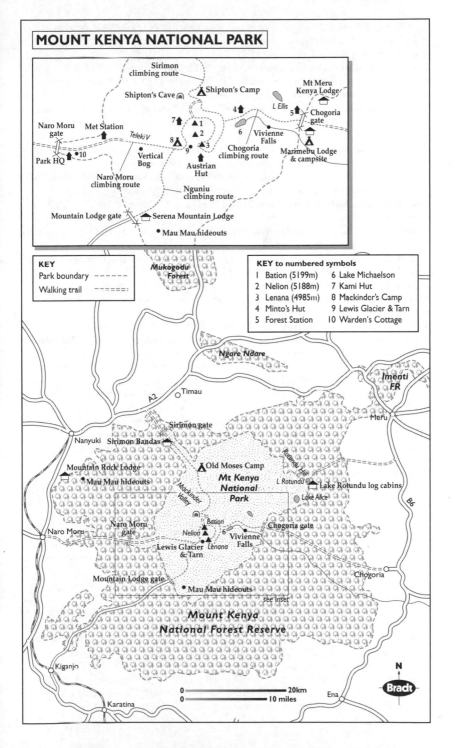

MOUNT KENYA NATIONAL PARK

Sirimon
climbing route

Shipton's Cave 🏚 ⛺ Shipton's Camp

Mt Meru
Kenya Lodge 🏠

L Ellis

Chogoria
gate ✕

Naro Moru
gate ✕

Met Station 🛖

Teleki V

7 🛖 ▲1

▲2

8 🛖

9 ● ▲3

4 🛖

6 ●

Vivienne
Falls

5 🛖

Chogoria
climbing route

Marimebu Lodge
& campsite ⛺

Park HQ 🏠 ●10

Vertical
Bog ●

Austrian
Hut 🛖

Naro Moru
climbing route

Nguniu
climbing route

Mountain Lodge gate ✕ 🏠 Serena Mountain Lodge

● Mau Mau hideouts

KEY
Park boundary – – – –
Walking trail ·········

KEY to numbered symbols
1	Bation (5199m)	6	Lake Michaelson
2	Nelion (5188m)	7	Kami Hut
3	Lenana (4985m)	8	Mackinder's Camp
4	Minto's Hut	9	Lewis Glacier & Tarn
5	Forest Station	10	Warden's Cottage

Mukogodu
Forest

Ngare Ndare

Imenti
FR

○ Timau

A2

Meru

Sirimon gate

Nanyuki Sirimon Bandas 🏠

Mountain Rock Lodge 🏠

● Mau Mau hideouts

▲ Old Moses Camp

**Mt Kenya
National
Park**

Mackinder
Valley

L Rotundu ●

Lake Rotundu log cabins 🏠

Ruaraki Hill

● Lake Alice

B6

Naro Moru
gate ✕

🏚 Bation
Nelion ▲ 6

Vivienne
Falls

Chogoria gate ✕

Naro Moru ○

Lewis Glacier
& Tarn ▲ Lenana

Chogoria ○

Mountain Lodge gate ✕

● Mau Mau hideouts

see inset

**Mount Kenya
National Forest Reserve**

○ Kiganjo

0		20km
0		10 miles

Ena ○

N

Bradt

○ Karatina

Base Camp Travel Galana Rd, off Argwings Khodhek Rd, PO Box 43369, Nairobi; tel: 020 577490; fax: 020 577489; email: info@basecampexplorer.com; web: www.basecampexplorer.com

Executive Wilderness Programmes PO Box 15014, Nairobi; tel: 020 891049; fax: 020 882723; or EWP, Haulfryn Cilycwm SA20 0SP, UK; tel: +44 (0)1550 721319; fax: +44 (0)1550 720053; email: ewp@ewpnet.com; web: www.ewpnet.com

East African Mountain Guides (**Savage Wilderness Safaris**) PO Box 44827, Nairobi; tel: 020 521590; fax: 020 501754; mob: 0733 735508; email: whitewater@alphanet.co.ke; web: www.whitewaterkenya.com

Ice Rock Mountain Trekking NCM Bldg, 4th Floor, Tom Mboya St, Nairobi, tel: 020 244608; email: icetrekk@kenyaweb.com; web: www.climbingafrica.com

Let's Go Travel Caxton House, Standard St, PO Box 60342, Nairobi; tel: 020 213033, 020 340331; fax: 020 336890; email: info@letsgosafari.com; web: www.letsgosafari.com

Real Wilderness Expeditions Wilson Njeru, PO Box 496, Chogoria; tel: 064 22260; mobile: 0733 553282

Mount Kenya Chogoria Guides Association based in the Joywood Hotel (see page 267) PO Box 62, Chogoria; mobile: 0733 262448

Mount Kenya Guides & Porters (on the track to the Naro Moru gate from the main road) PO Box 128, Naro Moru; tel: 062 62015

Mount Kenya Traverses PO Box 83, Chogoria; tel: 068 20781/2

Mountain Adventure next to Barclays Bank, PO Box 1180, Nanyuki; tel: 062 31887; email: tigerkami@yahoo.com

Mountain Rock Hotel PO Box 333, Nanyuki; tel: 062 62625; fax: 0176 62051

Naro Moru River Lodge PO Box 18, Naro Moru; tel: 062 62622; fax: 062 62211; email: mt.keny@africaonline.co.ke; web: www.alliancehotels.com

Serena Mountain Lodge PO Box 40690, 00100 Nairobi; tel: 020 711077; fax: 020 718103; email: cro@serena.co.ke; web: www.serenahotels.com

Tropical Ice Iain Allan, PO Box 57341, Nairobi; tel: 020 740811; fax: 020 740826; email: tropice@users.africaonline.co.ke

Wilderness Kenya The Clocktower, 72 Newhaven Rd, Edinburgh EH6 5QG, UK; tel: 0131 625 6635; fax: 0131 625 6636; email: neil@wildernesskenya.com; web: www.wildernesskenya.com

Organising guides and porters

When arranging guides and porters be aware that they should be members of the **Association of Mount Kenya Operators** and have identity cards to prove it, as there are plenty of rogue guides and porters. Porters carry 18kg, and you need to provide them with a rucksack. In addition you will have to pay for their transport to the park (or another day's wages) and their park entrance fees at around US$2 a day. Check out what's included in the price, as the charge will sometimes be inclusive of transport and park entry fees.

Cost guide

If arranging your own trip, rates for porters and guides and packages can vary considerably. The minimum you can expect to pay for a guide per day is US$6. For example, Mount Kenya Chogoria Guides Association, who are not the cheapest, have packages starting from US$125 per person per day for groups of five or more, which include guides and porters, transport to the park gate and park fees; daily rates are: guides US$12, porters US$9, cooks US$12, porter-guides US$16 and US$503 per group for a technical guide for Nelion and Bation. For a listing of guides and porters see above.

When to go

Generally, the best months on Mount Kenya are January and February, while August is fair; *avoid* May and November. However, the weather on the mountain is unpredictable at all times of year and even during the better months you may encounter heavy rain and snow, although severe storms are rare.

Health precautions

For trekking on the mountain you'll need to be reasonably fit, and being at altitude on the equator it's important to take precautions against sunburn and to wear UV sunglasses as snowblindness is common. In addition it's essential to maintain your liquid intake – between four and six litres a day – as dehydration heightens the possibility of hypothermia and altitude sickness. Also be aware in advance of the symptoms of acute mountain sickness, high-altitude pulmonary oedema and high-altitude cerebral oedema. These are given in the chapter on *Health and safety*, page 152, together with contents for a basic first-aid kit.

What to take

Clothing

It's important to have appropriate outdoor clothing – wearing several layers is the best option, as temperatures can range from –15° to 30°C and hypothermia can occur even at 10°C. Wool and synthetic materials are better than cotton and down due to the wet climate on the mountain. Take enough clothing for the duration of your trip and include plenty of socks, gloves, a woollen hat and a pair of thermals. In addition proper walking boots (well broken in) are advisable, together with a pair of trainers for camp, as it's normally wet underfoot.

Trekking equipment

Walking poles are useful, but not a necessity, and actually accelerate erosion on the paths, so if you carry them, use them sparingly. Depending on the time of year, you may require crampons and an ice axe on the Lewis glacier on Lenana. For mountaineering you will require specialist climbing equipment which is not mentioned here. The Mountain Club of Kenya gives advice on mountaineering, see page 124. If planning on hiring equipment, Naro Moru River Lodge has the best quality and choice, but no reservations can be made in advance.

Camping equipment

A limited amount of camping or climbing equipment is available in Nairobi. Apart from a tent and bed-mat, it's important to have a good sleeping bag capable of coping with temperatures down to –15°C. Gas cylinder stoves are recommended. No fires are permitted within the national park. Naro Moru River Lodge, page 241, can provide camping equipment for hire, but again, no reservations can be made in advance.

Food

Packet soups and dried foods are not generally available in Kenya and, due to the altitude, cooking takes longer, so pasta is preferable to rice; porridge is good for breakfast. The altitude affects appetite, but it's essential to eat carbohydrates and to maintain a good level of liquid intake – at least four litres a day, and preferably more; so plenty of hot brews – tea, chocolate and citrus fruit drinks – are recommended. As a precaution, it's wise to purify all drinking water.

Personal daypack

Even if in a guided group, if the mist comes down fast you can get separated. If porters are carrying your equipment, it's advisable to be prepared for an emergency, so carry water, high-energy snacks, warm and waterproof clothing, a space blanket, a basic first-aid kit, a map, compass, torch and mirror in your daypack.

Maps and guides

The most useful **map** is the 1:50,000 scale map and guide of Mount Kenya by Andrew Wielochowski and Mark Savage, available from West Col Productions (Goring, Reading, Berks RG8 9AA, UK), Stanfords in London and Nairobi bookshops. The most comprehensive **guidebook** for Mount Kenya is the *Guide to Mt Kenya and Kilimanjaro* edited by Iain Allan, published by the Mountain Club of Kenya, page 242, available through them or Nairobi bookshops. Other recommended guides are *Trekking in East Africa* by David Else, published by Lonely Planet and *The Mountains of Kenya*, a walker's guide, by Paul Clarke, also available in Nairobi.

Which route?

This is a matter of personal preference and how much time you have to spend. For **technical climbs** (not covered here) contact the Mountain Club of Kenya, page 242. Due to the height of the mountain, most people are likely to feel the **effects of altitude** over 4,000m, experiencing various symptoms such as headaches, which when extreme lead to acute mountain sickness or high altitude pulmonary oedema; see *Health and safety*, page 152. For a successful ascent it is important to acclimatise properly, and it's preferable to ascend no more than 700m a day. For those coming from sea level, it's advisable to spend at least four days at around 2,000m and a night at around 3,000m before the climb.

There are three main approach routes for the mountain – **Naro Moru**, **Sirimon** and **Chogoria**. Other routes do exist – Burguret, Timau and Meru – but they have not been maintained and are now difficult to follow. There's also the new **Nguniu route** opened by Serena Hotels (see page 240). Be aware that if attempting any of the routes other than the main three, or walking around the peaks, you'll require a permit from the park headquarters at Naro Moru, unless you're going on an organised trek. Of the three routes, Naro Moru is the most popular, giving the most direct access to Point Lenana, although it's tough going. The Sirimon route, although longer than the Naro Moru route, is less strenuous and has superb views of the main peaks, while the Chogoria route is the longest and toughest route, although scenically it's the most attractive.

Naro Moru route

From the park gate it's about 8km to the Met station, passing through thick forest to the bamboo zone and opening up to woodland draped in lichen at the **Met station** (3,050m). It's possible to get transport to this point from the youth hostel or Naro Moru River Lodge (page 241). If walking from the hostel, it will take about five hours. The climb up from the Met station is tough going, crossing an expanse known as the **vertical bog** before reaching the **Teleki Valley** where there are magnificent stands of giant groundsel and lobelia, to **Mackinder's Camp** (4,200m), a 5–6-hour walk. From here there are good views of the peaks. If you have the time, spend another day acclimatising at this altitude. Some treks leave at 02.00 to make the ascent on Point Lenana as dawn breaks, which certainly makes walking on the steep scree slope easier, as it's still frozen. From Mackinder's camp it's about an hour's walk to the scree slope, 3–4 hours to the top of the scree and **Austrian hut** (4,790m), and an hour to **Point Lenana** (4,985m) from there. Alternatively you can opt to stay at the Austrian hut next to the Lewis glacier, but you're likely to feel the effects of the cold and altitude with a splitting headache. From Austrian hut, the final ascent to Point Lenana entails walking up loose rocks and scree with a steep drop to the right and the Lewis glacier on the left, surrounded by dramatic mountain scenery with knife-edge ridges. If planning to go on the glacier, you'll need crampons and walking poles, and watch out for crevasses and the milky-green tarn below. In the early morning, the panoramic view from the top of the mountain is superb, looking down on to the bleached African plains some 3,000m below; even Kilimanjaro can be seen on a clear day. The descent from Point Lenana to the Naro Moru gate can be done in a day.

Sirimon route
From the park gate it's a steady 3–4-hour ascent on the moorland (not too wet underfoot) to **Old Moses Camp** (3,350m) – formerly called Judmaier Camp. From there it's about 5–6-hours' walking to the **Mackinder Valley** and **Shipton's Camp** (4,150m) with superb views of the mountain peaks. Normally another day is spent acclimatising at this level, with optional treks to Kami hut (4,425) and Hausberg Col (4,591m). It's an early start from Shipton's Camp to ascend **Point Lenana** (4,985m), about 4–5 hours. The descent can be via the same route, or alternatively via the Chogoria or Naro Moru routes.

Chogoria route
It's normal to spend the first night near the park gate, such as at Meru Mount Kenya Lodge (3,020m). As this is a camping route, campsites vary. Typically, you will walk for 3–4 hours, climbing steadily through rainforest and coming on to open moorland to a camp at **Lake Ellis** (3,500m). Leaving Lake Ellis, the trail has views of the **Vivienne Falls** on the way to the campsite at **Lake Michaelson** (4,000m), a 3–4 hour trek, not far from **Minto's hut** (porters only). An early start brings you to **Point Lenana** (4,985m), about a 4-hour trek. The descent can be via the same route, or alternatively via the Sirimon or Naro Moru routes.

Accommodation
For accommodation near the national park, look at the respective *Where to stay and eat* sections for **Naro Moru**, page 240, **Nanyuki**, page 253 and **Chogoria**, page 267. Within the national park, the camps and huts belong to different organisations. It's probably easiest to do all the booking through one agent like Let's Go Travel, page 101. If you have a rat phobia you may prefer to opt to take a tent as some of the less-used huts have furry residents. The main camps have accommodation for around 40 to 70 people. Two Tarn Hut, which is marked on some maps, no longer exists.

Selecting a campsite
In order to preserve the mountain habitat, aim to pitch camp in recognised campsites. When there is no obvious campsite, camp at least 50m away from water. For minimum impact it's preferable to camp on bare ground.

Naro Moru route
The Naro Moru River Lodge, page 241, owns the **Met Station** (a bunkhouse, costing about KSh500) and **Mackinder's Camp** (tents; costs about KSh600 per person) at the end of the Teleki Valley, while KWS is the booking agent for the **Warden's Cottage** at the park gate, see page 251, and **Austrian hut** (costs about KSh1,000 and a key needs to be collected from the rangers at the park gate).

Sirimon route
Kenya Wildlife Service is the booking agent for the **Sirimon bandas** at the Sirimon gate, see page 251, while Mountain Rock Lodge, Nanyuki, see page 252,

owns **Old Moses Camp** at the roadhead (costs US$7) and **Shipton's Camp** (costs US$8) in the Mackinder Valley.

Chogoria route
No huts are available on this route and it's compulsory to take a tent. Minto's hut is only for use by porters.

Mountain huts
There are six other mountain huts offering basic shelter, owned by the Mountain Club of Kenya, page 124 (costing about KSh50), which need to be booked and paid in advance.

Trekking on the mountain
National park fees
Park fees are US$15 a day, while guides and porters pay KSh100, and if certified only KSh50. You can enter the park only during daylight hours.

Go slowly
Ironically, it's the fit and competitive (and more commonly young men – sorry chaps) who are most prone to getting pulmonary oedema, so follow the maxim of the old Swahili proverb, *Haraka haraka haina baraka* – which roughly translates as 'To hurry is not a blessing'.

Ablution etiquette
Use soap and toothpaste minimally and at least 10m away from water sources. Human waste is a major water pollutant on the mountain. When available, use the existing toilets in the campsites. If none are available, select an area at least 30m from water and away from camps and trails. At low altitude, bury excrement in shallow holes, while at altitude, where vegetation cover is scant, UV radiation from the sun is the most efficient method for accelerating decomposition, so here it's preferable to scatter the excrement and not to bury it. In either case, all toilet paper should be retained and disposed of with other litter *off* the mountain.

In an emergency
If the weather suddenly turns bad and you become lost, or visibility is poor, find some shelter and keep as warm as possible. Do not attempt to head down the mountain, as once below the treeline you'll be difficult to find. Once visibility improves, attract attention by using the mirror in your daypack, or waving your space blanket if you see a plane overhead.

Mount Kenya National Park and Forest Reserve
PO Box 69, Naro Moru; tel: 061 21575
Open daily 06.30–18.00; park entry fees US$15; vehicle entry KSh200
The park has three main gates – the **Naro Moru** and **Sirimon gates** are accessed off the A2 Nairobi to Isiolo road, while the **Chogoria gate** is reached via the B6 Embu to Meru road.

The Naro Moru gate turn-off is at the village of Naro Moru, from which it's about 18km to the park gate. The turn-off to the Sirimon track is about 13km north of Nanyuki, from which it's about 10km to the park gate. The Chogoria gate is about 35km from the main turn-off on the B6 at Marima. From the Naro Moru and Sirimon gates there are around 20km of tracks within the park where you can drive (4WD recommended) as far as the 3,350m contour.

Conservation Mount Kenya was gazetted a national park in 1949 and covers an area of 71,500ha, most of it above the treeline. It includes the area above 3,200m and two small salients which extend along the Naro Moru and Sirimon tracks. Its unique Afro-alpine flora was recognised by UNESCO in 1978 when it was made an International Biosphere Reserve and this importance was compounded in 1997 when it was given World Heritage Site status. The boundaries of the World Heritage Site also include part of Mount Kenya National Forest Reserve which surrounds the national park. The forest reserve covers 199,500ha. While the park is well protected, the forest reserve has suffered severe deforestation due to illegal logging of camphor, cedar, olive and rosewood, charcoal production, clear felling for agriculture and a breakdown of the '*shamba* system' – an agroforestry practice, where annual agricultural crops are planted between tree seedlings until the young trees shade out the crops after about three years, after which the system is then used in a new area. A forest fire, thought to have been started by illegal squatters, raged for over a week, destroying 3,000ha of natural forest near Meru in 2003. As Mount Kenya is a vital water catchment area for the Tana and northern Ewaso Ng'iro rivers, increasingly attention is being paid to the conservation of its natural forests through organisations like the Working Forests Action Group, page 54, and the Bill Woodley Mount Kenya Trust, page 250, who work alongside the Kenya Wildlife Service and the Forest Department. The park itself now has over 15,000 visitors a year who create their own environmental impact, so when visiting the park, do bear this in mind and stick to the main trails.

Geomorphology Mount Kenya now stands at 5,199m. An extinct volcano which was active between 3.1–2.6 million years ago, it is likely that the summit once stood at more than 6,500m. Over the years, the volcanic crater rim eroded away, the present-day peaks – Batian, Nelion and Lenana – being the core of the original volcano. There are 12 remnant glaciers on the mountain, which have been receding rapidly during the last two decades, together with typical glacial features like moraine, U-shaped valleys and tarns.

Flora and fauna With its location on the Equator, Mount Kenya has a fascinating variety of plant-life and you cannot fail to be impressed by the giant groundsels and lobelias on the high moorland. The changes in altitude create distinctive plant zones and 13 species are endemic to the mountain. The **montane forest** begins around the 2,000m contour, dominated by cedar and podocarpus rising through **bamboo forest** at around 2,500m, extending into open woodland of *Hagenia abyssinica* draped in old man's beard – high-altitude lichen. Above 3,000m it's too cold for trees and the vegetation changes to **heathland,** with abundant everlasting flowers (*Helichrysum*), merging into **Afro-alpine moorland,** with giant groundsels 4m high, the rosette-shaped lobelias and grassy tussocks, before reaching bare rockface, scree and ice.

Inevitably, the **wildlife** on the mountain corresponds to the different habitats. Elephant, Cape buffalo, Sykes monkey, giant forest hog, black-fronted duiker, bushbuck and leopard are found in the forest, although you are more likely to see their spoor and droppings. On the moorland the Mount Kenya mouse shrew, endemic to the area, rats and rock hyrax are commonly seen around the campsites, the rock hyrax resembling giant guinea pigs. Surprisingly, they are the closest living relative to the elephant and have tusks, although these are not visible. (Be aware that due to food being left on the mountain or fed to the animals, in the past there's been a plague of rats which damaged the fragile vegetation.) Serval and golden cats have been seen on the moorland and buffalo, hyena and leopard occasionally venture into the open. The poisonous Mount Kenya bush viper and montane viper are rarely seen. The mountain has a rich **birdlife** of both forest and moorland species. Among

Met Bill Woodley's son, Bongo, in Mt Kenya Safari Club bar - 25/1/05 - who works as warden of Mt Kenya National Reserve.

THE BILL WOODLEY MOUNT KENYA TRUST
Susie Weeks

The Bill Woodley Mount Kenya Trust (BWMKT) is a Kenya-based organisation dedicated to helping preserve and protect Mount Kenya. Recognising that the natural resources and associated biodiversity of Mount Kenya are among the most important in Kenya, BWMKT was established in 1999 by Kenyans concerned about the high levels of habitat destruction on the mountain. Mount Kenya has the largest remaining forest zone in Kenya. Its ecosystem as a whole plays a critical role in water catchment for two main rivers in the country, the Tana and Ewaso Ng'iro, and it also contains several important threatened wildlife species. Although Mount Kenya's forests and alpine habitat are protected by law, unchecked illegal activity threatens their very existence. Population pressure has caused people to wantonly over-exploit the natural resources to obtain charcoal, timber, grazing and bushmeat and to encroach into the forest for crop cultivation, leaving some areas devoid of any form of natural vegetation. The trust concentrates its conservation projects at field level for maximum impact and assists government agencies such as the Forest Department and the Kenya Wildlife Service (KWS) in stemming illegal activities. The Bill Woodley Mount Kenya Trust's objectives and projects include:

- Reafforestation and the establishment of nurseries for indigenous trees
- Anti-poaching and the removal of snares and traps used for the bush-meat trade
- Fencing to reduce human/wildlife conflict
- Development of environmental education and research

Among the BWMKT's most important achievements to date are regular de-snaring operations, anti-poaching support for KWS, several ongoing tree-planting projects and elephant fencing. The de-snaring operations are implemented over a 20-day period and involve KWS and young Kenyan volunteers, who patrol specific areas of the national reserve. Snares and traps set to kill wildlife are destroyed and key poaching hotspots are identified for future monitoring. The teams also involve local communities in order to try to reduce the overall problem. It employs six wildlife guards on a permanent basis who constantly patrol an area of the mountain notorious for poaching activity. In addition it has raised funds to build a barrack block to house newly recruited KWS rangers who are helping to increase overall security. The trust supports community-based organisations and the Forest Department with tree nurseries and reafforestation efforts. This may be in the form of donations of badly needed equipment or the provision of seeds. It is also reafforesting degraded areas within the national reserve with indigenous trees, using a method called enrichment planting. Over 50km of fencing has been erected to protect communities from elephants destroying their crops and seedling plantations from destruction. As further fencing is underway the trust intends to establish an elephant corridor, which would allow elephants and other wildlife to move safely off the mountain to other suitable habitats.

Further information on the Bill Woodley Mount Kenya Trust is available on www.mountkenyatrust.com

the forest birds are the green ibis, Ayre's hawk eagle, the African long-eared owl and Hartlaub's turaco (hunted for its scarlet flight feathers used for making fishing flies). On the high moorland, the scarlet-tufted malachite sunbird is common, while Abbott's starling is rare and endangered. The Mackinder's eagle owl can sometimes be heard at night around the campsites. The wildlife in the national park is well protected, but in the forest reserve near the areas of settlement, friction is often caused by problem animals – usually elephant, buffalo, bush pigs and baboons – due to their crop-raiding tendencies. Electric fencing is proving to be a good solution to reducing the conflict between wildlife and the local people. However, conversely, much of the wildlife in these areas is also subject to illegal hunting, buffalo, bushbuck and bush pig being the main targets of the bushmeat trade.

Where to stay

Warden's Cottage (2 rooms, self-catering) Book through KWS, page 91
Situated near the Naro Moru gate, the cottage has been refurbished and offers comfortable accommodation, sleeping 4. There's an open fireplace in the sitting-room. Bedding and towels are provided and the kitchen is fully equipped.
Rates: from US$40–70 a day plus park and vehicle entry fees
Sirimon bandas (2 bandas, self-catering) Book through KWS, page 91
Located near the Sirimon gate, each banda is a self-contained unit with 2 rooms, sleeping 4, a fitted kitchen and brightly furnished sitting-room. In the adjacent house, there's a kitchen, sitting-room with a fireplace, dining-room and large veranda. Towels and bedding are provided and there's a resident caretaker. Game drives and walks can be arranged.
Rates: US$40–70 a day plus park and vehicle entry fees

For other accommodation see page 247.

NORTH TO NANYUKI AND ISIOLO

Heading north from Naro Moru, the A2 continues to skirt the slopes of Mount Kenya to the busy market town of Nanyuki, with its wide, tree-lined main street. It was established around 1907 as a settler town and remains an important centre for the ranching communities of Laikipia and Timau, as well as being a base for the Kenyan Air Force and British military training exercises. There's also a buoyant woodworking industry, mainly producing furniture. The road continues to climb up to Timau, passing one of the major homegrown horticultural enterprises (cut flowers, haricot beans and mange-tout that find their way to European supermarkets) and large wheat farms, while the views open up revealing a wonderful panorama stretching north to the blue hills of the Mathews range and the vast expanse of the northern frontier district, set against a backdrop of mountain moorland and the craggy peaks of Mount Kenya. From Timau, the road begins to descend, passing the Lewa Wildlife Conservancy on the left (see page 264) and hill *shambas* to the right, to the hot, dry plains of Isiolo.

Getting there and around

From Naro Moru the A2 continues on to the sizeable market town of **Nanyuki** (about 20km). After Nanyuki the road surface is potholed in sections, before climbing up to **Timau** (about 15km) and continuing about 30km, before bearing north at the B6 junction from Meru to **Isiolo** (about 25km); see *Chapter 13* on northern Kenya, page 351.

By bus

There's a regular bus service along the A2 between Nairobi and Isiolo, which stop at Naro Moru and Nanyuki, and a number of share taxis between Nairobi and Nanyuki.

By air

There's an airfield at Nanyuki with daily scheduled flights to Nairobi, Samburu and Masai Mara. This is also the base for Tropicair, see page 82, who arrange charters to northern Kenya.

By rail

No passenger service is available.

Getting organised

For **changing money**, Barclays (with ATM), Standard Chartered and Kenya Commercial banks as well as the main **post office** (open Mon–Fri 08.00–17.00, Sat 09.00–12.00) are situated on the main street. For **internet access** there are several internet cafés in town – one next to Barclays bank and another next to Mountain Rock Café, both on the main street. For **general provisions** visit the Settler's Store, while the **market** is on the west of town past the bus station. There's a **pharmacy** on the main street and in a **medical emergency** go to the excellent Nanyuki Cottage Hospital which also has a doctors' surgery (tel: 062 32666). In an emergency the **tourist helpline** is 020 604767. There are plenty of **petrol stations** in Nanyuki and petrol is also available in Timau. For **shopping**, visit Nanyuki Spinners and Weavers and Cape Chestnut.

South of Nanyuki
Where to stay and eat

Mountain Rock Lodge (cottages, camping) PO Box 333, Nanyuki; tel: 062 62625; fax: 062 62051; email: reservations@mountainrockkenya.com; web: www.mountainrockkenya.com
About 8km north of Naro Moru, signed to the right (1km off the main road), the hotel nestles on the forested foothills of Mount Kenya. It's primarily a base for climbing the mountain and offers a selection of mountain excursions and has a good collection of equipment for hire. The management is helpful and friendly. The main building has a lounge, a couple of bars and a dining-room, while there's also a beer garden and *nyama choma* barbecue area. The cottages have fireplaces and are simply furnished with en-suite bathrooms. The two spacious campsites have showers, toilets and good security. **On offer:** mountain climbing, birdwatching, horseriding, trout fishing, excursions to the Mau Mau caves.
Rates: from US$35 per person sharing; camping US$6
Trout Tree Restaurant (self-catering cottage, sleeps 8) tel: 062 62059; mobile: 0722 664830; email: troutree@wananchi.com; web: www.chardust.com/elk/troutree
Located 100m off the A2, after the Nanyuki airfield, and fishbone-signed to the left if heading north, this is a superb restaurant on the Burguret River about 13km south of Nanyuki. It's an ideal stop-off point between Nairobi and Samburu and excellent value (main courses from KSh450). Resembling a treehouse and imaginatively built around a huge fig tree, it overlooks trout ponds. Fresh trout, fillet steak and kebabs with home-grown salads are on the mouth-watering menu, and black-and-white colobus monkeys may sometimes be seen in the surrounding trees. A popular disco, the BoneZone, is held on the last Saturday of each month (entry KSh200). In addition, a self-catering guesthouse is available, with a spacious sitting-room with an open fireplace, a veranda, a kitchen with cooker and cutlery and 4 double rooms, a bathroom, shower and 2 flush toilets.
Rates: guesthouse from KSh6,000 per night

What to see and do
Crossing the Equator
Just south of Nanyuki the road crosses the Equator. If you stop you can watch a demonstration of the coriolis effect – in the northern hemisphere water runs anti-clockwise down the plug hole while in the southern hemisphere it does the opposite.

Stayed (in superior dble room, no.33)
25/1/05 - 27/1/05

NORTH TO NANYUKI AND ISIOLO 253

Nanyuki
Where to stay
Mount Kenya Safari Club (114 rooms in suites and cottages; swimming pool) Book
through Lonhro Hotels, page 91
About 15km east of Nanyuki, this is Kenya's most salubrious country hotel and enjoys
an international reputation. Set in beautifully kept tropical gardens with sweeping lawns
and colourful flowerbeds, the club was started in 1959 by William Holden, the
American actor, and since then has entertained a string of celebrities. The club still
retains an old-fashioned colonial opulence, and is one of the few places that insists on a *No it doesn't!*
jacket and tie for dinner. It has a couple of bars and restaurants and a lounge adorned
with hunting trophies. The rooms all have fireplaces, country-house-style furnishings
and en-suite bathrooms, and most have a veranda with views to the mountain. The food
and service are excellent. There's a chapel in the grounds that is popular for weddings.
On offer: 9-hole golf course, bowls, croquet, tennis, horseriding, trout fishing, William
Holden Wildlife Conservation Centre, animal orphanage, health centre, art gallery,
shop.
Rates: from US$175 full board per person sharing; daily membership KSh400
Sportsman's Arms (60 rooms, cottages, self-catering; heated swimming pool) PO Box 3,
Nanyuki; tel: 062 32347; fax: 062 22895; email: sarms@nanyukiafricaonline.com
Located about 500m east of the town centre, the Sportsman's Arms started as a settlers'
watering hole and has undergone extensive refurbishment to become a glitzy businessmen's
hotel. Set in 4ha of gardens, the rooms are spacious, smartly decorated with en-suite
bathrooms (including bidets), and have satellite TV while there are old and new cottages
with fireplaces and kitchenettes. It has the facilities you'd expect of a large hotel, with bars,
business centre, and good restaurants serving European and African cuisine. **On offer:** trout
fishing, boating on the manmade lake, horseriding, health club, Buccaneer disco.
Rates: rooms from KSh2,500 B&B per person sharing; self-catering cottages from KSh2,500

There are a number of **cheap lodgings** in Nanyuki, among them:

Sirimon Hotel opposite the Kanu grounds and near the bus station, tel: 062 32344
A friendly establishment with a restaurant. Rooms are basic but have a shower and toilet
and there's secure parking.
Rates: from KSh300
Jambo House Hotel Bazaar St; tel: 062 31894
Similar in standard to the Sirimon Hotel, with a bar and restaurant.
Rates: from KSh300
Equator chalet opposite the Kenya Commercial Bank on the main street
Recently opened, the rooms are reasonable with shower and toilet, and there's safe parking.
Rates: from KSh500
Nanyuki Youth Hostel on Market St
Very basic with cold showers, but cheap.
Rates: from KSh50 for a dorm bed

Where to eat
Apart from the hotels listed above, there are plenty of **cheap eats** in Nanyuki in
the town centre. Try the **Marina Grill**, **Muneera Restaurant** (good curries) and
the **Mountain Rock Café** for samosas and mandazis.

Cape Chestnut at the southern end of town near Nanyuki Cottage Hospital. Has good
snack meals (from around KSh250) with homemade soups, smoked trout, salads and cakes,
in a pleasant garden setting. There's also a gift shop, ideal for small presents, and a business
centre next door. *Closed Sundays.*

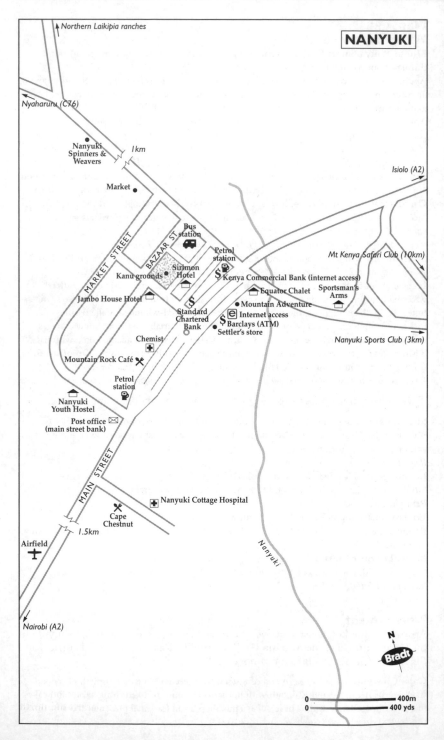

NANYUKI

Northern Laikipia ranches

Nyaharuru (C76)

Isiolo (A2)

Nanyuki Spinners & Weavers

1km

Market

MARKET STREET

BAZAAR ST

Bus station

Petrol station

Mt Kenya Safari Club (10km)

Kanu grounds

Sirimon Hotel

Kenya Commercial Bank (internet access)

Jambo House Hotel

Equator Chalet

Sportsman's Arms

Mountain Adventure

Standard Chartered Bank

Internet access

Barclays (ATM)

Settler's store

Nanyuki Sports Club (3km)

Chemist

Mountain Rock Café

Petrol station

Nanyuki Youth Hostel

Post office (main street bank)

MAIN STREET

Nanyuki Cottage Hospital

Cape Chestnut

1.5km

Airfield

Nairobi (A2)

Nanyuki

N

Bradt

0 ____ 400m
0 ____ 400 yds

What to see and do
Nanyuki spinners and weavers
On the western side of town about 1km down the Nyaharuru road, this is a women's co-operative producing woven materials and rugs at very reasonable prices. *Closed Sundays*

Nanyuki War Cemetery
There's a large cemetery to the east of town between the Sportsman's Arms and the Nanyuki Sports Club.

Climbing Mount Kenya
Mountain Adventure next to Barclays Bank (PO Box 1180, Nanyuki; tel: 062 31887; email: tigerkami@yahoo.com) can arrange mountain treks from US$60 a day. For more options on climbing Mount Kenya, please see page 242.

North of Nanyuki
Where to stay and eat
Kentrout Grill (self-catering cottages and bandas, camping by request) PO Box 14, Timau; tel: 062 41016 or book through Let's Go Travel page 101
It's about 3km down a track signposted to the right from Timau, to the fish farm. A popular stop-off point for buffet lunches (KSh800), with trout being the speciality, the restaurant is in a peaceful woodland setting, with black-and-white colobus monkeys, next to the Teleswan River. The cottages and bandas are comfortable with en-suite facilities.
Rates: from KSh2,150 half board per person; camping by negotiation. Restaurant open 11.00–17.00.
Timau River Lodge (cottages, camping; swimming pool) PO Box 212, Timau; tel: 062 41230
Located on the right about 2km from Timau, the log cabins are perched above a waterfall in a peaceful, picturesque setting. The rustic cabins sleep 2–4 and have en-suite facilities. There's an excellent bar and restaurant which specialises in north Indian cuisine and also caters for vegetarians. The campsite is sheltered by trees and provides hot showers, toilets and free firewood. **On offer:** mountain trekking, trout fishing, birdwatching and camel rides.
Rates: from KSh1,250 B&B per person; camping KSh300

LAIKIPIA PLATEAU AND RUMURUTI
Only now is Laikipia gaining recognition as a wildlife destination in its own right. Within Kenya its wildlife densities rank second to the Masai Mara. In addition, Laikipia boasts more endangered mammals than anywhere else in East Africa. Half of Kenya's black rhino are protected in the Solio, Lewa, Ol Jogi, Ol Pejeta and Ol Ari Ng'iro sanctuaries; it has the biggest elephant herds (over 3,200) outside the national parks and is one of the few places in Kenya where you can see Jackson's hartebeest. It's also home to about 25% of the world's population of Grevy's zebra and to other rare species like wild dog and sitatunga antelope. Many of the northern species of game are seen here – reticulated giraffe, Somali ostrich, Beisa oryx and gerenuk – while there are also healthy lion, leopard and cheetah populations and numerous impala and Grant's gazelle.

The Laikipia Plateau extends west from the foothills of Mount Kenya, to the wall of the Rift Valley at Lake Baringo, and north from Nanyuki and Nyaharuru to the lands of Samburu at Isiolo, merging with the Lerochi Plateau south of Maralal. It includes the small town of Rumuruti, with its handful of shops and a liquor store at the end of the tarmac on the C77 heading to Maralal. In the north the edge of the plateau drops abruptly to the northern frontier district. The greater

Laikipia area is the size of Wales and includes the entire Ewaso ecosystem, which extends from the Laikipia Plateau into northern Kenya as far as Samburu and the Mathews Mountains (see *Chapter 13*, page 351).

The land is divided into large, private, cattle ranches and community group ranches, while small-scale farmers occupy land on the foothills of the Aberdares and Mount Kenya, both being areas where wildlife conflicts with the needs of the local people. Over the past decade cattle ranching has diversified to embrace and develop wildlife tourism. In turn, ranchers have encouraged community group ranches along the foot of the plateau to tap the tourist potential of wildlife. Increasingly in this area of marginal rainfall, wildlife conservation and the income generated by tourism are more profitable than cattle and subsistence pastoralism. Perhaps the best example of this is **Lewa Wildlife Conservancy** (see page 264) which started as a cattle ranch and is now a non-profit-making trust focusing on conservation.

An umbrella body, the **Laikipia Wildlife Forum** (see page 62) was formed in 1992 to conserve the integrity of the Ewaso ecosystem and its members include conservation and research bodies as well as private and community-owned ranches. It brings a cohesion to new tourism and community developments as well as monitoring research programmes through Mpala Research Centre, the African Humanities and Biodiversity Centre and Lewa Wildlife Conservancy.

For the visitor, the appeal of Laikipia lies in the opportunity to escape the main tourist routes, where you can enjoy the wilderness and, taking that a step further, where you can walk, ride a bicycle, camel or horse, or be driven around in open vehicles. The lodges are expensive – you pay for the exclusivity – but the self-catering and camping options are reasonably priced, and there are new developments coming on stream. Kijabe, a community ecolodge, Soit Nasera and Sosian and the **Naibung Conservancy**, a joint venture between nine community group ranches and covering 8,000ha, are developing ecotourism activities.

Getting there and around

If driving, it is essential to have 4WD and to get precise directions when visiting the Laikipia properties, as roads are poorly marked and it's all too easy to get lost. The two major arteries in Laikipia are the C76 which bears west to connect with the B5 shortly before Nyaharuru and an unnumbered, but well-used road which heads north from the C76 a few kilometres out of Nanyuki, crossing the plateau and passing Mukenya (1,845m) before connecting with the C77 north of Rumuruti.

By bus

No buses operate in Laikipia, but buses and *matatus* operating between Nyaharuru and Maralal stop at Rumuruti.

By air

The majority of Laikipia ranches have private airstrips, as do Lewa Wildlife Conservancy and the community lodges of Il Ngwesi and Tassia.

By rail

No rail service is available.

Getting organised

It is best to get organised with money and provisions prior to going to Laikipia. **Petrol** is available at Nanyuki, Rumuruti and Nyaharuru, so fill up before going to Laikipia, and if in doubt carry extra fuel. By arrangement you may be able to purchase fuel at some of the ranches in an emergency, but do not rely on this. For other services – money, post office, medical and shopping – the best place is

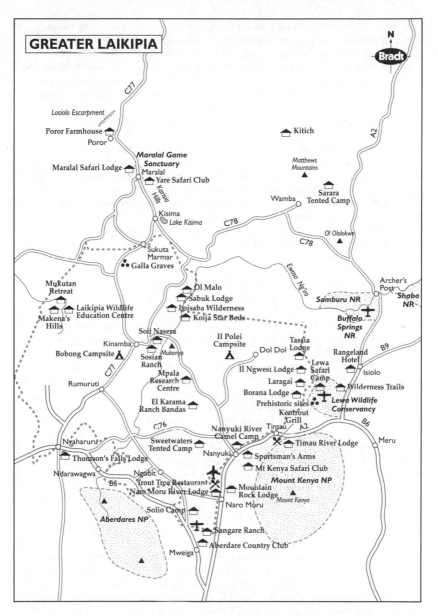

Nanyuki, or if coming from further afield, Nakuru or Nairobi. In an emergency the **tourist helpline** is 020 604767.

Where to stay and eat

Wilderness Trails (8 cottages; saltwater swimming pool) Book through Bush Homes of East Africa, page 90

This is a charming, private homestay on Lewa Wildlife Conservancy with Will Craig, whose family initiated the conservancy, and his wife, Emma. The 8 individual and twin cottages are sited in the garden, rooms having a fireplace and sitting-room area, an honesty bar, large four-poster beds and en-suite bathrooms. There's also a separate, communual sitting-room, in the garden, complete with comfortable sofas, Africana books and a log fire in the evenings, and a dining grotto with delicious food and organic, home-grown vegetables. **On offer:** day and night game drives, bush walks, bush breakfasts, horseriding, camel rides, jogging, tennis, visits to a Maasai cultural *manyatta* and prehistoric sites and fly-camping. *Rates: from US$365 full board per person sharing*

Lewa Safari Camp (12 tents; swimming pool) Book through Bush Homes of East Africa, page 90

The camp is located within Lewa Wildlife Conservancy (it belongs to the conservancy) and has views down towards the arid northern frontier district. The main building is a cedar wood cottage, expanded to include a bar and dining area and a sitting-room, with a log fire, overlooking a floodlit waterhole where black and white rhino, elephant and other wildlife come to drink. During the day, meals are often taken at the poolside. The tented rooms are well spread out with good views and have a private veranda, comfortable beds and en-suite shower rooms. **On offer:** day and night game drives, educational talks, guided walks, sundowners, horseriding, visits to prehistoric sites and a Maasai cultural *manyatta*.

Rates: from US$260 full board per person sharing. Closed April to mid-May and November.

Borana Lodge (6 cottages; swimming pool) PO Box 20139, 00200 City Square, Nairobi; tel: 020 607528; fax: 020 607529; email: bookings@borana.com; web: www.boranaranch.com

Located on Borana, a private 14,000ha commercial ranch devoted to the conservation of wildlife in its natural habitat, the lodge, made from cedar, natural stone and thatch, has an elevated position with expansive views across Laikipia to the north. It's run by Fuzz Dyer, who grew up on the ranch, and his wife Bimbi. The main building has a sitting-room-cum-bar with leather sofas, an open fireplace and large plate-glass windows maximising the view. There's also a smaller, cosy sitting-room, with plenty of books and interesting *objet d'art* and a grand, baronial dining-room providing delicious meals. The cottages are individually designed, with huge bedrooms, complete with a fireplace and sitting area, comfortable beds and en-suite bathrooms. There's a waterhole in the valley below which has interesting birdlife and is visited by elephants. **On offer:** day and night game drives, horseriding, excellent guided walks, sundowners, lake and fly-fishing, excursions to Lewa Wildlife Conservancy (the adjacent ranch) and Lake Rotundu on Mount Kenya.

Rates: from US$400 full board per person sharing. Children only welcome by special request.

Laragai (8 rooms; swimming pool) PO Box 20139, 00200 City Square, Nairobi; tel: 020 607528; fax: 020 607529; email: bookings@borana.com; web: www.boranaranch.com

Laragai is a timber and thatch house set within the 14,000ha Borana ranch. Although built in a traditional African style, its interior is more akin to an English manor house. There's a huge baronial drawing-room, with large, open fireplaces at either end, gilt-framed mirrors and chintz-covered sofas. It opens on to a veranda with views to the distant north. The rooms are in two separate buildings and are comfortably furnished with en-suite bathrooms. **On offer:** guided walks, day and night game drives, horseriding, bush meals, excursions to Samburu and Lewa Wildlife Conservancy, fly-fishing.

Rates: from US$400 full board per person sharing

Il Ngwesi Lodge (6 rooms; swimming pool; community ecolodge) Booking through Let's Go Travel, page 101; web: www.laikipiawildlife.com

It's an adventurous 4WD from Borana to reach Il Ngwesi, or alternatively a short flight from Nanyuki. This ecolodge opened in 1996 on the 14,500ha Il Ngwesi group ranch and is owned and hosted by the Il Ngwesi Maasai. It's spread out on a small hill at the base of the Mokogodo escarpment with superb panoramic views across arid plains to the sugarloaf mountain of Ol Ololokwe. The lodge is unique for its free-form architecture, which follows the twisted shapes of ancient Newtonia trees under a grass thatch. Rustically furnished, the 6 rooms are raised on stilts and open-plan (no glass or netting) with partitioned, flush 'loos with a view' and 'under the stars' showers. There's a bar-cum-dining mess area, a waterhole with a viewing platform and a leopard bait. Elephants and giraffe are regularly seen, a rhino has been translocated to the ranch and there's a pet kudu on the compound. **On offer:** bush walks with knowledgeable Maasai guides, game drives, candlelit dinners in a traditional *boma*, picnic breakfasts and camel treks.

Rates: self-catering, for exclusive use of whole lodge US$380; fully catered exclusive use US$265–480 depending on numbers; fully catered non-exclusive use US$190 per person

Tassia Lodge (6 rooms and kids' bunkhouse; swimming pool; community ecolodge) web: www.tassia.com. Booking through Let's Go Travel, page 101.

Tassia is reached by 4WD from Borana ranch or alternatively you can fly in. A sister project to Il Ngwesi, Tassia opened in 2001. Located on the 16,000ha Lekurruki group ranch, it is hosted by the Lekurruki Maasai, and here again one can savour the African wilderness in a tranquil setting. Perched like eyries and cut into the steep rock face, the rooms are open and have en-suite facilities with rustic furniture, and are sited for privacy and the views. The sitting and dining area looks down on to a plunge pool built into the rocks and there's a natural waterhole on the plains below. Although using similar building techniques and materials to Il Ngwesi, the architecture has evolved its own distinctive style. While some rooms are dictated by the solidity of natural rock forms, others rise like small lookout towers, and there's also a bunkhouse for children. **On offer:** bush walks with knowledgeable Maasai guides, day and night game drives, bush picnics, camel treks and visits to a Maasai cultural *manyatta*.

Rates: exclusive use, from US$190–360 full board depending on numbers

Nanyuki River Camel Camp (8 Somali houses, camping; picnicking) Camellot, PO Box 485, Nanyuki; tel: 062 32327, mobile: 0722 328622/361642; email: camellot@wananchi.com

Located 4km to the west of Nanyuki town, this camp was started by Chris and Nasra Field who previously worked with the charity FARM-Africa, working on outreach programmes among the camel-owning nomadic tribes of northern Kenya. The camp is based on the mobile camps they used, where natural materials proved more durable than tents. The aim is to give guests a 'nomad's experience', staying in traditional Somali houses made from woven palm mats attached to wooden frames, eating traditional meals, watching camels being milked (and sampling the milk) and learning how nomads survive in the arid environment. There is a separate dining banda and ablution block. There are several campsites along the riverbank. **On offer:** Camel rides, birdwatching in riverine forest, Boran and Somali dancing, authentic curios for sale and excursions to Sweetwaters Game Reserve.

Rates: US$30 half board per person; camping from US$8; picnicking US$4. Camel rides from US$10–25

Sweetwaters Tented Camp (30 tents; swimming pool) Book through Lonrho Hotels, page 91

The camp is situated within the 9,700ha Sweetwaters Game Sanctuary (which includes a chimpanzee sanctuary) on Ol Pejeta ranch, west of Nanyuki, signposted to the left off the Nyahururu road. Most of the tents, which are comfortably furnished with a veranda and en-suite bathrooms, overlook a waterhole, and some are raised on stilts. The restaurant (good variety of meals) and bar (with satellite TV) are in the original farmhouse. **On offer:** tree planting, guided bird and nature walks, camel rides, day and night game drives, excursions to the chimpanzee sanctuary and information centre, a Maasai cultural *manyatta*, and visits to Morani, the tame rhino.

Rates: from US$160 full board per person sharing

Ol Pejeta Ranch House (6 suites; swimming pool) Book through Lonrho Hotels, page 91

The ranch has been owned by the famous and the infamous in its time – Lord Delamere, Christina Onassis' father-in-law, Roussel, and now Adnan Khashoggi, the arms dealer. In the main house are Mr and Mrs Khashoggi's private suites (the de-luxe option, both being suitably 'over the top' with giant beds) and a couple of guest suites, together with a shared sitting-room with an open fireplace, while **Buffalo cottage** has 2 additional suites. **On offer:** escorted game walks, game drives, horseriding, tennis, and excursions in the sanctuary as above.

Rates: from US$175 full board per person sharing

Il Polei (community-run campsite) Book through Let's Go Travel, page 101

An hour's drive west of Nanyuki on the Dol Dol road, the camp is situated on the Il Polei group ranch where the Mokogodo Maasai have set aside 2,000ha of their 8,000ha ranch for wildlife and tourism; elephant, lion, greater kudu, leopard, gerenuk and Grevy's zebra come to water at the dam, and the cultural *manyatta* is well worth a visit. The campsite, with basic facilities, is suitable for 3 families and is situated under acacia trees overlooking a dry riverbed. You will need to be fully self sufficient and to bring everything, including drinking water. There is no water on site, but it can be fetched from the chief's office a few kilometres away, and firewood can be purchased.

Rates: KSh2,200 for the whole camp

El Karama Ranch (9 self-catering bandas) P Bag, PO Box 172, Nanyuki. Book through Let's Go Travel, page 101

A working stud for Sahiwal cattle, El Karama is a wonderfully picturesque ranch and the home of Guy Grant and his wife Lavinia, the artist and author of *On a Kenya Ranch*. The bandas, for 2–3 people, are situated on the Ewaso Ng'iro River (where you can swim) and are provided with basic beds, mattresses, a table, chairs, wash basin, bucket, shower, fireplace and firewood. Long-drop toilets are situated not far from the bandas and a watchman is on duty 24 hours. Hurricane lamps, bedding, cooking utensils, crockery, cutlery and glasses are available for hire. You'll need to bring all provisions and drinking water. **On offer:** by arrangement through the ranch office are wildlife walks with a tracker at 07.00 or 16.00 daily (KSh400), fishing for catfish or barbel (bring your own tackle), game drives (KSh1,000), horseriding (KSh2,000) and horse and camel treks.

Rates: from KSh1,000 per person (10% discount for 3 nights or more)

Loisaba Wilderness (7 cottages; swimming pool) Book through the Mellifera Collection, PO Box 24397, Nairobi; tel: 020 577381; fax: 020 577381; email: mellifera@swiftkenya.com; web: www.loisaba.com

The former home of Count Ancelotto, the lodge lies on the 25,000ha Colcheccio ranch, at the edge of the Laikipia Plateau, where the landscape ranges from open plains to thornscrub and rocky escarpments. The property has two permanent rivers and springs attracting a variety of wildlife with some exceptional viewing of leopard, lion and cheetah. The main house and the cottages are perched on a 300m cliff with expansive views across the plateau towards Mount Kenya. The rooms (on the small side) are in individual cottages with en-suite shower rooms, and a small deck, while the main house has a large sitting room with an open fireplace and comfortable leather sofas. During the day, meals are often taken at the pool house. **On offer:** day and night game drives, sundowners, guided walks, bush picnics, horseriding, camel riding, spa and health treatments, bush breakfasts, river rafting and fishing in season, helicopter excursions and options for a night in a star-bed.

Rates: from US$425 full board per person sharing

Koija star-beds (2 sets of 3 platforms, community-owned) Booking through the Mellifera Collection, PO Box 24397, Nairobi; tel: 020 577381; fax: 020 577381; email: mellifera@swiftkenya.com; web: www.loisaba.com

Located adjacent to Loisaba, and hosted by the Koija community, there are 2 star-bed venues. The first is Kiboko, where the raised platforms are on a hill overlooking a dam where game comes to water, while the second has platforms cantilevered out over the Ewaso Ng'iro river. The star-beds consist of a raised, half-thatched platform where beds (complete with four-poster mosquito netting) can be wheeled out on to the deck for stargazing. It's rather like sleeping on a trailer, as the wheels are 4WD in size and you have to climb up into the huge bed. Each platform has a flush toilet and shower to the rear. There's also a small, thatched, open mess area for meals and food is prepared in a traditional camp kitchen.

Rates: from US$425 full board per person sharing

Sabuk Lodge (5 cottages) Book through Cheli & Peacock, page 90.

Located in western Laikipia (not far from Loisaba Wilderness) Sabuk Lodge has a delightful setting perched 50m above a gorge where the Ewaso Ng'iro thunders through the rocks. The ranch has a variety of game, including greater kudu, reticulated giraffe, klipspringer, eland, lion and leopard together with good birdwatching. It's the home of professional safari guide Simon Evans, and a base for his camel safaris. The lodge is cosy and open plan with high thatched ceilings and a laid-back atmosphere, while service is attentive and friendly. The rooms are in stone-built and thatched cottages in the wilderness garden – simply furnished, they are novel in design, with free-form, open-air baths and views across the gorge. **On offer:** camel safaris, excellent guided bush walks with Laikipiak Maasai, birdwatching, swimming and fishing in the river.

Rates: from US$255 full board per person + US$30 conservation fee. Children welcome.

Ol Malo (4 cottages; swimming pool) Book through Bush Homes of East Africa, page 90

Located on a 2,000ha ranch in western Laikipia, about an hour's drive south of Maralal, Ol Malo – which means the 'Place of the Greater Kudu' – occupies a fabulous position on the escarpment edge, with views down to a waterhole, where leopard and elephant come to water, and extending across the Laikipia plains to Mount Kenya on the distant horizon. It's the home of Rocky and Colin Francombe who are congenial hosts and a fountain of knowledge about the local area. The main house has a cosy sitting-room with a log fire in the evenings and an open dining-room – delicious food, much of it home-grown – and veranda, while the rooms are in stone and olive-wood thatched cottages sited along the escarpment rim. Each has a private veranda, a spacious bedroom with a picture window and a sitting area, together with olive-framed beds and en-suite bathrooms. **On offer:** bush walks, camel treks, birdwatching, day and night game drives, bush picnics and sundowners, cultural visits to Samburu *manyattas* nearby and excursions to market towns and the Karisia Hills.

Rates: from US$415 full board per person sharing plus US$30 conservation fee

Bobong Campsite and Field Study Centre (camping and 3 self-catering bandas; small swimming pool) PO Box 5, Rumuruti; tel: 062 32718; fax: 062 32719; email: olmaisor@africaonline.co.ke

The campsite is situated in the southern corner of Ol Maisor, a cattle ranch owned by Amanda and John Perrett, and is readily accessed 100m to the left off the main Maralal road, 20km north of Rumuruti. The campsite, with superb views across the Ewaso Ng'iro floodplains, is next door to the Perrett's Farmhouse, complete with its pet cheetah and vervet monkey, and has basic facilities – rustic bandas sleeping 2 – and an ablution block with long-drop toilets and hot showers. Water, lighting and firewood are available, together with assistance in camp if required and there's good security. The camp is popular for field trips and family outings. **On offer:** bird walks and hides near the Rumuruti swamp, camel treks from a couple of hours to several weeks, guided walks and river fishing.

Rates: camping and bandas from KSh250. Child friendly.

Mukutan Retreat (3 cottages; swimming pool) PO Box 45593, Nairobi; tel: 020 520799; fax: 020 521220; email: mukutan@africaonline.co.ke; web: www.mukutan.com

Accessed to the west off the Nyaharuru–Maralal road, or by air, the retreat is located on the 40,500ha Ol Ari Ng'iro – which means the 'Place of Dark Waters' in Maa – ranch, owned by Kuki Gallmann who wrote *I Dreamed of Africa* and the location for the feature film of the same name starring Kim Basinger. It overlooks the Mukutan gorge with its waterfalls, palm trees and thermal hot springs. The ranch plays an important role in conservation and is the

THE LAIKIPIA PREDATOR PROJECT
Dr Laurence Frank

Lions are disappearing. Conflict between large carnivores and livestock-based communities is causing the rapid extinction of predators throughout Africa.

Recent surveys by scientists suggest that fewer than 23,000 lions remain in Africa, and those are primarily found in national parks. Outside parks, predators kill livestock, especially where uncontrolled poaching has reduced their natural prey. As guns and poison are widely available, lions, leopards, cheetahs, hyenas and wild dogs are heavily persecuted. Few parks are large enough to sustain these wide-ranging animals. Prides often wander across park boundaries and are shot or poisoned when they resort to killing goats or cattle.

In order to explore the ecology and conservation of African predators that conflict with man, the Laikipia Predator Project in northern Kenya was established in 1998. It is the first effort to study the ecology and behaviour of large African carnivores in a human-dominated landscape, with emphasis on finding practical alternatives to the killing of problem predators. Laikipia District is one of the few areas where commercial cattle ranchers, traditional herding tribes, and predators coexist. By studying the threat that predators pose to people's livelihoods, and the threats that human activities pose to predators, we are identifying management techniques for coexistence that can be applied to other parts of Africa.

Over 90 lions have been captured and released, 65 of which have been radio-collared. A similar number of other large predators, such as hyenas, have also been collared. Through radio tracking we can monitor their movements as well as the effects of human activities upon them. We collect data on habitat use, group size, reproduction, causes of mortality, disease and the habits of chronic livestock raiders. Our studies show that while traditional methods of livestock management are effective at reducing livestock losses, these can often be improved through modest modifications to better serve the interests of both the human community and the predators. We are working with commercial ranchers and traditional herdsmen to identify weaknesses in their current practices that can be improved at little or no cost. Livestock is most vulnerable at night, but well-maintained traditional thornbush *bomas* are highly effective at keeping predators at bay. In some areas, however, bush has been depleted through over-use, and we are experimenting with solar-powered electric fences and other modern, but affordable, methods to protect livestock. We need to expand our monitoring programme through buying a light aircraft and to expand our community outreach programme by employing a field officer to assist with predator problems and the education of Maasai communities. We are also extending our work to other areas of Kenya where coexistence between humans and large predators may still be possible.

Dr Frank is the director of the Laikipia Predator Project. If you would like to donate to the project, or for further information, please contact: Africa Program, Wildlife Conservation Society, 2300 Southern Boulevard, Bronx, New York 10460, USA; tel: (1) 718 220 1387.

base for the Gallmann Memorial Foundation, as well as having a black rhino sanctuary and the largest population of Cape buffalo on private land in Kenya. In addition, elephant, eland, waterbuck, lion, leopard and cheetah are readily seen, and birdlife is prolific with 400 species recorded. The varied landscape has around 800 indigenous plants, dramatic ridges, steep gorges, waterfalls, open savanna and indigenous forest containing troupes of black-and-white colobus monkeys. The retreat itself consists of three spacious stone-built thatched rondavels with verandas open to the view, spacious rooms lavishly furnished with authentic Swahili and Lamu furniture, double fireplaces and large bathrooms. The central lounge and dining area have a homely ambience with old chests, ethnic artefacts and *Africana* books, while food has an Italian emphasis with fresh produce from the ranch gardens. The emphasis is on being at one with nature – there is no generator and lighting is by solar or candle light. **On offer:** birdwatching, camel and horseriding, game viewing, swimming in natural pools, health spa, star-gazing from a roofless cottage near a waterhole, fishing for tilapia, black bass or crayfish, organised walks with local, knowledgeable guides, visits to the Gallmann Memorial Foundation Education Centre and projects.

Rates: from US$375 full board per person sharing; conservation fee US$30

Makena's Hills (8 tents; swimming pool) PO Box 45593, Nairobi; tel: 020 520799; fax: 020 521220; email: mukutan@africaonline.co.ke; web: www.mukutan.com

Also situated on the Ol Ari Ng'iro ranch, this permanent tented camp has views across the Rift Valley. The tented rooms are comfortably furnished with Oriental carpets and objets d'art, queen-size or four-poster beds, en-suite bathrooms and flush toilets. There's a central dining area and bar, satellite TV, a panoramic swimming pool and secluded viewpoints amongst clumps of trees for sundowners, meditation and yoga. There's a choice of Italian or Indian cuisine using home-grown produce. **On offer:** birdwatching, camel treks, lake fishing, guided walks, horseriding, visits to see the the Gallmann Memorial Foundation conservation projects, Pokot cultural visits, health spa with meditation and yoga, helicopter excursions, and shop.

Rates: US$330 full board per person sharing; conservation fee US$30

What to see and do

As the land in Laikipia is privately owned, activities vary with the individual properties and these are listed under the accommodation above. However, there are also opportunites for **cycling, riding** and **camel safaris**, and the **Lewa Marathon** is an annual fundraising event held within the Lewa Wildlife Conservancy (see *Chapter 6*, page 107, for further details and operators).

Research

Mpala Research Centre PO Box 555, Nanyuki; fax: 0176 32750; email: info@mpala.org; web: www.nasm.si.edu/mpala

A collaboration of Kenyan and US institutions, the centre is an international facility for researchers into the sustainable development of East Africa's savanna and semi-arid woodland habitats. If staying on a Laikipia property, you may well gain a brief insight into some of the ongoing research, such as the Laikipia Predator Project. Research facilities, accommodation and board for up to 15 visitors and a dormitory for ten students are available for researchers only.

Rates: on application

The Gallmann Memorial Foundation PO Box 63704, Nairobi; tel: 020 521220/ 520799; fax: 020 521220; email: info@gallmannkenya.org; web: www.gallmannkenya.org

Based on the 40,500ha Ol Ari Ng'iro ranch in western Laikipia, the Gallmann Memorial Foundation was founded by Kuki Gallmann in 1984 in memory of her

Paco
Ndaronse

uwrorJ (sp?)

Visited on 26/1/05 - Winston, Jeanne, Edwin, Heather, Elephant Dam. Saw large herd of elephants (25+) at lunch. Good seeing. Chimps worth seeing.

late husband Paolo and son Emanuele who both died tragically in Kenya. It aims to promote the development of natural resources in harmony with the conservation of wildlife and the environment. The foundation operates two education centres:

African Humanities and Biodiversity Centre
This provides research facilities and has 12 tents available for researchers, volunteers and students who are interested in carrying out postgraduate studies, such as in African humanities, ethno-botany, cosmology and astronomy, anthropology and forestry. The facility is also open to university summer camps and adult research trips.
Rates: from US$95 per person per day for full board with support services; conservation fee US$30

Laikipia Wilderness Education Centre
This tailor-makes a range of excellent field studies courses primarily for school and youth groups, both local and international.
Rates: from US$70 per person per day for organised groups for full board in a bunkhouse and inclusive of conservation fee.

Sweetwaters Game Reserve and Chimpanzee Sanctuary
Entry fee US$16
Reached via Nanyuki on a dirt road (17km) this 9,700ha sanctuary is on Ol Pejeta ranch. On arrival, you can obtain a map to drive around the sanctuary, where there's a good variety of game including lion and elephant. One of the main attractions is a visit to the chimpanzee sanctuary. A boat trip on the Ewaso Ng'iro River takes you through the 1km² sanctuary, with riverine forest and savanna, where there are 26 orphaned chimpanzees. Most of the chimpanzees came from the Jane Goodall Institute in Burundi where they were rescued from a miserable existence. Although chimpanzees are

not naturally found in Kenya, the sanctuary has formed a trust which aims to attract investment into the Jane Goodall Institute for conserving chimpanzees in the wild – there's a donation box at the sanctuary. Another star attraction at Sweetwaters is Morani, a tame rhino.

Lewa Wildlife Conservancy
Entry: US$35 per person (includes a guide) by prior arrangement only
Lewa Downs, Private Bag, Isiolo; tel: 064 31405; fax: 064 31405; email: lewa@bushmail.net; web: www.lewa.org
Lewa Wildlife Conservancy (LWC), was bought by the Craig family in the 1920s as a 18,000ha cattle ranch. Subsequently they sectioned off part of the ranch for the **Ngare Sergoi Rhino Sanctuary**, started by Anna Merz in 1983. In 1995, the Craigs handed over the management of the ranch to the LWC, a non-profit-making trust focusing on conservation. The conservancy works closely with KWS on poaching control, does research into wildlife conservation, has an active programme to stimulate development and economic growth in the area and has been the catalyst for developing the community lodges of Il Ngwesi and Tassia and a cluster of projects in the north such as Sarara and Kalacha (see pages 378 and 380). It employs a community development officer encouraging self-help groups, assists several primary schools and provides a clinic while a furniture workshop and rug-weaving centre provide additional employment. The game-viewing

STREAKING ELEPHANTS

One night, Ngalatoni, a matriarch elephant, led her family of 14 from Samburu National Reserve to the Il Ngwesi Community Wildlife Area bordering the Laikipia ranches to the south. Travelling in a direct line, through an area favoured by bandits and poachers, they covered 24km between 18.00 and 09.00, crossing the danger zone between these two safe havens under the cover of darkness. (Normally elephants only travel about 10km per day.) This feat has been termed 'streaking' by elephant researchers and has been discovered by the detailed monitoring of elephant movements through radio tracking.

Elephants are motivated by three main factors – finding food and water, socialising with other elephants, and avoiding danger. In 1995 Dr Iain Douglas-Hamilton and his elephant-research team pioneered a new system of radio-tracking relying on Global Positioning System (GPS) technology. These high-tech collars are programmed to measure the exact position, activity level and outside air temperature every three hours for later downloading to a remote receiver. Locating an elephant from the air, the data from the collar can be downloaded on to a computer in the plane when flying overhead. This information is then transposed on to a satellite map recording the movement patterns of the elephant, such as hot spots where they go to water, and streaking.

The data gathered from GPS radio tracking can illustrate the importance of elephant 'corridors' and migration routes, as well as specific detail on elephant behaviour, such as showing which elephants have crop-raiding tendencies. This information is vital for helping to limit the human–wildlife conflict between elephants and people. It is also essential for developing future conservation strategies for elephants, especially as the land over which elephants can roam is increasingly being reduced by the expansion of human settlement. The information gathered by GPS tracking can also assist with management problems relating to ecology and biodiversity.

Further information is available from **Save the Elephants**, PO Box 54667, Nairobi; tel: 020 891673; fax: 020 890441; email: save-eleph@net2000ke.com; web: www.savetheelephants.

opportunites are excellent, with the northern species of game – Grevy's zebra, reticulated giraffe and Somali ostrich, together with white rhino, elephant, lion, leopard, gazelle and sitatunga antelope. In line with its policy of high-income, low-volume tourism, LWC is only open to casual visitors by arrangement (contact LWC direct) between mid-morning and mid-afternoon in their own, neutral-coloured 4WD vehicle. Otherwise you'll need to stay at Wilderness Trails or Lewa Safari Camp within the conservancy or at Borana Lodge or Laragai on the adjacent Borana ranch (see page 258).

FROM THIKA EAST TO EMBU, CHOGORIA AND MERU

Embu is a provincial capital, but has a limited appeal, and much the same can be said for Meru – the main reason for taking this route being to climb Mount Kenya from Chogoria, or to visit Meru National Park. However, from Thika it's a scenic drive on a good road circumnavigating Mount Kenya, passing rice paddies and roadside *dukas* milling rice. The road then starts to climb, roller-coasting around the hills, with the odd steep descent to cross rivers, where *shambas* with brick-red soil grow a mixture of coffee, tea, napier grass, maize and beans, shaded by grevillea and eucalyptus trees. At Embu the road climbs through jacaranda avenues to the town, with its collection of shops and destitute street kids before continuing through rolling countryside and forested hills to Meru. A bustling town, Meru is surrounded by pockets of natural forest in the Imenti Forest Reserve. First impressions are somewhat intimidating, but in fact people are friendly enough. The town lies at the heart of the *miraa* market – a stimulant, known as *qat* in Arabia, much favoured among the long-distance truck drivers. The town itself is rundown with potholed streets and tragic, persistent, glue-sniffing street kids. (There does not appear to be any outreach charity helping them here.) About halfway between Embu and Meru is the turn-off to Chogoria, another popular route on the Mount Kenya circuit. The road north from Meru passes through mature natural forest, but there is evidence, too, of large areas clear-felled to make way for agriculture. Further north there are open views across the Nyambene Hills and the lands of Samburu.

Getting there and around
North of Thika, take the B6 (good tarmac road) northeast to Embu (90km). From Embu it's about 50km to the village of Marima where you can organise climbs for the mountain. The Chogoria turn-off is on the right, just after Marima, 5km along a dirt track which is impassable in wet weather. The B6 continues to Meru (78km) and the C91 turn-off to Maua and Meru National Park. From Meru the road continues round the mountain to join with the A2 at the Isiolo turn-off (about 25km).

By bus
There are several buses a day operating the Meru–Embu–Chogoria–Thika route, as well as the usual *matatus* and share taxis. Kensilver Bus is probably the best and details can be obtained through their Nairobi office on tel: 020 221839.

By air
There's an airstrip in Meru National Park, with a scheduled service between Nairobi and Samburu on Wednesdays, Fridays and Sundays. (If you're pushed for time, this is definitely the way to travel, cutting out the dreadful road.) In addition there are several private airstrips in the park.

Getting organised
For **changing money**, there are banks and post offices in Embu and Meru town centres, together with a number of **petrol stations**. In an emergency the **tourist helpline** is 020 604767.

Embu
Where to stay and eat
Highway Court Hotel Next to BP petrol station, PO Box 354, Embu; tel: 068 20046
A 3-storey hotel located on the main street not far from the bus station, the s/c rooms are spacious and clean. There's a restaurant downstairs serving basic fare and the staff are friendly and helpful.
Rates: rooms from KSh500–800 B&B
Izaak Walton Inn (50 rooms; swimming pool) Kenyatta Highway, PO Box 1, Embu; tel: 068 20128; fax: 068 30135; email: emugo@africaonline.co.ke; web: www.izaak_waltoninn.com

A former fishing lodge, built in 1948, this child-friendly inn is situated in 3.5ha of tropical gardens with mature trees and is well placed for visits to Mwea National Reserve. The rooms are in cottages in the garden, spacious and simply furnished with a telephone, en-suite bathroom and private veranda. There's a good choice of buffet-style food, from African to European and Chinese. Lunch and dinner cost KSh700. The lounge has satellite TV. **On offer:** squash, horseriding and activities for children.
Rates: from KSh1,800 B&B per person sharing

Mwea National Reserve
Reserve entry US$15
The easiest route, signposted, is via Embu (4WD required), heading southeast for about 14km on the B7. This small reserve (42km²) includes the confluence of the Tana and Thiba rivers and the Kaburu and Masinga hydro-electric dams. The reserve is owned by Mbeere County Council and managed by Kenya Wildlife Service. Attractive and peaceful, it includes large baobab trees, thick bush and open glades. The water attracts a **rich birdlife**, with a high number of raptors and waterfowl, and the rare Hinde's babbler endemic to Kenya. There are a couple of picnic sites at Gichuki Island and Hippo Point. Game is plentiful and includes elephant, buffalo, crocodile, hippo, vervet and Sykes monkey, waterbuck and lesser kudu, although the last is shy and not readily seen. A park map is available at the gate.

The reserve has a very basic **campsite** near the main gate, with no facilities.
Rates: US$8

Chogoria
Where to stay and eat
Joywood Hotel and Campsite PO Box 62, Chogoria; mobile: 0733 262448
This small hotel is located at Marima on the main road before the turn-off to Chogoria. It's also the base for the Mount Kenya Chogoria Guides Association. The service is welcoming and friendly and the s/c rooms have hot showers. There's a restaurant serving a mixture of African and Western food (meals around KSh400). The campsite has basic facilities, but hot showers and good security.
Rates: rooms US$10 B&B per person sharing; camping from KSh160
Marimebu Lodge and Campsite Near the forest station, Chogoria; tel: 064 22255
This small lodge is next to the forest station near the park gate and is of a similar standard to the Joywood Hotel. It has s/c rooms and a good campsite with hot showers.
Rates: rooms US$10 B&B per person sharing; camping from KSh190
Meru Mount Kenya Lodge (12 self-catering bandas and cottage) Book through Let's Go Travel, page 101
Located 26km from the Chogoria turn-off on the eastern slopes of Mount Kenya, the turn-off to the lodge is about 1km from the Chogoria park gate, from where it's another kilometre to the lodge. The road is rough and 4WD is essential. Facing the peaks of Bation and Nelion, positioned around a glade, with dams nearby attracting wildlife, the bandas have a small lounge/dining area with fireplace, a room with two single beds and an extra bed, a kitchen and bathroom. The cottage has two small twin rooms, a lounge, kitchen and bathroom. Hot water is provided by Tanganyika boiler. Electricity (at extra charge) is by generator. Bedding is provided but it is advisable to take extra blankets and to be fully self-sufficient.
Rates: from KSh1,000 per person
Lake Rutundu log cabins (2 self-catering cabins, sleep 4) Book through Let's Go Travel, page 101
Located on the northern slopes of Mount Kenya west of Meru. Access is by air or 4WD

to Rotundu Hill, after which it's a 15-minute walk to the cabins at the foot of Rotundu Hill. There are two rustic log cabins with a living/dining-room with a log fire, 2 rooms with en-suite bathrooms and a kitchen. Lighting is by hurricane lamps. Bedding, crockery and kitchen utensils are provided and there are staff to help. The cabins overlook Lake Rotundu, a small montane tarn where 2lb rainbow trout are 'average' and monsters of 6–8lb are frequently encountered. There's also fishing on Lake Alice, a 2-hour hike up the mountain. At 3,000m the cabins are on the moorland above the treeline, but there are walks in the cedar and podocarpus below, as well as through the alpine flora of giant groundsel and heather. **On offer:** walking, birdwatching, trout fishing with boat and ghillies.
Rates: from KSh375 per person (minimum 2 people)

Climbing Mount Kenya
This is one of the main routes for climbing Mount Kenya, and details of the route are given on page 247. For further options, see page 242.

The **Mount Kenya Chogoria Guides Association** (based in the Joywood Hotel, PO Box 62, Chogoria; mobile: 0733 262448) can arrange an assortment of treks on the mountain together with guides and porters. Packages start from US$125 per person per day.

Meru
Where to stay and eat
Pig and Whistle (17 rooms) PO Box 3160, Meru; tel: 064 31411
Originally built as the district commissioner's house, the Pig and Whistle is on a tree-covered hill, signposted to the left, when coming into town. A 1930s wooden building with a veranda and small, cosy bar, even if a little dilapidated it still retains its character and the staff are friendly and welcoming. The rooms are in cottages, in the unkempt garden, and although shabby are reasonably comfortable with telephone, TV and en-suite bathrooms. There's a large *nyama choma* joint at the bottom of the garden and there are plans to build a swimming pool.
Rates: from KSh750 B&B per person sharing
Meru County Hotel (50 rooms) PO Box 1386, Meru; tel: 064 20432; fax: 064 31264
A large hotel with several bars and restaurants, it's located on the main road so you'll hear the lorries all night, changing down gear to go over the speed bumps. The rooms are basic, but clean and spacious with comfortable beds, telephone and en-suite shower rooms. The service is friendly, if a little slow, and the food poor.
Rates: from KSh1,000 B&B per person sharing

What to see and do
Meru market
If you're interested in the *miraa* trade, the market is worth a visit. The Meru region is thought to grow the best *miraa*, and it's the dominant cash crop in the area, raising prices of up to KSh1,500 a kilo. A small plant, standing at about 50mm, it resembles miniature rhubarb, with its pink stems topped with bright green leaves. The outer stem is stripped off with the teeth and chewed, acting as a mild stimulant which becomes addictive over time. The main market is Somalia, and as the quality of the *miraa* diminishes within 48 hours, much of it is swiftly transported to Nairobi and then flown to Mogadishu.

Meru museum
PO Box 597, Meru; tel: 064 20482
Housed in the former district commissioner's office to the left of the main road in town, the museum has excellent **ethnographic exhibits** of the Meru people,

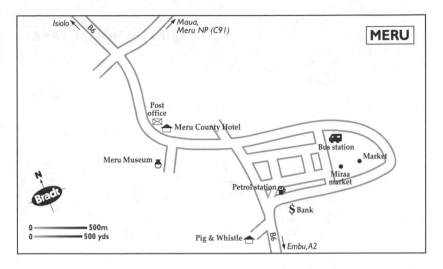

together with a well-displayed Meru homestead and an interesting demonstration garden of **indigenous plants** and their uses. Other exhibits include displays about **evolution**, **fauna** and **archaeology**. There's also a miserable collection of orphaned animals in cramped cages.
Open Mon–Fri 09.30–17.30; Sat 09.30–14.00; entry KSh200

Meru National Park

PO Box 11 Maua; tel: 064 20613
Open 06.00–18.30; entry US$27; vehicle entry KSh200
From Meru take the C91 tarmac road signposted to Maua (where there's petrol), winding through the Nyambene Hills to the small town of Kangeta (about 40km) after which it's about 5km to the turn-off to Meru National Park on the left (several kilometres before reaching Maua). This dirt road starts well, and there are encouraging piles of gravel at the roadside for grading, which apparently have been there for several years. The surface soon deteriorates appallingly, to bare rock in parts, and it's a bone-rattling drive through smallholdings growing maize, beans and *miraa* to the **New Murera Park gate** (28km). Once there, the park roads are a dream. The other main access is via **Ura gate** on the southern park boundary. There's a good network of roads within the park with most of the game viewing concentrated in the northwestern section. However, a good day trip is to **Adamson's Falls** on the Tana River (where you can fish for barble and catfish) in the southeastern corner of the park.

History The park was opened in 1968 and covers an area of 870km². It became famous for its association with the film *Born Free*, Elsa the lioness and the work of Joy and George Adamson. In its heyday it used to get 40,000 visitors a year. But during the late 1970s and 1980s Meru gained a reputation for poor security. Poaching and banditry (Somali *shifta*) were rife. In 1979, 80% of the rhino were decimated in six months, while from 1984–89 elephant numbers plummeted from 3,500 to 210. The park's problems were magnified in 1989 when five rhino were slaughtered, followed by a couple of French tourists and George Adamson (at Kora National Reserve, which borders Meru National Park to the east) being killed. The park fluctuated with the security situation, and then, in 1997, was hit

NB. Mark Jenkins obtained £8million from the French Government in 2006 for Meru NP.

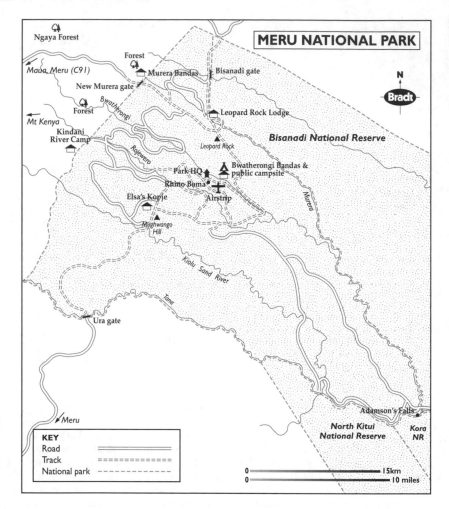

Ngaya Forest

Forest

Maua Meru (C91)

Murera Bandas

Bisanadi gate

MERU NATIONAL PARK

New Murera gate

N

Bradt

Forest

Bwatherongi

Mt Kenya

Leopard Rock Lodge

Kindani
River Camp

Bisanadi National Reserve

Rojewero

Leopard Rock

Park HQ

Bwatherongi Bandas &
public campsite

Rhino Boma

Murera

Elsa's Kopje

Airstrip

Mughwango
Hill

Kiolu Sand River

Tana

Ura gate

Meru

Adamson's Falls

KEY
Road
Track
National park

North Kitui
National Reserve

Kora
NR

0 ————— 15km
0 ————— 10 miles

hard by the bushmeat trade. Game counts revealed that meat animals had dropped by over two-thirds. Warthog, ground hornbill and ostrich disappeared altogether, while numbers of other species like oryx, Grevy's zebra and kongoni were severely dented.

The turnaround came with the appointment of Mark Jenkins as head warden in 1999 – a man with a mission, whose father was a former warden in the park. Security has been beefed up and the infrastructure improved. Morale is high among the KWS staff and the park is now increasingly a safe haven for wildlife. Visitors are trickling back. As game numbers had got so low, a translocation programme has been in operation to restock species so that they have a viable breeding population and to reintroduce animals which had been wiped out. A variety of plains game, elephant, rhino, Grevy's zebra and reticulated giraffe have been translocated to the park and there's a new rhino *boma*. In 2001, 56 elephants – nine different families – were translocated from Sweetwaters game reserve in Laikipia. A good reflection on the increase in plains game is seen in the growth in predator numbers, and 2003 saw the birth of a white rhino.

Flora and fauna Straddling the Equator the park is dominated by **savanna**, but includes **diverse woodland**. It's bisected by 13 **rivers** which flow roughly parallel towards the Tana River in the southeast, separated by lava flows, fed by mountain streams running off the Nyambeni Hills. The western section of the park is dominated by *Combretum* species, particularly *C. apiculatum*, merging with dense *Commiphora* and *Acacia* woodland in the southern part of the park and *Acacia* wooded grassland, with *A. tortilis* and *A. senegal* on the rocky ridges. A couple of **inselbergs** rise from the plains at Leopard's Rock and Mughwango. The park has 16 varieties of acacia alone, but it is the **riverine forest** that is most impressive – wonderful, mature tamarind, fig, newtonia and Cape mahogany trees draped in cascading creepers where giant and grey-headed kingfishers are common. Around the **swamps** are doum palms. The **birdlife** is excellent (about 280 recorded species). Among these are the black-faced sandgrouse (which carry water in their feathers for their chicks), vulturine and helmeted guineafowl, yellow-necked spurfowl, grey-headed bush shrike, Pel's fishing owl, African finfoot and Martial eagles. The **wildlife** is increasing and eland, gerenuk, Beisa oryx, Grant's gazelle, Grevy's zebra, reticulated giraffe, elephant, cheetah, prides of up to 16 lion, leopard and cheetah are regularly seen together with the elusive lesser kudu. The park is also active in **wildlife research** – nine elephants have radio collars and are being monitored, and there's an ongoing research programme on naked mole rats.

Where to stay and eat
Within the park
Leopard Rock Lodge (15 cottages; swimming pool) PO Box 208, Maua; tel: 020 862527; fax: 020 862527; email: leomico1@bushmail.net; web: www.merukenya.com
Recently refurbished, the lodge has extremely spacious large, thatched cottages decorated in a Lamu-cum-African theme, with rich furnishings and en-suite shower rooms. The main building has a lounge, bar and dining area facing on to the Murera River, a narrow, perennial stream surrounded by leafy bushes and doum palms. It's owned by a Frenchman, and there's a distinct French flair to the cuisine as well as African dishes and locally brewed beer. It has a novel swimming pool with a perspex end facing on to the Murera, where, in theory, you can look face to face at crocodiles basking on the river bank. **On offer:** game drives and bush walks, a pottery workshop, small natural history museum and Boran cultural centre.
Rates: from US$210 full board per person sharing. No children under 7 allowed.
Elsa's Kopje (8 cottages; swimming pool) Book through Cheli & Peacock, page 90
The lodge has a privileged position, located on Mughwango Hill, the site of George Adamson's original camp, and takes its name from Elsa the lioness of *Born Free* fame who was released here. From its elevation above the savanna plains the central lodge building and swimming pool are sited to maximise the sweeping views across the park. The cottages are the height of luxury – open plan but with gauze netting on the windows, four-poster beds and large bathrooms with giant baths and flush toilets, all with a view. There's plenty of privacy and good service. **On offer:** game drives and bush walks with excellent guides, night drives, fishing, massage and an open-air bath.
Rates: from US$320 full board per person sharing
National Park Bandas and Camping Book through KWS in Nairobi, page 91
Bwatherongi Bandas and Public Campsite (4 self-catering bandas, camping)
Situated near the park headquarters, this is an excellent shady campsite on the Bwatherongi River. It has basic facilities – showers and toilets – and there are 4 self-catering bandas, one double and 3 single which have a sitting-room, bedroom with a mosquito net and Tilley lamp, shower and flush toilet. Outside there's a barbecue area by the river. You'll need to be fully self-sufficient.
Rates: camping US$10; single bandas US$15; double bandas US$40; plus park and vehicle entry fees

Outside the park

Murera Bandas (4 self-catering bandas, dorm beds) Book through KWS, page 91
The Murera bandas are situated just before the New Murera gate to the Meru National Park. Each banda has 2 rooms with a double and single bed and there's an ablution block. A barbecue area replaces a kitchen and there's a caretaker who cleans and assists with making fires. You'll need to be fully self-sufficient and take your own linen. There's also a dormitory block with bunk beds and a central kitchen. **On offer:** birdwatching, game viewing, organised walks.
Rates: from US$30

Kindani River Camp (5 self-catering rondavels, sleeps 10) Book through Let's Go Travel, page 101
Located outside the western boundary of the park overlooking the Kindani River near the Kanjoo park gate, about 14km south of the New Murera park gate. The rondavels are comfortable with flush toilets and open-air showers. Linen and cutlery is provided, so you need only bring provisions and drinks. Access to the camp is by 4WD only, as the Rojewero River has to be forded. **On offer:** swimming in a natural pool, excursions to the park, game viewing, birdwatching.
Rates: from KSh750 per person

Bordering Meru National Park are the **national reserves** of **Kora**, **Bisanadi**, **Rahole** and **Mwingi**. Of these, the most accessible is **Kora** but at the time of writing the reserve was closed due to poor roads and concerns about security. If wanting to go there, special permission is required from the national park headquarters in Nairobi, page 191.

Specialists in tailor-made itineraries to Kenya and the Indian Ocean Islands together with personalised safaris to all of Central, Eastern and Southern Africa.

Steppes Africa

Steppes Africa Limited
51 Castle Street, Cirencester, Gloucestershire, GL7 1QD
Telephone: 01285 650011 Fax: 01285 885888
E-mail: safari@steppesafrica.co.uk
www.steppesafrica.co.uk

Footloose is the tailor made specialist for Kenya and East Africa
• Safaris, tours and hotels
• Mount Kenya and trekking
• Cultural and special interest tours
• Adventure travel, treks, climbs, safaris worldwide

FOOTLOOSE
ADVENTURE TRAVEL

Footloose Adventure Travel
Tel: 01943 604030
E-mail: info@footlooseadventure.co.uk
Web: www.footlooseadventure.co.uk

Travel Trust
Association
No. R4338

atta

The Rift Valley

The Rift Valley bisects Kenya from north to south, giving rise to spectacular scenery with dramatic escarpments and an intriguing necklace of freshwater and soda lakes. This chapter covers the freshwater lakes of Naivasha, Baringo and Kamnarok, the soda lakes of Elmentaita, Nakuru and Bogoria and their environs. The other lakes in the Rift Valley system are Turkana in the north (*Chapter 13*, page 351) and Magadi in southeastern Kenya (*Chapter 9*, page 197).

LAKE NAIVASHA AND ENVIRONS

In the 1930s, flying boats landed on Lake Naivasha en route between Durban (South Africa) and London. Several of the lakeside houses were home to the infamous 'Happy Valley' characters (read *White Mischief*, see page 468). Dominated by the yellow-barked acacia trees and surrounded by private ranches and huge flower farms, there's limited access to the lake frontage. It's a fertile farming area, with irrigated horticulture and agriculture, dominated by Delamere Dairies and numerous farms like Oserian growing cut flowers for the international market. Consequently the population has expanded with a buoyant migrant labour force. Along Moi South Lake Road are the houses for the estate workers – cheek by jowl and a sharp contrast to the grand houses at the lake's edge; nevertheless they show signs of increased prosperity, as there's a preponderance of television aerials.

Lake Naivasha is readily accessible to those on a modest budget, with excellent camping facilities and access to nearby attractions by boat, foot or mountain bike. There are, of course, plenty of highly salubrious and exclusive places to stay as well.

Getting there and around

Travelling from Nairobi (86km) there are two good tarmac roads snaking down the escarpment into the Rift Valley with fabulous views from the Kikuyu smallholdings at the top of the escarpment to the volcanic cones of mounts Longonot and Suswa, Lake Naivasha and the giant golfball of Longonot's satellite station in the dusty Kedong plains. The high road (A104) passes roadside fruit sellers – plums and apples in season – near Limuru and from the escarpment edge has look-out points and clusters of wooden *dukas* selling curios, sheepskins, Maasai blankets, jewellery, baskets and wooden carvings. (It's fine to stop during daylight hours, but not in the evening.) Naivasha is signposted to the left. The B3 from Limuru follows the line of the old escarpment road, through the rapidly reducing forests, passing a small Italian chapel at the foot of the escarpment (built by the Italian prisoners of war in 1943

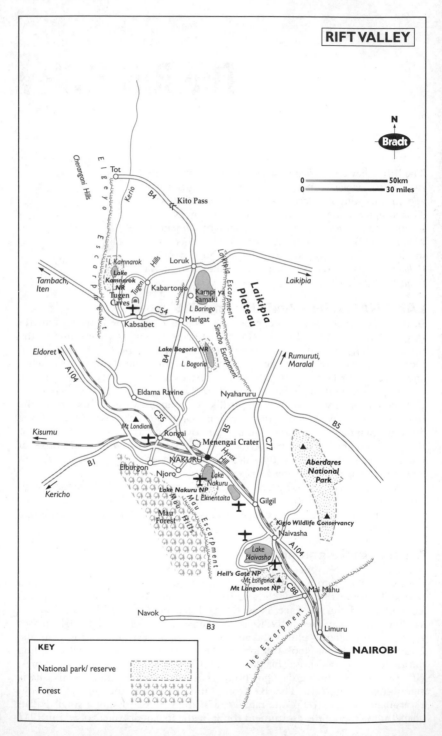

when they were building the road) and passing the Mai Mahu turning to Narok before continuing along the C88 to Naivasha.

By bus
There are regular buses and *matatus* from Nairobi to Naivasha and north to Nakuru. The bus station is off Kariuki Chotara Road. There are also frequent *matatus* along Moi South Lake Road to Fisherman's Camp, which leave from Kenyatta Avenue. Alternatively you can catch the shuttle service for Fish Eagle Inn (page 278).

By air
There are no scheduled flights, but there's a public airstrip off Moi South Lake Road, and plenty of private airstrips in the vicinity.

Getting organised
For **changing money**, Barclays (ATM) and Kenya Commercial banks are on Moi Avenue. The main **post office** is on Posta Lane, open Monday–Friday 08.00–17.00, Saturday 09.00–12.00. For **internet access** try La Belle Inn on Moi Avenue. There's a supermarket in the town centre and a good fruit and vegetable market off Biashara Road. A **travel agent**, Bates Travel, is on Moi Road next to Securicor at the north end of town. In an emergency the **tourist helpline** is 020 604767. There are **petrol stations** on the access roads into Naivasha, but note there are none around the lake.

Naivasha town
Where to stay
La Belle Inn Moi Av, PO Box 532, Naivasha; tel: 050 21007; fax: 050 21007; email: labelle_inn@yahoo.com
One of the original hotels in Naivasha, La Belle Inn still retains its historical charm. It's long been a popular stopover point between Nairobi and Nakuru and has a large veranda serving a good selection of snacks during the day, and the restaurant has good evening meals. It also has a lively bar, with satellite TV, and a bakery selling pies and cakes. The rooms are comfortable with en-suite bathrooms off a small courtyard and there's secure parking behind.
Rates: from KSh1,000 B&B per person sharing
Kafico Lodge Biashara St, PO Box 1246, Naivasha; tel: 050 21344
A large hotel in the town centre. Rooms are simple and clean.
Rates: rooms from KSh300
Kenvash Hotel (61 rooms) Posta Lane (off Moi Av), PO Box 211, Naivasha; tel: 050 30049; fax: 050 21503
A large, rather impersonal hotel, but the s/c rooms are comfortable.
Rates: from KSh900 B&B per person sharing
Naivasha Silver Hotel Kenyatta Av (near bus station), PO Box 939, Naivasha; tel: 050 20580; email: silverhotel@ebonykenya.org
The rooms, with hot water, are clean and comfortable. There's a bar and the Jolly Café serves wholesome African dishes.
Rates: from KSh800 B&B per person sharing
Sam's Holiday Inn (44 rooms) Sokoni Rd, PO Box 287, Naivasha; tel: 050 20810; fax: 050 21044
A large, lively hotel with TV and pool tables, with a restaurant serving African food. Rooms are basic but good value.
Rates: rooms from KSh250

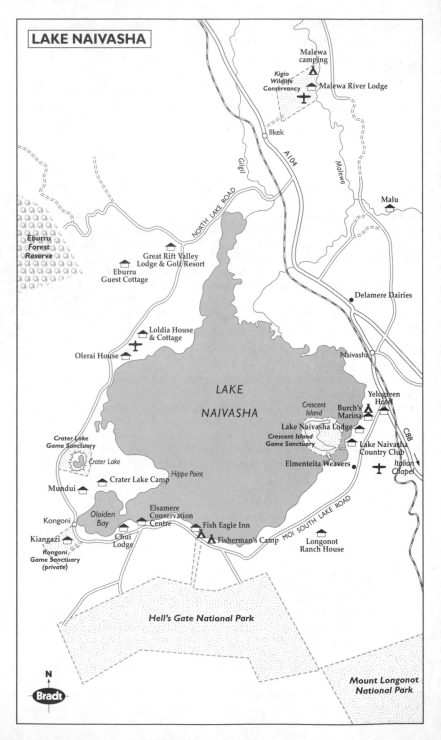

LAKE NAIVASHA

Where to eat

Most of the hotels listed above serve food. Other places to eat are:

Bright Moon Chinese Restaurant Moi Av (south of La Belle Inn), PO Box 1730, Naivasha; tel: 050 20746; email: mingyue@kenyaweb.com
A small, intimate family restaurant serving excellent, authentic Chinese cuisine. It also has a take-away service.
Rates: from KSh275 for a main course
Jim's Corner Dishes Station Lane (near La Belle Inn), Naivasha
A popular lunch spot serving tasty African dishes, stews a speciality, for around KSh200 or less.

Moi South Lake Road
Where to stay and eat

Yelogreen Hotel (small hotel and camping) PO Box 561, Naivasha; tel: 050 30269; fax: 050 30269
On the left at the roadside, about 0.5km from the turn-off to Moi South Lake Rd, the Yelogreen Hotel has a pleasant ambience and friendly management but is not near the lake. Rooms are s/c and meals are cheap and filling.
Rates: from KSh1,000 per person sharing; camping KSh150
Burch's Marina (4 self-catering bandas and camping) Box 40, Naivasha; tel: 050 21010.
About 3km from the turn-off to Moi South Lake Rd, the bandas and camping area are near the lake, but there's no view due to the papyrus. A pleasant campsite with good communal facilities, hot water night and morning and reasonable security. You'll need to bring all provisions with you. **On offer:** gift shop, boat hire.
Rates: bandas from KSh600; camping KSh200; boat hire from KSh1,500 an hour. Book in advance. Closed on Thursday.
Lake Naivasha Lodge (12 rooms) PO Box 685, Naivasha; tel: 050 20611; fax: 050 21156
About 4km from the turn-off to Moi South Lake Rd, this small lodge is surrounded by acacia trees. **On offer:** guided walks, birding, boating, horseriding, hippo-viewing platform, excursions to Hell's Gate National Park and Elsamere Conservation Centre.
Rates: from KSh2,300 B&B per person sharing
Lake Naivasha Country Club (49 rooms, swimming pool) PO Box 15, Naivasha; tel: 050 21160; fax: 050 21161; email: blocknaivasha@africaonline.co.ke; or book through Block Hotels, PO Box 40075, Nairobi; tel: 020 540780; fax: 020 545948
About 5km from the turn-off to Moi South Lake Rd, this is a delightful hotel set in spacious tropical gardens with well-kept lawns and large shady trees. It became famous in the 1930s as a staging post for the Imperial Airways' flying-boat service from Durban to London which used to land on Lake Naivasha. It still retains a colonial charm, with elegant public rooms and a large fireplace in the lounge. There's a boardwalk to the jetty for boat trips, and a small pagoda at the lakeside – a quiet, daytime retreat for birdwatching. **On offer:** boat trips, guided walks, birdwatching, fishing and excursions to Crescent Island, Hell's Gate and Longonot national parks.
Rates: from US$85 half board per person sharing
Longonot Ranch House (homestay; 6 double rooms and honeymoon suite) Book through Safaris Unlimited, PO Box 24181, 00502 Karen, Nairobi; tel: 020 891168; fax: 020 891113; email: samawati@safarisunlimited.co.ke; web: www.safarisunlimited.co.ke
About 12km from the turn-off to Moi South Lake Rd, Longonot Ranch House is located on Kedong ranch, a private 32,000ha game sanctuary, with expansive views of the surrounding area. There's plenty of wildlife on the ranch – eland, giraffe, zebra, impala, Thomson's and Grant's gazelle, kongoni, buffalo, cheetah, leopard, civet and genet cats. The rooms are comfortably furnished with en-suite bathrooms. **On offer:** boating, walking and horseriding.
Rates: from US$350 full board per person sharing

Fisherman's Camp (bandas, camping with tents for hire) PO Box 79, Naivasha; tel: 050 30088
About 17.5km from the turn-off to Moi South Lake Rd, Fisherman's Camp has a delightful location on the lakeside, with plenty of shady trees, and at night you can watch the hippos as they come out to graze. There's an excellent bar and restaurant serving good food, which copes well with the number of meals being ordered. The campsite itself is spacious and well-organised (hot showers and flush toilets). The downside is the noise, from ghetto-blasting weekenders and the British Army when they're in residence. (They have a private site adjacent, but use the bar and restaurant facilities.) **On offer:** boating (rowing and motor), waterskiing, bike hire, guided bird walks (Joseph Oluoko is recommended), guided tours to Hell's Gate National Park, Crater Lake, Crescent Island and Eburru Forest and lake fishing (bring your own rods).
Rates: camping KSh200; tent hire KSh200; bandas from KSh800; entrance only KSh100
Fish Eagle Inn (rooms, dormitory and camping; swimming pool) PO Box 1554, Naivasha; tel: 050 30306; fax: 050 21158; email: info@fish-eagle.com; web: www.fish-eagle.com
About 18km from the turn-off to Moi South Lake Rd, this is a friendly family hotel. Rooms are rather airless, being on the small side in dark décor, but are clean and comfortable. The campsite is infinitely more peaceful than Fisherman's Camp. There's a bar and restaurant and the executive rooms have satellite TV. **On offer:** internet café after 20.00, boating (rowing and motor), guided walks with a naturalist, health club, basketball court, pool table, mountain-bike hire and shuttle transport to Naivasha town.
Rates: rooms from KSh1,600 per person sharing; dormitory bed KSh400; camping KSh200
Elsamere Conservation Centre (8 rooms and cottages) PO Box 1497, Naivasha; tel: 050 21055, mobile: 0722 648123; fax: 050 21074; email: elsa@africaonline.co.ke
About 25km from the turn-off to Moi South Lake Rd, this is the former home of Joy Adamson of *Born Free* fame. The centre has a peaceful setting on the lakeshore opposite Crater Lake, and there's resident troop of black-and-white colobus monkeys. The rooms are nicely furnished with en-suite bathrooms. The homely meals are delicious, but there's no bar, so bring your own alcohol. There's an excellent Sunday buffet lunch and tea (KSh1,000, book in advance if possible) and afternoon tea daily (KSh350) between 15.00–18.00 for casual visitors. The small museum has a collection of Joy Adamson paintings and memorabilia of Elsa the lioness and the film, *Born Free*. **On offer:** video screenings of *The Joy Adamson Story*; museum visit and afternoon tea on the lawn; boat rides, trips to Crescent Island, guided walks, birdwatching (200 species recorded) and the Elsa Trust shop.
Rates: from US$140 full board per person sharing
Chui Lodge (6 cottages; swimming pool) PO Box 209, Naivasha; tel: 050 20792; fax: 050 30353; email: kongoni@africaonline.co.ke; web: www.kongoni.com
About 25km from the turn-off to Moi South Lake Rd, Chui Lodge is located in Kongoni Game Sanctuary, a private 8,000ha ranch with over 44 different mammals – among them white rhino, Grevy's zebra, kudu, topi, oryx, cheetah and leopard, although some would not occur naturally in this environment – and 300 recorded bird species. The main house and cottages are exquisitely designed using local stone, olive, leleshwa and marula wood and decorated with batiks. Each room is en suite with four-poster king-size beds and a private veranda. The food has an excellent reputation. Nestling in a grove of *euphorbia* trees overlooking a waterhole, there are views to the Mau escarpment. **On offer:** day and night game drives, guided game walks, bush breakfasts and lunches, sundowners, boat trips, visits to Hell's Gate National Park and flower farms.
Rates: from US$205 fully inclusive per person sharing. Closed May.
Kiangazi (6 rooms; swimming pool) PO Box 209, Naivasha; tel: 050 20792; fax: 050 30353; email: kongoni@africaonline.co.ke; web: www.kongoni.com

Also located in the Kongoni Game Sanctuary, Kiangazi is a luxurious, private house set in delightful gardens overlooking Oloidien bay and the Mau escarpment. The food is good and there's a satellite TV lounge and library. **On offer:** exclusive access to the sanctuary, boat trips, fishing, horseriding, tennis and excursions to Hell's Gate and Mount Longonot national parks and Crescent Island.
Rates: from US$150 full board per person sharing
Mundui (2 rooms; swimming pool; homestay) Book through Bush Homes of East Africa (page 90)
About 32km from the turn-off to Moi South Lake Rd, Mundui is the home of Sarah and Andrew Inniskillen. An elegant, double-storey 1920s house, it's set in delightful gardens facing on to Oloiden bay. One room is en suite while the other has a private bathroom, and the food is delicious. There's plenty of wildlife on the 500ha estate – eland, hippo, buffalo and giraffe – and over 280 recorded bird species. **On offer:** croquet and badminton, game and bird walks, boating, guided trips to Hell's Gate and Lake Nakuru national parks; private airstrip.
Rates: from US$300 full board per person sharing. Closed April, May and November.
Crater Lake Camp (10 tents) PO Box 24742, Nairobi; tel: 050 20613; email: crater@africaonline.co.ke
About 35km from the turn-off to Moi South Lake Rd, this is a charming permanent tented camp, with comfortable en-suite tents under thatch, surrounded by yellow-barked acacia trees set in the middle of the **Crater Lake Game Sanctuary**. The home-cooking is excellent and there's also a honeymoon suite, complete with a double jacuzzi overlooking the lake and crater. The Ndabibi Estate was once owned by Lady Diana Delamere, who inherited the land from her third husband, Gilbert Colville, and the graves of Diana, Gilbert and Lord Delamere are in the estate churchyard. **On offer:** camel rides, bush walks, sundowners on Leopard's Rock; visits to the Delamere graveyard, night game drives and a snake park.
Rates: from US$128 full board per person sharing; entry to sanctuary KSh100

North Lake Road
Where to stay and eat
This is a dirt road and deeply rutted in parts, so 4WD is advisable.

Great Rift Valley Lodge and Golf Resort (30 rooms, 14 2–4-bed cottages; swimming pool) Book through Heritage Hotels, page 91
About 11km from Naivasha on the Moi North Lake Rd, the resort overlooks Lake Naivasha with panoramic views to Mount Longonot and the Aberdares. It's primarily a golfing hotel, with an 18-hole championship course, but there's plenty for non-golfers and children too. Rooms are pleasantly furnished, with en-suite bathrooms and private balconies, and there's a very good restaurant. **On offer:** golf, tennis, escorted game and bird walks in Eburru Forest, boating and fishing on Lake Naivasha, horseriding, mountain biking, and excursions to parks and reserves. There's a gift shop and a private all-weather airstrip.
Rates: from US$170 full board per person sharing
Eburru Guest Cottage (4 rooms, self-catering) Book through Let's Go Travel, page 101
About 12km from Naivasha town on Moi North Lake Rd (follow the signs to Greenpark and pass through the Greenpark Development barrier) the cottage is on the forested slopes of Eburru. Quiet and peaceful, it has wonderful views of the surrounding area, but at 2,100m it gets chilly at night and can be miserable during July and August. A house servant is provided, but you need to do your own cooking and bring all provisions. **On offer:** walking on the farm (beware of buffalo) where you can see eland and zebra, and good birdwatching.
Rates: from KSh1,500 a night, depending on numbers
Loldia House and Cottage (4 rooms in house, 3 in cottage) Book through Governor's Camps, page 91

About 18km from Naivasha town on Moi North Lake Rd, Loldia ranch still belongs to a settler family who arrived by ox-wagon from South Africa over one hundred years ago. The house was built in the 1950s and retains its original features and furniture. There's a large fireplace and veranda. Rooms in the house are en suite, with views across Lake Naivasha, and the cottage has its own sitting room with an open fire.

Rates: US$275 full board per person sharing and ranch fee of US$15 per person

Olerai House (5 rooms) PO Box 54667, 00200 Nairobi ; tel: 020 334868; fax: 020 243976; email: oleraihouse@africaonline.co.ke; web: www.olerai.com

About 19km from Naivasha town on Moi North Lake Rd, Olerai is an enchanting, bougainvillea-clad farmhouse surrounded by yellow fever trees, with giant cushions spread outside on the lawn. There's a small sitting room, and delicious meals with an Italian flair (home-grown vegetables) are taken alfresco or under a pergola-covered courtyard to the accompaniment of Swahili musicians. This is where Iain and Orial Douglas-Hamilton wrote their book, *Among the Elephants* – their old office is now an elephant-themed bedroom. All rooms are imaginatively furnished and have en-suite bathrooms, with plenty of thoughtful extras. **On offer:** walks to the lake about half a kilometre away; birdwatching and gamespotting (several animals have been translocated here), gondola rides on the lake to see the hippo, otters and birdlife and lakeside excursions. There's a private airstrip.

Rates: US$440 full board per person sharing

What to see and do
Lake Naivasha

'Naivasha' means 'Rippling Water' in Maa. It's aptly named, as coming from Nairobi one sees the lake shimmering in the distance as the road descends into the Rift Valley from the top of the escarpment. A freshwater lake, it's currently about 20km long and 15km wide, but lake levels have fluctuated enormously over the years. In the early 1880s during the time of Joseph Thomson's travels it was reduced to a swamp, while in the 1920s lake levels were about eight metres higher than at present.

The lake itself is an **international Ramsar site**, and has prolific birdlife, from majestic fish eagles to tiny malachite kingfishers and there are also large concentrations of waterfowl, among them red-knobbed coot, African spoonbills and little grebe. Black bass and tilapia are caught in the lake, but illegal fishing methods gave rise to a temporary fishing ban in 2002, which has helped to increase fish stocks. There's a sizeable hippo population (about 600) and it's not uncommon to see hippo grazing in the moonlight, tearing at the grass like a team of giant lawnmowers. Within the papyrus reedbeds live Cape clawless otters. On the ranches around the lake wildlife is dominated by plains game – impala, waterbuck, Grant's gazelle and giraffe being common.

Conservation There are enormous environmental pressures on the lake, including an expanding lakeside population due to the migrant labour force on the flower farms leading to an increased demand for water; the increase in irrigation for horticulture and the subsequent filtering of nutrient discharge into the lake; poor sewerage causing pollution; over-fishing; and threats from invasive plants like the water hyacinth. Encouragingly, the landowners on the lakeside are active through the **Lake Naivasha Riparian Association** (PO Box 1011, Naivasha; tel: 050 21008; fax: 050 21009; email: kijabe@africaonline.co.ke; web: www.ncf.ca/~es202/naivasha), which is working on a number of conservation projects at grass-roots level in the area, assisting the government with management plans for the lake and striving to achieve a balance of interests between both people and wildlife using the lake's resources.

For those offering boating and birding excursions on the lake, see under *Where to stay* above.

Crescent Island Game Sanctuary

At the southeastern end of the lake, Crescent Island is actually a peninsula, the crescent being the remaining rim of a volcano. The sanctuary is best reached by boat – there are regular excursions from Lake Naivasha Country Club (page 277) although you can go by road through Sanctuary Farm. Walking in the sanctuary gives the opportunity to see gazelle, waterbuck and giraffe as well as fantastic birdlife.

Elmenteita Weavers

PO Box 85, Naivasha; tel: 050 30115
About 4km from the turn-off to Moi South Lake Road, Elmenteita Weavers is signposted to the right. There's a range of original designs and good quality colourful rugs, cushions and *kikois*, table linen, bedspreads, pottery and other gifts for sale in the showroom, and you can visit the workshop and see the weavers at work.
Open daily 09.00–17.30; Sun 09.00–17.00

Crater Lake Sanctuary

This sanctuary contains a small, steeply sided crater lake, with distinctive milky-green waters, surrounded by acacia forest where black-and-white colobus monkeys are often in residence. Around the lake you can find pieces of the shiny, jet-black stone, obsidian. There's an excellent nature trail to the lake (about a 2-hour walk) and there's also a 4WD driving circuit where you're likely to see buffalo, waterbuck and gazelle.
Entry KSh200

Hell's Gate National Park

PO Box 234, Naivasha; tel: 050 20284; email: hellsgatenp@africaonline.co.ke
Open daily; park entry US$15; vehicle KSh200
There are three entrances to the park: **Elsa gate**, the park headquarters, with a small information centre and bikes for hire (KSh500 a day, but they have only a few, so book in advance or hire one elsewhere) is 2km off Moi South Lake Road, about 20km from the turn-off to Naivasha town; **Olkaria gate** is 7km off Moi South Lake Road, near Elsamere; and **Narasha gate** exits to the south, eventually joining the B3 to Suswa and the Mara after about 12km. It's preferable to have 4WD.

A small park (68km²), Hell's Gate is scenically dramatic with ochre-coloured cliffs, volcanic plugs at Fischer's and central towers, the steep Njorowa Gorge and the extinct Hobley's and Olkaria volcanoes. It's well worth a visit and is one of the few national parks where you can go **walking**, **cycling** and **rock climbing** unaccompanied by rangers, although (as always) it's best to take a guide, especially if planning to walk in the lower gorge as the path is steep and difficult to find at times. **Note**: if walking or cycling, carry water. There are several **viewing circuits** off the main route – Twiga and Buffalo are in the eastern section of the park, and from here you can visit the **obsidian caves**. There's good game viewing, with the chance of seeing rock hyrax at Fischer's Tower, and klipspringers on the steep slopes around the Naiburta campsite, as well as more common savanna species – giraffe, gazelle, buffalo and kongoni. Occasionally lion venture into the park, so check on entry for recent sightings. However, it's the large birds that really stand out – Egyptian and Ruppell's griffon vultures, Verreaux's eagle, secretary birds and kori bustards are often seen. The park used

LEGEND OF FISCHER'S TOWER: HELL'S GATE NATIONAL PARK

This legend draws parallels with the biblical story of Sodom and Gomorrah, when Lot and his wife and daughters were told to flee for their lives, with instructions not to look back. In this case, a young Maasai girl leaves her home village for the last time as she sets forth to marry her warrior husband. Unwittingly, she turns to take one last look at the home she's leaving and is immediately turned to stone – the stone monolith of Fischer's Tower.

to have a breeding colony of lammergeyers (sometimes known as bearded vultures) on the cliffs, but they disappeared in 1984. Efforts are being made to reintroduce them.

At the western end of the park, you can visit a **Maasai cultural *manyatta*** and continue up the hill to the **geothermal power station**.

There are three **campsites** in the park (PO Box 234, Naivasha; tel: 050 20284; email: hellsgatenp@africaonline.co.ke; or book through KWS head office, page 91). The sites have pit latrines and a water tap, but the water supply is unreliable, so take your own. The best campsite is **Naiburta**, at the top of a bluff looking south over the park. It's an excellent lookout post for watching the game coming to water below. Other campsites are **Oldubai** on the Twiga circuit, **Narasha gate** and **Ol Karia**.

Rates: US$8 plus park entry fee US$15 and vehicle entry KSh200

Olkaria Geothermal Power Station

PO Box 785, Naivasha; tel: 050 21233

Africa's first geothermal power station, built in 1985, Olkaria's billowing clouds of steam and maze of enormous industrial pipes come as rather a rude shock after the wilderness of Hell's Gate. But for all that it makes little visual impact on the surrounding landscape. Owned by the Kenya Electricity Generating Company, the plant produces about 15% of Kenya's electricity supply which feeds into the national grid at Suswa. There are plans to expand the site to harness additional power. Geothermal energy comes from the natural heat stored in the earth's crust which rises to the surface in the form of fumaroles and hot springs. Deep wells are drilled to tap into the steam source and the steam is then piped to a powerhouse to drive the turbines. At Olkaria, the heat comes from hot magma bodies up to 6km below ground.

Open daily; free entry

Mount Longonot National Park

PO Box 234, Naivasha; tel: 050 20284; email: hellsgatenp@africaonline.co.ke

Open daily; park entry fee US$15; vehicle entry KSh200

Access is off the C88 about 12km south of Naivasha. The distinctive crater of Mount Longonot (2,886m) is a major feature in the Rift Valley near Lake Naivasha. Sharply etched in the early morning light, at other times it takes on a dark and brooding nature. The main attraction is to climb the deeply serrated cone to the ridge, a little strenuous in parts, particularly near the top, and then to circle the lip of the crater. The round trip takes about 4 hours. It's worth the effort, as the views from the top are superb. There has been the odd isolated incident in the past, so check security before climbing.

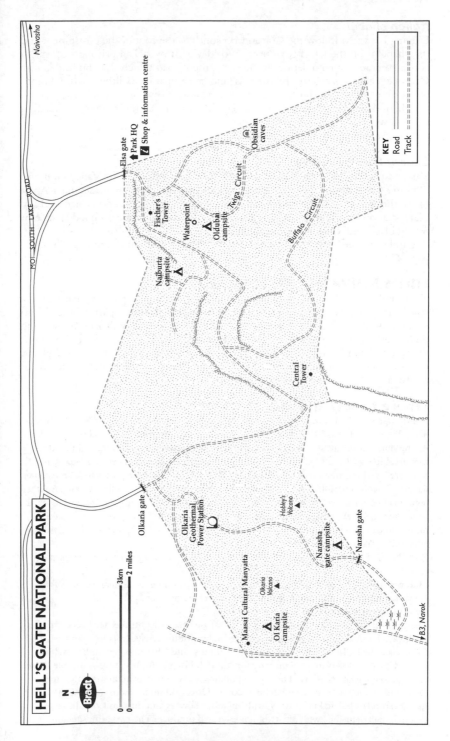

HELL'S GATE NATIONAL PARK

KEY
Road
Track

Naivasha

MOI SOUTH LAKE ROAD

Elsa gate
Park HQ
Shop & information centre

Fischer's Tower
Waterpoint
Oldubai campsite
Twiga Circuit
Obsidian caves

Naiburta campsite

Buffalo Circuit

Central Tower

Olkaria gate

Olkaria Geothermal Power Station

Maasai Cultural Manyatta
Olkaria Volcano
Ol Karia campsite

Hobley's Volcano

Narasha gate campsite
Narasha gate

B3, Narok

N

3km
2 miles
0
0

Italian chapel

Leaving Naivasha follow the C66 and B3 south to the foot of the escarpment and the chapel is on the left. Built during World War II by Italian prisoners of war to commemorate the completion of the escarpment road which they built, this tiny Catholic chapel has beautiful frescos and a campanile belltower. It fell into disrepair in the 1970s but has since been restored (by the orginal artist) and a couple of African women act as caretakers, lighting the altar candles and arranging fresh flowers.

Entry is free but a donation is appropriate

Eburru Forest Reserve

Situated on the northern side of the lake, not far from the Rift Valley Golf and Country Club, Eburru Forest is ideal for **walking**, but there are no set trails. Apart from the forest scenery and wildflowers, there are good views across Lake Naivasha towards Mount Longonot and the Aberdares. There's a good chance of seeing black-and-white colobus monkeys.

Guides can be arranged through the Rift Valley Golf and Country Club; see page 279.

FROM NAIVASHA TO NAKURU

The A104 from Naivasha to Nakuru is deeply potholed in parts, which makes a complete nonsense of driving on the left. Buses thunder past at speed and numerous, heavily laden lorries trundle their way north with *matatus* weaving their way in between. In 2003 funds had been allocated to upgrade the road, but the timing had still to be specified. The road climbs from Naivasha to Gilgil and then descends past Lake Elmentaita to Nakuru. Zebra are often seen at the side of the road.

Where to stay and eat

Malu (16 rooms in 4 cottages and 2 villas; self-catering treehouse; plunge pool) PO Box 536, Naivasha; tel: 050 30181; fax: 050 20272; email: malu@africaonline.co.ke

About 9km from Naivasha town, after Delamere shop, there's a sign to the right on the back road to Gilgil and Nyaharuru. Nestling in a 700ha estate with a pristine cedar forest, there are sweeping views over the Rift Valley. The rooms have four-poster beds and feather duvets. There's superb Italian cuisine in the restaurant and log fires in the evening. Another option is to cater for yourselves and stay in the treehouse overlooking the Malewa River (2 bedrooms en suite) which is fully equipped; you need only to bring provisions, although meals can be taken in the restaurant. **On offer:** guided walks through virgin forest, fishing, horseriding and mountain biking.

Rates: US$135 full board per person sharing; treehouse KSh11,500 a night (or catered option at lodge rate)

Malewa River Lodge (6 rooms, 2 campsites; river swimming; ecolodge) PO Box 446, Naivasha; tel: 050 30312; email: malewa@kenyaweb.com; web: www.malewariverlodge.com

The turn-off for the lodge is on the right, 17km from Naivasha off the A104 Nakuru Highway. This delightful ecolodge was designed by wildlife artist and conservationist, Chris Campbell Clause, who runs the lodge with his wife Christine. Set in the 1,400ha Kigio Wildlife Conservancy, a sanctuary for Rothschild's giraffe and plains game, the lodge faces on to the Malewa River. The central building has an open-plan dining- and sitting-room with a huge fireplace and 2 double rooms. Three additional rooms (also open) are in spacious rondavels, sited for privacy, with en-suite showers and flush toilets. The food is superb and imaginative, with plenty of home-grown produce. The two campsites are next

ROTHSCHILD'S GIRAFFE TRANSLOCATION
Chris Campbell Clause

In August 2002, eight female and two male Rothschild's giraffe were transported from Lake Nakuru National Park to Kigio Wildlife Conservancy in a high-sided lorry along a carefully selected route to avoid power lines and telephone wires. After a few days in a holding pen, they were released. A new sanctuary for Rothschild's giraffe was born and another successful conservation initiative implemented by the Kenya Wildlife Service, with financial assistance from the European Union Biodiversity Trust Fund, Tusk Trust UK and the Born Free Foundation.

Capturing and moving a giraffe is not easy. Rothschild's giraffe are larger than the Masai and reticulated giraffe, also found in Kenya, being in excess of 17ft tall. How do you go about this exercise? For several days the capture teams were camped in Nakuru, and each morning they drove out in search of a suitable animal. Sometimes one was found quickly and on other occasions, uncannily, not a giraffe was in sight. Once located, the vets were driven within range to shoot the immobilising drug into the flank of the targeted animal. Tension rose amongst the capture crews stationed in several vehicles, as this was the most dangerous time, following these long legged animals through all sorts of terrain, with the chance of hitting trees or driving into hidden holes.

After being darted, giraffe are inclined to get an adrenalin kick and start to behave erratically, sometimes running great distances. Was there enough dose or was there too much for the estimated body weight? Where would the giraffe run to, and for how long? Imagine how far a giraffe can run in a time period of eight to ten minutes before the drug takes effect, and the capture teams have to keep pace with the animal so that when it falls down, they can administer the antidote immediately. The blood pressure to the brain is immense in an animal with such a long neck, and if it lies on the ground for too long the pressure on the brain will be excessive and the giraffe may die. All these factors make the difference between a successful capture and a failure. Failure may mean death to an innocent animal.

Fortunately, the captures went according to plan, and the giraffe were successfully caught over a ten-day period. Having been immobilised and quickly revived, the giraffe has a hood placed over its head while a transport trailer is positioned next to the prostrate animal. Any escape route is cordoned off with ropes so that when the giraffe is allowed on to its feet, it is coaxed into the crate, loaded on to a trailer and moved to the holding pens a few kilometres away. Here the giraffe spent several days to limit the trauma experienced by their capture, before their final journey to the Kigio Wildlife Conservancy.

The Rothschild's giraffe translocation is the subject of a BBC documentary presented by the actress Joanna Lumley, called 'Born to be Wild'.

to the river, downstream. Well-run, they provide wood, hot showers and flush toilets. **On offer:** birdwatching, trout fishing, nature walks, night game drives, horseriding, abseiling, rock climbing, mountain biking, canoeing and rafting, cultural visits and voluntary work. There's a private airstrip nearby.
Rates: lodge from US$165 full board per person sharing; camping KSh300; activities extra

Lake Elementaita Lodge (33 rooms; swimming pool; camping) PO Box 66, Gilgil; tel: 051 850863; fax: 051 850833; email: lake-nakuru@gatewayonline.co.ke; web: www.lakenakurulodge.com
Located off the A104 on the left, about 32km south of Nakuru on Kikopey ranch, the lodge is a good stop-off point from the main road. It's the former residence of the English settler-peer, Lord Galbraith Cole, who built the house in 1916. It still retains some of its old features, with shady terraces (overlooking the large swimming pool) and an internal courtyard, but the square, modern furniture looks rather incongruous. There's a good restaurant and the rooms are in cottages in the garden, and all have en-suite showers and, as their brochure beautifully describes, 'dazzling-to-the-eye mosquito nets'. The staff are extremely friendly and helpful. **On offer:** nature walks and birdwatching (350 species) with the resident naturalist, horseriding, ox-wagon rides, visits to Lord Cole's memorial and a natural water spa which flows into the lake, an ostrich farm and the Kariandusi prehistoric site.
Rates: from US$110 B&B per person; camping KSh500 but no facilities and no water; activities extra

What to see and do
Kigio Wildlife Conservancy
A small, private game sanctuary where you can see the rare Rothschild's giraffe (see box, page 285).
Open daily; entry KSh100

Gilgil War Cemetery
About 3km out of Gilgil on the Nyharuru road, this is one of 40 cemeteries in Kenya maintained by the Commonwealth War Graves Commission. Beautifully kept, there are a couple of hundred graves from the East Africa Campaign of World War II and a few from the Mau Mau Emergency between 1959 and 1962.

Lake Elmenteita
As the A104 climbs up the hill beyond Gilgil, on the rise you look down on to the soda lake of Elmenteita, often fringed with the pink tinge of flamingos and the white of pelicans. It's surrounded by hills to the south, former volcanoes, giving a profile of a man's face, often referred to as 'Delamere's nose', being on part of the Delamere Estates on Soysambu. There's a turning on the left to the lake, about 3km along a dirt track. At the lake edge you can observe the birdlife (300 species recorded). Other options are to come via Lake Elmentaita Lodge.

Kariandusi prehistoric site
About 1.5km off the A104 on the right near Elmentaita the Kariandusi site was excavated by Louis Leakey between 1929 and 1947 and displays an assortment of Stone Age tools – predominantly axe heads and knives, some made from obsidian – between 1.4 million and 200,000 years old. There's also a small museum which gives a brief history of the Rift Valley and early man.
Open daily 08.00–18.00; entry KSh200

NAKURU AND ENVIRONS
Nakuru started as a railway station at the turn of the 20th century and is now Kenya's fourth-largest urban area, with a population of over a million. It is a surprising combination of agricultural market town, industrial manufacturer and provincial administrative centre. Spreading out along the railway line towards the lake is a fast-growing area of ramshackle huts, while the more prestigious houses are sited on the hill. Avenues of jacaranda and pepper trees line the road, but the

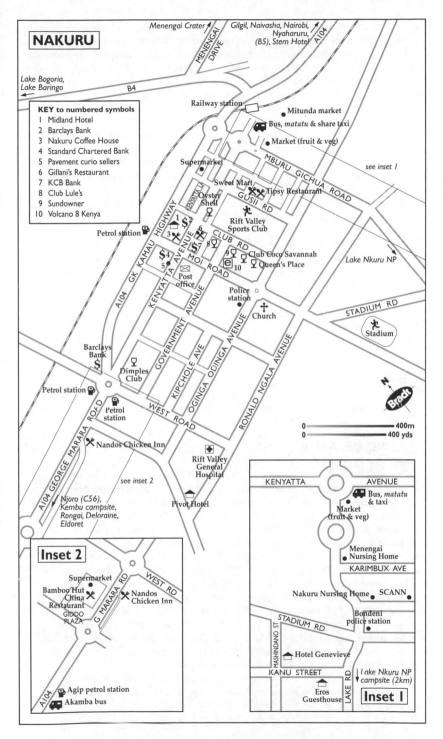

NAKURU

Menengai Crater
Gilgil, Naivasha, Nairobi,
Nyaharuru,
(B5), Stem Hotel
A104

MENENGAI DRIVE

Lake Bogoria,
Lake Baringo

B4

Railway station

Mitunda market

Bus, *matatu* & share taxi

Market (fruit & veg)

Supermarket

see inset 1

KEY to numbered symbols
1 Midland Hotel
2 Barclays Bank
3 Nakuru Coffee House
4 Standard Chartered Bank
5 Pavement curio sellers
6 Gillani's Restaurant
7 KCB Bank
8 Club Lule's
9 Sundowner
10 Volcano 8 Kenya

Sweet Mart

Tipsy Restaurant

MBURU GICHUA ROAD

Oyster
Shell

GUSII RD

Rift Valley
Sports Club

Petrol station

CLUB RD

Club Coco Savannah

Queen's Place

Lake Nkuru NP

Post
office

Police
station

Church

STADIUM RD

Stadium

Barclays
Bank

Dimples
Club

Petrol station

Petrol
station

N

Bradt

0 ——— 400m
0 ——— 400 yds

Nandos Chicken Inn

Rift Valley
General
Hospital

see inset 2

Inset 1

KENYATTA   AVENUE

Bus, *matatu*
& taxi

Market
(fruit & veg)

Menengai
Nursing Home

KARIMBUX AVE

Nakuru Nursing Home   SCANN

Bondeni
police station

Njoro (C56),
Kembu campsite,
Rongai, Deloraine,
Eldoret

Pivot Hotel

STADIUM RD

MASHINDANO ST

LAKE RD

Hotel Genevieve

KANU STREET

Lake Nkuru NP
campsite (2km)

Eros
Guesthouse

Inset 2

Supermarket

Bamboo Hut
China
Restaurant

GIDDO
PLAZA

WEST RD

G MARARA RD

Nandos
Chicken Inn

Agip petrol station

Akamba bus

town itself is rundown, with potholed streets and people leading a frenetic existence. Sadly, there's a high proportion of street children (see box piece on page 290). But it's also a lively place with an expanding middle class and, consequently, a burgeoning leisure market in the form of restaurants and clubs. On the outskirts, farm machinery outlets for combine harvesters and tractors line the road out to Rongai, with large grain silos on the skyline. (It's a major wheat-growing area.) Other industries include a tannery, blanket and battery manufacture, a Coca-Cola bottling plant and cooking-oil processing. There's an excellent fruit and vegetable covered market and a lively *mitunda* market next to it (but remember to take only small change and leave valuables behind). Next to Standard Bank on Kenyatta Avenue, the pavement is choc-a-bloc with curio sellers. There's an excellent selection of kiondo baskets, wooden carvings and kisii stone ornaments for sale at reasonable prices, although a bit of haggling is expected.

Located on the railway line, about 20km to the west of Nakuru are the small settlements of **Njoro** and **Rongai**, still a major farming area.

Getting there and around

Nakuru is at the hub of major transport routes. From the south comes the A104 from Nairobi, which branches west in Nakuru for Eldoret and roads to Kericho and Kisumu. The B4 heads north for Baringo, with the option to branch west to Eldama ravine and Kabarnet, while the B5 heads northeast to Nyaharuru. Within Nakuru itself, be aware of car tricksters if you leave a parked car. A squirt of oil on a back wheel is a favourite, with a plausible chap kindly pointing it out to you on your return, explaining how dangerous it could be, and how he has a friend who's a very good mechanic who can fix it … it's a good scam and it does happen.

By bus

There are regular buses to Nairobi, Kericho, Eldoret, Kisumu, Nyaharuru and Kampi ya Samaki (Baringo), as well as Peugeot 504 car taxis and *matatus*. Crossways

LORD DELAMERE
Andrew Nightingale

Lord Delamere first came to Kenya in 1897 and returned to settle in 1904. His first estate, Equator ranch, stretched from the Mau Forest to the Equator, his first home being on the lower slopes of the Mau. He chose the area around Njoro because of the ideal farming conditions found at high altitude on this section of the Uganda railway. He had grand plans for Njoro, hoping it would become the colony's administrative capital as it was the geographical centre of the British East Africa (Kenya) and Uganda Protectorates. He instigated Njoro township's unusual decagonal shape, basing the town layout on the American grid system.

Initially experimenting with sheep and cattle, which proved a failure, he put land under the plough, planting 800 acres of wheat in the hope of clearing his overdraft. The crop withered and rotted due to several varieties of rust and fungus. As a result, Delamere set up a plant-breeding laboratory. Having bred over 2,000 hybrids, he selected 32 varieties and turned Njoro into Kenya's cradle of wheat production.

Njoro remains a ramshackle town with spacious streets, and the plant-breeding station near Egerton University is still the nucleus of seed experimentation in Kenya.

speed taxis are recommended. The main bus station is adjacent to the market on the eastern side of town. The Akamba bus stage is on the A104 on the left, next to the Agip petrol station heading west on the A104.

By air
There's no public airstrip or scheduled flights, but there are plenty of private airstrips in the vicinity.

Getting organised
Barclays on Kenyatta Avenue and Standard Chartered Bank on Moi Road have **ATMs** and there's a **forex bureau** on George Marara Road. The main **post office** is on the corner of Moi Road and Kenyatta Avenue, open Monday–Friday 08.00–17.00, Saturday 09.00–12.00. For **internet access** try Volcano Eight Kenya on Government Avenue. There are several **supermarkets**; Uchumi in Kenyatta Lane is the best. Next door, Medika Chemists in Equator House has a good **pharmacy** and there are others in town. In a **medical emergency** go to the Rift Valley General Hospital in West Road (tel: 051 214503). The **police station** is on Oginga Odinga Avenue (tel: 051 42222) and the **tourist helpline** is 020 604767. There are plenty of **petrol stations** on the access roads into Nakuru.

Where to stay
Midland Hotel PO Box 908, Nakuru; tel: 051 212125; fax: 051 44517
A popular businessmen's hotel, with a lively outdoor restaurant serving a good selection of European and African food (about KSh450 main course). It's seen better days, but the rooms are comfortable with bathrooms en suite, the best being in the new wing.
Rates: from KSh1,000–1,850 B&B per person sharing
Hotel Genevieve (97 rooms) Mashindano St, off Kanu St, PO Box 127, Nakuru; tel: 051 211062; fax: 051 42143
This is a modern little hotel, with friendly management and attentive staff, located in a rather rundown area not far from Lake Nakuru National Park. There's safe parking and the rooms are clean and comfortable with en-suite bathrooms. There's a residents' lounge with a TV and video and a panelled dining-room with modern, functional furniture, and a bar area. It opened in 2002 and is popular with the business and conference fraternity.
Rates: from KSh1,500 B&B per person sharing
Pivot Hotel PO Box 1369, Nakuru; tel: 051 210226
All rooms are s/c – the best are from 1–15, being furthest away from the disco which is held nightly. There are good-value meals from KSh350.
Rates: KSh450 B&B per person sharing
Eros Guest House and Hotel Langa Langa Rd; PO Box 2198, Nakuru; tel: 051 44120; fax: 051 213428; email: eros@pioneer.africaonline.com
A small, efficient little hotel near Lake Nakuru National Park. Comfortable s/c rooms have instant hot water, a TV and telephone and there's secure parking. A small dining-room serves good *nyama choma*.
Rates: from KSh1,100 B&B per person sharing
Stem Hotel Off the A104 on the right, PO Box 1076, Nakuru; tel: 051 850135; fax: 051 851273; email: info@stemhotel.com; web: www.stemhotel.com
On the outskirts of Nakuru on the Nairobi side of town, the Stem Hotel is a useful transit stop. It's a busy hotel, and has no salient features, but the staff are friendly and the rooms reasonable. Its restaurant has a good choice of European, African, Oriental and Indian cuisine. The African dishes are recommended.
Rates: from KSh1,550 per person sharing

SCANN – STREET CHILDREN'S ASSISTANCE NETWORK OF NAKURU

Yasmin Galani

The Street Children's Assistance Network of Nakuru (SCANN) is a rehabilitation project which started in 2000. It's supported by various reputable charitable organisations, among them the Rotary Club, Lions Club, Round Table Club and Salvation Army. Its mandate is to provide all necessary assistance to street children many of whom are as young as four years old. The SCANN centre consists of three dormitories – each has a house-mother's quarters, dining-cum-all-purpose hall, kitchen, four classrooms and two staff houses. The centre has a capacity for 200 children. The project presently assists 127 children, all boys, aged between three-and-a-half and 17, and continues to admit more needy street children. Once admitted into the centre the children are counselled, detoxified of all glue and petrol fumes they have sniffed over the years and rehabilitated within the centre. They are then graded and admitted into a class. As soon as the child is settled, he is admitted into a government-funded public school where he continues with his education. Some of the older children, who have never had the opportunity of going to school, are sent on various apprenticeship courses, such as motor repairs, welding, bicycle repairing, plumbing and cooking. A number of children have completed their courses and are now in gainful employment and living independently. Although SCANN is a partnership of various charitable organisations, in view of the various other projects carried on by these clubs SCANN obtains very little financial assistance from the partner organisations. However it obtains valuable expertise from its experienced partners. The partnership also ensures that the project is long term and that funds are fully accounted for – transparency is paramount – and that accounts are audited by a qualified firm of reputable independent auditors.

Fundraising

It should be noted that SCANN is a 100% charitable project. No fees are charged, neither is any contribution expected from the children or their parents – they just don't have any! SCANN has held various fund-raising events in Nakuru and Nairobi. The SCANN children perform dances, songs and excellent acrobatics. The community has been impressed by the project and has been very supportive. The centre also raises funds through sponsorship. To sponsor a child for 12 months costs KSh15,000 (US$200 or £135). This ensures that the child is given all the necessities of life including food, shelter, clothing, education and health care.

The SCANN centre welcomes visitors to the project all day, every day. The SCANN centre is located in the Bondeni Area of Nakuru (not more than five minutes' drive from the town centre) along Shadrack Kimarel Avenue, opposite Kisulisuli Primary School. A mature adult wishing to provide voluntary services at the centre will be considered.

For further information, or if you would like to support a child, please contact SCANN, PO Box 14819, Nakuru; tel: 051 216118; email: totem@multitechweb.com.

Njoro and Rongai

Kembu Cottages, Farmstay and Campsite (camping; 2 rooms; 2 cottages sleep 2–4; self-catering and full board; swimming tank) PO Box 23, Njoro; tel: 051 61413, mobile: 0722 725003; email: kembu@net2000ke.com
Take the A104 west of Nakuru and turn-off after a few kilometres on to the C56 to Njoro. Turn right through Njoro town on to the C56 to Molo and Elburgon (or just ask for Nightingale's farm). About 8km out of town, you'll see avenues of eucalyptus trees and fields of horses. Kembu campsite is signposted on the left. If coming by public transport, take any *matatu* heading to Molo and ask to get off at Kembu campsite. The **campsite**, popular with overlanders, is well organised, with hot showers and thunderbox toilets. It's small and intimate, with an excellent restaurant serving good food, with a log fire in the evenings and a congenial bar where neighbours often congregate for a drink. On site there's also a bougainvillea-clad treehouse with a double bed (use facilities in campsite). The campsite is situated next door to Zoe and Andrew Nightingale's home, and they're usually around to advise on farm activities and local excursions. They offer full-board accommodation in their home – the Yellow Room (double bedroom with en-suite bathroom) is in the house and **Acacia Cottage** (1 room with double bed, lavish bathroom and private patio with French windows) is situated in the garden, while meals are taken in an open-air courtyard under an awning in the main house. Next door to the house is **Albizia Cottage** (2 rooms, kitchen, bathroom, sitting room with fireplace, large veranda and garden), a wooden bungalow built in the 1920s with self-catering and catered options. **Beryl's Cottage** (2 rooms, kitchen, breakfast deck, bathroom and sitting room with fireplace) is self-catering or you can eat at the restaurant. It's a 10-minute drive from Kembu. A small, enchanting wooden bungalow with quaint hexagonal wood-panelled rooms and glorious views across the valley, it was built in 1915 by Charles Clutterbuck for his daughter, the famous (and infamous) aviatrix, Beryl Markham, who was the first woman to fly the Atlantic solo. **On offer:** walking, horseriding and cycling on the 400ha farm, badminton, volleyball, darts and pool; visits to the school (they raised the funds to build the school), to a white-fronted bee-eater colony and around the working farm with race horses and dairy cows, and excursions to Lake Nakuru National Park and Lake Baringo. Next door there's a beauty parlour, Maintenance Matic 4WD workshop and Roving Rovers Land Rover hire (see page 87).
Rates: Camping US$3; treehouse KSh1,400; self-catering KSh4,000; farmstay KSh4,800. Tents and mountain bikes are available for hire.
Deloraine (6 rooms; homestay; swimming pool) Offbeat Safaris, Deloraine Estate, PO Rongai; tel: 051 32005; email: offbeat@africaonline.co.ke; web: www.offbeatsafaris.com
Continue past Rongai on the A104 for about 6km, and there's a sign on the right to Deloraine Estates. The grand, double-storey, colonial mansion, with capacious verandas, sweeping lawns and exotic herbaceous borders, is set in a 2,000ha farm on the lower slopes of Londiani Mountain (3,008m). Built in 1920 by Lord Francis Scott, the sixth son of the sixth Duke of Buccleuch, the house has entertained royalty in its time. On the veranda there's an old tea chest from Fortnum and Mason in London addressed to 'Lord Francis Scott, Rongai, Kenya Colony' – quite remarkable that it ever arrived. All the rooms are comfortably furnished with en-suite bathrooms. The house is hosted by Cindy and Tristan Voorspruy and is primarily a base for their riding safaris (page 123). **On offer:** horseriding on the farm (not for amateurs), croquet, tennis and excursions to local attractions; airstrip for light aircraft.
Rates: from US$220 full board per person sharing; day excursions extra

Where to eat

In addition to the hotel restaurants are the following:

Bamboo Hut China Restaurant Giddo Plaza, PO Box 16532, Nakuru; tel: 051 43734. This is one of the best licensed restaurants in town, serving a good selection of Chinese

food at a reasonable price. They also do some African specials – roast meat with noodles or rice.
Open daily 11.00–22.00

For **cheap eats** try **Tipsy Restaurant** on Gussi Road for a selection of curries and local food; **Nakuru Sweet Mart,** also on Gussi Road, a long-established favourite for Indian specialities; **Gillani's Restaurant** on Club Road (above the Gillani's supermarket); and **Nandos Chicken Inn** off George Marara Road for pizzas, and the **Nakuru Coffee House** on Kenyatta Avenue for fresh Kenyan coffee and good snacks.

Entertainment
Club Lule's on Club Avenue is the place to head for – there's a one-man guitar show on Tuesdays and Thursdays, Mugithi disco on Wednesdays and Fridays, family entertainment at the weekend and live bands at the end of the month. It also has secure parking, and good *nyama choma*. Other places to try are **Dimples Club** and **Oyster Shell** on Kenyatta Avenue, **Sundowner**, **Club Coco Savannah** and **Queen's Place** on Club Road and **Queen's Bridge** on Lake Road.

What to see and do
Hyrax Hill
PO Box 9535, Nakuru
An Iron Age stone enclosure and neolithic burial ground, excavations were begun by Mary Leakey in 1937. Of the three major areas of prehistoric settlement, the oldest dates back 3,000 years, while the most recent are only a couple of hundred years old. There's a small museum on site with ethnological exhibits of the Rift Valley and neolithic artefacts from the Hyrax Hill sites, including obsidian tools and a stone platter.
Open daily 09.30–18.00; entry KSh200

Menengai Crater
Immediately north of Nakuru, and giving a backdrop to the town, is an enormous caldera – Menengai – which is about 12km wide. Follow Menengai Drive from town, and it's around 4.5km to the crater rim. It's not advisable to walk this route as there have been muggings in the past. There's not a lot to see apart from the size of the crater, hyrax scuttling around in the rocks and thorny scrub on the crater floor, but there are good panoramic views of the lake.

Njoro Sports Club
This is a members-only club, but if you're in the vicinity, ask if you can have a look inside the clubhouse. The walls are adorned with royal portraits of King Edward VI and black-and-white photographs of Njoro flying rallies in 1918 and 1934.

Mau Forest
From Njoro, the C57 heads south to Mau Narok, along the Mau escarpment of the Rift Valley wall. East of the escarpment, the Mau Forest stretches east across a broad belt of highland between 2,000 and 2,700m as far as the tea country of Kericho. It's one of the last remaining near-continuous blocks of indigenous montane forest in East Africa covering about 270,000ha. Within the forest there remain a few clans of Ogiek hunter-gatherers, some of whom still retain a traditional way of life (see page 54). Remnants of this magnificent forest, with

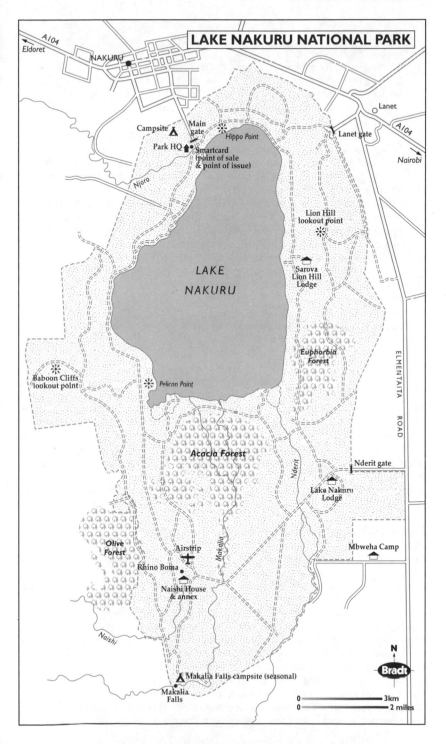

EGERTON'S CASTLE
Andrew Nightingale

Lord Egerton, fourth baron of Tatton, first came to Kenya in the 1920s. A keen hunter and photographer, he was enchanted by the country and bought 800ha of farmland near his friend Lord Delamere. On returning to England, he fell in love with a lady who would not consider marrying him, as she had been brought up to live in a castle, not a mud hut. Lord Egerton returned to Kenya and built a 52-room castle near Njoro, modelled on the family mansion in Knutsford, complete with oak panelling – the oak imported from England – and a magnificent ballroom. He apparently spent so long perfecting his castle, that by the time it was finished, his ladyfriend had fallen in love with someone else.

Lord Egerton then threw his energies into farming. He set up Egerton Agricultural College on 500 hectares of land near Delamere's plant-breeding station, now part of Egerton University. His entire family fortune was sunk into developing Kenya's agriculture, as he died in 1958 leaving no heir. The castle is a shadow of its former glory, but is open to the public. Egerton University, in association with the National Museums of Kenya, plans to renovate the castle as a Museum of Agricultural Development in Kenya.

Egerton's Castle is between Njoro and the A104. Ask at Kembu Campsite, page 291, for directions.

cedar, olive and podocarpus, may be seen from the road, but there's no formal access for visitors. A vital water catchment area, with some of the highest rainfall in the country, it feeds the Sondu and Mara river systems in the west, and the Njoro, Makalia and Enderit rivers in the east. The Mau Forest has suffered (and continues to suffer) from indiscriminate logging and forest clearance for settlement and in many areas indigenous forest has been replaced with plantations. **Friends of the Mau Watershed** (FOMAWA, PO Box 1977, Nakuru; email: fomawa1@yahoo.com) are making efforts locally to redress the destruction of the forest resource through providing assistance and information at grass-roots level.

Lake Nakuru National Park
PO Box 39, Nakuru; tel: 051 44069
Open daily; smartcard required; park entry fee US$30 and vehicle entry KSh200. Point of sale for smartcards at main gate (see page 41 for further details).
There are three entrances to the park – the **main gate** and the park headquarters are about 1km south of Nakuru town, while about 8km east of Nakuru, on the right off the A104, it's about 2km to **Lanet gate.** The **Nderit gate** is on the southeastern boundary, joining the Elmentaita road to Lanet. The park is accessible with 2WD. Covering an area of 188km², the centre of the park is dominated by the shallow soda lake, Nakuru, renowned for its concentration of lesser flamingos (up to 1.5 million at certain times of year) feeding on the algae. The lake was designated Kenya's first **Ramsar site** in 1990, its wetland being of international importance for waterfowl, among them greater flamingos and giant white pelicans, as well as Palaearctic migrants. The **birdlife** is superb with over 450 recorded bird species. **Game viewing** is good too – Burchill's zebra, impala,

Defassa waterbuck, Rothschild's giraffe, white and black rhino, leopard and tree-climbing lions may be seen. (There are no elephants.) You are virtually guaranteed to see white rhino, introduced from South Africa in 1977, grazing on the southern lakeshore, and the park has played a major part in rhino rehabilitation and breeding programmes (see page 48). There are hippo at **hippo point**. The terrain varies from open savanna around the lake to mature *acacia* woodland, and a superb *Euphorbia candelabra* forest on the eastern side of the park. There's a good **viewing circuit** with viewpoints and picnic spots – it's worth driving up to the top of **Baboon Cliffs**, from which you get an excellent view of the lake. A leisurely drive around the lake takes about three hours.

Where to stay and eat
Within the park
Sarova Lion Hill Lodge (67 rooms; swimming pool) PO Box 7094, Nakuru; tel: 051 85455; 051: 037 210836; email: um@lhill.sarova.co.ke; web: www.sarovahotels.com
Spread out on a hill, surrounded by *euphorbia* forest, the hotel is on the eastern side of the lake, which can be seen in the distance. The staff are extremely hospitable and there's a large public area with dining-room (good food), lounge, bar, terrace and gift shop. The rooms are located on the hillside behind the main hotel, with comfortable rooms and en-suite shower rooms. There's also a honeymoon suite.
Rates: from US$95 full board per person sharing, plus park and vehicle entry fees
Lake Nakuru Lodge (60 rooms; swimming pool) PO Box 561, Nakuru; tel: 051 85446
In the southeastern part of the park, this is a sizeable lodge in pleasant gardens, and views across to the lake. It's built around an old colonial house and has the usual hotel facilities. The rooms are en suite and comfortable.
Rates: from US$120 full board per person sharing plus park and vehicle entry fees
Naishi House and annex (2 rooms, sleeps 6; annex sleeps 2; self-catering) PO Box 39, Nakuru; tel: 051 44069 or book through KWS in Nairobi (page 91)
Known as the Old Warden's House, Naishi is comfortable, clean and well equipped with a sitting room, bathroom, kitchen with gas cooker, fridge and cooking utensils. Electricity is on between 19.00–22.00 and linen is provided.
Rates: from US$200–250 a night plus park and vehicle entry fees
Public campsites PO Box 39, Nakuru; tel: 051 44069 or book through KWS in Nairobi (page 91)
One is next to the main gate and the other (and nicest) at Makalia Falls at the southern end of the park. Both have water and pit latrines, but monkeys can be a nuisance.
Rates: US$10 a night plus park and vehicle entry fees

Outside the park
Mbweha Camp (camping only) PO Box 7112, Nakuru; tel: 051 210943; mobile: 0722 677449; email: mbwehacamp@yahoo.co.uk
Coming from Nairobi, turn left off the A104 to Elmentaita (at the oil tanks before Stem Hotel) for about 17km to the turn-off on the right through a barrier to Mbweya Camp (4WD in wet weather). Alternatively, if coming through Lake Nakuru National Park it's a 15-minute drive from the Nderit gate. Set in a 2,600ha conservancy, the campsite looks out across the Eburru and Mau ranges. There's a variety of plains game, good birdwatching (250 recorded species) and aardvark and leopard may be seen at night. The camp is well organised with good facilities – firewood, hot showers, toilets, a sunken bar (overlooking a small waterhole) and excellent wholesome meals (from KSh350) in the restaurant. **On offer:** nature walks, cycle rides (bikes for hire), game and night drives (camp vehicles available) and excursions to Soysambu. There's also a private airstrip.
Rates: camping KSh200; conservancy fee KSh100; activities extra

LAKES BOGORIA AND BARINGO
Getting there and around
Take the B4 (good tarmac road) out of Nakuru and just south of Marigat on the right is the road down to Lake Bogoria National Reserve's main gate at Loboi. For Lake Baringo, continue north on the B4 to Kampi ya Samaki. If travelling by public transport, there are several buses and *matatus* a day from Nakuru to Kampi ya Samaki. If going to Bogoria, get off at Marigat, from where there are several *matatus* in the afternoon to Loboi with transport back from Loboi in the morning. You can buy honey and fresh fruit at Marigat, but for more substantial provisions you'll need to stock up in Nakuru.

Lake Bogoria National Reserve
PO Box 64, Marigat; tel: 051 40746
Open daily 06.00–19.00; reserve entry fee US$15 and vehicle entry KSh200
There are three gates to the reserve – **Emos gate** is via Mogotio off the B4 (for experienced 4WD only), but the best route is to turn right off the B4 just before Marigat to the main entrance at **Loboi gate** at the northern end of the reserve. (**Maji Moto gate** is between Emos and Loboi gates on the western boundary.) At Loboi, there's a small **conservation centre** which is mostly used for educating schoolchildren. Originally called Hannington, after Bishop Hannington who passed through the area on his way to Uganda (where he was subsequently murdered), Bogoria is a soda lake, often fringed by a mass of flamingos. It's contained by the hills of the Siracho escarpment which run along the eastern shore, mirrored in ever-changing reflections by the dark green waters. There's minimal plains game, but this is one of the best places to see **greater kudu** in the dry acacia scrub. However, the 'must-see' are the naturally occurring **Loburu hot springs**, boiling geysers, erupting plumes of water and jets of steam at the lakeside; but be warned, the water is scalding hot and can boil an egg, so tread carefully. **Walking** and **cycling** are permitted from the Loboi gate to the hot springs, but if you wish to go further you'll need to obtain permission at the gate and to take a ranger escort.

Where to stay and eat
Within the reserve
Lake Bogoria National Reserve (3 campsites) PO Box 64, Marigat; tel: 051 40746
There are no camping facilities provided and the best campsite is **Fig Tree** at the south eastern end of the lake.
Rates: camping US$8 plus reserve and vehicle entry fees

Outside the reserve
Lake Bogoria Hotel (23 rooms, camping; swimming pool; spa pool) PO Box 208, Menengai West, Nakuru; tel: 051 40225; fax: 051 40748; email: lbogoriahotel@wananchi.com; web: www.bogoriasparesort.com
A moth-eaten stuffed lion in a glass cage in the entrance hall sets the tone and there's a rather dejected air about the place, although the en-suite, AC rooms in cottages at the back of the main building are perfectly adequate. There's a lounge with video blaring and full-size photo-murals of beech trees, while outside there's a terrace spa pool which taps into the warm waters feeding Lake Bogoria's hot springs. Service is friendly but slow. The hotel's main attraction is that it's only 5 minutes' drive from the entrance to Lake Bogoria National Reserve and it has a good swimming pool as well as the spa. The **restaurant** serves meals for casual visitors (US$13 for lunch). You can also camp within the compound, but no facilities are provided.
Rates: from US$80 full board per person sharing; camping KSh500 inclusive of use of large swimming pool and security.

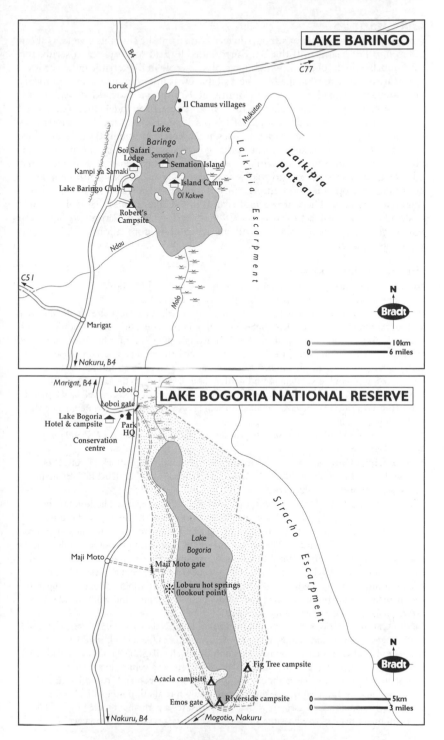

LAKE BARINGO

C77

Loruk

Il Chamus villages

Lake Baringo

Soi Safari Lodge

Semation I

Semation Island

Kampi ya Samaki

Lake Baringo Club

Island Camp

Ol Kokwe

Robert's Campsite

Ndau

C51

Molo

Marigat

Nakuru, B4

Laikipia Plateau

Laikipia Escarpment

Mukutan

N

Bradt

0 — 10km
0 — 6 miles

LAKE BOGORIA NATIONAL RESERVE

Marigat, B4

Loboi

Loboi gate

Lake Bogoria Hotel & campsite

Park HQ

Conservation centre

Maji Moto

Maji Moto gate

Lake Bogoria

Loburu hot springs (lookout point)

Siracho Escarpment

Fig Tree campsite

Acacia campsite

Emos gate

Riverside campsite

Nakuru, B4

Mogotio, Nakuru

N

Bradt

0 — 5km
0 — 3 miles

Lake Baringo

This large freshwater lake, a sea of pale terracotta from the silt in its waters, is about 10km north of Marigat off the B4. Surrounded by arid scenery, acacia scrub, and interminable flocks of goats (which have played a role in the terrible gulley erosion in the area), the lake is flanked by the Laikipia escarpment on its eastern boundary and supports a small fishing community at **Kampi ya Samaki** – Swahili for 'Fishing Camp' – a small village with a main street of wooden huts (shops sell household provisions and a couple of tearooms serve cheap meals) although it's expanding rapidly with new stone houses and a hotel. Although Baringo does not have park or reserve status, the enterprising local community has put up a barrier at the entrance to Kampi ya Samaki, which, when open, charges KSh200 entry. The lake itself is shallow, normally around 6m at its deepest, although levels continue to drop due to reduced run-off into the lake and siltation, causing increasing concern. There are several islands in the lake, some inhabited, a couple of which are accessible to tourists – Ol Kokwe, for Island Camp and Semation where you can rent a house – and an indigenous population of Il Chamus pastoralist fishermen.

Where to stay and eat

Robert's Campsite (campsite, bandas, self-catering cottages) PO Box 2, Kampi ya Samaki; tel: 053 51431; email: robertscamp@africaonline.co.ke
A long-established, well-run and popular campsite at the lake's edge, there are hot showers and toilets and firewood for sale (KSh80 a bundle). Hippo come out to graze at night, and there's a resident giant tortoise. There are 3 bandas (sleeping 2) set further back from the lake, which use the camp facilities, and 2 self-catering cottages, Hammerkop (sleeps 6) and Little Egret (sleeps 7), quaint wooden houses with a lake view, small sitting room, bathrooms, well-equipped kitchens and garden, both facing on to the lake. The Thirsty Goat bar and restaurant serves good wholesome meals, with an à la carte and snack menu. **On offer:** boat rides on the lake; small shop selling provisions; screen-printed materials and clothing for sale.
Rates: camping KSh300; bandas KSh1,600; cottages Ksh4,000 for 4 people and KSh500 per additional person

Lake Baringo Club (48 rooms; swimming pool) book through Block Hotels, Block House, Lusaka Rd, PO Box 40075, Nairiobi; tel: 020 535412; fax: 020 545954; email: blockreservations@net2000ke.com
The turning is off the B4 to the right, just after Robert's Campsite. The hotel is spread out along the lake's edge. There's a central reception area with a lounge and dining room, while the rooms – a good size with comfortable beds and en-suite shower rooms – are spread out in the garden. The restaurant serves excellent buffet-style meals. The main attraction is the superb birdlife – huge Verreaux eagle owls roost in the trees and the exquisite red and yellow barbet is readily seen. **On offer:** boat excursions on the lake, morning and evening birdwalks with the resident ornithologist (Benson Mugambi highly recommended), camel rides, slide show on Lake Baringo and wildlife videos.
Rates: from US$81 per person sharing full board

Island Camp (23 tents; swimming pool) PO Box 1141, Nakuru; tel: 051 374069; fax: 051 850858; web: www.island-camp.com or book through Let's Go Travel, page 101
To get to Island Camp's jetty you pass through the small village of Kampi ya Samaki and the turning's about 0.5km on the right where you can leave a vehicle in a secure compound. The boat ride takes about 20 minutes, passing hippo and crocodiles on the way. Located on Ol Kokwe Island, the camp is neatly spread out on the hillside under mature trees in landscaped gardens with stone paths. It's a permanent tented camp. The tents, all under thatch, have en-suite showers and toilets, privacy and lake views. There's

an open-plan bar and dining area, a more formal dining room (delicious food) and poolside snack bar. Apart from the magnificent birdlife, the colours are forever changing on the Rift wall on the Laikipia escarpment. It's a good place to unwind. **On offer:** waterskiing, windsurfing, guided walks, champagne breakfasts, boat trips, birdwatching (and feeding the fish eagle), Njemps (Il Chamus) village and hot springs.
Rates: from US$138 full board per person sharing; activities extra

Semation Island (self-catering, sleeps 8) Book through Richard Bonham Safaris, PO Box 24133, 00502 Nairobi; tel: 020 882521; fax: 020 882728; email: Bonham.Luke@swiftkenya.com
Small and exclusive, this delightful island retreat consists of a couple of cottages, with open views over the lake, lit by hurricane lamps at night. There's a sitting-room, bathroom, veranda and a separate, well-equipped kitchen block. The resident cook will prepare delicious meals, but you need to take all provisions. Alternatively, there's a fully catered option. **On offer:** boat trips around the lake. Excursions further afield can be arranged.
Rates: self-catering from US$250 a day; US$245 per person (4 or more) full board, inclusive of boat activities. Closed April and May.

Soi Safari Lodge (30 rooms; swimming pool) PO Box 45, Kampi ya Samaki; tel: 053 51242
Just opened when visited in 2002, this is a large, rather swish Asian-style hotel facing on to the lake, with an interesting use of stone, bamboo and ironwork. The rooms are self-contained with AC. The landscaping has a preponderance of concrete and no grass, but the pool is large with an open outlook to the lake.
Rates: US$45 half board per person sharing; pool KSh200

What to see and do
Birdwatching
Baringo is undoubtedly one of the best places for birdwatching in the country, with a bird list of over 400 which can double between October and December due to visiting winter migrants. Both white- and pink-backed pelican, cormorants, seven types of heron, ibis, African spoonbills and white-faced whistling ducks are among the birds seen, not forgetting the African fish eagles which will happily play their party piece, snatching fish proffered by the boatman. Excellent birdwalks are offered twice daily from Lake Baringo Club.

Visit to Njemps village
There's a small community of Il Chamus (more often known as Njemps) living on the northeastern shore, where you can visit the village for a small fee. It's well organised and, depending on the time of visit, you may see the primary school-children having a lesson under a tree, fish being smoked in a clay kiln, or get a health check from an old man with cataract-clouded eyes – a healer who douses using a well-worn pair of 'retread' sandals made from old tyres. The women gather around and display articles for sale – but there's no harassment to buy – and they have some charming clay sculptures of elephant and hippo. Related to the Maa peoples, the Il Chamus combine pastoralism with fishing, although they differ

---

SWIMMING ELEPHANTS
In 2002, a small herd of elephants swam across Lake Baringo, an event witnessed with astonishment, as most of the local residents had never seen an elephant before. It is thought that the elephants were following an ancient migration route from Kamnarok in the Kerio valley to the Laikipia plateau, crossing Lake Baringo in the process.

from other pastoralists as they eat fish which they catch from their *ambatch* (similar to balsa wood) rafts.

Rates: from KSh400 per person from Lake Baringo Club

Aridlands workshop

This is next to Robert's Campsite (page 298). The workshop employs 15 local women and beautiful, hand-printed cotton fabric and clothing are for sale in colourful, original designs.

Boat excursions and water activities

There are excellent boat excursions from the tourist venues on the lake (see under *Where to stay*, page 298). Most use the motorised *ssese* canoes (as used on Lake Victoria) and some have an awning which can give a welcome reprieve from the blazing hot sun. Crocodile and hippo are readily seen, together with the myriad birdlife. Waterskiing and windsurfing are offered at Island Camp and people do swim in the lake. There's not been an incident with crocodiles to date, although one suspects that falling lake levels and fewer fish might cause this to change, so do consult local knowledge first.

Rates: boat trips from KSh3,000 an hour for a boat (7 people) or KSh800 an hour per person from Lake Baringo Club. Also from Robert's Camp and Island Camp. See page 298.

North and east of Baringo

If you have your own 4WD transport, from Baringo you can travel north and east to Laikipia and Maralal (see *Chapters 10* and *13*, pages 255 and 363). Continue on the B4 from Baringo to Loruk, and turn right along a dirt road (fair condition) through scenic countryside to join the C77 road from Rumuruti to Maralal. Alternatively, you can continue north from Loruk (end of tarmac) on the B4 through the Kito Pass to Tot in the Kerio Valley. The views from the top of the Kito Pass are magnificent, but the road is appalling and you'll need to check security first. There's no public transport on this route and few vehicles.

KABARNET, THE TUGEN HILLS AND KERIO VALLEY

Tucked on the edge of the Tugen Hills, Kabarnet in many ways is more reminiscent of an Indian hill station, with a distinctive frontier-town atmosphere. Surrounded by columnar pine trees, it's the main administrative centre for Baringo district. Spread out on a steep hill, the centre is a quaint mixture of shops selling farm machinery and food, small hotels and wooden kiosks, while further out are the government offices and schools.

Getting there and around

From Baringo, take the B4 Nakuru road south for about 10km, turning right on to the C51 at Marigat. Alternatively, take the C51 (good tarmac road) from Eldoret to Iten (about 20km) which is at the top of the **Elgeyo escarpment**. As the road zigzags down to the hot Rift Valley floor, there are magnificent views east across the **Kerio Valley** to **Lake Kamnarock** and the **Tugen Hills**. It's a steep descent, passing the **Torok falls** cascading down the escarpment and further south is an enormous fluorspar mine. The road crosses the Kerio River at **Cheploch Gorge**. It's worth getting out to have a look, as the river plunges into a narrow gorge – reportedly it's safe to swim here, if you dare, as the water is too fast-flowing for crocodiles. Shortly after is the turn-off on the left to Lake Kamnarok National Reserve. The road continues to climb up the Tugen Hills to Kabarnet.

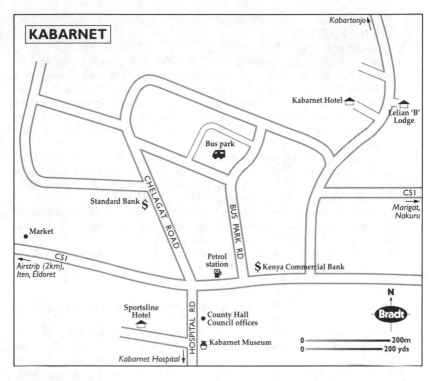

By bus

Kabarnet is not on a main bus route to Nairobi, but there are plenty of *matatus* running from the centre of town to Nakuru and Eldoret, most of which leave in the morning from Bus Park Road.

By air

There's a good tarmac airstrip at Kabarnet, but no scheduled flights.

Getting organised

There's a **bank**, a **post office**, small **supermarket**, a **hospital** and **petrol station** in the centre of town. In an emergency the **tourist helpline** is tel: 020 604767.

Where to stay

Kabarnet Hotel (30 rooms; swimming pool) PO Box 109, Kabarnet; tel: 053 22150
This hotel has a wonderful location looking out across the Kerio Valley, which more than makes up for its shabbiness. The friendly management is making efforts to brighten up the décor, and the rooms are comfortable with private bathrooms. Despite its size, there are few visitors, this being well off the main tourist route. There's a bar and dining room with a basic menu and a patio around the large swimming pool, which is icy cold.
Rates: from US$30 B&B per person sharing
Lelian 'B' Lodge PO Box 125 Kabarnet; tel: 053 22458
A friendly establishment with a large TV lounge-cum-dining-room serving good helpings of African food. The s/c rooms are basic but reasonably comfortable.
Rates: KSh500 B&B per person

THE RIFT VALLEY
Dr David Roden

While trekking across northern Kenya in 1893, the British geologist J W Gregory recognised the tremendous furrow he saw near Lake Baringo as a feature created where a slice of the Earth's crust dropped down as the crust on each side pulled apart. Molten magma escaped along the resulting cracks creating volcanoes and lava plateaux, both on the floor of the furrow and along the bounding faults. Gregory later used the term 'Rift Valley' to describe what he had seen.

In fact the Rift Valley system stretches approximately 5,500km southwards from Turkey and Jordan to Botswana and Mozambique. In eastern Africa it splits into eastern and western branches running through Kenya and Uganda respectively, with Lake Victoria occupying a depressed plateau between the two arms.

Nowadays, the processes involved in the Rift Valley formation are seen to have been much more complex than those described by Gregory. The Rift is the product of a combination of forces, mostly tensional but with crustal separation, anticlinal arching, sedimentary infilling and isostatic adjustment all playing a part over the last twenty million years. Take a Mars Bar, break it in half pulling apart the two portions, and you will have replicated some of these processes. Such a scenario is associated by some scholars with the break-up of the ancient continental mass of Gondwanaland, with the drifting apart of separate African and Indian crustal plates.

The eastern (or Gregory) branch of the Rift Valley dominates the physical geography of Kenya, running as a gentle S-shaped furrow north–south and gradually narrowing from a width of 200–300km in the Lake Turkana area to 30–60km wide further south. In actuality, the Rift Valley here is not one well-

Sportsline Hotel Hospital Rd, Kabarnet; tel: 053 21430
It has a good **restaurant** with basic fare and the s/c rooms are reasonable.
Rates: rooms from KSh400
Tugen Hills campsites District Council Offices, Town Hall Bldg, Hospital Rd, PO Box 159, Kabarnet; tel: 053 22189; mobile: 0722 829008 for details and location
There are plans to open campsites at Ossen and Saimo on the eastern ridge of the Tugen Hills, set on the edge of the forest with views across to Lake Baringo. There are no facilities at present, but you may be able to camp by arrangement if you get permission from the district council offices in Kabarnet.

Where to eat
Other than the hotels, there are a number of **cheap eats** and *nyama choma* joints in town, down the hill along Chelagat Road and Bus Park Road, but you'll need to go early as they close by 20.00.

What to see and do
Kabarnet Museum
Hospital Rd, PO Box 419, Kabarnet; tel: 053 21221
Established in the former district commissioner's residence, this is an interesting regional museum. Among the exhibits are **ethnological displays** of the Il Chamus (Njemps), Tugen and Pokot peoples of Baringo district and the **Lake Baringo environment**. **Indigenous trees** and plants in the garden are named, and there are plans for a snake display. Reference is also made to the

formed feature, but rather a series of troughs and basins between parallel fault lines, bounded by escarpments and uplifted crust of varying heights on either side of the troughs. In many places the high margins are further accentuated by volcanic activity (as in the Ngong Hills and the Aberdares) while some of the largest volcanic features have formed along lines of weakness running away from the main Rift as in mounts Elgon, Meru, Kenya and Kilimanjaro. Outpourings of magma also created extensive peripheral lava plateaux, such as the Uasin Gishu Plateau (between Eldoret and Kitale), the Laikipia Plateau and the Kericho Plateau. The valley floor is uneven, varying between 375 and 585m above sea level in the north and south respectively to about 2,000m in the Nakuru-Naivasha area, representing sedimentary infilling, localised uplift and collapsed remnants of earlier formations.

The valley floor is also broken by craters, among them Longonot and Menengai, by small scarps, and by a string of lakes where local barriers impeded drainage. Some lakes (Naivasha and Baringo) are freshwater; others, like Lake Turkana, are sodic. Upwarping of strata on both sides of the Rift has produced gentle slopes away from the escarpments, down which streams have often cut well-defined valley networks.

The Rift Valley escarpment in Kenya is at its most impressive in the northwest. Between Iten and Marich Pass, the Cherangani Hills, an uplifted remnant of an ancient platform, plunge 1,600m in little over three kilometres down to the Kerio Valley. The road from Nairobi to Naivasha also offers fine views of the Rift Valley system.

Dr David Roden is the director of the Marich Pass Field Studies Centre in western Kenya.

palaeontological sites of the area, the best known being at Chemera, Ngorora and Chesowanja.
Open daily 09.00–18.00; entry KSh200

Kapchemuso cave
Take the road C51 west for a few kilometres to the outskirts of town, past the museum, and follow the airport road to the right. It's about 10km at the most to the end of the airstrip from which there are superb views of the Kerio Valley. About 3km along the road is a track on the right for Kachemuso cave.

A 40-minute climb up a narrow, rocky path brings you to the cave's entrance. In the past, the cave was used by Tugen elders for planning battles against neighbouring tribes. According to the local Tugen people, the cave stretches back about 20km along narrow passages where sometimes you need to crawl. (For information on caving see *Chapter 6*, page 113.) During the rains, a waterfall cascades over the cave. If you are keen, you can continue climbing on to the ridge above, from which there are panoramic views of the Kerio Valley and the Elgeyo escarpment.

Lake Kamnarok National Reserve
PO Box 53, Kabarnet; tel: 053 22169
Open daily 07.00–18.30; reserve entry US$15 and vehicle KSh200
Access is 25km north off the C51 at Cheploch Gorge in the Kerio Valley to the west of Kabarnet. Alternatively, you can take the airport road from Kabarnet and

descend down the Tugen Hills to the reserve, about a 40-minute journey on a dirt road, and you'll need a 4WD. The reserve includes Lake Kamnarok, an ox-bow lake formed off the Kerio River. Elephants are often seen enjoying the swampy vegetation. The crocodiles here are said to be extremely hostile and there's a variety of waterfowl, among them herons and egrets.

Tugen Hills

There is an excellent tarmac road from Kabarnet running along the ridge of the Tugen Hills, passing though magnificent stands of mature virgin forest, with towering podocarpus and cedar trees. Just before the village of Ossen, on the left is a footpath to the **Ossen Footprints**. It's a short walk through the forest, vibrant with beautiful butterflies, birdsong and monkeys, to a weathered rock about 2m long where, with a liberal dash of imagination, you can distinguish a couple of fossilised ancient footprints. The road continues to **Kabartonjo,** where the former president, Daniel Arap Moi, went to school. The town is notable for its huge modern church with stained-glass windows. Winding up and down the steep, terraced hillsides the road continues to **Bartolimo**, after which it's a dirt road to Poi. A few kilometres after Bartolimo there's a road on the right which descends to the east, joining the B4 Baringo road just south of Loruk. This section is rough and steep in parts and requires 4WD.

Kipsaraman Museum

Community Museums of Kenya, PO Box 74689, Nairobi; tel: 020 729496
Follow the road from Kabarnet along the Tugen Hills. *Matatus* run regularly from Kabarnet to Kabartonjo. After Kabartonjo, there's a turning off along a dirt road on the right to **Rondinin.** After about 1km is the museum, built on a precipice overlooking the Lake Baringo basin. A community museum, funded with the help of the French government, it opened in 2002. The timber building, reportedly the original Fairview Hotel in Nairobi, was dismantled and reassembled on site to form one spacious room. The exhibits' main themes are palaeontology, geomophology and biodiversity conservation. It houses some of the region's famous fossil finds, the most recent 'big' find being the six-million-year-old hominid *Orrorin tugenensis*, dubbed 'Millennium man' as it was discovered in 2000 by a French–Kenyan team of palaeontologists. In fact, *'orrorin'* means 'original man' in Tugen, while *'tugenensis'* refers to the area. The displays have excellent illustrations of the various geological formations of the Tugen Hills together with the relevant fossil specimens – giant prehistoric pigs the size of a hippo, heads of elephant and crocodile, enormous paw prints, plants and wood. There are also pictorial displays of *Chemosit tugenensis*, the Nandi bear (see page 335). From the veranda there are superb views into the valley below where you can see the sites of the fossil finds. There are some 24 excavated sites and 240 geological sites in the region. Millennium man was discovered at Rondinin, 8km away, where in the future there are plans to open a fossil-site museum with tours to see fossils *in situ*. *Open daily 09.00–18.00; entry KSh200*

absolute Africa

Affordable overland truck camping safaris including the Masai Mara migration
Tours from 9 days to 77 days • For Ages 18 – 40s
www.absoluteafrica.com   email: absaf@absoluteafrica.com   Phone: +44 (0) 20 8742 0226

Western Kenya

The appeal of western Kenya lies in its varied landscapes and rich tribal cultures. Its main draw is the Masai Mara, a wildlife Mecca mingled with colourful, traditional Maasai pastoralists. It encapsulates the epitome of how you imagine Africa's wildlife to be: large herds roaming bleached plains, with rolling hills, endless vistas and dramatic skies. Apart from the Masai Mara, the remainder of western Kenya is little visited by tourists, but it's an ideal area for touring and hiking, often well off the beaten track. Highlights of the region include the Masai Mara National Reserve, the islands of Lake Victoria, Kakamega Forest, Mount Elgon, Saiwa Swamp and Ruma national parks, the Elgeyo escarpment and the Cherangani Hills.

MASAI MARA AND NAROK

Kenya's finest game-viewing area, the Masai Mara area covers not only the Masai Mara National Reserve, but also extensive game dispersal areas on the adjacent land. The Mara Reserve and the Mara Triangle make up the current national reserve. Transmara extends along the Oloololo (sometimes called Siria) escarpment and includes the Maasai group ranches of Kimentet, Kerinkani and Olorien to the west. The Maasai group ranches of Koyiaki, Oliopa (formerly Lemek) and Ol Chorro stretch north of the reserve to the Mau escarpment and Narok. In the Loita Hills to the northeast of the reserve is the Maasai group ranch of Maji Moto, while on the eastern reserve boundary is the Siana group ranch. This greater Mara area is as extensive as the reserve itself – Koyiaki and Oliopa alone cover about 526,000ha – where game viewing is equally prolific and it's less crowded, being off the main safari circuit. The Maasai group ranches have a variety of concession agreements with private operators and in some cases have formed wildlife trusts where they have set aside a section of their land as a no-grazing zone, specifically for wildlife. However, there are changes in land tenure afoot, from communal to individual ownership, which may have far-reaching effects upon the future of tourism and wildlife in the dispersal areas.

The small trading centre of **Narok** is the last place to get petrol and basic provisions before entering the reserve.

Getting there and away

The main route to the Mara is from Nairobi, a four- to five-hour drive. Take the A104 to Limuru, followed by the B3 to Narok (tarmac, but patchy in parts, with sections breaking up badly towards Narok). It's a stunning drive – down the escarpment, and then along the Rift Valley floor passing mounts Longonot and Suswa and climbing the foothills of the southern Mau up to the Maasai trading

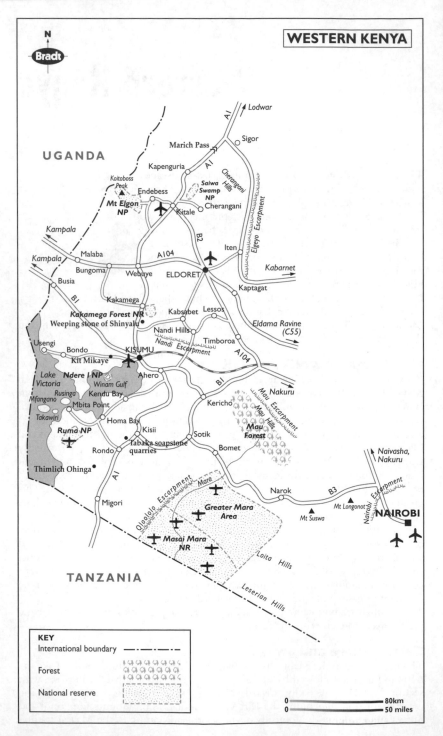

WESTERN KENYA

UGANDA

Lodwar

Marich Pass

Sigor

Kapenguria

Koitoboss Peak

Endebess

Mt Elgon NP

Saiwa Swamp NP

Cherangani Hills

Cherangani

Kitale

Elgeyo Escarpment

Kampala

Malaba

A104

Iten

Kabarnet

Bungoma

Webuye

ELDORET

Busia

Kaptagat

B1

Kakamega

Kabsabet

Lessos

Kakamega Forest NR

Weeping stone of Shinyalu

Nandi Hills

Eldama Ravine (C55)

Usengi

Bondo

KISUMU

Nandi Escarpment

Timboroa

A104

Kit Mikaye

Ahero

Nakuru

Ndere I NP

Winam Gulf

B1

Mau Escarpment

Lake Victoria

Rusinga

Kendu Bay

Kericho

Mau Hills

Mfangano

Mbita Point

Homa Bay

Mau Forest

Takawiri

Kisii

Sotik

Ruma NP

Tabaka soapstone quarries

Bomet

Rondo

Naivasha, Nakuru

Thimlich Ohinga

A1

Narok

B3

Nairobi Escarpment

Migori

Oloololo Escarpment

Mara

Greater Mara Area

Mt Longonot

NAIROBI

Masai Mara NR

Mt Suswa

Loita Hills

TANZANIA

Leserian Hills

KEY

International boundary

Forest

National reserve

0   80km
0   50 miles

town of Narok. From Narok, the most direct route is on the C12, passing the Loita Hills, to the Sekenani gate (a dirt road which gets difficult in wet weather). Alternatively you can continue on the B3 through wheat plantation schemes and turn-off on the C13 at Ngorengore to enter at the northern end of the reserve at the Musiara or Olololo gate. If coming from Kericho (it's an equally attractive drive, dropping down from the highlands with splendid views down to the Mara plains and south to Tanzania), follow the C23 and B3 to Bomet (good tarmac road), before dropping down to the small settlement at Ngorengore. For the last part of the journey the road scarcely exists in places, and you'll require 4WD. (Within the Masai Mara National Reserve 4WD is also recommended). Be aware that there is no public transport within the reserve.

By bus
Public transport is available to **Narok** – buses come via Kericho and Kisii through Bomet and continue on to Nairobi and also come on the same route from Nairobi. The bus station is in the centre of town and there are several buses daily. In addition there are plenty of *matatus*. If you wish to go to the Masai Mara, there's a local bus service, known as the *Dab-Dab*, which runs a couple of buses daily from Narok to Sekenani, normally leaving between 14.00–16.00. It costs about KSh200 and takes three hours. Ask to be dropped off at the junction just before the last bridge, next to the *dukas* on the left, from which you can get a guide to the campsites. The return *Dab-Dab* leaves early in the morning at around 06.00, so you'll need to take an escort from the campsite as you have to leave in the dark. There is no public transport in the Masai Mara National Reserve and organised excursions to the Mara are best arranged from Nairobi; none are available from Narok.

By air
There are seven airstrips in the Mara – Serena, Olkiombo, Siana, Musiara, Keekorok, Kichwa Tembo and Ngerende (Mara Safari Club), serviced by scheduled flights. Airkenya and Queensway fly twice daily from Nairobi and Blue Sky, Mombasa Air Safaris and Eagle Aviation from the coast (see page 82).

Narok
There is little attraction to staying in Narok, and accommodation is limited.

Getting organised
For **changing money**, there's Barclays and Kenya Commercial banks on the main street in Narok. Lodges and hotels in the reserve will exchange money, but at a premium rate. Narok also has a **post office** open Monday–Friday 08.00–17.00, Saturday 09.00–12.00 and for **internet access** try Sky Apple enterprises opposite the Commercial Bank. There's no **supermarket** and shops only have basic supplies and there's limited market produce. For major supplies stock up in Nairobi or Nakuru. The Kobil petrol station has a reasonably well-stocked mini-market. In an emergency, the **tourist helpline** is 020 604767. There are several **petrol stations** on the access roads into Narok, and surprisingly fuel is cheaper here than in Nairobi. You'll need to fill up with fuel in Narok, as there's none available in the reserve except at some of the large lodges.

Where to stay
Spear Hotel
It has basic s/c rooms and is conveniently located near the bus station.
Rates: from KSh300 per person

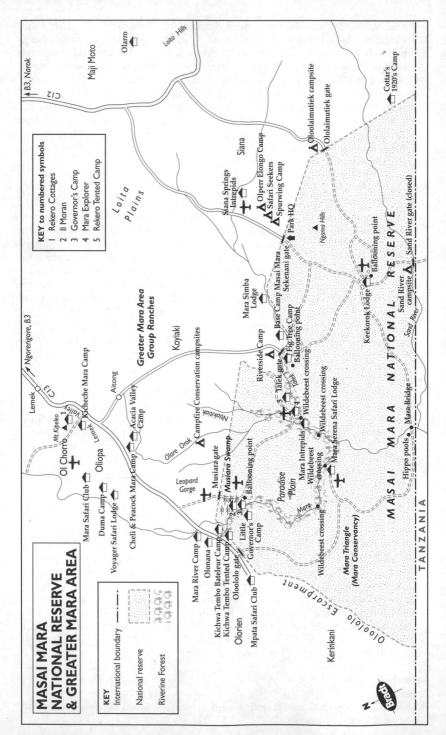

MASAI MARA
NATIONAL RESERVE
& GREATER MARA AREA

KEY
International boundary
National reserve
Riverine Forest

KEY to numbered symbols
1 Rekero Cottages
2 Il Moran
3 Governor's Camp
4 Mara Explorer
5 Rekero Tented Camp

Loita Hills
Maji Moto
Olarro
B3, Narok
C12

Siana
Siana Springs
Intrepids
Olperr Elongo Camp
Safari Seekers
Spurwing Camp
Park HQ

Oloolaimutiek campsite
Ololoaimutiek gate
Ololaimutiek gate
Cottar's 1920's Camp

Loita Plains

Greater Mara Area
Group Ranches

Koyiaki

Campfire Conservation campsites

Aitong
Acacia Valley Camp

Ngorengore, B3
Lemek
Kicheche Mara Camp
Mt Kipeleo
Lemek Valley
Ol Chorro
Oliopa
Cheli & Peacock Mara Camp

Mara Safari Club
Duma Camp
Mara Simba Lodge

Base Camp Masai Mara
Sekenani gate
Fig Tree Camp
Ballooning point

Ngomo Hills
Ballooning point

MASAI MARA NATIONAL RESERVE

Keekorok Lodge
Sand River campsite
Sand River gate (closed)

Sand River

Ntiakitiak
Olare Orok
Leopard Gorge
Musiara gate
Musiara Swamp
Ballooning point

Riverside Camp
Talek gate
Talek
Wildebeest crossing
Mara Intrepids
Wildebeest crossing
Mara Serena Safari Lodge

Paradise Plain
Mara
Wildebeest crossing

Voyager Safari Lodge
Mara River Camp
Olonana
Kichwa Tembo Bateleur Camp
Kichwa Tembo Tented Camp
Olololo gate
Olorien
Mpata Safari Club

Little Governor's Camp

Hippo pools
Mara Bridge

Mara Triangle
(Mara Conservancy)

Kerinkani
Oloololo Escarpment

TANZANIA

N
Bradt

③ Funzi Keys (9 rooms) www.thefunzikeys.com

Funzi Island

$500 full board.

④ Mawula Bay – Cheli + Peacock.

6/8/16 - Jia / sawula bo ? ?

① Blue Safari Club — 10 bandas

www.bluesafariclub.com

Manda Island.

$300 full board per person inc. of most activities.

② Kiwayu Safari Village — 18 bandas

check + Peacock.

Kiwayu

$1318 full board per person inc. of most activities.

Transit Hotel opposite the Kobil petrol station (tel: 050 22288)
There are reasonable s/c rooms and secure parking.
Rates: from KSh1,500 B&B per person sharing
Members Club Campsite (camping and bandas)
Located near the river, the campsite is reasonable with basic facilities. Camping is
preferable to the rather shabby bandas.
Rates: from KSh200

Where to eat

There are several **cheap eats** on the main street, serving local dishes such as
chapatis, *ugali, sukuma wiki* and stew, which are frequented by the Maasai (cost
about KSh75). Few Westerners deign to eat here, so you'll receive a few curious
looks, but the service is friendly. **Kim's dishes** and the **Three in One Bar and
Restaurant** are popular. The Total and Kobil petrol stations at either end of town
have a good selection of snacks at reasonable prices.

What to see and do
Narok Maa Cultural Museum
PO Box 868, Narok; tel: 050 22095
Coming from Nairobi, the museum is on the right at the entrance to Narok, near
the bank. It contains a small collection of ethnological exhibits of Maasai culture
which are interesting to compare with the traditional Maasai you encounter in the
Mara, together with a collection of photographs taken by Maasai women using
disposable cameras.
Open daily 09.00–17.30; entry: KSh200

Masai Mara National Reserve
*Open daily 06.30–19.00; Entry US$30; vehicle KSh500. **Note** entrance fees can be paid
at the lodges too. If travelling through the reserve to the Mara Conservancy (which is part of
the reserve), pay conservancy fees at the lodge and not at the gate. The entrance fee covers
access to the whole of the Masai Mara National Reserve as well as the group ranches
bordering the reserve. If camping on a private site in the group ranch areas, you may be liable
to an additional camping levy of around US$3.*
There are several entrances to the reserve. The main gate, and most popular, is
Sekenani gate on the northeast boundary, which is reached from Narok. Also on
the northern boundary are **Talek gate**, reached via Aitong from Narok, and the
Musiara and **Oloololo gates** which are the most accessible if coming from
western Kenya. On the eastern boundary is **Olaimutiek gate**, while **Sand River
gate** borders the Serengeti, but is currently closed. The southeastern section of the
reserve has sandy, lateritic soils with *murram* roads, accessible with high clearance
2WD, but the northern and western section of the reserve is on black cotton, clay
soils where 4WD is essential when it is wet.

Driving around
In the Mara Conservancy (Mara Triangle) section the roads are well-graded and
signposted, but in the remainder of the reserve, roads are poorly maintained and
signs, if they exist at all, can be confusing. There's a park map showing the circuits,
but it's easy to get lost. The best option is to take a guide from the gate. Outside
the reserve on the group ranches no map is available and you'll need to take a guide
or obtain foolproof directions.

THE MARA COUNT – IMPROVING CONSERVATION AND DEVELOPMENT IN THE MASAI MARA

Dr Robin S Reid and Michael Rainy

The Serengeti-Mara ecosystem supports the most diverse migration of grazing mammals on earth. The Mara, although only a quarter of the total ecosystem area, is crucial to the survival of the entire system because it is the source of forage for wildlife migrating from the Serengeti during critical points in the dry season. Three-quarters of the wildlife habitat in the Mara is in pastoral lands outside the reserve where wildlife faces growing human populations, expansion of wheat farming in wildebeest calving grounds and increasing tourism facilities. Since the mid-1970s, these pressures and drought have caused a 70% decline in wildlife both inside and outside the Masai Mara National Reserve. Pastoral peoples living in the Mara ecosystem make less from livestock than they did 20 years ago, and about half survive today on less than KSh70 (US$1) per day per person. If these trends continue, we estimate that the Mara will support very few wildlife and poorer pastoral peoples 20 years from now. What is needed is a unified effort, by all concerned, to join together to seek solutions. The Mara count is one such effort: a joint venture by the Maasai, conservationists, private industry, land managers and researchers to create an unparalleled set of information to form the foundation of future decisions to conserve wildlife and develop pastoral peoples. From the results we get from the count, we aim to clarify and accelerate efforts to improve the livelihoods of the Maasai and to protect the remaining wildlife populations of this rich ecosystem.

Mara count 2002

Thirty-five organisations supported 29 teams and 86 people to successfully count wildlife, livestock and people (and tsetse flies) at a 100m resolution across

History The Mara has only been inhabited by the Maasai for around 200 years, although there's evidence of Neolithic settlements in the Lemek Valley near Aitong. Nomadic pastoralists, their traditional lifestyle has changed little over the years, herding cattle, goats and sheep and co-existing with the wildlife.

In 1948, the western area known as the Mara Triangle was declared a National Game Reserve by the colonial government. This was extended in 1961 to incorporate land east of the Mara River. Land was excised in 1984 to form the reserve's present size of 1,500km². The reserve itself is managed by two district councils, Narok, which is responsible for the Mara Reserve east of the Mara River and Transmara, which covers the Mara Triangle west of the Mara River. The Masai Mara National Reserve, although a major national resource, has suffered over the years from serious mismanagement, with virtually no input into maintaining the reserve's infrastructure. Within the reserve, off-road driving has been rampant in the past, with the roads themselves being poorly signed and graded. There's been a laissez-faire attitude towards development, with the result that the number of lodges and camps with overlapping game-drive areas has created honey-pots for game viewing, giving the impression of overcrowding and numerous incidents of vehicles around the 'big five'. This has impacted particularly badly on the cheetah population, whose prime hunting time is during the peak game-viewing periods.

Efforts are at last being made to control new development and to limit environmental degradation and wildlife harassment. There's now a moratorium

more than 2,200km² of the Mara pastoral-wildlife ecosystem from November 9–16 2002. A similar count, over a smaller area, was completed in 1999.

What did the 1999 and 2002 counts tell us?

- Settlement numbers (*bomas*) grew by 11% between 1999 and 2002 in the group ranches but less than 1% of the pastoral land is farmed or fenced
- There is as much wildlife in pastoral grazing areas next to the reserve as in the reserve itself.
- Some species of wildlife, like elephant, eland and most carnivores, avoid people and livestock and are more common in the reserve.
- Other species (giraffe, impala, dik-dik) prefer to graze in pastoral lands.
- People and livestock attract wildlife by creating short grassy areas around settlements where forage nutrients are high and predators are visible to grazers.
- Wildlife diversity is greatest when the number of settlements is low to moderate; above or below this level, wildlife diversity is lower.
- Most of the tsetse flies are in the group ranches, probably because there are more shrubs and trees.
- Both livestock and wildlife populations grew strongly between 1999 and 2002 after high mortality during the 1999 drought.

Want to be involved?

If you would like to support future Mara counts (2004 or 2005), further information is available on www.maasaimaracount.org.

Dr Reid is a systems ecologist working with the International Livestock Research Institute in Nairobi and Mike Rainy is a human ecologist working with Bush Homes of East Africa, Nairobi.

on building new lodges in the reserve, a firewood collecting ban has been introduced (several camps and hotels are implementing ecotourism principles as set out by the **Ecotourism Society of Kenya** (page 56), off-road driving is discouraged and **Friends of Conservation** (PO Box 74901, Nairobi; email: foc@nbnet.co.ke) distributes leaflets to visitors drawing their attention to environmental and wildlife ethics.

In 2001, the Transmara County Council took an unprecedented move by employing a private company, the **Mara Conservancy** (PO Box 63457, Nairobi 00619; email: mara@triad.co.ke), to manage the Mara Triangle section of the reserve under their jurisdiction. It was a brave political move which has brought significant financial rewards. Conservancy fees are now paid at the lodges, and initial anti-poaching measures resulted in 300 wire snares being recovered and 26 poachers arrested within the first six months of operation. Roads and tracks are in the process of being upgraded and buildings renovated. Tourism earnings topped KSh10 million in the first year, with local communities receiving a ten-fold increase in income. The neighbouring group ranches of Kimentet, Kerinkani and Olorien also received a percentage share of earnings from game-viewing fees. At the same time, a **Mara Conservation Trust** has been formed to combat incompatible land use in the game dispersal areas of the Greater Mara. Its remit includes purchasing land, developing community-based ecotourism projects and establishing fuelwood plantations.

This partnership between professional environmental land managers and local landowners has the potential to be a blueprint for the sustainable use of the natural resource for the benefits of both people and wildlife in areas outside the Kenya Wildlife Service's national parks and reserves.

The Mara-Serengeti ecosystem forms the northern section of a vast ecosystem which stretches south into Tanzania, incorporating the Serengeti National Reserve, and north to the Loita plains, an area of some 25,000km². 'Mara' means 'dappled' in the Maa language. It's an apt description where savanna plains are bisected by the dark green of riverine forest, interspersed with quartz outcrops. The rich **grasslands**, dominated by red oat grass, *Themeda triandra*, are the feeding grounds for numerous migrating zebra, wildebeest and Thomson's gazelle, as well as Grant's gazelle, topi, eland, impala and buffalo. Clumps of gardenia bushes form petticoats around *Euphorbia candelabra* trees, a favourite haunt for lion, and lone *Balanites* trees are a popular roost for secretary birds, vultures and raptors on the open plains. Giraffes prefer the **savanna woodland**, dominated by numerous acacia species, such as the whistling thorn with its large ant galls, *A. drepanolobium,* and the wait-a-bit thorn, *A. brevispica*, while elephant enjoy the marshland and forested areas, also preferred by waterbuck and bushbuck. The tiny dik dik and black rhino inhabit acacia thickets. **Riverine forest** is at its best along the Mara River and its tributaries the Talek, Olare Orok and Ntiakitiak, whose headwaters lie in the Mau Forest to the north. There are magnificent stands of African greenhart, *Warburgia ugandensis*, African olive, *Olea africana* and various fig trees, which attract troops of monkeys and olive baboons and a variety of birds such as green pigeons and casqued hornbills when they're fruiting. Within the **rivers** are numerous pods of hippo, particularly at Hippo Pools south of Mara bridge and in the Mara River on Paradise plains near Governor's Camp, and large crocodiles. The most spectacular **wildebeest crossings** are on the Mara and Talek rivers in the northern section of the reserve. The predators are never far away from the plains game. Lion and cheetah are commonly seen on the savanna, while leopard prefer the riverine forest. There are numerous clans of spotted hyena, seen in the woodland areas in the northern section of the reserve, but they are more often heard, their eerie howls lingering on the night air. Of the smaller mammals, jackal, bat-eared foxes and mongooses are often seen around termite mounds.

Where to stay and eat
The Mara is not short of accommodation. Essentially there's a wide choice of large and small lodges, medium, small and exclusive permanent tented camps, small, seasonal, traditional bush camps and private, mobile bush camps. Public campsites are limited. A selection is presented here:

In the reserve
Governor's Camp (38 tents, 1 suite) Governors Camps, PO Box 48217, Nairobi; tel: 020 331871; fax: 020 726427; email: reservations@governorscamp.com; web: www.governorscamp.com
A beautiful location on the Mara River, with pleasant public areas and friendly, efficient staff, this is one of the oldest camps in the Mara. It's where the BBC *Big Cat Diary* team are based during filming, and many of the wildlife 'stars' can be seen in the vicinity. The tents are spread out along the river bank, sited closely together, with nine facing the greater Mara view. The generator has an early start (there are plans to replace it) so ask for tents furthest away. The tents are comfortably furnished with enormous en-suite shower rooms and flush

toilets, and each has a small veranda. The Justin suite is more spacious, and its bathroom includes a full-size bath. Food is excellent with buffet-style breakfasts and lunch and à la carte dinner. Being next to the Musiara marsh, it's a prime game-viewing area, with plenty of elephant and the marsh lions as expounded in Jonathon Scott's book of the same name. **On offer:** game drives in open (with an awning) 4WD vehicles – the guides are good, but still have a hang-up on the 'big 5' – shop, game walks, guide course, balloon safari, *manyatta* visit and day trips (or longer) to Mfangano Island, a sister camp, in Lake Victoria.

Rates: from US$260 full board per person sharing

Little Governor's Camp (17 tents) Book through Governors Camps, page 91
Little Governor's, being smaller, is less formal, and is a favourite from the Governor's Camps stable. Located a few kilometres from Governor's Camp on the Mara River, it has an open view over a waterhole where there's good birdwatching, as well as animals coming to water. The tents are well spread out and are comfortably furnished with en-suite shower rooms and flush toilets. There's an open bar-cum-dining tent, with meals and service on a par with Governor's Camp. **On offer:** activities as with Governor's Camp.

Rates: from US$260 full board per person sharing

Il Moran (10 tents) Book through Governors Camps, page 91
This is the most stylish and recent of the trio of Governor's Camps permanent tented camps. It's small and secluded, with spacious tents furnished with heavy antique furniture, thick-pile rugs and en-suite bathrooms complete with full-size bath and gold fittings, shower and flush toilet. Yet its location is not as spectacular as the two earlier camps. The open bar and restaurant tent overlooks the river, while food and service are excellent. **On offer:** activities as per Governor's Camp above.

Rates: from US$385 per person sharing

Mara Intrepids (30 tents, swimming pool) Book through Heritage Hotels, page 91
Located on a sweeping bend of the Talek River, the tents are set out along the riverbank. There's an excellent small natural history museum near the reception courtyard, with a path leading down to the main lodge. The staff are welcoming and friendly and the lodge has a strong ecotourism emphasis. A dining-room overlooks an open terrace shaded by trees (also used for alfresco dining), and there's a good selection of food including delicious home-made breakfast jams (try the passion-fruit curd). There's a small, rather public, swimming pool with a few sunloungers. The bar is adjacent to a viewing deck, where a leopard is baited on the other side of the river each evening. The tents are comfortable, with heavy reproduction furniture, four-poster beds, small en-suite shower rooms and a veranda. **On offer:** game drives in open 4WD vehicles with *superb* guides who have an in-depth knowledge of the flora and fauna of the area, bush walks, visits to community projects, Maasai dancing and lectures, Adventurer's Club for children, shop, ballooning, fishing excursions to Lake Victoria. Fuel is available.

Rates: from US$290 full board per person sharing

Mara Explorer (10 tents) Book through Heritage Hotels, page 91
This is the smartest of the Heritage Hotel's trio in the Mara, and guests are allocated a personal butler for their stay. The camp is situated on a secluded, thickly forested bend of the Talek River. There's a small lounge decorated with interesting African artefacts and a dining area adjoining the viewing deck above the river. Bush meals near the camp are a speciality. The tents are well spread out and have private verandas. They're decorated with an early explorer's theme – hand-carved mahogany furniture, old wooden chests, historic prints and Persian rugs – and shower rooms are en suite with flush toilets. **On offer:** game drives in open 4WD vehicles with excellent guides, bush walks, visits to community projects, bush banquets, ballooning and fishing excursions to Lake Victoria.

Rates: from US$400 fully inclusive per person sharing

Keekorok Lodge (84 rooms; swimming pool) Book through Block Hotels, page 90
The first lodge to be built in the Mara, Keekorok still retains a distinct character, being

constructed from cedar and the local, pink and grey Sand River stone. It's ideally placed for watching the wildebeest migration when it's in the southern section of the park near the Tanzanian border. The rooms are in bungalows, single storey blocks or chalets, comfortably furnished with en-suite bathrooms. The main reception areas face on to a terrace, overlooking a bougainvillea garden and swimming pool. There's a good choice of food and friendly service. A special attraction is the 300m raised walkway through riverine forest to a thatched lookout, with views of the Mara plains and a hippo pool. **On offer:** ballooning, game drives, bush walks, bird walks, Maasai dancing, wildlife videos. Fuel is available here.
Rates: from US$100 full board per person sharing

Rekero Tented Camp (6 tents) Book through Bush Homes of East Africa, page 90
Located close to the confluence of the Mara and Talek rivers, the camp nestles in riverine forest on the banks of the Talek. The camp is hosted by Jackson ole Looseyia, a remarkable Maasai guide, who trained in South Africa and has travelled to the UK promoting tourism to the Mara. His enthusiasm is contagious and you gain a fascinating first-hand insight into Maasai culture and the use of different plants, as well as viewing wildlife. The tents are spacious, lit by solar lanterns, and have en-suite showers and flush toilets. **On offer:** game drives and walking with Maasai guides; bush picnics and sundowners.
Rates: from US$300 full board per person sharing. Closed April, May and November.

Fig Tree Camp (35 tents, 27 cabins; swimming pool) Book through Mada Hotels, PO Box 40683, Nairobi; tel: 020 221439; fax: 020 332170; email: sales@madahotels.com; web: www.madahotels.com
Located near the Talek gate, this was one of the original camps in the game reserve. The tents (under thatch) and rooms, sited close together, have en-suite shower rooms and are simply furnished. There are two restaurants and bar areas serving buffet-style meals, and a there's a small lookout tower. **On offer:** day and night game drives, ballooning, bush walks, horseriding, lectures on the Mara, video room, shop.
Rates: from US$100 full board per person sharing

Mara Serena Safari Lodge (74 rooms; swimming pool) Book through Serena Hotels, page 91
Located in the Mara Conservancy (Mara Triangle) in the western section of the Masai Mara National Reserve the hotel, built on a ridge, has commanding views across the Mara. It's designed to emulate Maasai architecture, the central dining area having several large domed huts decorated with local artefacts. There's a wide selection of buffet-style food, with a choice of African, European and Indian dishes, together with barbecues. The rooms are comfortably furnished with en-suite bathrooms (with baths and showers). **On offer:** game drives, bush meals, hippo breakfasts, ballooning, Maasai dancing, wildlife films, shop, babysitting. Petrol is available.
Rates: from US$125 full board per person sharing. Child friendly.

Sand Rivers Campsite (camping only) Narok County Council, PO Box 60, Narok; tel: 050 22068; email: samkores@hotmail.com
This is the only public campsite within the reserve. It has basic facilities, with an ablution block and reasonable security, but you'll need to be self-sufficient and baboons can be a hazard.
Rates: from KSh500

Greater Mara area

Voyager Safari Lodge (78 rooms; swimming pool) Book through Heritage Hotels, page 91
The lodge is located on an open bend of the Mara River, close to the airstrip, with views of hippo and crocodiles. Rooms are in a collection of cottages in the grounds, each room being comfortably furnished with en-suite facilities. There's a large terrace overlooking the river, where displays of Maasai singing, dancing and jumping take place, a bar and dining

area. There's a good selection of table d'hôte and vegetarian cuisine. The swimming pool is set in a secluded walled garden. **On offer:** game drives in 4WD vehicles, bush walks, visits to community projects, Adventurer's Club for children, wildlife videos and presentations by local rangers and conservationists, shop, ballooning, fishing excursions to Lake Victoria.
Rates: from US$140 full board per person sharing

Mara River Camp (16 tents) Book through Savannah Camps and Lodges, page 91
One of the original permanent tented camps on the Koyiaki group ranch, it lies on a sweeping bend of the Mara River where there's a resident hippo population. Set out under the trees, the tents, sited close together, are spacious (can accommodate families of 4), rustically furnished and have en-suite showers and flush toilets. There's a dining tent serving wholesome meals, and friendly staff. There are resident Maasai naturalists in the camp. **On offer:** nature and bird walks, game drives in 4WD, Maasai lectures and cultural visits, ballooning, fishing trips to Lake Victoria, walking safaris.
Rates: from US$225 full board per person sharing

Kichwa Tembo Tented Camp (40 tents, 2 rondavels; swimming pool) Book through Conservation Corporation Africa – Kenya, PO Box 74957, 00200 Nairobi ; tel: 020 751545; fax: 020 750512; email: theresa@conscorp.co.ke; web: www.ccafrica.com
Located between the Musiara and Oloololo gates just outside the Masai Mara National Reserve, the camp is in a forested site on the Sabirongo River, at the foot of the Oloololo escarpment. Hemingway-style tents are spaced out along the river, shaded by ebony and fig trees. They have classic safari-style furnishings, and en-suite shower rooms with flush toilets. The main restaurant (good cuisine) is thatched with open views on to the Mara plains. **On offer:** game drives, bush walks, bush banquets, Maasai *manyatta* visits, Maasai dancing, library, shop.
Rates: from US$120 full board per person sharing

Kichwa Tembo Bateleur Camp (9 tents; swimming pool) Book through Conservation Corporation Africa – Kenya, PO Box 74957, Nairobi 00200; tel: 020 751545; fax: 020 750512; email: theresa@conscorp.co.ke; web: www.ccafrica.com
Adjacent to the main Kichwa Tembo Camp, Bateleur caters for exclusivity. It's well positioned to benefit from the forest canopy and expansive views across the Mara plains. The tents are more opulent, with wooden floors, ceiling fans, writing desks, four-poster beds and spacious en-suite bathrooms. There's a comfortable lounge area with leather sofas and fireplace. **On offer:** personal butler service, and the same activities as the main camp, above.
Rates: from US$240 full board per person sharing

Base Camp Masai Mara (formerly Dream Camp – 15 tents) Base Camp Travel, page 102
Among all the camps in Kenya, Base Camp Masai Mara, which opened in 1998, follows the most stringent of ecotourism principles. It's located next to the settlement of Talek, a few kilometres from the Talek gate entrance to the Masai Mara Game Reserve. A permanent, low-key, camp, the tents are on raised wooden platforms under a thatched roof. Rooms are rustically furnished with a small veranda, and have en-suite open-air showers, compost toilets and solar heating. Waste water feeds the trees planted around the compound. There's an open-plan dining-room, bar and tiny sitting room in the eves with superb views directly on to the Mara plains. A small viewing tower provides a good vantage point for watching the wildebeest migration, and the trees attract monkeys and an increasingly varied birdlife. A tree nursery has been started for the Maasai community, fertilised by the compost waste. **On offer:** entertaining bush walks with Maasai guides and visits to their *manyattas*, 4WD game drives, Maasai dancing and longer walks with fly-camping.
Rates: from US$105 full board per person sharing

Mara Safari Club (50 tents; swimming pool) Book through Lonhro Hotels, page 91
Located on a bend in the Mara River within the Ol-Choro Oiroua Conservation Area north of the Masai Mara National Reserve, the tents are spread out along the riverfront. All have a small, private veranda, comfortable four-poster beds and en-suite showers with flush toilets.

There are 7 luxury tents which have minibars, some with sunken baths, and the option to dine privately. The main building is cantilevered over the river, with good views of the hippo below. **On offer:** game drives, guided bush and bird walks, fishing, village visits to a Maasai *manyatta*, Maasai dancing and talks on the Mara ecosystem and Maasai culture.
Rates: from US$200 full board per person sharing
Rekero Cottages (4 cottages) Book through Bush Homes of East Africa, page 90
Located in the Lemek Valley, this is an enchanting, intimate homestay. The four cottages (3 double and 1 family cottage with 2 doubles) are set in a small garden in front of a waterhole, where elephants sometimes come to water, surrounded by thick olive forest. The rooms are comfortable with cottage-style furnishings and private bathrooms (shower only, flush loos). Nearby, there's a separate veranda with copious reference books and a dining-room (wholesome food with a good variety of garden salads) displaying some of Rainee Anderson's exquisite wildlife drawings (see illustrations in the guide). Hosted and guided by Gerard Beaton (whose parents started Rekero) and Rainee, guests have the option of relaxing or participating in various activities. **On offer:** walking on Mount Kipeleo with Maasai and Il Dorobo (Ogiek hunter-gatherer) guides with stunning views across the Mara plains, game drives in 4WD with open viewing hatches, visits to a Maasai *manyatta*. There's a private airstrip or access via Ngirende on scheduled flights an hour's game drive away.
Rates: from US$300 full board per person sharing. Closed April, May and November.
Acacia Valley Camp (5 tents, fully serviced or self-catering) Acacia Trails, PO Box 30907, Nairobi; tel: 020 608487; fax: 020 608487; email: acacia@swiftkenya.com
A traditional tented camp situated in a secluded valley on the Koyiaki group ranch. The tents are sited under sprawling shade trees and have private showers and toilets. The mess-cum-dining tent boasts a well stocked library and delicious meals are prepared from fresh produce. Self-catering guests are required to provide all their own food, drinks and transport and are responsible for their own activities during their stay. **On offer:** game drives, night drives and bush walks.
Rates: from US$300 full board per person sharing; self-catering US$400 for the camp
Cheli & Peacock Mara Camp (6 tents) Reservations Office, PO Box 39806, 00623a Parklands, Nairobi; tel: 020 604053; fax: 020 604050; email: safaris@chelipeacock.co.ke; web: www.chelipeacock.com
A seasonal tented camp surrounded by mature trees overlooking the Mara plains. The traditional-style safari tents are comfortable and spacious with en-suite showers, and safari short-drop toilets. Dining is normally alfresco, under the stars, and lighting is by hurricane lamps. **On offer:** Game drives, birdwatching, ballooning.
Rates: from US$280 full board per person sharing
Kicheche Mara Camp (11 tents) PO Box 15243, Nairobi; tel: 020 890541; fax: 020 891379; email: sales@kicheche.com; web: www.kicheche.com.
A low-key, traditional bush camp (excellent value) nestling in a grove of olive and croton trees in the northern Koyiaki area of the Mara. The tents, which have an animal theme, are comfortably furnished, with en-suite showers and flush toilets, a small veranda and hammocks. Lighting is by hurricane lamps and solar power. There's a *Nyati* tent, a spacious lounge area with a good selection of reference books. The staff are friendly and meals – delicious wholesome food – are eaten alfresco (or in the dining tent during bad weather) or you can dine separately if preferred. There's good game viewing nearby – cheetah, hyena and wildebeest and a pride of lions sometimes comes into camp – and the reserve proper is about an hour's drive away. **On offer:** game drives in 4WD vehicle, bush walks.
Rates: from US$105 full board per person if you have your own vehicle; otherwise, US$190 full board per person (this is one of the few places that does not charge a single supplement). Closed May.
Duma Camp (5 tents, fully serviced or self-catering) JMAR Safaris Ltd, PO Box 25326, 00603 Nairobi ; tel: 020 570239; fax: 020 570239; email: jenn@africaonline.co.ke; web: www.jmarsafaris.com

A traditional, secluded tented camp in the northwest of the Mara on the Oliopa group ranch, the tents are comfortably furnished with en-suite showers and flush toilets. The food enjoys an excellent reputation – the head chef was Kenya trained and then worked in a London hotel. If self-catering, you just need to bring provisions; the cook and staff are provided. **On offer:** game drives, river walks, nature walks with picnics, ballooning, fishing on Lake Victoria.
Rates: from US$350 full board per person sharing; self-catering is KSh20,000 per night for the whole camp
Olarro (8 cottages; swimming pool) Book through Archers Tours and Travel, PO Box 40097, 00606 Nairobi; tel: 020 3752472; fax: 020 3752476; email: archers@archers.co.ke; web: www.archers.co.ke
Set in the Loita Hills on the 60,700ha Maji Moto group ranch, the camp has superb panoramic views over the Mara plains. Lesser kudu and packs of wild dog can sometimes be seen on the ranch. The cottages, emulating African huts with thatched roofs, are spread out in the bush. The rooms, on the small side, have en-suite shower rooms and flush toilets. The main building has high thatched ceilings and attractive use of local stone. The lounge has an open fireplace, satellite TV and wildlife video shows. **On offer:** game drives in open Land Rovers, bush walks with Maasai guides on the ranch, day excursions to the Masai Mara National Reserve (35km away).
Rates: from US$300 fully inclusive per person sharing. Closed May and June.
Siana Springs Intrepids (38 tents; swimming pool) Book through Heritage Hotels, page 91 Located on the eastern edge of the reserve in a private group ranch, this permanent tented camp is surrounded by a woodland oasis in the Ngama Hills. Tree hyrax and bushbuck can be seen during the day, while genet cats come out at night. The tents are simply furnished and comfortable, with en-suite shower rooms and flush toilets. The public areas include a spacious terrace, often used for dining and performances of Maasai dancing, with views to the open plains. **On offer:** day and night game drives, bush walks, ballooning, fishing, bush picnics, wildlife lectures, children's Adventurer's Club, shop.
Rates: from US$265 full board per person sharing
Cottar's 1920's Camp (6 tents; plunge pool) Book through Mellifera Collection, page 91 This luxurious permanent tented camp is in a private concession on the southeast of the Mara Reserve, bordering Tanzania. Kenya's first theme camp, Cottar's has large white canvas tents with antique 1920s furniture and exotic rugs, private en-suite bathrooms and canopied verandas. Three of the tents have private sitting-rooms. Game drives are in an old jalopy or 4WD and each group is allocated a separate driver and guide. The Cottar family has been in the safari business for several generations and the camp library contains an interesting collection of memorabilia. **On offer:** day and night game drives, bush walks, aromatherapy massage and fishing. There's a private airstrip.
Rates: from US$550 fully inclusive per person sharing
Olonana (12 tents; swimming pool) Book through Abercrombie & Kent, page 101 A lavish, permanent, tented camp on the Mara River with good food and service, this is one of the best camps in the area. The main buildings are thatched and ethnic in design, but there's no scrimping on style – comfortable armchairs and a fireplace in the lounge, a library, dining-room and veranda overlooking the river with wallowing pods of hippo below. The tents are spacious with 2 queen-size beds, wooden floors with woollen rugs and large gauze windows, en-suite shower rooms (flush loos) and a veranda where you can have private meals. There's no set time for meals, so you can eat when and where you like. **On offer:** visits to a *manyatta*, watching Maasai bead-making, making bows and arrows, bush walks and game drives.
Rates: from US$340 full board per person sharing. Child friendly.
Campfire Conservation (mobile camps) Information from Bateleur Safaris, PO Box 42562, 00100 Nairobi; tel: 020 890454; fax: 020 891007; email: bateleur@alphanet.co.ke.
Campfire Conservation is the umbrella body for 14 upmarket, 4WD, private, mobile,safari operators which have exclusive campsites with small, traditional bush camps along the

Talek and Olare Orok rivers in the Koyiaki area north of the reserve. **On offer:** day and night game drives, bush walks, birdwatching, *manyatta* visits, bush picnics and dinners, ballooning, fishing trips to Lake Victoria.

Rates: prices vary according to operator and safari itinerary; ballpark figure around US$350–400 per day full board per person sharing

Mara Simba Lodge (84 rooms; swimming pool) PO Box 66601, Nairobi; tel: 020 444401; fax: 020 444403; email: marasimba@form-net.com; web: www.marasimba.com

A large, timber, thatched lodge overlooking the Talek River, where you can see hippo and crocodile. The spacious, airy bedrooms are in 6 blocks, and all have en-suite showers, fans and private verandas. The food is good (includes vegetarian menu) and the staff helpful and friendly. There's a fireplace in the bar for chilly evenings. The hotel has installed a water treatment plant, the recycled water being used for irrigation. **On offer:** resident naturalist giving lectures on ecology and Maasai culture, Maasai dancing, game drives, night game drives, walking safaris. Fuel is available.

Rates: from US$125 full board per person sharing; all activities extra

Mpata Safari Club (11 suites, 12 rooms; swimming pool) Book through Mpata Investments, PO Box 58402, Nairobi; tel: 020 310867; fax: 020 310859; email: mpatam@africaonline.co.ke

Set high on the Oloololo escarpment, the club rudely stands out above the Mara plains. It's a 5-star Japanese establishment, Japanese being the main clientele. It has good food and service, while the rooms are pleasant and have individual plunge pools. Its main drawback is its distance from the main game-viewing areas of the reserve – a good 2-hour drive. **On offer:** game drives, *manyatta* visits, ballooning, fishing.

Rates: from US$200 full board per person sharing, inclusive of game drives

Campsites

Riverside Camp tel: 050 2128

This is a well-organised campsite near the Talek gate on the northern boundary of the reserve. It provides hot water and flush toilets. There's a kitchen, bar and dining area. Tents are available for hire.

Rates: for camping KSh250; double tents KSh1,000 and tents with en-suite bathrooms KSh1,200

Oloolaimutiek Campsite

A popular campsite run by the Maasai near the Oloolaimutiek gate on the eastern boundary of the reserve. It has good security and firewood is provided. Water can be scarce, so bring your own supply and provisions.

Rates: from KSh200

Olperr Elongo Camp Book through Bike Treks, PO Box 14237, Nairobi; tel: 020 446371; email: info@biketreks.co.ke; web: www.biketreks.co.ke

A pleasant, well-run campsite about 1km from the Sekenani gate. Meals can be arranged and firewood is available. There are hot showers and flush toilets. **On offer:** excellent guided walks with the Maasai in the surrounding hills (cost KSh500).

Rates: from KSh250

There are a couple of **other campsites** near the **Sekenani gate** which have similar facilities – **Safari Seekers** (Ksh250) and **Spurwing Camp** (KSh250 or KSh500 for a tent).

What to see and do

While staying in the Mara, apart from the wonderful variety of wildlife and birds, the main draw is the annual **wildebeest migration** (page 132). Most lodges and camps can arrange **ballooning** (page 110), **Maasai** *manyatta* and **school visits** (the schools often being supported by trusts set up to raise funds from tourists) and **bush walks**. In addition, there are serious **horseriding** (page 123) and **walking**

safaris (page 130) in the dispersal areas outside the reserve, a **wildlife guide's course** (page 108), **aromatherapy massage** (page 122) and **fishing excursions** to Lake Victoria (page 120).

Koyiaki Guide School and Wilderness Walking Camp

Scheduled to open in 2004, a guide training school is being established to train Maasai guides from the Mara vicinity. Alongside this is a Wilderness Walking Camp. Further details of this community project are available from Rekero, as listed above.

KISUMU

Originally known as Port Florence, named after the chief engineer's wife when the railway reached the lake in 1901, Kisumu developed during the colonial era as the main trading port for the lake steamers which transported goods around the lake. Kenya's third largest town, after Nairobi and Mombasa, it was given city status during the railway centenary celebrations in 2002. It's an important regional centre for western Kenya and is dominated by an entrepôt of predominantly Asian businesses. The city appears rundown with a rather dilapidated air, an image no doubt brought about by its change in business fortunes over the years. (It was badly affected when the East African Community closed in 1997 and has not yet benefited from it being revived in 1999.) However, despite its shabbiness, it's a noticeably clean city (compared with other urban areas in Kenya) with a relaxed and friendly atmosphere.

The Kisumu area is bounded by Lake Victoria on the west, flanked by the Kisii and Kericho highlands to the south and the Nandi escarpment to the east, rising to the forested highlands of Kakamega to the north. Hot and humid, there are enormous sugarcane plantations east of the Kisumu–Kericho road, with a predominantly subsistence agriculture in the rest of the region. Other industries include a limestone quarry at Koru at the foot of the Nandi escarpment, and a hydro-electric power station in the hills to the west of Homa Bay.

Getting there and away

The main route to Kisumu is on the B1 from Kericho, a delightful drive from the highlands as the road drops to the sultry Kano plains and Lake Victoria. Other major routes are from Kitale via Webuye and Kakamega on the A1, the B1 from Busia on the Uganda border and the A1 from Kisii.

By bus

Kisumu is the transport hub for this part of Kenya. Akamba Bus has several services a day to Nairobi, the first at 09.00 and also offers a de-luxe service. The offices are on Alego Street. Kenya Bus has a daily service to Nairobi, while Coast Bus leaves at 09.00 to Nairobi, connecting with the night service to Mombasa. The bus and *matatu* stage is near the market, at the junction of Gumbi Road and Kenyatta Avenue.

By air

Flamingo Airlines has up to six flights a week from Nairobi to Kisumu return (page 82). **Kisumu Airport** (PO Box 13 Kisumu; tel: 050 41620) is on the B1 Busia road, about 12km from town. Taxis into town cost about KSh700. The town office is in Alpha House, Ground Floor on Oginga Odinga St (PO Box 1427 Kisumu; tel: 057 20081).

By train

The passenger train scheduled to run from Nairobi to Kisumu via Nakuru departs at 18.00 on Mondays, Wednesdays and Fridays, departing from Kisumu to Nairobi on Tuesdays, Thursdays and Saturdays, leaving at 18.00. The train service can be spasmodic, so do check trains are running in advance. The train station is near the ferry jetty – follow New Station Road off Oginga Odinga Street, or contact Kenya Railways (page 167).

By boat

A passenger ferry service used to run from Kisumu to Kendu Bay, but stopped due to water hyacinth congesting the channels, although services may resume again. Similarly there used to be passenger ferries to Uganda and Tanzania. There is talk of running a steamer service around the lake in the future. Ask at the jetty for information.

Getting organised

For **changing money**, Barclays, Standard Chartered and Kenya Commercial banks are situated in the centre of town and all have ATMs. The main **post office** is on Oginga Odinga Road, open Monday–Friday 08.00–17.00, Saturday 09.00–12.00. For **internet access** try the British Council on Oginga Odinga Road or the Imperial Plaza Café at the Imperial Hotel on Jomo Kenyatta Avenue. There's a well-stocked Nakumatt **supermarket** in Mega Plaza on Oginga Odinga Road. There's also a **pharmacy** in the Mega Plaza and plenty of others in town. In a **medical emergency** go to the Aga Khan Hospital on Otieno Oyoo Street (tel: 057 43516). The **police station** is on Olmolo Agar Road (tel: 057 4445) and the **tourist helpline** is 020 604767. If you need to extend a visa the **immigration department** is in the Reinsurance Plaza on Oginga Odinga Street. There are plenty of **petrol stations** on the access roads into Kisumu.

Where to stay and eat

Sunset Hotel (large hotel; swimming pool) PO Box 215, Kisumu; tel: 035 41100
A modern (1970s) 5-storey hotel, located at the lakeside, with expansive views of Lake Victoria and spectacular sunsets across the water. There's a good swimming pool. Hippo wallow in the shallows while impala graze the foreshore. The rooms are comfortable with en-suite facilities. The restaurant is popular for its buffet lunches which are good value.
Rates: from KSh2,000 B&B per person sharing

Imperial Hotel (large hotel; swimming pool) Jomo Kenyatta Av, PO Box 1866, Kisumu; tel: 057 41455; fax: 057 40345; email: imperial@africaonline.co.ke
The Imperial Hotel, a 6-storey building, faces on to the lake. There's a rooftop bar and the restaurant serves some of the best food in town (from KSh750 for dinner). The rooms have AC and are comfortably furnished with en-suite bathrooms. **On offer:** health club, internet café and small swimming pool.
Rates: from KSh2,400 B&B per person sharing

Hotel Royale Jomo Kenyatta Av, PO Box 1690, Kisumu; tel: 057 40924; fax: 057 44644; email: takawiri@net2000ke.com
This old colonial hotel has seen better days. It has a bizarre combination of faded grandeur with a modern casino. Facing on to the street, its spacious, raised veranda, under a huge awning, is a popular meeting point. The food has an Indian emphasis and there's an Indian barbecue on Wednesdays which is excellent value (KSh350). Rooms are adequate with en-suite facilities, and there's a nightclub and casino which can get noisy.
Rates: from KSh1,500 B&B per person sharing

YMCA Off Ang'awa Av, PO Box 1618, Kisumu; tel: 057 43192
A friendly establishment, with basic facilities. There's a small canteen selling cheap food, but water can be unreliable.
Rates: from KSh200 for a dorm bed

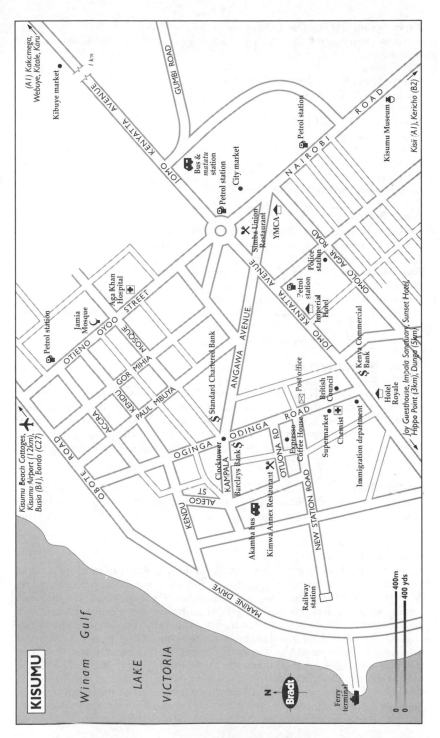

KISUMU

Winam Gulf

LAKE
VICTORIA

Bradt

N

Ferry terminal

0   400m
0   400 yds

Marine Drive

Railway station

New Station Road

Immigration department

Hotel Royale

Kenya Commercial Bank

British Council

Chemist

Supermarket

Post office

Expresso Coffee House

Otuona Rd

Odinga Road

Kimwa Annex Restaurant

Akamba bus

Clocktower

Barclays Bank

Kampala

Alego St

Kendu

Oginga

Acara Road

Obote Road

Kendu

Gor Mihia

Paul Mbuya

Oyoo

Otieno

Mosque Street

Jamia Mosque

Aga Khan Hospital

Standard Chartered Bank

Angawa Avenue

Petrol station

Kisumu Beach Cottages,
Kisumu Airport (12km),
Busia (B1), Bondo (C27)

Kibuye market

(A1) Kakamega,
Webuye, Kitale, Koru

1 km

Jomo Kenyatta Avenue

Gumbi Road

Bus & *matatu* station

Petrol station

City market

Petrol station

Simba Union Restaurant

YMCA

Nairobi Road

Police station

Petrol station

Imperial Hotel

Jomo Kenyatta Avenue

Omolo Agar Road

Kisumu Museum

Kisii (A1), Kericho (B2)

Joy Guesthouse, Impala Sanctuary, Sunset Hotel,
Hippo Point (3km), Dunga (5km)

Expresso Coffee House Otuona Rd, Kisumu
A popular café during the day, serving inexpensive fruit juices, curries, steaks and
beefburgers.
Closed evenings
Kimwa Annex Restaurant Otuona Rd, Kisumu
This has a good varied menu which includes local dishes like *githeri* and *matoke* (see page 465).
Open 24 hours
Simba Union Kenyatta Av near the market
Officially a Sikh Club for members, but non-members are usually welcome. Service can be
slow, so order your food and then come back if time's precious. The meals are worth the
wait: excellent Indian dishes with vegetarian options, fish and steak. They have good curry
dinners on a Friday.
Cost: from around KSh500 for a main course

Near Kisumu
Joy Guest House (5 rooms) Dunga, PO Box 9105, Kisumu; tel: 057 43406
A pleasant, family-run guesthouse with comfortable rooms.
Rates: rooms from KSh700 B&B
Kisumu Beach Cottages (bandas and camping) off Pipeline Rd, near airport, Kisumu; tel:
057 44006
A pleasant campsite across the Winam gulf, located near the airport next to the lake. The
restaurant serves basic meals (cost around KSh500) and boat trips can be arranged to Ndere
Island.
Rates: from KSh200 for camping and bandas

What to see and do
Markets
The **city market** on Nairobi Road is one of the best in western Kenya. Even if
you're not buying, it's worth a visit just to soak up the ambience of colour and
frenetic bustle, and to see the variety of foodstuffs for sale. It closes at around
18.00. On Sundays, the **Kibuye Market** on Jomo Kenyatta Highway draws people
from far and wide, and sells all manner of things, from secondhand clothes to
furniture.

Jamia Mosque
The Jamia Mosque on Otieno Oyoo Street was built in 1919. Pale green and white,
it has twin minarets. Surprisingly, Islam has had a foothold in Kisumu since the
19th century.

Kisumu Museum
Located on the Nairobi road, a short walk from town, this is an excellent regional
museum, with a comprehensive range of historical and ethnic artefacts, a Luo
homestead, reptile park and freshwater aquarium. The exhibits are well displayed
and informative, depicting different tribal groups of the region – Luo, Luhya,
Kipsigis and Nandi – and a range of traditional pottery and cooking implements.
Among the displays are a collection of pipes – smoked by both Luo men and
women – and photographs of Thimlich Ohinga, Kenya's equivalent of the Great
Zimbabwe ruins (see page 325) and the arrival of the railway at Port Florence in
1901. Central to the exhibition hall, and rather incongruous, is an amazing feat of
taxidermy of a lioness pouncing on a terrified wildebeest. The **snake house** is well
displayed, with black, red and brown spitting cobras, the forest cobra, Jameson's
and green mamba, puff adder, rock python and the evil-looking rhinoceros-horned